Interpreting
Canada's Past

Fifth Edition

Interpreting Canada's Past

A Pre-Confederation Reader

EDITED BY

Michel Ducharme

Damien-Claude Bélanger

J.M. Bumsted

OXFORD
UNIVERSITY PRESS

OXFORD
UNIVERSITY PRESS

Oxford University Press is a department of the University of Oxford.
It furthers the University's objective of excellence in research, scholarship,
and education by publishing worldwide. Oxford is a registered trade mark of
Oxford University Press in the UK and in certain other countries.

Published in Canada by
Oxford University Press
8 Sampson Mews, Suite 204,
Don Mills, Ontario M3C 0H5 Canada

www.oupcanada.com

First Edition published in 1986
Second Edition published in 1993
Third Edition published in 2005
Fourth Edition published in 2012

Library and Archives Canada Cataloguing in Publication
Interpreting Canada's past / edited by Michel Ducharme,
Damien-Claude Bélanger, and J.M. Bumsted. — Fifth edition.

Includes bibliographical references and index.
Contents: v. 1. A pre-confederation reader — v. 2. A post-confederation
reader.
ISBN 978-0-19-902025-6 (v. 1 : softcover).—ISBN 978-0-19-902026-3
(v. 2 : softcover)

1. Canada—History. 2. Canada—History—Sources. I. Ducharme,
Michel, 1975-, editor II. Bélanger, Damien-Claude, 1976-, editor
III. Bumsted, J. M., 1938-, editor

FC170.I57 2016   971   C2016-902882-8

Oxford University Press is committed to our environment.
This book is printed on Forest Stewardship Council® certified paper
and comes from responsible sources.

Printed and bound in the United States of America

1 2 3 4 — 20 19 18 17

Contents

Six ❧ Loyalists

Seven ❧ The Fur Trade in the Northwest

Preface

As with the fourth edition of *Interpreting Canada's Past*, it remains our intention to provide students of Canadian history with a collection of primary and secondary sources, a collection that represents the material historians use daily. Paying attention to current scholarship is essential, and bearing in mind the not-so-current interpretations of a particular theme is likewise part of the historian's job. The privilege of setting aside the work of historians and encountering voices from the eras under examination is another perk not usually available to students in lecture courses. We wanted once again to give those using the reader an opportunity to see how our understanding of the past is built upon evidence, carefully sifted and handled, and how sometimes these bits of evidence can lead historians to offer conclusions that prompt still more questions.

This reader has been conceived not as a replacement but rather as a complement to lectures and textbook chapters. It focuses on specific issues that may or may not have been discussed at length in class. The topics covered in this edition are varied and demonstrate the breadth of questions, approaches, methodologies, and primary sources inspiring Canadian historians, though we have chosen to privilege social issues, as the general trends in Canadian political and economic history are likely to be covered in lectures or other textbooks.

As with the previous editions, the emphasis is again on interpretation. The primary documents have been chosen so that students will take those first steps toward generating the kind of questions that are useful even outside the discipline of history: What does this document mean? Why did its creator want to express the ideas it contains? How reliable is it? What does it tell us about change? The historical interpretation selections have been simplified in this edition, with the assumption that students can dig deeper into each article or excerpt, dealing less in terms of who-did-what-when, but discovering more in terms of connections with the primary sources and the overall theme of each section. On the basis of user comments and classroom experience, we have retained the more popular selections and added ones that are entirely new, while also altering our lists of topics.

We thank the staff at Oxford, along with Len Kuffert and Jack Bumsted, for their vision for the readers and commitment through the previous editions. We also wish to thank Sean Graham, Aaron Boyes, and Gisèle Dubeau for their assistance.

Michel Ducharme, University of British Columbia

Damien-Claude Bélanger, University of Ottawa

Introduction to Primary and Secondary Sources

The work of historians is to understand the past or, to be more precise, to understand the lives of people who lived in the past. Just like undergraduate students working on their essays, MA students working on their theses, or PhD students working on their dissertations, professional historians have to design manageable research projects. In order to do so, they first select a topic and then focus their attention on historical questions that have not already been answered. Once they have decided which questions deserve exploration, they start looking for information to answer them. The first challenge they face is that their objects of study (i.e., the past) does not exist anymore. While the past has shaped the present, the present is different from the past.

In order to make sense of the past, historians have to use whatever evidence or testimonies they can find. They call this evidence, produced by the societies they are studying, primary sources or documents. It is by finding primary sources, analyzing them, and comparing them that historians can answer their research questions; they can find out how people lived in the past, establish causal relationships between facts and events, and develop their own interpretations about past societies. Depending on the objects of their inquiries, historians use different kinds of primary sources. Written documents are the most commonly used. Some of these written documents have been created by public institutions such as governments and courts of justice. Others have been produced by individuals or groups of individuals for a public audience: for instance, of political treatises, pamphlets, brochures, newspapers, and books such as novels, travel guides, or cookbooks. Other sources are private, created by individuals and private institutions and not been intended for public consumption. Internal documents from specific institutions such as voluntary associations, religious institutions, and charitable organizations are among these sources. Personal correspondence, journals, and diaries are also private, even if some have been made public over time. While many of these primary sources can be consulted in their original format, some have been reproduced on microfilms, republished, or digitized. Depending of the nature of these sources, historians can access them in archives (public or private), libraries, or online. Although most historians base their research on written documents, some use alternative primary sources such as artistic works (paintings, photographs, and cartoons, for instance) or even architecture and landscapes. Others focus on material culture such as old coins, clothing, and other artifacts. And lastly, historians can also use oral sources. These sources are especially useful to study societies with strong oral traditions such as Indigenous societies, or to think about more contemporary issues. What is important to remember is that all these sources are valid and valuable. The challenge for historians is to find the right sources to examine their own questions and to compare and confront those sources.

Regardless of the type of sources, historians need to analyze them carefully. They need to know exactly what these sources can and cannot tell them, as historians do not want to make unsubstantiated claims. In order to determine the limitations of their sources, historians must first question the documents themselves: What is the origin of these sources? Where are they coming from? Who created them? When were they created? Why were they created? Are they authentic? Once they have answered these questions, then historians can analyze their content: What do they say? What do they not say? What are their underlying assumptions? Lastly, historians can analyze these sources by putting them into dialogue, comparing them, and establishing how they relate to each other.

Once historians have collected all the primary sources they need (or that they can find), analyzed them, and compared them, then they can answer their questions and develop their own interpretations of the past. Their interpretations are embodied in what is known as secondary sources. These secondary sources, produced by historians, may take the form of monographs (books answering one question), book chapters, and journal articles, among other things. Historians use secondary sources for different reasons. They can use them to contextualize their topic, complement their own information, or situate their work within the overall historical production.

As the readers will notice, we have included in this collection a wide variety of primary sources: from artifacts to official documents, from travel accounts to novels and works of art, from personal diaries to transcription of speeches. All these sources include information that historians can use to understand the past. These sources have been paired to historical interpretations that offer an overview of the different questions asked by historians as well as the different approaches used to answer them. By reading these sources together, students will better understand the work of Canadian historians.

Chapter 1

Origins and Contact

READINGS

Primary Documents

Historical Interpretations

INTRODUCTION

As we look into the history of what is now called Canada, understanding the nature and the impact of the contact between Europe and North America requires an acknowledgement that the two sets of people in each contact zone viewed the world and approached knowledge in different ways. One way to appreciate this is to examine accounts of origin. Our first historical source consists of a Cree explanation for the presence of first peoples in the Americas. This narrative, like the biblical story of Adam and Eve, suggests a world with few people in it—a world in which people could communicate with powerful beings who directed and advised them, and who could help them find different places to live. Religious practices varied widely in pre-contact Canada, though most Indigenous people saw themselves as part of a cosmological order that included the land and its animals, the stars, and the sea. Rituals were often centred on maintaining balance between natural forces. Some of the artifacts illustrated here were used in Indigenous rituals, while others, like the famous pictographs from the shores of Lake Superior, represent Indigenous beliefs.

Contact between Europe and North America would profoundly alter the culture and society of both continents, and the historical studies included in this chapter show how it produced an array of consequences. As Ralph Pastore shows, for the Beothuk people of Newfoundland, contact with Europeans was a disaster. It caused the Beothuk to withdraw into the island's rugged interior, where food resources were few and subsistence was precarious. In his piece, Jean-François Lozier looks at a very different aspect of contact, which he terms "the transatlantic cosmetic encounter." He shows how many Indigenous people came to prefer imported vermilion for body painting over domestic red ochre, and consequently how the former became a valuable trade good throughout North America.

QUESTIONS FOR CONSIDERATION

1. Does the Cree narrative portray the new place to live as a reward, a punishment, or neither? What leads you to this conclusion?
2. Where does archaeology end and history begin?
3. Why is the question of how long Indigenous people occupied the land before contact an important one for scholars and society at large?
4. Why did the Beothuk avoid contact with Europeans?
5. What significance did Indigenous people give to body painting and how did contact with Europe change their use of pigments?

SUGGESTIONS FOR FURTHER READING

Keith Thor Carlson, *The Power of Place, the Problem of Time: Aboriginal Identity and Historical Consciousness in the Cauldron of Colonialism* (Toronto: University of Toronto Press, 2010).

Elaine Dewar, *Bones: Discovering the First Americans* (Toronto: Random House Canada, 2001).

E. James Dixon, *Bones, Boats & Bison: Archaeology and the First Colonization of Western North America* (Albuquerque: University of New Mexico Press, 1999).

Brian M. Fagan, *Ancient North America: The Archaeology of a Continent*, 3rd edn (New York: Thames & Hudson, 2000).

Gary Haynes, *The Early Settlement of North America: The Clovis Era* (Cambridge: Cambridge University Press, 2002).

Nina G. Jablonski, ed., *The First Americans: The Pleistocene Colonization of the New World* (San Francisco: California Academy of Sciences, Distributed by University of California Press, 2002).

Howard B. Leavitt, *First Encounters: Native Voices on the Coming of Europeans* (Santa Barbara, CA: Greenwood, 2010).

Ingeborg Marshall, *A History and Ethnography of the Beothuk* (Montreal and Kingston: McGill-Queen's University Press, 1998).

David J. Meltzer, *First Peoples in a New World: Colonizing Ice Age America* (Berkeley: University of California Press, 2009).

Primary Documents

1 From "Where the First People Came From," in C. Douglas Ellis, ed., *Cree Legends from the West Coast of James Bay* (Winnipeg: University of Manitoba Press, 1995), 2–5. Reprinted with permission.

So then, I shall tell another legend. I'll tell a story, the legend about ourselves, the people, as we are called. Also I shall tell the legend about where we came from and why we came . . . why we who are living now came to inhabit this land.

Now then, first I shall begin.

The other land was above, it is said. It was like this land which we dwell in, except that the life seems different; also it is different on account of its being cold and mild [here]. So then, this land where we are invariably tends to be cold.

So that is the land above which is talked about from which there came two people, one woman and one man . . . they dwelt in that land which was above. But it was certainly known that this world where we live was there.

Now then at one time someone spoke to them, while they were in that land of theirs where they were brought up. He said to them, "Do you want to go see yonder land which is below?"

The very one about which they were spoken to is this one where we dwell.

"Yes," they said, "we will go there."

"The land," they were told, "is different, appears different from this one where we dwell in, which you dwell in now during your lifetime. But you will find it different there, should you go to see that land. It is cold yonder. And sometimes it is hot."

"It fluctuates considerably. If you wish to go there, however, you must go see the spider at the end of this land where you are. That is where he lives."

The spider, as he is called, that is the one who is the net-maker, who never exhausts his twine—so they went to see him, who is called the spider.

Then he asked them, "Where do you want to go? Do you want to go and see yonder land, the other one which is below?"

"Yes," they said.

"Very well," said the spider. "I shall make a line so that I may lower you."

So then, he made a line up to—working it around up to, up to the top.

"Not yet, not yet even half done," he said.

Then he spoke to them, telling them, better for him to let them down even before he finished it the length it should be.

Then he told them, "That land which you want to go and see is cold and sometimes mild. But there will certainly be someone there who will teach you, where you will find a living once you have reached it. He, he will tell you every thing so you will get along well."

So he made a place for them to sit as he lowered them, the man and the woman.

They got in together, into that thing which looked like a bag.

Then he instructed them what to do during their trip. "Only one must look," he said to them. "But one must not look until you have made contact with the earth. You may both look then."

So, meanwhile they went along, one looked. At last he caught sight of the land.

The one told the other, "Now the land is in sight."

The one told the other, "Now the rivers are in sight."

They had been told however, that "if one . . . if they both look together, before they come to the land, they will go into the great eagle-nest and they will never be able to get out and climb down from there."

That's where they will be. That's what they were told.

Then the one told the other, "Now the lakes are in sight. Now the grass."

Then they both looked before they arrived, as they were right at the top of the trees. Then they went sideways for a short while, then they went into the great eagle-nest. That's where they went in, having violated their instructions. . . .

Then the bear arrived.

So he said to them . . . and they said to him, "Come and help us."

The bear didn't listen for long; but then he started to get up on his hind legs to go and see them. Also another one, the wolverine as he is called. They made one trip each as they brought them down.

But the bear was followed by those people.

That was the very thing which had been said to them, "You will have someone there who will teach you to survive."

This bear, he taught them everything about how to keep alive there.

It was there that these people began to multiply from one couple, the persons who had come from another land. They lived giving birth to their children generation after generation. That is us right up until today. That is why we are in this country.

And by-and-by the White People began to arrive as they began to reach us people, who live in this country.

That is as much as I shall tell.

2 Artifacts

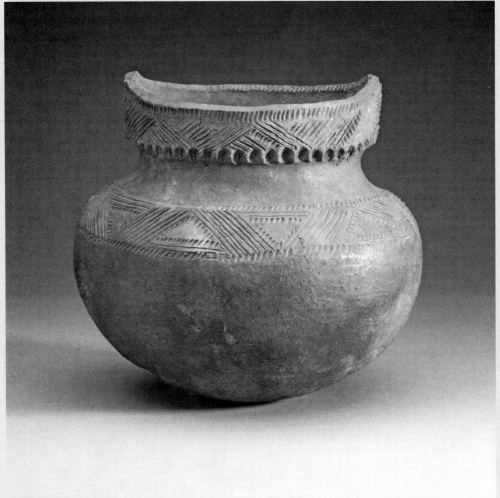

Artifact 1 This St Lawrence Iroquoian pot uses a fairly elaborate pattern of incised lines and indentations on the collar, with a similar incised design on the shoulder. It is 20 cm high and 20 cm in diameter.

Artifact 2 Distinctive pinched face-effigy pipes from the end of the Late Woodland period may represent a Huron shaman, or medicine man, named Tonneraouanont. The pipe has been broken at the base; the existing part measures 9.9 cm in height.

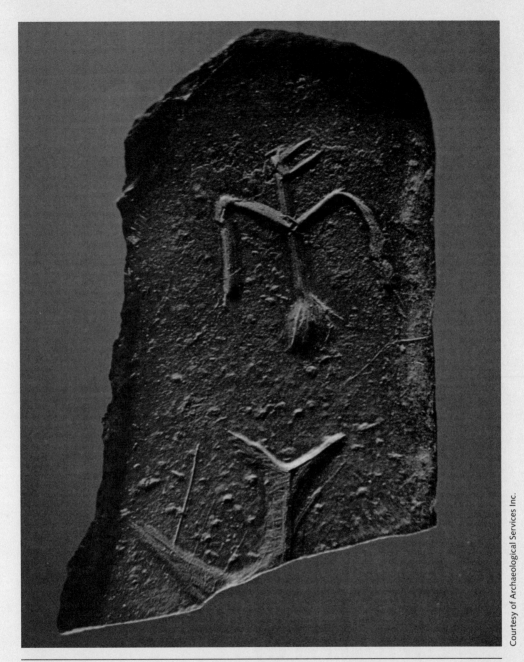

Artifact 3 Archaeologists excavating at the Peace Bridge Site recovered a fragment of a slate gorget that bears two incised Thunderbird images. They found the piece in an archaeological feature associated with the historic Neutral or New York Iroquois, from about 1650 CE.

Courtesy of Archaeological Services Inc., Photo by John Howarth

Artifact 4 This moose antler comb comes from Teiaiagon (Baby Point), a Seneca village near the mouth of the Humber River in Toronto. Dating to the 1680s, the comb has depictions of significant Aboriginal religious symbols including Mishipizhiw, the long panther-like being at the bottom with its head to the right and tail curled under its body to the left.

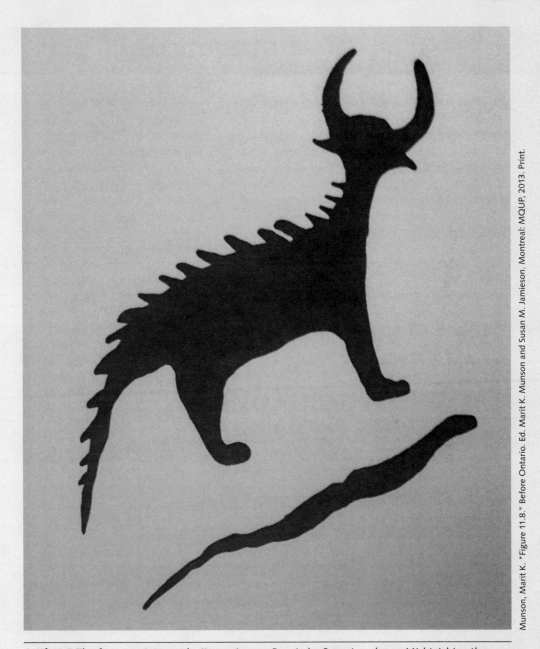

Munson, Marit K. "Figure 11.8." Before Ontario. Ed. Marit K. Munson and Susan M. Jamieson. Montreal: MQUP, 2013. Print.

Artifact 5 The famous pictograph site on Agawa Bay, Lake Superior, shows Mishipizhiw, the Underwater Lynx of Panther. One of the serpents who accompanies him is visible below.

Historical Interpretations

3 From Ralph Pastore, "The Collapse of the Beothuk World," *Acadiensis* XIX: 1 (1989): 52–71.

Until recently, the Beothuks, Newfoundland's Aboriginal people who became extinct in 1829, were a shadowy people whose origins, culture, and demise were little understood. In the past 15 years, however, archaeological, historical, and linguistic investigation has produced answers to a number of significant questions about them. It is now clear that the Beothuks were a hunting and gathering people of Algonkian stock,[1] whose ancestors in Newfoundland produced tools typologically similar to the late prehistoric Indian inhabitants of coastal Labrador and the Quebec North Shore.[2] It is also clear that, prior to the coming of Europeans, the Beothuk occupied, or at least used, all of the island of Newfoundland with the possible exception of the Avalon peninsula east of Trinity Bay. This island, despite its enormous size, has a simplified ecosystem characterized by a disproportionately small number of prey species relative to the large number of predators. Those predators included wolves, bears, lynx, marten, mink, weasels, otter, fox, and human beings. The major native interior prey species were caribou, beaver, and arctic hare (although the bones of the latter have never been identified from an archaeological site on the island). In essence, then, the island is a rather impoverished piece of the boreal forest in the mouth of the St Lawrence. Of course, the surrounding waters are much richer in available food. Most important of the marine mammals to native hunters were harbour, harp, grey, and hooded seals, and walruses, all of which were once found in abundance off the coasts. Other marine resources available to the Beothuks included cod, salmon, flounder, smelt, capelin, mussels, soft-shelled clams, and lobsters. A number of avian species also contributed to the Aboriginal diet including the now extinct great auk as well as murres and a wide variety of ducks and geese.[3]

The majority of prehistoric Beothuk sites are found along stretches of coastline that allowed them to exploit the resources of both the near shore and the interior of the island. This site distribution leaves the impression of a people who were not specialized in their hunting and fishing strategies,[4] an hypothesis strengthened by the few samples of prehistoric Beothuk food remains that have been recovered from archaeological sites.[5] A generalized subsistence pattern was probably necessary for the island's peoples because, despite the rich resources of the sea, prehistoric human populations in Newfoundland have always been vulnerable to changes in the availability of animal stocks. One of the most significant marine resources would have been the harp seal which is usually present, even today, in herds numbering more than a million. Yet there have been times in the historic period when, due to strong offshore winds, the unsuitability of the ice, or factors not yet understood, these seals unaccountably failed to arrive off the island's coast.[6] There is no reason to believe that prehistoric harp seal stocks would have been any more reliable. The most important land resource, caribou, may have been equally unreliable. A successful caribou hunt involved intercepting the animals primarily upon their fall migration.[7] Caribou movements are notoriously unpredictable and may be affected by factors as diverse as insects and ice storms. As illustrated in Figure 1, Newfoundland's Native peoples, like most hunting and gathering bands, had to time their own seasonal movements to coincide with the availability of their prey.

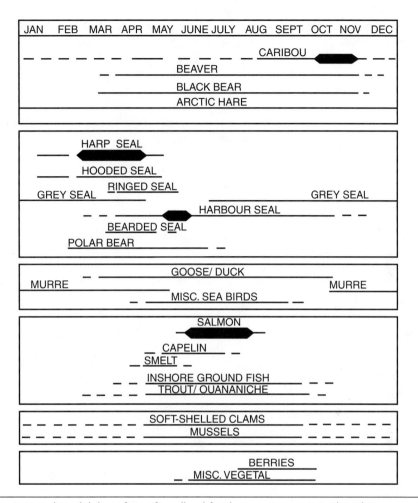

Figure 1 Seasonal availability of Newfoundland food resources. From Tuck and Pastore, "Extinctions."

If that prey was not there, hunters would have to fall back on less important substitutes. Unfortunately, the island of Newfoundland lacked many of "fall-back" species—the moose, deer, and porcupine—found on the mainland. Even less important prey species such as beaver and freshwater fish are much less abundant than on the mainland. Newfoundland Native groups, therefore, had little margin for survival if one of their major food resources, caribou or harp seal, failed. A few years of such failures might well cause the sort of extinctions that appear to be characteristic of Newfoundland's prehistory. Indeed,

archaeological research has demonstrated that in least three instances before the arrival of Europeans, prehistoric Native populations have become extinct—very likely because of changes in the availability of vital food resources.[8]

Although archaeology has provided at least the outlines of the prehistoric Beothuk subsistence pattern, it is not possible to determine the size of the Beothuk population at the time of European contact. Such a determination would require a systematic survey of the entire coast and much of the interior of the island as well as a program of excavation designed to reveal site size and population and, given the expense involved, such an undertaking is unlikely. Even the fortuitous discovery of archaeological sites is less likely in Newfoundland. Elsewhere, many archaeological sites are discovered because of modern building and road construction, but the island's poverty, sparse population, and rugged terrain make extensive activity of this sort highly improbable. In the absence of such a program of reconnaissance and excavation, estimates of Beothuk population can only be informed guesses. Perhaps the first recorded estimate was by Joseph Banks who noted in 1766 that Beothuks were "thought to be very few as I have been told not Exceeding 500 in number but why that should be imagind I cannot tell as we Know nothing at all of the Interior Parts of the Island nor Ever had the Least Connexion with them tho the french we are told had."[9] Although Banks believed that by the 1760s the Beothuks had retreated into the interior, there is evidence that they were still visiting the coast to hunt and fish, even if their permanent residence had shifted to the interior.[10] He was, however, correct in regarding that population estimate with some skepticism, for there really was no sound basis for estimating their numbers.[11]

Ignorance about the size of the Beothuk population at a time when the numbers of other Native peoples of the northeast were quite well known to whites is not surprising. Some time after about the second decade of the seventeenth century, the Beothuks followed a pattern of withdrawal from contact with Europeans which culminated in their extinction early in the nineteenth century. The tragedy of that extinction, unique in Canadian history, has attracted a great deal of attention from both scholarly and popular writers. The Newfoundland geologist, James P. Howley, whose remarkable collection of documents pertaining to the Beothuks was published in 1915, concluded that the Beothuks had been hunted and harassed to extinction. Although Howley discounted many of the more lurid

oral accounts of Beothuk persecution, his documentary collection was eagerly used by a number of popular writers, most notably Harold Horwood and Pierre Berton, to spin out a sensational tale of "the people who were murdered for fun."[12]

Given the fact that researchers limited to the documentary record were faced with a number of accounts, some trustworthy, others not, of Europeans killing Beothuks, it is perhaps not surprising that a monocausal explanation of the Beothuk demise was accepted. That would change after the results of James Tuck's archaeological investigations of a number of Newfoundland sites were published. He found that for thousands of years prior to the coming of Europeans, Newfoundland's inhabitants had depended upon the resources of the sea for most of their food. He also noted that when Europeans began to settle the island, of necessity they were drawn to the same resource-rich areas of the coastline that the Beothuks inhabited. As Tuck put it: "An unknown number of natives were actually killed outright by Europeans. But more important to the survival or extinction of the race, the remaining Beothuks were denied access to the coast and forced to try and survive on the resources of the interior."[13] In an important article published in 1977 Leslie Upton argued that "despite these tales of slaughter, common to all North American frontiers, the decrease in Beothuck population over a period of three hundred years was unspectacular." Positing a population of about 2000 at the time of European contact, Upton found nothing unusual about a rate of decline due to epidemic disease and loss of hunting territory that was, in fact, less than what other researchers had found for New England. In a suggestive comparison between the Micmac and the Beothuk experience Upton speculated that "the Beothuks died because they did not have enough contacts with the whites." He noted that the course of Beothuk–white relations had been remarkably different from that of other Indian peoples in

North America. Upton stated that "the Beothuk strategy of withdrawal has no parallel
elsewhere in the region, and its cause cannot
be known: epidemic disease may have been
the catalyst that prompted the decision."[14]
The problem with this explanation is that
every other Native people in North America
also suffered the ravages of epidemic disease;
none, however, withdrew so determinedly
from European contact.

Throughout North America, the lure that
drew Native peoples to European contact was
trade. The knives, axes, kettles, blankets,
and guns of the newcomers were immensely
desired by Indians. Elsewhere in North
America Indians endured disease, violence,
alcoholism, and an assault on their most
deeply held beliefs in order to trade furs for
European goods. The fact that the Beothuks
did not do so is remarkable, perhaps unique.
Since Upton's work, archaeologists working
on Beothuk sites have done much to suggest
a possible reason for the Beothuk failure to
participate in a fur trade.[15] In brief, it is argued that because of the unusual nature of
the early Newfoundland economy, the Beothuks did not *need* to enter into a fur trade
to obtain European goods—especially metal
objects. Once European fishermen began to
dry fish on shore, they left behind, each winter, flakes, wharves, stages, and a variety of
debris associated with an onshore fishery.
For the Beothuks, these seasonally abandoned fishing premises were treasure troves
of metal objects, particularly nails. Archaeological work at two Beothuk sites in Notre
Dame Bay, in fact, has resulted in the recovery of hundreds of nails (many of them modified into projectile points), as well as scraps
of iron and brass kettles, fish hooks, awls,
and numerous other metal pieces. Although a
marginal trade between European fishermen
and Beothuks may have existed in the sixteenth and early seventeenth centuries,[16] by
the latter date the Beothuks had been drawn
into a pattern of pilfering European goods
from seasonally abandoned fishing premises.

As a result, the first European settlers on the
island had to trap their own furs. The Newfoundland "furrier," as he was called, dates to
at least 1612–1613.[17] Although more research
is needed, the practice of whites trapping furs
in the seventeenth century appears to have
little parallel in the rest of North America.[18]
When whites were forced to trap their own
furs, there was, of course, even less possibility that a systematic fur trade would emerge
on the island between settlers and Beothuks.

The absence of fur traders in Newfoundland was paralleled by an absence of missionaries. Elsewhere in North America, one
of the more important ways in which Native
peoples were drawn into interaction with
Europeans was through the activities of missionaries. Newfoundland's seasonal fishery
and tiny year-round British population (estimated at about 1200 in the last quarter of the
seventeenth century),[19] however, could not
support a missionary effort to the Beothuks.
Nor is there any evidence that the colony of
Placentia, occupied by the French during
the period, 1662–1713, sent missionaries to
the Beothuks.[20] The other usual medium for
peaceful contact between Indians and whites
in the European colonies was the official assigned by the metropolitan powers to deal
with Native groups. Such officials generally
had two functions: to secure the assistance
or the neutrality of Indians, and to negotiate the sale of Indian land. But the British
Crown did not make the commanders of
the Newfoundland convoy governors nor did
it provide for the creation of magistrates who
would spend the winter on the island until
1724.[21] By then there was certainly no need
for Indian agents since the Beothuk pattern
of withdrawal was well established. Nor was
there any need to secure the assistance of the
Beothuks in the wars between Britain and
France. As a people who lacked firearms,
they would have counted for very little and,
in any case, the contest for supremacy in
Newfoundland would be won by the power
which had naval, not land, supremacy.

Without these Indian agents, fur traders, and missionaries, there was no one to stand between the Beothuks and the white settlers, their competitors for the resources of the coast.[22] Because the vast majority of those European occupiers left no written records, the historian of the Beothuk experience is forced to rely much more than usual upon archaeological data even for information as basic as the plotting of the Beothuk retreat from encroaching white settlement. In an attempt to delineate the shrinking world of the Beothuks, evidence from published and unpublished archaeological reports, site record forms on file in the Newfoundland Museum in St John's, and a few scattered documentary references, have been used to note the location of both prehistoric and historic Beothuk sites in Newfoundland and related sites in Labrador and Quebec.[23]

The question of what constitutes prehistoric Beothuk needs some explanation. It now is clear that the immediate prehistoric predecessors of the Beothuk on the island of Newfoundland were the possessors of the Little Passage complex. At two important sites in Notre Dame Bay, for example, there was no evidence of another occupation intervening between that of the Little Passage people and the Beothuks.[24] In addition, the strong resemblance between the stone tools used by both groups suggested a continuity over time. That hypothesis has been strengthened by a detailed attribute analysis of Beothuk and Little Passage stone projectile points which identified a number of trends in attributes extending from the prehistoric period to perhaps the beginning of the eighteenth century.[25]

On the other side of the Strait of Belle Isle, William Fitzhugh first identified a late prehistoric/early historic Indian presence extending along the coast of Labrador from Saglek Bay to the Quebec Lower North Shore, which he named the Point Revenge complex. "The geographic extent of Point Revenge occupation and its persistence into the historic period," he argued, "make it the most likely progenitor of the modern Indians of Labrador." He also noted that "sites related to Point Revenge in Newfoundland are thought to be ancestral to Beothuck culture, and on the Quebec north shore, prehistoric continuity into historic Montagnais is also suggested."[26] The posited relationship between Little Passage and Point Revenge is based both on a similarity of projectile point styles and an apparent preference in both cases for locating sites in similar areas. Little Passage and Point Revenge sites are often found in an inner coastal zone which suggests a subsistence pattern described by Fitzhugh as "Modified-Interior," i.e., a "generalized" rather than "specialized" dependency on coastal and interior resources.[27]

Although more research on both Little Passage and Point Revenge is needed, current evidence does suggest a relationship. [. . .] At present, James Tuck, the excavator of the Red Bay site, believes that the diagnostic artifacts of the two sites in the Strait of Belle Isle would fit generally within the assemblages recovered from prehistoric Beothuk (Little Passage) sites on the island. This should not be surprising. The much earlier Maritime Archaic and Palaeo-Eskimo traditions have been reported from both Quebec-Labrador and the island,[28] and it would be unusual if the Beothuks and neighbouring Quebec-Labrador groups were an exception to the general rule that related sub-Arctic hunter-gatherer cultures tend to be scattered over quite wide distances. Still, there are locations within these huge areas which were quite crucial for hunter-gatherers, and the Strait of Belle Isle would have been exactly such a place. It has quite rightly been referred to as a "resource funnel" for a variety of marine resources including many species of whales and seals.[29]

One explanation for the preponderance of sites in the island's northeast is illustrated by Figure 2 which shows the migration of harp seals and their breeding areas.[30] Clearly, Notre Dame Bay would have been very appealing to prehistoric Beothuk seal hunters. The attraction of the south coast is

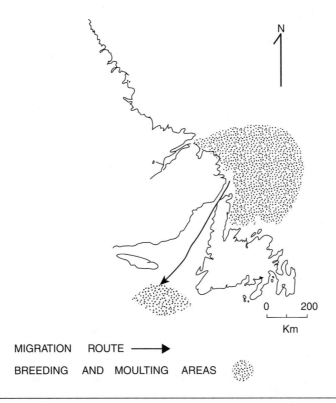

MIGRATION   ROUTE ⟶

BREEDING   AND   MOULTING   AREAS

Figure 2 Harp seal migrations. After A.W. Mansfield, *Seals of Arctic and Eastern Canada*, Bulletin No. 137. Fisheries Research Board of Canada (Ottawa, 1964), p. 12.

more difficult to explain, but since this coast tends to be ice-free all year long,[31] its coves and bays once had harbour and grey seals in abundance.[32] In addition, prehistoric hunters may well have been drawn to the south coast to hunt caribou in the winter since the largest winter concentrations of caribou on the island are to be found along the south coast and its interior.[33]

The pattern would be much clearer if it were possible to establish an age for each site, but in many instances the surviving material is simply not datable. In the far southeast, the Ferryland site is also the location of Lord Baltimore's colony, founded in 1621, and evidence of an Indian presence here lies beneath a stone wall attributed to Baltimore and is found with European artifacts which date to the late sixteenth century. In the far

northwest, material from Blanc Sablon in the Strait of Belle Isle is still undergoing analysis, but according to its most recent excavator, aboriginally produced stone tools have been found at the same level with European artifacts.[34] Preliminary work from the nearby site of Red Bay, a Basque whaling station occupied from ca. 1540 to ca. 1610, indicates an association of sixteenth-century Basque features with an Indian occupation. The stone projectile points produced by those Indians, both at Blanc Sablon and Red Bay, may in fact be a variant of those produced by historic Beothuks on the island. The island itself is clearly visible from the Labrador side of the narrow (20 km) Strait of Belle Isle, and it is inconceivable that Native groups on either side would have been prevented from traversing it throughout the year. Indeed, for much of the year travel by canoe across the Strait would be far easier than an inland journey of 20 kilometres by foot. The Strait of Belle Isle, in fact, should be viewed as a highway, not a barrier.[35]

Whatever the nature of the relationship between the historic Indians of Quebec-Labrador and those of the island, it is clear that both groups had access to European goods in a similar manner. That access is clearly indicated by the presence of Native hearths found at both Red Bay and Ferryland which are located in and among European structures. This has led the director of excavations at those sites to suggest that the Indians in question had been visiting the two locations to scavenge European iron from seasonally abandoned shore stations. The one site from the southwest corner of the island, in St George's Bay, was reported in 1594 by the master of the *Grace* of Bristol who found a Beothuk camp in that bay, along with the wrecks of two Basque ships. The other sites along the South Coast and Placentia Bay are either burials or archaeological sites, none of which can be dated with any confidence. The three sites from Trinity Bay are drawn from the account of John Guy who met a Beothuk group camped there in 1612, and from a work by an early Newfoundland entrepreneur who reported an encounter between Beothuks and European mariners around the turn of the seventeenth century. Only two sites are listed for Bonavista Bay, perhaps because of a lack of archaeological surveys in the area. Of these two, one is a burial, the other a living site. Unfortunately, neither has been dated with any precision.

The 28 sites in Notre Dame Bay and all but one of the 116 sites from the interior represent the Beothuk response to increased European utilization of Newfoundland. Most of these living sites date to the late eighteenth–early nineteenth centuries when the Beothuk presence in the bay was restricted to furtive fishing and hunting forays carried out under the guns of white settlers. Two of these sites,

Boyd's Cove and Inspector Island, however, have been dated to ca. 1650–1730, and merit special attention.[36] They are situated in eastern Notre Dame Bay and were occupied at a time when English permanent settlement ended in Bonavista Bay, and a French migratory fishery was carried on in the western portion of the bay. These two living sites were positioned in an area safely between the two zones of European exploitation from which it was possible to visit the seasonally abandoned French fishery to the west for European iron, and occasionally to steal from the English settlements and fisheries to the southeast.[37] These sites may well have been occupied at a time when Beothuk culture entered a period of florescence—when it was still possible to hunt and fish in safety, and still possible to acquire the iron from which to fashion the tremendously useful metal cutting and piercing tools that made their lives so much easier. Faunal analysis of the animal remains from the Boyd's Cove site bears this out. The wide range of species taken prompted the analyst Stephen Cumbaa to note: "At Boyd's Cove we have a glimpse of a people at ease in their environment and obviously exercising a fair degree of control over use of its resources. The contrasting picture we have a century later of a beleaguered and dwindling population ekeing out a living on the run from a dominant culture is all the sadder for the comparison."[38] The other sites in Notre Dame Bay represent archaeological sites, both living and burial, and bone ornament caches. None has been dated with any more accuracy other than to the historic period.

The sites clustered along the Red Indian Lake–Exploits River system represent the last refuges of the Beothuk. Many of these sites have been excavated, and they have produced a large quantity of knives, scissors, trap parts, and other European objects.[39] The abundance of European objects, coupled with the relative lack of stone tools, as well as the dates assigned to a number of artifacts from the Wigwam Brook site, support the evidence from the documentary record that this region was intensively occupied during the late eighteenth and early nineteenth centuries.[40] This was a period when the Beothuks were hindered by white settlement from access to the resources of the coast and were forced to try to subsist on the meagre resources of Newfoundland's interior. The nature of those last days is graphically revealed in the archaeological evidence. Animal bones from one late eighteenth–early nineteenth century site on the Exploits River, for example, revealed that not only were the Beothuks subsisting almost entirely upon caribou, but they were attempting to do so all year round.[41] One leading authority on caribou hunting has noted that in an area such as Newfoundland, where caribou migrate over short distances, it would have been possible for Aboriginal groups to prey on caribou year-round, but "humans usually found easier resources to harvest for part of the year, mostly anadromaous fish, beaver, or moose."[42] Moose, of course, were not introduced to the island until the late nineteenth century, and the island's fish and beaver populations are both much smaller than those on the mainland.[43] Conventional anthropological thinking has it that caribou "can theoretically supply all of the requirements of a human population, but the chances of this occurring are in fact extremely small."[44] In fact, Newfoundland's stark interior supported only 14 indigenous mammalian species, and there is no evidence in the archaeological record that any Aboriginal culture lived there for 12 months of the year. When the Beothuks were forced to do so, the results were tragic. Detailed analysis of a child's garments from a contemporaneous burial provides a graphic picture of Beothuk life during those last days. The shroud of one child (now in the Newfoundland Museum) was found to be a woman's legging, made from five pieces of skin, most of which had been patched and repaired. The child's moccasins exhibited similar careful patching and repairing; most surprising was the use of spruce root rather

than the usual caribou sinew to repair the moccasins. All of this suggests a people on the ragged edge of desperation who did not even have enough animal skins to clothe a child properly.[45]

This pattern of gradual Beothuk withdrawal from a territory which once encompassed almost all of Newfoundland and perhaps the Strait of Belle Isle to the banks of the Exploits River has been constructed largely on the basis of archaeological evidence. However, the same pattern is evident in the documentary record. For example, as late as 1612 John Guy noted the presence of Beothuks on the Avalon peninsula. Ten years later, the experienced sea captain Richard Whitbourne stated that although Beothuks from Bonavista Bay stole into Trinity Bay to pilfer "Hatchets, Hookes, Knives, and such like" he implied that they no longer lived in Trinity Bay.[46]

The Beothuks who had once lived in Trinity Bay appear to have travelled back and forth across the narrow isthmus of the Avalon peninsula to gain access to the considerable resources of Placentia Bay, especially the harbour seals.[47] The Beothuks may have also occupied that narrow neck of land in order to intercept caribou herds passing from the main part of the island to the isthmus.[48] The importance of that isthmus to the Beothuks is underscored by the presence of two large prehistoric Beothuk sites there. Thus, the year-round occupation of Trinity Bay by the English by 1675 and the French occupation of Placentia Bay by at least 1662 had the effect of denying these two important food sources to the Beothuk.[49] By 1694, de Brouillan, the commandant of the French garrison of Placentia, could write about "la découverte des sauvages qui habitent au sud de l'isle," clearly indicating that the French at Placentia had not been in contact with the Beothuks, if indeed they ever had, for some time.[50] De Brouillan's information was given to him by a band of Micmacs who had come to Newfoundland from Cape Breton. Their arrival in

Newfoundland meant yet another competitor for the island's resources. While it is possible that there were Micmacs in Newfoundland in the sixteenth century,[51] given the report by de Brouillan, it does not appear as if their presence on the south coast was intensive enough to disrupt Beothuk use of that portion of the island. However, it is clear that by the middle of the eighteenth century, Micmac use of the southern portion of the island from St George's Bay to Placentia Bay had denied yet another area of the island—and its caribou and seals—to its Aboriginal inhabitants.[52]

By the middle of the eighteenth century, then, the Beothuk range had shrunk considerably. The contraction of the Beothuk world would have meant more than just reduced access to food resources. Given the presence in a number of prehistoric Beothuk sites on the island of Ramah chert, a translucent silicate found only in Ramah Bay in northern Labrador, it can be assumed that a trade across the Strait of Belle Isle existed in prehistoric times. Since trade between band level societies also implies the exchange of marriage partners, it is possible that at the point in Beothuk history when contact with Indian peoples in Labrador was either lost or reduced, the subsequent reduced gene pool would have further imperiled the survival of the island's natives.

It is difficult to determine when contact with Labrador may have been interrupted. There is some evidence that the Basques who carried on a whale hunt in the Strait of Belle Isle, during the period ca. 1540 to ca. 1610, employed Native people at the shore stations.[53] Although there is some controversy—and no direct evidence—relating to the incidence of European epidemic disease among the Native peoples of the Northeast in the sixteenth century,[54] there are two factors about this Basque–Native contact which might have made the transmission of epidemic disease more likely. First, the distance from Europe to the Strait of Belle Isle was shorter than that to New England or the Maritimes,

thus increasing the likelihood that a disease carried by a crew member would not yet have run its course prior to landing. Second, if the Basques employed Indians in shore-based activities throughout the season, the prolonged close contact implied would have been more conducive to the spread of pathogens than would be the case in a fur trade where contacts between the two groups would have been of much shorter duration.

Assuming that the Indians of the Strait of Belle Isle survived the Basque whale fishery of the sixteenth century, they would have had to face an invasion of the Strait by Inuit in the seventeenth century. There is evidence that by the last half of the seventeenth century there was an Inuit population living in the region throughout the year,[55] and it is quite likely that Indian use of the Strait was either severely curtailed or ended. In 1705 Augustin LeGardeur de Courtemanche established a trading post at Brador, near Blanc Sablon, and it is significant that he had to bring a group of Montagnais families with him to hunt fur bearers and to prosecute a (salmon?) fishery.[56] The well-documented hostility between the Inuit and French traders and fishermen in the Strait of Belle Isle casts further doubt on the likelihood that normal communication between the Indian populations of the Island and Labrador could have persisted in the last half of the seventeenth and first half of the eighteenth century.[57] Those French posts were established to trade with the Montagnais whose persistence today underscores the hypothesis that it was the Beothuk decision to withdraw from the fur trade which was the most important factor in their demise. The effects of that decision, however, were reinforced by the growing exploitation of Newfoundland's resources by other ethnic groups. Although the spread of permanent English settlement on the island may have been the most important factor denying the Beothuks access to vitally needed coastal resources, to that equation must now be added the Basque and Inuit presence in the Strait of Belle Isle, the Micmac use of the southern third of the island, and the French base at Placentia. A complete understanding of all of the effects of these arrivals upon the Beothuks may not yet be attainable, but the pattern revealed by the distribution of Beothuk sites over time is clear enough. As contact with Labrador was lost, and as the various regions of the island were denied to the Beothuks, they were forced to withdraw to the island's impoverished interior where there could be but one outcome for them.

NOTES

An earlier version of this works was presented at the Seventh Atlantic Canada Studies Conference, Edinburgh, 4–7 May 1988. I am indebted to Laurel Doucette, Charles Martijn, Douglas Robbins and Jim Tuck for their comments.

1. John Hewson, *Beothuk Vocabularies: A Comparative Study* (St John's, 1978), pp. 135–46. Hewson also noted that the Beothuk language "appears to show" a "feature . . . normally considered diagnostic" of Central rather than Eastern Algonkian (p. 146). The present-day Naskapi-Montagnais of Labrador are also classified as part of the Central Algonkian subgroup.

2. Ralph T. Pastore, "Excavations at Boyd's Cove—1984: A Preliminary Report," in J.S. Thomson and C. Thomson, eds, *Archaeology in Newfoundland and Labrador, 1984* (St John's, 1985), pp. 322–37; and R.T. Pastore, "Investigations at Boyd's Cove: The 1985 Field Season, a Preliminary Report," in J.S. Thomson and C. Thomson, eds, *Archaeology in Newfoundland and Labrador, 1985* (St John's, 1986), pp. 218–32.

3. A.T. Bergerud, "Prey Switching in a Simple Ecosystem," *Scientific American* 249 (December 1983): 130–41; J.A. Tuck and R.T. Pastore, "A Nice Place to Visit, but . . . Prehistoric Human Extinctions on the Island of Newfoundland," *Canadian Journal of Archaeology,* 9 (1985): 69–80.

4. R.T. Pastore, "The Spatial Distribution of Late Palaeo-Eskimo Sites on the Island of Newfoundland," in *Palaeo-Eskimo Cultures in Newfoundland, Labrador and Ungava* (St John's, 1986), pp. 125–34.

5. David Simpson, "Prehistoric Archaeology of the Port au Port Peninsula," MA thesis, Memorial University of Newfoundland, 1986. Fieldwork under my direction in the summer of 1987 at a Beothuk site on an island in Notre Dame Bay revealed a prehistoric Beothuk midden made up of bones from a broad range of food species.

6. L. Chafe, *Chafe's Sealing Book: A History of the Newfoundland Sealfishery from the Earliest Available Records Down to and Including the Voyage of 1923* (3rd edn, St John's, 1924), p. 19.

7. Arthur E. Speiss, *Reindeer and Caribou Hunters: An Archaeological Study* (New York, 1979), p. 124.

8. Tuck and Pastore, "Extinctions."

9. A.M. Lysaght, ed., *Joseph Banks in Newfoundland and Labrador, 1766: His Diary, Manuscripts and Collections* (Berkeley, 1971), p. 132.

10. For example, see "The narrative of Lt John Cartwright's journey up the Exploits River, 1768," in J.P. Howley, *The Beothucks or Red Indians* (Cambridge, 1915), p. 33.

11. For a discussion of the debate on Beothuk population size, see Ingeborg Marshall, "An Unpublished Map Made by John Cartwright Between 1768 and 1773 Showing Beothuck Indian Settlements and Artifacts And Allowing a New Population Estimate," *Ethnohistory* 24 (Summer 1977): 223–49.

12. Harold Horwood, "The People Who Were Murdered for Fun," *MacLean's Magazine,* 10 October 1959; Pierre Berton, *My Country: The Remarkable Past* (Toronto, 1976).

13. James A. Tuck, *Newfoundland and Labrador Prehistory* (Ottawa, 1976), p. 75.

14. Leslie Upton, "The Extermination of the Beothucks of Newfoundland," *The Canadian Historical Review* 58 (June 1977): 133–53.

15. The following argument is a brief summary of the material presented in R.T. Pastore, "Fishermen, Furriers, and Beothuks: The Economy of Extinction," *Man in the Northeast* 33 (Spring 1987): pp. 47–62.

16. For example, in 1612 when the would-be colonizer, John Guy, encountered Beothuks in Trinity Bay, the Beothuks attempted to trade with the English by leaving behind poles with furs on them, but the English were not equipped with trade goods. As Cell noted, the Beothuks, unlike this particular group of Englishmen, appear to have engaged in a fur trade before. John Guy's Journal of a Voyage to Trinity Bay, 7 October 1612 to 25 November 1612, in Gillian Cell, ed., *Newfoundland Discovered: English Attempts at Colonization, 1610–1630* (London, 1982), p. 76.

17. "Occurrents in Newfoundland," 1 September 1612–1 April 1613, in David B. Quinn, ed., *New American World* (New York, 1979), IV, pp. 166, 169, 170, 172–5.

18. Although the Hudson's Bay Company did allow its men to trap privately at least by the eighteenth century (see for example Instructions of Joseph Isbister, Chief Trader at Albany Fort to John Yarrow, Master at Eastmain House, 15 September 1753, HBCA B.59/a/22, fo 4, extract provided by Toby Morantz), Morantz believes that such trapping by whites was "was on a very small scale."

19. Grant Head, *Eighteenth Century Newfoundland* (Toronto, 1976), p. 82.

20. See Ministère de la France d'Outre-Mer, Archives des Colonies, Serie C11C, Amérique du Nord, vols 1–7, Terre-Neuve (Plaisance), Microfilm in the PAC.

21. Keith Matthews, *Lectures on the History of Newfoundland, 1500–1830* (St John's, 1973), pp. 141–50.

22. Upton, "The Extermination of the Beothuks," p. 153.

23. Earlier results of this research were published in Graeme Wynn, Ralph Pastore, and Bernard Hoffman, "The Atlantic Realm" in R. Cole Harris, ed., *Historical Atlas of Canada,* I (Toronto, 1987). Results of archaeological research undertaken since the preparation of that volume have been incorporated in this work.

24. Ralph Pastore, "Excavations at Boyd's Cove, Notre Dame Bay—1983," in J.S. Thomson and C. Thomson, eds, *Archaeology in Newfoundland and Labrador, 1983* (St. John's, 1984), pp. 98–125; Ralph Pastore, "Excavations at Inspector Island, 1987: A Preliminary Report," in *Archaeology in Newfoundland and Labrador, 1987* (in press).

25. Fred Schwarz, "The Little Passage Complex in Newfoundland: A Comparative Study of Assemblages," Honours thesis, Memorial University of Newfoundland, 1984.

26. William W. Fitzhugh, "Indian and Eskimo/Inuit Settlement History in Labrador: An Archaeological View," in Carol Brice-Bennett, ed., *Our Footprints Are Everywhere: Inuit Land Use and Occupancy in Labrador* (Nain, Newfoundland, 1977), p. 14.

27. Schwarz, "The Little Passage Complex", pp. 43–7.

28. James A. Tuck, "Prehistoric Archaeology in Atlantic Canada since 1975," *Canadian Journal of Archaeology* 6 (1982): 203.

29. F.A. Aldrich, "The Resource Funnel of the Strait of Belle Isle," paper delivered to the International Symposium on Early European Settlement and Exploitation in Atlantic Canada, St John's, October 1979.

30. Based on A.W. Mansfield, *Seals of Arctic and Eastern Canada* (Ottawa, 1964), p. 12, and D.E. Segeant, "Migrations of Harp Seals *Pagophilus groenlandicus* (Erxleben) in the Northwest Atlantic," *Journal of the Fisheries Research Board of Canada* 22 (1965): 433–64.

31. Chesley Sanger, "The Evolution of Sealing and the Spread of Permanent Settlement in Northeastern Newfoundland," in J.J. Mannion, ed., *The Peopling of Newfoundland* (St John's, 1977), p. 139.

32. Even now there are major concentrations of harbour seals found from Placentia Bay to the southwest corner of the island. J. Boulva and I.A. McLaren, "Biology of the Harbor Seal, *Phoca vitulina,* in Eastern Canada," Department of Fisheries and Oceans Bulletin, No. 200 (Ottawa, 1979), p. 2.

33. During the period 1957 to 1967, the largest concentration of caribou was found along the south coast and its interior. A.T. Bergerud, "The Population Dynamics of the Newfoundland Caribou," Wildlife Society, Wildlife Monograph No. 25 (Washington, DC, 1971). Whether this was true in the prehistoric period is not known.

34. Jean-Yves Pintal, personal communication.

35. I am indebted to Marguerite MacKenzie, Memorial University Department of Linguistics, for this observation.

36. Pastore, "Fishermen, Furriers, and Beothuks" and "Excavations at Inspector Island, 1987." The Beothuk component at Inspector Island appears to date to ca. 1720–1730, although future analysis may result in modification of this conclusion.

37. Pastore, "Fishermen, Furriers, and Beothuks."

38. Stephen Cumbaa, "'Diverse Furres and Deeres Flesh'—Animal Use by a 17th Century Beothuk Population at Boyd's Cove, Notre Dame Bay, Newfoundland" (unpublished report, Zooarchaeological Identification Centre, National Museum of Natural Sciences, National Museums, Canada, 1984).

39. Don Locke, *Beothuck Artifacts* (Grand Falls, Newfoundland., n.d.); Helen Devereaux, "The Pope's Point Site," unpublished report, Newfoundland Museum, 1965; Helen Devereaux, "A Preliminary Report on the Indian Point Site, A Stratified Beothuk Site," unpublished report, Newfoundland Museum, 1970; Raymond LeBlanc, "The Wigwam Brook Site and the Historic Beothuk Indians," MA thesis, Memorial University of Newfoundland, 1973.

40. Marshall, "An Unpublished Map," pp. 223–49; Maps of the Red Indian Lake-Exploits River region drawn by Shanawdithit in 1829, in Howley, *The Beothucks,* pp. 238–45.

41. Frances L. Stewart, "Faunal Analysis of the Wigwam Brook Site, Newfoundland," Appendix 1, in LeBlanc, "The Wigwam Brook Site."

42. Speiss, *Reindeer and Caribou Hunters*, p. 138.

43. W.B. Scott, and E.J. Crossman, *Fishes Occurring in the Fresh Waters of Insular Newfoundland* (Ottawa, 1964); Thomas Northcott, "An Investigation of the Factors Affecting Carrying Capacity of Selected Areas in Newfoundland for the Beaver (*Castor canadensis caector* Bangs 1913)," MSc thesis, Memorial University of Newfoundland, 1964, p. 117.

44. Ernest S. Burch, "The Caribou-Wild Reindeer as a Human Resource," *American Antiquity* 37 (1972): 363, quoted in Speiss, *Reindeer and Caribou Hunters,* p. 139.

45. Ruth Holmes Whitehead, "I Have Lived Here since the World Began: Atlantic Coast Traditions," in Julia D. Harrison, ed., *The Spirit Sings: Artistic Traditions of Canada's First Peoples* (Toronto, 1987), p. 40.

46. Richard Whitbourne, *A Discourse and Discovery in New Found-land* (London, 1622), in Gillian Cell, ed., *Newfoundland Discovered* (London, 1982), p. 118.

47. Guy, "Journal," p. 72. Boulva and McLaren "Biology of the Harbour Seal," p. 2, found the largest concentration of harbour seals on the island in Placentia Bay.

48. The narrow necks of peninsulas are ideal for intercepting caribou migrations. M.A.P. Renouf, "Prehistoric Coastal Economy in Varangerfjord, North Norway," PhD thesis, Cambridge University, 1981.

49. Gordon Hancock, "English Migration to Newfoundland," in Mannion, ed., *The Peopling of Newfoundland,* pp. 16–7; Jean Pierre Proulx, *The Military History of Placentia* (Ottawa, 1979), pp. 9–12.

50. Jacques-François de Mombeton de Brouillan to the Minister of Marine, 25 October 1694, Archives des Colonies, C11C, II, 20.

51. The evidence for this is summarized in Charles A. Martijn, "Voyages des Micmacs dans la vallée du Saint-Laurent, sur la Cote-Nord et à Terre-Neuve," in Charles Martijn, ed., *Les Micmacs et la Mer* (Quebec, 1986), pp. 215–21.

52. Ralph T. Pastore, *The Newfoundland Micmacs,* Newfoundland Historical Society Pamphlet No. 5 (St John's, 1978), pp. 9–19.

53. Selma Barkham, "A Note on the Strait of Belle Isle during the Period of Basque Contact with Indians and Inuit," *Etudes/Inuit/Studies* 4, 1–2 (1980): 51–8.

54. Dean Snow and Kim Lanphear, "European Contact and Indian Depopulation in the Northeast: The Timing of the first Epidemics," *Ethnohistory* 35 (Winter 1988): 15–33; Bruce Trigger, *Natives and Newcomers* (Montreal, 1985), pp. 237–9.

55. Charles Martijn, "La présence inuit sur la Cote-Nord du Golfe St-Laurent à l'époque historique," *Etudes/Inuit/Studies* 4, 1–2 (1980): 105–25.

56. "Anonymous Memoir, 1715, Concerning Labrador," No. 1419, in Privy Council, *In the Matter of the Boundary Dispute Between the Dominion of Canada and the Colony of Newfoundland in the Labrador Peninsula* (Ottawa, 1927), VII, p. 3694.

57. François Trudel, "Les relations entre les Français et les Inuit au Labrador méridional, 1660–1760," *Etudes/Inuit/Studies* 4, 1–2 (1980): 135–46.

4   From Jean-François Lozier, "Red Ochre, Vermilion, and the Transatlantic Cosmetic Encounter," in Andrea Feeser, Maureen Daly Goddin, and Beth Fowkes Tobin, eds, *The Materiality of Color: The Production, Circulation, and Application of Dyes and Pigments, 1400–1800* (Farnham: Ashgate, 2012), 119–38. Reproduced with permission of Taylor & Francis Books UK.

The Europeans who approached North America from the final decade of the fifteenth century onwards could not help but notice that the inhabitants of this New World were scantily clad but abundantly decorated. The Taino encountered in the Caribbean islands by Columbus and his companions used pottery stamps coated with red, white, and black pigments to paint their bodies with lavish designs.[1] The Spanish explorers who in the decades that followed ranged into the North American southeast came across peoples with "their bodies, legs, and arms painted and ochred, red, black, white, yellow and vermilion in stripes" or, more commonly, "painted with a kind of red ointment."[2] The whalers and cod fisherman who began to visit the shores of Newfoundland too caught glimpses of men, women, and children whose bodies were painted red.[3] These, decidedly, were painted peoples.

Though the claim that it was due to early encounters with red-painted people that all Native Americans became "red-skinned" in Western eyes has been disproved in recent years, there is no doubting that body paint was of considerable socio-cultural importance among the inhabitants of the New World.[4] The same might be said, for that matter, of the inhabitants of the Old. Artificially whitened faces and reddened cheeks and lips were a common sight throughout early modern Europe. Leaving aside the related topics of tattooing and scarification, this article investigates the roots and ramifications of the meeting of Aboriginal and European skin-painting cultures—what might be termed the transatlantic cosmetic encounter—between the early sixteenth and late eighteenth centuries. In Europe this period was marked by the rise of face painting and of new pigments, which were accompanied by a heated polemic regarding the propriety of the painted face. On North America soil, painted faces also become a site of anxiety and innovation, with missionaries making tentative challenges to longstanding Indigenous practices and Indigenous practices making room for new transatlantic commodities. From locally sourced ochre, the following pages thus lead us to imported vermilion.

In Aboriginal North America, the search for good colours was assiduously pursued. To paint themselves, explained one commentator, the original inhabitants prepared colours "with several sort of Herbs, Minerals, and Earths, that they get in different parts of the Country where they Hunt and Travel."[5] The red pigments that dominated the palette might be extracted from a number of vegetal and mineral sources. In the east, bloodroot (*Sanguinaria canadensis*, also known as bloodwort of puccoon root) found widespread medicinal and decorative use. John Smith reported that the Powhatans of Virginia made great use of this root which they called *pocones* and "which being dried and beate in powder turneth red." It reduced swellings and aches, or, mixed with oil, was used to paint faces and garments.[6] Ochre was preferred, however, for the brightness of its hues and by its excellent colour fastness.

Ochre—the term can refer to a variety of red or reddish pigments processed from iron ores, mainly namely hematite and limonite—is associated with human activity in the archaeological record as early as the time of *Homo erectus*, approximately 300 000 BCE. The persistence of practices and regularity in patterns in the use of ochre in prehistoric and contemporary non-literate societies are such that one anthropologist describes it as being "like a red thread" woven through human history.[7] Red ochre has been found with regularity at the sites of the earliest human occupation throughout the US, much of Canada, and northern Mexico. Paleoindian habitation areas often reveal traces of ochre, while ochred human skeletal remains and associated red-stained artifacts are a common feature of that lithic period's burials and caches. So abundant was the use of powdered red ochre in the mortuary traditions of some regions that archaeologists speak of a "Red Paint People" on the north Atlantic coast (since renamed the "Moorehead Burial Tradition," circa 3000 BCE), and a "Red Ochre Culture" around the Great Lakes (circa 1000–500 BCE).[8] That ochre was used during this period to adorn the living, and not only the dead, can be inferred with confidence.

This prehistoric predilection for red ochre has been attributed by some to the substance's function as an external and internal healing agent: the iron salts found in ochre are effective antiseptics, have an astringent effect, and tend to arrest hemorrhaging.[9] More significantly perhaps, this predilection has been linked to a partiality, inferred from the prehistoric archaeological record and solidly documented by modern ethnography, for the colour red. Observing that all languages contain terms for black and white (or "light" and "dark") and that if a language distinguished a third colour it is necessarily "red," according to which the terms to describe these colours were the first to emerge in human languages everywhere. The other basic colour terms, yellow, blue, and green, appeared only at later stages, followed by terms for brown, orange, pink, purple, or grey.[10]

Victor Turner and others since have argued that the primacy of black, white, and red as basic colours follows from their cognitive relationship with body emissions—semen, milk, water, feces, blood—and with the associated physical experiences and heightened emotional states.[11] Linguistic evidence leaves no doubt of the connection between blood and the colour red among the Indigenous cultures of North America. In Proto-Algic, the reconstructed proto-language which would have been spoken from Atlantic Canada to the Rocky Mountains several thousand years ago and from which subsequent Algonquian languages derived, the word for red derives from a verbal root meaning "bleed" or noun meaning "blood." The connection persists in many modern languages: in Algonquin, *miskwi* means blood, and *misko* means red; in Mohawk, *onekwensa* means blood, while *onekwentara* means red.[12] Through its relationship with blood, the colour red is linked with physical and physiological excitement. It was closely connected with the rituals and symbol of life and death, of reproduction and violence, with festivities and joy. What one writer remarked of the inhabitants of the western Great Lakes in the 1860s—"Red is not only their joy, but also their favorite colour"—could have been said just about anywhere on the continent.[13]

* * *

Deposits of ochre—hematite, mainly—are abundant throughout North America. Bodies of water whose banks were known to be rich in ochre were often named accordingly: in the Algonquian-speaking northeast, names such as Aramoni, Olamon, Onaman, Oulaman, Osanaman, etc. dotted the landscape. European explorers and settlers in turn translated these diverse names into "Vermillon" Lake or River (in French, or Anglicized to Vermilion), or "Paint" River or Creek.[14] Depending on circumstances and cultural context, the ethnographic record suggests that specific sites of extraction might be kept secret from outsiders or shared with them. In recent years an otherwise friendly and co-operative Yuma informant explained to Paul Campbell that "no one divulges their source for red ochre." Meanwhile, Naskapi tradition held that all comers, regardless of their band affiliation, could take as much ochre as they needed for their personal use from the deposits near Lake Chibougamau, Quebec, without asking for permission from the band on whose hunting territory the resource was located or providing payment to them. The only constraint was that its sale was strictly forbidden.[15]

Restrictions on the sale of ochre or the divulgation of its source point to the highly sacred nature of this resource, which like most natural resources was thought to be controlled by supernatural beings. The extraction of ochre, accordingly, was generally accompanied by rituals and offerings aimed at honouring and appeasing these spirits. Several thousand years ago the Paleoindians who exploited the ochre deposits at the Powars II Site in Wyoming left behind successfully used stone projectile points and bifaces as an offering. In more recent times the Gwich'in or Loucheux of the Northwestern Territories, Yukon, and Alaska, were known to leave pieces of sinew when they extracted ochre from the earth. The Piegan Blackfeet of Montana would for their part "pray and sing and go through their religious activities."[16]

It is also possible that the processing of ochre had a ritual dimension. The technical components of this processing depended largely on the nature of the deposit. While ochre-bearing clays extracted from riverbanks required only minimal processing, stone-like chunks of ochre taken from the earth could be easily processed by scraping or crushing. Certain varieties of ochre may have been heat-altered, to facilitate their pulverization or to enhance their hues. Grease, water, sap, or spit was used as a binding agent before ochre was painted on the body, with more or less ceremony depending on the circumstances. The body-painting pottery stamps of the Taino had few if any parallels in North America, where paint was applied with hands, fingers, sticks, and rudimentary brushes. Fingers and sticks might then be used to scrape or remove paint to embellish designs with negative spaces.[17]

As might be expected, the practices and meaning associated with face and body painting varied form one Aboriginal culture

to another continent. For those peoples who usually went about naked or almost naked, full-body painting had the practical advantages of keeping away mosquitoes and gnats, and in northern climes to serve "in winter as a mask against the cold and the ice."[18] Additional layers of meaning, related to concerns with beauty, spirituality, and self-identification, were common. Among the Beothuks of Newfoundland, the ochring of every member of the band—conducted at a site that still bears the name Red Indian Lake—called for a ceremony, and the application of the first coat in infancy was regarded as a sign of initiation.[19]

While in some groups it was common for both women and men to paint themselves, the European newcomers discovered with some amusement that in the Eastern Woodlands it was to the men that paint tended to afford the greatest opportunities for self-expression. Women painted themselves sparingly in comparison, though it was customary for them too to paint their faces black to display grief in times of mourning. To European eyes, the garish designs adopted by men during celebrations, councils, and on the war path seemed to follow personal fancy. In attempting to describe the face paintings of the Iroquois one Jesuit drew on the vocabulary of facial features most familiar to him and to his European readers: some "appear artistically bearded," while others "seem to wear spectacles."[20]

When questioned about the meaning of such garish designs, warriors admitted to the quizzical foreigners that "not being master of their nature, their enemies could perceive on their face some air of pallor and of fear." Face paint concealed these signs of weakness, as well as "extremes of youth or age, which might inspire strength and courage in the adversary." Conversely, warriors found that paint "adds to their Courage and strikes a terror in their Enemies."[21] Though settlers were wont to believe that paint acted as a "disguise" which also concealed the identity of treacherous warriors, one Jesuit's statement that each warrior had "in this matter his own style of livery, so to speak, which he retains through life," suggests that the intent was quite the contrary.[22] While some warriors may indeed have sought to gain an advantage from the fact that paint covered up their identity, others used paint to proudly proclaim it.

Such personal "liveries" may very well have been inspired by visionary experiences. Though the spiritual significance of face and body painting tended to elude the European newcomers to the Eastern Woodlands and in the southwest during the early modern period, ethnographical information collected in the Plains in the late nineteenth and early twentieth centuries make it clear that colour and design preferences were generally inspired by visions and dreams in which supernatural entities imparted powers that protected the wearer from harm. Thus the Hidatsa chief Black Shield might "wet some gunpowder and paint his face" before going into battle, applying "white paint on his lips and eyes just as he has seen these things in his dream."[23] [. . .]

* * *

Although the European newcomers to North America found Indigenous manipulation of skin colour repulsive, or at the very least strange and unsettling, the practice was not entirely foreign to them. To those among them who had benefitted from a humanistic education, the classical authors offered a natural point of reference. After describing the painted breasts and arms of the Chiriguaná women of what is today Columbia, the sixteenth-century Spanish historian Gonzalo Fernández de Oviedo y Valdés had asked: "How can we blame them, when we look at other nations of the world who are now prosperous and live in a Christian republic, like the English of whom Julius Caesar writes?"[24]

The Jesuit Joseph-François Lafitau, who, after living among the Iroquois of what is now Canada between 1712 and 1717, penned *Moeures des Sauvages américains comparées aux moeurs des premiers temps* (1724) in an effort to provide reciprocal illumination of the customs of the inhabitants of the New World with those of the Old, found the adornment of the body with tattoos and paint to be a fecund point of comparison. On the subject of peoples who reddened their entire bodies, Lafitau was expansive. "As a rule," he writes, "the ancient writers tell us this about the [East] Indians, the Africans, the Picts, the Geloni, the Agathyrses and a number of other peoples," including the Ethiopians, about whom Pliny "assures us that they coloured themselves with vermilion from head to foot." Deducing that these people were doubtless the same who when about naked, Lafitau goes on to point out that even the Romans painted the statues of their gods during feasts in red, "because this colour better simulates that of fire," and that they did the same to the bodies of their victorious generals during their triumphal processions. Other societies, meanwhile, such as the Persians, had applied paint around the eyes. Noting that the inhabitants of North America had the habit of applying vermilion to their hair, Lafitau pointed out that "all the barbarian peoples of antiquity took pleasure in greasing it well and adorning it with artificial colours."[25]

Antiquity was not alone in offering points of comparison, for Europe itself has experienced a revival of face paint during the Age of Discovery. By most accounts, the cosmetic arts had been pushed out of fashion throughout most of the continent during the medieval period. While the Church followed the lead of Saint Augustine who, citing as precedent Saints Cyprian and Ambrose, exhorted against "women who colour, or discolour, their features with paint," the breakdown of trade routes restricted access to the cosmetic staples common in antiquity.[26] The Crusades and escalating activity of Italian merchants, who brought various perfumes, unguents, and recipes associate with beautification from the East, triggered a revitalization of cosmetic practices beginning in the thirteenth century.[27] [. . .]

Italy, unsurprisingly perhaps, emerged as the centre of the face-painting renaissance. Already in the early thirteenth century, the poet and jurist Cino da Pistoja could place in the mouth of an attentive mother the following admonition: "Never leave home without face paint, little girl."[28] If a tad of irony was implied, it nevertheless was an accurate reflection of what was becoming a prevailing fashion. [. . .] Caterina de'Medici was credited with bringing the practice of wearing white and red *fards* to France when she travelled there to become queen in 1533. In England, the preparation and use of what were called *fucus* increased dramatically during the second half of the century, as a result of the increased trade with the continent and of the example set by Queen Elizabeth who used them openly and increasingly with age. The *Siglo de Oro* also saw face paint become fashionable in Spain.[29]

By the early seventeenth century, the painted woman and the professional beautician had become familiar figures and—as with "Doctor Plaster-Face" in John Marston's play *The Malcontent*—stock characters on the stage.[30] Fashionable gentlemen were also wont to experiment with face paint.[31] The cosmetic convention was for women to whiten the skin of their faces and, as sartorial fashions evolved, shoulders and bosoms with variety of preparations centered on flour, alum, alabaster, talcum, etc. Because of their bright hues, because they clung well to the skin and because they did not require a heavy application, artists' pigments found new uses. White lead (lead carbonate or lead oxide), widely referred to as *ceruse*, generally came to be preferred to other whiteners.[32] [. . .]

* * *

Though women from all rungs of society indulged in white and red face paint to brighten their complexion, it emerged as a sign of aristocratic identity and a hallmark of the court culture which thrived in France and emanated from there throughout Europe. Given the theatrical way in which paint was worn at court, with white applied in a thick layer across the face so as to erase all signs of aging and disease, and red generously daubed on the lips and cheeks, there could be no question of its being intended to pass off as natural. Rather, paint was a power statement, a demonstration of the aristocratic elite's ability to force the boundaries of fashion beyond the norms of nature. To be sure, the face-painting excesses in vogue among the entourage of Louis XIV and Louis XV were widely exotic by comparison to those of the British court. In the mid-eighteenth century Horace Walpole was able to spot an Englishwoman at the Paris opera by the fact that she wore "no rouge."[33]

To wear or not to wear face paint was a question about which women across Europe had struggled for centuries. Italian, Spanish, French, and English men of letters, meanwhile, had expended profuse quantities of ink on the matter. Picking up the old patristic arguments which held that the use of cosmetics deformed God's work and contributed to shifting the emphasis away from the soul to the body, and fusing them with new humanist concerns about the relationship between nature, truth, artifice, and falsehood, these late medieval and early modern authors opposed an almost universally negative response to the cosmetic revival.

In England a puritanical current of reform, coupled with the death of that patron of face paint, Queen Elizabeth, and the perceived cosmetic excesses of the Jacobean period, unleashed a veritable flood of misogynistic polemics and satire, much of which took aim at cosmetic practices. John Donne and Richard Brathwait criticized the woman who took "the pencill out of God's hand" to hold it in her own "impudent hand." Thomas Tuke devoted an entire tract to the subject, entitled *Treatise against Painting and Tincturing of Men and Women* (1616).[34] Face painting was perceived to be a peculiarly feminine vice. Though men who indulged in face painting might be decried as effeminate fops—the enamored Benedick in *Much Ado About Nothing*, for example, is teased for washing, shaving, and painting his face—it was women who bore the brunt of the criticism.[35] [. . .]

Such misogynistic flights, which betrayed considerable anxiety with respect to women's lack of readability, appear to have been particularly virulent in England. Among their avalanche of complaints the English critics pointed to the fact that most cosmetics substances were imported and thus costly, but also foreign and corrupting.[36] Nonetheless, the critique of face painting was a theme which crossed national and linguistic boundaries. In Spain as well as in France, that bastion of face painting, men of letters disparaged and mocked the use of cosmetics.[37] Beyond that theological and moral arguments, critics everywhere pointed to the paradoxes of these substances which, though meant to enhance beauty, in fact damaged it. The corrosive effects of many ingredients used in face paint were already known in the fourteenth and fifteenth centuries, when the authors of some of the earliest treatises on beautification warned their readers against the deleterious effects of the very cosmetic recipes which they supplied. Still, though, it was widely known that substance such as white lead and vermilion (a compound of mercury, it will be remembered) were damaging to beauty and health, they continued to find wide use until the second half of the eighteenth century.[38]

* * *

Even if the meanings and practices of face and body painting in the New World mapped only imperfectly onto those of face painting in the Old, colonial commentators naturally recognized parallels between the two.

William Strachey thus remarked how the inhabitants of Virginia "annoynt" their bodies with colored dyes, "as doe out great Ladies their oyle of Talchum, or other Paynting white and redd." On one point of comparison, at least, Strachey found that the analysis favoured the locals. The Virginian woman was not as secretive with her cosmetic recipes as her English counterpart: she "preserves yt not yet so secret, and pretious unto her self, as doe out great Ladies . . . but they friendly communicate the secret, and teach yt one another."[39] More often than not, though, the newcomers tended to view Indigenous decorative habits as the result and proof of a collective deficiency in character. Like European women, Aboriginal men seemed overly preoccupied with their appearance. "The young people, absorbed in their vanity and desire to please, have recourse to art to embellish themselves," wrote Lafitau of the Iroquois. "[T]hey put infinite time on it and it occupies them as much as it does European ladies and much more than it does their own [women] who appear persuaded that charity, decorum and their domestic work require more modesty and simplicity."[40]

To the missionaries who wished to convert and civilize the "barbarous" inhabitants of the New World, face painting represented more or less of an obstacle to overcome. Roger Williams, the Protestant theologian and founder of the colony of Rhode Island, held opinions in line with those of the English polemicists of his time. It was with some regret indeed that he conceded that it was the "foolish Custome of all barbarous Nations to paint and figure their Faces and Bodies (as it hath been to out shame and griefe, wee may remember it of some of our Fore-Fathers in this [English] Nation)." In his *Key into the Language of America* (1643), Williams provided phrases by which his readers might attempt to dissuade the Narragansetts from painting themselves: "Cummachiteoûwunash kuskeésuchquash," meaning "You spoil your face"; and "Mat pitch cowahick Manit keesiteonckqus," meaning "The God that made you will not know you."[41] [. . .]

The Jesuit missionaries operating in the Saint Lawrence valley during the same period also attempted to rebuke their Montagnais, Algonquin, and Huron neophytes for the "mischievous custom" of face and body painting.[42] When he built and decorated a chapel in the mission-village of Lorette, near Quebec, patterned after the Santa Casa of Loreto in Italy, Father Pierre-Joseph-Marie Chaumonot was careful that the statue of Saint Mary be painted in flesh tones rather than in the dark tones that characterize the original in Loreto. "We did this for fear lest, if we exposed for the veneration of our Savages an image entirely black," explained Chaumonot, "we might cause them to resume the custom which we have made them abandon, of blackening and staining their faces."[43] In the decades that followed, however, the Jesuits of New France relaxed their attitudes toward face and body painting. Acknowledging the impossibility of effecting a wholesale transformation of Indigenous society, the missionaries came to believe that these customs, like other forms of adornment and dress, language, and music, were innocuous and compatible with the fundamentals of the Catholic faith. [. . .]

The Franciscan missionaries toiling in New Mexico similarly exhibited a great deal of tolerance of painting, even as they fought against idolatry and attempted to reform habits of nakedness. In 1714, the colony's Governor Juan Ignacio Flores Mogollón conducted an investigation into whether or not the Pueblos should be allowed to continue to paint themselves in a traditional manner. The friars to whom he turned for advice explained that the people of the Pueblos described the painted body as being akin to a "beautiful suit," and that "body paint is their fancy dress." Fray Salvador Lopez reminded the governor that the use of paint by their wards was little different from Spanish women's practice of painting their own faces with white shell powder. Because the Spanish used powder, colour, ribbons, and feathers "among themselves to adorn their bodies" and because this was not judged sinful, he reasoned that they could not prohibit the Pueblos from doing the same. "I have seen the painting and the plumes many times," declared Fray Antonio Miranda of the Pueblos, "and they have told me because among the Spanish it is not a bad thing to put on the hats, feathers and ribbons [that] . . . they don't use these things for bad things either."[44]

Anxieties about painted neighbours were not merely theological. Governor Flores's investigation had been prompted by the concern that Spaniards could not tell the friendly Pueblos apart from the other, "heathen" and hostile, inhabitants of the regions such as the Apaches. It was feared that the Pueblos, painted and dressed so as to be unrecognizable from the enemy, were free to mischievously steal livestock and murder settlers.[45] [. . .]

At the same time, colonists were only too happy to don the Aboriginal "disguise" when it suited their purpose. Taking to hearth the precept that "When in Rome . . . ," French and British officials and military men cultivated habits of self-presentation that allowed them to interact most fruitfully with their Aboriginal interlocutors. It was "dressed and painted after the manner of an Indian War Captain" that the trader and diplomat Sir William Johnson entered the city gates of Albany at August of 1746, at the head of a Mohawk delegation "likewise dressed and painted, as is usual when they set out in War." A willingness to display a face painted according to Indigenous conventions on certain key occasions, much like a familiarity with their languages, was a means of demonstrating solidarity with trading partners and allied warriors, of acquiring and maintaining a measure of influence among them.[46]

In difference circumstances, putting on the painted disguises allowed colonists to register political protest under the cover of anonymity. "I immediately dressed myself in the costume of an Indian," recalled George Hewes of his involvement in the Boston Tea Party of 1773. "[A]fter having painted by face and hands with coal dust in the shop of a blacksmith," he fell in "with many who were dressed, equipped and painted as I was," before reaching Griffin's wharf. This thinly veiled impersonation of "Indians" (Mohawks to be more precise) fooled no one. But then again, these colonists were less concerned with passing off as something other than what they were than about registering their protest in flamboyant and symbolic style. Painted faces and hands embodied both an expression of longstanding colonial anxieties centred on Indigenous neighbours beyond the frontier and of more recent anxieties centred across the Atlantic, on Great Britain. The painted Indian, representing the antithesis of King George's tyranny, was a convenient symbol of the emerging American identity.[47]

* * *

The rise of the transatlantic fur-trading markets in the seventeenth and eighteenth centuries transformed cosmetics use among the Indigenous peoples of North America. Mirrors, by facilitating the precise application of paint to one's own face, may have entailed a true revolution in face-painting practices, allowing for the more careful self-application of paint.[48] The introduction of copper vessels may have made the collection of manufactured pigments such as verdigris, red lead, and, more importantly, vermilion. By all accounts, Aboriginal consumers exhibited a marked preference for vermilion over ochre. As Lafitau explained, the locally sourced pigments produced "a rather nice red, but that is not worth our vermilion."[49]

When and how, exactly, the transatlantic trade in pigments began must remain a matter of conjecture. Oral tradition among the French residents of Canada during the mid-eighteenth century had it that

vermilion had been traded from the colony's earliest days. "Many persons have told me," reported the Swedish naturalist Pehr Kalm, in the mid-eighteenth century, "that they had heard their fathers mention, that the first Frenchmen who came over here got a great heap of furs from the Indians, for three times as much cinnabar [vermilion] as would lie on the top of a knife."[50] Though this suggests that vermilion had been traded since the first decade of the seventeenth century, it is not until the century's final decades that the earliest sure evidence of a transatlantic trade in red pigment emerges. In 1684, Cavelier de La Salle listed vermilion among the "small articles" which he was trading in the Great Lakes and asked for 50 pounds of it to be sent from France to "drive a profitable trade." By the turn of the century, the French chronicler Bacqueville de La Potherie stated that a "great commerce" in vermilion was conducted in Canada.[51] [. . .] Vermilion was abundantly traded and offered as diplomatic presents by French, British, and Spanish merchants in every frontier zone throughout the eighteenth century.

The rise of the transatlantic vermilion trade at the end of the seventeenth century may have something to do with technical advances. Since antiquity, vermilion had been derived from powdered cinnabar. "Vermilion mines" in Galicia continued to produce through the Middle Ages and early modern period.[52] A process for synthesizing vermilion from mercury and sulphur was recorded in Europe as early as the eighth century, plausibly after having been carried from China via Arabia. Form the twelfth century onwards, synthetic vermilion was used throughout Europe as an artist's pigment.[53] In the seventeenth century Amsterdam emerged as the centre of production of vermilion using the "dry" process, which involved combining mercury with molten sulphur and heating it to the point of sublimation.[54] In 1687, a German named Gottfried Schultz invented a new "wet" process which entailed heating a mixture of mercury and sulphur in a warm, caustic solution of ammonium or potassium sulphide. This more efficient and cheaper process was adopted in Amsterdam, which retained its dominance as a centre of vermilion production until the early nineteenth century.[55] [. . .]

Red lead, on the other hand, was something that Britain produced increasingly as the seventeenth and eighteenth centuries wore on. One source from 1670 mentions the presence of red lead mills at the lead mine in Cariganshire, and four decades later others are mentioned in Glamorganshire.[56] Given the lower value of red lead compared to vermilion, it is no surprise that it found its way into the hands of Britain's allies and trading partners in North America. Governor Dongan's 1684 enumeration of "Indian Goods" included not only vermilion, but also red lead. In 1711, Governor Robert Hunter of New York presented to Schagticoke headmen "5lb Red lead and half a pound of Vermilion for Paint." [. . .] Though lists of trading goods sometimes allude to both vermilion and red lead, and though they occasionally allude to "vermilion mixed" of "paint," there is good reason to believe that the pigments described simply as "vermilion" in the records were not always pure mercuric sulphide.

For traders there were good profit margins to be made in "vermilion," which by volume and weight was one of the most expensive commodities of the North American fur-trading market. The nineteenth-century historian François-Xavier Garneau's claim that "as much as 800 franc have been obtained for a pound of vermilion!" was most probably an exaggeration.[57] A pound of vermilion which cost Antoine Crozat only 5 livres in France was sold at his store in Mobile for more than three times as much in 1715.[58] The Hudson Bay Company's standard of trade through most of the eighteenth century hovered around 1 to 1.5 ounces (28 to 42 grams) of vermilion per beaver skin. To put this in perspective, a list of the value of various goods traded by the Hudson's Bay Company in 1749 indicates that a beaver skin could buy a full pound (450 grams) of heads, gunpowder, shot, or thread.[59] [. . .]

* * *

The impact of the introduction of vermilion on Indigenous customs is exceedingly difficult to ascertain. Evidence of ochre use for a variety of ceremonial purposes, including face and body painting, through the nineteenth century and in a limited context to this day, is abundant in the ethnographic record. Vermilion, it is plain, did not entirely replace ochre. The high cost of the imported pigment, like the fact that some groups lived at a great distance from trading posts and maintained relatively little contact with outside traders, may explain why ochre continued to be used. In addition, it is tempting to think that notwithstanding the oft-stated Indigenous preference for the vibrant hues of vermilion, some individuals and communities continues to prefer ochre because they could control the ritual dimensions of its extraction and thus maintain a relationship with the supernatural forces that inhabited the landscape. Imported vermilion or red lead, because it was decontextualized from the environment, may in some ritual circumstances have seemed rather poor ersatz.

The high price of vermilion should not be measured only in economic terms, for the impact of mercury- and lead-based pigments on the health of their Aboriginal users gives cause for pause. From the earliest days of the cosmetics revival, the deleterious effects of these substances were a concern to specialists. By the second half of the eighteenth century, these effects were almost universally recognized in Europe. With respect to women's use of vermilion on their cheeks, Antoine Le Camus' *Abedeker, ou l'Art de conserver la beauté* (1754) explains that it is "very dangerous; for by using it frequently they may lose their Teeth, acquire a stinking Breath, and excite a copious Salivation."[60] It was in no small part due to the intervention of medical professionals that the popularity of white and red face paint underwent a sharp decline in favour of a more naturalistic aesthetic. Still, in distribution and trade of vermilion in North America continued unabated. Perhaps the missionaries and officials who sought at various times to dissuade their Aboriginal wards and allied from painting themselves evoked this argument, but if that is the case it left no trace in the record. Only in 1902 do we find a Commissioner of Indian Affairs, William A. Jones, attributing "the majority of the cases of blindness among the Indians of the United States" to face painting in an attempt to bring about its end in the country's reservations.[61]

It was during the nineteenth and early twentieth centuries, rather than the seventeenth or sixteenth, that the most fundamental transformation of Aboriginal cosmetic culture occurred. On the one hand, the prized vermilion became more affordable and a wide variety of new pigments were introduced to the inventories of traders: Prussian blue, yellow lead chromate, green chromium oxide, ivory black or bone char, and zinc oxide of Chinese white.[62] On the other, new power dynamics undermined political and cultural autonomy as never before. In the years that followed the War of 1812, as the strategic importance of allied warriors waned, the British and American governments ceased to distribute presents of arms, ammunition, and other accessories of war among which vermilion had featured prominently until then. Warrior culture, for which imperial powers vying against one another had found uses in the seventeenth and eighteenth centuries, now represented a threat to the stability and progress of the American and British (later Canadian) nations in their westward expansion.

The nineteenth-century institution of reservations and increasingly rigid civilizing policies of the state allowed missionaries and government officials an unprecedented repressive power. The naturalistic shift taken by Western cosmetic culture left little room for the tolerance of Indigenous face- and body-painting customs, nor did the rising concern with hygiene. Missionaries now objected to these customs with reviewed vigour. Though vermilion continued to be traded well into the twentieth century to serve in various crafts, its use on the body was discouraged. Traders operating on many reservations were instructed not to sell pigments that could be used for face or body paint. At Metlakala in British Columbia, the factor was told that "No red paint or other articles of heathenism were to be offered for sale."[63] Painted peoples were now seen as belonging to the past.

NOTES

1. Julia Tavares, *Guide to Caribbean Prehistory* (Santo Domingo: Museo del Hombre Dominicano, 1978), 15–16; Lesley-Gail Atkinson, *The Earliest Inhabitants: The Dynamics of the Jamaican Taino* (Kingston, Jamaica: University of the West Indies Press, 2006), 148–9.

2. Edward Gaylord Bourne, ed., *Narratives of the Career of Hernando de Soto in the Conquest of Florida* (New York: Barnes, 1904), vol. 1, 108, 113; vol. 2, 56, 136.

3. Ingeborg Marshall, *A History of Ethnography of the Beothuk* (Montreal: McGill-Queen's University Press, 1998), 14–24.

4. James P. Howley seems to have been among the first to conclude, without supporting evidence, that the fifteenth-century explorers of Newfoundland called the locals "red," a claim which was repeated by the authoritative *Handbook of North American Indians*. See James P. Howley, *The Beothuks or Red Indians: The Original Inhabitants of Newfoundland* (Cambridge: Cambridge University Press, 1915), 2–3, 10; and Barrie Reynolds, "Beothuk," in William C. Sturtevant and Bruce G. Trigger, eds, *Handbook of North America Indians* (Washington,

DC: Smithsonian Institution, 1978–2008), vol. 15, 101, 107.

5. John Brickell, *The Natural History of North-Carolina* (Dublin: James Caron, 1737), 316. See also Joseph-François Lafitau, *Customs of the American Indians Compared with Customs of Primitive Times* (Toronto: Champlain Society, 1977), vol. 2, 32.

6. John Smith, *Generall Historie of Virginia, New England, & the Summer Isles* (Glasgow: James MacLehose and Sons, 1907), vol. 1, 55, 71, 76.

7. Ernst E. Wreschner, "Red Ochre and Human Evolution: A Case for Discussion," and Comments and Reply by Ralph Bolton, Karl W. Butzer, Henri Delporte, Alexander Häusler, Albert Heinrich, Anita Jacobson-Widding, Tadeusz Malinowski, Claude Masset, Sheryl F. Miller, Avraham Ronen, Ralph Solecki, Peter H. Stephenson, Lynn L. Thomas, Heinrich Zollinger, all in *Current Anthropology* 21, 5 (October 1980): 631–44; Erella Hovers et al., "An Early Case of Color Symbolism: Ochre Use by Modern Humans in Qafzeh Cave," *Current Anthropology* 44, 4 (August–October 2003): 491–522; Chris Knight, *Blood Relations, Menstruation and the Origin of Culture* (New Haven: Yale University Press, 1991), 435–49; Rebecca Morris, "A Shroud of Ochre: A Study of Pre-Contact Mortuary Ochre Use in North America" (unpublished Master's thesis, University of Leicester, 2007).

8. Michael D. Stafford et al., "Digging for the Color of Life: Paleoindian Red Ochre Mining at the Powars II Site, Platte County, Wyoming, U.S.A.," *Geoarchaeology* 18, 1 (2003): 71–90; D.C. Roper, "Plans Paleoindians Red Ochre Use and Its Possible Significance," *Current Research in the Pleistocene* 4 (1987): 82–4; D.C. Roper, "A Comparison of Contexts of Red Ochre Use in Paleoindian and Upper Paleolithic Sites," *North American Archaeologist* 12, 4 (1991): 289–301; D.C. Roper, "Variability in the Use of Ochre in the Paleoindian Period," *Current Research in the Pleistocene* 13 (1996): 40–2; Robert E. Ritzenthaler and George I. Quimby, "The Red Ochre Culture of the Upper Great Lakes and the Adjacent Areas," *Fieldiana Anthropology* 36, 11 (March 1962): 243–75; Morris, "A Shroud of Ochre."

9. On ochre as a healing agent, see Joseph Velo, "Ochre as Medicine: A Suggestion for the Interpretation of the Archaeological Record," *Current Anthropology* 25, 5 (1984): 674; A.R. Piele, "Colours that Cure," *Hemisphere* 23, 4 (1979): 214–17.

10. Brent Berlin and Paul Kay, *Basic Color Terms: Their Universality and Evolution* (Stanford CA: CSLI 1999).

11. Victor W. Turner, "Colour Classification in Ndembu Ritual," in Michael Banton, ed., *Anthropological Approaches to the Study of Religion* (New York: Praeger, 1966), 80–1; Knight, *Blood Relations*.

12. Paul Proulx, "Algic Color Terms," *Anthropological Linguistics* 30, 2 (Summer 1988): 135–49; Jean-Andre Cuoq, *Lexique de la langue Iroquoise* (Montreal: J. Chapleau, 1882), 33.

13. Johann Georg Kohl. *Kitchi-gami: Life among the Lake Superior Ojibway* (London: Chapman & Hall, 1860).

14. Jean-François Lozier, "Rouge Amérique: Le toponyme vermillon au Canada et aux Etats-Unis," unpublished paper presented at the annual meeting of the Canadian Society for the Study of Natives, Montreal, May 2010.

15. Paul Douglas Campbell, *Earth Pigments and Paint of the California Indians* (Los Angeles: Sunbelt, 2007), 32; Julian Lips, *Naskapi Law* (Philadelphia: American Philosophical Society, 1947), 443, 485.

16. Stafford et al. "Digging," 88; Richard Slobodin, "Kutchin," in William C. Sturtevant and Bruce G. Trigger, eds, *Handbook of North American Indians* (Washington, DC: Smithsonian Institution, 1978–2008), vol. 6, 517; Lloyd James Dempsey, *Blackfoot War Art: Pictography of the Reservation Period 1880–2000* (Norman: University of Oklahoma Press, 2007), 44–5.

17. See for example Reuben Gold Thwaites, ed., *Maximilian, Prince of Wied's Travels in the Interior of North America, 1832–1834* (Cleveland: A.H. Clark, 1906), vol. 22, 328.

18. Andrew White, "*A Briefe Relation of the Voyage unto Maryland,*" in Clayton Colman Hall, ed., *Narrative of Early Maryland* [1633–1684] (New York: Charles Scribner's & Sons, 1910), 42–3; George Percy, "Discourse," in Philip L. Barbour, ed., *The Jamestown Voyages under the First Charter, 1606–1609* (Cambridge University Press, 1969), 1: 130; *JRAD,* vol. 38, 253.

19. Marshall, *History,* 287–8.

20. *JRAD*, vol. 38, 249. See also *JRAD*, vol. 5, 23; John Heckewelder, *History, Manners, and Customs of the Indian Nations who Once Inhabited Pennsylvania and the Neighboring States* (Philadelphia: Historical Society of Pennsylvania, 1876), 203–5.

21. Claude Charles Le Roy Bacqueville de La Potherie, *Histoire de l'Amerique Septentrionale* (Paris: Jean-Luc Nion et François Didot, 1722) vol. 3, 43–4; *JRAD*, vol. 38, 253; Brickell, *Natural History*, 316; *NYCD*, vol. 3, 714.

22. Brickell, 316; *JRAD*, vol. 41, 111–13.

23. Alfred W. Bowers, *Hidatsa Social and Ceremonial Organization*, Smithsonian Institution, Bureau of American Ethnology, Bulletin 194 (Washington, DC: Government Printing Office, 1965), 239.

24. Quoted by Sabine McCormac in Frank Salomon and Stuart B. Schwartz, *The Cambridge History of the Native Peoples of the Americas: South America* (Cambridge: Cambridge University Press, 1999), vol. 1, 149.

25. Lafitau, *Customs*, vol. 2, 38.

26. Augustine of Hippo, *De doctrina christiana: On Christian Doctrine* (New York: Macmillan, 1958), 150, 157.

27. Jacques Pinset and Yvonne Deslandres, *Histoire des soins de beauté* (Paris: Presses Universitaires de France, 1960), 44–8; also see Denis Menjot, ed., *Les soins de beauté : Moyen Age— début des temps modernes. Actes du IIIe Colloque international, Grasse (26–28 avril 1985)* (Nice: Centre d'Etudes médiévales, 1987).

28. Quoted in E. Rodocanachi, *La femme italienne à l'époque de la Renaissance: Sa vie privée et mondaine, son influence sociale* (Paris: Hackette, 1907), 106.

29. Catherine Lanoë, *La poudre et le fard. Une histoire des cosmétiques de la renaissance aux Lumières* (Seyssel: Champ Vallon, 2008); Carroll Camden, *The Elizabethan Woman* (New York: Appel, 1952), 175–215; Neville Williams, *Powder and Paint: A History of the Englishwoman's Toilet* (London: Longmans, 1957); Farah Karim-Cooper, *Cosmetics in Shakespearean and Renaissance Drama* (Edinburgh: Edinburgh University Press, 2006); Jesús Terrón González, *Léxico de cosméticos y afeites en el Siglo de Oro* (Salamanca: Servicio de Publicaciones de la Universidad de Extremadura, 1990); Elizabeth Teresa Howe, "The Feminine Mistake: Nature, Illusion, and Cosmetics in the Siglo de Oro," *Hispania* 68, 3 (September 1985): 443–51.

30. John Marston, *The Malcontent*, ed. George K. Hunter (Manchester: Manchester University Press, 1988), 61–2.

31. James Cleland, *The Institution of a Young Nobleman* (Oxford: Barnes, 1607), 216; Annette Drew-Bear, *Painted Faces on the Renaissance Stage: The Moral Significance of Face-Painting Conventions* (Cranbury: Associated University Presses, 1994), 29–31, 73–82, 118; Frances E. Dolan, "Taking the Pencil Out of God's Hand: Art, Nature, and the Face-Painting Debate in Early Modern England," *PMLA* 108, 2 (March 1993): 224–39.

32. On the production of cosmetics in the early modern period, see Catherine Lanoë, *La poudre et le fard* and "La céruse dans la fabrication des cosmétiques sous l'Ancien Régeme (XVIe–XVIIIe siècles)," *Techniques and Cultures* 38 (2002), http://tc.revues.org/index224.html, accessed 15 January 2010; Moraig Martin, *Selling Beauty: Cosmetics, Commerce, and French Society, 1750–1830* (Baltimore: Johns Hopkins University Press, 2009).

33. Horace Walpole, *Letters of Horace Walpole, Earl of Orford, to Sir Horace Mann* (Philadelphia: Lea & Blanchard, 1844), vol. 2, 402.

34. George R. Potter and Evelyn M. Simpson, eds, *The Sermons of John Donne* (Berkeley: University of California Press, 1955), vol. 2, 343; Richard Brathwait, *Ar't asleepe Husband? A Boulster Lecture* (London: R. Bishop, 1640); Thomas Tuke, *A Treatise against Painting and Tincturing of Men and Women* (London: Tho. Creed and Barn. Allsope, 1616).

35. Drew-Bear, *Painted Faces,* 102.

36. Dolan, "Taking the Pencil," 229.

37. Lanoë, *La poudre et le fard* and "La ceruse"; Martin, *Selling Beauty,* 73–96; Howe, "The Feminine Mistake."

38. Lanoë, *La poudre et le fard* and "La ceruse"; Martin, *Selling Beauty,* 73–116; Rodocanachi, *La femme italienne,* 107.

39. William Strachey, *The Historie of Travell into Virginia Britania,* Louis B. Wright and Virginia Freund, eds (London: Hakluyt Society, 1953), 70–1.

40. Lafitau, *Customs*, vol. 2, 41.

41. Williams, *Key*, 192–3.

42. *JRAD*, vol. 18, 153; *JRAD*, vol. 29, 129; *JRAD*, vol. 59, 231.

43. *JRAD*, vol. 60, 93.

44. Quoted in Tracy Brown, "Tradition and Change in Eighteenth-Century Pueblo Indian Communities," *Journal of the Southwest* 46, 3 (Autumn 2004): 468–9.

45. Ibid.

46. *A Treaty between his Excellency . . . George Clinton . . . And the Six . . . Nations* (New York: James Parker, 1746), 8; Timothy J. Shannon's "Dressing for Success on the Mohawk Frontier: Hendrick, William Johnson, and the Indian Fashion," *The William and Mary Quarterly*, 3rd ser., 53 (January 1996): 13–42.

47. John Warner Barber, *The History and Antiquities of New England, New York, New Jersey, and Pennsylvania* (Hartford: H.S. Parsons & Co. 1842), 389; Bruce E. Johansen, *The Native Peoples of North America: A History* (Westport, CT: Praeger, 2005), vol. 2, 169–71.

48. *JRAD*, vol. 38, 253. Compare, tentatively with *JRAD*, vol. 4, 205.

49. Lafitau, *Customs,* vol. 2, 32 (retranslated by author).

50. Peter Kalm, *Travels into North America* (Barre: Imprint Society, 1972), 491.

51. *NYCD*, vol. 9, 220; Bacqueville de La Potherie, *Histoire,* vol. 1, 365; vol. 3, 43; Louis Armand de Lom d'Arce de Lahontan, *Mémoires de l'Amerique septentrionale en la ou la suite des voyages de M. le baron de Lahontan* (La Haye: Fréres l'Honoré, 1704), 70.

52. Jacques Savary de Brûlons and Philémon-Louis Savary, *Dictionnaire universel de commerce d'histoire naturelle & des arts* (Copenhagan: Claude Philibert, 1765), vol. 5, 879, 848.

53. Rutherford J. Gettens et al., "Vermilion and Cinnabar," *Studies in Conservation* 17, 2 (May 1972): 47–8; Pamela H. Smith, "Vermilion, Mercury, Blood, and Lizards: Matter and Meaning in Metalworking," in Ursula Klein and E.C. Spary, eds, *Materials and Expertise in Early Modern Europe Between Market and Laboratory* (Chicago: University of Chicago Press, 2010), 29–49.

54. A.F.E. Van Schendel, "Manufacture of Vermilion in Seventeenth-Century Amsterdam: The Pekstok Papers," *Studies in Conservation* 17, 2 (May 1972): 70–82.

55. Gettens et al., "Vermilion and Cinnabar," 50, *Encyclopédie méthodique* (Paris: Panckoucke, and Liège: Plomteux, 1789), vol. 6, 764; Jacques Accarias de Serionne, *La richesse de la Holland : Ouvrage dans lequel on expose l'origine du commerce & de la puissance des Hollandois . . .* (London: Compagnie [de Indes orientales], 1778), vol. 1, 66; Théodore Château, *Technologie du bâtiment spécialement destiné aux ingénieurs, architectes . . .* (Paris: A. Morel, 1866), vol. 2, 625.

56. William Henry Pulsifer, *Notes for a History of Lead* (New York: D. Van Nostrand, 1888), 56, 74, 276–83; David John Rowe, *Lead Manufacturing in Britain: A History* (Beckenham: Associate Lead, 1983), 5–18.

57. François-Xavier Garneau, *Histoire du Canada depuis sa découverte jusqu'à nos jours* (Quebec: P. Lamoureax, 1859), vol. 2, 153.

58. Review of Duclos' report by the Conseil de la Marine, September 1716, Archives nationales (France), Archives de la Colonie, C13A 4, fol. 271.

59. Elizabeth Mancke, *A Company of Businessmen: The Hudson's Bay Company and Long-Distance Trade, 1670–1730* (Winnipeg: Rupert's Land Research Centre, 1988), 56; *A Short State of the Countries and Trade of North America Claimed by the Hudson's Bay Company* (London: J. Robinson, 1749), 25–6.

60. Antonie Le Camus, *Abdeker au l'Art de conserver la beauté* (Paris: 1754) 82; Solange Simon-Mazoyer, "Le conflit entre les excès de la mode et de la santé au XVIIIe siècle, 'L'habillage' du visage," in Vincent Barra and Micheline Louis-Courvoisier, eds, *La médecine des Lumières Tout autour de Tissot* (Geneva: Georg, 2001), 41–53; Martin, *Selling Beauty*, 67–117.

61. Charles F. Lummis, "In the Lion's Den," *Out West* 16, 2 (February 1902): 189–91.

62. John Wesley Powell, *Fourth Annual Report of the Bureau of Ethnology, 1882–1883* (Washington, DC: Government Printing Office, 1886), 52.

63. Jean Usher, *William Duncan of Metlakatla: A Victorian missionary in British Columbia* (Ottawa: National Museums of Canada, 1974), 43, 67.

Chapter 2

Missionaries and Indigenous People

READINGS

Primary Documents

1 From *The Jesuit Relations and Allied Documents: Travels and Explorations of the Jesuit Missionaries in New France, 1610–1791*, Reuben Gold Thwaites, ed.

2 From *Word from New France: The Selected Letters of Marie de l'Incarnation*, Joyce Marshall, ed.

Historical Interpretations

3 From *Harvest of Souls: The Jesuit Missions and Colonialism in North America, 1632–1650*, Carole Blackburn

4 From *Bitter Feast: Amerindians and Europeans in Northeastern North America, 1600–1664*, Denys Delâge

INTRODUCTION

With the French determination to stay and colonize a corner of North America came a determination to make the Indigenous people living in what came to be called New France into faithful Christians. The belief system that had conquered Europe and had also led its faithful into battle during the Middle Ages was, by the mid-sixteenth century, undergoing its own crisis in the form of the Protestant Reformation. The Jesuit order that emerged as one of Catholicism's weapons during the struggle was well-suited (at least in the eyes of church leaders) to undertake missionary work in the new world. After their arrival in the early 1610s, the Jesuits and other orders took some time to set their missionary work in motion, not really becoming effective until the 1630s. Part of the problem for them was that the French colonial claim to the region was not yet at its strongest.

We include one primary source, the *Jesuit Relations*, which has been the richest account of the Jesuits' work. In the *Relations*, essentially a massive collection of reports, the missionaries reflect upon the successes and failures in their work, and try to describe some of the characteristics of life among a wide variety of Indigenous peoples. Their contact with the Huron, or Wendat, people was especially significant, as disease and the Wendat alliance with the French and Jesuits would result in the nation's destruction and dispersal by 1650.

The other primary source comes from the same era, but from a member of a female order, the Ursulines. The Ursulines arrived in Quebec in 1639. Their initial objectives were to convert and educate Indigenous girls. In order to do so, they opened the first learning institution in New France shortly after landing in the colony. Their convent soon afterward began to provide education to the daughters of the French colonists. The Ursulines eventually also provided care for the sick. As Roman Catholic nuns, the Ursulines took great pleasure in the news of religious conversions among Indigenous people.

We have scant evidence of suspicion among these missionaries that their work may have been harming its targets. Why would they doubt the faith when having faith in its eternal truth was part of their "job description"? The historical interpretations, looking into the records of these missionary groups, cast a different light on the interaction between missionaries and Indigenous peoples, interpreting the presence of missionaries as a disruption to the livelihoods and long-term physical and psychological or spiritual health of these societies. In her article, Carole Blackburn focuses on the resistance offered by the Hurons to the missionaries. For his part, Denis Delâge explains the reasons that led some Hurons to convert.

As you read the historical interpretations included here, try to hold these two perspectives in mind: the missionaries' eagerness to deliver salvation and the often tragic results of that effort. It is a theme that would be repeated much closer to our own time.

QUESTIONS FOR CONSIDERATION

1. The simplest and most obvious answer to the question "What motivated the missionaries?" is probably "faith." Is there a better answer—one that addresses missionaries' earthly goals for the Indigenous people they lived with?
2. What aspects of Indigenous life did those who compiled the *Jesuit Relations* consider worthy of their attention? Why?
3. Why do you think missionaries needed to live for extended periods among Indigenous people? Could they just have visited once in a while?
4. What might have led the Huron/Wendat to distrust the missionaries among them?
5. What might have led the Huron/Wendat to believe that a higher power favoured the missionaries?

SUGGESTIONS FOR FURTHER READING

Carole Blackburn, *Harvest of Souls: The Jesuit Missions and Colonialism in North America, 1632–1650* (Montreal and Kingston: McGill-Queen's University Press, 2000).

Robert Englebert and Guillaume Teasdale, eds, *French and Indians in the Heart of North America, 1630–1815* (Winnipeg: University of Manitoba Press, 2013).

Allan Greer, *Mohawk Saint: Catherine Tekakwitha and the Jesuits* (New York: Oxford University Press, 2005).

Kathryn Magee Labelle, *Dispersed But Not Destroyed: A History of the Seventeenth-Century Wendat People* (Vancouver: UBC Press, 2013).

Francis Parkman, *The Jesuits in North America in the Seventeenth Century* (many editions).

Jon Parmenter, *Edge of the Woods: Iroquoia: 1534–1701* (Winnipeg: University of Manitoba Press, 2014).

Thomas Peace and Kathryn Labelle, eds, *From Huronia to Wendakes: Adversity, Migration, and Resilience, 1650–1900* (Norman: University of Oklahoma Press, 2016).

Reuben Gold Thwaites, ed., *The Jesuit Relations and Allied Documents: Travels and Explorations of the Jesuit Missionaries in New France, 1610–1791* (73 vol. in 35) (New York: Pageant Books, 1959).

Bruce Trigger, *The Children of Aataentsic: A History of the Huron People to 1660* (Montreal and Kingston: McGill-Queen's University Press, 1976).

Primary Documents

1 From *The Jesuit Relations and Allied Documents: Travels and Explorations of the Jesuit Missionaries in New France, 1610–1791*, Reuben Gold Thwaites, ed. (Cleveland: Burrows, 1898), 103–21.

CHAPTER VII. OF THE HURONS WHO WINTERED AT QUEBEC AND SILLERY

The Seminary of the Hurons, which had been established at nostre-Dame des Anges some Years ago, in order to educate children of that nation, was interrupted for good reasons, and especially because no notable fruit was seen among the Savages; our experience in beginning the instruction of a people with the children, has made us recognize this fact. Here is an occasion which has obliged us to reëstablish a Seminary in a new fashion, as it were,—but easier, and in behalf of persons, older, and more capable of instruction. God grant that the incursions of the Hiroquois may not hinder us from continuing.

[104] A young man, of those who had formerly been at the first Seminary of the Hurons at Nostre Dame des Anges, happening to be in a great storm, in the midst of their great lake, made a vow to God, if he escaped, to lead a more regular and orderly life. His vow is heard,—he is delivered, contrary to every human probability; he goes to find our Fathers who were with the Hurons, and imparts to them his vow and his resolution. They think thereon; they deliberate; they finally resolve to take him out of his own country, where he was in greater danger, and to send him down here, so that he should be better aided, and that he might see the example of the French and of the Algonquins of Sillery. They gave him for companion another Huron young man, who desired to become a Christian;

both these arrived at Sillery last year, in the month of September. It was on that occasion that I again detained Father Jean de Brebeuf, who had wintered here in the preceding year, and who had not yet gone up again, in order to instruct them and to take charge of them. Several other Huron young men, who had come down to trade, presented themselves [105] also to us, in order to be received and instructed; but, the scanty provisions that we have not permitting us to admit any more, part of them were constrained to return to their own country, and the others, to join the Algonquins in order to go during the winter to the hunt or to the war with them.

Nevertheless, the charity of Monsieur the Governor and of the Hospital Mothers has given us means to add three to the first two, and to baptize those with us who were not baptized. With the help that I have mentioned, we have lodged and maintained four of them, and toward the Spring, a sixth, who came unexpectedly. Generally speaking, all have greatly edified us; they were always among the first at Mass and at prayers, and were the last to leave, both at evening and in the morning. They failed not to say their prayers, quite long, on both knees, whether they were at home or hunting in the woods. Several times in the day they went to the Chapel, to pray to God and salute the blessed Sacrament; they would take care not to begin anything [106] without having first made the sign of the Cross. All, since their baptism, have not failed to Confess themselves and receive Communion at least every Sunday; and several of them went to Confess themselves as soon as they thought they had committed any notable fault. Throughout the winter, they went every Sunday to Quebec, in order to attend high Mass, from which they have not been absent, whatever the state of the weather,— although the distance is about two leagues, and though they were usually obliged to start before daylight, during the rigor of the winter; but the desire of pleasing God, and

the satisfaction that they received in seeing the devotion of our French, assembled in the Church, caused them to find nothing difficult. Moreover, the peace and unity in which they have lived together, and with our French and the Algonquin Savages, and the services which they willingly rendered, showed well enough what the power of faith and of the divine grace can do when it has gained possession of even Savage hearts. The foregoing is what was common to all; here follows what is individual. The one who [107] gave occasion for the whole enterprise is a certain Armant Andewaraken, who has aided not a little, by his deeds and his words, in the instruction of the others, and in encouraging them to do well. Our Lord has imparted to him, at intervals, great desires for his salvation,—and sometimes even to forsake the world and to enter into Religion, which he knows very well, and separates from the common life; but it requires a long probation,—to be a Savage and to be a Religious are things which seem very repugnant; nevertheless, the grace of God, and time, will avail to compass everything. This young man came one day of last Winter to find Father Brebeuf, at the end of his Mass, and spoke to him as follows: "My Father, I have great desire to do right and to save myself; I have wholly resolved that, for I fear those fires which burn incessantly beneath the earth, and which are never extinguished. In order to attain what I desire, I would like to live always with you, and not return to the Hurons, where there is great difficulty in saving oneself,—the opportunities for sin are frequent in our villages, [108] and the liberty in them is great. I am nevertheless determined to obey, and to do everything which the Father Superior shall order. If he commanded me to go to the Hyroquois, I would go very willingly, without any escort; and even if he commanded me to cast myself, at the loss of life, into this river which passes yonder before us, I would do so at once." Thus he spoke, not looking at the thing which in itself is illicit, but simply at the command. "Moreover," he said, "let the Father Superior tell me what I ought to do; I am sure that it will be the will of God, and therefore I shall acquiesce therein. Archiendassé"—that is to say, Father Hierosme l'Allemant, who is Superior among the Hurons—"has addressed me to him. I know well that you have still other Superiors in France; but it is he who here takes the place of God, and who will tell me what I must do." The Father Superior sent him word that he greatly praised his design and his devotion; that he should persevere courageously; that we would always have a most special care for him; that, with reference to living down there with us, we would think of it, [109] and we would recommend the matter to God, and that he, on his part, should do the same. There was a consultation after prayers were done, and it was found best that he should return again to his own country,—that God-fearing, as he is, and assisted by our Fathers, this would be the best for him and for his fellow Countrymen. He has mightily applied himself to the mortification of his impulses and inclinations; often he felt himself prone to dispute, and sometimes he would grow angry at certain words; but straightway he would return to himself, and stop short in silence, remembering that he had resolved to do right. One day, having had some difference with one of our Frenchmen, he not only went straightway to Confess, but he went to ask pardon of the one whom he had offended, embracing him tenderly; and since then he has rendered him all the services in his power.

The first to profit by these examples has been a young man named Saouaretchi, who had come down with him; he is of an excellent disposition,—gentle, peaceable, obedient, industrious,—and endowed with a good mind, by means of which he has quickly [110] learned all the prayers. He was baptized on Christmas eve, in the Chapel of the Ursuline Mothers, and named Ignace, by Monsieur Martial Piraube. On the very night of that great Feast, he received his first Communion; and since that time he has always continued to confess himself and receive Communion every Sunday, with much devotion: his desire to be instructed has notably appeared in this point. His comrades, toward the beginning of Lent, having taken the resolution to go hunting for the Moose, he said that, for his part, he would not go; and that he had not come from so far in order to go hunting, but in order to know God, and learn to serve him, and that he made account of no other thing than that; that it was this which he aspired to carry away at his return, and not skins of Moose, or other things. His particular devotion has been to fast every Saturday, in order to prepare himself for Sunday Communion, and for the prompt performance of all that was commanded him. The Baptism of this young man causes us to hope for the Conversion of many others; [111] for, besides that he is very exemplary and very zealous, he belongs to one of the largest and most numerous families of the Hurons, which already is thoroughly attached to the faith, and which awaits, it seems, only the Baptism of this young man in order to plunge after him into those blessed waters.

About the middle of January, one of the other Hurons, who had gone to live among the Algonquins of the Island, and who until then had remained with them near the fort of Richelieu, came down to Sillery, expressly to be instructed in the faith. The village of which he is native is named Arrente,[1] and he is nephew to one of the Captains; but what commends him still more, is his extreme gentleness and docility in every respect. He has very good wit and judgment; mild and thoroughly obedient.

The Hospital Mothers have lodged and fed him, with a charity which embraces all sorts of nations. It is remarkable how much satisfaction he has given them in all the services which have been desired of him; these he has rendered with a cheerfulness, promptness, and constancy that [112] would cause shame to many Frenchmen. His affection toward the faith has made itself noteworthy,—not only in that he constantly came, evening and morning, to find the Father, in order to be instructed; but also in that, having been instructed in some new prayer or lesson, he would repeat and meditate upon it, and that so much and so long, that he knew it before going away. Hence there was no need of telling him the same thing twice over. He failed not to go into the Chapel of the Hospital every evening and every morning, in order to say his prayers there; and stayed there a good space of time. He was baptized at the Hospital, the 8th of March, and was named Pierre by Monsieur de Repentigny, who since then has ever shown him much affection.

About the middle of February, two other Huron young men—natives of the same village as the preceding, and impelled by the same desire to have themselves enrolled in the number of the Christians—also abandoned the Algonquins at the fort of Richelieu, in order to come in quest of Father de Brebeuf, so as to be instructed by him. [113] We received them, moreover, at our abode; for want of room we were constrained to lodge them with our workmen; one was named Atarohiat, and the other, Atokouchiouani. The longing to be baptized as soon as possible, so greatly kindled in them the desire to be instructed, that they had learned all the prayers and the Catechism in a very little while; and one of them, moved with this vehement desire to learn, was not willing to divert himself by going to the hunt with his Comrades, saying: "The time that we have for staying here is too short: I desire to employ it in obtaining instruction; and then, besides, I have not the happiest memory in the world. I have not come down here to go hunting; and, as for eating meat, if I had cared to eat any, I had only to stay with the Algonquins up there at Richelieu, where the hunt is much better than here."

Seeing that they knew the prayers well, they requested Baptism so ardently,—saying, among other things, that they feared lest, going often into the woods, upon the waters, and into other dangerous places, there might happen to them some misfortune,—[114] that finally it was granted them. It was in the Church of Quebec where they were baptized, very solemnly, the day of the Annunciation of our Lady, when they also received Communion for the first time, according to the custom of the Church. Monsieur de saint Sauveur[2] gave the name of Joseph to Atarohiat; and Monsieur de la Vallée, that of René to Atokouchiouani.

I have said that they had been baptized as solemnly as possible,—and this designedly, because that has much effect upon the minds of the Savages, and is to them, not a slight incentive to belief. To this end, after the baptism of these two latter, Father de Brebeuf—having led all the Hurons before Monsieur the Governor, in order to thank him for so much kindness and honor as he did them—asked them in his presence, all in succession, what that is which touched them the most, and most inclined them to embrace the faith. The first said, that what struck him chiefly was, to consider the omnipotence of God, with whom nothing is impossible; and to think of the [115] marvelous works which he has done, from the beginning of the world,—as, to have drawn so many creatures out of nothing; to have caused the children of Israel to pass through the red sea with dry feet; to have fed them with the Manna for the space of forty years; to have satisfied several thousand persons with five loaves and two fishes; to have raised Lazarus from the dead, four days after death; and countless other like wonders.

Another said that what touched him very strongly was, to see men and Religious maids leave their own country, where they were much at their ease, and without danger, in order to come to places where there is nothing but dangers and incredible

inconveniences,—and all that in order to instruct them, and win them to God.

But the most part answered that what mainly attracted their attention was, to see all that was done to honor God. "When we see," said they, "every one assemble here on Sundays and Feasts, in order to hear the Mass and to pray to God; when we see Confessions and frequent Communions, [116] observed with so much devotion; when we consider what is done for the Savages,—how fields are prepared for them, how houses are built for them, how they are assisted in body and soul,—that is what makes us say that faith is something important, and that what you teach is true." Toward Spring there arrived a sixth, who had been baptized in passing through Montreal, together with some Algonquins. He lodged, as a rule, at the Hospital, with Pierre, his Comrade, and tried to compensate with his fervor for the little time that he should have, and to become instructed before his Baptism. He has given every sort of contentment to Father Brebeuf, in the short time that he could have him for his Teacher. Such has been the status of our five or six Huron boarders, who no doubt would be more numerous if the means were greater. Howbeit, one thing has caused them fear and given them pain,—to wit, the return to their country; "For," they said, "while we shall be here among you, it [117] is hardly possible for us to offend God, seeing so many good examples of virtue, and no vices: but in our own country, it is quite the contrary,—one knows not what it is to do right; it is a chaos of confusion and of disorder." "And then,"

said the one last baptized, "there is as yet scarcely any one in our village, or in those round about, who has solidly embraced the faith. We are the first and the only ones." Thus they spoke, and represented the danger wherein they believed themselves to be, of offending the divine Majesty. In fact, they have just cause to fear, and we also; and if, indeed, some one of them should happen to stumble, we must not be surprised. Nevertheless, we hope in the divine goodness that it will preserve them, and that it will perfect what it has begun. They all went away toward the middle of June, in order to return to their own country, in the company of about six-score other Hurons, who had come for trade. This plan of Seminary is easy, and can be realized at small expense, and is excellent,—choosing a number of young men, of twenty [118] or twenty-five years, of good will and good intelligence, and training them one Autumn and one Winter among our French and our Algonquin Christians; causing them to see and to taste the profession of Christianity among us, and among people of their very country; and then sending them away, under the Guard and the guidance of our Fathers who are with the Hurons. But I know not whether the rage of the Hiroquois will not deprive us of this consolation; and them, of so great a good fortune. If the Hurons were won over, the nation of the Neutrals, and others neighboring, would hardly be slow to follow. The Hurons who have come for trade have told us that these who are being instructed are, at present, the principal men of the country.

NOTES

1. For location of Arent (Aronte), vol. x, *note* 23.
2. Jean le Sueur, a secular priest, came to Canada in 1634, with Giffard (vol. vi, *note* 8); his other title was derived from a parish in Normandy, which he had served, Saint Sauveur de Thury. In 1645–46, he was missionary at Côte de Beaupré, and later officiated in the chapel at Côteau Ste. Genevieve. In March 1646, he became joint proprietor, with Jean Bourdon, of the fief St. Francis (vol. xi, *note* 11). *The Journ. des Jesuits* frequently mentions him, up to 1660. One of the suburbs of Quebec is named St. Sauveur, for this priest.

2   From *Word from New France: The Selected Letters of Marie de l'Incarnation*, Joyce Marshall, ed. (Toronto: Oxford University Press, 1967), 122–6, 387–8. Copyright © Oxford University Press Canada 1970. Reprinted by permission of the publisher.

17. NEWS OF JOGUES

TO HER SON.

Quebec, 30 SEPTEMBER 1643

My very dear and well-loved son:

May the love and life of the King of nations consume your heart with the ardour with which he transports the hearts of our converts.

You ought now to have received the letters I wrote to you in the month of July last and in which I gave you a brief account of what happened last year in New France and in the new Church of Jesus Christ. [. . .]

But I must not waste time; let us begin to speak of our converts. The first foundations of the Church have been laid this year at Miscou,[1] which is a French settlement solely for traffic in furs. Ten leagues beyond the settlement, a chapel has been built and a large mission established for the Savages to the north, who have been drawn to the Faith by the conversation of our Montagnais Savages from Tadoussac. This mission promises great fruit, for the material is ready. It is about a hundred and fifty leagues from here, going in your direction.

A hundred leagues to this side of it is the Tadoussac mission, where marvels have been seen this year, a great many Savages, who live more than twenty days' journey by land away, having come there to be instructed and then baptized. They have such religious sentiments and perform such Christian acts that they make us ashamed and surpass us in piety. This is the fruit of the zeal of our good settled Christians, for they go in one direction and the other expressly to win souls to Jesus Christ. All these nations are from the regions to the north; and Tadoussac, where they assemble, is forty leagues or thereabouts from here, going towards Miscou.

Sillery is one league above Quebec and we are midway.[2] Some of our settled Savages are at Sillery and the others at Quebec, where trade is carried on.

Last year the Attikamegue nation came here to be instructed and more than half of them were baptized. The first baptism was held in our church, and the first marriage also, for when a man and woman are baptized they are at the same time united before the Church. Several others were afterwards baptized and married. I must confess that the joy my heart feels when I see a soul washed with the blood of Jesus Christ cannot be expressed.

These good people were instructed every day in our chapel. After Mass we made them a feast of peas or sagamite—Indian corn with dried plums—after which they spent almost all the day at our grille, to receive some instruction or learn some prayer. It was a prodigy to see with what promptness and facility they learned everything they were taught.

One poor woman, who had a slightly duller mind than the others, grew angry with herself and said as she prostrated herself, "I shall not get up, from this day, unless I know my prayers." She kept her mouth pressed against the ground all day and God so blessed her fervour that, when she arose, she knew everything she had wished to learn. Fervour is universal and we are overjoyed to see great men coming eagerly to see us so that we may teach them to make interior acts and jaculatory orisons, which they employ when required.

The chief of this nation was a great sorcerer and the most superstitious man alive. I listened to him uphold the virtue of his charms and superstitions, and soon afterwards he came to see the Father with whom he had disputed, bringing his charms and the drum he had used in his enchantments, and declared that he intended never to use them again. I am sending the drum to you so you may see how the devil beguiles and seduces this poor people with a child's device, for you will know that it is used to cure sickness, to predict things to come, and for similar extraordinary things. After this change of heart, we had the consolation of seeing all the drums of this nation sacrificed to God in a single day.

Later they all went back, hunting, to their own county [the upper St Maurice valley], so as to arrive there in the spring. And because they are newly instructed, one of our new Christian women of Sillery went with them in terrible snowy cold to make them repeat their prayers each day for fear they might forget them. We have learned that they are leading an admirable life.

It is a marvel to see the fervour of our good converts. They are not satisfied with believing in Jesus Christ, but their zeal so carries them away that they are not content and think they only half believe if all do not believe as they do. The chief of the Abnaki-ouois [Abenakis] left his country and his people to come to settle here so he could be instructed and afterwards win his people to the Faith of Jesus Christ. He was baptized yesterday and married to one of our seminarians, named Angèle, of whom the *Relations* spoke last year with great praise. His zeal will carry him even further for he is resolved to carry the Gospel into many other nations. "I shall not be content," he told me, "to bring my people and my young men to faith and prayer, but as I have been in several other nations and know their tongues, I shall make use of this advantage to go to visit them and bring them to believe in God."

It is not only the men that are on fire with this zeal. A Christian woman went to a very distant nation expressly to catechize those that live there and succeeded so well in this that she brought them all here, where they were baptized. She needed an apostolic courage to face the dangers to which she exposed herself in order to render this service

to Our Lord. We often see like fervour in our good converts who, to be quite truthful, put those that were born of Christian parents to shame.

There is no prominent person among the Hurons that does not wish to be a Christian. Four chapels have been built in their country this year and hitherto they would scarcely suffer one. The Iroquois, nevertheless, persecute this poor nation greatly. They captured and killed a great number of them two years ago and but a fortnight since they defeated their fleet again.[3]

You know that last year they captured the Reverend Father Jogues, some Frenchmen, and one of our seminarians. They killed the old men[4] and made captives of the others. The Reverend Father was beaten into insensibility and stripped naked upon his arrival in their country. His thumb was cut off and his index finger gnawed to the joint. The ends of his other fingers were burned and then he was made to suffer a thousand ignominies. As much was done to a Frenchman [Guillaume Couture], his domestic, and another [René Goupil], who was also in his service, had his head split by the blow of a hatchet.[5] The poor Father, believing that the same would be done to him, go down on his knees to receive the blow and offer his sacrifice, but nothing further was done to him. The same was done to the greater number of the captives as to the Father, and then all their lives were spared. Our seminarian, Thérèse, has suffered no injury and has courageously continued to profess the Holy Gospel and to pray in public. The Reverend Father is at present preaching the Gospel among the Iroquois; he is the first to have that honour, and God has so blessed his labour that he has baptized more than sixty persons in his captivity.[6]

I must speak a little of our seminarians, who give us all possible satisfaction.

One said to me a little while ago, "I often speak to God in my heart. I get great pleasure from naming Jesus and Mary. Ah, what beautiful names they are!"

We sometimes hear them conversing together about God and making spiritual colloquies. One day among others they were asking one another for what they believed they were most greatly obliged to God.

One said, "It is because he made himself a man for me and suffered death to deliver me from hell."

Another replied, "It is because he made me a Christian and placed me, by baptism, in the number of his children."

A little girl, who is but nine years old and has been receiving communion for a year and a half, raised her voice and said, "It is because Jesus gives himself to us as meat at the Blessed Sacrament of the altar."

Is this not delightful in girls born in barbarism?

They never fail to make their examination of conscience or to accuse one another of their offences, which they do with matchless simplicity. They sometimes ask to be punished so they can pay the penalty to God for their sins while they are still in this world.

When one of them had been punished, we asked her what she thought of the chastisement she had been given.

"I thought," she said, "that you must love me, since you punished me to bring me to my senses, for I have no sense yet. I, who have been instructed, am much much more guilty than my companion, who was not."

You see our employments. I beg you to be very mindful of the kingdom of Jesus Christ. Pray for the conversion of the Iroquois, who hinder it greatly and close the passages lest the more distant nations come here to be instructed. The Iroquet nation was not allowed to pass through the lands of these barbarians, who fired more than a hundred shots at them, but God so well protected them that there was not a single one of them wounded.[7]

I am writing to you at night because of the pressure of letters and the imminent departure of the vessels. My hand is so weary that I can scarcely govern it—it is this that makes me finish by begging you to excuse me if I do not reread my letter.

NOTES

1. The Jesuits had maintained two priests at Miscou—an island off the northeast coast of New Brunswick at the entrance to the Baie des Chaleurs—since 1634 for the benefit of the Frenchmen who came there in connection with the fur trade. Marie de l'Incarnation's use of the words "first foundations of the Church" refers to the building of the chapel and a mission devoted exclusively to the Indians.

2. The Ursulines had occupied their new monastery in the upper town of Quebec since 21 November 1642. It was situated just west of the fort and was the first building encountered by the Indians of Sillery as they came along rue Saint-Louis (Grande Allée). This is undoubtedly Marie de l'Incarnation's meaning, though her use of the word "milieu," middle, is somewhat ambiguous. At the time there was no direct access to Sillery from the lower town except by boat.

3. As the result of this most recent capture, of a fleet that was attempting to carry supplies to the Huron missions, the Jesuits in Huronia were deprived for the second year in a row of the necessities of food and clothing that they were accustomed to receive annually from Quebec.

4. According to Jogues's own account, only one old man had been killed.

5. Goupil was killed 29 September 1642 at Ossernenon (now Auriesville, New York), on the order of an old man, who was angered because Goupil had made the sign of the cross over a child. Couture was adopted by a Mohawk family to replace a dead relative, according to a common Indian custom.

6. News of these things had been brought to Quebec by Thérèse's uncle, Joseph Teondechoren, who had escaped with some of the other prisoners. Jogues himself had managed

to send a letter to France and to have others delivered to Quebec. Within weeks of his capture, Arendt van Corlaer, the Dutch commandant of Fort Orange (Albany, New York), had tried without success to ransom him from the Mohawks.

7. The *Relation* (JR XXIV) tells a different story. A group of Algonkian Iroquets, who had sought refuge at Montreal, was sent out to parley with some Iroquois that had approached the settlement. The Iroquois then fired upon them, though none of the Iroquets was injured. The Iroquets, who lived above Montreal between the St Lawrence and the Ottawa Rivers, had no occasion to traverse the Iroquois country.

Historical Interpretations

3   From Carole Blackburn, *Harvest of Souls: The Jesuit Missions and Colonialism in North America, 1632–1650* (Montreal and Kingston: McGill-Queen's University Press, 2004), 105–28, 153–5.

CONVERSION AND CONQUEST

The Jesuits hoped to promote the obedience and submission that was a necessary attribute of Christian life by reconfiguring Aboriginal social and political relationships. Conversion itself, however, and the Jesuits' ability to gain compliance most frequently occurred after a process of chastisement and humiliation that had been brought about by disease or the consequences of warfare. The Jesuits described the misfortunes that were increasingly experienced by Native people during the 1630s and 1640s as afflictions and crosses, and they wrote that these afflictions had an especially beneficial effect in inducing conversion and generating the humility and obedience that were appropriate to Christian behaviour. Le Jeune, for example, wrote that affliction "opens the eyes of the understanding" (14:183). He and other Jesuits argued that suffering was necessary in order to reduce the pride and independence that kept people from recognizing the necessity of submission and their obligations to God and the Jesuits. This understanding was pointedly expressed in the *Relation* for

the years 1642 and 1643, which stated: "Humiliations are the harbingers that mark the dwellings of the great God; and tribulation attracts us more strongly and with much more certainty than does comfort. It is necessary to abase the pride and the haughtiness of these people, in order to give admission to the faith" (25:39).

THE HAND THAT SMITES THEM

Shortly after the Jesuits arrived in Huron country, many of the villages were stricken with a disease of European origin. This was the first of a series of epidemics that further reduced the Huron population by almost half over a period of six years (Trigger 1987, 499). Although the Jesuits and other French also became ill during the initial epidemic, they recovered and remained relatively unaffected as the outbreaks of disease recurred. This was in sharp contrast to the inability of large numbers of Huron to withstand the diseases, and it suggested to many of them that the French had some effective means of prevention and cure. The Jesuits were accordingly asked to help stop the sickness—at which point, they took the opportunity to insist that all Huron pray and believe in God, presenting this as "the true and only means of turning away this scourge of heaven" (13:159). While many people were initially prepared to adopt the Jesuits' terms, most did not realize the exclusive nature of the priests' demands, and they continued to seek other remedies, leaving the Jesuits to accuse them of hypocrisy and backsliding (13:165, 177).

As the diseases continued unabated, the Jesuits' proposed cures were soon discredited, though most Huron continued to believe that the priests had the power to protect themselves from the illnesses—a belief that was reinforced when the Huron observed the Jesuits spending so much time with the sick yet remaining "full of life and health" (19:93). For the Huron, withholding assistance from someone who was ill violated community reciprocity, and as a sign of disregard for the welfare of others it could only be motivated by hostile intentions. Such behaviour was easily interpreted as a sign of complicity in a disease that had been caused by witchcraft, which was believed to be the most common cause of incurable illnesses and the most frequent expression of antisocial, hostile sentiments (Trigger 1987, 66–7). Although the residents of most Huron villages first sought to identify and eliminate possible witches among themselves, the majority came to the conclusion that the French, and particularly the Jesuits, were causing the diseases through sorcery.

This interpretation of the Jesuits as witches was encouraged by the priests' reputation as successful and potentially powerful supernatural practitioners. Evidence that the Jesuits possessed power had already been apparent in their success in praying for rain and their ability to predict lunar eclipses (15:139, 175), as well as by a number of the technologies they had brought from Europe. Brébeuf had been involved in a successful bid for rain during his first years with the Huron, before the English defeat of the French and the removal of the missionaries to France (10:43–9). This was not forgotten by those Huron who knew Brébeuf, and during the very dry spring and summer of 1635 they asked the Jesuits to pray for an end to the drought. The efforts of Huron *arendiwane* to do the same had been unsuccessful. One shaman in particular blamed the Jesuits for his failure and demanded, much to the chagrin of the priests, that they take down the cross they had erected in front of their cabin in Ihonatiria (10:37–43). The Jesuits not only refused to remove the cross but they twice enjoyed seeing their prayers and processions followed by a significant amount of rain, as well as by the admiration and respect of many people.

Suspicion about the Jesuits' involvement in the diseases also stemmed from the fact that most Huron did not completely understand the priests' intentions in wanting to live among them (17:125). While it was accepted that traders and warriors had occasion to live with allies or trading partners, the missionaries' evangelical purpose, based as it was on a universalist belief, had no precedent and consequently was open to local interpretation (Trigger 1987, 534). As the diseases spread, the Jesuits' teaching and habits were easily shaped into indisputable proof of hostile intentions and sinister activities, whose ultimate objective was the destruction of the Huron people.

This was particularly the case with behaviour that was culturally alien and either oddly inappropriate or more directly suggestive of the stinginess and unco-operative spirit which the Huron associated with witchcraft. The priests' habit of closing their door at certain times of the day for private meditation, for example, fell within the range of antisocial behaviour, and many Huron believed that the Jesuits needed this privacy in order to practice their sorcery (15:33). Their practice of speaking to those who were sick about death and the afterlife was similarly unusual and inappropriate (15:23, 69). Most people found the priests' continual references to death disturbing and morbid, and they suspected that the Jesuits were concerned not with an individual's recovery but solely with sending him or her to heaven. The Jesuits attempted to aid the sick as much as possible, hoping to advance the cause of Christianity by discrediting the cures offered by the shamans and setting an example of Christian charity (15:69). However, at the same time as they were diligently attempting to bring people some relief, their stern criticism of Native curing rites and their refusal to participate in them were viewed by most Huron as socially unco-operative behaviour and interpreted as further evidence that the priests actually wanted to prevent people from recovering. In this way, although the priests cast their behaviour in the benevolent idiom of Christian charity and sacrifice, the Huron interpreted it through the divergent idiom of harmful intent and sorcery. Some Huron even suggested that the Jesuits' wish to see them in heaven as soon as possible caused them to shorten the lives of those whom they felt were best prepared for the afterlife (19:241).

The unfamiliar material and technological features of the mission were similarly subject to interpretation by the Huron, who saw in them further evidence of the Jesuits' sorcery. The act of writing, especially, was subject to a variety of appropriations that challenged the Jesuits' own understanding and their expectation of its significance. Writing was the Jesuits' most potent technology, both as the source of their universal truths and because Native people admired their ability to communicate silently through pieces of marked paper. The Jesuits based much of their faith in the truth of Christianity and its universal relevance on the authority of their written tradition. In their attempt to persuade people to convert, they lost no opportunity to assert the value of the Bible as a written document containing the authentic and undistorted Word of God. They argued that while oral traditions were subject to the fallibility of memory and

the accumulation of lies and stories invented for the sake of entertainment, the basis of their own faith in the Word, not just spoken but recorded, was indisputable (11:153; 17:135). Le Jeune quickly identified the word used by the Montagnais to speak of the distant past, *nitatohokan*, as meaning "I relate a fable, I am telling an old story invented for amusement" (6:157). By comparison, when some Huron asked Brébeuf how the Jesuits "knew there was a Hell, and whence we obtained all that we told about the condition of the damned," he replied "that we had indubitable proofs of it, that we possessed it through divine revelation; that the Holy Ghost himself had dictated these truths to certain persons, and to our Ancestors, who had left them to us in writing, and that we still carefully preserved the books containing them" (13:51–3).[1]

The Jesuits' faith in the Bible as a written document was deeply embedded in an assumption that all truth and knowledge was textually dependent (Mignolo 1992, 318). The proof of God himself could be "read" in nature. As one of the priests explained, "The reality of a God was . . . so clear that it was only necessary to open the eyes to see it written in large characters upon the faces of all creatures" (13:173). I have already noted that the Jesuits' mission in New France depended, in large part, on an oral practice and that the early history of Christianity was itself strongly oral, relying on an oral praxis of preaching and teaching the Word. However, the Jesuits came to North America after the Renaissance, when an ideology of the letter had emerged which emphasized the primacy of writing as well as the physical form of the book itself, both as the essential repository of knowledge and as its principal means of transmission (Mignolo 1992, 311, 318). While Christ himself was originally the Word of God embodied (11:169), the authority of this Word came to be the authority of the Book. Indeed, in an especially interesting gloss on Christ's physical embodiment of textual authority, Le Jeune referred to Christ as "the living Book" (16:123). Writing, knowledge, and the material form of the book convened in an ideology and philosophy of writing that had considerable effect on interpretations of the New World and its peoples; the absence of a system of alphabetical writing quickly came to be interpreted as a sign of the absence of civilization and as evidence of the inferiority of New World peoples (Mignolo 1992, 317–18).

The priests knew that "the art of inscribing upon paper matters that are beyond sight" (15:121) visibly impressed the people they were trying to convert. Notes sent between Jesuits from one village to another caused the Native people to think that the priests could predict the future and read minds at a distance, something that only shamans could similarly claim to do (Axtell 1988, 93). In 1635 Brébeuf wrote that the Huron admired the lodestone, prism, and joiner's tools, "but above all . . . writing, for they could not conceive how, what one of us, being in the village, had said to them, and put down at the same time in writing, another, who meanwhile was in a house far away, could say readily on seeing the writing. I believe they have made a hundred trials of it" (8:113). He added: "This serves to gain their affections, and to render them more docile when we introduce the admirable and incomprehensible mysteries of our Faith; for the belief they have in our intelligence and capacity causes them to accept without reply what we say to them" (8:113).

However, while the technology of writing contributed to the aura of power and prestige which the Jesuits' were trying to cultivate, they could not control the whole meaning of the relationship between writing and power in the minds of Huron who suspected them of witchcraft. This relationship was quite different from the priests' understanding of the power of writing as a privileged vehicle of knowledge and the permanent repository and record of the Word of God. While it constituted proof that the Jesuits were figures of some unusual skills and power, it was

precisely this power that would have enabled the Jesuits to harm people by causing inexplicable diseases through sorcery. That the Jesuits represented themselves as men who had come to North America only for the good of the Huron was irrelevant, since the Huron believed that powerful individuals did not use their power for good or evil exclusively but could put it to use for both purposes.

Thus, although writing initially contributed to the respect with which the priests were treated, as fears of the Jesuits' sorcery grew it also came to be suspected as a means by which the Jesuits targeted people for illness or otherwise spread the contagion. Lalemant explained in 1639 that if the fathers "asked the name of some one, in order to write it in the register of our baptized ones, and not lose memory of it, it was (they said) that we might pierce him secretly, and afterward, tearing out this written name, cause the death, by this same act, of him or her who bore that name" (19:129). Similarly, when Fathers Antoine Daniel and Simon Le Moyne visited the eastern Arendarhonon villages, some inhabitants of the principal village of Contarea claimed to have seen these fathers in dreams, "unfolding certain books, whence issued sparks of fire which spread everywhere, and no doubt caused this pestilential disease" (20:33). Dreams were not random occurrences for the Huron; they were prophetic of events, as well as of the innermost desires of the soul, and the Huron paid close attention to them (Sioui 1994, 297). In these instances, the symbolic significance of writing and its associated technologies slipped their moorings in the Jesuits' ideology and received altered significance at the hands of the Huron. Accusations that linked writing to witchcraft subverted the Jesuits' position as benefactors concerned with saving people rather than destroying them. In this way, they displaced the equivalence which the Jesuits were trying to convey between themselves and health and life. These accusations also denied the ideology of the letter that informed the priests' reliance on the book. By contesting the authority of writing, Aboriginal people acknowledged its power but denied its hegemonic function as the embodiment of a universal truth; in this way, if only temporarily, they refused the translation of colonial signifying practices and the authority embedded in them.[2]

In other instances, the ritual and pictorial symbolism of Christianity was appropriated and resisted in ways the Jesuits could neither control nor possibly have predicted. Many Huron had initially interpreted and received baptism as a healing rite; but as the diseases intensified, the Jesuits' sacrament of life came to be viewed as one of the ways in which they perpetrated their witchcraft. Many people refused it on the grounds that it was certain to kill them or their children. Others incorporated a facsimile of baptism into their own healing rituals, to the great annoyance of the Jesuits. This particular innovation first occurred in 1637, when it was introduced by a shaman who had fasted for ten days in an attempt to acquire insight into the cause and cure of the prevailing disease, and it involved sprinkling water on the sick (13:237–43). It appeared again in 1639, after a Huron man had a vision of Iouskeha, a central Huron deity, in which Iouskeha blamed the Jesuits for the disease and prescribed a healing ritual that involved drinking ritually prepared water from a kettle (20:27–9). The Jesuits roundly condemned the vision as the work of demons who were trying to defend their territory against the Jesuits, and they described the practitioners of the prescribed healing rite as "masqueraders" and "physicians from hell" (20:31).

The Jesuits' vigorous condemnation of these acts suggests the degree to which they frustrated their objectives. These acts also show the ambivalence of Huron resistance. The Huron did not wholly reject the content of the Jesuits' practices or the authority linked to them, nor did their actions leave Huron and French cultural meanings and systems of signification intact, within imaginary bound-aries, with their contents unimplicated in each other (Bhabha 1994, 110). The Huron men and women who participated in these rites engaged the potential power of baptism as a healing ritual. In doing so, they allowed some of its significance while disallowing the Jesuits' monopoly over the meaning and potentially life-saving effects of the ritual and its water (20:29–31).

This time of illness and death was, understandably, fraught with the search for signs of the cause of disease. The life-size paintings of Christ and the Virgin Mary displayed by the Jesuits in their chapel in Ossossané were believed to possess magical qualities and to be two of the instruments through which the priests were causing illness among Huron who were unfortunate enough to have looked at the pictures (15:19). Paintings of hell, detailing the torments of the damned—intended to inspire fear and to encourage people to convert—were interpreted as literal representations of the sufferings of those whom the Jesuits had afflicted with disease. Le Mercier explained that "on the day of the baptism of Pierre Tsiouendaentaha," the Jesuits "exhibited an excellent representation of the judgment, where the damned are depicted,—some with serpents and dragons tearing out their entrails, and the greater part with some kind of instrument of their punishment" (14:103). While "many obtained some benefit from this spectacle," some "persuaded themselves that this multitude of men, desperate, and heaped one upon the other, were all those we had caused to die during this Winter; that these flames represented the heats of the pestilential fever, and these dragons and serpents, the venomous beasts that we made use of in order to poison them" (14:103).

In this instance, the Jesuits' teaching about heaven, hell, and punishment was deflected and was returned to the Jesuits with new and contrary meanings. Even the communion wafers became suspect. As a general principle, the priests had been careful to reveal the doctrine of transubstantiation (whereby the wafers became the body of Christ) only to the few Christian Huron whom they felt most trustworthy in the faith (15:33). In spite of this precaution, the host soon featured in a rumour suggesting that the Jesuits were causing the diseases through a corpse they had brought from France and were hiding in their residence (15:33).

Several years later, after the diseases had largely run their course, stories began to circulate among the Huron of dreams and visions through which people had learned that the Jesuits' teachings were not only wrong but were dangerous. In one story, the soul of a recently deceased woman returned, after having journeyed to heaven, to warn the Huron that all who had become Christian were being tortured in heaven as prisoners of war, by the French, just as war captives were tortured by the Huron and their enemies (30:29). This warning was especially subversive because it situated the Jesuits as enemies whose objective in making converts was to take prisoners, rather than as people who had come to give the secret of eternal life. It also completely overturned the division between heaven and hell, which many Native people found especially problematic. These incidents demonstrate the decentring that can occur when signs that are supposed to stand for the authority of the colonizers—or, in this case, the missionaries—are exposed to interpretation and appropriation by the colonized; they also illustrate competition for control over the interpretation of events and for what passes as the truth. As assertions of Native beliefs that make sense of Christian symbolism and Christian figures in the context of these beliefs, they are also an ideological response in kind to the Jesuits.

However much the Jesuits were required to argue over meaning with the Huron while they were in the Huron villages, their own understanding of the cause of the diseases was forcibly and categorically expressed in the pages of the *Relations*. It revolved around

the influence of the devil in inspiring the persecution against them (19:91) and the biblically precedented interpretation of disease as divinely instigated punishment and trial. After the initial accusation of witchcraft in 1636, Le Jeune wrote that the growing hostility toward the Jesuits was a positive sign that the demons—hitherto unchallenged as the masters of the country—had been "powerfully attacked, since they put themselves vigorously on the defensive" (11:41). A few years later, Father Le Mercier characterized the accusations and general hostility as part of "the war that the powers of darkness have openly declared against us" (14:109). The Jesuits described their work with the sick and their unflagging attempts to teach and baptize people in the midst of threats as a literal struggle against the forces of evil (17:191; 20:51). In view of the Jesuits' own understanding of their mission, the allegation that it was they who were manipulating supernatural powers for harm could only be understood and represented as a fundamental misinterpretation of their activities and proof of the blindness of their accusers. Jérôme Lalemant responded to the accusations brought against the Jesuits with righteous indignation, writing that the words of their accusers were "often only blasphemies against God and our mysteries, and insults against us, accompanied with incredible evidences of ingratitude,—hurling at us the reproach that it is our visits and our remedies which cause them to sicken and die, and that our sojourn here is the sole cause of all their troubles" (17:15).

The Jesuits soon came to represent the diseases as punishment sent by God in response to people's initial refusal to heed the Word and to accept their opportunity for salvation.[3] Once spoken in the New World, the Word of God erased the legitimacy of previous religious practices and, significantly, exposed Aboriginal people to their ignorance as well as to the full force of the consequences of their sin. The words spoken by the Jesuits left a permanent mark, inhabiting the spaces where they had been spoken with a kind of ominous finality. To ignore them and the truths they announced was to make the fatal choice between salvation and condemnation to greater punishment in this life and the next. In a letter to Mutio Vitelleschi, general of the Society of Jesus at Rome, Lalemant explained: "While they were sound in body, they did not hear; it therefore pleased God to pull their ears through a certain kind of pestilence, which spread over the whole country, and adjudged many to the grave" (17:227).

At the beginning of the epidemics, Le Jeune compared the situation in which the priests found themselves with the persecution suffered by the first Christians and, reversing the accusations made against the Jesuits, attributed the diseases to God's justice: "All the misfortunes, all the pests, wars, and famines which in the early ages of the infant Church afflicted the world, were formerly attributed to the faith of Jesus Christ, and to those who embraced or preached it. What occurred in this regard in the primitive Church can be seen every day in new France, especially in the Huron country. There is no black malice of which we are not accused. Here are the causes of it. As the contagion caused a great many Hurons to die, these people, not recognizing therein the justice of God, who takes vengeance for their crimes, imagined that the French were the cause of their death" (12:85).

While the Jesuits attributed all power over the diseases to God and continually urged the Huron to have recourse to the faith, most Huron abandoned Christianity completely in an attempt to dissociate themselves from the priests' teachings and, by association, from the diseases. The few who had converted and who remained Christian during the epidemics were warned by their relatives of the injustice of the Jesuits' God and his powerlessness to assist them or to preserve their lives (19:211, 235). But while resistance to the Jesuits became more imperative for the majority of Huron men and women, it situated them in a more perilous position according to the Jesuits' understanding of the epidemic and its causes. The Huron's rejection of Christianity as the only possible cure and their continual search for cures among those offered by the shamans and curing societies confirmed the Jesuits' in their belief that the devil influenced these people's behaviour (15:71). According to this view, such behaviour made them more deserving of retribution for denying the opportunity for their salvation. In the same way, the threats and accusations that the Huron made against the priests—who believed themselves to be there as the instruments of the Huron's salvation—compounded the "measure of their sins" (13:161) and, consequently, the measure of their punishment. The Jesuits met the active resistance of the Huron with an intensification of their threats of punishment, rhetorically moving the Huron's refusal to comply into the realm of the worst blasphemy. While the Jesuits and many Huron apportioned blame for the disease to each other they did so according to divergent cultural and ideological premises that enabled them to find significant, incontrovertible meaning in their respective actions. The result was a duel over signification, in which each became grist for the other's worst accusations as they struggled—if not for life and death itself—at least for the meaning of life and the cause of death.

The first serious outbreak of disease occurred during the autumn of 1636 and lasted through the winter. After this, the Jesuits moved their principal residence from the village of Ihonatiria, where many people had lost their lives to the disease, to the more southern and less afflicted village of Ossossané. The Jesuits had been publicly accused of practising witchcraft in Ihonatiria that winter and were aware that their lives were at risk. Le Mercier, the author of the Huron *Relation* for that year, identified one family as having been most active in these accusations. According to Le Mercier, it was when the priests' lives were most threatened that "the scourge fell upon that wretched family that had said the most against us. This chastisement had been for a long time due them on account of the contempt they had always shown for our holy mysteries" (13:217). Lalemant later explained that the move from Ihonatiria was necessary because its population was "nearly all . . . scattered or dead from the malady, which seems to be, not without reason, a punishment from Heaven for the contempt that they showed for the favour of the visit that the divine goodness had procured for them" (17:11). The following autumn, when it appeared that a council of confederacy headmen in Ossossané would sanction the Jesuits' death, Brébeuf reiterated the priests' assumption that their lives would be preserved or disposed of solely as God willed. Their deaths would prevent the salvation of those they were trying to save, and Brébeuf believed that if God allowed the Jesuits to be killed, this in itself would be a form of punishment: "And yet I fear that divine Justice, seeing the obstinacy of the majority of these Barbarians in their follies, may very justly permit them to come and take away the life of the body from those who with all their hearts desire and procure the life of their souls" (15:63).

Crop failures, the escalation of the war with the Iroquois, and famines were also represented as the punishments of God. When Jérôme Lalemant described the destruction of one of the outlying Huron villages by an Iroquois war party, he associated this disaster with the village's previous rebelliousness: "It was the most impious of the villages, and that which had been most rebellious against the truths of the faith in all these countries; and its inhabitants had more than once told the Fathers who had gone to teach them that, if there were a God who avenged crimes, they defied him to make them feel his anger, and that, for anything less than that, they refused to acknowledge his power" (26:175). Similarly, Father Dequen explained to the Montagnais residing at Sillery that the capture of a group of Huron traders and the Jesuit father

accompanying them, as well as "so many other misfortunes," were "the effects of God's anger, who was justly irritated by the wickedness of bad Christians and of the infidels who would not obey his word" (25:149).

Of course, the few who remained or became Christian during the epidemics were equally likely to suffer from the diseases. Similarly, as more people converted to Christianity after the diseases had run their course, they—like the non-Christians—were caught up in the punitive effects of escalating warfare and famine (25:105; 26:217). Inequities in the distribution of suffering are not unaccounted for in the Judeo-Christian tradition, and the Jesuits drew on well-established precedents when they represented these afflictions as having been sent by God for the improvement and redemption of those he had elected to save (26:217). Such was the argument offered to a group of Huron who complained that the Iroquois, who did not pray, were prospering and that since prayer had been introduced among the Huron, they themselves were perishing from warfare and disease. These Huron were told that God was behaving toward them "like a Father toward his child; if his child will not have sense, he punishes it, in order to give it some; having corrected it, he throws the rods into the fire. A Father does not put himself to so much trouble about his servants as about his children. God regards you as his children: he wishes to give you sense; he uses the Iroquois as a whip, in order to correct you, to give you faith, to make you have recourse to him. When you shall be wise, he will throw the rods into the fire; he will chastise the Iroquois, unless they reform" (25:37).

The Jesuits had precedents for this language and did not have to invent it for use in North America. However, such language assumes particular potency when used in a situation of evolving political and economic inequality, and in conjunction with what was frequently an aggressive rhetoric of political imperialism, which compared the spread of

Christianity in the New World to a territorial conquest. These Huron replied that they had enough sense and suggested it might have been better if God had begun with the Iroquois. The Jesuits advised them that their greater misfortunes were due to the greater love God bore them and that, however much the Iroquois appeared to be prospering, it was certain that, as unbelievers, they would not enjoy the rewards of the next life. The Jesuits' representation of suffering reflects an assumption that the appropriate response to it could only be submission and endurance, undertaken with an understanding of the presence of a superior will to which one must be subordinate, and with the hope of rewards to come (Bowker 1970, 54). This complete abnegation of the self, along with submission before a greater will, was a feature of the Jesuits' training. While the Jesuits' interlocutors frequently appeared unmoved by a God who apparently benefitted people through their affliction, for the Jesuits suffering reduced neither the possibility of God nor the justice of God. Those who endured with strength and patience would be recognized and potentially rewarded—"for one is approved if, mindful of God, he endures pain while suffering unjustly" (1 Peter 2:19).

When sent as trials, misfortunes were a tool for separating those who were firm in the faith and willing to submit from those who were not (32:189). It is significant that in the *Relations* these trials were frequently represented as a necessary and important step in the establishment of Christianity in North America, just as they had been in Europe and Asia, where the faith of Christians had been tested through political persecution. While describing the hardships suffered by the Montagnais in the vicinity of Quebec, Le Jeune asserted: "The Faith must propagate itself as it has been planted,—namely, in calamities. And because there are here no Tyrants who massacre our Neophytes, God provides for them otherwise, deriving proof of their constancy from their afflictions, sore

indeed" (16:219). The repeated use of this historical reference situates the experiences of Native peoples in the St Lawrence region—for whom the signature events of Christianity were the remote occurrences in the life of an unknown prophet referring to the deity of an unknown people in a remote and alien land—within the frame of a universal, exclusively Christian and ultimately hegemonic vision of global history. In 1643 Barthélemy Vimont described the general condition of the Christians of New France:

> The condition to which this nascent Church is now reduced is such as to bring to the eyes of all who love it tears both of sorrow and of joy. For, on the one hand, it is pitiful to see these poor peoples perish before our eyes as soon as they embrace the Faith; and, on the other, we have reason to console ourselves when we see that the misfortunes which assail them on all sides serve but to arouse a desire for the faith in those who had hitherto despised it, and to strengthen it and make it shine with still greater glory in the hearts of those who had already received it. We see very well that God is the Founder of this Church, as well as of the primitive one; for he has caused the former to be born, like the latter, in travails, and to grow in sufferings, in order to be crowned with her in glory. (25:105)

By the summer of 1649 most Huron villages had been destroyed or significantly depopulated by warfare and the accompanying famine and disease. The priests and surviving Huron took refuge on an island in Georgian Bay, where they were temporarily safe from Iroquois raiding parties but lacked provisions for the coming winter. "Then it was," according to Paul Ragueneau, that the missionaries "were compelled to behold dying skeletons eking out a miserable life, feeding even on the excrements and refuse of nature" (35:89).

Conditions reached such an extreme that people were reduced to exhuming bodies for food. Ragueneau nevertheless wrote: "It was in the midst of these desolations that God was pleased to bring forth, from their deepest misfortunes, the wellbeing of this people. Their hearts had become so tractable to the faith that we effected in them, by a single word, more than we had ever been able to accomplish in entire years" (35:91).

The upheavals in Huron society in the final years of the Jesuits' mission among them made them more dependent on the Jesuits and enabled the priests to exact at least an outward compliance with Christianity. Lalemant had foreshadowed this role of affliction in creating subject relations of dependency, when he wrote of the general condition of Christianity in New France in the *Relation* for the years 1643–44: "We have, however, great reason to praise God because he reaps his glory from the affliction of these poor peoples and makes it serve still more for their conversion. Although there is not in the world a nation poorer than this one, nevertheless there is none prouder than they. When they were prosperous, we could hardly approach them; the French were dogs, and all that we preached them were fables. But since affliction has humiliated them, and necessity has made them more dependent upon the French, and has made them experience the effects of Christian charity, their eyes are opened; and they see more clearly than ever that there is no other Divinity than he whom we preach to them" (25:111). Lalemant's comment also reveals the strong sense of cultural superiority that characterized Aboriginal people's initial response to Europeans.

The Jesuits also represented affliction as the enactment of a more final and inevitable justice. In the Huron report of 1640 Lalemant explained that many "villages and cabins were much more populous formerly, but the extraordinary diseases and the wars within some years past, seem to have carried off the best portion; there remaining only very few old men, very few persons of skill and management" (19:127). To this he added, "It is to be feared that the climax of their sins is approaching, which moves divine justice to exterminate them as well as several other nations" (19:127). People who resisted conversion or actively argued against the Jesuits and who then suffered misfortune or death frequently figured in the *Relations* as examples of God's justice, however far removed this would have been from these people's own interpretation of their death or misfortune. The punishments featured in these incidents are in sharp contrast to the joy and gratitude which the Jesuits generally associated with conversion. In 1634 Paul Le Jeune attributed the miserable death of a "blasphemer" to the "just and terrible vengeance of the great God" (7:283). Ten years later Lalemant described the punishment of three Algonkin men who had come down to Trois-Rivières and were "placing some obstacles against the expansion of the Faith" by openly retaining more than one wife (31:257). Lalemant asserted that these three "refractory ones" (31:257) were the victims of "a thunderbolt hurled from Heaven" (31:257), all dying ignoble or miserable deaths.

One of these men, on becoming ill, blamed Christianity and in so doing was said to have revolted "more than ever against the arm which struck him only to cure him" (31:263). The Jesuits warned him of the punishment that would come in the next life if he did not open his eyes and accept baptism, but he replied unrepentantly "that a Law which made men die was abominable" (31:261). He died in this refutation of the faith, a resistance that became, under Lalemant's pen, the "rage" that was "the Catastrophe of his life" (31:263). Another of these men especially annoyed the Jesuits by his persistence in attributing a recent outbreak of disease to the effects of Christianity, and when he too fell sick Lalemant described this as an attack by God (31:263). Lalemant referred to this man, who bore the name Joseph Oumosotiscouchie, as an apostate who was unusually "proud and insolent" because he had been given the name used by several former leaders in his country (31:261).

Oumosotiscouchie publicly denied the utility of prayer to heal, blaming his sickness on the faith, and he undertook to cure himself in a healing ceremony that involved the fulfillment of three dream wishes. On completion of the ceremony, he publicly claimed to be cured, at which point, according to Lalemant, "a violent fever seizes him in the midst of his triumph, prostrates him to the earth, throws him into a wreck and into torments so unusual that he foamed like one possessed. Those of his cabin—frightened, and fearing lest he might beat some one to death—having tied him, threw over him a blanket, so as to conceal his fury and his rage; behold my blusterer much humbled" (31:265). When the Jesuits and the surgeon arrived, they found the man "stone-dead" and all who had witnessed the event astonished at "so awful a spectacle" (31:265). This man was later "flung into a hole like a common sewer, for fear that he might infect the air with his body, as he had polluted it with his vices and his apostasy" (31:275). After this punishment, Lalemant stated with some satisfaction that no one "dared longer open his lips against the Faith; it was now spoken of only with a dread and respect that altogether pleased us" (31:267).[4]

Those who physically harmed Jesuits could also be situated in the *Relations* as victims of divine punishment. One man, for example, kicked a priest while the latter was baptizing a child, and "some time after that, he was carried off by a disease as grievous as it was strange" (14:227). The woman who cut off the thumb of Father Jogues while Jogues was a captive in an Iroquois village apparently "had no long career after that rage" (29:229). Likewise, wrote Lalemant: "They who gnawed his fingers and those of his companions, and who treated them with most fury, have been killed by the Algonquin in their latest combats" (29:229). The "same justice" was applied to the Iroquois who tortured Father Bressani when he was held captive among them, although this punishment was in the form of diseases that would "perhaps . . . give true health to that poor people" (29:229).

NOTES

[Editor's note: Parenthetical references in the text are to volume and page number in Reuben Gold Thwaites, *Jesuits Relations and Allied Documents*, 73 vols (Cleveland: Burrows Bros. 1896–1901).]

1. In an especially interesting literal play on the Jesuits' insistence that the Bible was the unmediated, directly transmitted Word of God, Le Jeune reported: "When I told them that we had a book which contained the words and teachings of God, they were very anxious to know how we could have gotten this book,— some of them believing that it had been let down from the Sky at the end of a rope, and that we had found it thus suspended in the air" (11:209).
2. Indeed, while the smallpox epidemics ultimately passed, Native critiques of writing were not without prescience of the larger ramifications of entering history. One man, upon being told that his people were dying as a result of the overconsumption of the brandy used in the fur trade, retorted: "It is not these drinks that take away our lives, but your writings; for since you have described our country, our rivers, our lands, and our woods, we are all dying, which did not happen until you came here" (9:207). The Jesuits denied these deleterious consequences of writing the New World into a history that embraced the inhabitants with alien pathogens at the same time as it was supposed to proffer them the means of salvation, by explaining to this man that they "described the whole world" without similarly harmful effects (9:207).
3. A recent attribution of these diseases to the Europeans' abandonment of the "laws of

nature" and more general alienation from the natural world (Sioui 1992, 3–7) is as embedded in the assumption of a universally applicable schema of laws, causes, and effects as the attributions of the Jesuits. While it may be meant to refute such statements as the priests initially made and to represent the real truth, it matches them in the assumption that the cultural and religious dictates of one people—including an understanding of the natural world and the appropriate human relationships with it—are not, in effect, creations but represent reality as a given, and that, as such, they can be universally binding as a yardstick with which to judge and understand the history, behaviour, and beliefs of other peoples.

4. Aboriginal people who reportedly resisted or abused Christianity were not the only victims of God's anger and punishment in the *Relations*. The Jesuits represented the untimely death of French Protestants in a similar manner (5:233; 6:105–7).

REFERENCES

Axtell, James. (1988). *After Columbus: Essays in the Ethnohistory of Colonial North America*. New York and Oxford: Oxford University Press.

Bhabha, Homi. (1994). *The Location of Culture*. London and New York: Routledge.

Mignolo, Walter D. (1992). "On the Colonization of Amerindian Languages and Memories: Renaissance Theories of Writing and the Discontinuity of the Classical Tradition," *Comparative Studies in Society and History* 34, 4: 301–30.

Sioui, Georges. (1994). *Les Wendats: Une civilisation méconnue*. Sainte-Foy: Presses de l'Université Laval.

Trigger, Bruce. (1987). *The Children of Aataenstic: A History of the Huron People to 1660*, 2 vols. Montreal and Kingston: McGill-Queen's University Press.

 From Denys Delâge, *Bitter Feast: Amerindians and Europeans in Northeastern North America, 1600–1664* (Vancouver: UBC Press, 1993), 178–94, 358–9. Reprinted with permission of the Publisher © University of British Columbia Press 1993. All rights reserved by the Publisher.

THE PROCESS OF CONVERSION

The faith must propagate itself as it has been planted, namely, in calamities.[1] So true are those words, *Sanguis martyrum semen est Christianorum*—"the blood of the Martyrs," if they may be so named, "is the seed and germ of Christians."[2]

The missionaries had begun to baptize the dying as soon as they arrived in Huronia,[3] and, accordingly, the number of baptisms fluctuated with epidemics.[4] In 1638 only one family had converted to Christianity, but by the following year the Jesuits boasted "fully 300 souls".[5] Between 1639 and 1640 they baptized about a thousand people, although among them "there [were] not twenty baptized ones out of danger of death."[6] The year 1641 marked a turning point, however, for, despite much stricter standards in evaluating the genuine nature of professions of faith, the number of converts grew. The year 1642 saw 620 baptisms, with both men and women filling the chapels each morning.[7] "The faith finds no distinction between the sexes," noted the missionaries.[8]

Among the 250 Hurons of the bark flotilla that went down to Trois-Rivières in 1648, nearly half (120) were converts. They prayed twice a day and travelled together "in the presence of the pagans."[9] Between the *Jesuit Relations* of 1647 and that of 1648, the Jesuits baptized "nearly thirteen hundred persons."[10]

Then came the final disaster, and conversions increased as Huron villages fell into the hands of the Iroquois. "More than 1300 persons" were baptized between July 1648 and March 1649, and "more than fourteen hundred" between March and August 1649.[11] "Thus the Christian Church was increased by more than two thousand seven hundred souls in thirteen months, without counting those baptized at the Breach [the storming of the Huron villages], and those who were made Christians in other places."[12]

For a time, the Jesuits had thought they would convert the Hurons by educating the offspring of sachem families and by systematically baptizing all children. However, such baptisms—often surreptitiously practised by means of a handkerchief or finger dipped in holy water—could not provide the foundation for a new, organized church.[13]

The Jesuits would have dearly liked to send a large number of Huron children to a residential school. This would not only win over children who might "aspire to the highest positions"[14] in their native land; it would provide hostages to consolidate trade and ensure the safety of the French in Huronia. The Huron women always managed to scuttle such a project, however.[15] In 1636, only five of the twelve children destined for instruction at Quebec actually went. The venture was a fiasco: only two children displayed any pliancy, and these later died. The missionaries complained that the other three were incapable of submitting to the discipline of the Jesuits. The young Hurons were taught how to perform "neat courtesies" and greet "our Frenchmen" by "humbly . . . touching their hats when meeting them."[16] However, the three recalcitrants "aimed at nothing but the enjoyment of their pleasures and the gratification of their senses." They secretly got hold of "a canoe-load of provisions . . . and one fine morning they stole away, taking with them everything they could."[17]

Efforts to educate Montagnais children were equally ill-fated. In 1636 the French governor reproached the Montagnais for refusing to entrust their children to the French, although they entrusted a certain number to Amerindian allies. [. . .]

By 1639 the Jesuits had virtually given up the idea of converting Huronia by teaching its children, and their seminary in Quebec was of no use in this respect. The Ursuline nuns of Quebec met with about as much success in their attempts to educate young Amerindian girls, although a few Montagnais families found it convenient to leave their daughters at the convent over the winter.[18] Several little girls were sent to France, where they were fashionable curiosities in aristocratic circles. Generally speaking, however, church authorities considered it impossible to "train" the children.

> The freedom of the children in these countries is so great, and they prove so incapable of government and discipline, that, far from being able to hope for the conversion of the country through the instruction of the children, we must even despair of their instruction without the conversion of the parents. And consequently, all well considered, the first matter to which we should attend is the stability of the marriages of our Christians, who give us children that may in good time be reared in the fear of God and of their parents. Behold the only means of furnishing the Seminaries with young plants.[19]

Such were the first in a series of repeated attempts at educating Amerindian children by both French and English throughout the seventeenth and eighteenth centuries. The results were always the same, and young Amerindians never adapted to the manners and discipline of European institutions. The reverse process—that is, the integration of young whites into Amerindian society—was usually successful.

The Jesuits' efforts prospered most in Ossossané, the principal village of the

Attignawantans. In 1648, it outstripped all other villages in the number and zeal of its Christians,[20] and it therefore offers the best example for observing the process of conversion. [. . .]

After 1639 the Jesuits concentrated their efforts on converting council members, "some Old Men, and the more prominent heads of families."[21] The missionaries had remarked that "one truly Christian Savage, who is zealous for the faith, accomplishes more among his people than do three Jesuits,"[22] and therefore felt that converting leaders would have a ripple effect. It is worth noting that the men generally won over the women and children.[23] The arguments given were the need to conform to the new morality and the desire to meet again in the afterlife. Nonetheless, their influence also indicated the growing power of men involved in trade over their wives and the community in general.

With an eye to winning over community leaders, the Jesuits tightened their grip on the sale of weapons and the price of trade goods. After 1642, the desire to own a firearm became a strong inducement to convert to Christianity. This was the year in which one Ahatsistari, reputed to be the bravest warrior of Huronia, was baptized. He had been asking for baptism for three years, but the Jesuits had hitherto refused because he could not "make up his mind to abandon some Superstitious practices that are customary among the Infidels."[24] Now at last he would be able to replace bow and arrow with firepower and confront the Iroquois on an equal footing. That same year, "some Infidels, who were about to go to war . . . began to think of their Souls as much as, if not more than, of their bodies."[25] The following year, the missionaries wrote that "the affairs of our Lord advance in proportion to the adversities which he sends us. Hardly could one find, hitherto, among our Christians two or three warriors; but, since the capture of that worthy Neophyte, named Eustache, the most valiant of all the Hurons, we have counted

in a single band as many as twenty-two Believers—all men of courage, and mostly Captains or people of importance. The use of arquebuses, refused to the Infidels by Monsieur the Governor, and granted to the Christian Neophytes, is a powerful attraction to win them."[26]

It is no surprise to find Jesuits succeeding in their efforts to convert the families and villages most involved in the fur trade, since the trading expeditions were what exposed the Hurons, more than anything else, to Iroquois guns. Ossossané was such a village. [. . .]

Initially, the Jesuits' efforts at conversion had come up against the Hurons' fear of being separated from their relatives and ancestors in the other world. "'For my part, I have no desire to go to heaven,' said one. 'I have no acquaintances there.'"[27] Dead relatives and friends had gone to the hunting and fishing grounds of the afterlife.[28] Once converts were sufficiently numerous, however, the process rapidly snowballed. The argument that had held people back now became an incentive to convert, and for some the fear of separation from their families was actually the prime reason.[29]

The year 1645 marked a watershed in Huronia. The following dialogue demonstrates the confrontation between converted and unconverted Huron chiefs. "'Then,' said the Elders, 'we must resign ourselves to seeing our Country ruined, since our chief Captains range themselves on the side of the Faith. How can we prevent this disorder?' 'You are thinking of it too late,' he replies; 'you should have opposed the progress of the Faith before it had entered our hearts. Now it will reign there in spite of you; and it will be easier to tear our souls from our bodies than to remove from our minds the fear of Hell-fire, and the desire for the happiness that awaits us in Heaven.'"[30]

[. . .]

The process of conversion may in part be accounted for by dependency and the multitude of constraints under which the Hurons lived. A firearm was worth a baptism, certainly, but this does not offer a satisfactory explanation of why a significant number of converts actually interiorized the new religion. Why, in the words of a converted chief to his peers, had the faith entered his heart?[31] What accounted for the proselytizing zeal of many converts?[32] Some of the answers can, it seems, be found by considering the question from two standpoints: one sociological, the other psychoanalytical.

In the first instance, might the blood of martyrs indeed be the seed of Christianity? In other words, might the sense of insecurity created by the accumulated disasters (epidemics and wars), as well as intensified labour, have provided fertile ground for Christian ideology? Since 1634, disease and war had been undermining Native societies and endangering the whole of Amerindian civilization. The mechanisms for transmitting tradition had been dislocated and relations between tribes thrown into disarray. Furthermore, war had contributed to the displacement and marginalization of entire populations.[33] A closer look reveals that it was often the people who had lost or suffered most who were the most receptive to the evangelical message. In 1639, the missionaries reported nearly 60 converts in Ossossané, "of whom many are Wenroronons from among those poor Strangers taking refuge in this country."[34] This was a reference to a tribe of the Neutral confederacy that had been defeated by the Iroquois and forced to abandon its territory. Six hundred arrived in pitiable condition to seek refuge among the Hurons, who took them in.[35] Was there a connection between the rate of conversion at Ossossané and the number of refugees? There does seem to be a correlation between their presence and a willingness to welcome the missionaries.

In the same year, fathers Garnier and Jogues made their first journey to the Petuns. At this time all doors were closed to them through fear of witchcraft, except that of a "stranger," a former captive who had originally been a member of the "nation which they call Atsistahronons, 'Nation of fire'."[36] The fathers met with an equally frosty welcome on their first journey to the Neutrals in 1640–41, except for in one village where several Wenroronon refugees were lodged.[37] It would seem that the refugees, in other words the most deprived members of the community, were the most willing to listen to what the missionaries had to say. In earlier days refugees would have been integrated into the tribe. With the upheaval of traditional Huron values, however, integration was predominantly religious. In 1642, for example, when an Iroquois attack threatened to overthrow the country, even the unconverted Ossossané villagers asked the Jesuits to baptize everyone.[38] The seed of doubt was already sown. It would seem that recurrent epidemics, intensified warfare, and the process of Huronia's gradual strangulation created not only the material conditions, but the ideological base for conversion. In 1644 Father Lalemant wrote of the Hurons, "As for the new Christians, their number has been much greater this year than in previous ones. Even the Infidels, who are humiliated and made more docile by affliction, seem to us to be less distant from God's Kingdom. Finally, the body of Christians, after heavy trials sent by Heaven, is becoming more considerable, and begins to be in the majority in some of the villages."[39]

Also in 1644, Father Vimont described the Amerindians' general situation in more or less similar terms. "Although there is not in the world a nation poorer than this one, nevertheless there is none prouder than they. When they were prosperous, we could hardly approach them; the French were dogs, and all that we preached them were fables. But since affliction has humiliated them, and necessity has made them more dependent upon the French, and has made them experience the effects of Christian charity, their eyes are opened; and they see more clearly than ever that there is no other Divinity than he whom we preach to them."[40]

Several years later, in 1656, Father Chaumonot met some Hurons who had become Iroquois captives, about whom he had this to say: "The Hurons of the Village of Contareia, who, because of their strong aversion to the Faith, never allowed themselves to be instructed, are already beginning to yield, lending an attentive ear to the Father's words. So true is it that *afflictio dat intellectum*."[41]

Considering the degree to which Amerindian societies had become profoundly destabilized, could the traditional religious system have given meaning to the way of life their members were now facing? Dependency, tension, hierarchization, the establishment of a destructive relationship between man and nature, the crumbling of a civilization, dispossession—all these were realities that shook the old explanations of the world, engendering anomie (that is, the weakening of normative standards of conduct and belief) at the heart of Huron society, and what Pierre Bourdieu calls "the expectation of a systematic message capable of giving a unified meaning to life by offering its chosen recipients a consistent vision of the world and human existence, and by giving them the means to integrate it systematically into their daily behaviour—a message therefore able to provide them with the justification to live as they do, that is, in a defined social position."[42]

Such an expectation can be divined from the changes taking place in the Hurons' mythical universe. Thus, Aataentsic, the moon-mother goddess, changed herself into a vengeful goddess, sending fatal epidemics to punish the Amerindians who for years had been waging war with increasing frequency.[43] In the main, however, unlike Christianity, the traditional systems of explanation could not, despite alterations, offer a coherent vision of societies where oppression was the dominant factor. The missionary offensive therefore took advantage (at least in the case of the most deprived) of an ideological destabilization

caused by the collapse of Amerindian societies. Pierre Bourdieu cites Max Weber on the historical origin of religions, to the effect that all requests for salvation are an expression of a "need," economic and social oppression being the most important, but not the only instance of such a need.[44] It might be said that, as of 1640, this request for salvation came as much from within, instigated by the oppression to which Amerindians were subjected, as from without, in response to external pressure applied by the missionaries. The missionaries' conversion strategies could not have succeeded without the Amerindians being socially predisposed to join the faith. The evangelical message focused on themes of original sin, sins committed, redemption, resignation (to hell on earth), and hope (for heaven in the afterlife). It conformed to the world view then held by many Amerindians who, as with all those who are "disinherited by the brutalities of society," had developed an apocalyptic vision of history.[45]

Epidemics and wars marked the overturning of the Amerindian world. The missionaries interpreted all the visible stigmata (disease and suffering) as signs heralding "divine election" and eternal bliss. In so doing—that is, by promising "posthumous subversion" of the social order[46]—the missionaries forced the objective recognition that history was irreversible and that European power had been legitimated. The terms in which they spoke symbolically reinforced a world view where subjugation was the norm, linked to "the ethos of resignation and renunciation instilled by the conditions of life."[47] This meant legitimation of the dependency of Amerindian societies and of the process whereby these societies were divided into classes. In fact, insofar as Amerindian societies were crumbling from within, the new religion was the answer both to those seeking compensation (the promise of salvation from suffering for the most deprived), and those seeking legitimation of the established order (the inculcation of a sense of dignity and rightful superiority among the dominant forces).[48]

The fur trade had changed the Hurons' manner of acquiring wealth. Sachems possessed the right to grant passage over trade routes and accorded these rights in exchange for gifts, as well as reserving for themselves a relatively large share of the trade goods. As it developed, the fur trade gave rise to an increasingly unequal acquisition of wealth, and fostered the appearance of a distinction between governed and governors, whereas they had previously been mingled in a collective "we".

> Formerly only worthy men were Captains, and so they were called *Enondecha*, the same name by which they call the Country, Nation, district,—as if a good Chief and the Country were one and the same thing. But today they do not pay so much attention to the selection of their captains; and so they no longer give them that name, although they still call them *atiwarontas*, *atiwanens*, *ondakhienhai*, "big stones, the elders, the stay-at-homes". However, those still hold, as I have said, the first rank as well in the special affairs of the Villages as of the whole Country, who are most highly esteemed and intellectually preëminent. Their relatives are like so many Lieutenants and Councilors.[49]

This dichotomy was not merely one of language; it reflected a socio-economic reality. In 1636, for example, on the occasion of the great feast of the dead, the "Old Men and the notables of the Country," according to Father Brébeuf, "took possession secretly of a considerable quantity" of beaver cloaks.[50] In 1644, the missionaries were congratulating themselves on having converted Barnabé Otsinonannhont, for "this man has always been one of the leading personages of his tribe, on account of his birth (for they have their nobility here, as well as in France) and are as proud of it."[51] Although the comparison is obviously exaggerated, it echoes another comment of 1648 about access to and symbolic value of curing rituals. "When the prescription is given, the Captains of the village hold a council, as in a matter of public importance, and deliberate whether they will exert themselves for the patient. And, if there be a number of sick who are persons of note, it is impossible to conceive the ambition and intrigue displayed by their relatives and friends to obtain the preference for them, because the public cannot pay those honors to all."[52]

Taken together, these comments are indicative of emerging class relations and clearly show that there was unequal access to material and symbolic goods. Hitherto, social relations within Huron society had been based on redistribution and sharing. With the advent of the fur trade, however, social relations based on redistribution developed at the expense of those based on sharing. We know that redistribution carries with it a specific tension, because it sets unequal acquisition against equal consumption. It is true that the function of many traditional rituals was to counteract unequal acquisition of wealth by guaranteeing redistribution of goods in the community. Should these redistribution mechanisms disappear, unequal consumption would follow, bringing with it new social relations—relations that had been latent from the beginning. The work of the missionaries helped create a framework for this new social relationship.

The missionaries urged the converts not to take part in the feast of the dead, curing rituals, banquets, and exchanges of goods organized in response to dreams.[53] For ideological and moral reasons, the Jesuits also asked the converts to live among themselves, apart from non-Christians. By doing this, the missionaries effectively severed the traditional bonds of solidarity within the community and cut converts off from the redistribution network. As "the Feasts, which are the chief pleasure of the country, are so many sacrifices to the Devil," all Christians had to shun them. This meant that those who were well off did not share their wealth, while for those without resources "it requires a very ardent Faith to banish oneself from them."[54] As can be seen, Christian precepts favoured the haves and penalized the have-nots. Moreover, some Amerindians quickly grasped the fact that Christianity cost them less and accordingly took advantage of it:

> "The Demons," said one of them, "command us to do impossible things. They do not give us what is necessary for a feast, and they require us to make one. Sometimes they compel us, if we would avoid some great misfortune, to offer what we do not possess, and cannot get. Does not this show that they either trifle with us, or that they are pleased to see us miserable? But the God of the Christians commands them to do nothing that is impossible for them; and, if they fail, it is of their own will. It is by this," he said, "that I recognize that he alone is the Master of our lives, since he desires only our good."[55]

Despite their special status, Christians could not easily escape the redistribution ceremonies. Any attempt to do so immediately led to charges of witchcraft by the unconverted,[56] charges that became more frequent after 1634.[57]

Christianity offered two concepts that legitimated such opting out. First, it introduced Amerindians to the idea that acts were private property, that is, the private concern of each individual: to each, in the afterlife, according to his or her works.[58] Then, on the symbolic level, it proposed the view of a world divided between the redeemed and the damned—a view expressed in terms of inclusion and exclusion, to which a social content could be easily added.[59] Christianity thus justified "the big stones" in opting out of redistribution mechanisms, thereby legitimating inequality

and privileged status. In fact, while the fur trade accentuated the relative importance of redistribution compared to reciprocity, the Christian religion effectively restricted redistribution of the social product.

In 1642, Father Jérôme Lalemant wrote that "the grace of baptism works powerfully in a heart."[60] Looking at individual behaviour, one is indeed struck by the profound effect of baptism, and the sometimes radical personality change in certain converts. Like the social structure, personality structure was equally affected by Christianity, and this made interiorization of the new religious values all the more effective. The new religion was thrust upon a society already in the process of destructuration—that is, the disintegration of social and cultural patterns of thought. This was aggravated by the society itself, and it touched individuals whose sense of security had been deeply shaken and whose personalities were undergoing a similar process. It was as though this religion were reprogramming and restructuring profoundly traumatized human beings. One cannot help drawing a parallel, hypothetically at least, with the methods of modern religious sects for converting individuals who are either socially marginal or in a (temporary) state of psychological instability. We are familiar with the effects of personality restructuring resulting from membership in an institution that provides the double security of human and dogmatic support.

What stands out primarily is the intensity of religious practice. Huron converts and the Christian Algonkins of Quebec and Miscou displayed an uncommon degree of zeal and fervour.[61] According to Marie de l'Incarnation, it was beyond description.[62] The missionaries noted that there was nothing half-hearted about the Amerindians' faith, and neither cold nor ice nor distance could deter them.[63] The new Christians were proselytizers as well, and despite all opposition worked ardently to win over friends and relations. Often they had greater success than the missionaries.[64]

The more active the converts, the more they opposed tradition; the greater the aggressivity and hatred displayed by their traditionalist compatriots, the greater their own conviction about their role as "public victims," martyrs to the faith.[65] Their self-image as members of the chosen few was strengthened by the many sufferings they were able to offer God as a passport to heaven.[66] By implication, pleasure was forbidden in this context of suffering. Take the case of the young girl who adopted a melancholy air in public in order to avoid "the licence which the young men here assume . . . 'When I go anywhere' (she said), 'I alter my appearance; I keep my eyes cast down, and my forehead wrinkled, and I try to look sad so that no one is encouraged to accost me.'"[67]

The new religion involved a highly negative self-image: that of the sinner who must redeem himself or herself. The following reply by an Attikamègue convert to Father Buteux offers convincing evidence of this: "*Question*: 'What thoughts hast thou about thyself?' *Answer*: 'That I am a dog, and less than a flea before God.'"[68] The convert was afraid of himself, afraid of his thoughts and desires.[69]

In these circumstances, it comes as no surprise to find converts flogging themselves to expiate their sins,[70] rolling in the snow to escape the "infernal flames" of temptation,[71] or scorching themselves with live coals.[72] It is true that traditional Huron civilization had forms of bodily discipline and self-repressive behaviour. Children were trained from a very young age, for example, to withstand the cold by being scantily clad.[73] Hurons (and Amerindians in general) were very hardy in this respect and always dressed less warmly than the French.[74] Boys were trained to hide their emotions. Men were expected to remain impassive in the face of pain or suffering,[75] to endure ritual fasting for a successful hunt, or to harden themselves to pain by applying brands to their bodies.[76] Such practices appear to have been the exception rather than the rule, however, and were intended to develop, rather than break down, bodily strength and resistance. Conversion, on the other hand, established conscious self-repression as a basic form of behaviour, accompanied by the massive introjection of the missionaries' directives.[77]

Guilt and self-conscious repression, combined with the ostentatious and proselytizing practice of their religion, epitomized the converts' behaviour. The evolution of the human animal to the human being (or *animal sapiens*) involves the conscious repression of basic instincts, beginning with a radical transformation of the original value system. According to Herbert Marcuse, this conversion of the pleasure principle to the reality principle can be defined as follows:[78]

FROM	TO
immediate satisfaction	delayed satisfaction
pleasure	restraint of pleasure
joy (play)	toil (work)
receptiveness	productiveness
absence of repression	security

Transformations within Huron society in the first half of the seventeenth century all resulted in the repression of the pleasure principle. Wars, disease, longer and more intensified labour, and finally the social division of labour, were all factors that brought new constraints and prepared the ground for establishing further controls that went beyond those traditionally required by Huron society. Christianity was to catalyze the need for an ideology and institutions to reinforce what Marcuse calls surplus repression. Theoretically, the inhibition of the pleasure principle in response to the imperatives of reality was aimed at guaranteeing greater individual security. The wars and epidemics that led to the disappearance of Huronia were accompanied by an observable inhibition of desire, a rise in surplus repression, and growing insecurity.

It is perhaps needless to add that constraints imposed in adulthood were not truly interiorized, the Huron super-ego having been formed in the context of the permissive upbringing characteristic of Amerindian civilizations.[79] However, the previously accepted instinctive tendencies were becoming increasingly incompatible with an ever more hostile reality. Although most constraints imposed on children were interiorized and belonged to the unconscious, among converts no prohibition imposed in adulthood could become an automatic, unconscious response. It could only give rise to a strong feeling of guilt accompanied by the need to adopt conspicuous forms of religious practice.

The concentration of religious capital in the hands of the missionaries brought about the correlative dispossession of the converted. The missionaries' conversion strategy aimed at removing the Amerindian's entire identity, so that "being oneself" gave way to identification with another, to "being like".[80] The religious specialist's view of the convert established his or her identity. It was a view that both structured and destructured the personality. Unable to escape the eye of their religious mentors, the most credulous converts lived a life of pretence, mimicking the desired behaviour. They wore a mask and played a part. What the missionaries had once condemned, they now praised. Behaviour previously considered pagan was no longer associated with witchcraft. Thus the application of live brands to the body became a Christian purification practice—an act that, by the same token, embodied the recognition and legitimation of the missionary. Indeed, the influence of spells, associated with the privilege of being Christian, was now publicly recognized.

NOTES

[Editor's note: *JR* refers to Reuben G. Thwaites, ed., *The Jesuit Relations and Allied Documents*, Cleveland: Burrows Brothers 1896–1901, 73 vols.]

1. *JR* (1639), 16:219.
2. *JR* (1648–9), 34:227.
3. *JR* (1639), 16:59–61, 17:61–3.
4. *JR* (1637), 13:167–9.
5. *JR* (1638–9), 15:187–9.
6. *JR* (1640), 19:123.
7. *JR* (1642), 23:23–5, 101–3.
8. *JR* (1645–6), 30:23.
9. *JR* (1647–8), 32:179, 33:69.
10. *JR* (1647–8), 33:69.
11. *JR* (1648–9), 34:227.
12. *JR* (1648–9), 34:227. See also (1648–9), 33:227, 34:83.
13. *JR* (1637), 12:89–91, 14:7–9, 41–3; (1639), 17:189–91; (1640), 19:219–27; (1662–3), 48:123.
14. *JR* (1636), 9:283–5; (1637), 12:47.
15. *JR* (1636), 9:283; (1637), 12:41.
16. *JR*, (1636), 9:283; (1637), 12:41, 75.
17. *JR* (1638), 14:231–3.
18. Marie de l'Incarnation, Mère. *Lettres historiques de la Vénérable Mère Marie de l'Incarnation sur le Canada*. Edited by B. Sulte. Quebec: L'Action sociale, 1927, letter of 3 September 1640, 23–4. Groulx, Lionel. "Missionnaires de l'Est en Nouvelle-France. Réduction et séminaires indiens." *Revue d'histoire de l'Amérique française* 3:1 (June 1949): 62–5. See also *JR* (1647–8), 32:213–15.
19. *JR* (1639), 16:251.
20. *JR* (1645–6), 29:257–9; (1647–8), 33:141–3.
21. *JR* (1639), 17:33, 95; (1642–3), 24:237–9.
22. *JR* (1640–1), 20:231, 21:147–9; (1642–3), 24:239–41, 25:25–7.
23. *JR* (1645–6), 29:277–9.
24. *JR* (1642), 23:27.
25. *JR* (1642), 23: 199–201.
26. *JR* (1642–3), 25:27. See also 24:233–9, (1644–5), 28:89–91.
27. *JR* (1637), 13:127, 14:15.
28. *JR* (1637), 13:141.
29. *JR* (1645–6), 29:277–9.
30. *JR* (1644–5), 28:87–9.

31. *JR* (1645–6), 28:87.

32. *JR* (1639), 17:53.

33. *JR* (1640), 19:127–9.

34. *JR* (1639), 17:37–9.

35. *JR* (1639), 17:25–7; (1640), 20:51–3.

36. *JR* (1639), 17: 57–61.

37. *JR* (1640–1), 21:235.

38. *JR* (1642), 23:105–7.

39. *JR* (1643–4), 27:69; see also 105–9.

40. *JR* (1643–4), 27:111.

41. *JR* (1655–6), 42:73.

42. Bourdieu, Pierre. "Une interprétation de la théorie de la religion selon Max Weber." *Archives européennes de sociologie* 12 (1971): 9.

43. *JR* (1637), 14:9.

44. M. Weber, *Wirtschaft und Gesellschaft*, 1:385, cited by Bourdieu, "Une interprétation de la théorie de la religion," 9.

45. Bourdieu, Pierre. "Genèse et structure du champ religieux." *Revue française de sociologie* 12: 3 (1971): 313.

46. Bourdieu, "Une interprétation de la théorie de la religion," 9.

47. Bourdieu, "Genèse et structure du champ religieux," 315.

48. Bourdieu, "Une interprétation de la théorie de la religion," 10.

49. *JR* (1636), 10:231–3.

50. *JR* (1636), 10:303.

51. *JR* (1643–4), 26:307.

52. *JR* (1647–8), 33:205.

53. *JR* (1642), 23:125.

54. *JR* (1642), 23:187.

55. *JR* (1642), 23:129.

56. *JR* (1635), 8:95.

57. CA, 424.

58. *JR* (1634), 6:181.

59. Bourdieu, "Genèse et structure du champ religieux," 298.

60. *JR* (1642), 23:193.

61. *JR* (1647–8), 32:195–219; (1650–1), 37:51–61.

62. Marie de l'Incarnation, *Lettres historiques*, 35, 52, 55.

63. *JR* (1647), 31:155, 32:49–53.

64. *JR* (1639), 17:51. See also Marie de l'Incarnation, *Lettres historiques*, 1 September 1639, 22.

65. *JR* (1645–6), 30:19–21; see also (1643–4), 26:217–57.

66. *JR* (1642), 23:109.

67. *JR* (1642), 23:73; see also (1638), 15:107; (1642), 23:63, 73, 193; (1643–4), 26:229; (1647–8), 32:215–19.

68. *JR* (1650–1), 37:59.

69. *JR* (1647–8), 32:217.

70. *JR* (1645–6), 29:75.

71. *JR* (1645–6), 30:39.

72. *JR* (1645–6), 30:39.

73. Sagard, Gabriel. *Histoire du Canada et voyages que les Frères mineurs récollets y on faicts pour la conversion des infidèles depuis l'an 1615*. Paris: Edwin Tross, 1866. 4 vols., 318; Sagard, Gabriel. *Le grand voyage du pays des Hurons*. Montreal: Éditions Hurtubise-HMH, 1976, 119 (171).

74. *JR* (1657–8), 44:281.

75. *JR* (1662–3), 48:169; (1645–6), 39:30.

76. *JR* (1637), 12:69–71.

77. Marcuse, Herbert. *Eros and Civilization*. Boston: Beacon Press, 1966, 16.

78. Marcuse, *Eros and Civilization*, 12, 38.

79. Marcuse, *Eros and Civilization*, 31–5.

80. Olivier, Christiane. *Les enfants de Jocaste, l'empreinte de la mare*. Paris: Denoël-Gonthier, 1980, 67; see also 32, 65–72, 162–5, 176, 181.

Chapter 3

The Seigneurial Regime in New France

READINGS

Primary Documents

Historical Interpretations

INTRODUCTION

The seigneurial system stands as one of the defining aspects of the colonial experience in New France. Under this system of land tenure, large land grants were made by the French Crown to prominent subjects called *seigneurs* who were required, in turn, to grant strips of land to tenants called *censitaires* (also known as *habitants*) in exchange for the perpetual payment of rent and dues. Land was not to be sold to the censitaires, who owned their farms, and they were tied to their seigneur through a complex system of mutual obligations. A seigneur could become wealthy if he succeeded in attracting censitaires to the land, and it was assumed that paternalism and self-interest would guide him to provide the services necessary for settlement and encourage his tenants to work hard.

The seigneurial system defined everyone's duties clearly, but it required a great deal of management. Was this seigneur doing his part? Was that tenant using land or resources without permission? The first primary source is an excerpt from a memoir written by the intendant Jacques

Raudot addressed to the French Minister of Marine in 1707. In his memoir, Raudot highlights many problems relative to the working of the seigneurial system in New France and suggests many reforms to make it more effective. When Peter Kalm travelled through New France in 1749, he noted another effect of the system: the orderly arrangement of tenants' houses that were not in a village, but situated to allow the tenants to exploit their land and the transportation corridors offered by the St Lawrence and its tributaries. He also noted the poverty among the censitaires, whose happiness was tied directly to how well or poorly their crops fared in a particular year. With tenants living in this fashion, it was almost inevitable that the system would influence the social interactions between tenants, between tenants and seigneurs, and between seigneurs. As Colin Coates demonstrates, for seigneurs, the priorities were enlarging their holdings and establishing themselves as indispensable to the colonial effort. They renamed geographical features in their seigneuries, served in the military (French and British), allocated land to tenants, sued tenants, and played the role of social elite very well, maintaining their positions despite the considerable upheaval that accompanied the Conquest. In the final selection, Allan Greer studies the importance of the rents due to the landlords, arguing that these rents could be quite burdensome to the censitaires. He shows that it was difficult for the latter to accumulate wealth in the way that seigneurs could and did. For most colonists, survival was the priority.

QUESTIONS FOR CONSIDERATION

1. What do you find most remarkable or surprising about the way the seigneurial system worked?
2. What were the main abuses of the seigneurial system in New France according to Raudot, and how could the Minister of the Marine remedy them?
3. It is fairly well known that lands within the seigneuries were laid out in relation to rivers. How might this distribution affect the way people socialized?
4. List some examples of the ways in which the Lanaudière family consolidated its power under the seigneurial system.
5. What kinds of dues did seigneurs extract from their censitaires? How lucrative were they for the former and burdensome for the latter?

SUGGESTIONS FOR FURTHER READING

Louise Dechêne, *Habitants and Merchants in Seventeenth-Century Montreal* (Montreal and Kingston: McGill-Queen's University Press, 1992).

Allan Greer, *Peasant, Lord & Merchant: Rural Society in Three Quebec Parishes 1740–1840* (Toronto: University of Toronto Press, 1985).

———, *The People of New France* (Toronto: University of Toronto Press, 1997).

Benoit Grenier, *Brève histoire du régime seigneurial* (Montreal: Boréal, 2012).

Gregory Kennedy, *Something of a Peasant Paradise? Comparing Rural Societies in Acadie and the Loudunais, 1604–1755* (Montreal and Kingston: McGill-Queen's University Press, 2014).

William Bennett Munro, ed., *Documents Relating to the Seigniorial Tenure in Canada, 1598–1854* (Toronto: The Champlain Society, 1908).

Marcel Trudel, *The Seigneurial Regime* (Ottawa: Canadian Historical Association, 1971).

Primary Documents

1   From Jacques Raudot, "Memoir of Jacques Raudot, Intendant, to M. de Pontchartrain, Minister of Marine, on the Growth of Seigniorial Abuses in Canada, November 10, 1707," D.C. Bélanger, trans. and ed.

Correspondance Générale, XXVI, 7.

My Lord,

The spirit of enterprise, which has always, as you know, far more deviousness and chicanery than truth and righteousness, has begun to appear here recently and increases daily in a most negative way. If we could curb its undesirable side, *this spirit could augur well for the future*, though the simple life of bygone years would be far better. But the past is past, and to my mind there is nothing more pernicious than this spirit and more harmful to the repose and the tranquility that one must give to the people of a colony, which can only be upheld and increased by the labour of its inhabitants, and which they must not be given the occasion to turn away from.

Since almost none of the commerce that they have conducted followed the rules, the notaries, bailiffs, and even judges are all ignorant, especially those who were trained in this colony, as they have for the most part worked their lands *without proper assurances from those who conceded them*, there is no property against which one cannot find a fault, no division which is uncontestable, no widow that could not sued into a common state,[1] and no guardian who could not be brought to court for the accounts that he kept for his wards. It is not that things were done in bad faith, but rather that ignorance and a lack of observance for the rules in all these affairs has produced disorder, which would become worse if those who are imbued with the spirit of enterprise, either of their own accord or under the council of others, brought various matters to court. There would be more trials in this country than there are persons; and

since judges are obliged to follow the law, which they are beginning to get a sense of, as they apply it to cases where ignorance of the law insured that it was not followed, they would be obligated to perpetrate a thousand injustices, which I would have been forced to do myself, My Lord, if I had followed the strict letter of the law in many of the cases that were brought before me.

For all these reasons, My Lord, I believe that you could not do greater good to the inhabitants of this country than if you could obtain from His Majesty *a declaration that would guarantee permanent ownership over land* following existing property lines for those *who have been in possession of said property for five years* or who have laboured therein or held a title, in any form, that validates all present divisions, and which would forbid parties from initiating legal proceedings regarding guardianship agreements and legal waivers that wives have had to make to their husband's community, and which would forbid judges from accepting cases of this nature. Also, My Lord, the declaration would validate all the decrees that have come to pass and all other acts, as well as contracts that have been passed up to the present and the rights that individuals have obtained from each other, *except in odious cases*, for instance in acts and contracts where evidence of usury, misconduct, or fraud is present, or in cases of appropriation through violence or abuse of authority.

Only in this way My Lord, can you put this country at peace and tranquility, which without this just precaution will always be unhappy and unable to grow, as its inhabitants, who should be busy cultivating their land, will instead be forced to occupy themselves with spurious litigation. I know this evil, My Lord, through all the business that is continually brought before me and which has overwhelmed me since I have arrived here; because these poor inhabitants have found me easy to deal with and do not need to dip into their purse to plead their case, scarcely a day goes by where I do not issue several ordinances to straighten out various matters that were concluded before I arrived. There are even those who, fearing trials, come to see me to ask that I prevent such trials from occurring, their ignorance making them fearful of the smallest threats from those who are as ignorant as they.

I am honoured to tell you, My Lord, that if His Majesty gives them the declaration that I have the honour to ask for them, it will be necessary to insure the ownership over land to its rightful owners that it contain a clause that covers cases of simple possession because formalities were often not followed here when land grants were made. Many *habitants* have toiled on the mere word of the *seigneurs*, others on simple bills that did not properly lay out the dues related to their grant. Out of this has come much abuse, where *habitants* who have worked without a valid title have been subjected to arbitrary rents and contracts, which they are forced to accept because otherwise they will lose the fruits of their labour. This has created a situation whereby in almost all of the *seigneuries'* rights and obligations are different; some pay in one way, others in another way, all following the whim of the *seigneur* who made the grant. They have even introduced in almost all the contracts *a retrait roturier that is not contained in the Custom of Paris*,[2] but that has become customary in this country and which stipulates that a *seigneur*, when land is sold, can take back the land that he granted *en roture* for the sale price, and in so doing they have abused of the *retrait conditionnel*[3] that is stipulated in the Custom of Paris and which is sometimes contained in contracts of sale where the seller reserves the right to buy back the property, though it is not established between *seigneurs* and tenants; this preference, My Lord, hinders all land sales.

There are concessions where the capons[4] that are paid to the *seigneurs*, are in fact paid in kind or in cash at the whim of the *seigneurs*; these capons are appraised at 30 sols but are only in fact worth 10 sols; the *seigneurs* then force their tenants to give them money, which is extremely burdensome for them because they often do not have the means to pay, because while 30 sols might not seem like a lot of money, it is in fact a great deal of money in this country where specie is rare, aside from the fact that it seems to me that whenever there are accounts payable, when there is a choice, that choice should be made to the advantage of the debtor, as owing specie is a burden when he cannot pay in kind.

The *seigneurs* have also introduced in their fiefs the right of the *four banal*,[5] which the *habitants* cannot profit from because their homes are often quite far from the *seigneur's* house, where this oven must be placed, and which cannot be placed anywhere more convenient, no matter what, because most homes are far from each other and it would not be possible to bring the dough to the oven in all seasons; in winter it would freeze before it could be brought there. The *seigneurs* are vexed by these circumstances and do not exercise their full banal rights at present, but they will no doubt turn these into a title that must be bought for a large sum, and in so doing they will acquire a right that does not in any way benefit the *habitants*. This is called, My Lord, to give oneself a title in order to cause future vexation. [. . .]

I thus believe, My Lord, according to your pleasure, that to bring some semblance of order and to give justice to the *habitants* in a way that the *seigneurs* have not done at present and to prevent future abuse, that it is necessary for His Majesty to *make a declaration that will reform* and that will settle for the future the rights and obligations that the *seigneurs* have given themselves and that they will give themselves in the future, and that His Majesty will order in the future; and that His Majesty will order that they only take by arpent granted, one sol of rent and one capon by arpent of frontage, or twenty sols, at the discretion of the debtor; that the preference clause that *seigneurs* have given themselves in the sale of *héritages roturiers* be removed; that the right of *four banal* be removed; that in areas where fishing is practised the seigneurial rights be diminished to a simple tenth, without further conditions; and that the *droit de banalité* be maintained, and that a

mill be built in all seigneuries within a year, without which the right will be considered to have fallen into disuse, and the *habitants* will not have to mill their grain at the seigneurial mill thereafter; without this, My Lord, we will never be able to get the seigneurs to build mills, a situation which causes much suffering among the *habitants*. [. . .]

I remain, with profound respect, My Lord, your most humble, your most obedient, and your most obligated servant,
Raudot
At Quebec, on this 10th of November 1707.

NOTES

1. That is, "no widow whose dower right might not be contested."
2. The *retrait rotutier* was the right of the seignior, when a habitant sold his farm, to exercise an option of buying in the land at the sale price.
3. The Custom of Paris recognized the *retrait conditionnel,* or *jus retraiteur,* whereby a dominant seignior might, within 40 days after any sale of a sub-seigniory, buy it in by tendering the sale price to the purchaser (*Coutume de Paris,* Article XX.).
4. The reference is to the seigniorial *rentes,* which were usually paid in poultry and grain.

5. The Custom of Paris (Article LXXI.) recognized the seignior's right to erect a seigniorial oven, and, when he had so stipulated in the title-deeds given to his censitaires, to compel the latter to make use of such oven at a fixed toll. This toll was usually one twenty-fourth of the bread. The nature and extent of this right is discussed in a paper on "The Droit de Banalité during the French Régime in Canada," in American Historical Association, *Report,* 1899, I. 205–28.

---

2 From Peter Kalm, *Travels into North America: Containing Its Natural History and a Circumstantial Account of Its Plantations and Agriculture in General . . .* (London: T. Lowndes, 1773), vol. 2, 242–4, 330–1.

All the farms in *Canada* stand separate from each other, so that each farmer has his possessions entirely distinct from those of his neighbour. Each church, it is true, has a little village near it; but that consists chiefly of the parsonage, a school for the boys and girls of the place, and of the houses of tradesmen, but rarely of farm-houses; and if that was the case, yet their fields were separated. The

farm-houses hereabouts are generally built all along the rising banks of the river, either close to the water or at some distance from it, and about three or four *arpens* from each other. To some farms are annexed small orchards: but they are in general without them; however, almost every farmer has a kitchen-garden.

[. . .]

The farm-houses are generally built of stone, but sometimes of timber, and have three or four rooms. The windows are seldom of glass, but most frequently of paper. They have iron stoves in one of the rooms, and chimnies in the rest. The roofs are covered with boards. The crevices and chinks are filled up with clay. The other buildings are covered with straw.

There are several *Crosses* put up by the road side, which is parallel to the shores of the river. These crosses are very common in *Canada*, and are put up to excite devotion in the traveller. They are made of wood, five or six yards high, and proportionally broad. In that side which looks towards the road is a square hole, in which they place an image of our Saviour, the cross, or of the holy Virgin, with the child in her arms; and before that they put a piece of glass, to prevent its being spoiled by the weather. Those crosses, which are not far from churches, are very much adorned, and they put up about them all the instruments which they think the *Jews* employed in crucifying our Saviour, such as a hammer, tongs, nails, a flask of vinegar, and perhaps many more than were really made use of. A figure of the cock, which crowed when *St. Peter* denied our Lord, is commonly put at the top of the cross.

The country on both sides was very delightful to-day, and the fine state of its cultivation added greatly to the beauty of the scene. It could really be called a village, beginning at *Montreal*, and ending at *Quebec*, which is a distance of more than one hundred and eighty miles; for the farm-houses are never above five arpens, and sometimes but three, asunder, a few places excepted. The prospect is exceedingly beautiful, when the river goes on for some miles together in a strait line, because it then shortens the distances between the houses, and makes them form exactly one continued village.

[. . .]

August 26th. [. . .] The common people in the country seem to be very poor. They have the necessaries of life, and but little else. They are content with meals of dry bread and water, bringing all other provisions, such as butter, cheese, flesh, poultry, eggs, &c. to town, in order to get money for them, for which they buy clothes and brandy for themselves, and dresses for their women. Notwithstanding their poverty, they are always chearful, and in high spirits.

August 29th. By the desire of the governor-general, marquis *de la Jonquiere*, and of marquis *de la Galissonniere*, I set out, with some *French* gentlemen, to visit the pretended silver-mine, or the lead-mine, near the bay *St. Paul*. I was glad to undertake this journey, as it gave me an opportunity of seeing a much greater part of the country than I should otherwise have done. This morning therefore we set out on our tour in a boat, and went down the river *St. Lawrence*.

The prospect near *Quebec* is very lively from the river. The town lies very high, and all the churches and other buildings appear very conspicuous. The ships in the river below ornament the landscape on that side. The powder magazine, which stands at the summit of the mountain on which the town is built, towers above all the other buildings.

The country we passed by afforded a no less charming sight. The river *St. Lawrence* flows nearly from south to north here; on both sides of it are cultivated fields, but more on the west side than on the east side. The hills on both shores are steep and high. A number of fine hills, separated from each other, large fields, which looked quite white from the corn with which they are covered, and excellent woods of deciduous trees, made the country round us look very pleasant.

Historical Interpretations

3   From Colin M. Coates, "Seigneurial Landscapes," in *The Metamorphoses of Landscape and Community in Early Quebec* (Montreal and Kingston: McGill-Queen's University Press, 2000), 13–31, 171–6.

Land was no longer free as air or light,
A fixed division mark'd each owner's right.

Ovid, *Metamorphoses*, 12

In the 300 years following Jacques Cartier's first sighting of the area that became the seigneuries of Batiscan and Sainte-Anne de la Pérade, the landscape underwent irrevocable change. In contrast to the shields of forests that had confronted the early European explorers and settlers, it became possible by the early nineteenth century to compare the land to European landscapes and to use European artistic conventions to capture it on paper. The changes that occurred were long-term ones caused by different perceptions and uses of the land. At least in the areas close to the St Lawrence, the landscape became essentially European, with a visible hierarchy of land use.

The appropriation of the landscape by French settlers involved the importing of new animal and plant species and obviously a new race of humans. This process entailed the distancing of the native animals, plants, and humans from the new settlements. There was a dual process in the transformation of the landscape. In the first place, the French colonial state and the seigneurs played important roles in an overall restructuring of the land; the respective importance of the seigneurs and the state varied over time. Even more important, the practical labour of generations of habitants irrevocably altered the bases of society.

REDEFINING THE LAND

Naming

One of the most important ways in which the colonial state initially made its presence felt in Batiscan and Sainte-Anne de la Pérade was through attempts to redefine the land, to draw and redraw borders around the areas.[1] The first act of appropriating the territories in the name of the French king was to name them (or properly speaking, rename them).

The origins of the word "Batiscan" are obscure, though it doubtless has an Amerindian derivation. Samuel de Champlain first mentioned "a river called Batiscan" in his account of his 1603 voyage.[2] Among the various geographical phenomena that he saw during his explorations, he found rivers particularly noteworthy. This interest illustrates the bias of the typical explorer, intrigued by geographical phenomena which demarcate journeys as well as those which promise future explorations.[3] However, the ambiguous chronology surrounding its mention in the account leaves open the possibility that the name does not necessarily refer to the same river as today. Indeed, Champlain's 1612 map placed the "contrée de bastisquan" to the west of the Rivière Saint-Maurice. By contrast, Marc Lescarbot's map of 1609 illustrated and named the "R. Batescan" in the same area as the present one. Even if, in reporting the earthquake of 1663, the Jesuits alluded to "the river which the barbarians call Batiscan,"[4] it was a French decision whether or not to adopt the name.

The river with the Algonquin name formed the symbolic locus of future French settlement. The title "Batiscan" was extended to the seigneury, indicating that early French interest in the area lay, not in the land itself, but in the river and the transportation that it provided into the interior and into fur-trading areas. Over time, French settlers populated the territory and placed more importance on the land than the river. They even occasionally domesticated the Aboriginal origin of the name. In 1783, for example, the habitants living along the river drew up a petition in which the name was given as "Baptiste Camp".[5]

In his account of the 1609 voyage and on his 1612 map, Champlain had named the river to the east of the Batiscan the Sainte-Marie. This name later came to refer to the seigneury on the west bank of the river, and the river itself took on the name of an island at the mouth, Île Sainte-Anne.[6] As in Batiscan, the river's name was extended to both the seigneury on the east bank and the parish, which included settlers on both sides. The names Sainte-Marie and Sainte-Anne, linked as they were to Christian beliefs and particularly to the Marian cult of the Catholic Counter-Reformation, illustrated another imperial aim: the propagation of the faith.

But the region owed its territorial names not only to explorers and their imperial initiatives. Local seigneurs also made their imprint. To distinguish it from the other Sainte-Annes in the colony, the seigneurial patronymic La Pérade gradually replaced *près Batiscan* (near Batiscan) in the eighteenth century. Likewise, in Batiscan the choice of the Jesuit pioneers for the parish names of Saint-François-Xavier and Saint-Stanislas surely reflect the order's ownership. Finally, when the Jesuits' agent sold businessman Thomas Coffin an *arrière-fief* (a fief within a larger seigneury) in Batiscan in 1795, it is not difficult to imagine the inspiration for the name

Saint-Thomas. In these ways seigneurs replicated for their own purposes the state's initial process of imposing names on the region.

Distributing Fiefs

Conceded as seigneuries at different times, Batiscan and Sainte-Anne illustrate two important moments in the distribution of fiefs during the seventeenth century. According to its charter, the Compagnie de la Nouvelle France was compelled to establish a French population in the colony. In 1636 it conveyed ten leagues of land downstream from the Rivière Saint-Maurice to Jacques de La Ferté, the king's confessor. Three years later, La Ferté conceded part of the immense tract in *arrière-fief* to the Jesuits. The shape of Batiscan seigneury resembled other land grants of the period: a long trapezoid with relatively little waterfront.[7]

Jacques de La Ferté "for the love of God" conveyed the area around the Rivière Batiscan to the Jesuits, the religious order leading the Counter-Reformation and one of the largest landholders in the colony. The Jesuits' deed stipulated the width of the seigneury—from one-quarter league beyond the Batiscan to one-quarter league beyond the Rivière Champlain—but left its depth ill-defined.[8] It may have been Champlain's reference to an Aboriginal population in the Batiscan area that led to the decision to concede it to the Jesuits. According to the deed, the seigneury was intended for Christianized Amerindians, but their lack of interest and hostility delayed settlement for decades. The Jesuits' intention was clearly to create a new France in the New World, preferably with converted Natives. However, agents of the order did not perform the ritual taking symbolic possession of the seigneury until 1662.

Batiscan seigneury represented one of the larger land grants in the colony. Nonetheless, the exact boundaries were not immediately defined. In 1667 the Jesuits claimed, in vague fashion, ownership of "a space of land

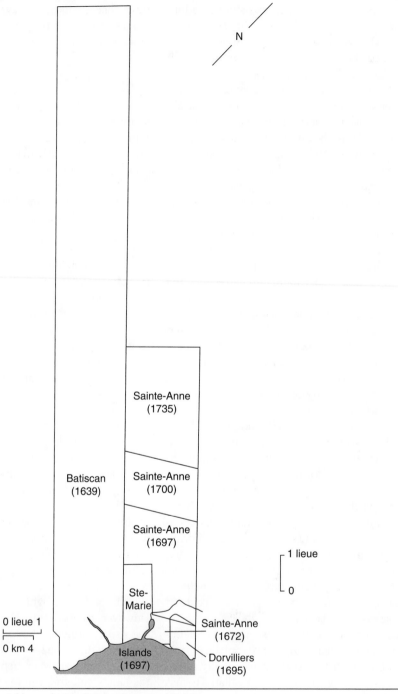

Figure 1 Seigneurial boundaries, Sainte-Anne and Batiscan

between the Rivière Batiscan and the Rivière Champlain."[9] Ten years later it was acknowledged that the breadth consisted of two leagues of river frontage from the east bank of the Rivière Champlain to a quarter league beyond the Rivière Batiscan.[10] The seigneury extended 20 leagues into the interior, representing some 282 240 arpents (1 arpent equals 0.342 hectares). Batiscan did not appear in the colonial census of 1663, but many settlers received land grants in the following decade.[11] According to the seigneurs, confirmed deeds of settlement had been delayed by two main factors, the Iroquois menace and the absence of established authority—"having no regular or established form of justice in the area."[12] From the beginning, European settlement required the authority of the colonial state.

Changes in royal policy account for the difference in size of the concessions of Batiscan and Sainte-Anne. After Louis XIV assumed direct control of the colony in the 1660s, he expressed the desire to limit the size of seigneurial grants and to curtail the granting of seigneuries to religious orders. The details of the granting of Île Sainte-Anne to Michel Gamelain, probably in 1666, are not known,[13] but it is clear that the seigneury extended over only a tiny area. Gamelain used this property to establish a fur-trade post, but he nonetheless did concede some land on the island.[14]

Intendant Jean Talon pursued the king's policy more thoroughly, granting smaller seigneuries, many of them to officers of the Carignan regiment.[15] This desire to facilitate the creation of a noble military-seigneurial class led to Talon's approval of the purchase of Gamelain's land by Edmond de Suève and Thomas de Lanouguère. In 1672 the intendant officially recognized the purchase and further conceded land to a depth of one league between the Rivière Sainte-Anne and the seigneury of Grondines to the two noble officers. As he stated, this grant was given "in consideration of the good, useful, and praiseworthy services that they have rendered to His Majesty in different places, both in Old France and in New France since they passed to the latter on His Majesty's order, as well as in consideration of the services that they intend to render in the future."[16] The intendant explicitly justified the officers' status as seigneurs by mentioning their service to the monarch. Members of the de Lanouguère family subsequently carved out a long career of service to their king, regardless of the throne on which he sat.

The co-owners of Sainte-Anne divided the seigneury into two distinct sections. In 1695 de Suève willed his half to Edmond Chorel de Champlain, who passed it into the hands of his brother, François Chorel d'Orvilliers. As in the western part of Sainte-Anne, the seigneurial family names over time came to identify the area. However, the seigneurs who owned the eastern section did not reside there. The d'Orvilliers family lived principally in Champlain seigneury during the French regime, and subsequent seigneurs of Sainte-Anne Est in the early nineteenth century were also absentee owners: Moses Hart, a merchant in Trois-Rivières, and Pierre Charest, a merchant at Saint-Joseph de Soulanges.[17]

From time to time boundary disputes set the seigneurial families of the two parts of Sainte-Anne against each other, but by the 1730s it was clear that de Lanouguère's son, Pierre-Thomas Tarieu de La Pérade, enjoyed greater local prominence. He and his mother had successfully petitioned for the extension of the original boundaries in 1697, 1700, and 1735.[18] The two smaller fiefs on either side, Dorvilliers to the east and Sainte-Marie to the west, found themselves bounded on the north by the expanded seigneury. By 1735 Sainte-Anne seigneury encompassed some 60 square leagues. Although the Tarieu de Lanaudière family was by no means always present at its seigneury, it seems to have participated actively in local issues. Like the

Jesuits in Batiscan, its members exercised their seigneurial privileges at certain times and provided a link to the world of the colonial state.

Hierarchy in the Landscape

In contrast to the Aboriginal occupation of the territory, the French landholding system entailed a hierarchical view of society. The king, in whom ultimate title rested, distributed tracts of land to seigneurs and preserved certain rights on that land, particularly concerning minerals and timber. The seigneur in turn distributed lots to tenants (*censitaires*) but placed limits on the tenants' control of their property.

When the seigneurs began to distribute land in their seigneuries, it was of course impossible for them to know that immigration would remain negligible over the next century. They could not know that future population growth and the concomitant increase of their seigneurial revenues would depend almost exclusively on natural demographic trends. Therefore in an examination of the way in which seigneurs preferred their landscape to take shape, the earliest years of French settlement are the most revealing.

The seigneurs' attempts to structure their space appear most clearly in their decisions concerning manors, mills, and churches. In both Batiscan and Sainte-Anne the early seigneurs first directed their proprietorial interest toward small islands in the St Lawrence, perhaps because these were more defensible. In Batiscan the *aveu et dénombrement* (list of landholdings) of 1677 designated Île Saint-Éloi, along with a nearby concession on the mainland, as the "demesne and seigneurial manor."[19] The first windmill, constructed in 1668, and the parish church were erected nearby on the mainland. Since this tract of land lay in the middle of the concessions along the St Lawrence, we can speculate that the Jesuits attempted thereby to provide a symbolic centre for the early seigneury, one

dominated by the religious power of the church, the practical economic functions of the windmill, and the legal authority of the seigneur. An early deed of concession referred to this area as "le village de batiscan," which, given the low density of settlement at that date, represented more a wish than a reality.[20]

In Sainte-Anne, Michel Gamelain first granted concessions on Île Saint-Ignace, at the mouth of the river. He reserved Île des Plaines for himself, and over time, subsequent seigneurs regained most of Île Saint-Ignace for themselves.[21] These islands would remain in the hands of the seigneurs for the next century and a half, but they chose to establish their manor on the mainland. Unlike Batiscan—or for that matter, neighbouring Sainte-Marie and Dorvilliers—none of the habitants' concessions fronted on the St Lawrence. In Sainte-Anne the seigneurs reserved this privilege to themselves, establishing their manor a short distance away from the river and only sharing the frontage with a common.[22] Consequently, from the perspectives afforded by the rivers, the seigneurs of Sainte-Anne dominated their landscape: anyone sailing along the north shore of the St Lawrence or travelling up the Sainte-Anne would first come into view of seigneurial lands. The Lanouguères enjoyed the clearest view of the St Lawrence from their land, while the principal axis for the habitants' concessions would be the Rivière Sainte-Anne.[23]

The seigneurs of Sainte-Anne also encouraged the founding of a village. Disputing the location of the parish church with the seigneur of adjacent Sainte-Marie, they were ultimately able to establish the church on the east bank of the river.[24] In 1691 de Suève granted to the parish land for a church and a presbytery and permitted the construction of a village on the remaining property, transferring the rents for this land to the church.[25] By the time of James Murray's 1760 map, a rather diffuse village had taken shape, largely to the south of the parish church.[26] It probably owed its existence in part to chance: it served as an important relay post along the royal road, one day's journey from Quebec. In general, the habitants in both Sainte-Anne and Batiscan avoided dense settlement.

Given the fact that Lanouguère, de Suève, and the Jesuits could not have known how slow the rate of settlement would be, we must speculate as to the nature of the ideal landscape that they wanted to establish. It was one in which the seigneurs wished to occupy central and strategic places. From the land that they maintained as a demesne, they could closely watch over the development of their respective seigneuries. The Jesuits' control centred around the church and the mill; that is, it was based on both religion and economy. The lay seigneurs of Sainte-Anne dominated the view of the St Lawrence and therefore the access to the external world.

After Gamelain's initial, and short-lived, focus on fur-trading activities, subsequent seigneurs turned their attention to a local agrarian economy. But the early attempts to structure the landscape illustrate their desire to assert their ascendancy and reveal the symbolism of land distribution.

SEIGNEURS AND THE STATE

The Lanaudière Family

The local elite ensured the connection of their society to the external world: seigneurs, priests, local state officials (judges, notaries, bailiffs, and militia captains), and military officials all played a role, but in Sainte-Anne the seigneurs enjoyed pre-eminence during the French regime. The colonial state relied on this noble elite to represent it in rural areas and provided privileged access to patronage and favours. For the Tarieu de Lanaudière family, this treatment persisted into the British regime.

For many seigneurial families, military commissions and concomitant fur-trade privileges provided the economic basis of their status. The Lanaudières always remained a military family. All the adult males up to the early nineteenth century held commissions in either the French or the British army, and a couple of the women were famous for their exploits with firearms too.[27] Through the five generations of Lanaudières who owned Sainte-Anne, the family profited from its connections to governing officials to obtain trade licences and other lucrative privileges.

After Sainte-Anne was granted to de Suève and Thomas de Lanouguère, the former managed the seigneury while the latter, with Governor Louis de Buade de Frontenac's support, participated in the fur trade and exercised the military command in Montreal.[28] From an early date the seigneurs defended their rights; in 1673 they appealed to their seigneurial judge to force their tenants to pay their dues.[29] After his death in 1678, Lanouguère's widow, Marguerite-Renée Denys, assumed control of the western half of the seigneury. A 1685 census enumerated 114 residents. In 1704 Denys abandoned, in exchange for annual payments of 400 livres, ownership to her second son, Pierre-Thomas, under the assumption that his long-absent elder brother was dead.[30]

In the 1720s and 1730s Pierre-Thomas and his wife Madeleine de Verchères initiated a number of court cases as they attempted to enforce their legal rights and ensure their social and economic prominence in the growing seigneury. In 1728, for example, they accused the local priest and several habitants of contravening the requirement to take grain to the seigneur's gristmill. The judgement in this case validated the seigneur's seizure of wheat and required the habitants to take their grain to the seigneurial mill in the future. To add prestige to the economic gain, the intendant ordered that the seigneur should serve as arbiter in any disputes over measurement.[31] In other cases, the family sought confirmation of its exclusive rights over fishing and hunting and for the privilege of first pew in the parish church.[32]

During this time it appealed to the government for other concrete recognitions of its status.

In 1731 Madeleine de Verchères requested, through the governor and the intendant, an increase in the royal pension that she received for her youthful heroism in defending her family fort at Verchères from the Iroquois.[33] Although Pierre-Thomas's application in 1729 for the position of chief road officer and his request the following year for a military promotion were not granted,[34] he continued to hold military posts, which he was able to use to profit from trade. Despite his activity outside the seigneury, Pierre-Thomas and in particular his wife were very active in local social relations. Their heirs, however, became less involved in the seigneury.

In the last decades of the French regime, Pierre-Thomas's son, Charles-François de Lanaudière, became even more closely tied to state officials in Quebec. Diarist Élisabeth Bégon described his wife as the intendant's "princesse".[35] Charles-François and his younger brother formed part of Intendant François Bigot's retinue, following him on his travels through the colony.[36] Charles-François, while serving as an officer in the colonial troops, earned the cross of the order of Saint-Louis in 1759. He served the governors on a number of occasions in a police capacity: compiling a roll of militiamen and requisitioning provisions from the peasantry for the sustenance of French troops during the Seven Years' War.[37] He also participated in the fur trade, establishing lucrative accounts with merchants in La Rochelle, selling seal furs and oil, and importing wine and brandy.[38] In 1750 Lanaudière was granted the seigneury of Lac-Maskinongé, presumably in recognition of the successes of his military career. The official favour that Lanaudière enjoyed in the period before the Conquest confirmed his status in society, but it also drew him away from the seigneury of Sainte-Anne. The estate inventory drawn up after the death of his first wife in 1762 noted that there was no seigneurial manor.[39]

After the Conquest, Sainte-Anne might have passed out of the hands of the Lanaudière family. Charles-François and his only surviving child, Charles-Louis, both sailed to France following the military defeat. However, they did not emigrate definitively. Charles-François, like others in his situation, discovered the difficulties of acquiring a good position in the French army, of maintaining his trade contacts in the newly redefined North America, and of establishing a son who lived more expensively than he could afford. With the direct trade to Canada blocked, Charles-François pursued trading possibilities through the French island of Miquelon off Newfoundland and through Louisiana, dealing in merchandise such as cloths, nails, and sealing lines, but this venture took many years to come to fruition and proved less lucrative than he had foreseen. Charles-François's subsequent correspondence with La Rochelle merchants focused on investing his capital in securities. He hesitated for a while about settling in France, but the news that Canadian officers found it difficult to acquire positions in the French army must have been discouraging.[40]

Charles-François returned to Canada in 1762, after the death of his first wife. Two years later he married Marie-Catherine Le Moyne de Longueuil, with whom he had ten children. Over time, his eldest son, Charles-Louis, developed an interest in Sainte-Anne seigneury, one which appeared to be tied up with noble sentiments and with an assertion of his position among his father's offspring.

[. . .]

Charles-Louis had returned to Canada by 1768, apparently because he was an inveterate gambler and had racked up so many debts that he had to leave France to escape his creditors. During his stopover in London he ran into more troubles and had to make a hasty return to Quebec.[41]

Back at home Charles-Louis de Lanaudière was able to acquire a position as aide-de-camp to General Guy Carleton, a position he relished. As he informed his father in 1770, "one cannot be happier than I am with my sire the general."[42] In this position, he returned to England and Europe on many occasions, during which he attempted to enhance his trading activities. [. . .]

According to Charles-Louis, a hunting trip with three English friends awakened his interest in the paternal estate of Sainte-Anne. The English aristocratic predilection for country estates and in particular for hunting privileges is well recognized.[43] Charles-Louis de Lanaudière undoubtedly came to share these tastes. He asked his father for title to the seigneury, which was granted to him less Île des Plaines (or Île Sainte-Marguerite) in an agreement signed in 1772.[44] Nonetheless, he did not establish permanent residency at Sainte-Anne. His activities led him to spend much of his time in Quebec, but the letters that Charles-Louis wrote from Sainte-Anne indicated that his presence at the seigneury was not restricted to any one season.[45] [. . .]

Despite his occasional notable appearances on his seigneury, Lanaudière paid much less day-to-day attention to its administration. He entrusted the management of the seigneury to the Gouin family. By the 1810s he was concentrating his demesne farming on sheep, hay, and wheat.[46] Nonetheless, he still maintained a paternalistic interest in his tenants.

Obviously, Lanaudière would have appreciated the steady, if not elevated, income that the seigneury provided. However, his main projects, such as fur-trading ventures, took place elsewhere.[47] But his principal field of activity was his connection with the new rulers of the colony. He was appointed to the sinecure of surveyor general of forests and rivers in 1771. He demonstrated his loyalty to the British crown in 1775 when he tried to raise militia to fight the American invaders and provided protection for Governor Carleton. Charles-Louis received his share of patronage and social recognition as a result, being appointed to the Legislative Council and to the position of overseer of highways.

Like British grandees of the period,[48] he saw the position of surveyor general as an opportunity to bend rules to his own profit. In 1778, for example, he sent a proposal to his cousin, François Baby, to cut timber from his seigneury and the neighbouring ones for sale in Quebec. Taking advantage of his position and his connections to the government, he suggested supplying the garrison in Quebec with wood: "As the government must use its authority to cut the wood—I propose this, if I can be given the parishes of Deschambault, Grondines, Sainte-Anne, and all of Batiscan—which never supply wood, with the power to command the men whom I will require for this work."[49] The government's ability to demand a corvée (required labour) would even release him personally from the necessity of hiring workers to cut the trees. He added in a subsequent letter, "in conducting government business, I must also do my own."[50] For Lanaudière, state and personal affairs were not just compatible; they were mutually reinforcing.

He and other members of the family continued to use whatever influence they could muster to support the colonial government. In the 1792 elections for the House of Assembly, for example, Lanaudière campaigned in favour of William Grant, a candidate who favoured strong British rule.[51] Almost two decades later, his half-brother Xavier-Roch presented himself for election in Sainte-Anne, an act which sister Agathe applauded in trying to convince her other brother Gaspard to do the same: "it is the duty of all men who are attached to their king to make this effort."[52]

The Lanaudière family, in particular Charles-Louis, had obviously made an easy transition to the new regime. It is possible that its members counted among the most successful French nobles in this regard.[53] In doing so, Charles-Louis adopted many of the viewpoints of the new rulers, in particular those concerning land tenure.

[. . .]

In 1790 Lanaudière submitted his opinions on seigneurial tenure to the Executive Council. After drawing a somewhat exaggerated picture of seigneurial privileges, he concluded, "The honorary, as well as pecuniary duties and dues are evidently complex, arbitrary, injurious. Can anything further be necessary to induce a benevolent monarch and nation to destroy them, and to grant in their stead that certain and determinate tenure of King Charles the Second, free and common socage, which the other subjects of His Majesty King George the Third enjoy, and with so much reason boast of."[54] The printing of Lanaudière's petition in 1791 in the *Gazette de Québec* launched a heated public debate with Abbé Thomas-Laurent Bédard over the advantages of free and common socage. Lanaudière reviewed the movement of settlers to other parts of North America and claimed that if he could not alter the tenure on his lands, "I ran the risk of remaining alone with my family and the few *habitans* who have settled themselves on it; and that the remaining part might lie uncultivated." Lanaudière continued his appeal by referring to the superiority of English social and economic conditions: "An english farmer discovers liberty in his very figure and air . . . He consumes more in one month than three fourths of your farmers [i.e., habitants], even of those at their ease, in six."[55] Of course, Lanaudière's wish was not granted. Nonetheless, he did not give up on his idea of abolishing seigneurial tenure on his lands.

In the meantime he defended his seigneurial privileges, for example, justifying his rights over the Sainte-Anne ferry by exhibiting his titles.[56] But in 1810 he renewed his petition, "having always ardently wished to hold his land in free and common socage in preference to feudal tenure."[57] In this light, Lanaudière occupies a rather singular place as an anti-seigneurial Canadian seigneur, preferring English land tenure to French.

A number of visitors to the colony met with Lanaudière and recorded his pro-British sentiments. John Lambert commented that Lanaudière "is sincerely attached to the British government, and in his conduct, his manners, and his principles, appears to be, in every respect, a complete Englishman."[58] He certainly was one noble with close connections to the government, and he tried to use these to his best advantage. As it had during the French regime, the Lanaudière family supported the colonial rulers and benefitted from its connections. For instance, just as the colonial government and the English elite tried to encourage hemp growing, Lanaudière addressed an appeal to his tenants to grow the plant, offering to purchase all their production at the highest market prices.[59] During his intermittent presences in Sainte-Anne, Charles-Louis worked hard to defend the policies of the British rulers. No French seigneur could have better represented the British colonial state.

The Jesuits

While a noble seigneur's ties to the state are readily apparent, the role of a corporate religious seigneur is more complex. The relationship between tenants and such a seigneur was obviously different from the personal connections that one might have with a powerful family. Nonetheless, the Jesuit owners of Batiscan were no less implicated in the running of the colonial state. In their general relations with the colonial government, they defended a specific elitist and state-oriented view of the social order, one in which religion represented the supreme virtue. Like that of the Lanaudière family, the history of the Jesuits' seigneurial title was linked to their relations with the colonial government.

Historians have shown that ecclesiastical seigneuries were managed with much astuteness and flexibility. This generalization applies to Batiscan also, at least during the French regime. The first concessions there date from 1664, and they multiplied thereafter. The Jesuits had begun to comply with the royal edicts compelling them to see to the settlement of their lands. According to the census of 1685, 261 people lived in the seigneury by that date.

Early riverfront concessions to individuals in the eastern part of the seigneury often accompanied grants of land in the western part. "The Jesuits," concludes the most detailed analysis of Jesuit policy in Batiscan, "could thus solidly establish the colonists by assuring them from the beginning a plot on which to settle their sons." An agent (*procureur général*) for the Jesuits' interests resided in Batiscan during the French regime. By the eighteenth century the order had taken advantage of a larger population base to enforce control over land-granting practices, not conceding land in pioneer zones until some clearing had occurred.[60] The seigneurial court, established definitively at Batiscan after 1726, provided a means for ensuring adherence to the Jesuits' policies. In 1745, for instance, the agent summoned Antoine Trottier to the court in order that he be dispossessed of land that he had worked without proper title for the previous five years.[61]

The Jesuits also constructed mills on their seigneury. A map from about 1726 depicts two windmills along the St Lawrence and a sawmill situated in the depths of settlement on the Rivière Batiscan. The Murray map of 1760 indicates the existence of a windmill on the St Lawrence and a watermill on the Batiscan. As shown by their land-granting policy and their construction of mills, the Jesuits' active role in the running of the seigneury continued up to the time of the Conquest.

Although the Conquest did not lead to a fundamental redefinition of land title and obligations in the old seigneuries, when the British abolished seigneurial courts, they destroyed a powerful instrument for enforcing the seigneur's will at the local level. Moreover, the Jesuits suffered more than other seigneurs when Canada was lost.[62] General Jeffery Amherst, the supreme British military commander in North America at the time of the Conquest, refused to grant protection to the property of the Jesuits and the Recollets until the Crown had pronounced on the future status of those orders in the colony. British aversion to the Jesuits in particular was reinforced by the movement in other countries to suppress the order. In 1764 a royal decree dissolved the Jesuits throughout France and its colonies. Nine years later Pope Clement XIV suppressed the entire order. The consequences for Jesuit properties in Canada were complex. In 1775 the British government outlined a policy concerning the Jesuits. Although the order was suppressed, the surviving members would be provided for during their lifetimes. Ultimately, this policy came to mean that they were to enjoy the profits from their properties, but that title would revert to the Crown on the death of the last member of the order.

Meanwhile, General Amherst had requested a grant of the Jesuit lands in recognition of his services to the Crown, and King George III had promised him this recompense. Subsequent attempts to acquire the titles persisted beyond his own lifetime. His nephew and heir, the second Lord Amherst, pressed the claim in the declining years of the last Jesuit, Father Jean-Joseph Casot. Ultimately, the second Lord Amherst received monetary compensation for the king's promise, but he never acquired title to the estates themselves. In 1800, upon Casot's death, the lands previously belonging to the Jesuits reverted to the Crown.

During this period of uncertainty over the disposition of the Jesuit estates (which launched a century-long political debate concerning the use of public funds for education and the relationship between church and state), the Jesuits continued to employ agents to manage their seigneuries. The principal agent for Batiscan, François-Xavier Larue, lived in Pointe-aux-Trembles, near Quebec. In general, the Jesuits now seem to have been less attentive to the management of Batiscan than in the period before the Conquest. However, they were more vigilant than the government itself would be when it ultimately took control.

Judging by the mills, the single most lucrative of the seigneurial privileges, the Jesuits through their agents continued to attend to their property. The 1781 *aveu et dénombrement* made reference to a mill in the process of being built in the seigneury.[63] The windmills along the St Lawrence were replaced over time by watermills along the Batiscan. A report prepared at the end of the Jesuits' administration noted two mills in operation, one built of stone on the northeast shore of the Rivière Batiscan at Sainte-Geneviève and the other built of wood on the Rivière des Envies.[64] The mills apparently remained functional and at least partially fulfilled the needs of the habitants: a seigneurial agent later reported that the mills "still worked and were in relatively good order at the time of the last Jesuit."[65] In providing relatively lucrative banal mills, the Jesuits maintained a traditional seigneurial monopoly, one that offered at least a minimum of required services to their tenants.

However, the Jesuits were much less attentive in their management of land grants in Batiscan seigneury. The numbers of titles conceded provide at least a general overview of their stewardship. From 1763 to 1790 only 22 concessions were awarded.[66] The Jesuits' agents were no longer facilitating settlement of the seigneury.

Another measure of the Jesuits' interest in their property is provided by their collection of seigneurial dues. Information concerning the amount collected is available for only a few scattered years. In 1768 the Jesuits acknowledged receiving 1291 *livres tournois* in rents. Thirteen years later, in 1781, different copies of the general recapitulation of the Jesuits' properties indicate between 988 and 1285 *livres tournois* in *cens et rentes*.[67] The reasons for the discrepancies in these figures, which relate to the same document, are not clear. It is possible that land-granting policy limited the amount of seigneurial dues paid up to that point. However, by 1790 the revenues had about doubled, although the population had increased by only about 40 per cent. Batiscan earned about £94 sterling in *cens et rentes*, or 2256 *livres tournois*. The banal mill earned another 1200 livres tournois. Even with this increase, Batiscan was not a particularly lucrative Jesuit seigneury: it provided less than 7 per cent of the total receipts for the estates, much less than other properties such as

La Prairie and Sainte-Geneviève near Montreal and Notre-Dame-des-Anges near Quebec.[68]

In the final years of life of the last Jesuit, the land-granting policy changed dramatically. A large portion of the seigneury fell into the hands of English-speaking entrepreneurs. In the 1790s the rhythm of concessions picked up markedly. Between 1795 and 1800, 83 concessions were granted, 53 in 1798 alone. Most of these involved small amounts of land and probably entailed the recognition of land already occupied by tenants. However, among the concessions were huge grants to businessman Thomas Coffin, made under the dubious circumstances surrounding the disposition of the Jesuits' properties. In 1795 Coffin received the *arrière-fief* of Saint-Thomas, comprising all of the seigneury north of the Rivière des Envies, in exchange for 300 sols annual rent. In 1798 he added three ill-defined "compeaux" of land, "being the remainders between conceded land, that he [Coffin] is obliged to have surveyed, and pay one 'sol' per arpent."[69]

This vast land grant, with its timber and iron resources, held much promise for profit, since Coffin and his partner, the deputy commissary general John Craigie, were able to establish a new ironworks. Not all colonial officials were pleased with such land grants. In July 1799, before the death of Father Casot, the attorney general, Jonathan Sewell, protested against the land grant, expressing to the agent, Desjardins, "the disapprobation of Government not only of that Concession but of all others (except perhaps the common Concession en roture to Habitans of small lots at the accustomary cens et rentes)."[70] Likewise, the local agent for the Jesuits' estates protested that Coffin had begun employing men to cut wood in the seigneury without permission.[71] Nonetheless, the owners of this Batiscan land were too well connected to be in danger of losing it.

When Father Casot died in 1800, title to the Jesuit estates reverted to the Crown, which appointed a commission to oversee the management of the property. Coffin and

Craigie soon acquired a new partner in the Batiscan ironworks, Thomas Dunn, a former administrator of the colony, who sat on the Board of Commissioners of the Jesuit Estates. Lord Amherst's brother-in-law, John Hale, who anxiously watched over the family's interests in the colony, resigned from the Board of Commissioners when it became apparent that the property was not likely to be turned over to Amherst.[72]

[. . .]

For their part, the Jesuits' role in Batiscan seigneury had changed over time. Following their active involvement in its administration during the French regime, the complicated post-1763 struggle over the order's estates in Canada led to an increasing indifference toward Batiscan. As title shifted from the Jesuits to the Crown, a large section of the seigneury fell into private hands.

CONCLUSION

Seigneurial control over the land was undoubtedly an important aspect of the changes in landscape. It gave the localities their broad outlines, though it did not strictly speaking determine the nature of land use. This responded more to the exigencies of small-scale, family-oriented agricultural production. Superficially, the landscape projected a seigneurial presence, even though this faded the closer and the later one looked.

Since the mid-eighteenth century, commentators have argued over the degree to which seigneurial tenure was incompatible with profitable economic development.[73] But as Françoise Noël has demonstrated, "seigneurial tenure . . . could be used by large proprietors to monopolize scarce resources."[74] The founding of the Batiscan ironworks rested upon seigneurial privileges granted in *arrière-fief* by an increasingly irrelevant seigneur.

Thus the lack of attention that seigneurs showed to their seigneuries could be equally determinant as when they did try to direct matters firmly. The increasing inattention during the British regime gave more rein to local elites to exercise control over social relations. It was during this latter period that the seigneurs had the least impact on the local landscape, marginalized as they increasingly became from local affairs.

NOTES

1. For the importance of naming and drawing boundaries in the appropriation of land, see Paul Carter, *The Road to Botany Bay: An Exploration of Landscape and History.* New York: Alfred A. Knopf, 1988.
2. H.P. Biggar, ed., *Works of Samuel de Champlain.* 6 vols. Toronto: Champlain Society, 1920–36, 1: 132.
3. Carter, *The Road to Botany Bay,* 47–54.
4. Reuben Gold Thwaites, *The Jesuit Relations and Allied Documents.* 74 vols. Cleveland: Burrows Brothers, 1896–1901, 48: 215.
5. Baby Collection, Université de Montréal (UM-Baby), mf. 2584, Requête des habitants de Baptiste Camp à François Baby, 15 février 1783. John Knox recorded the name as "Batiste camp" (Arthur G. Doughty, ed., *An Historical Journal of the Campaigns in North American for the Years 1757, 1758, and 1760.* By Captain John Knox. Vol. 2. Toronto: Champlain Society, 1914, 2: 478).
6. Raymond Douville, *Les premiers seigneurs et colons de Sainte-Anne de la Pérade, 1667–1681.* Trois-Rivières: Éditions du Bien Public, 1946, 9–10.
7. Marcel Trudel, *Les débuts du régime seigneurial au Canada.* Montréal: Fides, 1974, 20–1; Richard Colebrook Harris, ed., *Seigneurial System in Early Canada.* 2nd edn. Montreal: McGill-Queen's University Press, 1984, 23–5.
8. Fonds Seigneuries (FS), Archives nationales du Québec à Québec, vol. 3, Batiscan, Acte de Concession de Messire Jacques de La Ferté aux Pères Jésuites, 3 mars 1639.

9. National Archives of Canada (NA), France, Archives des colonies, Des limites et des postes, Transcriptions, MG 1 série c 11 E (mf. F-409), 14, Estat des Terres que les Reverends Peres Jesuistes Possedent en Canada suivant leurs declarations du 26e novembre 1667.

10. Archives nationales du Québec à Montréal (ANQ-M), Seigneurie Batiscan, P220/1, Aveu et dénombrement, 29 décembre 1677.

11. Philippe Jarnoux, "La colonisation de la seigneurie de Batiscan aux 17e et 18e siècles: L'espace et les hommes." *RHAF* 40, no. 2 (1986), 169.

12. "Ayant pas meme sur les Lieux aucune Justice formée ni assurée" (Terres et forêts, Biens des Jésuites (BJ), ANQ-Q, vol. 70, Title Deeds, Jesuits Estates, 82–4, Acte de Monsieur de Bouteroue Intendant pour suppleer au defaut d'insinuation des Donnations des fiefs Batiscan & Champlain, 27 nov. 1668).

13. Douville, *Les premiers seigneurs et colons*, 13–36.

14. C.-M. Boissonault, "Gamelain de La Fontaine, Michel," *Dictionary of Canadian Biography* (*DCB*), 1: 320–1.

15. Harris, *Seigneurial System*, 26–31.

16. "en Considera[ti]on des bons utils et louables services quil[s] ont rendus a sa ma[jes]te en differents endroicts tant en lancienne France que dans la nouvelle depuis quils y sont passez par ordre de sa ma[jes]te et en veue de ceux quils temoignent encore vouloir rendre cy apres" (FS, vol. 52, Sainte-Anne de la Pérade [Ouest], Acte de concession par Jean Talon, 29 octobre 1672).

17. Ibid., Sainte-Anne de la Pérade (est), Extrait d'un Contrat de vente par Moses Hart à Pierre Charay [sic] et uxor, 26 février 1816.

18. Hale Collection, National Archives of Canada (NA-Hale), vol. 2, Acte de foi et hommage, 23 décembre 1819.

19. ANQ-M, Seigneurie Batiscan, P220/1, Aveu et dénombrement, 1.

20. UM-Baby, MF. 2104–5, Contrat de concession d'une place au village de Batiscan, 13 septembre 1674.

21. Douville, *Les premiers seigneurs et colons*.

22. Carte de Catalogne, 1709, in Marcel Trudel, *Atlas de la Nouvelle-France/Atlas of New France*. Quebec: Presses de l'Université Laval, 1968, 169. This map does not, in fact, indicate the presence of a common in Sainte-Anne, though one was established.

23. Louis-Edmond Hamelin, "Le rang d'arrière-fleuve en Nouvelle-France," *Géographe canadien/Canadian Geographer* 34, 2 (1980): 113–14, notes that the St. Lawrence formed the principal axis for concessions in the majority of cases. Still, according to Catalogne's map of 1709, other seigneurs also assured themselves of the most prominent geographic positions.

24. Douville, *Les premiers seigneurs et colons*, 122–8.

25. NA, Sainte-Anne de la Pérade, Transcriptions, MG 8, F 83, 10–13, Copie du contrat de donation faite par feu messire de Suève, 8 aoust 1691.

26. National Map Collection (NMC), National Archives of Canada, NMC-10842, Murray Map (1760), section FI.

27. For the male Lanaudières' military activity, see P.-G. Roy, *La famille Tarieu de Lanaudière*. Lévis: [n.p.], 1922. As for the women, besides Madeleine de Verchères, Philippe Aubert de Gaspé discussed his aunt, Agathe de Lanaudière, in his Mémoires, 402–4.

28. Raymond Douville, "Lanouguère, Thomas de," *DCB*, 1: 417–18.

29. Douville, *Les premiers seigneurs et colons*, 56, 62.

30. FS, vol. 52, Sainte-Anne de la Pérade (Est) [sic], Acte d'abandon et cession de la seigneurie de Sainte-Anne par Marguerite-Renée Denys à Pierre-Thomas Tarieu de la Pérade (Greffe Genaple), 4 novembre 1704.

31. "Ordonnance qui déclare bonne et valable la saisie . . . ," in *Pièces et documents relatifs à la tenure seigneuriale*. Quebec: E.R. Fréchette, 1852, 120–4.

32. ANQ-M, Conseil supérieur, Registres, M9, (mf. 1197), vol. 28, folio 39r–v, Esmond et Jean Tessier et al. versus Thomas Tarrieu de la Pérade, 18 août 1721; vol. 32, folio 51v–52v, François Chorel Dorvilliers vs Thomas Tarrieu de la Pérade, 12 mars 1725.

33. NA, Nouvelle-France, Correspondance officielle, 3e série, MG 8, A1, vol. 12, 2657–8,

Lettre de Beauharnois et Hocquart au ministre, 15 octobre 1731.

34. Ibid., vol. 11, 2427–8, Lettre de Beauharnois et Hocquart au ministre, 25 octobre 1729; NA, France, Archives des colonies, Lettres envoyées, MG 1, série B, vol. 54, folio 423½, Lettre du ministre à Beauharnois, 4 avril 1730.

35. Élisabeth Bégon, *Lettres au cher fils: Correspondance d'Élisabeth Bégon avec son gendre (1748–1753)*. Montreal: Hurtubise HMH, 1972, 53.

36. Ibid., 72; Louis Franquet, *Voyages et mémoires sur le Canada*. Montreal: Éditions Elysée, 1974, 129, 141.

37. Baby Collection, National Archives of Canada (NA-Baby), vol. 1, 511a, Beauharnois à Lanaudière, 22 juillet 1744; vol. 3, 1722–3, Marquis de Vaudreuil à Mr de Lanaudière, 23 juillet 1759.

38. Ibid., vol. 30, 18725–61, Inventaire des biens de La communauté entre de La Perrade [Lanaudière] et feue Geneviève de Boishébert, sa première épouse, 5 juillet 1762 (according to this document, Lanaudière held some 63 000 livres in France in the hands of various merchants); Tarien de Lanaudière (TL), ANQ-Q, vol. 1, Accord entre M. de Lanaudière et M. Varin, 16 octobre 1753, and Cession de Gaultier, 4 avril 1754.

39. NA-Baby, vol. 30, 18759, Inventaire des biens de la communauté entre de La Perrade [Lanaudière] et feue Geneviève de Boishébert, sa première épouse, 5 juillet 1762.

40. Ibid., vol. 4, 2139–40, Thouron & Frères à Lanaudière, 22 avril 1764.

41. NA-Baby, vol. 5, 2652–8, Thouron & frères à Lanaudière, 10 mars 1768.

42. "On ne peux pas être plû heureux que je le sui avec Mr Le generalle" (ibid., 2968, Lanaudière à son père, 14 septembre 1770).

43. E.P. Thompson, *Whigs and Hunters: The Origins of the Black Art*. Harmondsworth: Penguin, 1977.

44. NA-Baby, vol. 30, 19052, Inventaire et procès-verbal de vente des biens de la succession de Lanaudière, avril 1788.

45. Letters in NA-Baby between 1774 and 1783 were written in March, July, September, October, and December.

46. Hale Family Collection (UT-Hale), Thomas Fisher Rare Book Library, University of Toronto, E.F. Hale to Lord Amherst, 17 September [1819].

47. NA-Baby, vol. 6, 3570–1, Lanaudière fils à Vercher, 24 juillet 1773.

48. Roy Porter, *English Society in the Eighteenth Century*. London: Penguin Books, 1977, 73–8.

49. "Comme nesséscairement il fautdra que le gouvernement fasse, Dotorité faire, faire le bois,—je propose sesi, si lon veux me dormer les paroisses—Déchambaut, grondine, *St anne* & tous batiscand—qui ne fournisse jamais du bois, avec pouvoir de commender Les hommes dont jorei besoin pour bucher" (NA-Baby, vol. 8, 4398–9, Lanaudière à M. François Baby, 17 septembre 1778; emphasis in original).

50. "En fesant l'affaire Du gouvernement il faut que je fasse les miéne" (ibid., vol. 8, 4406, Lanaudière à François Baby, 30 septembre 1778). Evidence that the enterprise was undertaken is shown by a further letter in the same collection (4736–7, Lanaudière à F. Baby, 6 mars 1781).

51. See the criticism of Charles de Lanaudière in the handbill *Commentaire sur le discours de l'honorable Chas. Delanaudiere (qui a paru hier)*, reprinted in John Hare, *Aux origines du parlementarisme québécois 1791–1793*. Sillery: Les Éditions du Septentrion, 1993, 177–9.

52. "Cest le devoir de toutes hommes quis est atachés a son rois de faire c'est [cet] effort" (TL, vol. 2, Agathe de Lanaudière à Gaspard Lanaudière, 2 avril 1810).

53. Roch Legault, "Les aléas d'une carrière militaire pour les membres de la petite noblesse seigneuriale canadienne de la révolution américaine à la guerre de 1812–1815." Mémoire de maîtrise, Université de Montréal, 1986, 113–15.

54. "Answers submitted by Charles de Lanaudière to various Questions relating to the Seigniorial System, October 11, 1790," in W.B. Munro, *Documents Relating to the Seigniorial Tenure in Canada, 1598–1854*. Toronto: Champlain Society, 1908, 273.

55. *Gazette de Québec*, 24 mars 1791; supplément, 28 avril 1791.

56. Archives nationales du Québec à Trois-Rivières (ANQ-TR), Cour de banc du roi (dossiers), T25, Terme de septembre 1808, no. 1, Pierre Bureau vs Jos. Riv[ar]d Lanouette et L'Honorable De Lanaudière.

57. "Ayant toujours ardemment désiré de tenir ses Terres en franc et commun Soccage en préference de Féodalité" (NA, Lower Canada Land Papers, RG 1 L 3 L, vol. 188 [mf. C-2538], 57763–4, Petition de Charles de Lanaudière à Sir James Craig, 21 décembre 1810).

58. John Lambert, *Travels through Canada and the United States of North America in the Years 1806, 1807 & 1808*. 2nd edn. London: C. Cradock and W. Joy, 1814, 461. Lord Selkirk was similarly impressed with Lanaudière: "a very gentlemanly old Canadian Officer, & a man of reflexion" (NA, Selkirk Papers, MG 19, E 1, Lord Selkirk's Diary, 19749).

59. *Gazette de Quebec*, 22 juillet 1802.

60. Jarnoux, "La colonisation," 173–5, quotation from 173. See also Raymond Douville, "Les lents débuts d'une seigneurie des Jésuits," *Cahiers des dix* 25 (1960): 249–76.

61. BJ, vol. 97, St-Agnian vs Antoine Trottier, 29 avril 1745. See also Collection des pièces judicaires et notariales (ANQ-Q), Mesager vs François Massicot, 6 avril 1748. Lavallée notes that the Jesuit seigneurs of La Prairie became more vigilant in the 1730s, launching a number of court cases for nonpayment of dues in the following decade (*La Prairie*, 100).

62. The following section dealing with the disposition of the Jesuit estates is summarized from Roy J. Dalton, *The Jesuits' Estates Question 1760–1888: A Study of the Background for the Three Seigneurial Regime in New France Agitation of 1889*. Toronto: University of Toronto Press, 1968, chaps. 1–6.

63. NA, Executive Council and Land Committee, RG 1, L 7, Jesuit Estates, vol. 38, 11, Extrait de l'aveu & dénombrement des Fiefs & Seigneuries des Jésuites, 12 décembre 1781.

64. BJ, vol. 96, Rapport de l'Etat actuel des Moulins situés en les Seigneuries qui appartenoient ci devant au Jesuites, dans le District des Trois-Rivières . . . (no date; probably July 1800).

65. "Marchoient encore et étoient en assez bon ordre Lors de lextinction des Jesuites" (ibid., vol. 103, Moulin de la Seigneurie, 1824–28, L. Guillet à John Stewart, 2 juin 1826).

66. Ibid., vol. 99, Liste des Concéssions qui ont été faites dans les Seigneuries qui appartenoient ci devant à l'ordre des Jésuites dans le District des Trois Rivières, en la Province du Bas Canada, depuis la conquête de ce pays, fait par l'agent des ditte Seigneuries dans le dit District en conséquence des ordres des Commissaires pour l'adminstration des dits Biens, Suivant une Lettre du secretaire en date du 18 janvier 1802.

67. NA, Earl Amherst Papers, MG 12, WO 34, packet 47 [mf. C-1215], Compte que rendent les Jesuites du Canada à Mr Guy Carleton, le 7 avril 1768; Executive Council and Land Committee, RG 1, L 7, Jesuit Estates, vol. 35, General Recapitulation . . . ; ibid., vol. 38, Extrait de l'aveu & dénombrement des Fiefs & Seigneuries des Jésuites, 12 décembre 1781; Haldimand Papers, MG 21 [mf. A-779].

68. UT-Hale, John Hale to Lord Amherst, 6 May 1802.

69. "Étant des restant entre des terres concédées, qu'il est obligé de faire mesurer, à payer un sol par arpent en Superficie" (BJ, vol. 99, Liste des concessions . . . 18 janvier 1802). The government finally was able to ascertain the extent of the three "grands compeaux" in 1828: 169 arpents behind the falls, 480 arpents behind the ironworks, and 420 arpents near the Rivière à Veillet (ibid., L. Guillet à J. Stewart, 24 septembre 1828).

70. Ibid., vol. 75, Lettres, 1787–1800, Jonathan Sewell to H. Ryland, 27 February 1800.

71. Ibid., vol. 99, Trépagny à Larue, 22 décembre 1799; vol. 257, Larue, 18 juin 1800.

72. UT-Hale, John Hale to Lord Amherst, 5 December 1800.

73. David Milobar, "The Origins of British-Quebec Merchant Ideology: New France, the British Atlantic and the Constitutional Periphery, 1720–70." *Journal of Imperial and Commonweath History* 24, 3 (1996): 370.

74. Françoise Noël, *The Christie Seigneuries: Estate Management and Settlement in the Upper Richelieu Valley, 1760–1854*. Montreal and Kingston: McGill-Queen's University Press, 1992, 136.

4   From Allan Greer, "The Feudal Burden," in *Peasant, Lord & Merchant: Rural Society in Three Quebec Parishes 1740–1840* (Toronto: University of Toronto Press, 1985), 122–39. © University of Toronto Press, 1985. Reprinted with permission of the publisher.

Were seigneurial and ecclesiastical exactions nothing more than a minor nuisance to the early Canadian peasantry? How exactly was wealth transferred from the agricultural producers to the dominant classes? Was the basis of appropriation fixed or was it at all changeable or arbitrary? Finally, how significant an impact did these feudal dues have on the habitant family economy? In attempting to answer these questions, I shall concentrate on the more problematic seigneurial economy.

SEIGNEURIAL DUES

The most important mechanism of transfer in most Canadian seigneuries was the "cens et rentes," an annual payment in money, produce, or labour, exacted on all lands in the "mouvance" at a rate proportional to the size of each lot. The cens alone was a small payment, considered a token of the "commoners'" form of tenure, which carried with it subjection to a number of dues, such as the "lods et ventes," outlined in the Custom of Paris. Rente was a lucrative charge added to and deliberately confused with the cens in order to subject the inhabitant to the penalties prescribed by law for late payment of the latter.[1] The term "rent" will be used here in the feudal sense, as it was in the past, to refer to the total of these two charges.

The annual rent on each lot was established at the time of concession and it could not legally be altered, although variations in the value of money and grain had the effect of changing the effective burden of this charge. The edict of 1711 moreover, in ordering seigneurs to make new concessions at the prevailing rates of cens et rentes, implied that a standard rate should apply in each seigneurie, if not throughout the colony, on lands granted at any time after that date. A legalistic bias has led some historians to assume that rents on new concessions therefore

remained stable during the French régime and only rose after the Conquest when a French government was replaced by a British one less sympathetic to the habitants. In fact, a clear pattern of ever-increasing rent scales on newly settled sections of the mouvance is evident in seventeenth-century Montreal.[2] Similarly, in St Ours, new rents rose steadily throughout the French régime, but remained stable after the 1750s, just the opposite of the pattern suggested by the traditional view. Apparently, the development of the region's agricultural productivity led seigneurs to insist on a proper share of the expanding peasant surplus.

But how did the seigneurs of St Ours manage to defy official policy in this way? An examination of St Ours concession deeds suggests that the rise was the outcome of a subtle policy of altering the combination of cash, produce, and livestock in the annual rents, substituting pseudo-equivalents so as to change the value of payments while appearing to alter only their form. Cash was substituted for capons, and then wheat was put in the place of the money; also area measurements were substituted for linear frontage. The switch to payments largely in wheat in the years after 1720 was partly a reflection of the emergence of an agricultural economy in the Lower Richelieu, but it was also a clever hedge against erosion of fixed money rents. The seigneurs' imposition of altered rates made a mockery of legislation intended to protect the peasantry; the eighteenth-century rise in grain prices, joined to biased alterations in the form of payment were such that, at early-nineteenth-century wheat prices, a 90-arpent farm conceded in the seventeenth century would owe about 6 livres per year, while one conceded after 1754 (this included the majority of St Ours farms) would owe 27 livres.[3] The trouble that the French régime seigneurs of St Ours took to adjust their rent scales suggests that they did not regard these revenues as "token payments".

Less is known about the evolution of cens et rentes in Sorel and St Denis. Toward the end of the French régime, the charge seems to have been a roughly equivalent combination of money and wheat to that exacted in St Ours, although every lot in Sorel owed an additional levy of one day's corvée labour.[4] (Note that corvée was simply a form of payment, labour rather than money or produce, and not a separate variety of seigneurial exaction, as many have suggested. The corvée in mid-eighteenth-century Sorel seems to have been an element of the cens et rentes, whereas Pierre de St Ours exacted a day's work from the habitants for use of a common pasture.) However, the seigneurs of Sorel and St Denis, both of them absentees probably anxious to simplify accounts and collection procedures, converted all charges in labour and kind to a single annual cash exaction. This change occurred around 1770 in Sorel and probably much earlier in St Denis, with the effect that rents there were greatly devalued by the long-term inflation of the eighteenth century. In the early nineteenth century, a 90-arpent farm was charged about 13.5 livres in St Denis, 18 livres in Sorel, and between 16 and 32 livres in St Ours, depending on the price of wheat.[5] The seigneur of St Ours tended to benefit in the long run by their adherence to rents in kind. The relative advantage of seigneur and habitant in each seigneurie changed, in opposite directions, with fluctuating grain prices. Moreover, the positions of the two parties reverse as one moves from St Ours to Sorel or St Denis; that is, a rise in wheat prices favoured St Ours seigneurs and Sorel habitants, while a price decline tended to favour Sorel seigneurs and St Ours habitants.

In addition to the cens et rentes, Canadian seigneurs benefitted from a variety of lucrative charges, including the lods et ventes, a mutation fine amounting to one-twelfth of the purchase price owed by the buyer of land in the mouvance. In France, and in some Canadian seigneuries, purchasers who paid promptly were charged a third or a quarter less than the legal rate, but this discount was not universal and St Ours seigneurs invariably demanded the full amount.[6] [. . .] To realize its full value, the right of lods et ventes required that a seigneur be aware of the details of land transactions in his fief and it was therefore closely tied, in its practical application, to the various official and unofficial aspects of his control over people and lands. In addition to his role as the main repository of land title records, the seigneur disposed of the retrait seigneurial to guarantee the proper reporting of prices. Of course the co-operation of the local notary, who officiated at transactions and kept their records, was invaluable, but what notary could risk offending the seigneur, normally his most important client?

Several minor exactions were added to the basic feudal rent and mutation fines. One of these was the annual fee for admission to the common pasture; such "droit de commune" was demanded of all Sorel habitants until the late eighteenth century and of the residents of the St Lawrence section of St Ours until the end of seigneurial tenure. The situation here was not what it was in Old Régime France, where commons were generally controlled by peasant communities whose possession was only partially usurped by aggressive seigneurial offensives.[7] [. . .]

Although they profited through the above-mentioned exactions from habitant grain-growing, livestock raising, and property sales, the seigneurs of the Lower Richelieu were not prepared to let even minor ancillary productions go untaxed. In Sorel, there was a levy on maple sugar-making as well as a fishing fee. In the eighteenth century, choice locations on islands in the St Lawrence were farmed out to habitants for 78 livres annually, as much as the rents of a dozen farms. A document dated 1809 mentions an exaction of two fish from each netful of shad caught.[8] There was no basis in law for this "droit de pêche," but this seems to have escaped the seigneurs' notice.

Seigneurs benefitted, not only from these direct exactions, but also from various monopolies, above all the "banalité" (grist mill monopoly), which will be discussed later. These privileges are quite different from the dues mentioned so far in that they were not lucrative in themselves, even though they could be used to enrich the seigneur at the habitants' expense. The banal mill was a protected enterprise with a captive market, but it did provide a service; the milling toll was therefore unlike the almost entirely parasitic cens et rentes as it went partly to defray expenses. Only a portion of this fee was profit for the seigneur and only part of that could be attributed to the effects of protection from competition.[9] Collecting the milling toll was a simple matter of withholding one-fourteenth of the grain processed, whereas seigneurs experienced considerable difficulty in securing payment of annual dues and mutation fines.

PAYMENT

Seigneurial dues were notoriously difficult to collect (frontier or no frontier, Canada was exactly like France in this respect).[10] Most habitants were a few years in arrears on occasion and many fell behind more seriously and were never able to get out of debt. Behind this backlog was probably a combination of inability to pay, unwillingness to pay, and a calculated postponement based on the knowledge that it was not worthwhile for the seigneur to take action to recover small debts. Some habitants lived so close to the edge of subsistence that chronic debt to the seigneur must have been almost unavoidable; whereas others, normally able to pay regularly, must have experienced temporary distress that put them slightly in arrears now and then. Most likely, there was

also a certain amount of passive resistance to seigneurial exploitation expressed in the failure to pay promptly. Figure 1 shows that only 15 per cent of Sorel's lands had rent arrears of more than four years in 1809. By 1855, however, this figure had risen to 25 per cent, reflecting the general distress of the seigneurie's habitants in the period when fur-trade employment had disappeared.[11] Accumulated arrears seem to have been disproportionately great in recently conceded lands, probably because many of them were not fully cleared and productive for several years. In Sorel, and presumably in other seigneuries, payments of current and overdue rents fluctuated from year to year with the harvests, the general economic situation, and the varying pressure exerted by the seigneur (see Table 1).[12]

Arrears of lods et ventes were more common and of much longer duration than arrears of rents. The former charge usually amounted to a relatively substantial sum due all at once, and many habitants found themselves unable to pay it for years, or even generations, even if they could make the more moderate rent payments year by year. "Quitte excepté les lods" is a recurrent phrase in the St Ours estate rolls. From the seigneur's point

Table 1 Seigneurial Rents and Arrears Paid, Sorel 1798–1805

Year	Annual Rent Due	Rent and Arrears Received	Percentage
1798	2 643	1 817	69
1799	2 787	1 988	71
1800	2 874	2 268	79
1801	2 930	1 523	52
1802	2 942	2 572	87
1803	3 407	3 564	105
1804	3 407	2 213	65
1805	3 407	2 493	73

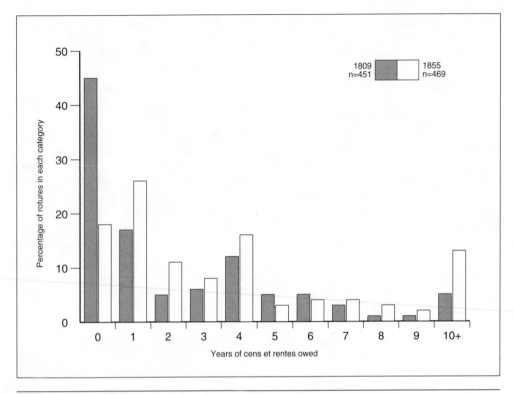

Figure 1 Arrears of Seigneurial Rent, Sorel, 1809 and 1855

of view then, the actual revenue in any one year was never even close to the total value of the dues to which he was legally entitled. By about 1840 the censitaires of Sorel and St Ours owed their seigneurs at least 92 000 and 71 158 livres respectively. Of course many of these arrears would never be paid at all. The notaries who drew up the inventory of 1841 following the death of François Roch de St Ours judged that one-third of the arrears of the seigneurie should simply be written off since they were owed on uncleared lots of very little value.[13]

Extracting payments of arrears from in-debted habitants was a delicate task requiring, on the part of the seigneur or his agent, a thor-ough acquaintance with the individuals and the productive capacities of their lands. If the seigneur was convinced that the debtor would never pay, he would generally take steps to have him removed so that the land could be turned over to a more promising candidate. This sometimes required an expensive and time-consuming lawsuit to obtain a judicial seizure.[14] Seigneurs naturally preferred the various procedures mentioned above—repos-session for failure to develop and "voluntary" abandonment—that weeded out undesir-ables with much less inconvenience. For less serious cases, they were inclined to show a certain amount of patience in the hopes of eventually recovering overdue rents. Pater-nalistic attitudes may have had something to do with it, but there were also more practical motives for forbearance. Since habitant ag-riculture was often quite unproductive and short harvests were common, rigid insistence on immediate payment would clearly be un-reasonable and self-defeating in many cases. As long as a habitant made a visible effort to make good back dues and as long as his farm was valuable enough to bear the debt, he could usually feel safe. In the end, a seigneur could take advantage of his position as legally privileged creditor to claim arrears from the estate when his debtor died. Prompter payment was certainly preferable, however, and seigneurs used a variety of strategies, threatening, cajoling, setting deadlines, and accepting payments in unusual forms, in order to wring as much as possible out of peasants who had the slimmest of surpluses and who were disinclined to part with them. Always it was the threat, implied or stated, of being deprived of their homes and livelihood that encouraged such marginal cases to turn over what they could.

[. . .]

Documents from St Ours suggest that seigneurial dues were acquitted in a great variety of forms. There were always a large number of habitants who apparently paid punctually and in the money and wheat specified in their title deeds but, for poorer censitaires, these commodities were only accounting abstractions. Products offered for rents and lods et ventes between the 1790s and the 1840s include oats, barley, peas, lumber, firewood, maple sugar, hay, cattle, and homespun cloth. Labour was also a common means of payment, even though officially there was no corvée in St Ours after about 1720. The estate rolls show that censitaires received a certain amount of credit for each day spent working on roads and fences or on the construction of a mill. When a gristmill on the Yamaska River was planned in 1814, the contract with the seigneur required the builder to employ, as far as possible, St Ours habitants who would be paid half their wages in cash and the other half in coupons to be applied to their accounts with the seigneur.[15] Once again it seems clear that the form in which feudal dues were officially set down was of no essential importance; what was appropriated was the surplus labour of the peasant, either in its raw form, or as agricultural produce or as produce converted into cash.

SEIGNEURIAL MONOPOLIES

As an outgrowth of seigneurial judicial powers, Canadian landlords enjoyed certain privileges and monopolies over the territories of their estates and the people who lived there; long after they had ceased to act as local judges, the seigneurs of Sorel, St Ours, and St Denis continued to insist on the lucrative perquisites of the position. The most important of these was the gristmill monopoly and it was more widespread and more stringent in Canada than it was in most parts of Old Régime France.[16] Here, it was often an important source of seigneurial revenues, and a real inconvenience to habitants. The Custom of Paris only allowed seigneurs to require their vassals to grind the wheat they needed for domestic consumption at the seigneurial watermill and only in cases where the right was sanctioned by written titles or ancient custom. A royal edict of 1686 enlarged the Canadian seigneur's rights in this regard by declaring banal every mill, whether water- or wind-driven, and without any need for stipulation in title deeds.[17]

Nevertheless, every St Ours deed mentioned the mill monopoly, in order to spell out the habitant's obligations and to specify penalties for infractions. The trend over the course of the eighteenth century was toward more extensive obligations and more stringent penalties. In the seventeenth century, only grain used for home consumption had to be ground at the seigneur's mill and the fine for processing flour elsewhere was the equivalent of the milling toll on the amount of grain. By the 1790s, the formula in concession deeds subjected all grain grown to the banalité, whether it was consumed at home or sent abroad, and piled penalty on top of penalty: not only would a fine equal to the milling toll be exacted, the illicit flour could also be seized and additional arbitrary fines imposed. This evolution in title deed clauses seems to reflect a wider trend toward a more careful and exacting style of estate management. Note, however, that, right from the beginning, the seigneurs of St Ours assumed the right to subject all varieties of grain to their monopoly even though the law of the land limited the banalité to wheat alone, and only to the amount needed for domestic consumption.[18]

There is a long-established myth in Canadian historiography to the effect that the law of 1686 giving all seigneurial mills monopoly privileges was as much a burden for the seigneurs as it was for the habitants, since it also forced the former to build mills within a year or forever forfeit their right of banalité.[19] In fact, many seigneurs easily retained their privileges even though they only opened a mill long after that date. Pierre de Sorel had a mill built in 1670, no doubt as much to contribute to the development of his estate as in anticipation of future profits, but Pierre de St Ours waited until 20 years after the law of 1686 before erecting a windmill, and his banal privileges were never revoked. Worse still, the absentee seigneurs of St Denis left their peasants with no mill until after the Conquest, noting all the same in concession deeds that granted lands would be, "sujette au moulin de ladte. seigneurie lorsqu'il y en aura un de construit."[20] Two small seigneurial mills, one wind-driven and the other water-driven, were eventually built in the late eighteenth century, but the seigneurs of St Denis found they did not even have to bother investing in milling facilities to profit from their banalité. [. . .]

After a period of severely fragmented ownership around the middle of the eighteenth century, the seigneurs of St Ours showed a greater willingness than their neighbours to establish their own mills and profit directly from the monopoly. This was partly because the fief was well supplied with good hydraulic sites, but also because the seigneurs generally lived on the estate for at least part of the year and took a personal hand in managing it. In addition to Pierre de St Ours's old windmill on the St Lawrence, there was a water-driven

mill on the Richelieu, built in 1773 and, following the development of the rear sections of the seigneurie, another watermill was established in 1815, this one on the Yamaska River. This last mill was the largest in St Ours and it contained three pairs of stones with bolts, as well as a fulling mill; in 1842 the building and machinery were insured for 10 000 livres.[21]

The milling toll in early Quebec was set by law at one-fourteenth of the grain ground but of course expenses claimed a considerable portion of the gross revenue. Mills were always leased out to a miller, either for a set annual rent or, more commonly, for a proportion of the proceeds; in various contracts this amounted to one-half, one-third, or one-quarter of the revenues.[22] The seigneur also had to pay for major repairs and for a portion of the operating expenses. This left, according to one optimistic estimate, about two-thirds of the milling tolls, or 4.8 per cent of all the grain processed, as the seigneur's net profit.[23] In Sorel, badly served by two decrepit windmills, net profits were only 160 minots of wheat (worth 480 livres) in 1782–3, but the big gristmills of St Ours were worth 1500 minots of grain (value about 3000–7000 livres) annually to their seigneur around 1840.[24]

[. . .]

A source of revenue to the seigneur, the banalité appeared from the habitant's point of view as a double restriction, preventing him both from having his grain ground where he wished and from establishing a gristmill of his own. In practice, it was the latter restriction that was most effectively enforced and economically most important. Although they always insisted on their right to prevent habitants from taking unground grain outside the fief, seigneurs were unable to police movements of this sort; contraventions seem to have been common.[25] On the other hand, it was impossible for interlopers to build unauthorized gristmills and escape detection. Two St Denis residents built mills on their own land but the seigneur promptly sued them and, in an out-of-court settlement, imposed the annual tribute mentioned earlier as the price of allowing them to continue operations; a less accommodating seigneur might have had the offending mills razed, with the full backing of the law. The lack of competition did not affect the cost of services to the habitant, since this was set by law at a moderate rate. On the other hand, the quality of flour and the regularity of service may have suffered. More serious was the inconvenience of having to carry grain to seigneurial mills that were, for many users, far from home. In France, only peasants within a certain distance, usually one league, were subject to the mill monopoly but, in Canadian seigneuries, which were generally quite vast, there was no such limit and farmers had to transport their grain many leagues to the banal mill.

[. . .]

FEUDAL EXACTIONS AND THE PEASANT HOUSEHOLD ECONOMY

If we add the ecclesiastical payments to the seigneurial dues enumerated here, it becomes clear that eighteenth-century habitants were subject to a diverse array of rents, tithes, fees, and fines. And yet, according to many historians, these all added up to an aggregate "feudal burden" that was paltry indeed.[26] The people of the Lower Richelieu, on the other hand, were more inclined to take these matters seriously. We have seen the heated disputes that often arose between priests and parishioners over pew rents and assessments for construction projects. Think also of the great pains that seigneurs took to adjust rent scales and to levy the full mutation fine on every imaginable transaction, and of the risks that many habitants ran in allowing backrents to accumulate even when they were in danger of losing their farms. These exactions

mattered both to exploiters and to exploited because the wealth at stake was significant.

What exactly was the material weight of feudalism on the peasantry? This is a question that has beddeviled historians of both Canada and Europe; many have attempted estimates but results have always been controversial and generally unsatisfactory.[27] Source deficiencies—the absence of reliable figures on agricultural production and aristocratic revenues—are only part of the problem. More serious are a number of thorny conceptual issues, many of them connected to the diversity of the forms of feudal exactions. It is very difficult to construct a single index out of the various dues when some were paid in cash, some in kind, and others in labour. Furthermore, some—tithes, pew rents, and seigneurial rents, for example—were due on a regular annual basis, while others—mutation fines and ecclesiastical assessments, for instance—had to be paid only on certain occasions. A further problem has to do with the fact that many payments to priests and seigneurs were at least partially compensation for a genuine service. Mill tolls fall into this category since only part of the fee can be attributed to the seigneur's privileged position. Finally, there is the question of whether the demands of the state—taxes, military service, road work—should be counted as part of the feudal burden. All this makes it next to impossible to measure the feudal economy with any precision or to make meaningful comparisons between different periods or between different countries.

Beyond these methodological dilemmas loom some options more theoretical than technical. Researchers wishing to determine the economic importance of feudalism must consider the questions, important for whom? and according to what criteria? The tendency is often to ignore the distinctions between capitalist and pre-capitalist economies and treat seigneurs and habitants as though they were landowners and agricultural entrepreneurs. From this point of view it makes sense to divide seigneurial revenues by the area of the censive to find a rate of seigneurial exactions amounting to so many livres per arpent. A similar procedure consists of estimating peasant agricultural income and dividing by the total of seigneurial and ecclesiastical revenues; this gives a percentage figure representing the proportion of habitant harvests absorbed by the feudal classes. This would be fine if the agriculturalists in question were genuine farmers engaged in a profit-making enterprise, selling all or most of what they grew and paying ground-rent as one of the expenses of doing business. Eighteenth-century habitants were of course nothing of the sort; they were peasants and their economy centred on production for domestic consumption. Thus there was a fairly inflexible minimum supply of many crops that habitant families needed to survive and to reproduce themselves. Ignoring this basic characteristic of pre-capitalist agrarian society allows one to conclude that "seigneurial dues . . . were very low, representing 10 per cent of the produce of their concessions,"[28] but it does not tell us much about the realities of the feudal economy since the 'produce" of peasant lands remains an abstract quantity. In fact, the figure of 10 per cent does not seem so low, especially when we realize that it does not include the tithe or other ecclesiastical dues, but that is not the point. The problem with this approach is that we do not know what the loss of 10 per cent of its harvest would mean for an habitant family, whether, for example, this would simply leave it with a little less wheat to sell or whether it would threaten its very survival by cutting into the stock needed for seed and for subsistence.

A better way of evaluating feudal exactions is therefore to consider them in relation to habitant *surpluses*. This requires estimating, not only how much peasants grew annually, but also how much they needed to retain in order to last the year. Because of the methodological and source difficulties mentioned above, I am not in a position to set up a complete

"model" of the habitant economy in the eighteenth century but I do have enough information to make a rough estimate of production, surplus, and exactions for wheat alone. Thus, only one aspect of Lower Richelieu agriculture is covered, although wheat was surely the most important element. Data [from the 1765 census on grain sown] can now be used to estimate the wheat production of all the habitants of St Ours. Census figures on the population of adults and children, along with information from deeds of gift on flour consumption, allow us then to calculate roughly the amount of wheat needed for home consumption. Taking the difference between production and consumption gives the estimated wheat surplus of each habitant family in the parish. It is then a simple matter to evaluate the impact on this surplus of the tithe and the wheat portion of seigneurial rents (see Table 2).[29]

According to this model then, almost half (44 per cent) of the wheat grown by the habitants of St Ours in 1765, beyond what was needed to maintain the growers, would have been owed to the local seigneur and curé just to pay those feudal exactions that were set down in terms of wheat. This of course does not give us a complete picture of the relationship between peasant surpluses and aristocratic exploitation. Habitants raised many products other than wheat, but most of these were exclusively for domestic use and therefore not part of a saleable surplus. On the other hand, many important feudal dues—mutation fines, pew rents, church assessments, and the cash portion of seigneurial rents, to name a few—do not enter into our calculations. If anything therefore, this partial estimate underestimates the feudal burden.

It should be noted that this is a "model" and not a detailed description of reality. In fact, harvests varied greatly from year to year, and so therefore did the relative weight of fixed dues; the seed-yield figure of 1:5.8 is simply one historian's estimate of the "normal"

Table 2 Habitant Surpluses and Feudal Exactions, Wheat Only, St Ours 1765

"Habitant" households		99
Production		
(a) grain sown	2098 minots	
(b) wheat sown (2/3a)	1399 minots	
(c) yield per seed	5.8	
(d) wheat harvested (b x c)	8112 minots	8112 minots
Deductions		
(e) wheat seed for next year	−1399 minots	
(f) mill toll (1/14)	−358 minots	
(g) total	−1757 minots	−1757 minots
Domestic consumption		
(h) adult population	238	
(i) boys under 15	158	
(j) "girls"	134	
(k) adult rations (h+i/2+3j/4)	417.5	
(l) consumption (12k)	5010 minots	−5010 minots
(m) surplus d − g − l		1345 minots
Exactions		
(n) wheat portion seign. rent	276 minots	
(o) wheat tithe (d/26)	312 minots	
(p) total	588 minots	588 minots
Feudal exactions = 588/1345 = 44% of habitant wheat surplus		

return. Also, some families no doubt ate more wheat than others and thus the 12-minot ration would not have been strictly uniform. [. . .] But, for the moment it is important to recognize that, imprecise and partial though this aggregate model may be, it does indicate that feudal dues deprived the Lower Richelieu peasantry of a substantial portion—probably more than half—of its agricultural surpluses.

Beyond this "average" experience, individual returns from the 1765 census make it clear that the production, surplus, and feudal burden varied greatly from one St Ours household to the next. For half the cases it is impossible to compute the percentage of wheat surpluses drained by tithe and seigneurial rent, since 48 of the families had no surplus at all once the exactions were subtracted. Of these households, 11 grew less than five minots of wheat per "adult equivalent"; evidently marginal grain-growers, these families may have been artisans or day-labourers. The other 37 who apparently lacked a wheat surplus must have had to scramble to get by, perhaps making do with less bread than their neighbours or earning a little money as hired hands at harvest time. These are no doubt the habitants who let their rents go unpaid for long stretches and who paid the seigneur, when they could, in lumber, cloth, and labour. Feudal dues must have been a serious problem for these families, but also for those, slightly better off, who grew enough in good years to retain a small surplus after they had paid the landlord and the curé. Table 3 shows that the wealthier half of the St Ours peasantry generally owed a substantial portion of their excess wheat to the aristocrats. Only 2 paid less than 10 per cent, whereas 28 paid more than 30 per cent of their surplus, some losing their entire surplus to feudal dues. For a handful of the richest peasants, on the other hand, tithes and rents were a much less significant drain. The three largest producers had a net wheat surplus after deductions, exactions and consumption of 110, 122, and 122 minots respectively. After them came ten others with 50 to 100 minots surplus. Feudal dues did not exceed 20 per cent of the excess of any of these 13 prosperous families. They normally had substantial quantities of grain to sell and were the section of the community that grain dealers were most interested in.

Table 3 Proportion of Wheat Surplus Devoted to Tithe and Seigneurial Rent (Wheat Only) by Habitant Household, St Ours 1765

	Households	Per cent
No surplus left after exactions	48	48
Exactions require 0–10% of surplus	2	2
Exactions require 10–20% of surplus	21	21
Exactions require 20–30% of surplus	11	11
Exactions require 30–50% of surplus	11	11
Exactions require 50–100% of surplus	4	4
Exactions require 100% + of surplus	2	2
TOTAL	99	99

This "model" of wheat surpluses by household demonstrates, not only the differing impact of feudal exactions, but also the variety of economic positions within the Lower Richelieu peasantry. As to the economic impact of feudal dues, it seems fair to conclude that they were an obstacle to the accumulation of capital in peasant hands. Certainly tithes, rents, and assessments did not absolutely prevent a habitant from amassing wealth, but generally they were a significant drain and particularly so for modest habitants like the Allaires who had a good deal of trouble in keeping above the subsistence line.

If extra-economic exactions and a prevalence of subsistence agriculture are the two primary characteristics of the feudal economy, here then is one connection between them. The first feature tended to reinforce the second by depriving peasants of part of the fruits of their labour. Seigneurial and ecclesiastical dues helped prevent the formation of an agrarian bourgeoisie by working against the accumulation of capital in habitant hands. Instead, a large portion of the agricultural surplus was delivered to priests and landlords who showed little inclination to invest their revenues in the land. Farms therefore remained relatively small and unproductive. Obviously feudal exploitation was not the only factor responsible for this state of affairs. The limited market for agricultural produce in the early years of the Lower Richelieu settlement also discouraged investment and egalitarian inheritance customs counteracted any long-term concentration of property. Moreover, the limitations on peasant ownership inherent in seigneurial tenure could be an obstacle to enterprise in some cases. Thus, although it would be an exaggeration to say that tithes, rents, and so on by themselves prevented the development of agriculture, it is nevertheless clear that they were a real burden for the habitant household, one that added its influence to other factors in making large-scale market-oriented production unlikely.

In other words, many of the basic characteristics of Lower Richelieu social and economic life were mutually reinforcing. The habitant majority lived and worked in family units, with household production organized mainly around the direct satisfaction of household consumption needs. This self-sufficient peasantry found a significant portion of its surplus drained off to support local priests and seigneurs, the latter constituting a local aristocracy whose political ascendancy guaranteed its economic privileges. This combination of peasant self-sufficiency, together with aristocratic appropriation through extra-economic compulsion, is the basically "feudal" configuration that is essential to an understanding of this rural society.

NOTES

1. Louise Dechêne, "L'évolution du régime seigneurial au Canada: le cas de Montréal aux XVIIe et XVIIIe siècles," *Recherches sociographiques* 12 (May–August 1971): 152.

2. Ibid.; cf. William Bennett Munro, *Documents Relating to the Seigniorial Tenure in Canada, 1598–1854* (Toronto: Champlain Society 1908) 74.

3. The assumption here is that wheat is valued at 10 livres per minot and that the hypothetical farm measures 3 arpents frontage by 30 arpents depth. The earliest concessions were fixed at one sol per arpent of area plus one capon (value 10 sols in 1709) for each arpent of frontage. The rate applied from 1754 on was one sol per arpent plus one-half minot of wheat for each 20 arpents (PAC, St Ours seigneurie, vol. 1, concession deeds). The evolution of rents in the seigneurie of Longueuil was almost exactly parallel, except that the rise in rates occurred rather earlier. Louis Lemoine, "Une société seigneuriale: Longueuil: méthode, sources, orientations" (MA thesis, Université de Montreal 1975) 145.

4. PAC, de Ramezay papers, pp. 1532–42, estate roll, Sorel, n.d. (1761–3).

5. ANQM, St. Denis seigneurie, 22RS7, list of arrears, 1840; PAC, Sorel seigneurie, vol. 11, estate roll, 1795.

6. PAC, Sorel seigneurie, vol. 12, accounts of the seigneurie of Sorel, 1840–7. Cf. William Bennet Munro, *The Seigniorial System in Canada: A Study in French Colonial Policy* (Cambridge: Harvard University Press 1907), 96; Dechêne, "L'évolution du régime seigneurial," 157–8.

7. Marc Bloch, *French Rural History: An Essay on Its Basic Characteristics*, trans. J. Sondheimer (Berkeley: University of California Press 1966), 180–9; Régine Robin, *La Société française en 1789: Sémur-en-Auxois* (Paris: Plon 1970), 153–4; Pierre de Saint-Jacob, *Les paysans de la Bourgogne du Nord au dernier siècle de l'ancien régime* (Paris: Université de Dijon 1960), 75–92, 377–80.

8. PAC, Haldimand papers, Add. Mss 21885, pt. 2, fols. 217–18; PAC, RG8, C, 278: 196–7, petition of Jean-Baptiste Veilleux, 22 July 1809.

9. Louise Dechêne makes this point in "L'évolution du régime seigneurial," 164. Other historians, on the other hand, include mill tolls, sometimes with operational expenses deducted, in lists of seigneurial revenues. This gives a misleading impression of the weight of seigneurial exactions. Habitants would have had to pay a charge to have their grain ground into flour even if there had been no seigneurial régime and it is difficult to say how much, if any, they would have saved had they not been subject to the banalité. Cf. Marcel Trudel, *The Seigneurial Régime,* Canadian Historical Association booklet 6 (Ottawa: CHA 1956), 13; R.C. Harris, *The Seigneurial System in Early Canada: A Geographical Study* (Madison: University of Wisconsin Press 1966), 78.

10. Cf. Jean Bastier, *La féodalité au siècle des lumières dans la région de Toulouse (1730–1790)* (Paris: Bibliothèque nationale 1975), 274–9.

11. PAC, Sorel seigneurie, vol. 13, "Rent Roll of His Majesty's Seigniory of Sorel for the year 1809," 24 March 1810; ibid., "Sorel Seigniory, abstract of arrears," 31 March 1858.

12. PAC, RG8, C, 279: 131, "Report on the Accounts of Mr Robert Jones Agent of His Majestys Seigniory of Sorel" (amounts shown are in livres).

13. ANQ, AP.G.–288 PAC, MG11, Q, 240–1: 190–5.

14. The disadvantages of this procedure did not stop the seigneur of St Ours from successfully suing ten habitants between 1839 and 1842. *Pièces et Documents relatifs à la tenure seigneuriale, demandés par une adresse de l'Assembée législative, 1851* (Quebec: E.R. Fréchette 1852), 150.

15. Ibid., agreement between Charles de St Ours and Bazile Bourg, 2 November 1815.

16. Dechêne, "L'évolution du régime seigneurial," 164.

17. François-Joseph Cugnet, *Traité de la Loi des Fiefs* (Quebec: Guillaume Brown 1775), 36–7.

18. Munro, *The Seigniorial System* 117–19.

19. Trudel, *The Seigneurial Régime,* 15; Harris, *The Seigneurial System,* 72.

20. ANQM, gr. Deguire, concession par M. de Contrecoeur à Jacques Coder, 8 December 1758.

21. Azarie Couillard-Desprès, *Histoire de la seigneurie de St-Ours,* 2 vols. Montreal: Imprimerie de l'institution des sourds-muets 1915–1917, vol. 1: 292–3; PAC, St Ours seigneurie, vol. 5, agreement between Charles de St Ours and Bazile Bourg dit Canic, 2 November 1815; ibid., vol. 10, Aetna Insurance Company, policy no. 3580, Mme R. de St. Ours, 11 November 1842.

22. ANQM, gr. Jehanne, lease by Monsieur de la Bruyère Montarville to Gabriel Chabot, 1 October 1779; ANQM, gr. Michaud, lease by Mr de la Bruyère Montarville to Sr Joseph Bourque dit Canique, 21 October 1799; PAC, St Ours seigneurie, vol. 5, agreement between Charles de St Ours and Bazile Bourg dit Canic, 2 November 1815.

23. PAC, Haldimand Papers, Add. Mss 21885, pt. 2, fol. 217–18, "Etat actuel des rentes et autres revenus de la seigneurie de Sorel, suivant les deux dernières Recettes en 1782 et 1783."

24. Ibid.; ANQ, St Ours collection, estate inventory of François Roch de St Ours, 19 June 1841. The seigneur's cash revenues cannot be estimated with any precision since a variety of grains with different values were ground.

25. *Edits, ordonnances, déclarations et arrêts relatifs à la tenure seigneuriale, demandés par une adresse*

de l'Assemblée Législative, 1851 (Quebec: E.R. Fréchette, 1852), 139–40; PAC, documents légaux des seigneuries, vol. 971, testimony of Joseph Mignault, 16 June 1860.

26. See Fernand Ouellet's critical discussion of this position in two articles: "Libéré ou exploité! Le paysan québécois d'avant 1850," *Histoire sociale/Social History* 13 (November 1980) 339–68; "La formation d'une société dans la vallée du Saint-Laurent: d'une société sans classes à une société de classes," *Canadian Historical Review* 62 (December 1981): 407–50.

27. Harris, *Seigneurial System* 78; Lise Pilon-Lê, "L'endettement des cultivateurs québécois: une analyse socio-historique de la rente foncière (1670–1904)" (PhD thesis, Université de Montréal 1978) 168–9; Guy Lemarchand, "Féodalisme et société rurale dans la France moderne," in *Sur le féodalisme,* 86–105 (see also Jacques Dupâquier's comments in ibid. 107); Albert Soboul, "Sur le prélèvement féodal," in *Problèmes paysans de la révolution (1789–1848): études d'histoire révolutionnaire* (Paris: François Maspero 1976), 89–115; Bastier, *La féodalité au siècle des lumières,* 258–9.

28. W.J. Eccles, *France in America* (Vancouver: Fitzhenry and Whiteside 1973), 79.

29. Only 99 of the 107 local households are included in this "model," the remaining 8 being eliminated either because data were evidently missing from their entries or because they had no land and were therefore apparently priests, artisans, or labourers. The assumptions underlying this estimate are that two-thirds of the census-recorded grain sown was wheat, that the seed-yield ratio of wheat was 1: 5.8, that the 11 037 arpents held by these 99 families were subject to the prevailing rate of seigneurial rent which included a levy of "one half minot of wheat for every 20 arpents," that adults required 12 minots of wheat a year (the lowest individual ration commonly found in eighteenth-century pensions alimentaires), while children needed only half that amount and "girls" (unmarried females not differentiated by age in the census) ate, on the average, three-quarters of an adult ration.

Chapter 4

The Expulsion of the Acadians

READINGS

Primary Documents

1   From "1755 Council Minutes," in *Acadia and Nova Scotia: Documents Relating to the Acadian French and the First British Colonization of the Province, 1714–1758*, Thomas B. Akins, ed.

2   From "Extracts from Col. John Winslow's Journal," in *Report Concerning Canadian Archives for the Year 1905*

Historical Interpretations

3   From "Île Royale, New England, Scotland, and Nova Scotia, 1744–1748," in *An Unsettled Conquest: The British Campaign Against the Peoples of Acadia*, Geoffrey Plank

4   From "The Decision to Deport," in *From Migrant to Acadian: A North American Border People, 1604–1755*, N.E.S. Griffiths

INTRODUCTION

In today's society, we venerate the ideals of harmony and trust, yet—collectively at least—we frequently fail to embody them. Eighteenth-century colonial North America was one place where similar failures occurred. The early eighteenth century brought significant change to the continent as French-speaking residents of Acadia (today's Nova Scotia and New Brunswick) found themselves under British control, thanks to a peace treaty in which the French "traded away" this territory. The 1713 Treaty of Utrecht gave the British a region that, a century earlier, had been one site of French colonial hopes. The new owners expected loyalty, but had demonstrated little patience with their Roman Catholic subjects elsewhere and knew little about the local Indigenous people. As in most conflicts, each side had some merit to its case. Acadians who largely wished to go about their lives unaffected by questions of colonial jurisdiction were urged to swear allegiance to the British monarch. Those who had to govern the region faced a population of Acadians who seemed to be stubbornly refusing to acknowledge British power and hoping for a return to the French fold.

For over 40 years, this was the pattern: an uneasy co-existence. In 1755, it came as a rather rude shock to the Acadians when longstanding suspicions about their disloyalty were followed up by British action. When the Acadians failed to convince British administrators that they had not been covertly aiding the French, they were handed an expulsion notice. Harmony and trust were impossible in Acadia with the larger conflict between colonial powers affecting the way that governors and governed related to one another.

The deportation was a process that lasted from 1755 to 1762. The Acadians of Minas Bassin and Beaubassin were the first to be evicted, followed by the ones from Louisbourg and Île St-Jean. In total, nearly 12 000 Acadians were deported to the Thirteen Colonies, Britain, and France. The primary documents describe that moment to show us the resolve of Governor Charles Lawrence along with Acadian disbelief and desperation. As for the historical interpretations, Geoffrey Plank discusses how the British authorities were reassessing their attitudes toward cultural and religious diversity in Nova Scotia after the Scottish uprising of 1746 and the War of the Austrian Succession. Naomi Griffiths argues, however, that the Deportation was not the result of a long-planned program, but of the decision of the local then–Lieutenant-Governor Lawrence. When the Acadians left, they went or were sent to a variety of places, none of which had agreed to accommodate them.

QUESTIONS FOR CONSIDERATION

1. What sort of behaviour did the British seem to expect from the Acadians?
2. What do the Acadians appear not to understand about their situation, and how are British suspicions confirmed later in the summer of 1755?
3. Do you think that the Acadians posed a real threat to British rule in Nova Scotia?
4. How different are Griffiths's and Plank's interpretations about the influence of British politics in the decision to deport Acadians?
5. Do you agree with Griffiths that the expulsion had not been planned long in advance?

SUGGESTIONS FOR FURTHER READING

Jean Daigle, ed., *The Acadians of the Maritimes: Thematic Studies* (Moncton: Centre d'études acadiennes, 1982).

John Mack Faragher, *A Great and Noble Scheme: The Tragic Story of the Expulsion of the French Acadians from their American Homeland* (New York: W.W. Norton & Co., 2005).

N.E.S. Griffiths, *From Migrant to Acadian: A North American Border People 1604–1755* (Montreal and Kingston: McGill-Queen's University Press, 2005).

Christopher Hodson, *The Acadian Diaspora: An Eighteenth-Century History* (Oxford: Oxford University Press, 2012).

A.J.B. Johnston, *Endgame 1758: The Promise, the Glory and the Despair of Louisbourg's Last Decade* (Sydney, NS: Cape Breton University Press, 2007).

Earl Lockerby, "The Deportation of the Acadians from Ile St. Jean, 1758," *Acadiensis* XXVII (Spring 1998): 45–94.

Jon Parmentier and Mark Power Robinson, "The Perils and Possibilities of Wartime Neutrality on the Edges of Empire: Iroquois and Acadians between the French and British in North America, 1744–1760," *Diplomatic History* 31, 2 (April 2007): 167–206.

Geoffrey Plank, *An Unsettled Conquest: The British Campaign Against the Peoples of Acadia* (Philadelphia: University of Pennsylvania Press, 2001).

Primary Documents

1   From "1755 Council Minutes," in Thomas B. Akins, ed., *Acadia and Nova Scotia: Documents Relating to the Acadian French and the First British Colonization of the Province 1714–1758* (Halifax, 1870), 247–57.

At a Council holden at the Governor's House in Halifax on Thursday the 3rd July 1755.

PRESENT—

The Lieutenant Governor.

Councs.: Benj. Green, Jno. Collier, Willm. Cotterell, Jonn. Belcher.

The Lieutenant Governor laid before the Council the two following Memorials, Signed by the Deputies and a number of the French Inhabitants of Minas and Pisiquid, and delivered to Capt. Murray the Commanding Officer there, by whom they had been transmitted to His Excellency.

[Translated from the French.]

"MINES June 10th. 1755."

"To His Excellency CHARLES LAWRENCE, Governor of the province of Nova Scotia or Acadie, &c. &c.

"Sir,—

"We, the Inhabitants of Mines, Pisiquid, and the river Canard, take the liberty of approaching your Excellency for the purpose of testifying our sense of the care which the government exercises towards us.

"It appears, Sir, that your Excellency doubts the sincerity with which we have promised to be faithful to his Britannic Majesty.

"We most humbly beg your Excellency to consider our past conduct. You will see, that, very far from violating the oath we have taken, we have maintained it in its entirety, in spite of the solicitations and the dreadful threats of another power. We still entertain, Sir, the same pure and sincere disposition to prove under any circumstances, our unshaken fidelity to his Majesty, provided that His Majesty shall allow us the same liberty that he has granted us. We earnestly beg your Excellency to have the goodness to inform us of His Majesty's intentions on this subject, and to give us assurances on his part.

"Permit us, if you please, Sir, to make known the annoying circumstances in which we are placed, to the prejudice of the tranquillity we ought to enjoy. Under pretext that we are transporting our corn or other provisions to Beausejour, and the river St. John, we are no longer permitted to carry the least quantity of corn by water from one place to another. We beg your Excellency to be assured that we have never transported provisions to Beausejour, or to the river St. John. If some refugee inhabitants at the point have been seized, with cattle, we are not on that account, by any means guilty, in as much as the cattle belonged to them as private individuals, and they were driving them to their respective habitations. As to ourselves, Sir, we have never offended in that respect; consequently we ought not, in our opinion, to be punished; on the contrary, we hope that your Excellency will be pleased to restore to us the same liberty that we enjoyed formerly, in giving us the use of our canoes, either to transport our provisions from one river to the other, or for the purpose of fishing; thereby providing for our livelihood. This permission has never been taken from us except at the present time. We hope, Sir, that you will be pleased to restore it, especially in consideration of the number of poor inhabitants who would be very glad to support their families with the fish that they would be able to catch. Moreover, our guns, which we regard as our own personal property, have been taken from us, notwithstanding the fact that they are absolutely necessary to us, either to defend our cattle which are attacked by the wild beasts, or for the protection of our children, and of ourselves.

"Any inhabitant who may have his oxen in the woods, and who may need them for purposes of labour, would not dare to expose himself in going for them without being prepared to defend himself.

"It is certain, Sir, that since the savages have ceased frequenting our parts, the wild beasts have greatly increased, and that our cattle are devoured by them almost every day. Besides, the arms which have been taken from us are but a feeble guarantee of our fidelity. It is not the gun which an inhabitant possesses, that will induce him to revolt, nor the privation of the same gun that will make him more faithful; but his conscience alone must induce him to maintain his oath. An order has appeared in your Excellency's name, given at Fort Edward June 4th, 1755, and in the 28th year of his Majesty's reign, by which we are commanded to carry guns, pistols etc. to Fort Edward. It appears to us, Sir, that it would be dangerous for us to execute that order, before representing to you the danger to which this order exposes us. The savages may come and threaten and plunder us, reproaching us for

having furnished arms to kill them. We hope, Sir, that you will be pleased, on the contrary, to order that those taken from us be restored to us. By so doing, you will afford us the means of preserving both ourselves and our cattle. In the last place, we are grieved, Sir, at seeing ourselves declared guilty without being aware of having disobeyed. One of our inhabitants of the river Canard, named Piere Melançon, was seized and arrested in charge of his boat, before having heard any order forbidding that sort of transport. We beg your Excellency, on this subject, to have the goodness to make known to us your good pleasure before confiscating our property and considering us in fault. This is the favour we expect from your Excellency's kindness, and we hope that you will do us the justice to believe that very far from violating our promises, we will maintain them, assuring you that we are very respectfully,

Sir,

Your very humble and obt. servants,"
Signed by twenty-five of the said inhabitants.

"MINES, June 24, 1755."
"To his Excellency CHARLES LAWRENCE, Esq., Governor of the province of Nova Scotia or Acadie.

"Sir,—

"All the inhabitants of Mines, Pisiquid and the river Canard, beg your Excellency to believe that if, in the petition which they have had the honor to present to your Excellency, there shall be found any error or any want of respect towards the government, it is intirely contrary to their intention; and that in this case, the inhabitants who have signed it, are not more guilty than the others.

"If, sometimes, the inhabitants become embarrassed in your Excellency's presence, they humbly beg you to excuse their timidity; and if, contrary to our expectation, there is anything hard in the said petition, we beg your Excellency to do us the favour of allowing us to explain our intention.

"We hope that your Excellency will be pleased to grant us this favour, begging you to believe that we are very respectfully,

    Sir,

    Your very humble and very obedient servants,"

    Signed by forty-four of the said inhabitants in the name of the whole.

The Lieutenant Governor at the same time acquainted the Council that Capt. Murray had informed him that for some time before the delivery of the first of the said memorials the French Inhabitants in general had behaved with greater Submission and Obedience to the Orders of the Government than usual, and had already delivered into him a considerable number of their Fire Arms, but that at the delivery of the said Memorial they treated him with great Indecency and Insolence, which gave him strong Suspicions, that they had obtained some Intelligence which we were then ignorant of, and which the Lieutenant Governor conceived might most probably be a Report that had been about that time spread amongst them of a French Fleet being then in the Bay of Fundy, it being very notorious that the said French Inhabitants have always discovered an insolent and inimical Disposition towards His Majesty's Government when they have had the least hopes of assistance from France.

The Lieutenant Governor likewise acquainted the Council that upon his receipt of the first Memorial, he had wrote to Captain Murray to order all those who had Signed the same, to repair forthwith to Halifax to attend him and the Council thereon, and that they were accordingly arrived and then in waiting without.

The Council having then taken the Contents of the said Memorials into Consideration, were unanimously of Opinion That the Memorial of the 10th of June is highly arrogant and insidious, an Insult upon His Majesty's Authority and Government, and deserved the highest Resentment, and that if the Memorialists had not submitted themselves by their subsequent Memorial, they ought to have been severely punished for their Presumption.

The Deputies were then called in and the Names of the Subscribers to the Memorial read over, and such of them as were present, ordered to Answer to their Names, which they did to the number of fifteen, the others being Sick, after which the Memorial itself was again read, and they were severely reprimanded for their Audacity in Subscribing and Presenting so impertinent a Paper, but in Compassion to their Weakness and Ignorance of the Nature of our Constitution, especially in Matters of Government, and as the Memorialists had presented a subsequent one, and had shewn an Appearance of Concern for their past behaviour therein, and had then presented themselves before the Council with great Submission and Repentance, The Council informed them they were still ready to treat them with Lenity, and in order to shew them the falsity as well as Impudence of the Contents of their Memorial, it was ordered to be read Paragraph by Paragraph, and the Truth of the several Allegations minutely discussed, and Remarks made by the Lieutenant Governor on each Paragraph, to the following Effect, vizt.

It was observed in Answer to this Paragraph of their Memorial of the 10th of June

"That they were affected with the Proceedings of the Government towards them."

That they had been always treated by the Government with the greatest Lenity and Tenderness. That they had enjoyed more Privileges than English Subjects, and had been indulged in the free Excercise of their Religion. That they had at all times full Liberty to consult their Priests, and had been protected in their Trade and Fishery, and had been for many Years permitted to possess their Lands (part of the best Soil of the Province) tho' they had not complied with the Terms, on which the Lands were granted, by Taking the Oath of Allegiance to the Crown.

They were then asked whether they could produce an Instance that any Privilege was denied to them, or that any hardships, were ever imposed upon them by the Government.

They acknowledged the Justice and Lenity of the Government.

Upon the Paragraph where

"They desire their past Conduct might be considered."

It was remarked to them that their past Conduct was considered, and that the Government were sorry to have occasion to say that their Conduct had been undutifull and very ungratefull for the Lenity shown to them. That they had no Returns of Loyalty to the Crown, or Respect to His Majesty's Government in the Province. That they had discovered a constant disposition to Assist His Majesty's Enemies, and to distress his Subjects. That they had not only furnished the Enemy with Provisions and Ammunition, but had refused to supply the Inhabitants, or Government, with Provisions, and when they did Supply, they have exacted three times the Price for which they were sold at other Markets. That they had been indolent and Idle on their Lands, had neglected Husbandry, and the Cultivation of the Soil, and had been of no use to the Province either in husbandry, Trade or Fishery, but had been rather an Obstruction to the King's Intentions in the Settlement.

They were then asked whether they could mention a single Instance of Service to the Government. To which they were incapable of making any Reply.

Upon reading this Paragraph,

"It seems that your Excellency is doubtfull of the Sincerity of those who have promised fidelity, That they had been so far from breaking their Oath, that they had kept it in spight of terrifying Menaces from another Power"

They were asked What gave them Occasion to suppose that the Government was doubtfull of their Sincerity? and were told, that it argued a Consciousness in them of insincerity and want of Attachment to the Interests of His Majesty and his Government. That as to taking their Arms, They had often urged that the Indians would annoy them if they did not Assist them, and that by taking their Arms by Act of Government, it was put out of the Power of the Indians to threaten or force them to their Assistance. That they had assisted the King's Enemies, and appeared too ready to Join with another Power, contrary to the Allegiance they were bound by their Oath to yield to His Majesty.

In Answer to this Paragraph,

"We are now in the same disposition, the purest and sincerest, to prove in every Circumstance Fidelity to His Majesty in the same manner as we have done, Provided that His Majesty will leave us the same Liberties which he has granted us"

They were told that it was hoped, they would hereafter give Proofs of more sincere and pure dispositions of Mind, in the Practice of Fidelity to His Majesty, and that they would forbear to Act in the manner they have done, in obstructing the Settlement of the Province, by Assisting the Indians and French to the distress and Annoyance of many of His Majesty's Subjects, and to the Loss of the Lives of several of the English Inhabitants. That it was not the Language of British Subjects to talk of Terms with the Crown, to Capitulate about their Fidelity and Allegiance, and that it was insolent to insert a *Proviso*, that they would prove their Fidelity *Provided* that His Majesty would give them Liberties.

All His Majesty's Subjects are protected in the Enjoyment of every Liberty, while they continue Loyal and faithfull to the Crown, and when they become false and disloyal they forfeit that Protection.

That they in particular, tho they had acted so insincerely on every Opportunity, had been left in the full Enjoyment of their Religion, Liberty and Properties, with an Indulgence beyond what would have been allowed to any British Subject, who could presume, as they have done, to join in the Measures of another Power.

They were told in answer to the Paragraph where,

"They desire their Canoes for carrying their Provisions from one River to another and for their Fishery"

That they wanted their Canoes for carrying Provisions to the Enemy, and not for their own use or the Fishery, That by a Law of this Province, All Persons are restrained from carrying Provisions from one Port to another, and every Vessel, Canoe or Bark found with Provisions is forfeited, and a Penalty is inflicted on the Owners.

They were also told in Answer to the following Paragraph,

"They Petition for their Guns as part of their Goods, that they may be restored to defend their Cattle from the Wild Beasts, and to preserve themselves and their Children, That since the Indians have quitted their Quarters, the Wild Beasts are greatly increased"

That Guns are no part of their Goods, as they have no Right to keep Arms. By the Laws of England, All Roman Catholicks are restrained from having Arms, and they are Subject to Penalties if Arms are found in their Houses.

That upon the Order from Captain Murray many of the Inhabitants voluntarily brought in their Arms, and none of them pretended that they wanted them for defence of their Cattle against Wild Beasts, and that the Wild Beasts had not increased since their Arms were surrendered. That they had some secret Inducement, at that time, for presuming to demand their Arms as part of their Goods and their Right, and that they had flattered themselves of being supported in their Insolence to the Government, on a Report that some french Ships of War were in the Bay of Fundy. That this daring Attempt plainly discovered the falsehood of their Professions of Fidelity to the King, and their readiness has been visible upon every Intimation of force or Assistance from France, to insult His Majesty's Government, and to join with his Enemies, contrary to their Oath of Fidelity.

Upon reading this Paragraph,

"Besides the Arms we carry are a feeble Surety for our Fidelity. It is not the Gun that an Inhabitant possesses, which will lead him to Revolt, nor the depriving him of that Gun that will make him more faithful, but his Conscience alone ought to engage him to maintain his Oath."

They were asked, what Excuse they could make for their Presumption in this Paragraph, and treating the Government with such Indignity and Contempt as to Expound to them the nature of Fidelity, and to prescribe what would be the Security proper to be relied on by the Government for their Sincerity. That their Consciences ought indeed to engage them to Fidelity from their Oath of Allegiance to the King, and that if they were sincere in their Duty to the Crown, they would not be so anxious for their Arms, when it was the pleasure of the King's Government to demand them for His Majesty's Service. They were then informed that a very fair Opportunity now presented itself to them to Manifest the reality of their Obedience to the Government by immediately taking the Oath of Allegiance in the Common Form before the Council. Their Reply to this Proposal was, That they were not come prepared to resolve the Council on that head. They were then told that they very well knew these Six Years past,the same thing had been often proposed to them and had been as often evaded under various frivolous pretences, that they had often been informed that sometime or other it would be required of them and must be done, and that the Council did not doubt but they knew the Sentiments of the Inhabitants in general, and had fully considered and determined this point with regard to themselves before now, as they had been already indulged with Six Years to form a Resolution thereon. They then desired they might return home and consult the Body of the People upon this subject as they could not do otherwise than the Generality of the inhabitants should determine, for that they were desirous of either refusing or accepting the Oath in a Body, and could not possibly determine, till they knew the Sentiments of their Constituents.

Upon this so extraordinary a Reply they were informed they would not be permitted to Return for any such purpose, but that it was expected from them to declare on the Spot, for their own particular, as they might very well be expected to do after having had so long a time to consider upon that point. They then desired leave to retire to consult among themselves, which they were permitted to do, when after near an hour's Recess, They returned with the same Answer, That they could not consent to take the Oath as prescribed without consulting the General Body, but that they were ready to take it as they had done before, to which they were answered, That His Majesty had disapproved of the manner of their taking the Oath before, That it was not consistent with his Honour to make any conditions, nor could the Council accept their taking the Oath in any other way than as all other His Majesty's Subjects were obliged by Law to do when called upon, and

that it was now expected they should do so, which they still declining, they were allowed till the next Morning at Ten of the Clock to come to a Resolution. To which Time the Council then adjourned. . . .

The Council being met according to Adjournment, the french Deputies who were Yesterday Ordered to Attend the Council, were brought in, and, upon being asked what Resolution they were come to in regard to the Oath, They declared they could not consent to Take the Oath in the Form required without consulting the Body. They were then informed that as they had now for their own particulars, refused to Take the Oath as directed by Law, and thereby sufficiently evinced the Sincerity of their Inclination towards the Government, The Council could no longer look on them as Subjects to His Britannick Majesty, but as Subjects of the King of France, and as such they must hereafter be Treated; and they were Ordered to withdraw.

The Council after Consideration, were of Opinion That directions should be given to Captain Murray to order the French Inhabitants forthwith to Choose and send to Halifax, new Deputies with the General Resolution of the said Inhabitants in regard to taking the Oath, and that none of them should for the future be admitted to Take it after having once refused so to do, but that effectual Measures ought to be taken to remove all such Recusants out of the Province.

The Deputies were then called in again, and having been informed of this Resolution, and finding they could no longer avail themselves of the Disposition of the Government to ingage them to a Dutifull Behaviour by Lenity and perswasion, Offered to take the Oath, but were informed that as there was no reason to hope their proposed Compliance proceeded from an honest Mind, and could be esteemed only the Effect of Compulsion and Force, and is contrary to a clause in an Act of Parliament, I. Geo. 2. c 13. whereby Persons who have once refused to Take the

Oaths cannot be afterwards permitted to Take them, but are considered as Popish Recusants; Therefore they would not now be indulged with such Permission; And they were thereupon ordered into Confinement.

2 From "Extracts from Col. John Winslow's Journal" [1755], in *Report Concerning Canadian Archives for the Year 1905* (Ottawa: S.E. Dawson, 1906), vol. II, Appendix A, Part III, 19–29.

Septr. 3rd—This Day had a Consultation with the Captains the Result of which was that I Should Give out my Citation to the Inhabitants to morrow Morning.

1755, September the 4th—This Morning Sent for Doctor Rodion and Delivd him a Citation to the Inhabitants with a Strict Charge to See it Executed, which he Promist Should be Faithfully Done.

September 5th—Att Three in the afternoon The French Inhabitants appeard agreable to their Citation at the Church in Grand Pré amounting To 418 of Their Best Men upon which I ordered a Table to be Sett in the Center of the Church and being attended with those of my officers who were off Gaurd Delivered them by Interpretors the King's orders In the Following words:

GENTLEMEN,—I have Received from his Excellency Governor Lawrance, The Kings Commission which I have in my hand and by whose orders you are Convened togather to Manifest to you his Majesty's Final resolution to the French Inhabitants of this his Province of Nova Scotia, who for almost half a Century have had more Indulgence Granted them, then any of his Subjects in any part of his Dominions. what use you have made of them, you your Self Best Know.

The Part of Duty I am now upon is what thoh Necessary is Very Disagreable to my Natural make & Temper as I Know it Must be Grevious to you who are of the Same Specia.

But it is not my Business to annimedvert, but to obey Such orders as I receive and therefore without Hessitation Shall Deliver you his Majesty's orders and Instructions vizt.

That your Lands & Tennements, Cattle of all Kings and Live Stock of all Sortes are Forfitted to the Crown with all other your Effects Saving your Money and Household Goods and you your Selves to be removed from this his Province.

This it is Preremtorily his Majesty's orders That the whole French Inhabitants of these Districts, be removed, and I am Throh his Majesty's Goodness Directed to allow you Liberty to Carry of your money and Household Goods as Many as you Can without Discomemoading the Vessels you Go in. I shall do Every thing in my Power that all Those Goods be Secured to you and that you are Not Molested in Carrying of them of and also that whole Familys Shall go in the Same Vessel, and make this remove which I am Sensable must give you a great Deal of Trouble as Easy as his Majesty's Service will admit and hope that in what Ever part of the world you may Fall you may be Faithful Subjects, a Peasable & happy People.

I Must also inform you That it is his Majesty's Pleasure that you remain in Security under the Inspection & Direction of the Troops that I have the Honr. to Command.

and then declared them the Kings Prisoner's.

And Gave out the following Declaration. GRAND PRÉ, September 5sh, 1755.

All officers and Soldiers and Sea Men Employed in his Majesty's Service as well as

all his Subjects of what Denomination Soever, are hereby Notified That all Cattle vizt.
Horsses, Horne Cattle, Sheep, goats, Hoggs
and Poultry of Every Kinde, that was this Day
Soposed to be Vested in the French Inhabitants of this Province are become Forfeited to
his Majesty whose Property they now are and
Every Person of what Denomination Soever is
to take Care not to Hurt, Kill or Destroy anything of any Kinde nor Rob Orchards or Gardens or to make waste of anything Dead or
alive in these Districts without Special order.
Given at my Camp the Day and Place abovesd.
JOHN WINSLOW.

To be Published Throhout the Camp and
at Villages where the Vessels lye.

After Delivering These Things I returned
to my Quarters and they the French Inhabitants Soon Moved by their Elders that it was
a Great Grief to them that they had Incurred
his Majty's Displeasure and that they were
Fearfull that the Surprise of their Detention
here would Quite over Come their Familys
whome they had No Means to apprise of
these their Maloncolly Circumstances and
Prayd that parte of them might be returned
as Hostages for the appearance of the rest and
the Biger number admitted to Go home to
their Families, and that as some of their Men
were absent they would be obliged to Bring
them in. I informed them I would Consider
of their Motions and reporte.

And Immediately Convened my officers,
to advise, who with Me all agreed that it would
be well that they them Selves should Chuse
Twenty of their Number for whome they would
be answerable vizt Ten of the Inhabitants of
Grand Pré & Village & other Ten of the River
Cannard and Habitant and they to acquaint
the Families of their Districts how Maters
where and to assure them that the women &
children should be in Safety in their absence in
their Habitations and that it was Espected the
Party Indulged Should take Care to Bring in
an Exact Account of their absent Bretheren &
their Circumstances on the Morrow.

Historical Interpretations

3   From Geoffrey Plank, "Île Royale, New England, Scotland, and Nova Scotia,
1744–1748," in *An Unsettled Conquest: The British Campaign Against the Peoples of
Acadia* (Philadelphia: University of Pennsylvania Press, 2001), 106–22. Reprinted with
permission of the University of Pennsylvania Press.

In 1739, after a series of disputes arising out
of Spanish efforts to regulate trade in the
Caribbean, Britain went to war with Spain.
Sir Robert Walpole had tried to settle his government's differences with Spain peacefully,
but domestic opposition to his foreign policy
forced his hand. The Walpole ministry's opponents rallied a significant portion of the
British public in support of war with Spain in
part by associating the interests of British merchants abroad with the political liberties of
Britons at home. They cited the government's
willingness to negotiate with the Spanish as
evidence of Walpole's corruption and an indication that he was willing to sacrifice British
liberty and subordinate himself to the Catholic powers to advance his own political ends.
At public rallies and in the press, the supporters of war called themselves "patriots," and by
linking domestic liberty with power overseas,
they created a new, broader base of political
support for British imperial expansion.[1]

The inhabitants of North America's eastern maritime region followed these events

with great interest, assuming that the Anglo-Spanish conflict would broaden into a larger conflagration and that Britain and France would soon be at war. One result was a precipitous decline in the number of New England fishermen visiting Canso. The New Englanders feared a French attack on the island, and many abandoned it after 1739. It turned out that the fishermen were right, though Europe's diplomats staved off war between the British and the French longer than the colonists anticipated. The War of the Austrian Succession, Britain's war with France, began only in 1744, after Walpole had been driven from power. It started far from the coasts of Nova Scotia, but the French on Île Royale exploited the outbreak of hostilities almost immediately by joining forces with Mi'kmaq allies and attacking the British settlement on Canso after the word arrived from Europe that war had been declared.

In response to the attack on Canso, Massachusetts entered the conflict, first by sending reinforcements to defend the garrison at Annapolis Royal, and then in 1745 (acting alongside forces from elsewhere in New England) by seizing Louisbourg. The New Englanders sent most of the French colonial population of Île Royale to France, but the French military remained active in the region nonetheless, particularly in the eastern part of peninsular Nova Scotia.

The fighting disrupted the conditions that had allowed for relative peace in Nova Scotia over the previous 18 years by forcing almost all the inhabitants to answer questions that many of them had previously been able to avoid. The Mi'kmaq and the English-speaking colonists, especially on the Atlantic coast, had to define in clearer terms the meaning of Mi'kmaq claims to the land. The Acadians throughout the province had to determine under what circumstances they were obliged to support the British colonial government or resist demands made on them by the government's French and Mi'kmaq opponents. Persons of mixed ancestry, and others whose way of life defied simple categorization as "French," "British," or "Indian," had to decide for official purposes in which community they belonged.

Almost every facet of daily life became politically significant. Growing crops and raising livestock in certain areas served the war efforts of the Mi'kmaq and the French and left the Acadians vulnerable to British reprisals. Other activities such as worshipping alongside Native warriors or French soldiers, dancing with the men or helping Mi'kmaq women care for their children, acquired new importance in the context of the war. And even those who avoided contact with the fighting men or their families had reason to monitor and re-evaluate their habits because the British used behavioural cues to determine whether a person was Mi'kmaq. From 1744 onward the Massachusetts government offered prizes for the scalps of the Native people.

The New England colonists who participated in military action in and around Nova Scotia in some respects closely resembled those of earlier generations who had fought in the maritime region, and the War of the Austrian Succession only served to intensify existing patterns of interracial violence. But in other respects the mid-eighteenth-century New Englanders were very different from their predecessors. Partly under the influence of the new brand of imperial patriotism, which had spread across the Atlantic since the start of the war with Spain, many New England colonists saw their actions as part of a larger imperial project, one they embraced without the misgivings of the old Puritans. Following their victory at Louisbourg the colonists celebrated in a way they had never done before.[2]

After 1745 political developments in Britain helped recast the terms of the debate surrounding the Acadians. In 1746, in the aftermath of an uprising in Scotland on behalf of the Stuart claimant to the throne, the British government debated a series of measures designed to pacify broad stretches of the Scottish Highlands and culturally assimilate the Highlanders. Ideas originally developed as a solution for perceived problems in Scotland were considered as policy options for the Acadians. Perhaps the most important idea that reached America in this way was a proposal to move suspect populations within the British Empire. Before the pacification of the Highlands, those who had proposed moving the Acadians imagined that they would be expelled altogether from the British colonies (as the New Englanders sent the French colonists from Île Royale to France in 1745). But from 1746 forward, under the influence of proposals developed in the Scottish context, the debate shifted as policy makers considered forced migrations designed to incorporate the Acadians into the communal life of British North America.

In the years following the outbreak of the War of the Austrian Succession, events far from Nova Scotia had profound effects on the lives of the peoples of the province. This article highlights the influence of groups who came to the colony from elsewhere in the British and French Empires. It begins with the decision of the French colonial administrators on Île Royale to attack the British fishery at Canso, and proceeds with an analysis of the military response of the New Englanders and the impact of the imperial war on the lives of the Mi'kmaq and the Acadians.

When the French colonial authorities began the large-scale settlement of Île Royale in 1714, they had hoped that the island colony would attract most, if not all, of the Mi'kmaq and the Acadians. The French succeeded in convincing some Acadian families to move, though fewer than they expected. Similarly, Île Royale attracted fewer Mi'kmaq than the French would have preferred, and many of those who went only visited. Nonetheless, even without a wholesale migration of Mi'kmaq and Acadians from Nova Scotia, the French colony on Île Royale prospered. By the early 1740s, Louisbourg alone had nearly 2000 inhabitants; three-quarters were civilians, including the families of soldiers, fishermen, colonial officials, merchants, artisans, and labourers. The island as a whole had a population approaching 5000.[3]

Though the French could not entice all the Mi'kmaq or Acadians to move to Île Royale, various French missionaries and colonial officials remained interested in the affairs of the peoples of Nova Scotia. They continued to think of the Acadians as compatriots, and they thought of the Mi'kmaq as a client people, dependent on the French for pastoral care, trade, and a measure of political direction. As early as 1734, Joseph Saint-Ovide de Brouillan, the governor of Île Royale, made tentative plans to retake Nova Scotia in the event of a war.[4] His advisors assured him that all of the Acadians and most of the Mi'kmaq would greet the French forces as liberators. Subsequent administrators continued to hold similar views.[5] The outbreak of the War of the Austrian Succession presented the colony's officials with an apparent opportunity to bring the Mi'kmaq and the Acadians back within the borders of the French Empire. Instead of asking them to move, the French would try to shift the boundary and drive Britain's colonial administration away.

The French attack on Canso was intended as a first step toward recapturing all of Nova Scotia. There were several reasons for striking the fishing settlement first. Driving the British from Canso foreclosed any possibility that the island could be used as a base for privateers. The French also hoped to cripple the British fishery in the North Atlantic and thereby acquire a larger share of the world market in fish. Canso seemed vulnerable, and since some of the British settlers there had well-furnished homes, the possibility of plunder made it easier for the French to recruit volunteer troops in Louisbourg. Furthermore, many of the Mi'kmaq continued to resent the British presence on the Atlantic coast, and thus the attack on Canso helped secure a wartime Franco-Mi'kmaq alliance.[6]

The decision to start with an attack on the fishing settlement appears in retrospect to have been a strategic mistake, however, because it had the effect of bringing New Englanders into the conflict from the moment the fighting began.[7] Though they had lost Canso, New England's fishermen and privateers could reach the waters off Nova Scotia from other bases, and the Atlantic fishing banks soon became a battle zone, as New Englanders sought retaliation against the French, and the French responded in kind. In a matter of months hundreds of fishing vessels were taken or destroyed.[8] Within Massachusetts, fishermen supported Governor William Shirley's decision to reinforce the garrison of Annapolis Royal, and fishermen were among the earliest proponents of his project to seize Île Royale.[9]

More than anyone else it was Shirley who defined and directed New England's response to the renewal of conflict in the maritime region. In many ways he personified an increasingly dominant, cosmopolitan outlook among active members of New England's political elite.[10] He was an English-born lawyer who had trained in London; he had lived in Massachusetts only since 1731, and remained equally at ease on both sides of the Atlantic Ocean. Shirley secured the Massachusetts governorship in 1741 with the help of his patron, Secretary of State Thomas Hollis-Pelham, the duke of Newcastle, and he entered office at a time when Massachusetts was badly divided. Economic disruptions associated with the war with Spain, political struggles over the emission of paper money, and religious upheavals associated with revivalism had combined to divide the colonial population into a complex set of mutually antagonistic groups.[11] Shirley never gained the support of all the colonists, but, as several historians have shown, his military ventures gave him the patronage power he needed to secure political support from the competing factions and govern Massachusetts effectively.[12] Self-interested merchants and office-seekers

supported Shirley and his campaign against the French, as did a broad cross-section of the colonial public, including evangelical preachers, conservative Congregationalists and Anglicans, fishermen, and young men eager to advance their prospects through military service and the acquisition of land. The New England churches abandoned their earlier reticence and endorsed Shirley's actions.[13] It helped that the French and the Mi'kmaq appeared to be the aggressors.

The early reports of combat appearing in the Massachusetts newspapers emphasized the participation of Mi'kmaq warriors and presented them in the worst possible light. In June 1744 a correspondent to the *Boston Gazette* indicated that the Mi'kmaq who took part in the attack on Canso had pleaded with the French for permission to slaughter the English-speaking residents of the town and that the French had struggled to restrain them.[14] Similar stories were repeated often during the war and served to convince many New Englanders that the Mi'kmaq were innately irrational and violent.[15]

Such beliefs had long circulated in Massachusetts, and they inspired the New England colonists during the War of the Austrian Succession to adopt a stance toward the Mi'kmaq similar to the one they had adopted in their previous wars. But in 1744 and 1745 the colonists were mobilized for war in the maritime region on an unprecedented scale.

On 20 October 1744 the government of Massachusetts officially declared war on the Mi'kmaq.[16] Five days later the Massachusetts General Court offered a bounty of £100 (provincial currency) for the scalp of any adult male member of the Mi'kmaq nation. For the scalps of women and children, the legislature offered £50.[17] Similar rewards were available for Mi'kmaq prisoners taken alive. Recognizing that it would be difficult to identify scalps by tribe, on 2 November Shirley announced that he would grant a reward for any "Indian" killed or captured east of the St Croix River, regardless of his or her language group. By necessity he made an exception for Native warriors serving under the Anglo-American military command.[18]

There is no record of Jean-Baptiste Cope's activities during the war, but the mission near his home on the Shubenacadie River became a centre of Mi'kmaq resistance. The resident missionary at the Shubenacadie mission, Jean-Louis Le Loutre, served as the principal intermediary between the French forces and the Mi'kmaq on peninsular Nova Scotia. It was Le Loutre who informed the Mi'kmaq in the interior of Nova Scotia of the plan to strike at Canso, and, acting on the advice of the governor of Louisbourg, he also sent them directions to lay siege to Annapolis Royal in the weeks immediately after that attack. Le Loutre accompanied Mi'kmaq warriors to the British colonial capital and played an active role as an advisor to the Mi'kmaq in the first three years of the war.[19] Pierre Maillard, another missionary working among the Mi'kmaq, also travelled with the bands on the peninsula of Nova Scotia and at Île Royale. He provided advice and delivered speeches aimed at strengthening the warriors' discipline and resolve.[20] After disease struck the Mi'kmaq in 1746, the missionaries told them that the British had deliberately infected them by distributing contaminated cloth.[21]

Le Loutre and Maillard may have argued more strenuously than necessary, because the scalp-bounty policy, by itself, was enough to foreclose easy reconciliation between the Mi'kmaq bands and the British. At least among those living within the traditional bands, almost all of the Mi'kmaq supported the war effort. They were fighting not just for land but for survival, and men, women, and children overcame severe hardships to keep the warriors afield. [. . .]

After their seizure of Louisbourg, the New Englanders transported the French-speaking population of Île Royale to France.[22] That decision inspired a brief debate within the provincial council of Nova Scotia over the possibility of similarly expelling the Acadians, though the option was ultimately rejected as impractical.[23] Proponents of deportation argued that the Acadians had not taken valid oaths of allegiance and that their refusal to contemplate military service undermined the credibility of their professed loyalty to Britain. The councilmen also cited the Acadians' recent behaviour. Those who favoured removing them argued that they had helped supply the French army and Mi'kmaq warriors and refused to sell provisions to the British except at exorbitant prices. The Acadians had seemed slow to inform the British about French and Mi'kmaq military preparations, and the councilmen assumed that they provided the French and the Mi'kmaq useful intelligence. Along with providing information and logistical support, the Acadians behaved in ways that boosted enemy morale. According to a report of the provincial council, when Mi'kmaq warriors and French soldiers first laid siege to Annapolis Royal, Acadian "men, women and children frequented the enemy's quarters at their mass, prayers, dancing and all other ordinary occasions."[24]

As the debate over expelling the Acadians made clear, the outbreak of armed hostilities increased the political ramifications of many aspects of the Acadians' lives. When Acadian merchants and farmers raised the price of food, the men in the garrison interpreted the action as a show of support for the king of France. When Acadian women danced with French soldiers, provincial councilmen took it as evidence of sedition. In part because their daily behaviour came under scrutiny, many Acadians who had formerly worked closely with the provincial government fled Annapolis Royal when the fighting began.[25] [. . .]

Acadian men and women reacted to the pressures of living in wartime in various ways, and it is difficult to generalize about their behaviour. A few young men left their homes and went to fight alongside Mi'kmaq warriors.[26] Others hired themselves out as civilian workers for the British army.[27] At least one merchant who had formerly traded with the British garrisons offered his services to the French military and spent the war ferrying men and equipment to French-controlled regions at the eastern end of the Bay of Fundy.[28] [. . .]

If there was anything "typical" about the Acadians' pattern of behaviour, it was that almost none of them could hold a consistent political stance. [. . .]

By 1746 the policy debates surrounding the Acadians had changed. Early in the conflict, Shirley and various members of Nova Scotia's provincial council had contemplated mass deportations or large-scale retributive raids, especially against the Acadian villagers at the eastern end of the Bay of Fundy, who seemed to have given the most assistance to the French and their Native allies.[29] In 1745, writing to his commander on Île Royale, Shirley had wistfully complained, "It grieves me much that I have it not in my power to send a part of 500 men forthwith to Menis [Minas] and burn Grand Pré, their chief town, and open all their sluices, and lay their country waste."[30] But by the winter of 1746 Shirley had shifted his efforts and began to seek ways to gain the Acadians' co-operation and ultimately win their hearts.

Several factors contributed to this change in thinking. In the previous summer a French fleet sent to recapture Louisbourg foundered on the Atlantic coast of Nova Scotia, and from that time forward the British military position seemed more secure, particularly at Annapolis Royal. Disease had swept through the Mi'kmaq community, killing hundreds and weakening the military power of the survivors.[31] Equally important, the New Englanders within the garrison at Annapolis Royal gradually changed their outlook toward the Acadians. Given more time to interact with the villagers outside the context of an immediate military crisis,

they began to believe that they could gain the Acadians' friendship. The soldiers depended on Acadian farmers and merchants for food and firewood, and the social environment encouraged the men to seek the company of Acadians outside the context of trade.

In the first year of the war relations between the garrison and the community had deteriorated. Most of the Acadians in Annapolis Royal had shunned the English-speakers in their village when French or Mi'kmaq forces were in the area. In any event there were fewer English speakers in the French-speaking village; most of the married officers and soldiers at Annapolis Royal had sent their wives and children to Boston for protection, and the departure of their families helped cut the men off from the Acadian community, at least temporarily.[32] Over time new bonds were formed, however, and by the last two years of the war, official British discussions of the Acadians returned repeatedly to the issue of intermarriage between the soldiers and Acadian women.[33]

Overcoming significant cultural obstacles, by 1747 a few New England soldiers managed to court and marry Acadian women in Annapolis Royal.[34] According to reports that reached Shirley, the women who married the New England men were punished with excommunication from the Catholic Church. Shirley complained bitterly about the church's reaction. Though he hoped that the women would leave the church eventually, he knew that church-imposed sanctions would humiliate them and isolate them from their neighbours; excommunication was a strong deterrent to intermarriage. Shirley objected not only for the sake of the soldiers and their spouses, but also because he believed that the church's policy deterred British settlement in Nova Scotia. Almost certainly exaggerating the influence of the policy, he claimed that it "has had so general an effect as to prevent the settlement of any one English family within the province."[35]

When Shirley referred to "English" families, he meant families in which the husband spoke English. This is evident, not only in the context of his concern over the marital fortunes of the soldiers, but also in light of long-term proposals he was developing to promote marriages between Acadian women and English-speaking settlers in Nova Scotia. Intermarriage became a central feature of Shirley's project to transform the Acadians culturally. He wanted to convert them to Protestantism, teach them English, and make them loyal British subjects. As part of that program, he wanted to change the composition of the Acadians' families by encouraging soldiers to settle permanently in Nova Scotia and providing Acadian women with incentives to marry English-speakers and Protestants. He also wanted to force the Acadian women to send their children to English-language schools so that their descendants would become, as he succinctly put it, "English Protestants".[36]

Shirley advanced this plan in response to the experiences of the soldiers at Annapolis Royal. Though only a few marriages had taken place between the men of the garrison and Acadian women, he saw those unions as a model for social development in the entire colony. In 1747 Shirley began designing a project to intermingle soldiers and Acadians throughout the eastern Bay of Fundy region, to facilitate integration and gradual assimilation. Annapolis Royal gave him inspiration, but he was also responding to contemporary events in Britain, where the ministry was engaged in a similarly forceful effort at cultural assimilation.

During the winter of 1745, Charles Stuart led an uprising in Scotland in an effort to place his father on the British throne. Though he was ultimately defeated, he received considerable support in certain parts of the Scottish Highlands. Charles was a Catholic and he had counted among his supporters a disproportionate number of Catholics and "nonjurant" Anglicans, communicants in a conservative wing of British Protestantism. It also seemed from the perspective of British policy makers that his support had been strongest among impoverished Highlanders who came from remote pastoral regions where the clans maintained their own juridical traditions and where a considerable amount of economic activity depended on barter and other forms of non-monetary exchange. After defeating the Stuart forces, the British government adopted a set of measures designed to "pacify" the Scottish Highlands by destroying the economic and cultural conditions that they believed underlay support for Charles.[37]

Beginning in 1746, Parliament outlawed Highland dress, made it illegal for the Highlanders to carry weapons, abolished the local court system, and confiscated the property of all those who had fought for the Stuart cause. Missionaries were sent to the Highlands along with land speculators and other investors with the aim of establishing model towns where, through a combination of educational work, economic coercion, and government regulation, the Highlanders could be converted to authorized forms of Protestantism and taught to participate in the market economy. One individual involved in the pacification program summed up the theory as follows: "Make then the Highlanders as rich and industrious as the people of Manchester and they will be as little apt to rebel."[38]

In 1746 Admiral Charles Knowles, who had helped guard the sea lanes to Britain during the Stuart uprising, became governor of British-occupied Île Royale.[39] After he moved to America he continued to participate in the policy debates surrounding the pacification of Scotland, and he brought William Shirley into the debates. Knowles endorsed an idea advanced by William Augustus, duke of Cumberland, that entire Highland clans should be sent to America, and he suggested that space should be cleared for them in Nova

Scotia. The Acadians, he argued, could be moved to make room.[40]

When he first learned of this proposal Shirley opposed it, but after a raid against New England troops stationed in Minas in the winter of 1746–7, he entered into an extensive correspondence with Knowles, and the two men worked out a plan to relocate at least part of the Acadian population.[41] They agreed to abandon the idea of replacing the villagers with Highlanders, but endorsed the general theory behind that plan, that shifting peoples within the empire would be an effective way to control them. In a joint letter to the secretary of state they recommended using military force to expel the most "obnoxious" Acadians and replace them with Protestant immigrants. [. . .] The governors predicted that the introduction of immigrants, and the creation of a cosmopolitan society, would transform the Acadians and turn them into loyal subjects. They did not believe that all of the newcomers had to come from Great Britain. Citing the history of Pennsylvania, they claimed that Swiss and German settlers could serve effectively as promoters of British imperial culture.

In spite of his original misgivings, Shirley soon discovered that he liked the idea of directing the process of migration with the purpose of transforming Acadian society, and he began developing more elaborate plans. In the summer of 1747 he proposed sending 2000 New England troops to the isthmus of Chignecto, to clear the region of its inhabitants and settle on the vacated land. The dispossessed Acadians would be taken to New England and placed in scattered towns in Rhode Island, Connecticut, Massachusetts, and New Hampshire.[42] If everything proceeded as Shirley anticipated, the New England settlers in Nova Scotia would intermingle and intermarry with the Acadians. Similarly, the relocated Acadian families would get absorbed into New England.[43] Shirley was ready to proceed with this experiment, but his superiors in London stopped him. As long as the war with France continued, the ministers opposed the relocation program on the grounds that it would divert scarce resources from other projects, and when the war ended in 1748 the military justification for moving the Acadians lost its force.[44]

The Treaty of Aix-la-Chapelle ending the War of the Austrian Succession ceded Île Royale back to France.[45] The cession was controversial in Britain and even more so in Massachusetts, where hundreds of families had lost husbands, sons, and fathers in military service on the island.[46] The Massachusetts government had also nearly bankrupted itself and destroyed the value of the provincial currency financing the Louisbourg expedition, an aborted 1746 expedition to Canada, and the reinforcement of Nova Scotia.[47] After the terms of the treaty were announced Shirley tried to soften the blow by getting the ministry to reimburse the Massachusetts government for its expenses. He also asked the imperial authorities to sponsor an effort to resettle and fortify Nova Scotia so that it could be prosperous, secure, and self-sufficient. A central element of Shirley's project was to assimilate the Acadians into a new, cosmopolitan, British colonial society, and he hoped to accomplish this feat by directing a series of large-scale migrations.

In the winter of 1748 Shirley commissioned a survey of the eastern end of the Bay of Fundy. He wanted to identify hills and islands appropriate for forts, and farmland that could be confiscated to support new immigrants.[48] [. . .] Shirley sent his surveyor's report to London in February 1749, along with a proposal to resettle Nova Scotia with farmers from England, Germany, Switzerland, and other parts of Europe. He did not intend to send any of the Acadians out of Nova Scotia to make room for the new settlers. He suggested instead that some of the Acadians should be moved within the colony. Shirley considered short-distance moves necessary, because he wanted to intermingle European immigrants with Acadians. If all the current inhabitants of Nova Scotia were allowed to stay where they were, the province would remain divided, with a geographically separate French-speaking Catholic community.[49]

The proposal to settle Nova Scotia with Protestants from continental Europe helped Shirley politically in Massachusetts. At least since 1747, in serialized publications and newspapers, the governor's opponents in Boston had complained that the Louisbourg expedition and the reinforcement of Annapolis Royal had drained New England's labour supply.[50] Citing treatises on political economy, they had generalized from recent experience and argued that population density was the source of economic and military strength. By scattering the population, any effort to expand the territories of the British Empire in North America risked leaving the existing colonies underpopulated, poor, and vulnerable.[51]

[. . .]

British political elites as well as New Englanders had taken an interest in Île Royale in the long months of negotiation leading up to the conclusion of the Treaty of Aix-la-Chapelle.[52] It was a measure of the new importance of imperial issues in British politics that the government's opponents in Parliament and in the press hoped to exploit the cession of the island back to France as an embarrassment to the ministry. In an effort to limit political damage at home, alleviate the social ills associated with demobilization, and placate restive New Englanders, in 1749 the Board of Trade appointed Edward Cornwallis, a veteran of the pacification of the Scottish Highlands, as governor of Nova Scotia, and Parliament allocated a large sum of money to encourage Protestant settlement in the colony.[53] The British government offered veterans free transportation, land, tools, and a year's worth of provisions, and asked nothing in return except that they take the trip to Nova Scotia. It offered the same terms to carpenters, bricklayers, and other labourers with economically valuable skills.[54] In 1749 the ministry spent over £40 000 to encourage the settlement of province.[55] In addition to recruiting in England, agents of the government travelled to France, the valley of the Rhine, and Switzerland in search of Protestants willing to move.[56]

The Board of Trade directed Cornwallis to establish a Protestant town at Chebucto Harbor (present-day Halifax) and then disperse some of the new colonists in Acadian-dominated regions around the Bay of Fundy.[57] The board also instructed him to make sure that the new townships included both Protestants and "French Inhabitants" (Acadians), "to the End that the said French Inhabitants may be subjected to such Rules and Orders as may hereafter be made for the better ordering and governing the said Townships."[58] The governor was also told to establish "Protestant schools," "to the end that the said French inhabitants may be converted to the Protestant religion and their children brought up in the principles of it."[59] Following Shirley's advice, the Board of Trade directed Cornwallis to encourage intermarriage between Acadians and Protestants, and to apprehend, try, and punish any Catholic priest who censured his parishioners for marrying out of the faith.[60] If everything had gone as the ministers wished, within a few generations the Acadians would have converted to Protestantism and joined the new colonists as equals in a single society.

The project of resettling Nova Scotia with a diverse Protestant population, and the articulation of the plan to absorb Acadians into the cultural mix, reflected political developments beyond the shores of the colony. In many parts of the British Empire, public officials were rethinking what it meant to be a British subject and trying to devise new ways to incorporate persons of varying cultural backgrounds into a single political community. The eighteenth-century "British" nation had always been an aggregation of peoples with distinctive histories and traditions. As Linda Colley has argued, the promoters of British nationalism accommodated themselves to the existence of cultural differences in part by concentrating on a few ideals that Britons were presumed to share, such as opposition to Catholicism and loyalty to the Crown.[61] The opening of the British colonies to Protestant immigrants from continental Europe reflected a growing confidence that such settlers would adopt these minimal necessary attributes of "Britishness". Nonetheless, the recent events in the Scottish Highlands served as an object lesson on the dangers that could arise when culturally distinct communities within the realm refused to adhere to the necessary ideals.

NOTES

1. See Kathleen Wilson, "Empire, Trade and Popular Politics in Mid-Hanoverian Britain: The Case of Admiral Vernon," *Past and Present* 121 (1988): 74–109; Gerald Jordan and Nicholas Rogers, "Admirals as Heroes: Patriotism and Liberty in Hanoverian England," *Journal of British Studies* 28 (1989): 210–4.

2. See *Boston Evening Post*, July 8, July 15, 1745; *Boston Postboy*, July 8, 1745; Charles Chauncey to William Pepperell, July 4, 1745 in *Collections of the Massachusetts Historical Society* 1st ser. 1 (1792): 49; Thomas Hubbard to Pepperell, in *Collections of the Massachusetts Historical Society* 6th ser. 10 (1899): 308–9; Daniel Edwards to Roger Wolcott, July 9, 1745, in *Collections of the Connecticut Historical Society* 11 (1907): 334–7.

3. Christopher Moore, "The Other Louisbourg: Trade and Merchant Enterprise in Ile Royale, 1713–1758' *"Histoire sociale/Social History* 12 (1979): 79–96; John Robert McNeill, *Atlantic Empires of France and Spain: Louisbourg and Havana, 1700–1760* (Chapel Hill: University of North Carolina Press, 1985), 20–4.

4. McNeill, *Atlantic Empires of France and Spain*, 84.

5. See George Rawlyk, *Yankees at Louisbourg* (Orono:University of Maine Press, 1967), 6.

6. Ibid., 2–4.

7. For accounts of the attack, see David B. Flemming, *The Canso Islands: An Eighteenth-Century Fishing Station* (Ottawa: Parks Canada, 1977), 45; William Shirley to Newcastle, July 7, 1744, in Charles Henry Lincoln, ed., *Correspondence of William Shirley* (New York: Macmillan, 1912), 1:133; J.S. McLennan, *Louisbourg from Its Foundation to Its Fall, 1713–1758* (London: Macmillan, 1918), 111; Mascarene to Philipps, June 9, 1744, Add. Mss. 19,071, doc. 45; *Boston Postboy*, June 11, 1744.

8. For accounts of New England vessels taken, see *Boston Evening Post*, June 11, June 25, 1744; *Boston Newsletter*, September 20, 1744; *South Carolina Gazette*, July 4, 1744. For New England's attacks on the French fishery, see *Boston Evening Post*, September 24, October 22, November 26, 1744; *Boston Gazette*, August 21, 1744; *Boston Newsletter*, August 16, September 20, September 27, October 25, 1744; *Boston Postboy*, September 24, October 22, 1744; *New York Gazette*, October 1, 1744; William Douglass, *A Summary, Historical and Political, of the First Planting, Progressive Improvements, and Present State of the British Settlements in North America* (2 vols. Boston: Evans 6307/6663, 1749/1751), 1:339.

9. See Alexander Hamilton, "The Itinerarium of Dr. Alexander Hamilton," in *Colonial American Travel Narratives*, ed. Wendy Martin (New York: Penguin, 1994), 261. See also Rawlyk, *Yankees at Louisbourg*, 37, 38; John A. Schutz, *William Shirley: King's Governor of Massachusetts* (Chapel Hill: University of North Carolina Press, 1961), 90. It was a fisherman who

first alerted Boston of the attack on Canso, but the printer of the *Boston Evening Post* chose not to publish the story because it was "looked upon as fishermen's news." Only after a merchant confirmed the report was it placed in the paper. *Boston Evening Post*, May 28, 1744. For the reaction of the legislature, see *Journals of the House of Representatives of Massachusetts* 21: 8–11, 29, 42; *Boston Postboy*, June 4, 1744; *Boston Newsletter*, June 14, 1744.

10. See Schutz, *William Shirley*.

11. Ibid., 23–44; Rosalind Remer, "Old Lights and New Money; A Note on Religion, Economics, and the Social Order in 1740 Boston," *William and Mary Quarterly* 3d ser. 47 (1990): 566–73.

12. See, for example, Schutz, *William Shirley*, 80–103; Bernard Bailyn, *The Origins of American Politics* (New York: Vintage, 1967), 116–17; but see William Pencak, *War, Politics, and Revolution in Provincial Massachusetts* (Boston: Northeastern University Press, 1981), 115–47.

13. Nathan Hatch, "Origins of Civil Millennialism in America: New England Clergymen, War with France, and the American Revolution," *William and Mary Quarterly* 3d ser. 31 (1992):492–508.

14. *Boston Gazette*, June 26, 1744.

15. See, for example, *Boston Newsletter*, June 6, 1745; *Boston Evening Post*, July 29, 1745.

16. *Boston Evening Post*, October 22, 1744.

17. *Journals of the House of Representatives of Massachusetts* 21: 99, 106–7; *Boston Evening Post*, November 5, 1744.

18. *Boston Evening Post*, November 11, 1744; using a contemporary term, Shirley called the St Croix the Passamaquodi River.

19. Normand Rogers, "Abbé Le Loutre," *Canadian Historical Review* 11 (1930): 105–28; Jean-Louis Le Loutre, "Autobiography," translated by John Clarence Webster, in John Clarence Webster, ed., *The Career of the Abbé Loutre in Nova Scotia* (Shediac: Private printing, 1933), 33–50, 35; See also Rawlyk, *Yankees at Louisbourg*, 7–11.

20. Pierre Maillard, "Lettre," in Abbé Henri-Raymond Casgrain, ed., *Les Soirées canadiennes* (Quebec: Brousseau, 1863), 289–426, 322–28; Webster, *Career of the Abbé Le Loutre*, 10.

21. "Motifs des sauvages mickmaques et marichites des continuer la guerre contre les Anglois

depuis la dernière paix," in Gaston du Bosq De Beaumont, ed., *Les Derniers jours de l'Acadie* (Geneva: Slatkine-Megariotis, 1975), 248–53, 251.

22. Ian K. Steele, "Surrendering Rites: Prisoners on Colonial North American Frontiers," in *Hanoverian Britain and Empire: Essays in Memory of Philip Lawson*, Stephen Taylor, Richard Connors, and Clyve Jones, eds (Rochester: Boydell Press, 1998) 152–3; *Boston Evening Post*, July 15, July 22, August 5, September 2, October 21, 1745; *Boston Postboy*, July 22, September 9, September 30, 1745; *Boston Newsletter*, September 12, 1745.

23. Mascarene to Shirley, December 7, 1745, CO 217/39, doc. 316, Public Record Office (hereafter PRO); Shirley to Newcastle, December 23, 1745, RG1, vol. 13, doc. 21, Public Archives of Nova Scotia (hereafter PANS); Shirley to Newcastle, February 11, 1746, RG1, vol. 13A, doc. 5, PANS; see Barry Morris Moody, "A Just and Disinterested Man: The Nova Scotia Career of Paul Mascarene, 1710–1752" (PhD diss., Queen's University, 1976), 334–42.

24. "State of the Province of Nova Scotia," November 8, 1745, CO 217/39, doc. 320, PRO.

25. For accounts of the general wartime migration to French-controlled territory, see Andrew Hill Clark, *Acadia: The Geography of Early Nova Scotia to 1760* (Madison: University of Wisconsin Press, 1968), 278, 285, 291; Muriel K. Roy, "Settlement and Population Growth in Acadia," in *The Acadians of the Maritimes: Thematic Studies*, Jean Daigle, ed. (Moncton: Centre d'Etudes Acadiennes, 1982), 151–2; Jean Daigle, "Acadia from 1604 to 1763: An Historical Synthesis," in *Acadia of the Maritimes: Thematic Studies from the Beginning to the Present*, Jean Daigle, ed. (Moncton: Chaire d'Etudes Acadiennes, 1995), 36.

26. Report of Jean Luc de La Corne, September 28, 1747, RG1, vol. 3, doc 89, PANS; Statement of Honore Gautrol, December 13, 1749, in Thomas B. Akins, ed., *Selections from the Public Documents of the Province of Nova Scotia* (Halifax: Charles Annand, 1869), 177; *Boston Evening Post*, January 15, 1750; John Salusbury, *Expeditions of Honour: The Journal of John Salusbury in Halifax, Nova Scotia, 1749–53*, Ronald Rompkey, ed. (Newark: University of

Delaware Press, 1980), 76; Edward Cornwallis to Board of Trade, March 19, 1750, CO 217/9, doc. 188, PRO.

27. Mascarene to Philipps, June 9, 1744, Add. Mss. 19,071, doc. 45; Mascarene to Secretary of State, June 15, 1748, CO 217/40, doc. 22, PRO; Mascarene to Gorham, August 6, 1748, Add. Mss. 19,071, doc. 119; Mascarene to ?, September 29, 1749, Add. Mss. 19,071, doc. 99.

28. Mascarene to Shirley, spring 1745, in Placide Gaudet, "Acadian Genealogy and Notes," in *Report Concerning Canadian Archives for the Year 1905* (Ottawa: National Archives of Canada, 1906), 38; Council minutes, May 2–4, 1745, in Charles Bruce Fergusson, ed., *Minutes of his Majesty's Council at Annapolis Royal, 1736–1749* (Halifax: Public Archives of Nova Scotia, 1967), 68–70; Council minutes, November 14, 1746, in Fergusson, *Minutes*, 94; Shirley to Newcastle, May 22, 1746, in Lincoln, *Correspondence of William Shirley*, 1: 150; see also E.B. O'Callaghan, ed., *Documents Relative to the Colonial History of the State of New York* (15 vols. Albany: Weed, Parsons, 1850–83), 10: 155; "Relation d'une expedition faite sur les anglois dans le pays de l'Acadie, le 11 fevrier 1747, par un détachement de canadiens," in Abbé Henri-Raymond Casgrain, ed., *Collection des documents inédits sur le Canada et l'Amérique* (3 vols. Quebec: L.-J. Demers and Frère, 1888), 2:10–16, 15; "Journal de la compagne du détachement de Canada à l'Acadie et aux mines, en 1746–47" in Casgrain, *Collection*, 2: 16–75, 47, 51–52. For evidence of the merchant's earlier co-operation with the government, see Mascarene to William Douglass, July 1740 and August 20, 1741, Mascarene Family Papers; Abbé Henri-Raymond Casgrain, *Pèlegrinage au pays d'Evangéline* (Quebec: L.-J. Demers and Frère,1888), 519; Council minutes, August 17, 1736, in Archibald M. MacMechan, *Original Minutes of His Majesty's Council at Annapolis Royal, 1720–1739* (Halifax: Public Archives of Nova Scotia, 1908), 361–62.

29. See Mascarene to Deputies of Mines, Pisiquid and River Canard, October 13, 1744, in Akins, *Selections*, 137; Shirley to Board of Trade, October 16, 1744, in Lincoln, *Correspondence of William Shirley*, 1:150; Shirley to Newcastle, October 16, 1744, RG1, vol. 12, doc 37, PANS.

30. Shirley to Pepperell, May 25, 1745, in *Collections of the Massachusetts Historical Society* 6th ser. 10 (1899): 219.

31. "Journal de la campagne," 1746–47, in Casgrain, *Collection*, 2: 16–75, 44, 48; *Boston Evening Post*, December 1, 1746; see also *Boston Evening Post*, November 3, November 17, 1746; William C. Wicken, "Encounters with Tall Sails and Tall Tales: Mi'kmaq Society, 1500–1760," PhD diss, McGill University, 1994, 184–205. For a vivid description of the epidemic, see "Journal," July 25, 1748–September 14, 1748, AC, F3, vol. 50, doc. 447, National Archives of Canada (NAC).

32. *Boston Evening Post*, May 28, 1744.

33. See, for example, Shirley to Newcastle, October 20, 1747, RG1, vol. 13A, doc. 32, PANS; Shirley to Newcastle, November 21, 1746, RG1, vol. 13, doc. 33, PANS; Charles Knowles and Shirley to Newcastle, April 28, 1747, RG1, vol. 13A, doc. 25, PANS; Shirley to Newcastle, July 8, 1747, RG1, vol. 13A, doc. 27, PANS.

34. See "Journal de la campagne," 1746–47, in Casgrain, *Collection*, 2: 16–75, 48.

35. Shirley to Newcastle, October 20, 1747, RG1, vol. 13A, doc. 32, PANS.

36. Shirley to Newcastle, November 21, 1746, RG1, vol. 13, doc. 33, PANS; Knowles and Shirley to Newcastle, April 28, 1747, RG1, vol. 13A, doc. 25, PANS; Shirley to Newcastle, July 8, 1747, RG1, vol. 13A, doc. 27, PANS.

37. See Allan I. Macinnes, *Clanship, Commerce, and the House of Stuart, 1603–1788* (East Lothian: Tuckwell Press, 1996), 210–41; Charles W.J. Withers, *Gaelic Scotland: The Transformation of a Cultural Region* (New York: Routledge, 1988).

38. "On the subject of civilising the Highlands," 1748, GD248654/1, Scottish Record Office.

39. John Knox Laughton, "Knowles, Sir Charles," in *Dictionary of National Biography* (DNB) (London: Oxford University Press, 1882) 11:293; see also Laughton, "Martin, William" (DNB), 12:1185; Jeremy Black, *Culloden and the '45* (New York: St. Martin's Press, 1997), 89, 124–5.

40. Shirley to Newcastle, November 21, 1746, RG1, vol. 13, doc. 33, PANS. See Duncan

Forbes, "Some Considerations on the Present State of the Highlands of Scotland," in Duncan Warrand, ed., *More Culloden Papers* (Vol. 5. Inverness: R. Carruthers and Sons, 1930), 5:98–103; W.A. Speck, *The Butcher: The Duke of Cumberland and the Suppression of the '45* (Oxford: Blackwell, 1981), 168; John Prebble, *Culloden* (London: Penguin, 1967), 232.

41. Brenda Dunn, *The Acadians of Minas* (Ottawa: Parks Canada, 1985), 19; *Boston Evening Post*, November 24, 1746, March 2, March 9, September 28, 1747; *Pennsylvania Gazette*, December 16, 1746, March 3, March 10, 1747; Report of Pierre de Chapt, Chevalier de la Corne, September 28, 1747, RG1, vol. 3, doc. 89, PANS; Report of Jean Baptiste Le Guardier de Repentigny, November 1, 1747, RG1, vol. 3, doc. 90, PANS; *Journals of the House of Representatives of Massachusetts*, 23: 313–15, 319; Knowles and Shirley to Newcastle, April 28, 1747, RG1, vol. 13A, doc. 25, PANS; see also Knowles to Shirley, May 24, 1747, HM 9712, Huntington Library.

42. Shirley to Newcastle, July 8, 1747, RG1, vol. 13A, doc. 27, PANS.

43. Shirley to Newcastle, July 8, 1747, RG1, vol. 13A, doc. 27, PANS.

44. John Russell, duke of Bedford, to Newcastle, September 11, 1747, RG1, vol. 13A, doc. 30, PANS; Newcastle to Shirley, October 3, 1747, RG1, vol. 13A, doc. 31, PANS.

45. Jack M. Sosin, "Louisbourg and the Peace of Aix-la-Chapelle, 1748," *William and Mary Quarterly* 3d ser. 14 (1957): 516–35. The final decision to cede Île Royale back to France was not made until the end of the negotiations in 1748, but the ministry had considered the island a bargaining chip from the moment it learned of New England's conquest. See Newcastle to ?, August 18, 1745, Add. Mss. 32,705, doc. 65.

46. More than 1000 New England men died, most of disease after an epidemic struck the New England garrison at Louisbourg after the French surrendered. See George Rawlyk, *Nova Scotia's Massachusetts: A Study of Massachusetts–Nova Scotia Relations, 1630 to 1784* (Montreal: McGill-Queen's University Press, 1973), 177; Gary B. Nash, *The Urban Crucible: Social Change, Political Consciousness, and the Origins of the American Revolution* (Cambridge, MA: Harvard University Press, 1979), 172; William Pencak, *War, Politics, and Revolution in Provincial Massachusetts* (Boston: Northeastern University Press, 1981), 127; Gary B. Nash, "Failure of Female Factory Labor in Colonial Boston," *Labor History* 20 (1979): 165–88. For London newspaper pieces urging the retention of Île Royale, see General Advertiser, February 21, 1746 (quoted in the *Boston Evening Post*, June 2, 1746); *General Evening Post*, July 26, 1746 (quoted in the *Boston Evening Post*, October 13, 1746); *Daily Gazetteer*, October 16, 1746 (quoted in the *Boston Evening Post*, March 2, 1747); *British Spy*, October 25, 1746 (quoted in the *New York Evening Post*, January 19, 1747); *London Magazine*, December 1746 (quoted in the *Maryland Gazette*, July 28, 1747).

47. The value of the province's notes dropped by one-half. See Douglass, *Summary*, 1: 357; *Boston Evening Post*, September 25, 1749.

48. Mascarene to Joseph Gorham, August 6, 1748, in Adam Shortt, V.K. Johnston, and Gustave Lactot, eds., *Documents Relating to Currency, Exchange and Finance in Nova Scotia, with Prefatory Documents, 1675–1758* (Ottawa: J.O. Patenaude, 1933), 274–6.

49. "Report by Captain Morris to Governor Shirley," 1749, in *Report of the Archives Branch for 1912, 79–83*; Shirley to Bedford, February 18, 1749, RG1, vol 13, doc. 45, PANS; see also Mascarene to Board of Trade, October 17, 1748, CO 217/32, doc. 103, PRO.

50. See especially Douglass, *Summary; Independent Advertiser.*

51. See, for example, *Independent Advertiser*, February 8, 1748; William Douglass, "To the Publishers of the *Independent Advertiser*," *Independent Advertiser*, July 4, 1748; *Independent Advertiser*, February 13, 1749. Political economists had been advancing this argument against imperial expansion at least since 1670. See Roger Coke, *A Discourse of Trade* (London, 1670. Reprint, New York: Arno Press, 1972), 7; *The Royal Fishery Revived* (London, 1670).

52. See, for example, *London Evening Post*, March 27–29, 1746.

53. James Henretta, *"Salutary Neglect": Colonial Administration under the Duke of Newcastle* (Princeton: Princeton University Press, 1972): 287–90. See also *Pennsylvania Gazette*, October 28, 1748; *Boston Evening Post*, May 1, 1749; Instructions for Edward Cornwallis, May 2, 1749, in Gaudet, "Acadian Genealogy and Notes," 49–51.

54. *Boston Evening Post*, May 1, 1749.

55. *Boston Evening Post*, June 5, 1749; Cornwallis to Bedford, March 9, 1750, CO 217/33, doc. 17, PRO.

56. Winthrop Pickard Bell, *The "Foreign Protestants" and the Settlement of Nova Scotia: The History of a Piece of Arrested Colonial Policy in the Eighteenth Century* (Toronto: University of Toronto Press, 1961), 284.

57. Instructions for Cornwallis, May 2, 1749, in Gaudet, "Acadian Genealogy and Notes," 49–51.

58. Ibid., 49.

59. Ibid., 51; see also Board of Trade to the Society of the Propagation of the Gospel (SPG), C/Can NS 1, iv, Records of the SPG.

60. Instructions for Cornwallis, May 2 1749, in Gaudet, "Acadian Genealogy and Notes," 51.

61. Linda Colley, *Britons: Forging the Nation, 1707–1837* (New Haven: Yale University Press, 1992).

4   From N.E.S. Griffiths, "The Decision to Deport," in *From Migrant to Acadian: A North American Border People, 1604–1755* (Montreal and Kingston: McGill-Queen's University Press, 2005), 431–64, 574–81.

One of the earliest historical accounts, as distinguished from the contemporary reports in newspapers, of the events of 1755 was published by Abbé Guillaume Raynal in 1766.[1] In his opinion, the Acadians had been deported because of the prevailing climate of the time, a period of "national jealousies, and of that greed of government which devours country and man."[2] But, Raynal concluded, the British had committed a great crime in removing an innocent pastoral people from their lands. Two years later, a work by a certain William Burck appeared in translation in Paris. He believed that, while the deportation was justifiable, in terms of the Franco-British conflict at the time, it involved actions that any "humaine and generous heart only takes with regret."[3] These differing opinions, one an explicit condemnation of a crime, the other a regretful verdict that what had taken place had been a cruel necessity, were only the first of many, increasingly bitter, disagreements over how the deportation of the Acadians should be judged.[4] By the middle of the twentieth century, more than 200 articles, books, and pamphlets had been published on the subject and since then a great many more have seen the light of day.[5] As was the case with Raynal and Burck, a significant number of the authors have made their judgment of what happened in 1755 the pivotal question of their work, spending relatively little time on a close analysis of the way in which the decision was reached or the immediate situation in the region at the time when the actual decision was made. The emphasis has been placed less on what is usually the first step of historical inquiry—"How did this happen?"—than on a search to discover the guilty. [. . .]

My approach is different. The focus in what follows is upon the actual experiences of those who lived in Nova Scotia in 1755, whether British administrators, French officials, military officers, or the Acadians themselves. More than anything else, this analysis has sought to present the realities of everyday eighteenth-century life for people of the North Atlantic world. In many ways, the argument I have with a number of colleagues rests as much upon an interpretation of the norms of eighteenth-century life as it does upon questions of ideology. The crucial debate turns

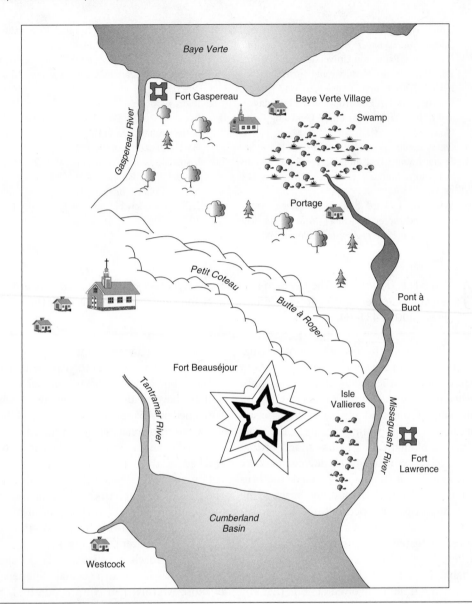

Map 1 The region of Beauséjour, 1755. Redrawn from a map by Louis de Courville (1755), reproduced in Stanley, *New France*.

upon whether the deportation was the result of a planned policy flowing from ethnic hatred or something that occurred as a consequence of local military action at a time of intense rivalry between competing empires. My interpretation suggests that short-term decision making is central to what happened, the personal convictions of the individuals in question being the framework for their actions but of less immediate significance than the immediate problems that had to be solved.

Of major influence upon the course of events leading to the deportation was the way in which the relationship between Lawrence and the Acadians developed between the late summer of 1754 and the capture of Beauséjour on 16 June 1755. Throughout these months, whenever Lawrence considered the problem of Nova Scotia security, the reliability of the Acadians during an attack by the French was always a major concern for him. The information Lawrence received about the international situation, the knowledge he had of the balance of power between Massachusetts and Île Royale, Louisbourg and Boston, and his opinion of the reality of Acadian neutrality governed many of his reactions to Acadian matters. The Acadians' response to his internal administration of the colony, toward requests made by his forces for food and labour, as well as the intelligence he received about the strength of the forts at Beauséjour and Gaspereau were major considerations in his thinking. When the steps he took to bolster his command of the colony showed some success, Lawrence was encouraged to continue along the same lines. His organization of the forts, the co-operation of the Acadians with requests for wood for the local garrisons, tentative peace proposals from the Mi'kmaq, and some lessening of the trade between Acadian farmers and Louisbourg and Port Lajoie—all confirmed Lawrence's belief in the wisdom of his tactics. From August 1754 on, one can see Lawrence becoming more and more confident in his office. He began to take decisions without waiting for less than clear-cut directions to reach him from London. This penchant for independent action was strengthened by Governor Shirley's support of his plan to attack Beauséjour as well as by their common interpretation of the freedom of action accorded them by the imperial authorities.

In many ways, of course, Lawrence had no alternative but to act independently, decisively, and with dispatch on matters that were brought either directly to his attention or to his notice through meetings of the Council: [. . .] it usually took five months, and often more, before Lawrence received an answer to his letters to London. But Nova Scotia was ruled by a governor and Council, which he appointed to advise him. Lawrence was charged with the day-to-day administration of a sparsely settled colony, with a minimum of troops and his few councillors. Together, they were responsible for the way in which the civil administration of the colony was carried out and for the security of its settlements. The questions confronting them involved not only the usual difficulties of colonial administrations with matters of local government but also the complex relationship of the British administration with the Mi'kmaq and the Acadians. As well, there was the constant problem of France's strength on the borders of the colony and its influence upon the Acadian population. While clashes with French land forces during the last months of 1754 were rare, two priests, Le Loutre at Beauséjour and Henri Daudin at Pisiquid, did everything in their power to stir up both the Mi'kmaq and the Acadians against the British.[6] [. . .]

Information about events in North America had arrived in London and Paris throughout the spring and summer of 1754. The reaction in London was both stronger and more immediate than that of France. The influence of Governor Dinwiddie of Virginia and Governor Shirley of Massachusetts was far greater upon the course of British politics than that of any French North American colonial official on French policies. As well, at this time, the French were more deeply concerned with European affairs than with matters across the Atlantic, whereas the British saw North American issues of considerable moment. [. . .] The Duke of Newcastle, who had come to power in March 1754, had considerable sympathy with the colonists. [. . .] There is no doubt that there was a general consensus among the political elite that British interests, whether in Europe or in North America, had to be defended. The debate between the different factions centred, of course, upon how, when, and where action should be taken.

Newcastle had chosen Sir Thomas Robinson as secretary of state and leader of the House of Commons.[7] On 5 July 1754 Robinson wrote to both William Shirley and Charles Lawrence. [. . .]

Both Lawrence and Shirley considered that these letters gave them the liberty to mount a joint expedition against the French in the Saint John valley and in the Chignecto isthmus. For Lawrence, Massachusetts co-operation was crucial. Without Shirley's permission to raise volunteers from Massachusetts, without loans from Apthorp and Hancock, Boston merchants and bankers, Lawrence had neither the manpower nor the money to undertake any major military enterprise, let alone one that would require at least an additional 2000 men to serve in Nova Scotia. Shirley [. . .] was convinced that war was imminent and [. . .] believed that, should Nova Scotia be lost, "the Eastern parts of the Province of Massachusetts Bay, and the whole Province of New Hampshire . . . together with the Rivers of St. John's, Pentagoet, and Kennebeck with the whole fishery to the Westward of Newfoundland" would soon be in French hands. It was this conviction that fuelled Shirley's support of Lawrence and ensured a sympathetic reception for the latter's request for assistance when it reached him in the first week of December.

[. . .]

Shirley's rhetoric on the opportunity for "ridding the Province of its dangerous Neighbours, with all the Mischiefs that threaten'd it from their remaining so near"[8] was not the sole argument in favour of Massachusetts endorsing the governor's proposal for raising 2000 volunteers. There was also the matter of the immediate financial benefits to Boston merchants, since it was they who would provide supplies and services for the men. There would also be further economic advantages to the Commonwealth, flowing from the terms under which the men would serve. They were promised "the King's Bounty Money, pay, uniform, Cloathing (the most that can be got here) and Arms, and have everything provided for them which is necessary for their comfortable Subsistence." The question of security and the possibility of financial gain proved useful arguments for John Winslow, who was given the rank of lieutenant-colonel and put in charge of recruiting for the new regiment. [. . .] The commander-in-chief of the expedition remained Lieutenant-Colonel Monckton, aged 29, a regular army officer who would end his career as a lieutenant-general, governor of Portsmouth, England, and an MP.[9] [. . .]

During the months that Monckton had spent in Boston, overseeing the preparations for the expedition, Lawrence had been considering what would follow the capture of Beauséjour. The lieutenant-governor had been aware that those Acadians who had lived in the area, some only since Beaubassin had been set on fire in 1750, would present political difficulties. Many of the Acadians had established farms on land which had previously been under British supervision but which had not yet been surveyed. As a result, the Nova Scotian administration considered their title to the land dubious at best. As far as Lawrence was concerned, the attitude of these Acadians could be expected to be the same as that of those who had asked to be re-admitted to British-controlled territory: argumentative, disputatious, and motivated by a strong belief that they had political rights that the British must respect. But, as will be seen, Lawrence in January 1755 was still unclear as to what would be the appropriate measures to take once the fort was captured. When he had written to the Board of Trade at the beginning of August 1754, he had tentatively stated that, should these Acadians refuse the unmodified oath of allegiance, when the opportunity to take it was given to them, he was of the opinion that it would be "better if they were away."[10] The lieutenant-governor had hedged this suggestion by remarking that he "would be very far from attempting such a step without your Lordships approbation." The Board of Trade did not compose a response to this letter until 29 October 1754.[11] Their dispatch arrived in Halifax at the beginning of January 1755.[12] It was not, in any way, a clear directive for decisive action. [. . .] The best advice they could offer was that the matter should be referred to Chief Justice Jonathan Belcher, who had taken the oaths of office at the Council meeting of 21 October 1754.[13] [. . .] In sum, in shaping his policy toward the Acadians, Lawrence was left to his own devices and to what guidance and recommendations members of the Council could offer.

Their lordships were aware, of course, of the parameters within which Lawrence would work. He was a successful regular army officer, whose career showed the extent to which he accepted the ideas of the politically and socially powerful of the time. Eighteenth-century society, French or British, Germanic or Hispanic, was hierarchical and brutal and paid considerable attention to hereditary rights.[14] Government measures taken to control dissidents differed from state to state but were, without exception, ruthless, without mercy. [. . .] In Britain, transportation of the indigent, vagrants, and children without visible means of support had begun in the reign of James I. In 1617, for example, a hundred children were dispatched from London to Virginia, their passages paid for by collections from various parishes, where they were considered a burden.[15] [. . .] For those transported as punishment, bonded service could be little better than slavery. The English Civil War provided the greatest impetus to the practice of removing difficult subjects from the care of the home government to the colonies. In 1648, when Cromwell's forces were unquestionably victorious, transportation for the defeated Stuart forces became commonplace.[16] From this time on, the English colonies in North America, as well as in the West Indies, received diverse groups of

dissidents, Scottish covenanters, youngsters from Ireland, and Scottish military exiles. The return of the monarchy did not end the practice. [. . .] Thus, by the middle of the eighteenth century, British authorities, civil and military, colonial and imperial, were accustomed to transporting a motley collection of subjects, under varying regulations, from one jurisdictional area of the realm to another.

Further, Lawrence would have been aware not only of the general use of transportation but of the deportation of some 2000 French and Acadian inhabitants of Île Royale to France in 1745 and of the forced French relocation of a minimum of 1500 Acadians from the Beaubassin area to Île Saint-Jean after 1750. And so there was nothing original, in late 1754 and early 1755, in Lawrence considering deporting the Acadians in the Beauséjour region, and it is clear from his correspondence with Monckton that the lieutenant-governor was, indeed, thinking seriously about such a possibility. In a letter to Monckton written on 30 January 1755, Lawrence told him that, once the fort had surrendered, he would not have the oaths of allegiance proposed to "the French Inhabitants" of the Chignecto area "as their taking them would tye our hands and disqualify us to extirpate them, should it be found (as I fancy it will) ever-after necessary."[17] Lawrence, at this point, was in the process of making up his mind over the best way to secure Nova Scotia. He was hopeful of populating the Beaubassin area with English-speaking Protestants, concluding his letter to Monckton with the suggestion that, if any of the Massachusetts troops had the "least disposition" to settle in the lands that were already controlled by the British but had been deserted since the burning of Beaubassin, they should be told that they would receive "all the encouragement" he had the power to offer. [. . .]

At the same time [Lawrence's] attitude toward the Acadians was reinforced by the appointment of the chief justice, Jonathan Belcher, as a Council member. It was Belcher who, on the day that Nova Scotia Council resolved to deport the Acadians, wrote the legal and political defence of the action.[18] Belcher had been born in 1710 to an established New England family, his mother's father having been lieutenant-governor of New Hampshire. His other grandfather had been a successful Boston merchant and member of the Massachusetts Council. His own father was governor of Massachusetts and New Hampshire from 1730 to 1741 and governor of New Jersey from 1747 to 1757.[19] [. . .] Until his appointment as the first chief justice of Nova Scotia, at the age of 44, Belcher had spent his working life outside North America but his childhood and early adulthood had been as a privileged member of the New England elite. [. . .]

The absence of any major discussion about the Acadians during this period by the Council is no indication of the actual relationship that existed at the time between the Acadians within Nova Scotia and the British administration. The rancour of the previous autumn continued. News about the lives of relatives on the Chignecto isthmus and along the Memramcook, the Petitcodiac, and the Shepody, where Le Loutre was active, served to sharpen Acadian ambivalence. Le Loutre was engaged not only in overseeing the building the dyke on the Aulac River in the Beauséjour area but also in encouraging the construction of smaller dykes on the Memramcook and the Shepody.[20] His aim was to stabilize the Acadian settlements, within the territory controlled by the French, by strengthening the development of traditional Acadian farming practices. At the same time, he worked to persuade the Acadians to recognize his authority to confirm their rights to the lands they farmed. The Acadians were hesitant, especially those who had their lands granted to them before 1710. Many had no wish to accept greater regulation of their affairs from any source, whether from

the military at Beauséjour or from Le Loutre personally.[21] As well, the abbé demanded that they swear loyalty to Louis XV, their "legitimate sovereign,"[22] a demand that the French government had made ever since 1751 with respect to the Acadians who came under their control.[23] [. . .] All this activity seemed to presage French determination to remain an effective power in the region and perhaps the possibility of French reoccupation of Nova Scotia.

But the most important determinant of the attitude of many of the Acadians, in the spring of 1755, must have been the manner and policies of the French officials in the region. There were four administrators, the most senior being Augustin de Boschenry de Drucour, who had arrived to take charge at Louisbourg in 1754. That same year, Gabriel Rousseau de Villejouin had been appointed as major and commandant of Île Saint-Jean. Charles Deschamps de Boishébert et de Raffetot, who had played such an important role in the engagement at Grand Pré in 1747, was at mouth of the Saint John River as commandant of Fort La Tour, and Louis Du Pont Duchambon de Vergor was the commandant of Beauséjour. [. . .] Vergor was joined at Beauséjour by the appointment that same year, 1754, of Louis-Thomas Jacau de Fiedmont as the chief engineer for the fort, and Louis-Léonard Aumasson de Courville as notary for the Acadian settlements in the area. Jacau left an account, from a military perspective, of the fall of Beauséjour and Gaspereau which, as Webster points out, sought to place the blame everywhere except upon his own shortcomings as the man in charge of the defences of the fort for the two previous years.[24] The memoir of Aumasson de Courville is a much longer work and includes a wide variety of comments on Vergor and Le Loutre.[25] Together with the journal of Thomas Pichon (Tyrell), a British spy who had somehow attached himself as a commissary officer to Beauséjour, these works provide a vivid picture of the disorganization among the officers stationed there and the general state of disrepair of the fort in 1755.[26] Vergor himself was convinced until the day the British force arrived that there would be no major fighting in the region that year, so nothing had been done to prepare a defence against an attack.[27] There had been no concerted effort during the last weeks of winter and the first weeks of more clement weather to recruit Acadians to strengthen the fort or to assemble those who had been given militia responsibilities.

So, before the anchoring of the Boston fleet in Annapolis Bay, little had taken place that would have alerted the Acadians to the possibility of a major outbreak of warfare in their lands. Evidently, only the vaguest of rumours about the recruitment of volunteers in Massachusetts for an expedition against Beauséjour had reached the Acadian population. Certainly, the possibility of a major disruption of Acadian life throughout the Acadian villages of Nova Scotia would not have entered their minds. As Lawrence prepared to make Nova Scotia a completely secure outpost of the British empire in North America and to establish once and for all British control of the colony, the Acadian population, as a whole, still believed that British administrators of Nova Scotia continued to take Acadian reactions into account when making policy decisions. The existence of Halifax, of a Protestant population within the colony that was more than ten times what it had been a decade before, was not something that had made the Acadians consider any revision of their political stance. For the majority of the population, the need to alter their religious beliefs and linguistic heritage in order to remain on their lands would have unimaginable. Even if the French never reclaimed Nova Scotia, the strong French presence in the region meant visible support for Acadian retention of their customs and traditions. French control of Île Royale and Île Saint-Jean did not appear to be weakening at this time, especially after the return of Louisbourg to France in 1748. Since then, the build-up of French forces in the Chignecto area had served to strengthen the conviction, among the British as well as among the Acadians, that France was prepared to defend its presence in the area and probably had plans to expand the territory under its control.

The rapid conquest of Beauséjour [in June 1755], followed by the fall of Fort Gaspereau, and the lack of any immediate French response fundamentally altered the military situation in the region. As a consequence, the political options for the British administration at Halifax were broadened and those of the Acadians narrowed. [. . .]

The establishment of Halifax and the founding of Lunenburg had presaged a decision, on the part of London, to make Nova Scotia as much a British colony as the other British colonies in North America. From the moment he was appointed as lieutenant-governor, Lawrence was eager to make this decision a reality. We have a great deal of information on how Lawrence saw his own policy. He wrote, at length, to Governor Shirley of Massachusetts, to other governors of British colonies in North America, and to the authorities in London. By the summer of 1754, Lawrence had decided that those Acadians who refused to take an unqualified oath of loyalty to the British crown were a major stumbling block to fulfilling his plans.[28] At the same time, he saw that the French control of the Chignecto isthmus was both a constant encouragement to those Acadians who were dissatisfied with the British government and a potential military threat to British control of Nova Scotia. While the attack on Beauséjour was taking place, his view of the unreliability of Acadian neutrality was strengthened. As has been previously mentioned, Lawrence had taken steps to prevent any major aid being sent to Beauséjour by the Acadians under his jurisdiction. He also had made an attempt to disarm the Acadians of the Minas Basin and Captain Murray had issued orders to this effect from Fort Edward in the first week of June.[29] As well, a number of Acadian canoes were confiscated. The extent to which the Acadians complied has been a matter of debate among historians but the evidence shows that the majority of them did surrender at least some of their guns. Judge Isaac Deschamps, who was in Pisiquid at the time, stated that just under 3000 guns had been brought in.[30] The strongest evidence for their compliance, however, is the petition of the Acadians for the return of their guns, which was presented to Captain Murray on 10 June and forwarded to Lawrence within the week. It is hardly likely that the Acadians would have taken time and effort to ask for their guns back had they not given up sufficient to make the request worthwhile.

[. . .]

On 24 June the Acadians arrived with another communication to the captain, this one much shorter and signed by 44 of the settlers "in the name of them all."[31] Obviously, the news of Beauséjour's capitulation on 16 June had reached the Minas Basin for in this communication "the Inhabitants of Mines, Pisiquid and the river Canard" begged Lawrence to understand that "if there shall be found any error or want of respect towards the government" in their recent memorial this was "intirely contrary to their intention."[32]

It is unlikely that this memorial would have reached Lawrence until just before the Council meeting of 3 July. Certainly, he could not have received it before 25 June, on which day he sent a dispatch to Monckton about the treatment to be accorded to the Acadian settlers in the Chignecto area. In this communication, Lawrence showed his continued concern for the security of the colony, his exasperation with the settlers in the Chignecto isthmus, and the policy he wished to pursue toward them as well as the uncertainty he had about implementing that policy. He was convinced that "unless we remain in possession undoubtedly

the French will return and re-establish and we can never expect a lasting peace with the Indians, without first totally extirpating the French who incite make war . . . "
[. . .] There is no doubt that Lawrence had a great wish to solve the Acadian problem, once and for all, but he hesitated over the imposition of truly Draconian measures. As well, he obviously considered that an unqualified oath of allegiance was something which would have to be taken into account. [. . .] Thus, on 3 July 1755, when Lawrence met with 15 Acadian leaders from the Minas area who had been summoned to Halifax to explain their reasons for the petition of 10 June, the lieutenant-governor was a man still unsure of the military security of his colony, wanting unequivocal proof that the Acadians had accepted the reality of British government of Nova Scotia and of their role as British subjects. He was also aware that, however inconvenient it might be, the Acadians had some civil rights under British law.

Nevertheless, Lawrence had written to the Board of Trade, four days before this Council meeting, about what he intended to do with the Acadians settled in the isthmus. His dispatch first reported the surrender of Beauséjour and Gaspereau and then went on to state that "the deserting French" were surrendering their arms, after which they were "to be driven out of the country," although they might very well be put to repairing Fort Beauséjour, now renamed Fort Cumberland, before they were sent into exile.[33] While there is no evidence that, at this point, Lawrence contemplated the wholesale deportation of the Acadian population, the possibility of the dispersal of a significant number of Acadians was definitely in his mind.

The attitude of the Acadians at the Council meeting of 3 July was in keeping with their past behaviour over close to a century. It did nothing to make Lawrence reconsider his position. [. . .] In fact, as the minutes of the Council meetings throughout the month of July 1755 show, Lawrence and his advisors considered the Acadians not only politically unreliable but also socially impertinent, lacking in proper deference to their betters.

It is not surprising, then, that the atmosphere at the Council meetings in the first week of July was one of mutual incomprehension.[34] Colonel Lawrence chaired this and all other Council meetings during July. There were four other Council members present on the meetings of the 3rd and 4th of the month. [. . .] None of them had any personal acquaintanceship with the Acadians, knowing them only as a French-speaking, Catholic people who claimed to be different from the French but whose behaviour in the face of French intrusions on the borders of the colony was, at best, unreliable.

It was clear from the outset that the councillors found the Acadians' rhetoric deeply offensive. Before the Acadians were called into the meeting, Council members had come to the unanimous conclusion that the memorial was "highly arrogant and insidious, an insult upon His Majesty's Authority and Government, and deserved the highest Resentment . . . "[35] Once the Acadians were present, it became quickly apparent that the two parties were at complete odds. The Acadians had composed their petition in the belief that Lawrence and the Council regarded them as people to be accorded consideration. The inhabitants had tried to explain, in the second paragraph of their communication, their difficulties. "Permit us, if you please, Sir, to make known the annoying circumstances in which we are placed, to the prejudice of the tranquillity we ought to enjoy," words that showed that, in their own eyes, they had every right to complain to those governing them.[36] They went on to ask the Council to take their past conduct into consideration as proof of their loyalty to the British. To this, the councillors answered that "their past Conduct was considered, and that the Government were sorry to have occasion to say that their Conduct had been undutifull and very ungrateful for the Lenity shown to them."

From that point on, the minutes show that the councillors were united in demonstrating to the Acadians that the latter had shown a "constant disposition to Assist His Majesty's Enemies, and to distress his subjects."

[. . .] Toward the end of the meeting, the essence of the administration's position became clear: the Acadians were told that their loyalty and obedience could best be properly demonstrated by "their immediately taking the Oath of Allegiance in the Common form before the Council." Until this point, and including the request for the oath, the members of Council, while more abrasive than their predecessors, had acted much as former administrations had done. But when the Acadians responded, as they had done in the past, by saying that "they had not come prepared to resolve the Council on that Head," they were then informed that for "these Six Years past, the same thing had often been proposed" and that they must have "fully considered and determined this point with regard to themselves before now." The Acadians next asked to return and "consult the Body of the People . . . as they were desirous of either refusing or accepting the Oath in a Body." The councillors rejected this reply as "extraordinary" and gave them an hour to consult among themselves. On their return, the Acadians were of the same mind but offered to take the oath "as they had done before." The councillors answered that "His Majesty had disapproved of the manner of their taking the Oath before" and that any such compromise was now unacceptable. At this point the meeting was adjoined until the next day at ten o'clock.

The next morning, the Acadians repeated their decision that they could not take the oath without consulting their communities. At this point, Lawrence and the Council, composed of the same people as the day before, informed the Acadians that they had now provided enough evidence to make the Council consider them "no longer as Subjects of His Britannick Majesty, but as

Subjects of the King of France, and as such they must hereafter be Treated; and they were Ordered to Withdraw."[37] The minutes record that the Council members then decided among themselves that Captain Murray should order the "French Inhabitants forthwith to Choose and send to Halifax new Deputies with the General Resolution of the said Inhabitants in regard to taking the Oath, and that none of them should for the future be admitted to Take it after having once refused to do but that effectual Measures ought to be taken to remove all such Recusants out of the Province." The 15 Acadians were now required to return to the meeting and were told of this decision. They then offered to take the oath but were informed that "they would not be indulged with such Permission, And they were thereupon ordered into Confinement."

It is striking that the Council decided, at this point, that refusal to take the oath of allegiance as offered would deprive the Acadians of their status as British subjects. In fact, it was a judgment that even Belcher and Lawrence would not repeat. It went against the tradition of international law, which had been accepted, particularly in the case of the Acadians after Utrecht, by both France and Great Britain, that peoples whose territories changed governments through treaties became unequivocally subjects of their new rulers.[38] In also went against all previous arguments by British administrators, including Cornwallis, on the status of Acadians. Finally, it contradicted English legal tradition since before the Tudors, as it had evolved with the linking of Wales and Ireland to England. By the time of Henry VIII, those born on territory ruled at the moment of their birth by England were considered as natural-born subjects.[39] The majority of the Acadian population within peninsular Nova Scotia had by this time, 42 years after Utrecht, been born on British territory. Belcher's influence on the matter is difficult to assess. His experience in Ireland ought to have prevented him making

a judgement that the Acadians' status as subjects depended on an oath of allegiance. By the end of month, when he wrote a defence of the decision to deport the Acadians en masse, he based his opinions upon the question of their loyalty as subjects, rather than upon their position as aliens. This is the argument that would be used in the future to defend the deportation.

The legal argument over the link between the oath of allegiance and the rights of the Acadians as British subjects had little import for the immediate circumstances of the Acadians in July 1754. At that time, their fate depended upon the designs of Lawrence and the Council, designs that become clear when the complete records of the Council meetings for 4, 14, and 15 July are read. The brief minutes of the meeting of 4 July alone leave some question in one's mind as to whether the decision to remove out of the province those who refused the oath referred to just certain individuals from the Minas area or to the Acadians as a whole. [. . .]

On 9 July, Admiral Edward Boscawen dropped anchor in Halifax harbour. On 14 July, Lawrence called another Council meeting; it was attended by the same people who had attended the meetings of 4 and 5 July.[40] Lawrence informed the Council that he had received instructions, which had been sent from the secretary of state to all governors on 15 April, requesting them to co-operate with Admiral Boscawen and provide him with all obtainable intelligence.[41] [. . .] At the meeting that took place on the 15 July, once more attended by those members who had been present at the meetings earlier in the month but with the addition of the two admirals, Lawrence laid out "the proceedings of the Council in regard to the French Inhabitants, and desired their opinion and advice thereon."[42] The admirals agreed that "it was now Time to oblige the said Inhabitants to Take the Oath of Allegiance to His Majesty, or to quit the Country." At this meeting, it was also decided that it was "absolutely necessary

for the Good of His Majesty's Service and the Security of this His Province, to retain in pay the Two Thousand New England Troops . . . "
[. . .]

The support of the admirals for Lawrence was precisely that: support. Obviously, they had not arrived in Nova Scotia with instructions to take over the administration of the colony, nor did they have either the requisite knowledge or the interest to do so. What they did provide was an agreement by senior British naval personnel that the policy being pursued by the administration of Nova Scotia seemed sensible, considering the overall military situation. Boscawen's presence at Halifax until October 1755, and the presence of the fleet in the region, obviously encouraged Lawrence.[43] But Lawrence remained the person in charge of the colony and ultimately the one responsible for its security. [. . .]

Lawrence wrote to the Board of Trade, presenting his view of the situation that confronted him. Neither in this dispatch nor in any other of his letters to London did Lawrence suggest that anyone else was responsible for the evolution of his policy toward the Acadians. Of course, he sought, and gained, the approval of the Council at each stage of its development; it was not a policy that the lieutenant-governor had fashioned against the general beliefs and attitudes of his advisers. However, essentially, it was his policy and the administrations of Cornwallis and Hopson had shown that it would have been possible to pursue another course. One of its most important antecedents was Shirley's proposal after the capture of Louisbourg in 1745, but no dispatch from London, whether from the Board of Trade or from any of the secretaries of state, suggested anything similar. Ever since 1713 the policy of the British government was one of determined refusal to admit that there was any great necessity to resolve the issue, one way or another, of the oath of allegiance. Further, Britain had consistently argued against sending the Acadians out of the colony and these arguments

were repeated again in a letter from the secretary of state, Robinson, to Lawrence on 13 August 1755.[44] In it Robinson wrote that "it cannot, therefore, be too much recommended to you, to use the greatest Caution and Prudence in your Conduct, towards these neutrals, and to assure such of Them, as may be trusted, especially upon their taking the Oaths to His Majesty and His Government, That they may remain in quiet Possession of their Settlements under proper Regulation . . . " This dispatch was in reply to one sent by Lawrence on 28 June 1755, in which he had broached the possibility of deporting Acadians, primarily from the Beauséjour region. Unfortunately, Robinson's dispatch arrived in Halifax only in late October 1755. As has already been mentioned, Lawrence's dispatch of August 1754, in which he pleaded for guidance on the issue, had received no other answer than that the problem he raised was, indeed, interesting and he should seek the advice of Belcher, the newly appointed chief justice of the colony.

Now, on 18 July, Lawrence reported his actions to his superiors.[45] It is a highly intelligent dispatch and guilty less of direct lying than of suppressing evidence and suggesting misleading implications. In relating what had happened at the Council meetings of 4 and 5 July, he omitted to mention that he had not, in fact, informed the Acadians clearly, before the final request to take an unqualified oath of allegiance, that their refusal would see them imprisoned and deported to France at the first opportunity. Moreover, he concluded the dispatch by saying that he was "determined to bring the Inhabitants to compliance, or rid the province of such perfidious subjects." There is no evidence whatsoever to suggest that Lawrence was then determined to exile not only the 15 men from the Minas Basin but also the Acadians who had settled in the Chignecto area, let alone all the Acadians settled elsewhere. Indeed, the information in his dispatch concerning the incarceration of the deputies on George's Island, until they could be sent to France, increases the impression that Lawrence was considering only a small group of the population for exile. It is possible, of course, that Lawrence was convinced that the Acadian population, especially those of the Annapolis region, would not prove obdurate.[46] The dispatch of 18 July, however, quite plainly ruled out any possibility of negotiation with those who did prove recalcitrant. Any softening of this position became less than likely when rumours of Braddock's defeat reached Halifax on 23 July.[47]

In the meantime, of course, from the moment the men from Minas had been detained at Halifax, the Acadian communities had been forced to consider their position on the oath. They responded to the demand for their presence at Halifax, 30 men from Annapolis Royal arriving there on 25 July and 70 from the Minas settlements on 28 July. The written response brought by the Annapolis group emphasized their past conduct, asserting that "several of us have risked our lives to give information to the government concerning the enemy; and have also, when necessary, laboured with all our heart on the repairs of Fort Annapolis."[48] The memorial stated that the deputies had been "charged strictly to contract no new oath."[49] [. . .] Their answer was discussed at the Council meeting of 25 July. [. . .] On this occasion, the Acadians were told clearly that "if they once refused the Oath, they would never after be permitted to Take it, but would infallibly lose their Possessions." They were then dismissed but required to attend another Council meeting on Monday, 28 July.

The same men were present at this meeting as had been in attendance three days earlier. Belcher presented to this meeting a memorial bringing together his ideas as to why the Acadians should be expelled. It was not sent to London until the spring of 1756.[50] It was a mean-minded document, full of historical inaccuracies and of specious arguments. In it the Acadians were accused of outright and continuous support of the French since

1713, and it was implied that all British administrators since 1713 had acted contrary to "the spirit and letter of His Majesty's Instructions." Belcher went on to assert that, to allow the Acadians to take the oath once they had refused to do so, would defeat "the Intention of the Expedition to Beau Sejour." He went on to say that the Acadian presence "may retard the Progress of Settlement . . . since the French at Lunenburgh and the Lunenburghers themselves . . . are more disposed to the French than to the English." In any case, Belcher wrote, even if the Acadians did take the oath, "it is well known, that they will not be influenced" by it "after a [papal] Dispensation."[51] He concluded by remarking that the presence of Massachusetts forces in the colony had provided an opportunity to remove the Acadians which, "once the armament is withdrawn," would be lost. At that point, the Acadians would "undoubtedly resume their Perfidy and Treacheries and with more arts and rancour than before." Belcher therefore advised that "all the French inhabitants may be removed from the Province" from "the highest necessity which is lex temporis, to the interests of His Majesty in the Province."

And so, when the Acadians were called before the Council on 28 July, their fate had already been decided. [. . .]

There had been no attempt made, in any of the Council meetings, to persuade the Acadians that taking the oath would guarantee them the peaceful possession of their lands. From the beginning, Lawrence had treated the Acadian population as a liability and something to control by fear. His policy had been one of accusation and demand. He had a fundamental disbelief in the possibility of the Acadian population being of any value to Nova Scotia and thus his communications with the various settlements were always threatening: "this will happen if you do not conform to my orders." Such a policy was bound to be less than successful, given that the Acadians had heard threats of exile and eviction from British administrators before. For more than 40 years, such threats had been no more than words. It was unlikely that the Acadians were disposed to take Lawrence seriously at this point, even with the presence of much greater military resources in the colony than they had ever known. As well, their forced exile would have seemed an almost unimaginable possibility—they could not conceive of a worse fate than transportation to France. Thus, the Acadian delegates unanimously refused the request to take the oath. They were sent into confinement and the minutes record that "as it had been before determined to send all the French Inhabitants out of the Province if they refused to Take the Oaths, nothing now remained to be considered but what measures should be taken to send them away, and where they should be sent to." The final paragraph of the minutes of this momentous meeting noted that, "after mature Consideration, it was unanimously Agreed That to prevent as much as possible their Attempting to return and molest the Settlers that may be set down on their lands it would be most proper to send them to be distributed amongst the several Colonies on the Continent, and that a sufficient Number of Vessels should be hired with all possible Expedition for that purpose."

An understanding of the sequence of events that led to the deportation leaves unanswered a great many questions. But it goes a long way to answering how such a catastrophe, the destruction of an established community of people, who had built a thriving society over more than a century and a half, occurred. It even goes some of the way to disentangling the complex of ideas and decisions that turned the possibility of the removal of Acadians from Nova Scotia, broached at the time of the Treaty of Utrecht, into the reality of exile. Insistence upon the context of eighteenth-century European life leads to a greater place being given to the contemporary realities of communication through time and across space. It provokes questions about

how the belief and opinions of the elites affected the actions of those who lived on the periphery of the European empires in North America. Above all, the reconstruction of who actually did what and when brings to the fore the political and social conventions that were widespread at the time.

The Acadian deportation, as a government action, was of a pattern with other contemporary happenings, from the deportations after the 1745 rebellion in Scotland to actions on the European continent during the War of the Austrian Succession. It was, in many ways, quintessentially an act of a time when the state rested its authority upon the hereditary right of the monarch and when, as Dummett and Nicol have pointed out, there was "a vertical relationship between monarch and individual, not a horizontal one between the members of a nation or the citizens of a body politics."[52] But this conclusion, that the Acadian deportation was not essentially an extraordinary incident, does little more than scratch the surface of the questions posed. There are at least three ways in which the events of 1755 were significantly different from the other such occurrences. First, as we have seen, the possibility of removing the Acadians from the colony had been a matter of discussion by both French and English from the time of Treaty of Utrecht in 1713.[53] It had a long history as a proposition whereas the other deportations were the immediate consequence of particular actions, the solution to recent and immediate problems. Secondly, the actual pressure for the deportation came as much from a neighbouring territory as from within the jurisdiction itself. The Commonwealth of Massachusetts and its governor, Shirley, were as fully implicated in the event as were the officials in place in Nova Scotia. Further, as has already been mentioned but bears repeating, the final authority, London, had consistently argued against such action since 1713 and reiterated this argument once more in a letter sent from Whitehall on 13 August 1755. Thirdly, the enterprise itself was significantly different from the deportations that followed the Monmouth and Jacobite rebellions. Those were organized after battles had been fought against those sent into exile and were the result of judgments made in a law court about individuals. As well, the number deported was, in each case, only a fraction of the communities concerned. The Acadian deportation involved the removal of almost an entire society, which had been judged as a collectivity. People were dispatched to other communities with a letter of recommendation by the man in charge of the operation, suggesting that, since the deportation would divide Acadian strength, "they May be of some Use as Most of them are Healthy Strong People; And as they Cannot easily collect themselves together again, it be out of their Power to Do any Mischief And they May become Profitable and it is possible, in time Faithful subjects."[54]

Finally, of course, the greatest difference between the Acadian deportation and the other events is what happened afterwards: neither Jacobite nor Huguenot went into exile with the capacity to retain a coherent identity. The Acadians did. They had always been involved in shaping their own lives. In 1713, when "Acadia or Nova Scotia" was transferred to Great Britain, the Acadians themselves, as much as the French or the English, decided that they would remain as subjects of the British empire rather than move to Île Royale, territory that the French still held.[55] In fact, the Acadians' stance represented two political beliefs that confronted the principles of hereditary power. The first was their conviction that they were indeed a people, distinct from the French of France and therefore with different political ambitions. The second belief was that, despite the actions of empires and the decisions of princes, the Acadians had every right to debate and present ideas about how and where they should live to those who claimed them as subjects. However skeptical others have been about the existence of Acadian identity, the Acadians themselves never seem to have doubted it. In considering their history, one has to give this "obstinacy" its due, particularly when "what happened next," the aftermath of the deportation, is examined. The Acadians had not been a collection of uneducated, illiterate, and ignorant peasants—the goods and chattels of others—before July 1755.

NOTES

1. *Histoire philosophique et politique de l'établissement des Européens dans les deux Indes*, 1766 edn, 7 vols.
2. "des jalousies nationales, de cette cupidité des gouvernements qui dévorent les terres et les hommes": ibid., 6:364.
3. "font telles qu'un coeur humain & généreux ne les adopte jamais qu'à regret": William Burck, *Histoire des colonies européennes dans l'Amérique en six parties* . . . (Paris: Merlin 1767), 2 vols, 2:319. My translation.
4. For a collection of opinions on the issue, see N.E.S. Griffiths, *The Acadian Deportation: Deliberate Perfidy or Cruel Necessity?* (Toronto: Copp Clark 1969).
5. For the nineteenth-century debate, see Francis Parkman, *Montcalm and Wolfe* (2 vols. Boston: Little, Brown 1884) and *A Half-Century of Conflict* (2 vols. Boston: Little 1897); and H.R. Casgrain, *Un pèlerinage au pays d'Evangéline* (Quebec: Demers 1887). The debate was continued in the twentieth century by a great number of writers, most recently by Robert Sauvageau, *Acadie: La guerre de Cents Ans des Français d'Amérique aux Maritimes et en Louisiane, 1678–1769* (Paris: Berger-Levrault 1987); Yves Cazaux, *L'Acadie: Histoire des Acadiens du XVIIe siècle à nos jours* (Paris: Albin Michel 1992); and Geoffrey Plank, *An Unsettled Conquest: The British Campaign against the Peoples of Acadia* (Philadelphia: University of Pennsylvania Press, 2001). The bibliographies produced by the Centre d'Études Acadiennes, at the Université de Moncton, New Brunswick, are the first place to begin a survey of this literature. See, in particular,

Inventaire général, vol. 2, *Bibliographies acadienne . . .* à 1975 (n.d.), and various supplements. Worthwhile consulting, too, is N.E.S. Griffiths, "The Acadian Deportation: A Study in Historiography and Literature" (MA thesis, University of New Brunswick 1957), which provides a critical survey of what was published before 1956.

6. A full account of their actions is found in Micheline Dumont-Johnson, *Apôtres ou agitateurs: la France missionnaire en Acadie* (Trois-Rivières: Boréal Express 1970), 116–28.

7. Robinson had been secretary to the embassy at Paris from 1723 to 1730 and plenipotentiary at the peace negotiations leading to the Treaty of Aix-la-Chapelle in 1748. He was appointed a member of the Board of Trade in 1748–49. See Alan Valentine, *The British Establishment, 1760–1784: An Eighteenth Century Biographical Dictionary* (Norman: University of Oklahoma Press 1970), 2:743–4.

8. For Governor Shirley's speech in February 1755, see *Doc. Hist. St. Maine*, 12:350–62.

9. I.K. Steele, "Robert Monckton," *Dictionary of Canadian Biography (1974)*, 4:540–2.

10. National Archives of Canada (NAC), CO 217, 15, Lawrence to the Board of Trade, 1 Aug. 1754; Thomas Beamish Akins, ed., *Acadia and Nova Scotia: Documents relating to the Acadian French and the first British colonization of the province, 1714–1758* (Cottonport: Polyanthos 1979. Rpt of Halifax: Charles Annand 1869 edn), 213.

11. NAC, CO 218, 5, Board of Trade to Lawrence, 29 Oct. 1754; partially printed in Akins, *Acadia*, 235–7.

12. NAC, CO 217, 15, Lawrence to the Board of Trade, 12 Jan. 1755.

13. NAC, CO 220, NS (B), 8, f.126, Council minutes.

14. A short corrective to present-day visions of the eighteenth century as a time of highly civilized and compassionate behaviour, epitomized by the glorious music of Bach and Mozart and the paintings of Fragonard, is found in M.S. Anderson, *War and Society in Europe of the Old Regime, 1618–1789* (Montreal and Kingston: McGill-Queen's University Press 1998). See also R.R. Palmer, *Age of the Democratic Revolution: A Political*

History of Europe and America 1760–1800 (2 vols. Princeton: Princeton University Press 1964).

15. Abbott Emerson Smith, *Colonists in Bondage: White Servitude and Convict Labor in America, 1607–1776* (New York: W.W. Norton 1971), 148.

16. Ibid., 92.

17. NAC, Vernon-Wager Papers, printed in Griffiths, *The Acadian Deportation*, 108. It is clear from the body of Lawrence's correspondence that he is using the word "extirpate" to mean "to clear away persons from a locality" and not in the sense of "to kill". See *Oxford English Dictionary*.

18. Included in a letter of 14 April 1756 from Secretary Fox to the Lords of Trade, printed in PAC *Report*, 1905, app. B, 63–5. As lieutenant governor of Nova Scotia, Belcher displayed a harsh attitude toward the Acadians: see C.J. Townshend, "Jonathan Belcher, First Chief Justice of Nova Scotia," *Collections of the Nova Scotia Historical Society* XVIII (1914), 25–57.

19. Susan Buggey, "Jonathan Belcher," *Dictionary of Canadian Biography* (DCB), 4:50–4.

20. See Abbé de L'Isle-Dieu to Pontbriand, 25 March 1755, in "Lettres et mémoires de l'abbé de l'Isle-Dieu," RAPQ, 1935–36.

21. Pichon to Surlaville, 12 Nov. 1754, in Gaston Du Boscq de Beaumont, *Les derniers jours de l'Acadie (1748–1759), correspondances et mémoires: extrait du portefeuille de M. le Courtois de Surlaville, lieutenant-général des armées du roi, ancien major des troupes du l'Île Royale, mis en ordre et annotés* (Genève: Slatkine-Megariotis Reprints 1975), 130.

22. "légitime souverain": R. Rumilly, *Histoire des Acadiens* (2 vols. Montreal: Fides 1955), 1:436.

23. John B. Brebner, "Canadian Policy Towards the Acadians in 1751," *Canadian Historical Review* 12, 3 (1931): 284. This includes the proclamation of La Jonquière on the subject, as does Griffiths, *The Acadian Deportation*, 82–3.

24. See excerpts and analysis in J.C. Webster, *The Forts of Chignecto: A Study of the Eighteenth Century Conflict between France and Great Britain in Acadia* (Shediac 1930), 58–60.

25. Aumasson de Courville, *Mémoires sur le Canada, depuis 1749 jusqu'à 1760*, LHSQ ed. (Quebec: Imprimerie de T. Cary 1838).

26. For an account of Pichon's career, with references to those of his papers held in PANS, see J.C. Webster, *Thomas Pichon, "the Spy of Beauséjour," an Account of his career in Europe and America* (Sackville: Tribune Press 1937). For a précis of the sort of information that Pichon sent the British, see T.A. Crowley, "Thomas Pichon," *DCB*, 4:630–2.

27. J.C. Webster, ed., *Journals of Beauséjour: Diary of John Thomas, journal of Louis de Courville* (Halifax: Public Archives of Nova Scotia 1937), 16, 17, and 100.

28. Akins, *Acadia*, 212–14.

29. PAC *Report*, 1905, app. B, 60; a description of the disarming is in *Coll. Doc. Inédits*, 1:138–9.

30. See, in particular, the evidence of Judge Isaac Deschamps in NAC, Brown Papers, Mss. 19073, item 52; and Grace M. Tratt, "Isaac Deschamps," *DCB*, 5:250–2.

31. "Signé par quarante-quatre des susdits habitants, au nom de tous": Council minutes, 5 July 1755, ff.166–7, printed in full in French in PAC *Report*, 1905, app. A, pt. 3, and in English in Akins, *Acadia*, 249–50.

32. "si dans la Requette qu'ils ont eu l'honneur de présenter à votre Excellence il se trouvoit quelque faute ou quelque manque de respect envers le gouvernement, que c'est contre leur intention . . .": ibid.

33. NAC, CO 217, 15, Lawrence to the Lords of Trade, 28 June 1755.

34. John Brebner believes that the British, clearly irritated, attempted to make the Acadians declare themselves unequivocally: *New England's outpost: Acadia before the conquest of Canada* (Hamden: Archon 1927), 215ff. L.H. Gipson maintains that the British judiciously presented their position to the Acadians: *The British Empire before the American Revolution* (New York: Alfred A. Knopf 1942), 6:255ff.; Emile Lauvrière is convinced that the meeting was a Machiavellian inquisition, designed to make the Acadians appear guilty: *La tragédie d'un peuple: histoire du peuple acadien de ses origines à nos jours* (2 vols. Paris: Editions Brossard 1922), 1:428ff.

35. NAC, CO 220, NS (B), 8, Council minutes, 3 July 1755; printed in Akins, *Acadia*, 250.

36. "Permettez-nous, s'il vous plaît, d'exposer ici les circonstances genantes dans lesquelles on

nous retiens au prejudice de la tranquillité dont nous devons jouir": ibid.

37. NAC, CO 220, NS (B), 8, Council minutes, 4 July 1755; printed in Akins, *Acadia*, 256.

38. See N.E.S. Griffiths, *From Migrant to Acadian: A North American Border People 1604–1755* (Montreal and Kingston: McGill-Queen's University Press), chapter 6 for a discussion of the decision by French jurists that the British crown was justified in demanding an oath of allegiance.

39. Anne Dummett and Andrew Nicol, *Subjects, Citizens, Aliens and Others: Nationality and Immigration Law* (London: Wiedenfeld and Nicholson 1990), 45.

40. Ibid., 14 July 1755; printed in Akins, *Acadia*, 257.

41. NAC, CO 218, 5, Secretary of State Robinson's circular to all governors, 15 April 1755.

42. NAC, CO 220, NS (B), 8, Council minutes, 15 July 1755; printed in Akins, *Acadia*, 258–9.

43. W.A.B. Douglas, "Nova Scotia and the Royal Navy, 1713–1766," PhD thesis, Queen's University 1973, 242.

44. CO 5, 211, British Library (BL), Mss. 19073, f.42, Robinson to Charles Lawrence, 13 Aug. 1755; printed in full in Griffiths, *The Acadian Deportation*, 111.

45. NAC CO 217, 15, Lawrence to the Lords of Trade, 18 July 1755.

46. In much the same way that officials in France were shaken in 685 when Protestants chose exile rather than conversion.

47. Brought by one of the ships, the brig *Lily* out of New York. See J. Macdonald, "The Hon. Edward Cornwallis," *Collections of the Nova Scotia Historical Society*, vol. XII, p. 42.

48. "nous pouvons bien assurer votre Excellence que plusieurs d'entre nous se sont risqué la vie pour donner connoissance au gouvernement de l'ennemis et aussi lorsqu'il a été nécessaire de travailler pour l'entretien du Fort d'Annapolis . . . nous nous y avons porter de tout notre coeur": NAC, CO 220, NS (B), 8 Council minutes, 25 July 1755; PAC *Report*, 2, app. A, pt. 3, app. C, 61.

49. "nous leurs enjoignons de ne contracter aucun nouveaux serment": ibid., 61.

50. This memorial was not sent to the Lords of Trade until 24 Dec. 1755. It was included in

a dispatch from Belcher, the main body of which was concerned with the need for an assembly for Nova Scotia: NAC, CO 217,16; printed in full in PAC *Report*, 1905, 2, app. A, Pt. 3, app. C, 63–5.

51. Belcher obviously believed that the Catholic hierarchy might proclaim that oaths sworn to a Protestant monarch were not binding. Such a position was extreme, but, when one recalls that Belcher had lived in United Kingdom during the Stuart rebellion of 1745, which had been openly financed by France, it becomes understandable.

52. Dummett and Nicol, *Subjects, Citizens, Aliens*, 22.

53. For the French view, and their wish to have the Acadians as settlers on Île Royale, see NAC, AC, IR, C11B, 1, f.123, Costebelle to the minister, 1715; for the English view, and their fear that the departure of the Acadians would strip Nova Scotia of its population, see NAC, NS/A, 5:1, Caulfield to the Lords of Trade, 1715.

54. NAC, CO 217, 15, Lawrence, "Circular letter to the governors of certain colonies," 11 Aug. 1755; printed in PAC *Report*, 1905, 2, app. B, 15–16.

55. See Antoine Bernard, *Le drame acadien depuis 1604* (Montreal: Clercs de Saint Viateur 1936), 247–85.

Chapter 5

Integrating the Province of Quebec in the British Empire

READINGS

Primary Documents

Historical Interpretations

INTRODUCTION

The Treaty of Paris (1763) ended the Seven Years' War and affirmed the British conquest of New France. Although the British had reason to celebrate their victory over the French, their celebration was short-lived. The conquest of the French colony in North America quickly created problems for the British government, now responsible for the entire region. Some of these issues had to do with the Indigenous rebellion led by Pontiac, south of the Great Lakes. Others concerned British policies toward the Thirteen Colonies to the south. The decisions made by the British government to prevent American expansion westward, to tax the American colonists without their consent, and to leave troops in the colonies, even without any external threat, exasperated the colonists and eventually pushed them on the path of rebellion. The conquest of New France and its integration into the British Empire also raised the issue of diversity within this empire. British identity had been created after 1707 in opposition to France and rested on Protestantism and commerce. The integration of the *Canadiens,* French Roman Catholic subjects who were mainly peasants, into the Empire represented a huge challenge for the British authorities and for the British American merchants (called *Bostonnais* by the Canadiens) who came to the colony after the Conquest.

The first set of primary documents includes a dispatch from James Murray, governor of the newly created Province of Quebec, to the lords of trade who managed colonial affairs for the British government. In it, Murray complains about the fanaticism demonstrated by local British traders toward French subjects. His sympathy is clearly with the latter. This set also includes a petition from the British local merchants to the king that illustrates their attitude toward their French fellow subjects. The second document comprises excerpts from an epistolary novel written by Frances Brooke, a British author who lived in Quebec for a few years in the 1760s. Close to the British traders (also called the English party), Brooke used her characters to express their and her prejudices toward French subjects. Many of these attitudes were tenacious and would poison French–English relationships in the colony for decades to come.

In his article, Donald Fyson revisits the period and argues that, despite the existence of prejudices, the period that led to the integration of the Province of Quebec within the British Empire was one of "mutual adaptation". Both French and English subjects learned to live with the other, make compromises, and collaborate. John Crowley discusses the issue of integration from an altogether different perspective. He explains how the British visually appropriated the new colony through the arts. He shows us how depictions of landscape can do more than entertain or highlight an artist's talents. He demonstrates that the territory formerly known as New France becomes British as it is visually catalogued, just as other parts of the empire were. Thinking critically about the way visual representations operate can perhaps help us understand more clearly the limitations of our written and oral sources.

QUESTIONS FOR CONSIDERATION

1. Do you consider literature and works of art to be reliable historical documents? What about photographs?
2. What kinds of prejudices are illustrated in the traders' petition and Brooke's novel? What important aspects of eighteenth-century British identity do they highlight?
3. Why did Murray dislike the people he called "the Licentious Fanaticks Trading" so much?
4. According to Fyson, how did British authority treat their new French and Roman Catholic subjects in the Province of Quebec? How did the new subjects adapt to the British regime? How did the British merchants adapt to the new colony?
5. Regardless of who controlled the land, what was the purpose of producing images of a colony?

SUGGESTIONS FOR FURTHER READING

Fred Anderson, *Crucible of War: The Seven Years' War and the Fate of Empire in British North America, 1754–1766* (New York: Knopf, 2000).

Phillip Buckner and John G. Reid, eds, *Revisiting 1759: The Conquest of Canada in Historical Perspective* (Toronto: University of Toronto Press, 2012).

———, eds, *Remembering 1759: The Conquest of Canada in Historical Memory* (Toronto: University of Toronto Press, 2012).

A.L. Burt, *The Old Province of Quebec*, 2 vols (Toronto: McClelland & Stewart, 1968).

Nancy Christie, ed., *Transatlantic Subjects: Ideas, Institutions, and Social Experience in Post-Revolutionary British North America* (Montreal and Kingston: McGill-Queen's University Press, 2008).

Donald Fyson, *Magistrates, Police, and People: Everyday Criminal Justice in Quebec and Lower Canada, 1764–1837* (Toronto: University of Toronto Press, 2006).

José Igartua, "The Merchants and Négociants of Montréal, 1750–1775: A Study in Socio-Economic History," PhD thesis, Michigan State University, 1974.

Philip Lawson, *The Imperial Challenge: Quebec and Britain in the Age of the American Revolution* (Montreal and Kingston: McGill-Queen's University Press, 1994).

Dale Miquelon, *Society and Conquest: The Debate on the Bourgeoisie and Social Change in French Canada, 1700–1850* (Toronto: Copp Clark Publishing, 1977).

Primary Documents

1   From "Governor Murray to the Lords of Trade, Quebec 29th Octr 1764," and "Petition of the Quebec Traders" in *Documents Relating to the Constitutional History of Canada 1759–1791*, vol. 1 (Ottawa: J. de L. Taché, 1918), 231–4.

GOVERNOR MURRAY TO THE LORDS OF TRADE

QUEBEC 29th Octr 1764

MY LORDS

The inclosed papers will shew you the situation of affairs here and how necessary it is for me to send Mr Cramahé to London that your Lordships may have the most Minute and Clearest Acc^t of every thing relating to this Province. An immediate Remedy seems necessary. To any thing I can write doubts may arise and misrepresentations may be made (which I find too frequently to be the case) the necessary delay to clear up such Doubts and misrepresentations by letters, may be dangerous. Mr Cramahé will answer every purpose, if properly attended too, he is thoroughly informed of all I know, no Man has the good of this Colony more at heart, no Man is more zealous for the Kings service and certainly there doth not exist a Man of more Integrity and Application.

Little, very little, will content the New Subjects but nothing will satisfy the Licentious Fanaticks Trading here, but the expulsion of the Canadians who are perhaps the bravest and the best race upon the Globe, a

Race, who cou'd they be indulged with a few priveledges which the Laws of England deny to Roman Catholicks at home, wou'd soon get the better of every National Antipathy to their Conquerors and become the most faithful and most useful set of Men in this American Empire.

I flatter myself there will be some Remedy found out even in the Laws for the Relief of this People, if so, I am positive the populer clamours in England will not prevent the Humane Heart of the King from following its own Dictates. I am confident too my Royal Master will not blame the unanimous opinion of his Council here for the Ordonnance establishing the Courts of Justice, as nothing less cou'd be done to prevent great numbers from emigrating directly, and certain I am, unless the Canadians are admitted on Jurys, and are allowed Judges and Lawyers who understand their Language his Majesty will lose the greatest part of this Valuable people. [. . .]

I have the Hon^r to be with the greatest truth & regard.
My Lords,
Your Lordships' mo. Ob^t, &^{ca}.
The Lords of Trade & Plant^n, (Signed)
JA MURRAY
[. . .]

PETITION OF THE QUEBEC TRADERS

To the King's Most Excellent Majesty
The Humble Petition of Your Majesty's most faithful and loyal Subjects, British Merchants and Traders in behalf of themselves and their fellow Subjects, Inhabitants of your Majesty's Province of Quebec
MAY IT PLEASE YOUR MAJESTY.

Confident of Your Majesty's Paternal Care and Protection extended even to the meanest and most distant of your Subjects, We humbly crave your Majesty's Gracious Attention to our present Grievances and Distresses.

We presume to hope that your Majesty will be pleased to attribute our approaching your Royal Throne with disagreeable Complaints, to the Zeal and Attachment we have to your Majesty's Person and Government, and for the Liberties & Priviledges with which your Majesty has indulged all your Dutifull Subjects.

Our Settlement in this Country with respect to the greatest part of us; takes it's date from the Surrender of the Colony to your Majestys Arms; Since that Time we have much contributed to the advantage of our Mother Country, by causing an additional Increase to her Manufactures, and by a considerable Importation of them, diligently applied ourselves to Investigate and promote the Commercial Interests of this Province and render it flourishing.

To Military Government, however oppressive and severely felt, we submitted without murmur, hoping Time with a Civil Establishment would remedy this Evil.

With Peace we trusted to enjoy the Blessings of British Liberty, and happily reap the fruits of our Industry: but we should now despair of ever attaining those desirable ends, had we not Your Majesty's experienced Goodness to apply to.

The Ancient Inhabitants of the Country impoverished by the War, had little left wherewith to purchase their common necessaries but a Paper Currency of very doubtfull Value: The Indian War has suspended our Inland Trade for two years past, and both these Causes united have greatly injured our Commerce.

For the redress of which we repose wholly on your Majesty, not doubting but the Wisdom of your Majesty's Councils will in due time put the Paper Currency into a Course of certain and regular Payment, and the Vigour of Your Majesty's Arms terminate that War by a peace advantageous and durable.

We no less rely on your Majesty for the Redress of those Grievances we suffer from the Measures of Government practised in this your Majesty's Province, which are

The Deprivation of the open Trade declared by your Majesty's most gracious Proclamation, by the Appropriation of some of the most commodious Posts of the Resort of the Savages, under the Pretext of their being your Majesty's private Domain.

The Enacting Ordinances Vexatious, Oppressive, unconstitutional, injurious to civil Liberty and the Protestant Cause.

Suppressing dutifull and becoming Remonstrances of your Majesty's Subjects against these Ordinances in Silence and Contempt.

The Governor instead of acting agreeable to that confidence reposed in him by your Majesty, in giving a favourable Reception to those of your Majesty's Subjects, who petition and apply to him on such important Occasions as require it, doth frequently treat them with a Rage and Rudeness of Language and Demeanour, as dishonorable to the Trust he holds of your Majesty as painful to those who suffer from it.

His further adding to this by most flagrant Partialities, by formenting Parties and taking measures to keep your Majesty's old and new Subjects divided from one another, by encouraging the latter to apply for Judges of their own National Language.

His endeavouring to quash the Indictment against Claude Panet (his Agent in this Attempt who laboured to inflame the Minds of the People against your Majesty's British Subjects) found by a very Worthy Grand Inquest, and causing their other judicious and honest Presentments to be answered from the Bench with a Contemptuous Ridicule.

This discountenancing the Protestant Religion by almost a Total Neglect of Attendance upon the Service of the Church, leaving the Protestants to this Day destitute of a place of Worship appropriated to themselves.

The Burthen of these Grievances from Government is so much the more severely felt, because of the natural Poverty of the Country; the Products of it been extremely unequal to support its Consumption of Imports.

Hence our Trade is miserably confined and distressed, so that we lye under the utmost Necessity of the Aids of Succours of Government, as well from Our Mother Country as that of the Province, in the Place of having to contend against Oppression and Restraint.

We could enumerate many more Sufferings which render the Lives of your Majesty's Subjects, especially your Majesty's loyal British Subjects, in the Province so very unhappy that we must be under the Necessity of removing from it, unless timely prevented by a Removal of the present Governor.

Your Petitioners therefore most humbly pray your Majesty to take the Premises into your gracious Consideration, and to appoint a Governor over us, acquainted with other maxims of Government than Military only; And for the better Security of your Majesty's dutiful and loyal Subjects, in the Possession and Continuance of their Rights and Liberties, we beg leave also most humbly to petition that it may please your Majesty, to order a House of Representatives to be chosen in this as in other your Majesty's Provinces; there being a number more than Sufficient of Loyal and well affected Protestants, exclusive of military Officers, to form a competent and respectable House of Assembly; and your Majesty's new Subjects, if your Majesty shall think fit, may be allowed to elect Protestants without burdening them with such Oaths as in their present mode of thinking they cannot conscientiously take.

We doubt not but the good Effects of these measures will soon appear, by the Province becoming flourishing and your Majesty's People in it happy. And for Your Majesty and your House your Petitioners as in Duty bound shall ever pray, &ca &ca

Saml Sills	John Danser.	Geo. Allsoopp.	Alex^r McKenzie
Edwd Harrison	Ja^s Jeffry.	Wm Mackenzie	Geo. Measam
Eleaz^r Levy	Ja^s Johnston.	B Comte.	J^n A. Gastineau
Ja^s Shepherd	Thos Story.	Peter Faneuil.	Ph. Payn.
John Watmough.	Danl Bayne	Geo. Fulton.	
John Ord.	John Purss.		

2 From Frances Brooke, *The History of Emily Montague* (London: Printed for J. Dodsley, in Pall Mall, 1769), 4 vols.

LETTER 22: FROM A. FERMOR TO MISS RIVERS (SILLERI, SEPT. 25)

I have been rambling about amongst the peasants, and asking them a thousand questions, in order to satisfy your inquisitive friend. As to my father, though, properly speaking, your questions are addressed to him, yet, being upon duty, he begs that, for this time, you will accept of an answer from me.

The Canadians live a good deal like the ancient patriarchs; the lands were originally settled by the troops, every officer became a seigneur, or lord of the manor, every soldier took lands under his commander; but, as avarice is natural to mankind, the soldiers took a great deal more than they could cultivate, by way of providing for a family: which is the reason so much land is now waste in the finest part of the province: those who had children, and in general they have a great number, portioned out their lands amongst them as they married, and lived in the midst of a little world of their descendants.

[. . .]

The corn here is very good, though not equal to ours; the harvest not half so gay as in England, and for this reason, that the lazy creatures leave the greatest part of their land uncultivated, only sowing as much corn of different sorts as will serve themselves; and being too proud and too idle to work for hire, every family gets in its own harvest, which prevents all that jovial spirit which we find when the reapers work together in large parties.

Idleness is the reigning passion here, from the peasant to his lord; the gentlemen never either ride on horseback or walk, but are driven about like women, for they never drive themselves, lolling at their ease in a calache: the peasants, I mean the masters of families, are pretty near as useless as their lords.

You will scarce believe me, when I tell you, that I have seen, at the farm next us, two children, a very beautiful boy and girl, of about eleven years old, assisted by their grandmother, reaping a field of oats, whilst the lazy father, a strong fellow of thirty two, lay on the grass, smoking his pipe, about twenty yards from them: the old people and children work here; those in the age of strength and health only take their pleasure.

A propos to smoking, 'tis common to see here boys of three years old, sitting at their doors, smoking their pipes, as grave and composed as little old Chinese men on a chimney.

[. . .]

They [the Canadiens] sow their wheat in spring, never manure the ground, and plough it in the slightest manner; can it then be wondered at that it is inferior to ours? They fancy the frost would destroy it if sown in autumn; but this is all prejudice, as experience has shewn. I myself saw a field of wheat this year at the governor's farm, which was manured and sown in autumn, as fine as I ever saw in England.

I should tell you, they are so indolent as never to manure their lands, or even their gardens; and that, till the English came, all the manure of Quebec was thrown into the river.

[. . .]

Adieu! I am tired of the subject.

Your faithful,

A. Fermor.

LETTER 72: FROM WILLIAM FERMOR TO THE EARL OF —— (SILLERI, FEB. 20)

My Lord,

Your Lordship does me great honor in supposing me capable of giving any satisfactory account of a country in which I have spent only a few months.

As a proof, however, of my zeal, and the very strong desire I have to merit the esteem you honor me with, I shall communicate from time to time the little I have observed, and may observe, as well as what I hear from good authority, with that lively pleasure with which I have ever obeyed every command of your Lordship's.

The French, in the first settling this colony, seem to have had an eye only to the conquest of ours: their whole system of policy seems to have been military, not commercial; or only so far commercial as was necessary to supply the wants, and by so doing to gain the friendship, of the savages, in order to make use of them against us.

The lands are held on military tenure: every peasant is a soldier, every seigneur an officer, and both serve without pay whenever called upon; this service is, except a very small quit-rent by way of acknowledgement, all they pay for their lands: the seigneur holds of the crown, the peasant of the seigneur, who is at once his lord and commander.

The peasants are in general tall and robust, notwithstanding their excessive indolence; they love war, and hate labor; are brave, hardy, alert in the field, but lazy and inactive at home; in which they resemble the savages, whose manners they seem strongly to have imbibed. The government appears to have encouraged a military spirit all over the colony; though ignorant and stupid to a great degree, these peasants have a strong sense of honor; and though they serve, as I have said, without pay, are never so happy as when called to the field.

They are excessively vain, and not only look on the French as the only civilized nation in the world, but on themselves as the flower of the French nation: they had, I am told, a great aversion to the regular troops which came from France in the late war, and a contempt equal to that aversion; they however had an affection and esteem for the late Marquis De Montcalm, which almost rose to idolatry; and I have even at this distance of time seen many of them in tears at the mention of his name: an honest tribute to the memory of a commander equally brave and humane; for whom his enemies wept even on the day when their own hero fell.

I am called upon for this letter, and have only time to assure your Lordship of my respect, and of the pleasure I always receive from your commands. I have the honor to be,

My Lord,

Your Lordship's, &c.

William Fermor.

LETTER 117: FROM WILLIAM FERMOR TO THE EARL OF —— (SILLERI, APRIL 8)

Nothing can be more true, my Lord, than that poverty is ever the inseparable companion of indolence.

I see proofs of it every moment before me; with a soil fruitful beyond all belief, the Canadians are poor on lands which are their own property, and for which they pay only a trifling quit-rent to their seigneurs.

This indolence appears in every thing: you scarce see the meanest peasant walking; even riding on horseback appears to them a fatigue insupportable; you see them lolling at ease, like their lazy lords, in carrioles and calashes, according to the season; a boy to guide the horse on a seat in the front of the carriage, too lazy even to take the trouble of driving themselves, their hands in winter folded in an immense muff, though perhaps their families are in want of bread to eat at home.

The winter is passed in a mixture of festivity and inaction; dancing and feasting in their gayer hours; in their graver smoking, and drinking brandy, by the side of a warm stove: and when obliged to cultivate the ground in spring to procure the means of subsistence, you see them just turn the turf once lightly over, and, without manuring the ground, or even breaking the clods of earth, throw in the seed in the same careless manner, and leave the event to chance, without troubling themselves further till it is fit to reap.

I must, however, observe, as some alleviation, that there is something in the climate which strongly inclines both the body and mind, but rather the latter, to indolence: the heat of the summer, though pleasing, enervates the very soul, and gives a certain lassitude unfavorable to industry; and the winter, at its extreme, binds up and chills all the active faculties of the soul.

Add to this, that the general spirit of amusement, so universal here in winter, and so necessary to prevent the ill effects of the season, gives a habit of dissipation and pleasure, which makes labor doubly irksome at its return.

Their religion, to which they are extremely bigoted, is another great bar, as well to industry as population: their numerous festivals inure them to idleness; their religious houses rob the state of many subjects who might be highly useful at present, and at the same time retard the increase of the colony.

Sloth and superstition equally counterwork providence, and render the bounty of heaven of no effect.

I am surprized the French, who generally make their religion subservient to the purposes of policy, do not discourage convents, and lessen the number of festivals, in the colonies, where both are so peculiarly pernicious.

It is to this circumstance one may in great measure attribute the superior increase of the British American settlements compared to those of France: a religion which encourages idleness, and makes a virtue of celibacy, is particularly unfavorable to colonization.

However religious prejudice may have been suffered to counterwork policy under a French government, it is scarce to be doubted that this cause of the poverty of Canada will by degrees be removed; that these people, slaves at present to ignorance and superstition, will in time be enlightened by a more liberal education, and gently led by reason to a religion which is not only preferable, as being that of the country to which they are now annexed, but which is so much more calculated to make them happy and prosperous as a people.

Till that time, till their prejudices subside, it is equally just, humane, and wise, to leave them the free right of worshiping the Deity in the manner which they have been early taught to believe the best, and to which they are consequently attached.

It would be unjust to deprive them of any of the rights of citizens on account of religion, in America, where every other sect of dissenters are equally capable of employ with those of the established church; nay where, from whatever cause, the church of England is on a footing in many colonies little better than a toleration.

It is undoubtedly, in a political light, an object of consequence every where, that the national religion, whatever it is, should be as universal as possible, agreement in religious worship being the strongest tie to unity and obedience; had all prudent means been used to lessen the number of dissenters in our colonies, I cannot avoid believing, from what I observe and hear, that we should have found in them a spirit of rational loyalty, and true freedom, instead of that factious one from which so much is to be apprehended.

It seems consonant to reason, that the religion of every country should have a relation to, and coherence with, the civil constitution: the Romish religion is best adapted to a despotic government, the presbyterian to a republican, and that of the church of England to a limited monarchy like ours.

As therefore the civil government of America is on the same plan with that of the mother country, it were to be wished the religious establishment was also the same, especially in those colonies where the people are generally of the national church; though with the fullest liberty of conscience to dissenters of all denominations.

I would be clearly understood, my Lord; from all I have observed here, I am convinced, nothing would so much contribute to diffuse a spirit of order, and rational obedience, in the colonies, as the appointment, under proper restrictions, of bishops: I am equally convinced that nothing would so much strengthen the hands of government, or give such pleasure to the well-affected in the colonies, who are by much the most numerous, as such an appointment, however clamored against by a few abettors of sedition.

I am called upon for this letter, and must remit to another time what I wished to say more to your Lordship in regard to this country.
I have the honor to be,
My Lord, &c.
Wm. Fermor.

LETTER 138: FROM WILLIAM FERMOR TO THE EARL OF —— (SILLERI, MAY 12)

It were indeed, my Lord, to be wished that we had here schools, at the expence of the public, to teach English to the rising generation: nothing is a stronger tie of brotherhood and affection, a greater cement of union, than speaking one common language.

The want of attention to this circumstance has, I am told, had the worst effects possible in the province of New York, where the people, especially at a distance from the capital, continuing to speak Dutch, retain their affection for their ancient masters, and still look on their English fellow subjects as strangers and intruders.

The Canadians are the more easily to be won to this, or whatever else their own, or the general good requires, as their noblesse have the strongest attachment to a court, and that favor is the great object of their ambition: were English made by degrees the court language, it would soon be universally spoke.

Of the three great springs of the human heart, interest, pleasure, vanity, the last appears to me much the strongest in the Canadians; and I am convinced the most forcible tie their noblesse have to France, is their unwillingness to part with their croix de St. Louis: might not therefore some order of the same kind be instituted for Canada, and given to all who have the croix, on their sending back the ensigns they now wear, which are inconsistent with their allegiance as British subjects?

Might not such an order be contrived, to be given at the discretion of the governor, as well to the Canadian gentlemen who merited most of the government, as to the English officers of a certain rank, and such other English as purchased estates, and settled in the country? and, to give it additional lustre, the governor, for the time being, be always head of the order?

'Tis possible something of the same kind all over America might be also of service; the passions of mankind are nearly the same every where: at least I never yet saw the soil or climate, where vanity did not grow; and till all mankind become philosophers, it is by their passions they must be governed.

The common people, by whom I mean the peasantry, have been great gainers here by the change of masters; their property is more secure, their independence greater, their profits much more than doubled: it is not them therefore whom it is necessary to gain.

The noblesse, on the contrary, have been in a great degree undone: they have lost their employs, their rank, their consideration, and many of them their fortunes.

It is therefore equally consonant to good policy and to humanity that they should be considered, and in the way most acceptable to them; the rich conciliated by little honorary distinctions, those who are otherwise by sharing in all lucrative employs; and all of them by bearing a part in the legislature of their country.

The great objects here seem to be to heal those wounds, which past unhappy disputes have left still in some degree open; to unite the French and English, the civil and military, in one firm body; to raise a revenue, to encourage agriculture, and especially the growth of hemp and flax; and find a staple, for the improvement of a commerce, which at present labors under a thousand disadvantages.

But I shall say little on this or any political subject relating to Canada, for a reason which, whilst I am in this colony, it would look like flattery to give: let it suffice to say, that, humanly speaking, it is impossible that the inhabitants of this province should be otherwise than happy. I have the honor to be,
My Lord, &c.
William Fermor.

Historical Interpretations

3 Modified version of Donald Fyson, "The Conquered and the Conqueror: The Mutual Adaptation of the *Canadiens* and the British in Quebec, 1759–1775," in *Revisiting 1759: The Conquest of Canada in Historical Perspective* (Toronto: University of Toronto Press, 2012), 190–217. © University of Toronto Press, 2012. Reprinted with permission of the publisher.

In much of the historiography of post-Conquest Quebec, the period from 1759 to 1775 is often presented as an unfortunate interlude leading up to the Quebec Act. The 1759–64 military regime, for example, while often mentioned, has been the subject of relatively little detailed study and no satisfactory overview, while the first decade of civil rule is presented largely as a time of confusion and conflict, only resolved by the Act itself and the subsequent recasting of politics and governance in the colony. This reading re-evaluates those critical years from the perspective of the European settlers in the new colony of Quebec, both Canadien and British. By

focusing on everyday practices and structures rather than on political discourse, it highlights the practical and utilitarian nature of the mutual adaptation that characterized the newly conquered society. [. . .]

This reading is thus built around the notion of mutual adaptation, as it allows for a richer, more nuanced view of the process by which the Canadien and British populations reacted to and attempted to shape the new realities that followed the military conquest of 1759–60 and the diplomatic cession of 1763. Mutual adaptation fundamentally implies compromise, which implies complexity. It thus inevitably undermines the

simplistic conflict perspective that has dominated much of the long-popular miserabilist
take on the Conquest that comes out of contemporary nationalist politics.[1] But mutual
adaptation should also not be taken to imply the sort of happy fusion of the races that
one finds in the jovialist take of much older
mainstream historiography, both francophone and anglophone, epitomized by works
such as Abbé Maheux's *Ton histoire est une
épopée*,[2] and which in turn drew on contemporary anti-nationalist or avowedly federalist
political leanings. For, to paraphrase the old
Chicago school schema proposed by Robert
Park (without adopting its laissez-faire and
sometimes uncritical perspective), the mutual
adaptation of different groups can include
varying degrees of conflict, co-operation, accommodation, and assimilation.

A further binary opposition that has often hindered analysis of the post-Conquest
period is the simplistic division between
French and English (or British) that un-
derlies much analysis. Of course, there
were two "national" European groups in
Quebec following the Conquest, along with the
various Native groups, as well as two main
European languages and two main strains
of Christianity, so the distinction is not entirely unwarranted (even if the "English" or
"British" were in fact a much more complex
group, composed of people born in England,
Scotland, Ireland, the American colonies, and
so on). Even if one accepts the distinction,
these two groups were not in any way unified,
with the Canadiens divided between elites
(themselves fragmented into overlapping seigneurial, clerical, and commercial groups)
and ordinary inhabitants (both urban and
rural), while the British colonists were frac-
tured between colonial administrators (supported by the army) and civilians, the latter
in turn composed not only of merchants, as
is often erroneously asserted, but also a wide
range of others.[3] It is perhaps not necessary
to adopt a sociological approach and apply a
fine analysis of the different fragments of the

post-Conquest population. But in considering
mutual adaptation following the Conquest,
one must at the least take into account three
main collective actors—the colonial administration (including the military), the Canadien
civilian population, and the British civilian
population—while being aware of the further
divisions within these groups. It is the failure
to address all of these groups adequately, and
especially the Canadiens, that led political
historians such as A.L. Burt, Hilda Neatby,
or, more recently, Philip Lawson to pay little
attention to mutual adaptation: their overwhelming focus on British political actors in
the immediate post-Conquest period too often led them to present relatively simplistic
views of the Canadiens as essentially conservative and passive actors.[4]

The period from the fall of Quebec in 1759
to the coming into force of the Quebec
Act in 1775 is an excellent laboratory for
studying the possibilities and limits of mutual adaptation between people of two formerly antagonistic national groups. It was,
after all, a time when the effects of the war
were still being felt directly, when anti-
Catholic provisions such as the Test Acts
were theoretically in force, when—again in
theory at least—English public and private
law had entirely replaced French, and when
the British (both colonial administrators
and civilians) generally thought they could
easily anglicize (or perhaps more accurately,
"Briticize") the Canadiens. But this was only
the theory. This reading, drawing on several
of my earlier studies as well as new research,
focuses briefly on three areas in which mutual adaptation became a necessity for both
the Canadien and British population of
the colony: the Catholic question, political
praxis, and the law.

One of the thorniest issues in the immediate post-Conquest period was that of the
civil rights of Catholics. The apparent exclusion of Catholics from public life following
the Conquest is one of the most-often publicly
cited "facts" regarding the period, proof of the

ill designs of the Conqueror. And indeed, the limited toleration of Catholicism in Quebec agreed to in the 1763 Treaty of Paris and the theoretical imposition of English penal laws, such as the Test Acts and their accompanying oaths and declarations (most notably the Oath of Supremacy and the Declaration against Transubstantiation, both objectionable to Catholics), marked a radical policy shift from the military regime. Following the terms of capitulation of both Quebec City in 1759 and Montreal in 1760, there was apparent broad toleration of Catholicism. To the extent that military government allowed it, Catholics were also appointed to significant positions of trust, with prominent Canadien merchants in Montreal; for example, serving as judges in the town's principal civil court, that of the militia captains, while Canadien militia captains elsewhere took on similar roles.[5] With the beginning of civil government, the rules of the Protestant supremacy applied, and continued to apply through to the emancipatory Quebec Act. Or did they?

The ideological debates and political discussions within the British community and the imperial government regarding the Catholic question have been fairly well explored by scholars, as have the legal arguments as to whether the penal laws applied to a newly conquered colony—the opinion of British law officers from 1765 was that they did not.[6] What has been less well explored is the actual application of the anti-Catholic provisions explicit and implicit in the transfer of sovereignty in 1763. One problem stems from a general misunderstanding of the scope and nature of the penal laws and their application to Quebec. The legal situation was fuzzy at best. For example, if the penal acts formed part of the public law of Britain applicable to the colony, as colonial administrators in Quebec initially assumed and were more or less told by their superiors in London,[7] they should have come into force immediately on Quebec's becoming a British colony, in February 1763, following the signing of the Treaty of Paris.

These laws at the very least would have disabled Catholics from acting as judges and holding other remunerated government positions, following the provisions of the original Act of Supremacy of 1559. And yet, in the colony, nothing changed through to the establishment of civil government in August 1764, 18 months later. For example, Canadiens continued to act as judges in the militia courts, in apparent direct contradiction of the Act of Supremacy. Already, then, the strict application of the penal acts was dubious.

There were other misapprehensions concerning penal laws in the colony as well. Take the often-cited Quebec grand jury presentment of October 1764. In it, the British grand jurors objected to the presence of Catholic jurors as "an open Violation of our most sacred Laws and Libertys, and tending to the utter subversion of the protestant Religion and his Majesty's power authority, right, and possession of the province to which we belong." They supported this by citing both the Treaty of Paris and British law:

> By the Definitive Treaty the Roman Religion was only tolerated in the province of Quebec so far as the Laws of Great Britain admit, it was and is enacted by the 3[d] Jam[s] 1st Chap[r] 5th Section 8th no papist or popish Recusant Convict, shall practice "the Common Law, as a Councellor, Clerk, Attorney, or Sollicitor nor shall practice the Civil Law, as Advocate or proctor, nor practice physick, nor be an apothecary, nor shall be a judge, Minister, Clerk or Steward of or in any Court, nor shall be Register or Town Clerk or other' Minister or Officer in any Court . . . but be utterly disabled for the same."[8]

Reading this, one might conclude, as many have done, that, under British law, Catholics were indeed excluded from juries and essentially from all administrative positions. The problem is that the grand jury or, rather, the author of the presentment appears deliberately to have misrepresented the law. The act in question referred only to "popish recusant convicts," not to papists in general as the wording of the presentment suggested. Hence, as long as Catholics were not convicted of being popish recusants, there was no bar, under this act at least, to their serving as jurors or in any of the other positions noted.[9] Further confusion can be found in the precise terms of the 1763 commissions and instructions to Murray as governor. These explicitly imposed the full range of anti-Catholic oaths and declarations only on members of the Council, on any future Assembly, and, arguably, on judges, justices of the peace, sheriffs, "and other necessary Officers and ministers" for the administration of justice.[10]

The legal situation was thus in no way clear-cut, and this left much room for manoeuvre by colonial administrators such as Murray and Carleton in adapting themselves to the local situation. And in this respect, they had much adapting to do. In essence, it was impossible for the colonial administration to draw its personnel only from among the colony's Protestant adult males, who numbered perhaps 200 at the end of the military regime, excluding the army, and perhaps 750 in 1775.[11] From a purely practical perspective, Murray and Carleton had to look elsewhere to compose the state apparatus necessary for running a colony of perhaps 65 000 to 70 000 European inhabitants at the beginning and 90 000 at the end of the period under consideration here. And the only possible pool was the Canadien population.

As a result, colonial administrators seem to have interpreted the restrictive provisions in as narrow a sense as possible, and the imposition of the various provisions of the penal laws appears to have been limited essentially to those instances specifically laid out in the commissions and instructions. [. . .]

In practice, there was no general bar to Catholics in the public service. In the legal system, Murray apparently believed that his commission required him to appoint only Protestants as justices of the peace, as did influential members of his council,[12] but he did not apply the same criteria to court clerks, bailiffs, and the like, even though a strict reading of his commission would have required that as well. Thus, Catholics were excluded only from the magistracy; all other positions, such as court clerks and court bailiffs, along with judicial auxiliaries such as notaries and lawyers, were not subject to the penal act exclusions. As a result, in the legal system, which was the one significant part of the colonial administration specifically targeted by the instructions, while the judges and magistrates were all Protestants (though not all British), the clerkships of the Common Pleas, the most active of the two higher courts, initially were split between British and French clerks, and the bailiffs attached to these courts were about three-quarters Canadien. Further, no limits were placed on Catholics acting as lawyers or notaries, such that about 50 per cent of the former and 90 per cent of the latter were Canadiens in the period under question. In sum, the penal laws were no bar to the creation of a legal system that, rather than being entirely dominated by Protestants, was instead a hybrid.[13] This flexibility was carried to the point of directly contradicting the explicit provisions of the governors' commissions: in the late 1760s, Governor Carleton appears to have appointed at least two Catholic Canadiens, Guillaume Guillimin in Quebec City and Louis-Joseph Godefroy de Tonnancour in Trois-Rivières, to act as judges of the Prerogative Court, essentially an administrative instance for the settling of inheritances, guardianships, and the like.[14]

Why this recourse to Catholics? Partly it was a question of numbers. But partly, as well, it was the need for colonial administrators to rely on local knowledge. Guillimin and Godefroy de Tonnancour had both held high judicial appointment in New France, the first as a judge and the second as king's attorney. The first two Canadien clerks of the Common Pleas, Jean-Claude Panet in Quebec City and Pierre-Méru Panet in Montreal, had also been legal professionals under the French regime; equally important, both had been the clerks of the equivalent military regime courts in their respective districts and thus could ensure judicial continuity. A significant number of the Canadien bailiffs employed by the courts in the 1760s, especially in Quebec City, had been bailiffs, under the French regime. And as for the notaries and the lawyers, since there was considerable continuity in the law as actually practised, at least on the civil side, it was natural that many of those who had practised before the Conquest, especially among the notaries, and had continued to practise under the military regime simply continued after the new system was set up in 1764. In many senses, they had far less adapting to do than the colonial administrators and new British subjects.

Nor were Catholics ever systematically excluded from juries. Under the 1764 ordinance setting up the courts, they could be jurors in the superior Court of King's Bench. There was confusion as to their capacity to act as jurors in the other courts (the Common Pleas and the Courts of Quarter Sessions of the Peace), until a July 1766 ordinance declared them able to act. However, the ordinance was clearly only declaratory of a de facto situation, since Canadiens had been acting as jurors since the very beginning of the operation of the civil courts. The 1764 Quebec Quarter Sessions grand jury presentment, given above, is one indication; but so too is the first jury listed in full in the Montreal Quarter Sessions register, in April 1765, which consisted of six British and six Canadien jurors. Similarly, the first jury listed in Quebec City's Common Pleas register, in January 1766, well before the ordinance, was composed of ten Canadiens and one British juror, along with one ambiguous case.

Beyond the legal system, Catholics also occupied many other positions in the colonial administration. Catholics were generally absent from the ranks of those with salaried and highly lucrative positions. But this was not a question of Catholic exclusion, but rather of metropolitan domination, much as under the French regime. Even then, at least two lucrative positions, those of the chief road inspectors, or *grand voyers*, were filled by Canadiens, with salaries of £100 each. The rationale given by the Council for these posts, which were in direct contradiction of the provisions of the Act of Supremacy, are instructive. The appointments were described as being "the more necessary as the persons presently employed in that office are men who can be trusted to furnish government with Intelligence from the distant parts of the province; all the Protestants and people of property and Understanding residing in the great Towns;" more specifically, "they will be able to give from time to time an Account to the government of the State and Situation of the Canadian Inhabitants."[15] In other words, British colonial administrators needed the local knowledge that the *grand voyers* could provide. The Canadien presence among the lower ranks of the colony's civil employees thus derived from mutual adaptation and mutual interest, rather than the altruism that has been postulated by some apologists of the British colonial administration.[16] But the apparent ready integration of Catholics into a supposedly Protestant and anti-Catholic state suggests a great deal of religious pragmatism on both sides [. . .]. Overall, the religious issue was not at all omnipresent in the daily administration of the colony whatever its place in transatlantic discourse and debate. And Canadiens were happy to accept the positions open to them, not the least because most were lucrative to a greater or lesser degree, or at the very least were a source of power.

A similar examination of everyday practices can also refresh our understanding of the nature of politics in the colony. Generally, political analysis of the period following the Conquest focuses on high politics, such as the debates around the calling of an assembly, with a tripartite struggle between British colonial administrators, British merchants, and, to a lesser extent, Canadiens. There is no denying that this was a highly conflictual period, with the many shifting groups in the new colony jockeying for position. But broadening our view beyond high politics reveals a series of intertwined adaptive processes: Canadiens adapting to new British political institutions, British institutions being adapted to Canadien practices, and the British population adapting to Canadien institutions.

At a macro level, authoritarian political structures were retained both under the military regime and under civil government, as an adaptation of political and administrative structures inherited from New France. Under the military regime, Murray presided over a paternalistic, intrusive, and controlling government, much as under the French regime. [. . .] And while this sort of moralistic paternalism largely disappeared under civil government, authoritarianism remained. In this context, it was the British civilian population that appears to have had the greatest difficulty adapting to this situation, especially that part of it used to the relative political liberty of the American colonies. Conflicts between British merchants and colonial administrators got the better of Murray, among others, and led to many of the merchants supporting the revolutionaries during the invasion of 1775–6.

But the continuing use of French structures ran deeper than the flavour of authoritarianism. On a symbolic level, for example, post-Conquest colonial administrators, both military and civilian, continued to occupy French-regime loci of power such as the Château St-Louis, the Jesuit college, or the Recollet church in Quebec City, drawing on symbolic capital built up by their French predecessors—all very familiar to the colony's Canadien inhabitants, but potentially disconcerting to British colonists who, for example,

might find themselves being judged in former Catholic religious buildings.[17] As well, the British colonial administration based its spatial conception of the colony's territory essentially on the Catholic parish. Already under the military regime, the Catholic parish was firmly established as the territorial referent used by governors.[18] And despite the governors' instructions explicitly directing them to have the colony "accurately surveyed, and divided into Townships, Districts, Precincts or Parishes" and also divided into counties,[19] the Catholic parish remained the colony's fundamental administrative structure under civil administration, at least outside the towns. This was ironic for an imperial state based on Protestant supremacy, as the Catholic parish was defined essentially by the Catholic Church, without significant intervention by the colonial administration. Once again, the British colonial administration adapted itself to the structures already in place, rather than creating its own.

Consider as well the language of everyday administration. Despite the very common misconception, scholarly as well as popular, that French lost all status following the Conquest, it remained as much the language of the state in Quebec as English, at least at the everyday level experienced by the colony's population. Under the military regime, for example, the linguistic adaptations were not of the Conquered to the Conqueror, but the opposite: orders and ordinances were published in French, records such as those of the military courts or the order books of the governors were kept in French by French-language clerks and secretaries, and in general it was the British who talked to the French in their own language, rather than, vice versa. This stemmed not from any particular charitable desire to do justice to the king's new subjects, but from the simple necessity of communicating with these subjects and the more basic fact that far more British knew French than the Canadiens knew English, at least among the elites.

The military regime was of course a particular time, before the British could be sure they were going to retain the colony and while the British population was very small. And yet, de facto bilingualism continued after the establishment of civil government in 1764. Legislation, proclamations, and other official documents were published in both English and French in the *Quebec Gazette* and in handbills and broadsides, giving a continued boost to official translation.[20] In the legal system, while surviving criminal court records are mainly in English, the main civil court, the Common Pleas, kept dual French and English registers and produced documents such as summons and the like in both English and French. And notarial records, the basis for most landed property transactions in the colony, remained almost entirely in French. In sum, French continued to be very much a language of officialdom, regardless of its official status, and the British population simply had to adapt.

The examination of the phenomenon of interpreters, fundamental to mutual adaptation, adds to this impression. While interpretation has yet to be studied in any detail in the immediate post-Conquest period, it seems that both British and Canadiens acted in this capacity: in a small sample of 24 interpreters mentioned in the *Parchemin* database of notarial records between 1760 and 1769, 13 were apparently francophones and 11 anglophones. At the same time, in all cases where this is explicitly mentioned in notarial records, the interpreter was acting for the anglophone rather than the francophone party, indicating British linguistic adaptation rather than vice versa.

Another example of mutual adaptation, in the sphere of very local politics, was the institution of parish bailiffs.[21] Under the military regime, the British military governors had maintained the pre-existing French system of militia officers, though shorn of their military role so as to leave only their administrative functions. Thus, the main representatives of

the military state in the countryside were the Canadien militia captains, to whom governors such as Murray, Gage, and Haldimand directed their orders for firewood or hay provisioning, impressment of labour, arrest of deserters, and the like.[22] In this respect, the military regime did not depart in any significant fashion from the French regime that preceded it. Under the civil government put in place in the colony from 1764, however, the militia was abolished, and colonial administrators were faced with the necessity of establishing some sort of structure to allow them to maintain a degree of administrative presence and control in the countryside. This was not possible through the normal English mechanism of justices of the peace, as magistrates had to be Protestants and there were few Protestants established outside the two main towns. The solution was to adapt another English structure, the parish constable, although renaming them as "bailiffs," or *baillis* in French. Thus, under the 1764 ordinance setting up the courts, each parish in the colony was to have a bailiff and two sub-bailiffs, with a variety of administrative and judicial duties, notably with regard to road maintenance and the execution of court orders. On the whole, they were to serve as replacements of the militia captains under the military regime, though with more limited functions; at the same time, they represented the English model of decentralized local governance.

The importance of the bailiffs for the political life of the Canadien population after the Conquest stems from the fact that, under the terms of the ordinance, these local officials were to be elected annually by an assembly of the parish householders, at least outside the main towns (where the bailiffs were generally appointed by the resident justices of the peace). The assembly elected six candidates and sent the list to Quebec, where the colonial administration selected three—in practice, almost always the first three on the list, thus reproducing the parish assembly's choice. Here we thus have a form of local "democracy" (in the limited eighteenth-century sense of the word) and interplay between the colonial administration and the population that went directly against the more centralizing spirit of the French regime. And yet, the Canadien population adapted very well to this newly opened political field. The positions, especially those of head bailiff, were often sought after, as they brought power and prestige—bailiffs, for example, had a special pew in the parish church, much like the militia captains before them. And there were contested elections, conflicts between different elite factions, interventions by seigneurs and clergy, and petitions and counterpetitions sent in to the central administration—in short, all the characteristics of developed electoral politics, but played out on such a local level that it has entirely escaped the attention of historians.

In this instance, the Canadiens adapted themselves very well to this new British institution, but in some respects that institution was also adapted to them. The use of parish assemblies, for example, tapped into local traditions of participatory "democracy" already in place under the French regime. In some parishes at least, parishioners met to elect church wardens or to make other decisions regarding parish affairs; the French regime *grand voyers* regularly assembled parish inhabitants to make decisions regarding road layout and repairs, with matters sometimes put to a vote; and under the French civil law system, issues such as the election of trustees for minor children were decided by a family assembly composed of relatives and friends. The new British system of elected local officials no doubt functioned partly because of these pre-existing traditions, which also continued after the Conquest. Similarly, after the system of parish bailiffs was in theory abolished with the coming into force of the Quebec Act in 1775, the launching of the American invasion, and the restoration of the militia by Carleton, the Americans in some of the occupied parishes instituted a system of

local elections for militia captains, to replace those appointed by the British governor. They, like a number of historians, might have thought they were introducing the Canadiens to local democracy for the first time and were thus instrumental in their political education.[23] But they were wrong: parish elections already had been going on for a decade, and local democracy for much longer.

[. . .]

A final example of mutual adaptation concerns the relationship of the Canadien and British populations to the law, and to each other through the law. The legal situation following the Conquest was complicated. The military regime saw the de facto preservation of French civil law, which continued to be applied in the military courts, while courts martial and military law were used for more serious criminal offences. The Proclamation of 1763 was taken by some to have swept away all of French law and replaced it with English law, while others supposed this change to have concerned only public law, including criminal law. Finally, the 1764 ordinance that set up a new court system, modelled on English precedents, allowed partial continuation of French law and said nothing of important aspects of the legal system such as notaries, who continued as before.[24] In this ever-shifting environment, mutual adaptation was a fundamental necessity, since right from the Conquest the colony experienced a mix of both French and British laws, legal structures, and legal practices. It thus involved both the adaptation of the Canadien population to English law—notably English criminal and public law—and to British-style courts, and the adaptation of the British population to French civil law and practice.

[. . .] With regard to the civil law, the Canadiens actually had relatively little adapting to do since, despite the apparent replacement of French civil by English common law, the former remained largely in effect throughout the period. Under the military regime, civil and minor criminal cases in Montreal and Trois-Rivières were judged by the merchants who were militia captains, while in Quebec City the court was composed of British military officers.[25] The courts in the two main towns, however, applied French civil law, aided by their clerks, the Panets.[26] The work of the courts was also taken up almost entirely by cases brought by Canadiens. Even before the Quebec City court, run by British military officers, virtually every case concerned Canadiens, and in 90 per cent of them they were the only parties.[27] As Murray remarked in one of his orders, "We are pained to see that for trifles the *habitants* pursue one another in cases that make them lose more time in their labours than the subject of the case."[28]

The shift to civil government produced no particular change in this situation: the vast majority of plaintiffs and defendants before the courts continued to be Canadien. Even in the criminal courts, if we look at the level of the justices of the peace where most cases were heard, Canadiens made up about two-thirds of plaintiffs in the Montreal Quarter Sessions between 1765 and 1773, and one-half in the Quebec City court; furthermore, most of the cases in which they were involved concerned only other Canadiens. British plaintiffs were certainly overrepresented, given that they made up only a tiny proportion of the population, but there was no Canadien boycott. As for the civil courts, Canadiens were involved in perhaps 90 per cent of the cases in the superior sessions of the Common Pleas in Montreal and 80 per cent in Quebec City; and in 70 per cent of the Montreal cases and 60 per cent of those in Quebec City, all parties were Canadien. Given that Canadiens appear to have been even more dominant in the inferior terms of the court,[29] the notion of a boycott is not at all tenable.

Take also, the example of juries, a new feature introduced under British rule. Canadiens are often portrayed as having mistrusted this new structure: elites because it was too democratic and ordinary Canadiens because it took too much time. But there is no evidence of anything but a rapid adaptation to the jury system. On the criminal side, Canadiens were as assiduous in acting as jurors as their British counterparts, and perhaps more so.[30] And in civil cases, where jury use was optional, thus reflecting the willingness of at least one party to have recourse to it, Canadiens were regularly involved in jury cases, and not only at the behest of British opponents. Of a sample of 53 jury cases in the Quebec City Common Pleas records between 1764 and 1775, 25 apparently concerned only British parties, 15 only Canadien parties, and 13 were mixed—hardly evidence of Canadien reticence to have recourse to juries, even though British parties were evidently far more likely than Canadiens to submit their differences to juries.

All in all, it is clear that Canadiens adapted to the new judicial realities that followed the Conquest, though whether or not this was an easy process remains to be studied in depth, at least for the civil courts. But what of the British population? The attitudes of the new British colonists toward the law and the courts have been examined in depth, and especially the political discourse of that part of the British population that clamoured for the full and exclusive introduction of English civil law.[31] In terms of the criminal law, there was, of course, little adaptation to make, since it largely followed British forms, But the civil law was a different story, and shows to some extent both the willingness of the British population to adapt and the limits of that adaptation.

Take, for example, British attitudes toward the notarial system, which was relatively alien to them, given the usual English system of private deeds and registration. Using the *Parchemin* database, which contains descriptions of all extant notarial acts in Quebec up to the 1780s, I have constructed a sample of 273 notarial acts apparently involving the new post-Conquest British population under the military regime.[32] Despite the preliminary nature of the sample, it allows for some observations. First, during the initial occupation of Quebec City, while the military fate of the colony was not yet decided, the new British colonists made no use of the notarial system, even though it manifestly continued to operate. Once the final capitulation of Montreal was signed in September 1760, however, it took very little time for British colonists to begin to interact with the Canadien population via the notarial system. The first notarial document described in the database that involved a British party was the lease of a house in Montreal by the widow of a Canadien merchant to Edward Best, an English merchant, on 18 September, only 10 days after the capitulation of the city. This was followed by a number of others soon afterward. Based on a systematic sample of the notarial acts in the database, one can estimate that, between 1761 and 1764, there were in all something over 700 acts involving British parties.[33] Given a British adult male civilian population of a couple of hundred, that would have meant three or four notarial acts each, on average, suggesting that it is far too simple to talk of British dislike and avoidance of this fundamental aspect of French civil law.

At the same time, there is every indication that, for the British, the notarial system served almost exclusively as an interface with the Canadiens, since only seven among the 273 identified acts involved agreements exclusively between British parties. The situation was similar for the military regime courts, where British parties were involved in about 10 per cent of the 4000 or so cases in the Quebec City court, but almost all of these cases involved Canadiens as well. [. . .] Nevertheless, right from the beginning, British colonists in no way systematically avoided either the French notarial system or military courts that applied French law in French; rather, they adapted themselves

to French practices while carrying out legal interactions among themselves through other means, such as private deeds.

As for the period of civil government, though much remains to be examined, an impressionistic survey suggests that, even when English law was imposed in the colony and a few anglophone notaries began practising according to English forms, British parties still did not desert the French notarial system. The same is true of British recourse to the Court of Common Pleas, which at least in part applied French law and forms, notably in cases involving Canadiens.[34] Had the British been entirely averse to adapting to French civil law, they might have been tempted to direct all of their cases to the King's Bench, which apparently applied English law exclusively, or perhaps to the justices of the peace (whose application of civil law has yet to be studied). And yet, this does not seem to have been the case. Again using the samples of Common Pleas cases, British parties were involved in 30 per cent of cases in Montreal and 40 per cent in Quebec City, they were about as likely to be plaintiffs as defendants, and between 10 per cent and 20 per cent of all cases involved British parties only. While many of these cases were decided according to basic rules of equity that conformed to English practice, especially those that concerned only British parties, other cases involved British suitors in complex arguments around French civil law. In some, it was the British parties who appealed to French law. Evidently, the relationship of British colonists with French civil law was more complex than simple avoidance.

All of the above suggests once again a simple conclusion: the process of mutual adaptation of the Canadien and British populations of Quebec in the immediate post-Conquest period, between 1759 and 1775, was far more complex than indicated by simplistic miserabilist and jovialist interpretations, and involved more than overriding ethnic conflict or the harmonious fusion of races. The Canadien and British populations in general, and their elites in particular, seem to have adopted the philosophy that, on a practical level, "adaptation is the better part of valour," even while continuing their political fights to shape post-Conquest Quebec state and society to their liking. How else to explain the colonial administration's partial relaxation of the penal laws, and the Canadien population's willingness to fill the space thus provided; or the complexity of the political sphere when one extends one's vision down to the local, everyday level; or the evidently supple approach to law and justice by the two groups. Pragmatism, utilitarianism, and instrumentalization played a part that was at least as important as the ideological debates historians have so often retained.

NOTES

1. As in the work of Michel Brunet, such as *Les Canadiens après la Conquête 1759–1775: de la révolution canadienne a la révolution américaine* (Montreal: Fides, 1969); or that of Gilles Bourque, notably *Question nationale et classes sociales au Québec, 1760–1840* (Montreal: Parti Pris, 1970).

2. Arthur Maheux, *Ton histoire est une épopée*, vol. 1, *Nos débuts sous le régime anglais* (Quebec: Charrier & Dugal, 1941).

3. On the splits within the British population, see notably A.L. Burt, *The Old Province of Quebec*, vol. 1 (Toronto: McClelland & Stewart, 1968). On the diversity of the British civilian population, see, for example, Honorius Provost, *Les premiers anglo-canadiens à Québec: essai de recensement, 1759–1775* (Quebec: IQRC, 1984).

4. Burt, *Old Province of Quebec*; Hilda Neatby, *Quebec: The Revolutionary Age, 1760–1791* (Toronto: McClelland and Stewart, 1966), 30–124 passim; and Philip Lawson, *The Imperial Challenge: Quebec and Britain in the Age of the American Revolution* (Montreal and Kingston: McGill-Queen's University Press, 1989).

5. José Igartua, "The Merchants and Négociants of Montréal, 1750–1775: A Study in Socio-Economic History" (PhD thesis, Michigan State University, 1974), 174–99; and Marcel Trudel, *Histoire de la Nouvelle-France X: le régime militaire* (Montreal: Fides, 1999), 155–84, are the only detailed examinations of the operation of these courts.

6. See notably Burt, *Old Province of Quebec*, vol. 1, 66–159 passim; Vincent T. Harlow, *The Founding of the Second British Empire,* 1763–1793 (London: Longmans, 1952–64), 664–714 passim; Neatby, *Québec,* 30–124 passim; Lawson, *Imperial Challenge,* 43–52, 96–103; and Peter M. Doll, *Revolution, Religion, and National Identity: Imperial Anglicanism in British North America, 1745–1795* (Madison, WI: Fairleigh Dickinson University Press and Associated University Presses, 2000).

7. As in Egremont to Murray, 13 August 1763, in *Documents Relating to the Constitutional History of Canada, 1759–1791*, 2nd edn, Adam Shortt and Arthur G. Doughty, eds (Ottawa: Historical Documents Publication Board, 1921), 169.

8. *Documents Relating to the Constitutional History of Canada* (hereafter cited as DRCHC), 214–15.

9. This was pointed out in the *Report to the Lords of the Committee for Plantation Affairs* of 2 September 1765, in DRCHC, 241–2.

10. DRCHC, 173–7 (Commission), 182–3 (Instructions).

11. In 1775, according to an analysis of the names presented in Provost, *Premiers anglo-canadiens à Québec,* there were about 325 civilian adult male anglophones in Quebec City; allowing for a similar number in Montreal and perhaps a hundred elsewhere, that would give perhaps 750 altogether.

12. Murray to Halifax, 15 October 1764, DRCHC, 210; Adam Mabane to Council, LAC, R10808-5-1, 6 February 1766.

13. On these issues, see Donald Fyson, *Magistrates, Police, and People: Everyday Criminal Justice in Quebec and Lower Canada, 1764–1837* (Toronto: University of Toronto Press, 2006), chaps. 1–4.

14. There is no official record of their appointment, but they are identified as judges of the prerogative court in various sources, including notarial records. On Guillimin's activity, see Jean-Philippe Garneau, "Droit, famille et pratique successorale: les usages du droit d'une communauté rurale au XVIII siècle canadien" (PhD thesis, Université du Québec à Montréal, 2003), 245–8.

15. LAC, R10808-5-1, 27 November 1765 and 2 December 1765.

16. Maheux, *Ton histoire est une épopée,* 52–80.

17. See Fyson, *Magistrates, Police, and People,* 313–19.

18. See, for example, "Ordonnances, ordres, reglemens et proclamations durant le gouvernement militaire en Canada, du 28e oct. 1760 au 28e juillet 1764," Université de Montréal, Collection Melzack (hereafter cited as Murray Melzack), 11 December 1762; available online at http://calypso.bib.umontreal.ca/cdm4/index_murray.php?CISOROOT=/murray.

19. *DRCHC,* 192, 194, 311, 313.

20. Patricia Dumas, "La naissance de la traduction officielle au Canada et son impact politique et culturel sous le gouvernement militaire et civil du général James Murray, Québec (septembre 1759 à juin 1766)" (MA thesis, York University, 2004).

21. This is explored in Fyson, "Paroisse et l'administration étatique sous le Régime britannique (1764–1840)," in *Atlas historique du Québec: La paroisse,* Serge Courville and Normand Séguin, eds (Ste-Foy, QC: Presses de l'Université Laval, 2001), 25–37; idem, *Magistrates, Police, and People,* 141–2; and idem, "Canadiens and British Institutions of Local Governance in Quebec, from the Conquest to the Rebellions," in *Transatlantic Subjects: Ideas, Institutions and Social Experience in Post-Revolutionary British North America,* Nancy Christie, ed. (Montreal and Kingston: McGill-Queen's University Press, 2008), 58–66.

22. For a summary overview of their role, see Trudel, *Régime militaire,* 85–116.

23. Pierre Tousignant, "La genèse et l'avènement de la Constitution de 1791" (PhD thesis, Université de Montréal, 1971), 19, citing Gustave Lancôt and Marcel Trudel.

24. For useful overviews, see Michel Morin, "Les changements de régimes juridiques consécutifs à la Conquête de 1760," *Revue du Barreau* 57, 3 (1997): 689–98; and John A. Dickinson, "L'administration chaotique de la justice après la Conquête: discours ou réalité?" in *Canada: Le rotte della libertà,* Giovanni Dotoli, ed. (Fasano, Italy: Schena, 2005), 117–27.

25. For an overview of the Court structure, see Trudel, *Régime militaire,* 155–84.

26. On the law applied in the Montreal courts, see Igartua, "Merchants and Négociants of Montréal," 174–99, which is, as far as I know, the only detailed examination of the actual operation of the courts.

27. From an analysis of an index of parties appearing before the Quebec Military Council, Bibliothèque et archives nationales du Québec (hereafter cited as BANQ), Instrument de recherche 303016, kindly supplied to me in electronic form by Rénald Lessard.

28. "Nous avons vu avec peine que pour des bagatelles les habitants se suscitent Les uns les autres des procès qui leur font perdre plus de temps dans leurs travaus, que l'objet devant"; Murray Melzack, 14 October 1762.

29. The figures for the superior sessions are based on an analysis of a sample of the case descriptions of Superior Court dossiers: for Montreal, as presented in the *Thémis* 3 database by Archiv-histo, and for Quebec, as in BANQ's *Pistard* database, kindly provided to me by Rénald Lessard. The figures for the inferior sessions are based on a database concerning the Montreal court for 1771, kindly supplied to me by Jean-Philippe Garneau. These are evidently very preliminary observations.

30. Of 102 trial jurors identified in the Montreal Quarter Sessions register between 1765 and 1769, 58 were apparently *Canadiens.*

31. See, for example, Evelyn Kolish, *Nationalismes et conflits de droits: le débat du droit privé au Québec, 1760–1840* (LaSalle, QC: Hurtubise HMH, 1994), 29–43.

32. The sample was constructed based on examining all descriptions in the database from the fall of Quebec (September 1759) to the end of 1760; all acts passed the 15th day of the month for the period 1761–4; all descriptions that explicitly mentioned that one of the parties was English, Irish, Scottish, etc.; all acts whose descriptions mentioned an interpreter; and a search for the names William, John, James,

Edward, and Peter, as well as names beginning with Mc.

33. Based on a systematic sample of all acts passed on the 15th day of the month for the period 1761–4; given the relatively small sample size

(a little under 4 per cent of all acts), this figure should be treated with caution.

34. S. Morley Scott, "Chapters in the History of the Law of Quebec, 1764–1775" (PhD thesis, University of Michigan, 1933).

4 John E. Crowley, "'Taken on the Spot': The Visual Appropriation of New France for the Global British Landscape," *Canadian Historical Review* 86, 1 (2005): 1–28. Reprinted with permission from University of Toronto Press (www.utpjournals.com).

During the British invasion, occupation, and colonization of New France, artists appropriated the conquests visually with topographic renderings of the empire's new landscapes. Officers in the invasion forces made drawings of landmarks along the St Lawrence, linking military events with striking physical features. During the occupation they portrayed the conquered province's capital as an exotic urban landscape. After the Treaty of Paris, military surveyors sought out the province's scenic attractions as they simultaneously mapped new British domains. Artistically inclined imperial agents represented the new British province as a place of natural beauty with a picturesque indigenous culture. They sent a visual message—to the king, ministers and aristocrats, parliamentary politicians, fellow officers and officials, their families, the viewing public at exhibitions—about a landscape whose scenic attractions and rustic tranquillity mitigated its appropriation by conquest.

The artists who created this imperial landscape claimed to have drawn their scenes first-hand—"taken on the spot"—in order to give them visual authenticity. These drawings conformed with a developing topographical imperative that required verisimilitude from representations of specific places of scenic interest.[1] Such topographic art cannot be taken for granted as artistically natural just because it was naturalistic. As Victoria Dickenson has shown, throughout the early modern period of colonization European artists lavishly represented the natural world of North America, but their empirical naturalism neglected landscapes and focused on studies of natural history. Until the arrival of topographic landscape artists with British forces in the 1750s, European representations of North American landscapes usually depended on artists' imaginations, with deliberately schematic and symbolic results.[2]

This paper analyzes post-conquest British representations of New France as part of the creation of a global British landscape, with Canada as a distinctive part. According to these representations, the sublime aspects of Canada's scenery confirmed the grandeur of the imperial project against New France, while the picturesque landscapes of towns, farms, and shorelines promised an easily governed population readily subject to British improvements. This aesthetic message is curiously harmonious with Allan Greer's summary of a revisionist historiography that considers "French Canada" as a "ceded colony" rather than a "conquered nation," "ruled by a different set of outsiders who happened to be British."[3] In Canada's early landscape art as in its historiography, the conquest becomes a hazy background to localized multicultural scenes.

[. . .]

The British landscape of conquests in North America would differ markedly from preceding French representations of imperial New France. The topographical imperative for landscape art was much stronger for British than for French artists. The indigenous inhabitants—crucial both to the French Empire's fur trade and strategic survival—predominated as subjects for artists of

New France. But French prints of Amerindians usually showed figures either as isolated studies or in schematic rather than identifiable settings. First-hand authority was less important than artistic skill and creativity, and French representations of North American peoples often set them in imaginary landscapes.[4] Few images nominally of colonial New France purported to show how its landscape actually looked. The French colonists' favourite art form, votive images, often referred miraculous events to particular places in New France, but it was the event, not the place, that required faithful representation. The often reprinted view of Niagara Falls in Louis Hennepin's *Nouvelle découverte d'un très grand pays situé dans l'Amérique entre le Nouveau Mexique, et la Mer Glaciale* (1697)

was an exception proving the rule. An anonymous engraver in Utrecht derived it from Hennepin's textual description (Figure 1), and there were no follow-up renderings by French artists on the spot.

French strengths in the visual representation of colonial landscapes were mainly cartographic and architectural. For the visual representation of colonial landscapes, French military engineers and architects applied their highly professional surveying and drafting skills to architectural plans, sections, and elevations and to town plans and models. With the exception of the models, these renderings of buildings deliberately abstracted them architecturally and isolated them from their settings. Printed representations of French colonial landscapes as they might

Figure 1 No first-hand renderings of Niagara Falls survive from the period of French rule in Quebec. Louis Hennepin, *Nouvelle découverte d'un très grand pays situé dans l'Amérique entre le Nouveau Mexique, et la Mer Glaciale* (Utrecht: Guillaume Broedelet, 1697), facing 44. Library and Archives Canada, C-004236.

actually be viewed were restricted to town views. These iconic views placed a premium on identifiably representing a town's most important buildings, and they often figured in architectural politics to secure royal favour. As landscapes, they typically presented a comprehensive, wide angle view of the respective town and invariably looked toward the commercial frontage of a port. They emphasized generic metropolitan connections, not creole colonial social life. Their authenticity was at a discount because metropolitan publishers often reissued them with a few imaginative updatings rather than go to the expense of engraving freshly taken views. In contrast to architectural drawing and cartographic surveying, topographical imperatives for landscape art were weak in New France.[5]

The topographical imperative did not preclude artistic licence. Topographic landscape artists intended their representations to be "picturesque". *Picturesque* meant literally "like a picture," and the pictures most often in mind were those of the Roman Compagna painted by three seventeenth-century artists: Claude Lorrain, Salvator Rosa, and Gaspard Poussin. They had painted idealized landscapes as settings for Roman historical and mythological scenes, with panoramic perspectives, strong contrasts of light and dark, irregular terrain, and cultural nostalgia in architecture and figures' dress. [. . .] As eighteenth-century British artists increasingly took an interest in their country's scenery, they adapted the idealizing style of the picturesque for their topographic representations. The popularity of the style encouraged the Reverend William Gilpin to make a series of tours, beginning in the 1760s, looking for picturesque scenery in the remoter parts of Britain, such as south Wales, Derbyshire, the Lake District, and Scotland. His enormously popular guidebooks located the exact spots where sensitive viewers could observe picturesque scenery.[6]

British topographic landscape art masked relations of power by privileging scenic representations over ones showing social,

economic, or political relations.[7] Humphry Repton, Britain's foremost landscape architect in the late eighteenth and early nineteenth centuries, forthrightly asserted that aesthetically motivated "appropriation" naturalized landowning and absolved it from charges of exploitation. Therefore the picturesque style also suited "the creation of imperial space" that has interested so many cultural historians over the past quarter century.[8] Empires, like nations, are works of politically imaginative representation.[9] As an "instrument of cultural power" in the politics of imperialism, landscape art "naturalizes a cultural and social construction, representing an artificial world as if it were simply given and inevitable."[10] Cultural historians now take for granted that the fine arts perform such political work: "Members of the dominant groups invariably use art as a device to explain and justify their power, to express the mystique of rulers, and to illustrate their knowledge and command of the natural world."[11] Imperial landscape art linked three crucial developments in eighteenth-century British culture and politics: 1) the creation of a British identity available to peoples throughout the British Isles and in settler colonies, 2) the imperial assertion of this identity through commercial expansion and strategic success, and 3) the commodified representation of these identities and successes to a viewing public.[12] Viewing imperial spaces in the picturesque style helped both colonists and metropolitans to maintain their identity and self-respect as civilized and civilizing Britons.[13] The picturesque style simultaneously created differences (topographically) and familiarity (aesthetically) among imperial spaces in ways that naturalized their appropriation as British rather than alien environments.[14]

Colonial landscapes claiming topographical accuracy became frequent at the same time that Britain extended its imperial interests through conquests and accessions on a global scale—in Canada, the trans-Appalachian West, India, and the Pacific. The Seven Years'

War, with its outcome for Great Britain of a global territorial empire over non-British peoples, critically changed governmental relations between the metropole and its new peripheries. The regular army stationed troops in the Indian subcontinent and the interior of North America for the first time, increased their numbers in Ireland and the West Indian slave colonies, and sent massive forces to put down the rebellion in the thirteen colonies that became the United States.[15]

In accordance with this militarization of the empire, army and naval officers produced most of the topographical art representing Britain's new imperial landscapes. Yet their artistic creations sent home a curiously anti-triumphalist message. Their aesthetically appealing representations of previously alien places helped legitimize imperial projects that were subjects of lively controversy in British politics: the eradication of the Scottish clans, the assimilation of a French-Catholic population in Quebec, the maintenance of peace between First Nations and European settlers in the trans-Appalachian West, the acquisition of additional Caribbean colonies dependent on slave labour, the regulation of a nascent empire in Bengal, the intrusion of disease-ridden naval expeditions into unspoiled Polynesia, and the penal transportation of free-born Britons to Botany Bay. Mary Louise Pratt's interpretation of "anti-conquest" themes in visual representations of Europeans' travel and natural history—"taking possession without subjugation or violence," as a bourgeois public sought to "secure their innocence in the same moment as they assert European hegemony"—reduces the paradox of such anti-triumphalist landscapes of imperial conquests.[16] They mystified colonization with an apolitical appreciation of scenery.

[. . .]

In the wake of Britain's far-flung assertions of rule and territory, artists created works of topographic landscape art informing the metropolitan viewing public of its new imperial domains. [. . .] In Canada,

British officers in the invasion forces during the Seven Years' War produced the first extensive landscape and genre art of European colonies in North America. [. . .]

Military art of the Seven Years' War spanned the aesthetic spectrum, from the sublime through the picturesque and beautiful to the grotesque. Pictures could make the mayhem of battle "awesome" and "tremendous"—terms straight out of Edmund Burke's aesthetics of the sublime. A typical battle-scene print, *Britain's Glory, or the Reduction of Cape Breton* (1758), showed mortar bombs in mid-air, ships' cannon and shore batteries blasting each other, and assault troops taking cannon fire at point-blank range—all to exhilarating rather than gruesome effect. Thomas Davies, then a young artillery lieutenant, drew a fiercely illuminated nocturnal scene of the "plundering and burning of the city of Grymross, Capital of the Neutral Settlements, on the River St. John's in the Bay of Fundy, Nova Scotia." Representations of heroism raised the military genre to the highest realm of art: moralized history. Benjamin West's *Death of General Wolfe* became the most celebrated British painting of the eighteenth century because he aesthetically elevated a glorious contemporary scene to comparison with classical models. In popular art, the symbolic conventions of Victory represented the defeated as a beautiful, distressed woman. On a medal for distinguished service in the capture of Louisbourg, a British soldier and sailor stand on either side of a globe—oriented to eastern North America—as it crushed a female personification of France.[17] The triumphalism of military art was virtually a tautology.

Yet in the context of New France—over the course of the British conquest and occupation—British officers deployed a demilitarized, anti-conquest art for a benignly civilian, picturesque representation of a defeated enemy's landscape. The creation of Quebec's scenic landscape for the British viewing public began during the British invasion of 1759. Captain Hervey Smyth, an adjutant to General James Wolfe, made drawings "on the spot" as the British expedition sailed up the St Lawrence to Quebec. The resulting series of engravings, *Six Views of the Most Remarkable Places in the Gulf and River of St Laurence* (1760), dedicated to William Pitt, Britain's strategist in the Seven Years' War, traced the campaign through a landscape at least as impressive for its scenic as its military interest. Every print juxtaposed British military force with arresting landscapes. The scene at the French settlement at Miramichi, "destroyed by Brigadier Murray detached by General Wolfe for that purpose," forthrightly showed soldiers with bayonets ready for assault, but their pathetic object was set in a vast forested valley. The tumultuous waterfall at Montmorency and the steep hills framing the valley at Cape Rouge warranted

inclusion for their sheer scenic interest, but Smyth's engravings also reported their crucial tactical importance in the siege of Quebec (Figure 2). The scene at Montmorency showed Wolfe's disappointing attack "on the French Intrenchments near Beauport, with the Grenadiers of the Army, 31 July 1759," while that of Cape Rouge portrayed how "from this place 1500 chosen troops at the break of Day fell down the River on the Ebb of Tide to the place of Landing 13 Sept. 1759." Smyth also designed a separate print elaborately showing the geography of events on that fateful day. The print centred on the defile and cliffs at Anse-au-Foulon that Wolfe's troops climbed during the critical early stage of the attack. Despite a key to 17 points of tactical importance, the print emphasized Quebec's most striking landscape features—its cliffs and broad river basin.

Figure 2 The visual record of the invasion balanced military events with picturesque landscapes. William Elliott after Hervey Smyth, *View of the Fall of Montmorency and the Attack Made by General Wolfe on the French Intrenchments near Beaufort* (London: Thomas Jeffreys, 1760). Library and Archives Canada/W.H. Coverdale collection of Canadiana Manoir Richelieu collection/C-041389.

Smyth placed the crucial battle scene to the side of the middle ground. At the climactic moment in Britain's conquest of New France, he implied, the landscape of the new imperial domain visually congratulated British military accomplishments there.[18]

This muted triumphalism carried over to the next series of British prints about Quebec, *Twelve Views of the Principal Buildings in Quebec* (1761), by Richard Short, purser aboard HMS *The Prince of Orange*. Short forthrightly showed how extensively the British bombardment had wrecked the town. To underline their reportorial quality, several of the prints stated that they depended on drawings "made on the spot" and noted where the artist stood to draw them. The series moved from square to square within the town, providing its first thorough topographical description. Only two pictures had a heavy military presence. One showed British troops being rowed toward Quebec from Point Levy. The other showed three ranks of troops drawn up before the Recollets' church—with a sunrise metaphorically bringing a new day to the town. The rest of the pictures showed British sailors, soldiers, and officers casually taking stock of the surrendered town in the company of townspeople. Numerous carts, carriages, and porters marked the unobstructed continuation of daily life, as French religious and judicial officials moved freely about the town (Figure 3). Besides a few broken statues, the interior scenes of rubble in the Jesuits' and Recollets' churches barely hinted at iconoclasm: The devotional paintings and altarpieces and altar furnishings were miraculously intact.[19]

Short's tranquil presentation of Quebec corresponded with General James Murray's post-conquest assessment of the "new subjects"

Figure 3 Short's topography of Quebec's wrecked institutions implicitly asked what would replace them. Antoine Benoist after Richard Short, *A View of the Bishop's House with the Ruins as they appear in going up the Hill from the Lower to the Upper Town* (London: Richard Short, 1761). Library and Archives Canada/W.H. Coverdale collection of Canadiana Manoir Richelieu collection/C-041514.

for Lord Egremont, secretary of state. Murray painted a picture of cross-confessional succour in the aftermath of the conquest, as female Catholic religious tended to the wounded and ailing British soldiers, while later in the winter British officers and men drew up a subscription to relieve the starving inhabitants. As people from each nation gained trust in the others, Murray implied, a liberation had succeeded a conquest: "Such uncommon generosity towards the conquered . . . convinced these poor deluded people how grossly they had been imposed upon . . . the daily instances of lenity, the impartial justice which had been administered, so far beyond what they had formerly experienced, have so altered their opinion with regard to us . . . that, far from having the least design to emigrate into any other of the French colonies, their greatest dread is lest they should meet with the fate of the Acadians and be torn from their native country."[20] In emphasizing the beauty of newly acquired domains and the picturesqueness of their inhabitants, artists encouraged the metropolitan viewing public to consider the expanded empire as benign realms of amenable subjects. Such landscapes made it difficult to imagine Canadian insurgency.

Frances Brooke's *History of Emily Montague* (1768) played a crucial post-war role in familiarizing Britons with their new colony's scenic and social landscape. It was an epistolary novel with a typically romantic plot. A sensitive but dutiful man (Colonel Ed. Rivers) learns to follow his heart to happiness. With the help of a vivacious mutual friend (Arabella Fermor), supplemented by a surprise dowry from his fiancée's long-lost father, he finds happiness by marrying a sentimental but intelligent woman (Emily Montague). Brooke lived in Canada while she wrote the novel. Her husband had been a garrison chaplain with British invasion forces at Louisbourg and Quebec. After the peace, she joined him at Quebec for most of the period between 1763 and 1768.

She and her husband socialized with Governor Murray, his council, leading merchants, and seigneurial families, and her fluency in French gave her a familiarity with Canadian society that she conveyed in her novel.[21]

Brooke's novel was distinctive for its topographical presentations of colonial landscapes.[22] As Rivers sailed upriver to Quebec, he "felt a kind of religious veneration, on seeing rocks which almost touch'd the clouds, cover'd with tall groves of pines" (3). His description of Quebec and environs recalled Richard Short's prints: "The island of Orleans, the distant view of the cascade of Mormorenci, and the opposite village of Beauport, scattered with a pleasing irregularity along the banks of the river Saint Charles, add greatly to the charms of the prospect" (4). Arabella described the river leading to the Montmorency Falls with the care of a topographic print: "Paint to yourself a stupendous rock burst as it were in sunder by the hands of nature, to give passage to a small, but very deep and beautiful river; and forming on each side a regular and magnificent wall, crowned with the noblest woods that can be imagined" (23–4). Arabella compared the cultivated landscape favourably with the ease and visual amusement of an English landscape garden.

For a romantic novel with such a picturesque setting, *Emily Montague* had a strong undercurrent of imperial politics. Brooke dedicated *Emily Montague* to Governor Guy Carleton and began the novel's narrative just before he arrived. Her husband had favoured Carleton as a replacement for Governor Murray, whom he increasingly saw to be insufficiently supportive of an Anglican establishment. Sir William Fermor, a retired military officer and father of Arabella, Emily's coquettish but shrewd confidante, wrote thirteen of the novel's letters. Sir William's letters were anything but coquettish: they were political disquisitions on Canada, sent to a nobleman in Britain. He explained the seigneurial system ("military, not commercial"), the "peasants" ("love war and hate labour . . . resemble the savages, whose manners they seem strongly to have imbibed"), religion ("extremely bigoted . . . [a] great bar, as well to industry as population"), Canadians' agriculture (they "just turn the turf once lightly over, and, without manuring the ground, or even breaking the clods of earth, throw in the seed in the same careless manner, and leave the event to chance"), and prospects for improvement ("these people, slaves at present to ignorance and superstition, will in time be enlightened by a more liberal education, and gently led by reason to a religion which . . . is so much more calculated to make them happy and prosperous as a people") (177–8). "Enlightened," "liberal," and "gentle" British rule, Brooke implied, was the strategy for Quebec's happiness and prosperity.

[. . .] Brooke forthrightly linked her novel's sentimentally picturesque representations of Quebec with the new colony's value to the empire. Canada was not the "Irishman's Prize" of sarcastic journalists: It had rich underutilized economic resources in its land and people, which would be mobilized by Britain's commercial empire.[23]

In linking Canada with the global British landscape, Brooke established three metonymic scenes of Quebec: the contented habitant, the calèche, and Montmorency Falls. Rivers saw a georgic potential—for economic development that would enhance scenic beauty—where other British observers scornfully dismissed an improvident land and people: "Nothing is wanted but encouragement and cultivation; the Canadians are at their ease even without labour; nature is here a bounteous mother, who pours forth her gifts almost unsolicited: bigotry, stupidity, and laziness, united have not been able to keep the peasantry poor" (20). The calèche stood for the enviable capacity of the Canadians to enjoy their landscape in "little excursions of pleasure," even in winter. The Montmorency Falls provided the prime scenic destination for leisurely sleigh riding:

The torrent [in winter], which before rushed with such impetuosity down the deep descent in one vast sheet of water, now descends in some parts with a slow and majestic pace; in others seems almost suspended in mid air; and in others, bursting through the obstacles which interrupt its course, pours down with redoubled fury into the foaming basin below, from whence a spray arises, which, freezing in its ascent, becomes on each side a wide and irregular frozen breastwork; and in front, the spray being there much greater, a lofty and magnificent pyramid of solid ice. (127–8)

At the novel's conclusion, Rivers and Emily reluctantly gave up their plans to settle in Canada and returned home at his mother's request. To his surprise Rivers found that he still appreciated the English countryside: "I point out every fine prospect, and am so proud of my country, that my whole soul seems to be dilated. . . . the numerous herds and flocks on the side of the hills, the neatness of the houses, of the people, the appearance of plenty; all exhibit a scene which must strike one who has been used only to the wild graces of nature. Canada has beauties; but they are of a different kind" (251). Their return enabled them to think of Canada as part of a global British landscape: The inevitable comparisons heightened their appreciation of its scenic distinctiveness.[24]

Topographic landscape art helped Britons visualize their new Canadian landscape in the broad context of a North American empire. Thomas Davies published a series of engravings of waterfalls—on the Niagara, Passaic, Cohoes, and Genessee rivers—which he had drawn after the fall of Montreal when Lord Amherst sent him to survey the upper St Lawrence and the rivers that flowed from New York into Lake Ontario.[25] Waterfalls had both strategic and scenic significance. They posed critical tactical problems along wartime communication routes, while their visual variety made them picturesquely attractive. More ambitiously, the *Scenographia Americana: Or, a Collection of Views of North America and the West Indies* (1768) presented a 28-print series of topographical landscapes in an arc across eastern North America from Montreal to Guadeloupe. Now the drawing master at the Royal Military Academy at Woolwich, Paul Sandby compiled the collection from "Drawings taken on the spot, by several officers of the British Navy and Army." The *Scenographia Americana* traced the geography of Britain's strategy during the Seven Years' War. The series began in Canada with views of Montreal, Quebec, and Louisbourg, plus Hervey's five sights from the invading fleet in 1759. It then moved southward for views of Boston, New York, and Charleston—reminders that the war in North America had been about the security and growth of Britain's colonies there. Sandby also engraved six of Governor Thomas Pownall's drawings of dramatic landscape features in the middle colonies—the falls on the Passaic River in New Jersey, the highlands of Tappan Zee at the mouth of the Hudson, the Catskill Mountains further upriver, and the Great Cohoes Falls on the Mohawk River in northern New York. Pownall had drawn these impressive sights as part of a strategic survey of terrain for Britain's war with France in North America. From continental North America the *Scenographia* then shifted theatre to the Caribbean—just as the war had—and concluded with six views of Havana, one of Dominica, and three of Guadeloupe. Scenic attractiveness, as well as success by British arms, united these places in their connection to Britain's global landscape.[26]

British atlases complemented the *Scenographia* cartographically in placing Britain's new North American empire in a global context. The hundred maps in Thomas Jefferys and Robert Sayer's *General Topography of North America and the West Indies* (1768) covered both the Atlantic and Pacific coasts (including recent Russian explorations in the northern Pacific) and related them to the nearest African, Asian, and European coasts. Most of the maps described areas of British conquests during the Seven Years' War—in Cuba, Florida, the Lesser Antilles, and Guyana. Twelve of them described the former New France—charts of the St Lawrence, plans of Quebec and Montreal, and maps of Acadia and the fur trading country west of Hudson Bay and the Great Lakes.

The most important visual survey of Britain's new continental empire in North America was the *Atlantic Neptune* (1777–84), a monumental coastal charting initiated shortly after the Treaty of Paris. In 1763 the Admiralty directed Joseph Frederick Wallet DesBarres to chart the coastal waters of Nova Scotia and Cape Breton Island. In 1764 the Board of Trade appointed Samuel Holland as surveyor general of Quebec and of the Northern District (i.e., north of the Potomac River) and William De Brahm as surveyor general of the Southern District. In 1769 the board ordered them to co-operate with DesBarres in charting their respective coasts. For the first time the Atlantic coast of North America would have a continuous series of navigational charts based on direct hydrographic surveys: from the tidal reaches of the St Lawrence in the west and the Strait of Belle Isle in the north, around Cape Breton Island and Nova Scotia, along the Atlantic seaboard of the British-settled colonies, and reaching south and westward to include the new British colonies of East and West Florida.[27] New France would be seamlessly integrated with the colonies of British settlement and accessions from Spanish America.

The strategic importance of this project was self-evident—it made the Royal Navy's patrolling of a lengthy imperial coastline safer and more thorough—but its aesthetic priorities are more surprising. As DesBarres compiled and revised the *Atlantic Neptune*, he added scenic aquatints (the first ones of North American landscapes) to the conventional charts and profiles dictated by his commission. The scenes often included waterfront activities as staffage, giving them a genre quality: careened ships being cleaned, lighters landing cargo on beaches, even—in a bit of reflexivity—boats making soundings for a chart. Most of the prints were of Nova Scotian scenes because that was where DesBarres mainly worked, and he respected the topographical imperative by only illustrating places he had actually seen. Often coloured by hand, these views—over 130 of them—went well beyond the Admiralty's directions for a coastal survey. DesBarres's views gave a self-commissioned priority to British landscape aesthetics of the beautiful, the sublime, and the picturesque, as Edmund Burke and William Gilpin had defined them. Scenes drawn from near shore had picturesquely gnarled trees and varied rock formations. Some views even contradicted the cartographic project in order to represent impressive landscapes: the ships setting some of the scenes were so numerous that they obscured the coastal profile, and a few views were from land to sea—not a useful perspective for navigating a ship (Figure 4). Ships carried the *Atlantic Neptune* as a navigational aid, but DesBarres also aimed the work at armchair sailors interested in imagining themselves along

Figure 4 DesBarres' favourite subjects for landscapes were rocky promontories—features that navigators had little interest in seeing up close. "A View of the Plaister Cliffs, on the West Shore of Georges Bay," *Atlantic Neptune* (London: Joseph Frederick Wallet DesBarres, ca. 1779). Library and Archives Canada/W.H. Coverdale collection of Canadiana Manoir Richelieu collection/C-040998.

Britain's new imperial coastline, especially so that they could follow events in the rebellious colonies.[28]

The outcome of the War of American Independence made Quebec Britain's largest, and potentially most important, colony in North America. Yet its imperial features received less visual emphasis than representations of its georgic potential, picturesque culture, and genteel leisure. Quebec's invitation of scenic tourism in a landscape simultaneously sublime and picturesque implied a happily governed colony, welcoming immigrants and encouraging imperial resources.

The watercolours and prints of James Peachey epitomized these trends, and in the mid-1780s they accounted for most of the representations of Quebec to British metropolitan viewers. In the early 1770s he had worked with Samuel Holland's survey of the Northern District; then he returned to England to produce maps for the *Atlantic Neptune*. He went back to Quebec in 1780, where he gained patronage as a draftsman for the governor of Quebec, General Frederick Haldimand. He flattered Haldimand's taste by painting a series of watercolours of the area around the governor's country house on the bluff above Montmorency Falls. Haldimand counted himself a connoisseur of landscape: He built a Chinese-styled viewing seat upstream as well as a viewing lodge perched on stilts over the head of the falls.

Peachey also flattered his patron's benign rule with watercolours of the Quebec countryside. They showed a peaceful province whose cottages, outdoor ovens, horse-drawn sleighs, and habitants and Amerindians in colourful costumes marked it as distinctively Canadian (Figure 5). Peachey's views

Figure 5 Georgic symbols of Quebec's prosperous agricultural potential—notably bridges built at Haldimand's behest—complemented the province's picturesque landscape. James Peachey, *A View of the Bridge Built over the River Bertier by Order of General Haldimand in 1781* (1785). Library and Archives Canada/W.H. Coverdale collection of Canadiana Manoir Richelieu collection/C-045559.

of Quebec and Montreal played down their fortifications. His *View of the City of Quebec* (ca. 1785) showed the citadel and outworks indistinctly in the background, while the foreground and middle ground showed a farm with large, well-fenced fields, heavily laden hay wagons, a well-maintained house and barn, and leisurely farm workers. *A View of the Citadel at Quebec* (1784), taken from the Heights of Abraham, showed outworks now fenced for pasture.[29]

[. . .]

In late 1784 Peachey returned to Britain with Haldimand and immediately began to publicize his landscapes of Quebec. Besides exhibiting paintings at the Royal Academy, he published aquatints of Montreal and Quebec and a series of coloured etchings of the area around General (now Sir Frederick)

Haldimand's country house. These showed Montmorency Falls, from above and below, in summer and winter, as well as the river above the falls. Despite the awesome majesty of the falls, rapids, and cliff-lined river, the scenes' numerous gentlefolk out walking and fishing demonstrated that the Quebec landscape was readily approachable.

When Thomas Davies returned the third time to North America in 1786, now as a lieutenant colonel commanding artillery in Quebec, he elaborated on Peachey's themes. His watercolours returned to a favourite subject, waterfalls, but now he chose sites on rivers easily reachable from the city rather than ones important for military campaigns as in 1759–60 (Figure 6). Along these waters, habitants and gentlefolk fished, picnicked, and walked their dogs. His scenes of the countryside studied distinctively

Figure 6 Davies helped to create a regional, genre landscape of Quebec. Thomas Davies, *Chaudière Falls near Quebec* (1792). Library and Archives Canada/George Heriot collection/C-013313.

Canadian features of the landscape: hunters returning with a canoe on a wagon, weirs set along tidal marshes of the St Lawrence, farmsteads strung along the road of the first *rang*, the church at Château-Richer, a traverse of a portage on the Ottawa River, and the annual encampment at Pointe-Lévis for First Nations peoples to receive their obligatory presents. His less frequent urban scenes showed a reconstructed Quebec with many of its old ways represented—female religious in habits, dog-drawn watercarts, one-horse carriages—with the British presence barely hinted at by an officer overseeing the scene, a single sentry, and three stands of guns for soldiers out of the picture.[30] Scenic, social, and political tranquillity implicitly complemented each other in reassuring ways for Britain's imperial presence in North America.

Elizabeth Posthuma Simcoe extended the British imperial landscape into areas of the Great Lakes uncolonized while part of New France. She arrived in Canada in 1791 as the wife of Lieutenant Colonel John Graves Simcoe, the first lieutenant-governor of the new Province of Upper Canada. During her nearly five years in the Canadas she sometimes wintered at Quebec, but she spent the rest of the time at her husband's bases in Upper Canada, first at Newark (later Niagara-on-the-Lake), then at York (formerly and eventually Toronto).[31] She recorded landscapes of the Canadas in several diaries and sketchbooks. She regularly revised her diaries and made finished watercolours from her drawings to send to her four older daughters, whom she had left in England, and to a friend, Mary Anne Burgess, a notable author (she updated *Pilgrim's Progress*) and illustrator of natural history. Though she never published her landscapes, she publicized them by private circulation. She had an artistic fellowship with British officers such as Peachey, Holland, and George Bulteel Fisher, with whom she compared and copied drawings (40, 55, 58, 74, 108). She drew maps for her

husband's reports, and she gave King George III 32 watercolours on birchbark of scenes in the Canadas.[32]

Elizabeth Simcoe sought and found a picturesque Canada. In her diary "picturesque" described dozens of scenes that caught her eye. Besides editorializing aesthetically with terms such as "beautiful," "prettiest sight imaginable," "very fine sight" (76), "very fine scene" (107), and "sweet view" (184), she recommended the visual interest of Canadian scenes by comparing them with landscapes her correspondents already knew from European art and literature. An "old-fashioned" Quebec inn "resembled my idea of a Flemish house" (38); the "pretty vale" at Sillery was just as Emily Montague described it (59); the "Lake-like" St Lawrence put her in mind of how "Spenser, Ariosto etc., dwelt on the delight of sailing in a Boat on Lakes" (64); as she rode toward Niagara Falls she "was struck by the similarity between these Hills & Banks & those of the Wye about Symond's Gate & the lime Rock near Whitchurch in Herefordshire" (76); a mill under construction "has the appearance of a Sketch of a Ruin in Italy" (190). In providing positive comparisons between Canada and aesthetically prestigious European landscapes, Simcoe made a new part of the empire recognizable, familiar, and desirable for appropriation.

Simcoe constantly evaluated the landscape along her travels and frequently made scenic excursions. Within four days of arriving at her new home at Navy Hall near the mouth of the Niagara River, she went to see Niagara Falls. She was not disappointed: "The fall itself is the grandest sight imaginable from the immense width of waters & the circular form of the great fall" (Figure 7). She immediately appreciated the artistic challenge of capturing the falls' distinctive features, "the whole centre of the circular fall being of the brightest green & below it is frequently seen a Rainbow." She venturesomely descended to Table Rock to get the full effect of "the prodigious Spray which arises from

Figure 7 Elizabeth Simcoe painted Niagara Falls many times. *Niagara Falls* (ca. 1795). Archives of Ontario/Niagara Falls [ca. 1785] by Elizabeth Simcoe/I0007030/47-11-1-0-178.

the foam at the bottom of the fall [and] adds grandeur to the scene" (76–7). Happily for Simcoe, areas near where she lived in Upper Canada—the Niagara River, the eastern and western ends of Lake Ontario, and between the escarpment and the lake at York—provided her with ample opportunities to paint landscapes in both picturesque and sublime styles.[33]

In counterpoint to her husband's geopolitical strategies, Elizabeth Simcoe presented Upper Canada as a sub-boreal English landscape garden.[34] Her pictures showed a fascination with the scenic harmony between European settlement and heavily forested areas along wilderness shorelines: mills on the Gananoque and Napanee, tents on the heights above Queenston, houses in park-like water meadows along the upper St Lawrence, and rustic Castle Frank with its pedimented facade supported by Greek

columns of pine logs. The familiar picturesque style of her landscapes helped her metropolitan correspondents imagine Britain's imperial outposts in North America.

[. . .]

In Canada, as elsewhere in the empire, representations of picturesque, sublime, and georgic scenes in British colonies mitigated the forthrightness of their conquest and/or military rule. The supposed authenticity of topographic landscape art gave Britons at home confidence to identify with Britain's new possessions overseas, while the familiar picturesque style of these imperial landscapes diverted attention from the controversies surrounding them. Artists' representation of imperial landscapes harmonized the empire's implicit mayhem with its scenery. The sublime glory of British arms was reinforced by the picturesque landscape in which they had prevailed, and vice versa.

NOTES

1. Dean MacCannell, *The Tourist: A New Theory of the Leisure Class*, 2nd edn (Berkeley and Los Angeles: University of California Press, 1999), 91–107.

2. Victoria Dickenson, *Drawn from Life: Science and Art in the Portrayal of the New World* (Toronto: University of Toronto Press, 1998), 105–39.

3. For revisionist historiography of New France and the conquest, see Allan Greer, "Comparisons: New France," in *A Companion to Colonial America*, ed. Daniel Vickers (Maiden, MA: Blackwell Publishers, 2003); id., *The People of New France* (Toronto: University of Toronto Press, 1997), quoted 115.

4. Claude-Charles Bacqueville de la Potherie, *Histoire de l'Amérique septentrionale*, 4 vols (Paris: Jean-Luc Nion and François Didot, 1722); Joseph François Lafitau, *Moeurs des sauvages ameriquains comparée aux moeurs des premiers temps* (Paris: Sauguin l'aîné and Charles-Estienne Hochereau, 1724).

5. Luc Noppen and Marc Grignon, *"L'art de l'architecte": Three Centuries of Architectural Drawing in Québec City* (Quebec: Musée du Québec and Université Laval, 1983), 27–53, 114–36.

6. Malcolm Andrews, *The Search for the Picturesque: Landscape Aesthetics and Tourism in Britain, 1760–1800* (Stanford, CA: Stanford University Press, 1989).

7. John Barrell, *The Dark Side of the Landscape: The Rural Poor in English Painting 1730–1840* (Cambridge: Cambridge University Press, 1980); Ann Bermingham, *Landscape and Ideology: The English Rustic Tradition, 1740–1860* (Berkeley and Los Angeles: University of California Press, 1986).

8. Daniel Clayton, "The Creation of Imperial Space in the Pacific Northwest," *Journal of Historical Geography* 26 (2000): 327–50.

9. Benedict Anderson, *Imagined Communities: Reflections on the Origin and Spread of Nationalism*, rev. edn (London: Verso, 1991); Beth Fowkes Tobin, *Picturing Imperial Power: Colonial Subjects in Eighteenth-Century British Painting* (Durham, NC: Duke University Press, 1999).

10. W.J.T. Mitchell, "Introduction," in *Landscape and Power*, ed. W.J.T. Mitchell (Chicago: University of Chicago Press, 1994), 1–2.

11. John M. MacKenzie, "Art and the Empire," in *The Cambridge Illustrated History of the British Empire*, ed. P.J. Marshall (Cambridge: Cambridge University Press), 296.

12. Linda Colley, *Britons: Forging the Nation 1707–1837* (New Haven, CT: Yale University Press, 5992); Kathleen Wilson, *The Island Race: Englishness, Empire and Gender in the Eighteenth Century* (London: Routledge, 2003); John Brewer, *Pleasures of the Imagination: English Culture in the Eighteenth Century* (Chicago: University of Chicago Press, 1997), 201–51, 449–63, 615–61.

13. Colin M. Coates, "Like 'The Thames towards Putney': The Appropriation of Landscape in Lower Canada," *Canadian Historical Review* 74 (1994): 317–43 (Repton quoted 322).

14. Douglas Cole and Maria Tippett, "Pleasing Diversity and Sublime Desolation: The Eighteenth-Century British Perception of the Northwest Coast," *Pacific Northwest Quarterly* 65 (1974): 1–7.

15. P.J. Marshall, "Empire and Authority in the Later Eighteenth Century," *Journal of Imperial and Commonwealth History* 15 (1987): 105–22.

16. Mary Louise Pratt, *Imperial Eyes: Travel Writing and Transculturation* (London: Routledge, 1992), 38–85 (quoted 7, 57).

17. R.H. Hubbard, ed., *Thomas Davies in Early Canada* (Ottawa: Oberon, 1972), 9; Bruce G. Wilson, *Colonial Identities: Canada from 1760 to 1815* (Ottawa: National Archives of Canada, 1988), 24–7 (victory medals); Dennis Montagna, "Benjamin West's *The Death of General Wolfe*: A Nationalist Narrative," *American Art Journal* 13 (1981): 72–88.

18. *A View of the Landing Place above the Town of Quebec*, Pierre-Charles Canot after Francis Swaine after Hervey Smith (London, ca. 1760).

19. *Twelve Views of the Principal Buildings in Quebec, from Drawings, Taken on the Spot, at the Command of Vice-Admiral Saunders*, Pierre Grignon et al. after Richard Short (London, 1761).

20. "General Murray's Report on the State of the Government of Quebec in Canada, June 5, 1762," in *Documents Relating to the Constitutional History of Canada 1759–1791*, ed. Adam Shortt and Arthur G. Doughty (Ottawa: King's Printer, 1907), 60.

21. Laura Moss, "A Literary Biography of Frances Moore," in *The History of Emily Montague by Frances Brooke: A Critical Edition*, ed. Laura Moss (Ottawa: Tecumseh Press, 2001), 355–64. Parenthetical references are to this edition.

22. Later travellers often noted how their first-hand visual impressions confirmed their expectations from reading Brooke's novel. Pam Perkins, "Frances Brooke, Emily Montague, and Other Travellers: Representing Eighteenth-Century North America," in *History of Emily Montague*, 421–36.

23. Cf. Philip Lawson, "'The Irishman's Prize': Views of Canada from the British Press, 1760–1774," *Historical Journal* 28 (1985): 575–96.

24. Cecily Devereux, "'One Firm Body': 'Britishness and Otherness' in *The History of Emily Montague*," in *History of Emily Montague*, 459–76.

25. R.H. Hubbard, ed., *Thomas Davies c. 1737–1812* (Ottawa: National Gallery of Canada, 1972), 28, 30, 54–6, 138–45, plates I–VI.

26. I.N. Phelps Stokes, *The Iconography of Manhattan Island 1498–1909*, 6 vols (New York: Robert H. Godd, 1915), 1:281–95.

27. G.S. Ritchie, "Introduction," in *The Sea Chart*, Derek House and Michael Sanderson, eds (New York: McGraw-Hill Books, 1973), 11–13.

28. Richard L. Raymond, *J.F.W. DesBarres: Views and Profiles* (Halifax: Dalhousie University Art Gallery, 1982); G.N.D. Evans, *Uncommon Obdurate: The Several Careers of J.F.W. DesBarres* (Toronto: University of Toronto Press, 1969), 9–26.

29. *James Peachey, in Archives Canada Microfiches*, 2 (Ottawa: Public Archives, 1975–1976); W. Martha E. Cooke and Bruce G. Wilson, "James Peachey," *Dictionary of Canadian Biography* (*DCB*), 4:612–14; Stuart R.J. Sutherland and Madeleine Dionne-Tousignant, "Sir Frederick Haldimand," *DCB*, 5:887–904.

30. Hubbard, *Thomas Davies in Early Canada*, 41–61; id., "Art of Thomas Davies," 34–8; id., *Thomas Davies*, 118–30.

31. S.R. Mealing, "John Graves Simcoe," *DCB*, 5:754–59; Edith G. Firth, "Elizabeth Posthuma Gwillim Simcoe," *DCB*, 7:361–3; Mary Beacock Fryer, *Elizabeth Postuma Simcoe 1762–1850: A Biography* (Toronto and Oxford: Dundurn Press, 1989).

32. Tom Gerry, "Extremes Meet: Elizabeth Simcoe's Birchbark Landscapes," *Queen's Quarterly* 106 (1999): 589–601. Mary Quayle Innis, ed., *Mrs Simcoe's Diary* (Toronto: Macmillan of Canada, 1965). Parenthetical references are to this edition.

33. Canada, "The Visual Diary of Elizabeth Simcoe: A Journey through Upper and Lower Canada," http://collections.ic.gc.ca/elizabeth-simcoe (accessed 27 January 2005).

34. Malcolm MacLeod, "Fortress Ontario or Forlorn Hope? Simcoe and the Defence of Upper Canada," *Canadian Historical Review* 53 (1972): 177.

Chapter 6

Loyalists

READINGS

Primary Documents

Historical Interpretations

INTRODUCTION

The characteristic of loyalty that distinguished some North Americans from others during and after the American Revolution is often invoked to explain some of the most significant differences between Canadians (especially Upper Canadians and Maritimers) and Americans, and the resulting divergence in their values. The decision made by the Loyalists to leave the new republic and seek safety, food, and comfort in other parts of the British Empire certainly affected their lives. However, was loyalty to the British monarch during and after the revolution the only factor that mattered in their decision? Might they have been just as loyal to, or eager to maintain, the positions they held as merchants or tradesmen regardless of who ruled over them?

In her diary entries, Sarah Frost, a woman of no great fortune, reflects on the choice she and her fellow Loyalists made, knowing that even though the road ahead looked daunting, to remain in the new United States would have been far worse. The prospects for remaking their lives after being identified with the oppressive British regime were such that the only card they had left to play was loyalty, and the language of loyalty was relocation. The documents petitioning for land and compensation from the Crown show that those who left the US to settle in British North America wanted the Crown to know that they expected to be accommodated and rewarded in proportion to their service.

The historical interpretations here reveal that the experiences of Loyalists were hardly uniform. Janice Potter sketches the clear gender divisions within the group that settled in what would become eastern Upper Canada (ultimately Ontario) in the early post-revolutionary period. However, the reasons that led the Loyalists to emigrate into what became Upper Canada were more complex than it may seem at first. In his contribution, James W. St G. Walker discusses the fate of the Black Loyalists in Nova Scotia. Even if the British authorities had promised them freedom if they joined the fight against the rebellion, the British never considered granting them equality. Relocated to poor areas, given smaller lots than white settlers, and treated as second-rate subjects, their lives in Nova Scotia were so difficult that many black settlers eventually left North America altogether for Sierra Leone.

QUESTIONS FOR CONSIDERATION

1. Do you think Frost would have known any of the people who created the petition (Document 2), and why?
2. What was the purpose of the petition?
3. To what degree do you think the Loyalists were acting in their own interests?
4. Does Potter think that Loyalist women gained anything beyond political calm by coming to the area that is now eastern Ontario?
5. What were the challenges faced by the free black settlers in Nova Scotia after the American Revolution?

SUGGESTIONS FOR FURTHER READING

Jerry Bannister and Liam Riordan, eds, *The Loyal Atlantic: Remaking the British Atlantic in the Revolutionary Era* (Toronto: University of Toronto Press, 2013).

Ann Gorman Condon, *The Envy of the American States: The Loyalist Dream for New Brunswick* (Fredericton: New Ireland Press, 1984).

Jane Errington, *The Lion, the Eagle, and Upper Canada: A Developing Colonial Ideology* (Montreal and Kingston: McGill-Queen's University Press, 1994).

Barbara Graymont, *The Iroquois in the American Revolution* (Syracuse, NY: Syracuse University Press, 1972).

Maya Jasanoff, *Liberty's Exiles: American Loyalists in the Revolutionary World* (New York: Vintage Books, 2012).

Stephen Kimber, *Loyalists and Layabouts: The Rapid Rise and Faster Fall of Shelburne, Nova Scotia, 1783–1792* (Toronto: Doubleday Canada, 2008).

Norman Knowles, *Inventing the Loyalists: The Ontario Loyalist Tradition and the Creation of Usable Pasts* (Toronto: University of Toronto Press, 1997).

Neil MacKinnon, *This Unfriendly Soil: The Loyalists Experience in Nova Scotia, 1781–1791* (Montreal and Kingston: McGill-Queen's University Press, 1986).

Janice Potter-MacKinnon, *While the Women Only Wept: Loyalist Refugee Women* (Montreal and Kingston: McGill-Queen's University Press, 1993).

James W. St G. Walker, *The Black Loyalists: The Search for a Promised Land in Nova Scotia and Sierra Leone 1783–1870* (Toronto: University of Toronto Press, 1992).

Ruth Holmes Whitehead, *Black Loyalists: Southern Settlers of Nova Scotia's First Free Black Communities* (Halifax: Nimbus Publishing, 2013).

Harvey Amani Whitfield, *North to Bondage: Loyalist Slavery in the Maritimes* (Vancouver: UBC Press, 2016).

Primary Documents

1

From "The Diary of Sarah Frost, 1783," in Walter Bates, ed., *Kingston and the Loyalists of the "Spring Fleet" of 1783* (Fredericton: Non-Entity Press, 1980), 30–2.

Friday, June 6.—We are still lying at anchor waiting for other vessels of our fleet. My father will come on board in the morning if my husband can go and fetch him. I do so long to hear from my dear mother and my brothers and sisters. We have had a very bad storm this evening. Our ship tossed very much, and some of the people are quite sick, but I am in hopes the storm will soon abate. It grows late as I conclude for the night, hoping to see "Daddy" in the morning.

Saturday, June 7.—My husband went on shore and brought father on board to breakfast. Soon after breakfast he returned on shore, for he expected to go home in the same boat he came down in, but hearing there was a vessel coming from Stamford today, he concluded to stay and return in it, so he came on board again to dine.

Sunday, June 8.—We are still lying at anchor in the North River. We expected to sail tomorrow for Nova Scotia, but I believe we shall remain at Staten Island or Sandy Hook for some days, or until our fleet is all got together.

Monday, June 9.—Our women, with their children, all came on board today, and there is great confusion in the cabin. We bear with it pretty well through the day, but as it grows towards night, one child cries in one place and one in another, whilst we are getting them to bed. I think sometimes I shall be crazy. There are so many of them, if they were as still as common there would be a great noise amongst them. I stay on deck tonight till nigh eleven o'clock, and now I think I will go down and retire for the night if I can find a place to sleep.

Tuesday, June 10.—I got up early, not being able to sleep the whole night for the noise of the children. The wind blows very high. My little girl has been very sick all day, but grows better towards evening.

Wednesday, June 11.—We weighed anchor in the North River about six o'clock this morning, and sailed as far as Staten Island, where we came to anchor. I went on shore with Mr. Goreham and his wife, and Mr. Raymond and his wife, and my two children. We picked some gooseberries. We staid but a short time. In the afternoon I went ashore again with Mr. Frost and several others.

Thursday, June 12.—Nothing seems to be worth mentioning today. We are so thronged on board, I cannot set myself about any work. It is comfortable for nobody.

Friday, June 13.—It is now about half after three in the morning. I have got up, not being able to sleep for the heat, and am sitting in the entry-way of the cabin to write. It storms so I cannot go on deck. My husband and children are still sleeping. Through the day I am obliged to lie in my berth, being quite ill.

Saturday, June 14.—I am something better this morning. My husband brings me my breakfast, which I relish. We are still lying at Staten Island. We expected to sail this morning.

Sunday, June 15.—Our people seem cross and quarrelsome today, but I will not differ with any one, if I can help it. At half-past twelve our ship is getting under way—I suppose for Nova Scotia. I hope for a good passage. About five o'clock we come to anchor within six miles of the lighthouse at Sandy Hook. How long we shall lie here I don't know, but I hope not long. About six o'clock this evening we had a terrible thunder storm, and hail stones fell as big as ounce balls. About sunset there came another shower, and it hailed faster than before. Mr. Frost went out and gathered up a mugful of hail stones. Such an instance I never saw before on the 15th day of June.

Monday, June 16.—*Off at last!* We weighed anchor about half after five in the morning, with the wind north-nor'west, and it blows very fresh. We passed the lighthouse about half after seven. We have twelve ships belonging to our fleet besides our commodore's. Two hours later a signal was fired for the ships all to lie to for the *Bridgewater*, which seems to lag behind, I believe on account of some misfortune which happened to her yesterday. At 9 a.m. we have a signal fired to crowd sail. Again we are ordered to lie to. I don't know what it is for, as the *Bridgewater* has come up. It is now two o'clock, and we have again got under way. The mate tells me they have been waiting for a ship to come from New York, and she has overhauled us. We have now got all our fleet together: we have thirteen ships, two brigs, one frigate. The frigate is our commodore's. The wind dies away. It is now three o'clock, and the men are fishing for mackerel. Mr. Mills has caught the first one. I never saw a live one before. It is the handsomest fish I ever beheld. . . .

Monday, June 23.—It grows brighter towards noon, and the fog disappears rapidly. This afternoon we can see several of our fleet, and one of our ships came close alongside of us. Mr. Emslie says we are an hundred and forty miles from land now. The wind becomes more favorable, the fog seems to leave us and the sun looks very pleasant. Mr. Whitney and his wife, Mr. Frost and myself have been diverting ourselves with a few games of crib.

Tuesday, June 24.—The sun appears very pleasant this morning. Ten ships are in sight. The fog comes on, and they all disappear. We have been nearly becalmed for three days. A light breeze enables us to sail this evening two miles and a half an hour.

Wednesday, June 25.—Still foggy; the wind is fair, but we are obliged to lie to for the rest of the fleet. The commodore fires once an hour. The frigate is near us, and judging by the bells, we are not far from some of the other ships, but we can't see ten rods for the fog. We have *measles* very bad on board our ship.

Thursday, June 26.—This morning the sun appears very pleasant. The fog is gone to our great satisfaction. Ten of our ships are in sight. We are now nigh the banks of Cape Sable. At nine o'clock we begin to see land, at which we all rejoice. We have been nine days out of sight of land. At half after six we have twelve ships in sight. Our captain told me just now we should be in the Bay of Fundy before morning. He says it is about one day's sail after we get into the bay to Saint John's River. Oh, how I long to see that place, though a strange land. I am tired of being on board ship, though we have as kind a captain as ever need to live.

Friday, June 27.—I got up this morning very early to look out. I can see land on both sides of us. About ten o'clock we passed Annapolis; after that the wind all died away. Our people have got their lines out to catch codfish, and about half after five John Waterbury caught the first one for our ship.

Saturday, June 28.—Got up in the morning and found ourselves nigh to land on each side. It was up the river St. John's. At half after nine our captain fired a gun for a pilot; an hour later a pilot came on board, and at a quarter after one our ship anchored off against Fort Howe in St. John's River. Our people went on shore and brought on board spruce and gooseberries, and grass and pea vines with the blossoms on them, all of which grow wild here. They say this is to be our city. Our land is five and twenty miles up the river. We are to have here only a building place of forty feet in the front and a hundred feet back. Mr. Frost has now gone on shore in his whale boat to see how the place looks, and he says he will soon come back and take me on shore. I long to set my feet once more on land. He soon came on board again and brought a fine salmon.

Sunday, June 29.—This morning it looks very pleasant on the shore. I am just going ashore with my children to see how I like it. *Later*— It is now afternoon and I have been ashore. It is, I think, the roughest land I ever saw. It beats Short Rocks, indeed, I think, that is nothing in comparison; but this is to be *the city*, they say! We are to settle here, but are to have our land sixty miles farther up the river. We are all ordered to land to-morrow, and not a shelter to go under.

---

2 "The Petition of 55 Loyalists," 22 July 1783, and "A Memorial of Samuel Hakes and 600 Others," 15 August 1783, in *Vindication of Governor Parr and His Council* (Halifax: 1783).

THE PETITION OF 55 LOYALISTS (22 JULY 1783)

The affairs at Nova Scotia and New York went on amicably among the Loyalists till August 1783, when it was discovered that the Rev. John Sayre, with fifty-four other persons, had privately presented to Sir Guy Carleton the following letter:

NEW-YORK, JULY 22, 1783.

SIR,

Your Excellency's kind attention and offers of your support to us demand our warmest thanks, which we beg the favour of you to accept.

The unhappy termination of the war obliges us, who have *ever been steady in our duty, as loyal subjects*, to leave our homes; and being desirous of continuing to enjoy the benefits of the British constitution, we mean to seek an asylum in the province of Nova Scotia.

Considering our several characters, and our former situation in life, we trust you will perceive that our circumstances will probably be the contrast to which they have been heretofore; especially as, from our respective occupations, we shall be unable *personally* to obtain the means of a tolerably decent support, unless your Excellency shall be pleased to countenance us by your recommendation in the following proposals; which are, with the utmost deference, submitted to your Excellency's consideration.

1. That a tract or tracts of land, free from disputed titles, be laid out for us in Nova Scotia, in such part of that province as

one or more gentlemen, whom we propose to send forward for that purpose, being first approved of by your Excellency, shall pitch upon for us.

2. That this tract be sufficient to put us on the same footing with field-officers in his Majesty's army, with respect to the number of acres.
3. That, if possible, these lands may be exonerated of quit-rents.
4. That they be surveyed and divided at the expence of Government, and the deeds delivered to us as soon as possible, remitting the fees of office.
5. That, while we make this application to your Excellency, we wish not to be understood as soliciting a compensation for the losses we have sustained during the war, because we are humbly of opinion, that the settling of such a number of Loyalists of the most respectable characters, who have *constantly* had great influence in his Majesty's American dominions, will be highly advantageous in diffusing and supporting a spirit of attachment to the British constitution, as well as to his Majesty's royal person and family.

We have only to add our earnest request of your Excellency's aid and support in carrying this matter into execution, as soon as it shall comport with your leisure; and to assure your Excellency, that we are, with great respect, your Excellency's most humble and obedient servants,

Signed by, Addison, Henry (and 54 others). . . .

A MEMORIAL OF SAMUEL HAKES AND 600 OTHERS (15 AUGUST 1783)

The Loyalists about this time (mid-August) discovered the art and designs of the Fifty-five: a meeting of them was held immediately; when they agreed upon . . . a Memorial to the Commander in Chief:

The Memorial of the Subscribers,
Humbly sheweth,
That your Memorialists, having been deprived of very valuable landed estates, and considerable personal properties, without the lines, and being also obliged to abandon their possessions in this city, on account of their loyalty to their Sovereign, and attachment to the British constitution, and seeing no prospect of their being reinstated, had determined to remove with their families, and settle in his Majesty's province of Nova-Scotia, on the terms which they understood were held out *equally* to all his Majesty's persecuted subjects.

That your Memorialists are much alarmed at an application which they are informed Fifty-five persons have joined in to your Excellency, soliciting a recommendation for tracts of land in that province, amounting together to *two hundred and seventy-five thousand acres*, and that they have dispatched forward Agents to survey the unlocated lands, and select the most fertile spots and desirable situations.

That, chagrined as your Memorialists are at the manner in which the late contest has been terminated, and disappointed as they find themselves in being left to the lenity of their enemies, on the dubious recommendation of their leaders, they yet hoped to find an asylum under British protection, little suspecting there could be found, among their fellow-sufferers, persons ungenerous enough to attempt engrossing to themselves so disproportionate a share of what Government has allotted for their common benefit, and so different from the original proposals.

That your Memorialists apprehend some misrepresentations have been used to procure such extraordinary recommendations, the applications for which have been most studiously concealed, until now that they boast its being too late to prevent the effect.

Nor does it lessen your Memorialists surprize to observe, that the persons concerned (several of whom are said to be going to Britain) are most of them in easy circumstances, and, with some exceptions, more distinguished by the repeated favours of Government, than by either the greatness of their sufferings, or the importance of their services.

That your Memorialists cannot but regard the grants in question, if carried into effect, as amounting nearly to a total exclusion of themselves and families, who, if they become settlers, must either content themselves with barren or remote lands, or submit to be tenants to those, most of whom they consider as their superiors in nothing but deeper art and keener policy.—Thus circumstanced,

Your Memorialists humbly implore redress from your Excellency, and that enquiry may be made into their respective losses, services, situations, and sufferings; and if your Memorialists shall be found equally entitled to the favour and protection of Government with the former applicants, that they may be all put on an equal footing; but should those who first applied be found, on a fair and candid enquiry, more deserving than your Memorialists, then your Memorialists humbly request that the locating their extensive grants may at least be postponed, until your Memorialists have taken up such small portions as may be allotted to them.

And your Memorialists, as in duty bound, shall ever pray, &c.
New-York, Aug. 15, 1783.

Signed by Samuel Hake,
and above 600 others.

Historical Interpretations

3 From Janice Potter, "Patriarchy and Paternalism: The Case of the Eastern Ontario Loyalist Women," *Ontario History* 81, 1 (1989): 3–24. © Ontario Historical Society (www.ontariohistoricalsociety.ca) and Janice Potter. Any alteration of its content or further copying in any form whatsoever is strictly prohibited unless otherwise permitted by law.

Although the American Revolution did not alter the legal or political rights of women, it changed their lives dramatically in other ways.[1] With the men away fighting, women were forced to shoulder the burden of running the farm, the estate, or the business, and as a result there was less rigidity in the sexual division of labour, women gained confidence in their abilities, and men had more respect for women and their contributions to society. Those experiences were reinforced by public recognition of women's contribution to the Revolution and by the ideology of the Revolution. For example, boycotts of British cloth meant that wearing homespun became a sign of patriotism and that spinning, one of the most time-consuming and clearly feminine domestic chores, was raised in status. Moreover, there was an anti-patriarchal aspect of the Revolution that fostered less authoritarian and more reciprocal relationships between men and women. Republican ideology, with its emphasis on voluntary consent, also allowed more scope for women. There was "greater mutuality and reciprocity" in marriages and in some cases "more egalitarian marital relationships."[2] The belief in the need to raise a moral and upright citizenry also enhanced the status of motherhood and made it easier for women to obtain an education, since it was they who would be raising the children. The result was more confident, self-reliant women, some of whom decided not to marry, and a society that valued more highly the domestic sphere generally and women specifically.

But what was the situation of Loyalist women, whose actions did not receive the same recognition and for whom there was no equivalent to republican ideology? The existing material on Loyalist women includes books about individuals, papers about specific groups, such as Loyalist women who filed claims for compensation, and an interesting thesis discussing Loyalist women in general terms.[3] This paper, however, considers in a preliminary way the effect of the Revolution on one specific group of Loyalist women—those who lived on the frontiers of New York, New England, and Pennsylvania and eventually settled in the townships created along the St Lawrence River and Lake Ontario between Longueuil and the Bay of Quinte in what is now eastern Ontario.

Despite the diversity of their ethnic origins, the eastern Ontario Loyalist women shared a common background characterized by paternalism and patriarchy, and their experiences during the Revolution were similar. Virtually all went through several stages in the course of becoming refugees: they were harassed or persecuted, they were forced to flee to British bases for protection, they lived under British military rule in what might be called refugee camps, and with aid from the British they were eventually resettled.

Information about these women can be found in the few personal letters and diaries that have survived, in the claims Loyalists made for compensation from the British government, and in the records of the Patriot committees that interrogated Loyalists and of the British authorities who had to supervise and provision them. And, from records such as military registers, provisioning lists, returns of Loyalists, and land grants, it is possible to compile a reasonably precise statistical profile of the eastern Ontario Loyalists.

The 1786 census reveals that the 1800 families, or 4661 individuals, living along the St Lawrence River and the eastern end of Lake Ontario were an ethnically diverse group that included many recent immigrants. Of the eastern Ontario Loyalists whose birthplace is known, about 45 per cent were foreign and about 45 per cent American-born.[4] Many of the American-born belonged to ethnic groups that had retained their native language, group cohesiveness, and other aspects of their culture. The largest of the ethnic minorities were the Germans, who accounted for about 30 per cent of the total and of whom one-quarter were immigrants and the rest Americans of German ancestry. About 5 per cent were Dutch, mostly more traditional members of the Dutch Reformed Church who had kept their culture and language.[5] Another group of American-born Loyalists who had retained their distinctive culture were the Mohawk Indians, who had played an important military role in the Revolution.

The largest of the immigrant groups, constituting 24 per cent of the total, were the Scots. Many were Highlanders and Jacobites who had emigrated because of poverty and the enclosure of their lands. In the colonies they retained their Gaelic language, Catholic religion, and other aspects of their culture.[6]

Whether American- or foreign-born, the vast majority of eastern Ontario Loyalists had lived on the frontiers of colonial society and were farmers. Over 70 per cent came from the northern New York counties of Tryon, Charlotte, and Albany. About 2 per cent came from each of New Jersey, Connecticut, and Pennsylvania, and many of the Pennsylvanians were from the frontier settlements along the Susquehanna River.[7] They had all been part of the mass movement to the frontiers after the Seven Years' War.

A common theme in the social relationships of many eastern Ontario Loyalists was paternalism. Paternalism has been variously defined as interference with people's liberty for their own good and as the determination by one person what is in the best interests of another. A paternalistic relationship need not be harsh, however, and can even be co-operative in that it is a close and affectionate relationship in which the dependent party feels the need for guidance and is willing to exchange some independence for security.[8] But in such a relationship there is a hierarchy or at least inequality—there are superiors and subordinates, leaders and followers—and the dominant party feels an obligation to protect the interests of the subordinate in return for loyalty and deference.

Eighteenth-century paternalism was exemplified in the relationship between some New York landlords and their tenants. In spite of the rush to the frontiers for land, not all colonial Americans managed to acquire land of their own. In the case of the eastern Ontario Loyalists, only 20 per cent had held their land in freehold, and some had shared land or squatted on disputed land, but the vast majority had been tenants on the northern New York manorial estates owned by families like the Johnsons; indeed, at least 20 per cent of the Loyalist claimants who settled in what is now eastern Ontario had been tenants of the Johnsons.

The Johnsons ran their 20 000-acre estate like quasi-feudal lords. They helped their tenants financially, burned the debtor bonds of over-extended tenants, and helped artisans like Richard Mandevell, a "Breeches Maker" who later settled in eastern Ontario, establish themselves in the local village. They also built roads, schools, and mills; introduced sheep and new crops; and at Johnstown, the county seat, established a county fair and built the local jail, courthouse, and Anglican church.[9]

In return for looking after the interests of their tenants, the Johnsons expected loyalty and deference—letters to them from tenants and others, for example, often began, "May it Please your Lordship". When the Revolution came, the Johnson's tenants formed an armed guard to protect their landlord, and when he fled to Canada, they followed.[10]

There were also other paternalistic relationships between eastern Ontario Loyalists and various authorities. Many of the colonists, of German Palatinate or French Huguenot ancestry were Protestants who had fled to England in search of religious freedom and who revered George III as a defender of Protestantism. The Highlanders were accustomed to an authoritarian society, and their family and clan structure was patriarchal. And the Mohawk, although they considered themselves an independent people, spoke of the king as a father and looked to the British government to protect them from the rapaciousness of the powerful New York landlords who spent much of the eighteenth century defrauding the Indians of their land. [. . .]

The social and family structure in which these Loyalists and other colonial Americans lived was also patriarchal if we take patriarchy to mean "the manifestation and institutionalization of male dominance over women and children in the family and the extension of male dominance over women in society in general. . . . [It] implies that men hold power in all the important institutions of society and that women are deprived of access to such power."[11] Colonial American society was patriarchal in several senses. Women could not participate in the political process, they could not get a higher education, and men controlled the most basic commodity in the society—land. Not only was the title to the family's property in the man's name, but a widow who remarried lost ownership of her property to her new husband. A married woman's identity was subsumed in that of her husband's. "A married couple," in the words of one historian, "became like a legal fiction: like a corporation, the pair was a single person with a single will"—the husband's. Even within the household it was common for the man to make all of the major decisions about finances and even about raising the children, and in any marital separation the man retained custody of the children.[12]

Patriarchal relationships, like paternalistic ones, did not mean that there could not be affection between husband and wife. To cite one example, a 1776 letter from Alexander McDonald, a captain in the Royal Highland Emigrants stationed in Halifax, to his wife in the colonies began, "My dear Susannah" and ended tenderly, "I have no time to write more. . . . Kiss the children for me and believe the one forever to be yours." Yet the patriarchal nature of the relationship was revealed in the instructions he gave her about all aspects of her life: "Keep the Child always clean and well dress'd and you must appear in yr best Colours yourself." Of a fellow soldier, he wrote, "Keep the old gentleman always at a distance from you and never let him again appear in the House."[13]

The subordination of women in the colonial American family was revealed in the diary of Dothe Stone, sister of the eastern Ontario Loyalist, Joel Stone. As Dothe's list of births illustrates, marriage and childbirth were central to women's lives. The average woman was married in her early twenties to a man from one to five years older; she could expect to be pregnant within 12 months, and her childbearing years became a cycle of pregnancy, birth, and lactation.[14]

The birth and care of children, combined with women's other tasks, meant that their life centred on the home. The family farm was the basic economic and social unit on the frontier, and although some women did have to help with clearing and farming the land, women's jobs were more often milking the cows, taking care of the chickens, planting and tending the garden, and harvesting the

orchard. As well, they cared for the house, salted beef and pork, preserved fruit and stored vegetables, made cider and cheese, and dried apples. A major chore was making clothing: Dothe writes of spending days with her sisters at spinning wheels. Whereas her husband might get away from home by going fishing or hunting or by travelling to town for supplies or to do business, the woman, especially if she had small children (which was almost always), was tied to the home.[15]

Colonial women found security in what was familiar to them—their homes, their families, and their circle of community friends and relatives. Dothe wrote fondly of her favourite room, her "once loved chamber," and her diary is full of excitement when describing social events, such as weddings, or gatherings at which a fiddler led the party in singing and dancing. Dothe also relied heavily on female companionship. Tasks like spinning were done in the company of other women; women helped each other in childbirth and child rearing, and most of them lived in the same house as, or close to, other female relatives. [. . .] Home, family, and female companionship were what mattered most to colonial women. [. . .]

Relationships within the colonial family were patriarchal, and even women themselves spoke of their own inferiority and dependence. Widows, like the strong-minded Patriot, Mary Fish, for example, described themselves as "a poor weak and helpless creature, [who] could do nothing but lie at the foot of mercy and look for direction." "What," she asked rhetorically, "Could a feble [sic] woman do."[16] Statements like these do not necessarily mean that women inwardly accepted the notion of their helplessness and inferiority. What they do mean, however, is that the social norms were such that women felt the need to express their feminine dependence and weakness.

But the notions of female helplessness and dependence were brought into question by the Revolution, which posed new challenges for Patriot *and* Loyalist women and forced many to adopt new roles. To Loyalist women, attached to their homes and local surroundings, accustomed to the security of friends, relatives, and neighbours, and used to relying on men to direct their lives and make important decisions for them, the Revolution was a shattering experience. Patriot women, it is true, were left to manage the family and farm or business in their husbands' absence; but at least most remained in their homes and communities. Many Loyalist women, however, lost everything they valued most. Their families were scattered and the men who had directed their lives, gone. Many were also wrenched from all that was familiar—their homes, their relatives, and their communities. What all Loyalist women shared was their experiences as refugees, which were far more challenging than those of most Patriot women.

The pattern was set in May 1776, when Sir John Johnson fled from his northern New York estate with 170 tenants to escape arrest by the Patriots and to seek refuge in Canada, leaving behind his wife, Lady Mary Watts Johnson, who was pregnant and already the mother of two children under two. Mary, or Polly, who was from a prosperous New York city merchant and banking family, had married Sir John in 1773 at the age of 19 and moved north to live in Tryon County. When her husband fled, Polly could not accompany him because of her condition, the hastiness of his departure, and the extraordinary rigours of the trip. Disappointed at the escape of Sir John, the Patriots forced her to turn over the keys to "every place"; her husband's private papers were seized, his "books distributed about the country," and their home, Johnson Hall, plundered and "made a Barrack." Lady Johnson was held hostage in Albany, although she was in touch regularly with her husband through "Indian and white men . . . sent through the Woods." After some 20 months in captivity, Lady Johnson escaped, travelling through enemy territory in the cold winter. Although she finally reached the British base in New York City, her youngest child died as a result of its traumatic experiences.[17]

Within months of Lady Johnson's escape the war that was to rage on the frontier for more than four years began, and the hostages in this vicious conflict were the women and the children. As the Patriots attempted to assert their control over the region by forcing suspected Loyalists to take oaths of allegiance or join the militia, many able-bodied Loyalist men were either arrested or followed Sir John Johnson's lead by escaping to British lines, reluctantly leaving their families behind. Once in Canada, most had to join the various Loyalist regiments that collaborated with the Indians to launch retaliatory raids on the American frontier. For the British, the raids had a military purpose; to harass the enemy and destroy food supplies for Patriot forces. For many Loyalist soldiers, the raids were an opportunity to seek revenge on their foes in the colonies, find new recruits, make contact with their families, and occasionally bring the families back to Canada. For the families, the raids complicated their already troubled lives by intensifying Patriot hatred of the Loyalists and compromising them even further, since the families often harboured or helped the raiding parties. As the raiding parties retreated to the safety of Canada, they left their families behind.[18]

With the men in their lives gone, Loyalist women were forced to assume new responsibilities, and some even actively engaged in the war effort. For example, three women were implicated in a plot to kidnap the mayor of Albany, and one, an Indian woman, confessed to having lured the mayor to the woods by reporting that she had found a dead body there.[19] Another woman was arrested and jailed along with 20 men for "having assisted in the destruction of Currey Town."[20] Women were arrested and some imprisoned for taking part in robberies, which were especially common at the manor of Rensse-laerwyck in the late 1770s.[21] Loyalist women also provided intelligence and passed messages between the British in New York City and Canada.[22]

Two eastern Ontario Loyalist women who were unusually active in the war effort were associated with the Mohawk Indians. This is not surprising in light of the status of women in the matrilineal Mohawk society, where children belonged to the mother's rather than the father's clan and women chose and deposed the chiefs. The local economy of the predominantly agrarian Mohawk was controlled by the women, who were responsible for planting, harvesting, and distributing the crops. Mohawk matrons were also influential in war councils and in determining the fate of captives.[23]

One very influential Mohawk woman was Molly Brant, or Konwatsi'tsianienni. A member of a high-ranking Mohawk family, sister of the famous Mohawk chief, Joseph Brant, and a matron who had a great influence in the matrilineal Iroquois society, Molly Brant "was a person of great prestige in her nation and throughout the Confederacy." Her power and influence were heightened after 1759, when she became the wife in all but name of Sir William Johnson, superintendent of Indian affairs, with whom she had eight children. Equally at home in the Indian village, in the war council, as the charming and gracious hostess at Johnson Hall, or in running Johnson's huge estate during his frequent absences, Molly Brant was a remarkable woman.[24]

She helped many Loyalists escape to Canada, provided intelligence to the British, and played a decisive part in fostering the ties of loyalty, self-interest, and history that underpinned the Mohawk support for the British during the Revolution. After her home was plundered by the Patriots and she was forced to flee with her family to the safety of the Iroquois villages, Brant came to Canada in 1778 and moved from one British base to another, cementing the Mohawks' loyalty to the British. Daniel Claus, Indian agent and son-in-law of the late Sir William Johnson, said of Molly Brant, "One word from her is more taken notice of by the five nations than a thousand from any white man without Exception." The commanding officer at Carleton Island attributed the good behaviour of the Indians there to Brant's influence: "The Chiefs were careful to keep their people sober and satisfy'd, but their uncommon good behaviour is in a great Measure to be ascribed to Miss Molly Brant's influence over them, which is far superior to that of all their Chiefs put together, and she has in the course of this Winter done every thing in Her power to maintain them strongly in the King's interest." Brant's stature was recognized by the British government, which awarded her one of the largest pensions ever given to any Indian and built her a house at present-day Kingston, where she spent her last years.[25]

Another woman influential among the Mohawk was Sarah Kast McGinnis, an American-born Palatine German, who as a child in northern New York lived with the Mohawks, was adopted by them, and learned their language. In the 1740s Sarah married an Irishman, Timothy McGinnis, who became involved with Sir William Johnson in the fur trade and as a captain in the Indian Department. After her husband was killed in the Seven Years' War, the widow McGinnis carried on his trading business.[26]

When the Revolution broke out, both sides courted Sarah because of her close association with the Iroquois, the Patriots offering her 12 shillings York currency a day and a guard of 15 men. But Sarah and her family sided with the British and worked to cement the Iroquois' loyalty, actions that caused them to be persecuted by the Patriots. In 1777, as news spread of Burgoyne's expedition from Canada through northern New York, the Patriots considered it necessary to neutralize

Loyalists like Sarah and her family. In Sarah's case, this involved arresting her son-in-law and then confiscating all her property. Sarah, her daughters, and grandchildren watched helplessly as their belongings were sold at public auction; they were then arrested and "so harshly used" that one granddaughter died. When the Patriots mistakenly concluded that the British had the upper hand in the region, Sarah and her family were released. Before they could be recaptured, they "escaped at night with only what they could carry on their backs" and left for Canada with British troops, although Sarah had to leave behind a son "who was out of his senses and bound in chains . . . and who some time afterward was burnt alive."[27]

After arriving in Canada, Sarah agreed to a British request to return to northern New York, winter with the Iroquois, and try to counter the harmful effects of Burgoyne's defeat. On her arrival at "the most central village of the Six nations," the Indians "flocked to her from the remotest villages and thanked her for coming . . . to direct and advise them in that critical time." Soon after her arrival, the Patriots sent messages to the Iroquois, "with a most exaggerated account of General Burgoyne's disaster" and "belts," inviting them to join the Patriots along with "threats" in case the Indians refused. In response to the Patriot overtures, the Indians "consulted with" Sarah and sought her "opinion and advice": "Then after that with an Authority and privilege allowed to women of Consequence only among Indians, [she] seized upon and cancelled the [Patriot] Belts, telling them such bad news came from an evil Spirit and must endanger their peace and union as long as it was in their sight and therefore must be buried underground."[28] When Sarah spent this long and difficult winter in the Indian villages, she was 64 years old.

Although Sarah Kast McGinnis's relationship with the Indians and her active participation in the Revolution were extraordinary, her other experiences were typical of those of other Loyalist women. As able-bodied Loyalist men on the frontiers either were arrested or fled, leaving their families behind, the sins of the fathers and husbands were visited on the wives and children. Patriot committees and mobs assumed, unless there was evidence to the contrary, that families were accomplices in the guilt of one member. If one member of a family fled or was arrested, the rest were vulnerable either to official interrogation by committees or to unofficial harassment by mobs or Patriot neighbours.

The case of the Cartwright family was not unusual. The father, Richard, Sr., a prosperous innkeeper, landowner, and deputy postmaster of Albany, had shown his support for the Patriots in 1775 when he gave money to the Patriot expedition against Ticonderoga. But his daughter, Elizabeth, who was married to a British soldier and lived in Niagara, was in touch with his son, Richard, Jr., and when the local committee of correspondence discovered this in February 1777, it forced Richard, Jr., to give security for his future good behaviour. By October 1777 he could no longer give this guarantee, and with his young niece, Hannah, he left on a difficult journey through the northern New York wilderness to Canada. The parents, tainted by the Loyalism of their children, were mistreated, their property was confiscated, and within a year of their son's departure they were taken under guard to the border.[29]

The Cartwrights' experiences were shared by many Loyalist women who had to live with the consequences of their husbands' actions. With the men in their lives gone, the women not only had to assume responsibility for running the farm and taking care of their families, but also had to deal with Patriot harassment or persecution and in many cases they were forced to leave their homes to seek refuge behind the British lines. [. . .]

The severity of the treatment meted out to Loyalist women depended on their husbands' connections and reputation among the dominant faction in the community. The case of two Vermont Loyalist women illustrates this point. Sarah Bottum was the wife of Justus Sherwood, a Vermont landowner, speculator, and entrepreneur in the timber business. Originally from Connecticut, Justus had received his land in Vermont from the New Hampshire government, and he supported Ethan Allen and his brothers, the dominant faction in the disputed territory. When Justus fell afoul of the local Patriots for refusing to take an oath of allegiance and allegedly corresponding with the British, he was threatened with execution and imprisoned, although he escaped and fled to Canada. The Patriots ransacked the Sherwoods' cabin and destroyed some of their belongings, but Sarah could look to her parents for help, and she was allowed to remain in Vermont until she decided to seek permission from the Patriots to join her husband in Canada.[30]

The treatment of another Vermont Loyalist, Mary Munro, was much harsher because her husband belonged to an unpopular faction in Vermont. John Munro, originally from Scotland, had been granted large tracts of land by New York, and this put him at odds with the dominant faction in Vermont, whose land grants came from New Hampshire. Munro became even more unpopular when he was appointed justice of the peace and given the unenviable task of imposing law and order on Ethan Allen and the Green Mountain boys, who harassed New Yorkers in Vermont. When the Revolution came and Munro supported the British, the Council of Safety drove him from his home and seized all his property, except "a few personal articles left for the support of his wife." Unlike Sarah Sherwood, who had the support of her family, Mary Munro was treated very harshly by her neighbours and shunned by her own family. She wrote to her husband of her plight:

I am in a poor state of health and very much distresst. I must leave my house in a very short time and God knows where I shall get a place to put my head in, for my own relations are my greatest enemies. . . . They have distrest me beyond expression. I have scarcely a mouthful of bread for myself or children. . . . Is there no possibility of your sending for us? If there is no method fallen upon we shall all perish, for you can have no idea of our sufferings here . . . my heart is so full it is ready to break.

Luckily, Mary Munro and her eight children did make their way to Canada within a few months of this letter.[31]

Flight may have represented an end to persecution for many Loyalist women; yet, it was also difficult for them to leave their homes and cut their ties with their families, friends, and communities. Simon Schwartz, the son of tenants of the Johnson family, who described his father's flight to Canada with Sir John in 1776 and the harassment of other family members, stressed that his mother had left only when she had to; she "would not come in [to Canada] before the House & builds [sic] were burnt." Women like Mrs. Schwartz usually had no choice but to leave. If they left voluntarily, it was usually because their property had been confiscated or their homes destroyed and there were no relatives or neighbours to protect them.

Some Loyalist women simply fled, but many others sought permission to leave from Patriot committees. Either permission was granted and the women escorted to the frontiers, or they were exchanged for Patriot prisoners being held in Canada. Mary Cruger Meyers had been alone with seven children under 13 since the summer of 1777, when her husband, John Walden Meyers, left to join Burgoyne. In October 1778 she and another Loyalist woman requested permission to go to New York.[32] After being dispossessed of their property, the wives of Loyalists in Tryon County petitioned the local Patriot committee to be either taken care of or allowed to join their husbands. Their latter request was eventually granted.[33] When women left, they could only take children under 12 with them; boys 12 and over were considered capable of bearing arms and had to be left behind.[34] Those going to British lines also had to pay all the costs of being escorted there and take 14 days' provisions with them.[35]

By the late 1770s, however, many Loyalist women were forced to leave. Some were sent to Canada because they were destitute and "subsisted at public Expense". A more common reason for removing the women was that they had assisted the enemy. When their husbands, relatives, or friends returned to the frontiers from Canada to gather intelligence, to recruit, or to raid, the women provided food, shelter, and other forms of assistance, which only further incriminated them in the eyes of the Patriots. Rachel Ferguson and her daughters, for example, were brought before the local Patriot committee in 1779 "for harbouring and entertaining a Number of Tories who came down from Canada with an inte[n]tion of Murdering the Defenceless Inhabitants on the Western Frontiers."[36] For their efforts the Ferguson women were jailed and later forced to leave.

By July 1780 it was official policy in New York to "remove families of persons who [had] joined the Enemy." The families were given 20 days to prepare for their departure, their goods and chattels were to be sold to pay the costs, and any who ignored the edict were to "be liable to be proceeded against as Enemies of this and the United States."[37] Some women asked for and received a reprieve; but this required that "sundry well affected inhabitants" had to testify that the woman had "behaved herself in a becoming manner."[38] In other words, it was up to the woman to prove innocence by having well-known Patriots testify on her behalf. In the absence of such testimony, the woman was assumed to share the guilt of her husband.

Exile was the last stage in a process that profoundly altered the role and responsibilities of many Loyalist women. Like their Patriot counterparts, Loyalist women assumed the responsibility for running the household and farm in the absence of their husbands. But Loyalist women also had to endure harassment, persecution, and often poverty because of the actions of their husbands. Most difficult of all, perhaps, was the necessity of abandoning their homes, relatives, and communities. [. . .]

Women were also forced to take more responsibility for looking after themselves and families. A group of New York Loyalist women who had established themselves near Saratoga petitioned the Patriots in 1780 for permission to go to Canada; in 1781 they were still on the frontier and regarded as a serious enough threat that they were ordered to move to the interior. The 16-year-old daughter of John McDonell, a Scots Loyalist from Tryon county, "was obliged to hire herself to an old Dutch woman to spin in order to prevent starving." And there was the case of Elizabeth Bowman, who, after her house on the Susquehanna River had been sacked by the Patriots and her husband and eldest son carried off, was left to care for eight children. The Indians helped them through the winter, and in the spring she moved to the Mohawk River and joined other Loyalist women to grow corn and potatoes. When the British rescued them in the fall and took them to Canada, there were 5 women, 31 children, and one pair of shoes.[39]

Exile marked the end of one stage of Loyalist women's refugee experience and the beginning of another. The women had left the American colonies as disaffected citizens considered a threat to the security of the new nation. In British territory they were burdens, mouths to be fed and bodies to be clothed and housed. When they reached Canada, they were usually destitute and the British unprepared for their arrival. In 1777 an officer in Niagara described the refugees flocking to that base: "They are almost naked and have been so long hiding in the woods, and almost famished that it is distressing to behold them. . . . I am informed that 50 are on their way, but so weak they can scarcely crawl. I wish your excellency's direction on how to dispose of them."[40] From Crown Point, a base at the other end of the outer perimeter of British defences, came similar accounts of the arrival of Loyalists who "had fled from persecution," especially in the winter when the lakes and rivers could be crossed by sleigh. Often British officials were uncertain what to do with the refugees, and families arriving in Niagara were often sent on to Montreal.[41]

When the women arrived at the bases, they were in need of food, clothing, and shelter. Most had been stripped of their property and many of their possessions before their flight. The journey itself across the wilderness of northern New York was gruelling. Reaching Canada involved either crossing one of the many lakes in an open boat or perhaps a sleigh in winter, or travelling along rugged trails since "there [was] no road by land to go with a carriage." Sir John Johnson and his tenants who fled from northern New York in 1776 travelled for 19 days, during which they almost starved, going nine days without provisions, except "wild onions, Roots and the leaves of beech trees." When they reached Canada, their shoes were worn through and their clothes ragged.[42]

Sarah Bottum Sherwood's greatest ordeal during the Revolution was her trip to Canada, which began with a wagon ride over trails to the shores of Lake Champlain. Next was a boat trip across the lake and a 30-mile trek through the bush to the closest British outpost. When Sarah undertook the trek, it was November; she had with her a slave, a child of three, and a baby; and she was seven months pregnant. But she succeeded and was re-united with her husband.[43]

When Loyalists arrived at British bases, penniless and exhausted by the rigours of their journey, they were at the mercy of paternalistic and patriarchal British military regimes. Even Sarah McGinnis, the tough 64-year-old who had wintered with the Iroquois in 1777, was "in dire need" in Montreal

the following year. Her daughter was "so scantily lodged" that her mother could not stay with her. She was also refused firewood by the officer in charge, who said that only the governor could make such a decision. Sarah and her family were left "without any money or income except what they could earn by the needle."[44] Thus, Loyalists had to look to the British government to provide shelter, clothing, and rations and at the end of the war to chart their future.

The British government took care of its charges but expected deference and service in return. The British regimes were military ones that dealt quickly and harshly with dissenters. In return for their keep, men had to fight in the Loyalist regiments and women had to do washing and other domestic chores for the army. Questioning of the regime was neither common nor tolerated. When a group of Loyalists in Quebec petitioned the governor for more aid, for example, they were informed that if the governor's plans for them were not acceptable, they could go to Nova Scotia.[45]

Patriarchy and paternalism were also apparent in the last phase of the Loyalists' experience—their resettlement in what is now eastern Ontario. Under the direction of British officials, the Loyalists were transported into the interior and provided with food, clothing, agricultural equipment, and seeds. They were settled on land surveyed by British officials, and British army officers were there to preserve order and ensure that the governor's instructions were obeyed. Although the new communities were on the frontier, from the beginning there was a structure and hierarchy. In a society where land ownership was central to status, the size of one's land grant varied according to one's military rank, the British government compensated Loyalists for their losses on the basis of the value of their former assets in the American colonies, and Loyalist officers received half pay after their regiments were disbanded.[46]

Thus, when Loyalist women reached British lines, they were re-integrated into a

paternalistic and patriarchal power structure. Within this paternalistic order there
was a hierarchy. There were those who
needed to be cared for and those responsible
for administering the care, those in leadership roles and those who were clearly subordinates. Deference to authority was built
into the military regimes, and deference was
accorded to those dispensing benevolent care
and expected of those receiving it. Even more
so than the civil regimes in the American
colonies, the military regimes in Quebec and
New York City had no place for women and
even shunned them as extra mouths to be
fed and families to be housed. Women could
only fit into such paternalistic and patriarchal power structures as subordinates needing care and protection.

This subordination was reflected in the
Loyalist women's petitions for rations, subsistence, or compensation for losses. The very
act of petitioning those in authority for aid
cast all Loyalists in the role of supplicant;
"the formulation of a petition," in the words
of Linda Kerber, "begins in the acknowledgement of subordination."[47] Moreover, many
Loyalist petitions were stylized litanies of loyalty, service, and sacrifice. But there was a difference in the substance of women's petitions:
women based their claim to British assistance
on their feminine frailty and on the service
of their husbands. In fact, some did not even
petition on their own behalf but had men
request aid for them. When Catherine Peck,
wife of one of Sir John's tenants who had fled
to Canada in 1776, arrived in New York City
"in hope of getting a Passage to Canada" and
found herself and her child "destitute of any
Sort of Support," it was an official from Indian Affairs who appealed to British officials
to assist her.[48] Even Molly Brant, who had
been so active in maintaining the loyalty of
the Mohawk, had to seek male help when it
came to approaching the British for support.
She sought advice from her brother in 1779,
and in 1780 two members of the Johnson
clan and another associate discussed helping

Molly and her daughters to get a pension
from the British.[49] Of the 26 eastern Ontario
Loyalist women who sought compensation
from the British for their losses, four had men
file their claims.[50]

Whether Loyalist women petitioned
themselves or had others do it for them, what
was stressed was their weakness, helplessness, and dependence. Citing a "numerous,
small and helpless family" as his main burden, one Loyalist appealed to the governor of
Quebec for subsistence, while another asked
for aid for his "chargeable family". The Loyalist Jean McConell summed up perfectly
the notion of female incapacity when she described herself as "feeble" and added that she
also had "a family of daughters".[51] Feeble and
helpless were the adjectives used most often
by Loyalist women to describe themselves.[52]

These professions of feebleness were
very much at odds with Loyalist women's recent experiences. The case of Phoebe Grant,
or Grout, illustrates this point nicely. When
her husband and son joined Burgoyne in
1777, the "rebels" seized his property and
"effects" and turned her "and three helpless
Female children Out of Doors destitute."
She then had to "fly" to Quebec "for protection". Within days of her arrival in Quebec,
her husband drowned and she was "obliged
to provide for herself and her three children without an allowance from government
which ceased on the death of her husband."
After her husband's death she did "everything in her power to support herself," even
though she was "in a country far from a single
Friend and a stranger to the language." When
Phoebe finally had to throw "herself and poor
family at your Excellency's feet praying" for
subsistence, she could not revel in her accomplishments and seek praise for even surviving such ordeals; all she could do was tell her
story as a tale of suffering and depict herself,
in her own words, as "a Feeble Woman".[53]

Why did Loyalist women describe themselves as feeble or helpless when their recent
experiences suggested just the opposite?

One reason was a practical reality. What the British needed from the Loyalists were able-bodied males to raid the frontiers, spy on the Patriots, bring in new recruits, supply British troops, or build fortifications. What they did not need or want was women and children, who, it was assumed, could perform none of these services and would be a burden to the British because they had to be fed, clothed, and housed. Thus, the only way for women to appeal to the British was to cite their husbands' valued services, rather than their own undervalued ones, and to invoke the paternalism of the military regimes by stressing their vulnerability and need for protection.

Another reason, however, was that when they reached British lines, Loyalist women confronted a well-defined power structure in which there were clearly prescribed social roles. In the colonies during the Revolution, traditional relationships were disrupted and lines of authority far from clear. Women could and did do things they might have never dreamed of doing in peacetime, and their actions were of necessity considered socially acceptable, if only because the boundaries of socially acceptable behaviour are more flexible in wartime. However, at British bases lines of authority were not only clear, but were better defined than they had been in the colonies. Though there had been elements of paternalism and patriarchy in the pre-Revolutionary experiences of many Ontario Loyalists, the British regimes were much more patriarchal and paternal. And women could fit into such a power structure only as frail subordinates.

But the fact that women used the language of enfeeblement does not mean that they themselves accepted their own weakness. They were supplicants who had to petition for assistance, and "the rhetoric of humility is a necessary part of the petition as a genre, whether or not humility is felt in fact."[54] Women had no choice but to stress their dependence and helplessness; whether they actually believed it is another matter.

Yet, whether or not women accepted their own weakness is beside the point. The language they used expressed accurately their position in the power structure. Whether or not they were weak and dependent, they were assumed to be so for all public purposes and were outwardly treated as such. On the other hand, the consistent use of certain words cannot be divorced from one's attitudes about oneself: if women were forced by circumstances to reiterate their helplessness again and again, how long was it before they came either to accept that helplessness was basic to their femininity or to allow their actions to be limited by their supposed weakness? The fact that the eastern Ontario Loyalist women were never allowed to speak of their achievements with pride meant that they never received in any measure the recognition accorded to Patriot women.

It is ironic that many eastern Ontario Loyalist women, though they overcame greater obstacles and met more devastating challenges during the Revolution than their Patriot counterparts, received less recognition. As well as having to take charge of their families and farms in the absence of their husbands, Loyalist women were dispossessed of their property, thrown out of their houses, and even jailed by the Patriots. They had to leave what was most dear to them—their homes, their relatives, and their friends—and travel through the wilderness to the British lines.

Yet these remarkable and heroic accomplishments were never recognized. When they reached British lines, they had to fit once again into a patriarchal power structure in which their inferiority and dependence were assumed. Needing British support, they had to stress their dependence and weakness to appeal to the paternalism of the British regime. Only their suffering and their husbands' service counted with the British. Whereas republicanism at least potentially offered more scope to women, paternalism assumed inequality and deference. There were the weak and the strong, the leaders and the followers. Within such a framework, women could only be the weak followers.

Not only were the accomplishments of eastern Ontario Loyalist women not recognized by the British; they were also ignored by later generations. After the Revolution, myths grew up about the Loyalists' undying devotion to the British Empire or their upper class backgrounds, and tales were told of the men's heroism. Virtually ignored, however, were the heroic feats of the Loyalist women. Whereas the contributions of Patriot women, such as their spinning of homespun cloth, became part of the American folklore, the memories of the travails and victories of the eastern Ontario Loyalist women died with them.

These women were also ignored by Canadian historians, who, by focusing on the Revolutionary war on the frontier as it was run by the British and fought by the Loyalist regiments, have overlooked the essential fact that the war was a civil war in which women and children were of necessity participants. The experiences of the eastern Ontario Loyalist women and their part in the civil war that raged on the frontiers are an important part of Canadian history. Recognition of their accomplishments is long overdue.

NOTES

1. Mary Beth Norton, *Liberty's Daughters: The Revolutionary Experience of American Women, 1750–1800* (Boston: Little, Brown, 1980); Linda Kerber, *Women of the Republic: Intellect and Ideology in Revolutionary America* (Chapel Hill, NC: University of North Carolina Press, 1980). For another view, see Joan Hoff Wilson, "The Illusion of Change: Women and the American Revolution," in Alfred F. Young, ed., *The American Revolution: Explorations in the History of American Radicalism* (DeKalb: Northern Illinois University Press, 1976), pp. 383–446.

2. Jay Fliegelman, *Prodigals and Pilgrims: The American Revolution against Patriarchal Authority, 1750–1800* (Cambridge: Cambridge University Press, 1982); Norton, *Liberty's Daughters*, pp. 235, 229; Jacqueline S. Reinier, "Rearing the Republican Child: Attitudes and Practices in Post-Revolutionary Philadelphia," *William and Mary Quarterly*, 3rd ser., 39 (1982): 150–63.

3. See, for example, Mary Beacock Fryer, "Sarah Sherwood: Wife and Mother, an 'Invisible Loyalist,'" in *Eleven Exiles: Accounts of Loyalists of the American Revolution*, Phyllis R. Blakely and John N. Grant, eds (Toronto: Dundurn, 1982), pp. 245–64; Mary Beth Norton, "Eighteenth-Century American Women in Peace and War: The Case of the Loyalists," *William and Mary Quarterly*, 3rd ser., 33 (1976): 386–409; Katherine M.J. McKenna,

"'Treading the Hard Road': Some Loyalist Women and the American Revolution" (MA thesis, Queen's University, 1979).

4. M.S. Waltman, "From Soldier to Settler: Patterns of Loyalist Settlement in 'Upper Canada,' 1783–1785" (MA thesis, Queen's University, 1981), p. 58.

5. Waltman, "From Soldier to Settler," p. 60; Walter Allen Knittle, *Early Eighteenth Century Palatinate Emigration: A British Government Redemptioner Project to Manufacture Naval Stores* (Baltimore: Dorrance, 1937); Eula C. Lapp, *To Their Heirs Forever* (Picton: Picton Publishing Co., 1970); Alice P. Kenney, *Stubborn for Liberty: The Dutch in New York* (Syracuse: Syracuse University Press, 1975); "The Albany Dutch: Loyalists and Patriots," *New York History*, 42 (1961).

6. Waltman, "From Soldier to Settler," p. 62; I.C.C. Graham, *Colonists from Scotland: Emigration to North America, 1707–1783* (Ithaca: Cornell University Press, 1956); Hazel C. Mathews, *The Mark of Honour* (Toronto: University of Toronto Press, 1965).

7. Waltman, "From Soldier to Settler," pp. 39–42.

8. Gerald Dworkin, "'Paternalism,'" in Rolf Sartorius, ed., *Paternalism* (Minneapolis: University of Minnesota Press, 1983), pp. 19–34; Donald Van De Veer, *Paternalistic Intervention: The Moral Bound of Benevolence* (Princeton: Princeton University Press, 1986), pp. 16–23;

John Kleinig, *Paternalism* (Totow, NJ: Rowman and Allaneld, 1984), pp. 4–5; Jack D. Douglas, "Co-operative Paternalism versus Conflictual Paternalism," in Sartorius, *Paternalism*, pp. 171–200; David Roberts, *Paternalism in Early Victorian England* (New Brunswick, NJ: Rutgers University Press, 1979), pp. 4–6.

9. Abbott Collection, Ms. 420, Letter and Reference for Richard Mandevell, Sir William Johnson, 11 June 1771, quoted in Robert William Venables, "Tryon County, 1775–1783: A Frontier in Revolution" (PhD thesis, Vanderbilt University, 1967), pp. 72, 64; Edward Countryman, *A People in Revolution: The American Revolution and Political Society* (Baltimore: Johns Hopkins University Press, 1981), pp. 21, 33.

10. Countryman, *A People in Revolution*, p. 33.

11. Gerda Lerner, *The Creation of Patriarchy* (New York: Oxford University Press, 1986), p. 239.

12. Kerber, *Women of the Republic*, p. 120; Joan R. Gundersen and Gwen Victor Gampel, "Married Women's Legal Status in Eighteenth-Century New York and Virginia," *William and Mary Quarterly*, 3rd ser., 39 (1982): 114–34.

13. NAC, Fraser Papers, MG 23, B 33, Alexander McDonald to his wife, in "Letters Extracted from the Letter Book of Capt. Alexander McDonald of the Royal Highland Emigrants written from Halifax, Windsor and Cornwallis between 1775 and 1779."

14. Archives of Ontario [hereafter AO], Joel Stone Papers, Dothe Stone Diary, 1777–1792 [hereafter Stone Diary]; Joy Day Buel and Richard Buel, Jr., *The Way of Duty: A Woman and her Family in Revolutionary America* (New York: Norton, 1984); Robert V. Wells, "Quaker Marriage Patterns in a Colonial Perspective," in Nancy F. Cott and Elizabeth Peck, eds, *A Heritage of Her Own: Toward a New Social History of American Women* (New York: Simon and Shuster, 1979), pp. 81–106; Norton, *Liberty's Daughters*, pp. 71–72; Laurel Thatcher Ulrich, *Good Wives: Image and Reality in the Lives of Women in Northern New England, 1650–1750* (New York: Knopf, 1982).

15. See, for example, Stone Diary; Norton, *Liberty's Daughters*, pp. 3–14.

16. New Canaan Historical Society, Noyes Family Papers, pp. 39–47, Mary to Joseph and Rachel Fish, 6 August 1769, 30 May 1772, privately owned, quoted in Buel, *The Way of Duty*, pp. 62–63, p. 67.

17. NAC, Claus Papers, C-1478, vol. 1, Sir John Johnson to Daniel Claus, 20 January 1777.

18. Jack M. Sosin, *The Revolutionary Frontier, 1763–1783* (New York: Holt, Rinehart and Winston, 1967).

19. Victor Hugo Palsits, ed., *Minutes of the Commissioners for Detecting and Defeating Conspiracies in the State of New York: Albany County Sessions, 1778–1781*, 3 vols (New York: J.B. Lyon, 1909), 13 August 1781, vol. 2, 762–63.

20. Ibid., 25 July 1781, vol. 2, 751–52.

21. Ibid., 4 September 1778, vol. 1, 224; 20 May 1778, vol. 1, 122; 17 June 1778, vol. 1, 146; 3 August 1779, vol. 1, 398; 3 October 1778, vol. 1, 252.

22. Ibid., 8 November 1780, vol. 2, 563; 29 January 1781, vol. 2, 624; 9 June 1781, vol. 2, 733.

23. Barbara Graymont, *The Iroquois in the American Revolution* (Syracuse: Syracuse University Press, 1972), pp. 17, 21–23.

24. Graymont, *The Iroquois in the American Revolution*, p. 47; *Dictionary of Canadian Biography*, vol. 4, 416–19; H. Pearson Gundy, "Molly Brant, Loyalist," *Ontario Historical Society Papers and Records*, 45 (1953): 97–108.

25. NAC, HP, vol. 21, p. 774, Daniel Claus to Governor Haldimand, 30 August 1779; NAC, HP, vol. 21, p. 787, Captain Frazer to Haldimand, 21 March 1780.

26. NAC, HP, vol. 21, p. 774, Daniel Claus to Governor Haldimand, 5 November 1778.

27. NAC, HP, vol. 27, p. 302, Petition of Sarah McGinn, Audit Office 14.

28. Ibid.

29. Janice Potter and George Rawlyk, "Richard Cartwright, Jr," *Dictionary of Canadian Biography*, vol. 5, 167–72.

30. *PAO Report*, Claim of Justus Sherwood; Ian Cleghorn Pemberton, "Justus Sherwood, Vermont Loyalist, 1747–1798," (PhD thesis, University of Western Ontario, 1973); Mary Beacock Fryer, *Buckskin Pimpernel: The Exploits of Justus Sherwood, Loyalist Spy* (Toronto: Dundurn, 1981), "Sarah Sherwood: . . . ," *Eleven Exiles*, pp. 245–64; Queen's University Archives, H.M. Jackson, *Justus Sherwood: Soldier, Loyalist and Negotiator* (Kingston: n.p., 1958).

31. AO, John Munro Papers, Undated document; NAC, HP, series B, vol. 214, p. 35.

32. Palsits, *Minutes of the Commissioners*, 1 October 1778, vol. 1, 248.

33. "Petition of sundry women wives of tories for relief," n.d. Tryon County Committee of Safety Papers, in Kerber, *Women of the Republic*, p. 50.

34. Palsits, *Minutes of the Commissioners*, 1 August 1778, vol. 1, 190.

35. Ibid., Introduction, vol. 1, 57.

36. Ibid., *Minutes of the Commissioners*, 21 September 1778, vol. 1, 237–8; 8 September 1779, vol. 1, 441.

37. Ibid., vol. 3, 795.

38. See, for example, the case of Elizabeth Hogel, in Palsits, *Minutes of the Commissioners*, vol. 2, 540.

39. Palsits, *Minutes of the Commissioners*, 29 October 1780, vol. 3, 558; 30 April 1781, vol. 3, 696; NAC, HP, vol. 73, p. 54, John McDonell to Mathews, 20 March 1780; "A Letter from Mrs. Elizabeth Bowman Spohn," in J.J. Talman, *Loyalist Narratives from Upper Canada* (Toronto: Champlain Society, 1946): 315–22.

40. NAC, Colonial Office 42 [hereafter CO 42], vol. 36, B 33, pp. 2–3, R.B. Lernoult to Haldimand, 28 April 1777.

41. CO 42, Q13, vol. 36, B 33, Sir Guy Carleton to Lord G. Germaine, 27 May 1777; NAC, Claus Papers, vol. 25, C 1485, Taylor and Diffin to Daniel Claus, 11 November 1778, Claus Papers.

42. Claus Papers, C 1478, vol. 1, Johnson to Claus, 20 January 1777.

43. Fryer, "Sarah Sherwood: . . . ," *Eleven Exiles*, pp. 245–64.

44. NAC, HP, vol. 21, p. 774, Claus to Haldimand, 19 November 1778.

45. NAC, HP, vol. B 211, pp. 133–4, Memorial: Michael Grass and Loyalists from New York, Sorel, January 1784; NAC, HP, vol. B 63, pp. 109–10, Mathews to Stephen DeLancey. 2 March 1784.

46. H.V. Temperley, "Frontierism, Capital and the American Loyalists in Canada," *Journal of American Studies*, 13 (1979): 5–27.

47. Kerber, *Women of the Republic*, p. 85.

48. NAC, British Headquarters Papers, vol. 16, microfilm, reel M-348, [Name illegible] to Lt. Col. Roger Morris, 22 April 1779.

49. NAC, Claus Papers, C 1478, Mary Brant to Joseph Brant, 5 October 1779; C 1485, Captain Frazer to Daniel Claus, 26 June 1780.

50. Lydia Van Alstine, Flora Livingston, widow Obenholt, Margaret Hare.

51. NAC, HP, vol. 21, p. 875, Petition to Haldimand, 3 January 1783; HP, vol. 21, p. 874, Petition of George Christie, 16 December 1778; HP, vol. 21, p. 874, Petition of Jean McDonell, 30 November 1782.

52. Mary Beth Norton, "Eighteenth-Century American Women in Peace and War: The Case of the Loyalists," *William and Mary Quarterly*, 3rd ser., 33 (1976): 386–409.

53. NAC, HP, A 776, Phoebe Grout, Petition.

54. Kerber, *Women of the Republic*, p. 85.

4   Modified version of James W. St G. Walker, "Freedom Denied," in *The Black Loyalists: The Search for a Promised Land in Nova Scotia and Sierra Leone 1783–1870* (Toronto: University of Toronto Press, 1999), 40–63. © University of Toronto Press, 1999. Reprinted with permission of the publisher.

THE BONDAGE OF DEPENDENCE, 1783–91

The Nova Scotia that offered a haven to fleeing American slaves was not itself innocent of the evils of slavery. It has been reported that slaves participated in the building of Halifax in 1749, and one of them, Peter, with his wife and daughter, was included in the muster of original settlers. A list of settlers there in 1750 contained at least 14 different persons specified as "Negro".[1] A slave girl named Louisa, the first in Annapolis County, was sold in July 1767 for £15. That year throughout Nova Scotia the census showed 104 slaves in a total population of 3,022, the largest number, 54, being in the city of Halifax. Returns later in the 1770s included small numbers of slaves, one of them owned by the Reverend

James Logon, Nova Scotia's first Presbyterian minister.[2]

It was only with the arrival of the Loyalists, however, that slavery assumed any numerical significance in the province. An estimated 1,232 slaves, often designated "servants" or "servants for life," were brought by Loyalists from the former American colonies.[3] Shelburne in particular, host to the largest body of Loyalists, received hundreds of slaves along with the free blacks being settled there. Shelburne settler Andrew Barclay brought 57 slaves with him; Stephen Shakespeare brought 20, and Charles Bruff 15. Simeon Perkins had two male "servants" and later added a female. The new settlement of Digby counted slaves as well as free blacks among the first pioneers to arrive there in 1783, and some slaves were carried as far as Cape Breton.[4] John Wentworth, former governor of New Hampshire, appointed Surveyor-General of the King's Woods in 1783 and later to become governor of Nova Scotia, included black slaves among the baggage he salvaged from his American estate. Finding them less useful in Halifax, he sent 19 slaves to his cousin Paul Wentworth to be employed on the latter's plantation in Dutch Guiana. "They are all American born and well seasoned," Wentworth wrote to his cousin's agent, "and all are perfectly stout, healthy, sober, industrious and honest. . . . The Women are stout and able, and promise well to increase their numbers."[5]

Other Halifax residents, unwilling like Wentworth to support uneconomic slaves, would sometimes turn "their slaves out of doors to maintain themselves and family, if the family should be so large as to become burthensome to the Master." Then if the slaves' services were required again, or if an opportunity arose to sell them, the master could reclaim them at will. Still others sent six slave children, ranging in age from 5 to 19 years, to the black school established by the Associates of the late Dr Bray. Perhaps they were moved by a genuine humanitarian sentiment, or they may have been seeking to increase their slaves' earning capacity so that they could join that large group of enterprising slave owners who were able to rent their slaves out, particularly if they possessed marketable skills, and pocket the salary that would normally have been paid to the worker.[6] Though many Nova Scotians, most prominent among them Chief Justice Thomas A. Strange and Attorney-General S.S. Blowers, sought to make perpetual bondage illegal, slavery remained a fact throughout the 1780s and 1790s. It was legally recognized that slaves could be bequeathed as part of an estate, and when Provincial Secretary Richard Bulkeley's slave James was married his status was duly recorded in the Halifax Marriage Bonds.[7]

The presence of so many free blacks in Nova Scotia after 1783 naturally presented a problem to slave owners. With slave and free mingling in schools and markets it was difficult to maintain the notion, in the slave's own mind, that he deserved to be in servitude because of his colour. It was equally difficult for whites to identify a wandering black as a runaway, since a black face could no longer be assumed to be a badge of bondage. Birchtown became a haven to which slaves from all over the province could flee,[8] and once safely hidden there it was extremely unlikely that a master could retrieve them. Advertisements were placed in the newspapers, characteristically accompanied by a representation of a black fugitive carrying a stick, offering rewards for the return of a runaway.[9] Despite the relative insignificance of slavery in the province, and the difficulties involved in retaining a slave at all and then keeping him economically employed, still Nova Scotia was a slave society displaying the crude traits of all such societies. This placed severe limitations on the freedom and opportunities of the Black Loyalists. In a society conditioned to thinking of blacks as slaves, their claims for equality were not always to be taken seriously by white individuals or even by white officialdom. American slavery, fundamentally, had meant the exploitation of black labour. To the Nova Scotian of European descent, therefore, blacks were usually considered to be nothing but a source of labour. It was this economic attitude taken by white people, rather than any identifiable belief in racial interiority, that was to cause the most discriminatory situations experienced by Black Loyalists during the 1780s.

Ironically, labour was in scarce supply during the decade following the Loyalist influx. With most people pioneering their own farms, larger landowners and urban employers were pressed for workers to make their assets productive. As a consequence wages rose until, according to Legislative Assembly Member Alexander Howe, they were "higher than in any other Part of the World." Governor Parr complained to Lord Sydney of the "High Price" of "Every kind of labour in this Country," and even the Rector of St Paul's reported the "exorbitant price of Labour" in a letter to England. A petition to the Secretary of State from a group of large proprietors noted that "The greatest inconvenience which [we] lye under at present is the scarcity of Labourers," and that the demand had driven wages into the range of 2s. 6d. to 4s. per day for unskilled workers.[10]

The existence of a large body of free blacks, forced into the labour market through their lack of land or other means of support, appeared to offer a solution to the labour shortage. They had no choice but to offer their skills and muscles to the nearest employer, and as prevailing opinion considered them an exploitable labour pool, in desperate supply from any other source, they were in a poor position to bargain for the privileges and bounties freely accorded to white Loyalists. [. . .] White employers came to depend on the cheap services of the Black Loyalists until they formed "in many Parts of this Province, the Principal Sources for Labour and Improvement."[11] Besides providing the only group of inexpensive workers the Black

Loyalists, being landless, had to buy their food in the open market and therefore helped to increase the prices that could be charges for the staple items of diet. Their value as a buying force in a slim market was noted in the Preston–Dartmouth area, where their departure in 1792 caused a serious decay in local trade, and in Shelburne, where the threat of a black exodus brought about a decline in the price of potatoes from 1s. 3d. to a mere 2½ d. per bushel.[12] It did not escape official notice that the free blacks, in such circumstances, constituted a valuable addition to the provincial economy.

The intention of the British government had been that no Loyalist should be required to become a wage-labourer in order to survive. Provisions were promised to Loyalists, partly as a reward for their loyalty and a compensation for their losses, but primarily to sustain them during their first few years in Nova Scotia until their new farms should become productive and enable them to support themselves. Official policy was that all Loyalists should receive, free from government, full rations for their first year as refugees, two-thirds rations for the second year, and one-third rations for the third year.[13] In the meantime, it was presumed, they would be clearing their land, planting first crop and awaiting a harvest of their own.

[. . .]

Though the Black Loyalists had been given the same promises of government support, and though their claim for government protection was subsequently confirmed by Whitehall,[14] generally speaking they fared as badly with provisions as they had with land. John Clarkson reported to William Wilberforce in 1791 that he could "bring innumerable witnesses (all of whom were parties concerned) who have not received one year's provisions though they were allowed three . . . nay, many of these have neither received a mouthful of provisions, or so much as an implement of husbandry (though these articles were allowed also)."[15]

When the disbanded Black Pioneers first arrived at Digby in May 1784 Sergeant Thomas Peters was placed in charge and it was to him that government provisions were to be delivered. Digby Commissary Thomas Williams eventually issued 12 096 pounds of flour and 9 352 pounds of pork, representing 80 days' full rations for 160 black adults and 26 children, but this was not done until December 1784 and Williams stated bluntly, "it is all they are to git for the winter." Though Peters may have taken delivery of another 61 days' worth of rations for distribution among the Pioneers, the flour and pork above-mentioned was sent not to Peters but to the Reverend Edward Brudenell. Brudenell, once described as "a particular friend of the Governor's," was one of those Digby agents later to come under criticism for his inefficiency and favouritism. Rather than distributing the rations directly to the blacks, Brudenell stored them in a cellar belonging to one Richard Hill and gave them out only to those blacks who performed work on the township's roads. Most of the people, with no other means of support, agreed to do so, and 11 980 pounds of the flour and 9 209 pounds of the pork were eventually handed over to them by agent John Donnally. No further supplies were ever issued.[16] The Digby blacks, therefore, received provisions only for a few months, not for the three years they had a right to expect; and for these they were forced to work. This labour requirement was not a condition placed on white Loyalists in Digby in order to receive their government support.

David George was given six months' provision by Governor Parr in July 1784, and if he received no further supplies it may be that he failed to fulfill the labour requirement. In Shelburne all Loyalists, whatever their colour, were expected to perform six days of statute labour annually in exchange for rations that "were issued daily to all and sundry."[17] However, since most of the blacks were already engaged in labour through their companies of Pioneers, and gaining their subsistence

thereby, the statutory labour period simply meant that they worked those days without pay. Unlike the whites, they did not receive provisions on the basis of their status as Loyalists plus six days' work. The blacks of Preston were also expected to "Work a Proportion of Time on the Road,"[18] and it may have been in exchange for rations inferior to those granted to whites, as was certainly the case in Halifax. "Codfish, molasses and hard biscuit were the principal items" in the Halifax Loyalist diet, with occasional additions from "a very limited supply of meat." But this was for whites only. "Meal and molasses sustained the negroes."[19] In St John at least some of the blacks evidently were issued with government provisions, though these supplies ceased before 1785.[20]

There were also many disappointed white Loyalists who were inadequately supplied with provisions. They had left most of their possessions in the United States, and some of them owned little else than the clothes on their backs. In 1785 Parr wrote to General Campbell for "any Kind of Clothing or Blankets in the King's Stores" that could be distributed to the destitute Loyalists in his care. Time and again the harassed governor had to request extra supplies, since so many of the people were completely dependent on the Royal bounty. The partial allowances issued after the first year were not enough, as few people were yet in a position to contribute to their own support. Some destitute souls, with no food or clothing but confident in the government's generosity, were actually taking credit with local merchants against the eventual receipt of their provisions. By the time those provisions arrived, the recipients would again be destitute.[21]

In Halifax the earliest Loyalists were housed, in winter, in tents, bark shelters, and public buildings, and fed on the streets. Others had to remain in the cramped holds of their transport vessels, unable to find any room ashore.[22] Every available building in Annapolis, including the church, was used for shelter, yet hundreds of people remained without a roof. Some of the more fortunate families there had "a single apartment with sods, where men, women, children, pigs, fleas, bugs, mosquitoes and other domestic insects, mingle in society."[23] Many of those people, moreover, were not receiving the authorized issue of provisions. [. . .]

Clearly, the blacks had no monopoly on poverty and unfulfilled promises. The numbers of Loyalists and the confusion they caused meant that the limited resources of the province could not be strained to satisfy all. But once again the Black Loyalists fared worst in a generally bad situation. Without farms and without provisions they had no choice but to grasp at any opportunity, however unfair, to keep themselves alive. Though almost all the whites were settled within three years of their arrival or, if not, at least had the option, in many cases, of returning to the United States, the blacks continued to depend on whatever they could earn in a labour market prepared to take advantage of them. No deliberate conspiracy is suggested but it is possible that many agents in charge of land and provisions, aware that black services as labourers might not be available if they were to become self-supporting, were inclined, as Brudenell evidently was, to place them last on the list of recipients in both cases.

One common fate of Black Loyalists with neither land of their own nor government support was that they were "obliged to live upon white-mens property which the Govr has been liberal in distributing—and for cultivating it they receive half the produce so that they are in short in a state of Slavery."[24] Akin indeed to slavery or serfdom, the system of "share-cropping" tied the tenant to the land of another and to the landowner himself. The proprietor could take his percentage from the gross produce of the land, leaving his tenant with responsibility for seeding and cultivating a new crop, and therefore, on the marginal farmlands of Nova Scotia, with no hope of accumulating any savings to begin a farm

of his own. John Clarkson wrote of one such tenant that the system had "reduced them to such a state of indigence, that in order to satisfy their landlord and maintain themselves, they have been obliged to sell their property, their clothing, even their very beds."[25] [. . .] Of that majority of Black Loyalists who received no land or did so only in uneconomic quantities, hundreds became tenants in circumstances such as these.

For those incapable or unprepared for life as a tenant farmer, a favourite choice was to become a servant or day labourer in an urban centre, particularly Halifax. Those with enough land on which to build a house, particularly if they were near the sea, would supplement the produce of a small garden with seasonal fishing. This was the case the Preston blacks, who contributed to their region's meagre food by selling fish in the local markets. [. . .]

The ever-present Atlantic, of course, offered other opportunities besides fishing. Birchtowners Luke Jordan, Thomas Godfrey, and John Thomas were among those from their community to become members of ships' crews. Black Anthony sailed out of Liverpool on the merchant ship *Goodfortune* as a crewman at 35s. per month. When the schooner *Pilgrim* was lost only one man aboard, Black Jack, "was qualified to Navigate a vessel." Mulatto Jack Peterson commanded 40s. per month as a ship's cook, a salary matched by ordinary seaman Black Philip. Black Harry, Prince Harris, and Black Boston were evidently of exceptional talents, the latter eventually gaining a sailor's salary of 75s. per month. Small wonder that many graduates of the Shelburne black school "have taken to follow the sea."[26] Perhaps the experience of so many black veterans as pilots during the American war qualified them for equal pay afloat. Certainly sailing was one area of employment into which, short of the press gang, black workers could not be coerced. Joining the ships freely, and their navigational skills in great demand in a maritime province, they were also free to bargain for a just wage.

It was noted previously that large numbers of the former slaves had been trained in specific skills on their home plantations. In Nova Scotia they often had an opportunity of following their own trades. Boston King was a carpenter and boat-builder in Shelburne, one of 21 men in Birchtown who described themselves as carpenters. Twelve more were sawyers, of masons, coopers, and caulkers there were three each, and two blacksmiths, a tailor, a sadler, a baker, a shoemaker, a blockmaker, a barber and a weaver. [. . .] If Boston King's experiences were at all typical, however, pay rates on shore fell far short of those within a sailor's grasp, and employment was much less regular. Even a skilled carpenter could expect no more than one shilling for a day's work.[27]

There seems to have been considerable resistance on the part of many white people to any black attempts at equality or self-improvement. When David George first arrived in Shelburne to preach and teach he "found the White people were against me." He persisted in his efforts "but the White people, the justices, and all, were in an uproar, and said that I might go out into the woods, for I should not stay there." At Tracadie the Acadian Roman Catholics kept both relief and religion from the blacks, and a white from Digby reported haughtily that the blacks there "are so wonderfully proud-spirited, that the females think they must dress, when they attend Church, in quite a superior stile to white Ladies."[28] Evidently Loyalist Nova Scotia had a "place" for black people, and though it was usually an improvement on condition of slavery still it meant that a black's true function was a lowly worker to serve the white establishment. Of course whole classes of white people were in an equivalent position in Europe and North America, but the blacks of Nova Scotia derived their class from their colour and its associations with slave labour. [. . .] The vulnerable blacks were fair game

for any exploitive employer, and to keep them so a society dominated by class interests had to restrict their independence.

White workers were equally resentful of the Black Loyalists' vulnerability, but as is so often the case they blamed not those responsible the oppression but the blacks who accepted the lower wages and thereby monopolized certain categories of work. On 26 July 1784 Benjamin Marston reported from Shelburne:

> Great Riot today. The disbanded soldiers have risen against the Free negroes to drive them out of Town, because they labour cheaper than they—the soldiers. [27 July] Riot continues. The soldiers force the free negroes to quit the town— pulled down about 20 of their houses.[29]

Two days later Simeon Perkins heard the news "that an Extraordinary mob or Riot has happened at Shelburne. Some thousands of Assembled with Clubs and Drove the Negroes out of the Town." To David George's Shelburne home "40 or 50 disbanded soldiers . . . came with the tackle of ships, and turned my dwelling house, and every one their houses, quite over." Later they came and beat him with sticks and drove him into a swamp. Along with others of his colour George sought refuge in Birchtown, but even here they were unsafe. While the force of the riot continued in Shelburne for at least 10 days, incursions into Birchtown were reported for up to one month.[30]

Although they, like other post-war immigrants, were entitled to government support and grants of land, the ordinary soldiers had to wait until their betters were served first. In the meantime they were forced into the labour market with the blacks, but employers were unwilling to pay standard wages as long as blacks could be had at one-quarter the price. Governor Parr blamed Nova Scotia's first race riot exclusively on the soldiers' delay in obtaining land, and indeed he placed responsibility directly on Surveyor Marston, who was dismissed for not preparing the grants more quickly.[31] Parr was undoubtedly correct in assessing the riot's cause as the soldiers' inability to support themselves. The incident is important not so much as an illustration of racial hostility than as an indication of how serious was the economic predicament of those Nova Scotians who had not received lands on which to support themselves.

Outside Shelburne, and without its black companies and organized labour corps, individual blacks often lacked the opportunity to enter a competitive workforce. For them the choices were between starvation and indentured servitude, sometimes termed apprenticeship. Indenture was an established system in Nova Scotia long before the arrival of free blacks, and conditions among white indentured servants differed little from that of outright black slaves. They were liable to the same harsh punishments, the same pervasive authority of a master, as were blacks, but usually for a limited and specified term. James Walch, a white, the indentured servant to Patrick Wall, was sentenced to ten lashes with the cat-o'-nine tails by Shelburne magistrates merely for applying to be discharged from his master's service. Runaways were sought through advertisements and returned to their masters, though the court seems have presumed the right to punish them, rather, than leaving it to the individual who happened to hold the indenture. There is at least one case on record in Shelburne in which a master, Edward Elliott, was charged with maltreating his apprentice.[32]

Many Black Loyalists had to accept positions as indentured servants since there was often no other way to ensure support. The master might then hire them out, as was done with slaves, and retain his servants' earnings as compensation for the subsistence he guaranteed.[33] For the blacks, indenture or apprenticeship was not infrequently the route to a return to actual slavery. Impoverished black parents, unable to sustain their families, would bind their children out for limited terms. When the indenture had run its course, however, the master might claim the child as his legitimate slave or demand of the parents payment for the child's board, during the period of indenture, before turning him free. Molly Roach met such a demand from a Mr Jenkins of Green Harbour when she went to reclaim her child, and Caesar Smith's daughter Phoebe, put to work by a Mr Newman in the dock yards, was claimed as a slave.[34]

The case of Lydia Jackson is perhaps informative, for it was recorded as a typical example of the experience of many unfortunate Black Loyalists. Lydia was living in great distress in Manchester when Henry Hedley invited her to work for him. After several days he demanded payment for her board or, as an alternative, her indenture to him for seven years. Though Lydia refused the seven-year term she was eventually persuaded to place her mark on an agreement for a one-year term. Hedley, however, took advantage of her illiteracy to substitute a term of 39 years in the articles of indenture. She was then sold for £20 to a Dr Bulman of Lunenburg who, with his wife, beat her with fire tongs and kicked her in the stomach, though Lydia was then eight months pregnant. A court case on her behalf, brought by a Lunenburg attorney; was dismissed by the magistrates. After three years with Bulman Lydia learned of his intention to sell her as a slave in the West Indies. To avoid this fate was worth the risk of capture and punishment as an escapee, so she left Bulman's farm and fled to Halifax. John Clarkson, the passionate Abolitionist who interviewed Lydia Jackson, said he had met "many others of a similar nature," and cited five by name.[35]

Though it evidently happened on occasion, an indentured servant could not legally be sold to anyone outside Nova Scotia. The Shelburne court ordered the cancellation of the indenture of Robert Conner when his master, John Harris, was apprehended in an attempt to sell his black servant to a non-resident. The courts took a similar stand when whites detained or attempted to sell black children without holding the properly authorised documents of indenture. Timothy Mahan tried to sell a boy he claimed had been given him by the boy's parents, but the magistrates declared that this did not constitute an indenture. James Cox was ordered to set a boy at liberty whom he claimed, but could prove, to be legally indentured.[36]

These attempts to enslave free blacks were stopped by the authorities, but the fact that attempts were made at all may be taken as an indication of the insecurity in which the Black Loyalists lived. In fact the fear of being returned to slavery was a prominent reason offered by numerous people anxious to leave Nova Scotia in 1791. Apprenticeship was only one threat. Direct kidnapping for sale in the United States or the West Indies was another. Shelburne was particularly vulnerable, and many blacks were seized there illegally and carried off as slaves.[37] In 1789 this situation drew the attention of the Legislative Assembly where, in a draft bill, reference was made to the need to prevent the practice of carrying free blacks "out of the Province, by force and Strategm, for the scandalous purpose of making property of them in the West Indies contrary to their will and consent."[38]

Above all, there remained the threat of being claimed, in the courts and with the full sanction of the law, as a legal slave. Four Black Loyalists, all of them with war service, were claimed by Captain Hamilton on the grounds that he had owned them years before in North Carolina. In Halifax Michael Wallace granted Hamilton a warrant to seize the four in question and sell them in the Bahamas. Fortunately their ship put in to Shelburne, where they managed to have word carried to the court that they were being held without a hearing. Presiding judge Isaac Wilkins decided that Hamilton's claim was insufficient, and the blacks were set free.

Black Loyalists Pero and Tom were claimed by Joseph Robins, and though they were not freed at least Robins was required to bring further proof, within one year, of his ownership. Mary Postell was brought to court and claimed, together with her children, by Jesse Gray. While Black Loyalists Scipio and Dinah Wearing were in court testifying in Mary's behalf, their home was set on fire and one of their children killed. Mary had been the slave of a rebel officer and still had General Birch's Certificate in her possession, but again the court granted the alleged master one year to prove his ownership.[39] These people had been free for 10 or more years and could produce documents and witnesses in their own support, but this was not automatically accepted by the law as constituting free status. If a master could prove a prior claim, of however long standing, the black was liable to be returned to slavery.

Such were the sufferings, insecurity and injustice inflicted upon Black Loyalists by their fellow-refugees in the land of their new liberty. As conditions in Nova Scotia became worse during the late 1780s, and all sorts and conditions of men were brought low by famine and disease, the blacks' position fell correspondingly lower. Hailed as an example of what could be achieved by good and faithful citizens under properly constituted authority, the province failed to develop as quickly or to become as prosperous as most people had expected in 1783. Roads remained unmade and farms uncleared, and trade was not diverted to Halifax and Shelburne in the volume anticipated. In May 1788 the province was still not producing its own food, and a law had to be passed permitting the importation of essential supplies such as food, livestock and lumber, from the United States.

[. . .]

Shelburne, meanwhile, was suffering unique problems of its own. [. . .] In a city of traders, there was no one with whom to trade. Business stagnated, resulting in unemployment and removal to areas with a healthier economy. From its heyday during the period 1784 to 1787, when its population reached 10 000 and it was not only the largest British American city but the fourth largest city anywhere in North America, Shelburne experienced a sharp decline. [. . .]

The conditions of famine in 1789 and the decline of Shelburne naturally struck hardest at the black people of the district. Unemployment wiped out the black companies of Birchtown. Many were forced to indenture their families and some even sold themselves as slaves. Blacks died of starvation and exposure after parting with all their belongings in exchange for temporary nourishment. Birchtown, like Shelburne, lost some of its most ambitious residents as they left in search of employment and food. Always at a bare subsistence wage, the black labourers had no savings or property to cushion their fall.[40] Only those with farms or with jobs in the fisheries, and of course the indentured servants and share-croppers, were able to make a meagre living in Shelburne County. Those who drifted to Halifax met conditions scarcely better. The shortage of food and retarded trade affected the capital city too, and few jobs were available. Soon it became impossible for a Halifax resident to walk the streets without being approached by a black beggar.[41] No part of Nova Scotia remained unaffected. [. . .]

But for the charity of their white neighbours and certain well-wishers in England, many more blacks would have died of starvation or exposure during those harrowing years. [. . .]

Public support was also available to paupers in Nova Scotia, though not always generously. In 1789 the people of Halifax preferred to contribute the passage money for 20 white paupers to return to England, rather than maintain them on relief in Nova Scotia. Various acts were passed by the Assembly during the 1780s and 90s to provide for the support of the poor and the maintenance of a poor house, and commissioners and overseers were appointed to ensure that the allocated budget was wisely spent. [. . .]

Black paupers were often included on the relief rolls. Sometimes black vagrants in Shelburne were sent by the court to Birchtown, there to subsist on whatever charity that impoverished community might be able to afford them. A proclamation of that court in 1786 ordered the overseers to be more attendant to the binding out of poor black children, though some black adults appear to have been allowed to remain free while on relief. It was possible for citizens to take black paupers from the poor house as indentured servants, if they reimbursed the overseers for their past support by the public.[42] [. . .]

The life of the Black Loyalist was filled with fear, for his continued freedom, for his subsistence, and for his peace from the interference of discriminatory acts by white individuals and officials. A last desperate move on the part of Shelburne merchants to sustain their economy by making their city a free port for trade with the United States, brought the blacks' fear to a climax in that they expected their former American masters would then be able to enter British territory and reclaim them as slaves.[43] Seldom was it possible, from his very arrival in Nova Scotia, for a Black Loyalist to feel secure in the freedoms and privileges of a British subject.

Either as veterans or as Loyalists, the free blacks had a right to expect treatment as full citizens. They had been promised as much, and these promises were reinforced by statements of officials in London and Halifax.[44] On the one hand, they were required to perform the duties of citizenship, on the other, their rights fell short of equality. Clarkson recorded that the blacks were required to pay taxes, and for Sydney County at least the poll tax returns indicate that some of them did so. A black militia company was formed in Halifax which Governor Wentworth described as "an able, daring, and faithful Body of Men," and he also praised the Black Pioneers attached to the Royal Nova Scotia Regiment.

The Digby militia had its black company as well, "of good able Stature and Countenance as any other Men."[45]

While fulfilling these responsibilities, the blacks were "entirely deprived of the privileges of British subjects, particularly trial by jury."[46] From New Brunswick Governor Thomas Carleton gave the opinion that the blacks, "having come within the British Lines with no other View than to escape from the service of their American masters, cannot be considered as intituled to claim anything from Government further than personal protection and freedom from servitude" and therefore "they have not been admitted to vote in Elections for Representatives the General Assembly."[47] In addition to their lack of the vote and trial, the blacks often suffered restrictions on their private lives as well. In Shelburne hand bills were published by the magistrates "forbidding Negro Dances, and Negro Frolicks in this Town." When this bylaw was contravened the offending blacks were charged with "Riotous behaviour" and sent to the house of correction. A second offence might mean being "ordered out of their home for keeping a disorderly house."[48]

When a black was brought before the court for breaking a law, the treatment he received at the hands of the justices was not always equal to that for whites convicted of the same crime. In Guysborough County (Lower Sydney County) between 11 October 1785 and 8 February 1791 no white suffered corporal punishment. Theft slander, assault, "keeping a house of ill fame," even riot, were punished by fines. But when a Black Loyalist woman, Sarah Ringwood, stole some butter, she was "ordered for Punishment to receive Thirty nine stripes on her naked back, at the Public Whipping Post in Manchester." Another black woman, Eleonar Bourke, received the same punishment plus a week's imprisonment "for being a Vagrant, Idle, Disorderly Person." This was during the famine of 1789. In one year four black men

were whipped for stealing food, and another black woman "for abusive, Lewd and Indecent behaviour."[49]

The Shelburne court records bear cruel testimony to the harsh inhumanity of the late eighteenth century. Prince Frederick received 78 lashes and a month's hard labour for stealing a pair of shoes, Daniel Anderson 39 lashes and John Russel 100 lashes for thefts valued at one shilling each. One black woman named Dianna, convicted on two counts of petty larceny, suffered the incredible sentence of "Two hundred lashes at the Cart's Tail, next Saturday, at 12 o'clock, at noon, for the first Offense, and One hundred and fifty lashes on the following Saturday, at the Cart's Tail, for the second offense." The unfortunate Alicia Wiggins received 39 lashes in April 1792 for theft, and in July, for a second offence involving 3s. 11d. worth of used clothing, she was sentenced to be hanged. Alicia pleaded a stay of execution on the grounds of pregnancy but "twelve Matrons or discreet women," on examining her, found that she was "not four months gone with child," so she was executed as ordered. All these sentences were inflicted on black people. As in Guysborough County, Shelburne whites were often, though not always, fined for similar offences. [. . .][50] In Halifax County punishments generally were milder, and even blacks were allowed to pay fines for their misdemeanours. [. . .][51]

Without doubt the last two decades of the eighteenth century represent a heartless and difficult period in the history of Nova Scotia. No man or woman of low station could avoid the constant threat of physical suffering. It also appears quite evident that for black Nova Scotians, as a group, the threat was greater and more frequently realized than for any others. In a slave society they took their status not from the body of Loyalists, to which they belonged, but from the mass of slaves whose African race they shared. In many ways their life as freemen was not altogether different from the life of slavery that they had left behind. As share-croppers, indentured servants, or subsistence day-labourers they were still completely dependent upon white people and subject to the whims and prejudices of their white employers. The law deemed them equal privileges and services yet expected as much of them as of any other resident, and when they strayed they were corrected greater severity. They were regarded as little more than physical beings, whose function was to fill the lowest levels of the labour force.

The Black Loyalists faced, with other Loyalists, all the hardships of a pioneering situation in a new country. They were also pioneering in a sense unique to themselves. The vast majority of them had been born and raised in slavery, a condition which sapped

their initiative, resourcefulness, and self-reliance. An attitude of dependence had developed in these people, long accustomed to direction in labour and sustenance in living. Now they were expected to find some inner spring of resourcefulness within themselves, and to fend for themselves in a climate calling for expensive shelter and with a scarcity of food. More than any other group of immigrants the blacks needed special assistance during a period of transition for their new lives as free and self-supporting citizens. Instead, that same "slave mentality" was perpetuated and reinforced by their experiences in Nova Scotia. They continued to feel dependent on whites, in the economic sphere, neither encouraged nor capable to strike out on their own.

NOTES

1. T. Watson Smith, "The Slave in Canada," *Collections of the Nova Scotia Historical Society* 10 (1898): 9; T. Akins, "History of Halifax City," *Collections of the Nova Scotia Historical Society* 8 (1895): Appendix F, p. 246, "List of Families, original settlers, 1749."

2. Charlotte Isabella Perkins, *The Romance of Old Annapolis Royal* (Annapolis, 1934), 108; Public Archives of Nova Scotia (PANS), vol. 443, "A General Return of the Several Townships in the Province of Nova Scotia for the first day of January 1767" and "Poll Tax and Census Rolls, 1767–1794"; W.R. Riddell, "The Slave in Canada," *Journal of Negro History* V, 3 (July 1920): 362.

3. Smith, "The Slave in Canada," 23, 32.

4. J. Plimsoll Edwards, "The Shelburne That Was and Is Not," *Dalhousie Review* (April 1922): 132; C.B. Fergusson (ed.), *The Diary of Simeon Perkins,* vol. III, 1790–96, (Toronto, 1961), pp. 50, 196, 394; Isaiah W. Wilson, *A Geography and History of the County of Digby, Nova Scotia* (New Haven and Montreal, 1971), 74; C.W. Vernon, *Bicentenary Sketches and Early Days of the Church in Nova Scotia* (Halifax, 1910), 237.

5. Sir Adams Archibald, "Life of Sir John Wentworth, Governor of Nova Scotia 1792–1808,"

Collection of the Nova Scotia Historical Society XX (1921): 53, letter of John Wentworth, 24 February 1784.

6. PANS, Family Papers. Clarkson, Clarkson's Mission to America, p. 230, diary entry for 7 December 1791; *An Account of the Designs of the Associates of the late Dr Bray, with an Abstract of their Proceedings, Abstract for 1787,* p. 31; Simeon Perkins, *Diary of Simeon Perkins,* eds H.A. Innis, D.C. Harvey, and C.B. Fergusson (Toronto, 1948–67, 4 vols), vol. III, p. 85.

7. Riddell, "The Slave in Canada," pp. 367–9; I. Allen Jack, "The Loyalists and Slavery in New Brunswick," *Transactions of the Society of Canada* (2nd Series), IV (1898): section II, pp. 142, 149–50; PANS, Shelburne Records, Early Wills 1784–92, will of Thomas Robinson, 10 August 1787; New Brunswick Museum (NBM), Hazen Collection, Shelf 88, Box 2, Folder I, "Schedule of Goods and Chattels" accompanying will dated 2 May 1791; NBM, Jarvis Papers, Shelf 86, Box 21, Items 19 and 20, sale certificates; Public Archives of Canada (PAC), MG 23 D1, Lawrence Collection, vol. 19, Business Papers, memo of 9 February 1805; PANS, Marriage Bonds, 1763–99, 20 May 1794.

8. PANS, Shelburne Records, General Sessions, 5 July 1791.

9. For example, *Royal Gazette and Nova Scotia Advertiser,* 7 September 1790, 1 March, 7 June, 5 July, 19 and 22 November 1791, 10 and 17 January, 19 May 1792.

10. Public Records Office (PRO), CO 217/68, Howe to Quarrell, 9 August 1797; PANS vol. 47, doc. 51, Parr to Sydney, 17 October 1785; Society for the Propagation of the Gospel (SPG), Dr Bray's Associates' Minute Books, vol. III, 1768–1808, 3 February 1785, quoting Breynton to Associates, 15 November 1784; PRO, CO 217/64, Proprietors of Lands to Henry Dundas, 16 May 1793.

11. PRO, CO 217/68, Howe to Quarrell, 9 August 1797.

12. PANS, Bishop Charles Inglis, Letters, 1791–99, number 3, p. 58, memo to the Archbishop of Canterbury, 3 May 1794; Clarkson's Mission, p. 109, letter to Henry Thornton, 6 November 1791.

13. PANS, vol. 366, doc. 33, George Rose to Haldimand, 17 March 1784.

14. PANS, vol. 359, doc. 65, "The Humble Petition of the Black Loyalists," 21 August 1784; PANS, vol. 33, doc. 12, Sydney to Parr, 5 October 1784; Clarkson's Mission, pp. 98–100, diary entry for 31 October 1791.

15. Ibid., p. 188, Clarkson to Wilberforce, 27 November 1791.

16. PRO, CO 217/63, Bulkeley to Dundas, 19 March 1792, enclosure, "Enquiry into the Complaint of Thomas Peters, a Black Man," evidence given before the enquiry by Thomas Peters, 16 and 19 November 1791; Appendix E, Thomas Williams to the Secretary to Dr Brudenell, 11 December 1784; Appendix G, "State of the Provisions sent the Rev. Mr Brudenell for the use of the Blacks at Digby"; PANS, vol. 394, doc. 52, Morris to Major Studholme, 20 August 1783.

17. David George, "An Account of the Life of Mr. David George (as told to Brother John Rippon)," *Baptist Annual Register,* vol. I (1790–3), 478; PANS, Shelburne Records Special Sessions, 6 August 1787 and 23 September 1789; Edwards, "The Shelburne that Was," p. 189.

18. PANS, Halifax County Quarter Sessions, 1766–1801, 7 June 1791.

19. James S. MacDonald, "Memoir of Governor John Parr," *Collections of the Nova Scotia Historical Society* XIV (1910): 54.

20. Public Archives of New Brunswick (PANB), Colonial Correspondence, New Brunswick, III, Carleton to Dundas, 13 December 1791.

21. PANS, vol. 137, Parr to Campbell, April 1785, Parr to Commodore Sawyer, 29 June 1785, Parr to Campbell, 18 and 30 November 1785; PANS, vol. 367½, doc. 34, Stephen Tuttle to Major Matthews, 26 April 1784.

22. James S. MacDonald, "Memoir of Governor John Parr," *Collections of the Nova Scotia Historical Society* (1910), 47, 52, 55, 56.

23. SPG Journal, vol. 23, p. 284, Jacob Bailey to Society, November 1783; Vernon, *Bicentenary Sketches,* p. 145, quoting Jacob Bailey. See also Duncan Campbell, *Nova Scotia in its Historical, Mercantile and Industrial Relations* (Montreal, 1873), 165–71.

24. British Museum (BM), Add. Ms. 41262B, Clarkson Papers, II, fol. 8.

25. Clarkson's Mission, pp. 66–7, diary entry for 22 October 1791.

26. PRO, CO 217/63, "List of the Blacks of Birch Town"; *Diary of Simeon Perkins,* III, pp. 107, 116, 171, 285; *Diary of Simeon Perkins,* IV, pp. 213, 233, 235, 265; Bray Minutes, III, 1 November 1802, Rowland to Associates, 3 May 1802.

27. Boston King, "Memoirs of the Life of Boston King, a Black Preacher, Written by Himself, During his Residence at Kingswood-School," *Arminian Magazine* XXI (March, April, May, June 1798): 210; PRO, CO 217/63, "List of the Blacks of Birch Town."

28. David George, "Life," p. 478; Rawlyk, "The Guysborough Negroes: A Study in Isolation," *Dalhousie Review* (Spring 1968): 26–7; SPG, Bray Associates, Canadian Papers, Elkana Morton to Associates, 20 June 1817.

29. W.O. Raymond, "The Founding of Shelburne and Early Miramichi, Marston's Diary," *Collections of the New Brunswick Historical Society,* vol. III (1907), 265.

30. *Diary of Simeon Perkins,* II, p. 238; Raymond, "Marston's Diary," p. 265; David George, "Life," pp. 479–80; PANS, Shelburne Records, General Sessions, 21 August 1784.

31. PANS, vol. 47, doc. 29, Parr to Sydney, 6 September 1784.

32. PANS, Shelburne Records, Special Sessions, 8 September 1785, General Sessions, 12 April 1786, 5 April 1791.
33. Cf. *Diary of Simeon Perkins,* II, pp. 85–7.
34. Clarkson Papers, II, fols. 15 and 19.
35. Clarkson's Mission, pp. 197–201, diary entry for 30 November 1791.
36. PANS, Shelburne Records, General Sessions, 1, 2 and 3 November 1791.
37. Clarkson Papers, II, fol. 8, "Reasons given by the free Blacks for wishing to leave Nova Scotia," and fol. 22.
38. PANS, Unpassed Bills, 1789.
39. PANS, Shelburne Records, Special Sessions, 5 August 1785, General Sessions, 12 April 1786, 5 April, 8, 11 and 19 July 1791. See also the cases of "a Negro wench Molly," 12 April 1786, and "James Singletory, his wife and child," Special Sessions, 25 August 1785.
40. Boston King, "Memoirs," pp. 209–10; SPG, Bray Associates, Canadian Papers, Blucke to Associates, 22 December 1787.
41. Clarkson's Mission, pp. 294–5, diary entry for 27 December 1791; BM, Add. Ms. 41262A Clarkson Papers, I, Clarkson to Hartshorne, 13 December 1791.
42. PANS, Shelburne Records, Special Sessions, 25 August 1785, General Sessions, 10 April 1786, 6 May 1788, 17 July 1793. See also NBM, Simonds, Hazen and White Papers, Items 238, 239 and 241, indentures of black children by the Overseers of the Poor, St John, 1787.
43. Clarkson's Mission, pp. 94–5, diary entry for 29 October 1791.
44. PANS, vol. 33, doc; 12, Sydney to Parr, 5 October 1784; PANS, Minutes of the Legislative Council, 1782–90, 9 October 1783.
45. Clarkson Papers, II, fols. 15 and 21; PANS vol. 444½, Poll Tax Returns, Sydney County, 1791 and 1793; Parlimentary Papers (PP) 1796–97, vol. 102, no. 889, Wentworth to Portland, 29 October 1796.
46. Selina Thompson, "The Nova Scotians," letter number 3, *The Harbinger,* May 1812; PRO General Correspondence, America, FO 4/1, fols. 419–20, Thomas Peters to Lord Grenville, n.d. (received 26 December 1790).
47. PANB, Colonial Correspondence, New Brunswick, III, Carleton to Dundas, 13 December 1791.
48. PANS, Shelburne Records, Special Sessions, 12 and 19 May 1785, General Sessions, 3 July 1799.
49. PANS, Quarter Sessions, Guysborough County, 1785–1800, 10 October. 1787, 12 August 1789, 8 February, II and 13 August, 3 November 1791.
50. PANS, Shelburne Records, Special Sessions, 24 February, 9 June 1785, General Sessions, 3 November 1784, 14 April 1789, 12 April 1792; White Collection, VI, doc. 553, "Proceedings of the Court of Oyer and Terminer," Shelburne, 3 July 1792.
51. PANS, Halifax County Quarter Sessions, 1755–1801; MacDonald, "Memoir of Governor John Parr," p. 64.

Chapter 7

The Fur Trade
in the Northwest

READINGS

Primary Documents

1   From *Narrative of the Captivity and Adventures of John Tanner*, John Tanner

2   From *A Sketch of the British Fur Trade* (1815), in *The Collected Writings of Lord Selkirk 1810–1820*, vol. 2, Lord Selkirk

Historical Interpretations

3   From "The Woman Who Married a Beaver: Trade Patterns and Gender Roles in the Ojibway Fur Trade," Bruce M. White

4   From *Making the Voyageur World: Travellers and Traders in the North American Fur Trade*, Carolyn Podruchny

INTRODUCTION

The fur trade has generated much historical research and commentary. The great economic historian Harold Innis viewed it as one of the activities that pushed European domination of North America northward and westward, but it also created a meeting place and a site for cultural exchange between Europeans and Indigenous people. The fur trade gave birth to the Métis nation, as European men formed bonds of affection and partnership with Indigenous women, and it was of course a major commercial activity that helped structure the pre-Confederation Canadian economy.

It is clear that the fur trade moved the territory that would become the Dominion of Canada closer to the industrial age, as the companies involved sought to make their ventures predictable and steadily profitable through the efficient deployment of their capital. In other words, they sought to make what might seem like the rather disordered, outdoor pursuit of animal skins into something organized and predictable. However, as we see in the primary documents, a fur trade post was not exactly akin to a modern-day convenience store. It had to respond to the needs of those bringing the furs to the posts, needs that usually included credit and sometimes winter accommodation.

As competition became most intense between the Hudson's Bay Company and its rivals, colonial endeavours (such as those at Red River) were directly affected. Account books and chronicles can tell us a great deal, but historians have done much more recently to flesh out our understanding of the social relationships created and sustained via the trade. In his piece, Bruce White examines gender roles in the Ojibway fur trade. He notes that the Ojibway did not practise a rigid division of labour and that women played a key role in the fur trade, most notably as providers of food and supplies, but also as marriage partners for European traders. We learn also, thanks to Carolyn Podruchny, how rich the culture of the fur trade was. It created its own rules, its own atmosphere, and most certainly changed the course of North American history.

QUESTIONS FOR CONSIDERATION

1. What does Tanner's account tell us about trade practices in the Northwest?
2. What is Lord Selkirk's opinion of the way that the NWC ran their business? Did he admire them or reject their way of doing things?
3. Thinking about both the primary and secondary documents, what sort of personality type do you think might be suitable for a career with the Hudson's Bay Company or one of its rivals?
4. Did Podruchny's account of voyageur life change your assumptions about what such a career might be like?
5. Did the fur trade alter gender roles among the Ojibway?

SUGGESTIONS FOR FURTHER READING

Jean Barman, *French Canadians, Furs, and Indigenous Women in the Making of the Pacific Northwest* (Vancouver: UBC Press, 2014).

Theodore Binnema, Gerhard J. Ens, and R.C. Macleod, eds, *From Rupert's Land to Canada: Essays in Honour of John E. Foster* (Edmonton: University of Alberta Press, 2001).

J.M. Bumsted, *Lord Selkirk: A Life* (East Lansing, MI: Michigan State University Press, 2009).

D. Francis and Toby Morantz, *Furs: A History of the Fur Trade in Eastern James Bay, 1600–1870* (Montreal and Kingston: McGill-Queen's University Press, 1983).

Patricia Alice McCormack, *Fort Chipewyan and the Shaping of Canadian History, 1788–1920s* (Vancouver: UBC Press, 2010).

Laura Lynn Peers, *Gathering Places: Aboriginals and Fur Trade Histories* (Vancouver: UBC Press, 2010).

Carolyn Podruchny, *Making the Voyageur World: Travelers and Traders in the North American Fur Trade* (Toronto: University of Toronto Press, 2006).

Stephen A. Royle, *Company, Crown, and Colony: The Hudson's Bay Company and Territorial Endeavour in Western Canada* (New York: Palgrave Macmillan, 2011).

Claiborne A. Skinner, *The Upper Country: French Enterprise in the Colonial Great Lakes* (Baltimore: Johns Hopkins University Press, 2008).

Sylvia Van Kirk, *"Many Tender Ties": Women in Fur Trade Society, 1670–1870* (Toronto: University of Toronto Press, 1992).

Primary Documents

1   From John Tanner, *Narrative of the Captivity and Adventures of John Tanner* (New York: G. & C. & H. Carvill, 1830), 181–4.

Mr. Henry had traded ten years at Pembinah; he was succeeded by a Mr. McKenzie, who remained but a short time, and after him came Mr. Wells, called by the Indians Gah-se-moan, (a sail,) from the roundness and fullness of his person. He built a strong fort on Red River, near the mouth of the Assinneboin.

The Hudson's Bay Company had now no post in that part of the country, and the Indians were soon made conscious of the advantage which had formerly resulted to them from the competition between rival trading companies. Mr. Wells, at the commencement of winter, called us all together, gave the Indians a ten gallon keg of rum, and some tobacco, telling them, at the same time, he would not credit one of them the value of a single needle. When they brought skins, he would buy them, and give in exchange such articles as were necessary for their comfort and subsistence during the winter.

I was not with the Indians when this talk was held. When it was reported to me, and a share of the presents offered me, I not only refused to accept any thing, but reproached the Indians for their pusillanimity in submitting to such terms. They had been accustomed, for many years, to receive credits in the fall; they were now entirely destitute not of clothing merely, but of ammunition, and many of the ———— of guns and traps. How were they, without the accustomed aid from the traders, to subsist themselves and their families during the ensuing winter?

A few days afterwards, I went to Mr. Wells, and told him that I was poor, with a large family to support by my own exertions, and that I must unavoidably suffer, and perhaps perish, unless he would give me such a credit as I had always, in the fall, been accustomed to receive. He would not listen to my representation, and told me, roughly, to be gone from his house.

I then took eight silver beavers, such as are worn by the women, as ornaments on their dress, and which I had purchased the year before at just twice the price that was commonly given for a capote; I laid them before him, on the table, and asked him to give me a capote for them, or retain them as a pledge for the payment of the price of the garment, as soon as I could procure the peltries. He took up the ornaments, threw them in my face, and told me never to come inside of his house again.

The cold weather of the winter had not yet set in, and I went immediately to my hunting ground, killed a number of moose, and set my wife to make the skins into such garments as were best adapted to the winter season, and which I now saw we should be compelled to substitute for the blankets and woollen clothes we had been accustomed to receive from the traders.

I continued my hunting with good success, but the winter had not half passed, when I heard that Mr. Hanie, a trader for the Hudson's Bay people, had arrived at Pembinah. I went immediately to him, and he gave me all the credit I asked, which was to the amount of seventy skins. Then I went to Muskrat River, where I hunted the remainder of the winter, killing great numbers of martens, beavers, otters, &c.

Early in the spring, I sent word by some Indians to Mr. Hanie, that I would go down to the mouth of the Assinneboin, and meet him there, to pay my credit, as I had skins more than enough for this purpose.

When I arrived at the Assinneboin, Mr. Hanie had not yet passed, and I stopped to wait for him opposite Mr. Well's trading house. An old Frenchman offered me a lodging in his house, and I went in and deposited my peltries under the place he gave me to sleep in. Mr. Wells, having heard of my arrival, sent three times, urging me to come and see him. At last, I yielded to the solicitations of my brother-in-law, and crossed over with him. Mr. Wells was glad to see me, and treated me with much politeness; he offered me wine and provisions, and whatever his house afforded. I had taken nothing except a little tobacco, when I saw his Frenchman come in with my packs. They carried them past me into Mr. Well's bed room; he then locked the door, and took out the key.

Immediately his kindness and attentions to me relaxed. I said nothing, but felt not the less anxious and uneasy, as I was very unwilling to be deprived of the means of paying Mr. Hanie his credit, still more so to have my property taken from me by violence, or without my own consent. I watched about the house, and at length found an opportunity to slip into the bed room, while Mr. Wells was then taking something from a trunk. He tried to drive me, and afterwards to push me out, but I was too strong for him. After he proceeded to this violence, I did not hesitate to take up my packs, but he snatched them from me. Again I seized them, and in the struggle that ensued, the thongs that bound them were broken, and the skins strewed about the floor.

As I went to gather them up, he drew a pistol, cocked it, and presented it to my breast. For a moment I stood motionless, thinking he would certainly kill me, as I saw he was much enraged; then I seized his hand, and turned it aside, at the same moment drawing from my belt a large knife, which I grasped firmly in my right hand, still holding him by my left. Seeing himself thus suddenly and entirely in my power, he called first for his wife, then for his interpreter, and told them to put me out of the house.

To this, the interpreter answered, "You are as able to put him out as I am." Some of the Frenchmen were also in the house, but they refused to give him any assistance. Finding he was not likely to intimidate or overcome me by violence, he had recourse once more to milder measures. He offered to divide with me, and to allow me to retain half my peltries for the Hudson's Bay people.

"You have always," said he, "belonged to the north west; why should you now desert us for the Hudson's Bay!" He then proceeded to count the skins, dividing them into two parcels; but I told him it was unnecessary, as I was determined he should not have one of them.

"I went to you," said I, "last fall, when I was hungry and destitute, and you drove me, like a dog, from your door. The ammunition with which I killed these animals, was credited to me by Mr. Hanie, and the skins belong to him; but if this was not the case, you should not have one of them. You are a coward; you have not so much courage as a child. If you had the heart of a squaw, you would not have pointed your pistol at my breast, and have failed to shoot me. My life was in your power, and there was nothing to prevent your taking it, not even the fear of my friends, for you know that I am a stranger here, and not one among the Indians would raise his hand to avenge my death. You might have thrown my body into the river, as you would a dog, and no one would have asked you what you had done; but you wanted the spirit to do even this."

He asked me if I had not a knife in my hand. I then showed him two, a large and a small one, and told him to beware how he provoked me to use them. At last, wearied with this altercation, he went and sat down opposite me in the large room; though he was at considerable distance, so great was his agitation, that I could distinctly hear his heart beat. He sat awhile, then went and began to walk back and forth in the yard. I collected my skins together, and the interpreter helped me to tie them up; then taking them on my back, I walked out, passed close by him, put them in my canoe, and returned to the old Frenchman's house, on the other side.

2 From Lord Selkirk, *A Sketch of the British Fur Trade* (1815), in J.M. Bumsted, ed., *The Collected Writings of Lord Selkirk 1810–1820*, vol. 2, *Writings and Papers of Thomas Douglas, Fifth Earl of Selkirk* (Winnipeg: Manitoba Record Society, 1987), 48–55.

I. Remarks on the respective systems adopted in Canada prior and subsequent to the Cession of that Colony to Great Britain.— General View of the Canadian Fur Trade.—

Origin and Constitution of the North-West Company of Montreal.

The commercial benefits which were expected to accrue from the Fur Trade in Canada, formed the principal object in the original settlement of that colony.[1] For a long period that branch of trade furnished the chief employment of the colonists; but of late years the progress of population, and the increase of wealth, have given rise to other and more valuable branches of traffic.[2] The Fur Trade, however, still constitutes an important branch of Canadian commerce. An inquiry into the principles on which this trade has been conducted may be interesting, in many respects, not only to those who are connected with the colony, but to all who have turned their attention to the commercial resources, and colonial prosperity, of the British Empire: and the inquiry may be the more important, because the mode in which the Fur Trade is conducted does not appear to be generally understood, or justly appreciated, even in Canada.

While that province was in the possession of France, the Fur Trade was carried on under a system of exclusive privileges.[3] In each district of country, or nation of Indians, a licence was granted by the governor of the province, assigning to some favoured individuals the privilege of trading within the prescribed limits. The persons who obtained these privileges were generally officers of the army, or others of respectable family connection. Whatever were the motives in which this system originated, there can be no doubt that it contributed, in a very great degree, to the main object of the French government in their transactions with the Indian nations of America: *viz.* to establish and extend their political influence.[4] Whoever possessed the exclusive trade of a district was the only person to whom the Indians could apply for such articles as an intercourse with Europeans had introduced among them; and, independent of the ordinary transactions of barter, the natives had frequently occasion to solicit favours which they could only expect from the indulgence of the privileged traders. These were generally men of liberal education, who knew how to promote the views of government; and they had the greater anxiety on this head, as it was well known that if any of them abused their privileges, or otherwise failed in promoting the general objects expected from them, their exclusive rights would be withdrawn. The conduct of the traders was at the same time closely watched by the Missionaries, whose anxious attention was directed to prevent the abuses which had been found to arise from the sale of spirituous liquors among the savages; an object in which they appear to have been in general zealously seconded by the Provincial Government.[5]

This system appears to have been wisely adapted to increase the comforts, and improve the character, of the natives; as a proof of which, we need only compare the present state of the Indians in Canada, with that in which they stood immediately after the conquest of that province by Great Britain, at which period populous villages existed in many districts, where at present we meet only two or three wandering families, and these addicted to the most brutal excesses, and a prey to want and misery.

A few years after the conquest of Canada, the former system of traffic with the Indians was laid aside, as inconsistent with the received principles of freedom of trade; and, with the exception of one district, no more exclusive privileges were granted. After the trade was thrown open to the public, the first adventurers who arrived in the Indian country made very large profits, and this circumstance soon gave rise to a keen commercial competition, the result of which, however, was very different from that which would have taken place in a civilized country, where the effect of rivalship tends only to compel the trader to supply his customers with better goods, and on more reasonable terms.[6] Among the Indians it was found that a profuse supply of spirituous liquors was a shorter and more certain mode of obtaining a preference, than any difference in the quality or price of the goods offered for sale.[7] The ungovernable propensity of the Indians to intoxication is well known, and it is easy to imagine the disorders which would arise, when this propensity was fostered by unbounded temptation. But, to comprehend the full extent of the mischief, it must be recollected, that these rival traders were scattered over a country of immense extent, and at such a distance from all civil authority, as to lead them to believe that the commission of almost any crime would pass with impunity. In such a situation every art which malice could devise was exerted without restraint, and the intercourse of the traders with each other partook more of the style of the savages by whom they were surrounded, than of the country from which they had sprung. The only difference was that their ferocity was mixed with a greater portion of cunning. Direct personal violence was perhaps seldom resorted to, because it was more easy to succeed when the object was disguised, and effected through the agency of the Indians. Those of the natives who had formed a connection with one trader might be led by him to believe the most atrocious calumnies of another, and to credit the most absurd tales of his hostile and wicked designs; and, under the influence of continued intoxication, there was no pitch of fury to which an Indian might not be roused, nor any act of ferocity which he might not be impelled to commit. Mr. Henry, one of the first British subjects who engaged in the Canadian Fur Trade, in the very interesting account which he has published of his Travels and Adventures, observes, that on his arrival at the Grand Portage on Lake Superior, in the year 1775, "he found the traders in a state of extreme reciprocal hostility, each pursuing his own interests in such a manner as might most injure his neighbour. The consequences," he adds, "were very hurtful to the morals of the Indians." (Page 239).[8] The same facts are stated more at large by Sir Alexander M'Kenzie, who, in his Account of the Fur Trade, (prefixed to his Voyage through North America,) states, that "this trade was carried on in a very distant country, out of the reach of legal restraint, and where there was a free scope given to any ways or means in attaining advantage. The consequence was, not only the loss of commercial benefit to the persons engaged in it, but of the good opinion of the natives, and the respect of their men, who were inclined to follow their example; so that with drinking, carousing, and quarrelling with the Indians along their route, and among themselves, they seldom reached their winter quarters; and if they did, it was generally by dragging their property upon sledges, as the navigation was closed up by the frost. When, at length, they were arrived, the object of each was to injure his rival traders in the opinion of the natives as much as was in their power, by misrepresentation and presents, for which the agents employed were peculiarly calculated. They considered the command of their employer as binding on them, and however wrong or irregular the transaction, the responsibility rested with the principal who directed them:—this is Indian law." (*Page x.*)[9] The agents here alluded to, were the Coureurs des Bois, whom the Author had previously described, (*page ii.*) as French Canadians, who, by accompanying the natives on their hunting and trading excursions, had become so attached to the Indian mode of life, that they had lost all relish for their former habits, and native homes. Of these people the Author remarks, that they often brought home rich cargoes of furs, but that during the short time requisite to settle their accounts with the merchants, and procure fresh credit, they generally contrived to squander away all their gains. He adds, that "this indifference about amassing property, and the pleasure of living free from all restraint, soon brought on a licentiousness of manners, which could not long escape the vigilant observation of the missionaries, who had much reason to complain of their being a disgrace to the christian religion, by not only swerving from its duties themselves, but by thus bringing it into disrepute with those of the natives who had become converts to it." Sir Alexander M'Kenzie goes on to state, that from this conduct of the traders and their servants, the winter was passed among them in a continual scene of disagreement and quarrels; that the natives could entertain no respect for persons who conducted themselves with so much irregularity and deceit; that from the consequences of this licentious conduct, the traders were in continual alarm, and frequently laid under contribution by the Indians,—in short, that matters were daily becoming worse and worse, so that the merchants who furnished the traders with goods, and participated in their adventures, became disgusted with their ill success, and were with difficulty persuaded to continue their advances. The same Author specifies a few

individuals, who, from greater precaution and good sense, were more successful than others, but observes, that these partial advantages "could not prevent the people of Canada from seeing the improper conduct of some of their associates, which rendered it dangerous to remain any longer among the natives. Most of them who passed the winter at the Saskatchawan, got to the Eagle Hills, where, in the spring of the year 1780, a few days previous to their intended departure, a large band of Indians, being engaged in drinking about their houses, one of the traders, to ease himself of the troublesome importunities of a native, gave him a dose of laudanum in a glass of grog, which effectually prevented him from giving further trouble to any one, by setting him asleep for ever. This accident produced a fray, in which one of the traders and several of the men were killed, while the rest had no other means to save themselves but by a precipitate flight, abandoning a considerable quantity of goods, and near half the furs which they had collected during the winter and spring. About the same time, two of the establishments on the Assiniboin River were attacked with less justice, when several white men and a greater number of Indians were killed. In short, it appeared that the natives had formed a resolution to extirpate the traders; and, without entering into any further reasonings on the subject, it appears to be incontrovertible, that the irregularity pursued in carrying on the trade has brought it into its present forlorn situation." (*Page xiii, xiv.*) "The traders," he adds, "were saved from the indignation of the natives, only by the ravages of the smallpox, which at this period spread among the Indians like a pestilence, and almost depopulated the country. By this calamity, the traders were rescued from personal danger, but the source of their profits was cut off, and very few peltries were to be obtained. Even such of the natives as escaped the contagion, were so alarmed at the surrounding destruction, that they were dispirited from hunting, except for their own subsistence." In this deplorable state of things, it is not wonderful that the traders should have been (as the Author states) very much reduced in number, and that the merchants in Canada, who supported them, having foreseen that the continuance of such proceedings would be altogether fatal to their interests, should have been inclined to form a junction for carrying on the trade in partnership. Accordingly, during the winter 1783–4, these merchants formed an Association under the name of The North-West Company, in which the leading persons were Messrs. B. and J. Frobisher, and Mr. Simon M'Tavish, by whose influence chiefly the coalition had been brought about. The main principle of the arrangement was that the separate capitals of the several traders were to be thrown into a common stock, in consideration of which, each individual held a proportionable share of the combined adventure. In the arrangement of this co-partnership, difficulties were found, from the claims of some individuals (chiefly Messrs. Pangman and Gregory), who were not satisfied with the shares assigned to them, and who, refusing to concur in the coalition, continued to carry on a separate trade. This retarded for some time the formation of a general union, and, after that was effected, it was again dissolved by differences of a similar nature. This led, in the year 1798, to a great secession from the North-West Company, and to the formation of a New Company (known in Canada by the name of The X.Y. Company), which traded for some years in competition with the former establishment. A coalition, however, was at length effected between these rival bodies in the year 1805, at which time the North-West Company took its present shape.—The means by which this Association acquired a preponderance which has enabled the Company to secure to themselves so extensive and lucrative a trade, will be found well deserving of public attention.[10]

After the junction of the Old and New North-West Companies, the whole concern came to be divided into a hundred shares, of which a considerable proportion is held by the mercantile houses in London or Montreal, which had contributed the capital for the companies; and other shares are held by individuals who are termed *wintering partners*, and who take upon themselves the charge of managing the affairs of the Company in the interior. Of seventy-five shares assigned to the Old Company, thirty are held by one house at Montreal, the successors of those who planned the original coalition in 1783. Of twenty-five assigned to the New Company, eighteen or nineteen are appropriated to the different houses in Montreal or London, which had contributed a capital for the undertaking. All the remaining shares are distributed among the wintering partners, some of whom possess one share, and some two. The partners hold a general meeting every summer, at the rendezvous at Fort William, at the Grand Portage on Lake Superior, where all matters are decided by a majority of votes, every share giving one vote, and the absentees voting by proxy. At this meeting, the operations to be carried on during the succeeding year are arranged, and the station to be assigned to each individual is determined; the accounts of the former year are settled; and every partner brings a statement of the transactions of the department which has been under his charge.

When a wintering partner has served for a certain number of years, he is at liberty to retire from the concern; and, without doing any further duty, to receive not only his share of the capital of the Company, but also, for seven years, to draw one-half of the profits of the share which he had held. Upon his retiring, the vacancy is filled up by the election of a new partner. The candidates for this situation must have served the Company for a certain number of years as clerks, of whom a great number are employed under the direction of the wintering partners, and are entrusted with the command and immediate management of one or more trading posts situated in the interior. The election of a new partner is decided, like the other affairs of the Company, by the majority of votes at the general annual meeting of the partners: and, as the conduct of the new partner may affect in a material degree the personal interest of every one who has a right to vote in the election, it is not likely that the choice should fall upon a person destitute of those qualifications which are considered requisite for promoting the common interest. No candidate can have much chance of success, unless he be well acquainted with the nature of the trade, the character and manners of the Indians, and the mode of acquiring influence with them. He must also be of an active disposition, and likely to pursue with perseverance and vigour any object that can tend to promote the interest of the Company. The hope of obtaining the envied station of a partner, being kept alive among all the senior clerks, excites among them an activity and zeal for the general interests of the concern, hardly inferior to that of the partners themselves. They act under the immediate inspection of those who have a direct interest in the result of their management, and are sensible that all their ability must be exerted to secure the favour of their superiors. Every wintering partner watches closely the conduct of the clerks who are under his immediate command; he is excited to this vigilance, not merely by the common interest in which he participates as a partner, but also by feelings of personal responsibility. He comes to the general meeting to give an account of the transactions of his department; and the praise or the censure of his associates is dealt out to him, in proportion to the profit or loss which has occurred in the trade under his direction, and to the success, or failure, of the plans entrusted to his management.

Nothing certainly could be devised more admirably calculated than this system, to infuse activity into every department of so extensive a concern, and to direct that activity, in the most effectual manner, and with complete unity of purpose, towards the common interest. But however much this community of interest

among all the partners, and the responsibility thus imposed upon each individual, tend to keep alive an active attention to the Company's affairs, it must be admitted that they are by no means calculated to produce much respect for the rights of others:—On the contrary, the very nature of the Association, and the extensive range which their operations embrace, cannot fail to produce an *esprit de corps* not very consistent with the feelings of propriety and justice.—This observation will be found particularly applicable to the wintering partners. In the common intercourse of civilized society the necessity of maintaining a fair character in the estimation of the public forms a continued check to that inordinate stimulus of self-interest which too often causes individuals to deviate from the principles of honour and honesty. But a wintering partner of the North-West Company is secluded from all society, except that of persons who have the same interests with himself; and if, in the pursuit of these, he should be induced to violate the rules of justice, he must feel that he is not likely to be judged with extreme rigour by the only persons for whose approbation he is solicitous. The civilized world is at so great a distance, that he cannot be very deeply affected by the chance of his conduct meeting with public reprobation; and he naturally flatters himself that his proceedings will never be investigated, or that if they should, there are so many persons to share in the responsibility, that it cannot fall very heavily on himself. In these remote situations, the restraints of law cannot operate as in the midst of a regular society.—When a plaintiff has to travel thousands of miles to find the court from which he is to seek redress, and when witnesses are to be brought from such a distance, at a vast expense, and to the total interruption of their ordinary pursuits, it must be a case of extraordinary importance, which would induce even a wealthy man to encounter the difficulty of obtaining it.[11] Every wintering partner, therefore, must naturally be aware of the extent of his power over individuals who are not rich enough to contend with the whole

Association of which he is a member; and if under these circumstances, acts of injustice and oppression be committed against weaker neighbours, however greatly they are to be regretted, they cannot form a subject of much surprise.

Thus, from the very nature and organization of the Company, a conclusion may reasonably be drawn as to the line of conduct which they are most likely to pursue. That indeed may be varied in a certain degree by the personal character of the individuals at the head of the concern; but even supposing that these were men of the most honourable principles, and incapable of countenancing a systematic violation of justice, it would be with the greatest difficulty that they could restrain this tendency in others.

NOTES

[Editor's note: The reference numbers in the text are Selkirk's page references to the original books.]

1. Modern scholars might dispute Selkirk's assertion here; see, for example, Marcel Trudel, *The Beginnings of New France 1524–1663* (Toronto, 1973).

2. In general, see Fernand Ouellet, *Social and Economic History of Quebec, 1760–1850* (Toronto, 1980).

3. For a general description of the workings of the French fur trade, see Harold A. Innis, *The Fur Trade in Canada* (rev. edn, Toronto, 1956). But consult also William J. Eccles, "A Belated Review of Harold Adams Innis's *The Fur Trade in Canada*," *Canadian Historical Review* 60 (1979): 419–44.

4. Most modern scholars would agree that Selkirk here overemphasizes the extent to which the French were able to exercise their monopoly through licensing.

5. Again, Selkirk overemphasizes the success of the government in controlling matters, especially in the so-called Brandy Trade. See, for example, J.E. Lunn, "The Illegal Fur Trade Out of New France, 1713–1760," *Canadian Historical Association Annual Report* (1939): 61–76.

6. For modern scholarly accounts of the changes in the fur trade after 1763, consult E.E. Rich, *The Fur Trade and the Northwest to 1857* (Toronto, 1967), 130–85; Arthur J. Ray, *Indians in the Fur Trade: Their role as hunters, trappers and middlemen in the lands southwest of Hudson Bay 1660–1870* (Toronto, 1974), 94 ff.

7. For recent analyses, see Ray, *Indians in the Fur Trade*, and Arthur J. Ray and Donald Freeman, *"Give Us Good Measure": An Economic Analysis of Relations between the Indians and the Hudson's Bay Company before 1763* (Toronto, 1978), 192–7.

8. Alexander Henry, *Travels and Adventures in Canada and the Indian Territories between the years 1760 and 1776* (New York, 1809).

9. Alexander Mackenzie, *Voyages from Montreal, on the River St. Laurence, through the Continent of North America, to the Frozen and Pacific Oceans; in the Years 1789 and 1793; With a Preliminary Account of the Rise, Progress, and Present State of the Fur Trade of that Country . . .* (London, 1801).

10. For the North West Company, see Marjorie Wilkins Campbell, *The North West Company* (Vancouver, 1983); Gordon Charles Davidson, *The North West Company* (New York, 1967); W. Stewart Wallace, ed., *Documents Relating to the North West Company* (Toronto, 1934); L.R. Masson, ed., *Les bourgeois de la Compagnie du Nord-Ouest . . .* (Quebec, 1889–1890).

11. The British government attempted to deal with these questions in 1803 with the passage of the so-called Canada Jurisdictions Act, which made the courts of Upper and Lower Canada responsible for the obtaining of justice in the western territories. This legislation, of course, became one of the major bones of contention between the Hudson's Bay Company (which denied that the act applied to territory in their charter) and the North West Company backed by the Canadian government (which insisted the act did apply). In general, see A.S. Morton, "The Canada Jurisdiction Act and the North-West," *Transactions Royal Society of Canada* 3rd ser., 32 (1938): 121–38.

Historical Interpretations

3 From Bruce M. White, "The Woman Who Married a Beaver: Trade Patterns and Gender Roles in the Ojibwa Fur Trade," *Ethnohistory* 46 (Winter 1999): 109–47. © 1999 The American Society for Ethnohistory. All rights reserved. Republished by permission of the copyright holder, and the present publisher, Duke University Press (www.dukeupress.edu).

In 1904, Kagige Pinasi (John Pinesi), an Ojibwa (Anishinaabe)-French man living at Fort William on the north shore of Lake Superior, told anthropologist William Jones a story about a young woman who married a beaver. With blackened face she went to fast for a long time during a vision quest. She saw a person in human form who spoke to her. He asked her to come live with him. She did and eventually agreed to marry him. She was well provided with food and clothing and soon gave birth to four children.[1]

She soon noticed something very odd that led her to realize for the first time that she had married a beaver. From time to time the woman's husband or children would leave with a human being who appeared outside their house. "And back home would they always return again. All sorts of things would they fetch—kettles and bowls, knives, tobacco, and all the things that are used when a beaver is eaten; such was what they brought. Continually they were adding to their great wealth." They would go to where the person lived and the person would kill the beavers. Yet the beavers were never really killed. They would come back home again with the clothes and tobacco that people gave them. The beavers were very fond of the people and would visit them often. The woman herself was forbidden to go by her husband, but this is what she heard.

Eventually the woman's husband died and she returned to live with human beings. She lived a long time after that and often told the story of what happened while she lived with the beavers. She always told people that they should never speak ill of a beaver or they would never be able to kill any: "If anyone

regards a beaver with too much contempt, speaking ill of it, one simply [will] not [be able to] kill it. Just the same as the feelings of one who is disliked, so is the feeling of the beaver. And he who never speaks ill of a beaver is very much loved by it; in the same way as people often love one another, so is one held in the mind of the beaver, particularly lucky then is one at killing beavers."

[. . .]

A primary purpose of such accounts is educational. Ojibwa elders told stories like this, usually in winter, to teach young people about the world while entertaining them.[2] As such, these narratives are also a useful way for outsiders to learn about the people's world view and understand their view of their history.[3] Kagige Pinasi may have had a variety of reasons for wishing to instruct William Jones by telling him this story. Jones's biographer, Henry M. Rideout, spoke of the informant as "an old chief" and an experienced trapper who made Jones examples of animal traps. He also told Jones a number of odd experiences he had had hunting and trapping with his sons. He also recounted, for Jones's transcription, more than 50 stories, which Jones praised for their artistry. Jones wrote that the man developed a fondness for him—the anthropologist was of Fox and British-American ancestry—and tried to convince him to "come and live here, take to myself a wife, and be one of the people." Telling Jones this story of a kind of intermarriage may have been a form of subtle encouragement.[4]

Beyond Kagige Pinasi's own personal motives, this story is, like all Ojibwa stories, interesting on many levels. It instructs young people, especially girls, on the importance of the vision quest, the means through which an Ojibwa person obtained a relationship with powerful beings who would be helpful to her and could chart a unique course for her life. Further, it is a basic description of and commentary on the co-operative arrangements that many Ojibwa people believed existed between different kinds of beings in the world. Ojibwa people who hunted, fished, or gathered plants had to be aware of their reciprocal obligations with the natural world and give back something to the animals, fish, or plants from which they harvested. In taking small plants in the woods, or bark from the trees, people often left a gift of tobacco. After a bear was killed, they held an elaborate ceremony of thanks and gave presents to the bear. The beaver story shows that reciprocity was necessary to keep the system operating. Without gifts and respect, animals would not be so helpful to humans. They would hold themselves back and not allow themselves to be used by people. Without gifts and respect, the system would cease to function.[5]

Ojibwa people also applied the principle of reciprocity to their dealings with people, including non-Indians. In their earliest interactions with the French and the British, the Ojibwa made use of the same gifts, ceremonies, and words that they used in dealing with animals, plants, and other beings.[6] The logic of approaching Europeans in this way was solid; interaction with Europeans was important because of the valuable technology Europeans brought with them. [. . .]

Dealing with animals differed, of course, from dealing with Europeans. The Ojibwa quickly worked out a variety of strategies that were specific to the newcomers. For example, they gave different things. The story of the woman who married the beaver describes a reverse fur trade. In the European fur trade, Indian people gave furs in return for tools, kettles, and tobacco, but this story tells of a relationship in which people gave tools, kettles, and tobacco to beavers in return for the animals' furs.

There is yet another striking feature of the story: it delineates an intermediary role for women in the interaction between people and animals, suggesting a role for women in the interaction between the Ojibwa and Europeans. This story is not an origin tale.[7] For the people in the story, the relationship was a well-established, functioning system. Yet the story explains the system and how it works through the experiences of a woman. If the story was intended to teach, in Lyotard's words, "positive or negative apprenticeships," there was clearly a special message in it for young women about what was possible. Women, it would appear, have power to cross boundaries, explaining one world to another, in this case through a marriage relationship. This power had implications for the workings of the fur trade.

GENDER AND FUR TRADE HISTORIOGRAPHY

Many accounts of the fur trade imply that trade took place mainly between native and European men, with women playing an adjunct role. [. . .]

Despite broad examinations of the role of women in the fur trade, detailed and focused studies of gender relations in the Ojibwa fur trade have yet to be done. Discussion of the role of Ojibwa men and women in the fur trade has come largely in the context of ethnographic and historical studies of Ojibwa women. In such work, the differing roles of men and women in relation to the fur trade have been interpreted in light of theories about the autonomy and power of Ojibwa women—the control of women over their own activities and the power they exerted in the society as a whole.[8]

[. . .]

GENDERED PATTERNS OF TRADE

[. . .] From the seventeenth century on, the fur trade was important to the Ojibwa, who had a continuing, though variable, interest in obtaining European merchandise to use in their daily lives, in hunting, cooking, and religious ceremonies.[9] Trade goods offered material benefits, increased status, and much more. But from the beginning, traders accommodated Ojibwa demand by bringing a rich assortment of goods, including cloth, blankets, utensils, tools, silver jewellery, thread, and beads. In return, traders needed more from the Ojibwa than furs. They also needed a rich variety of products that only women could provide. All these factors meant that both Ojibwa men and women had a variety of roles to play and methods of exerting power and influence over the trade process.

The major role of women in the fur trade was not evident in the earliest years of French–Ojibwa interaction, when canoe-loads of people from the western Great Lakes went east to Montreal to trade their furs with the French. It may be that women were involved in these expeditions, although most accounts suggest that the participants were mainly men.[10] Later, however, when the location of trade shifted to native villages, women became crucial to the trade.

In the context of the trading post and the village, Ojibwa men and women had distinct and often different relationships with traders. The fur trade was never simply an exchange of furs for trade goods. It included a variety of other kinds of transactions. Traders needed to get food from native people; without it, they could not survive the winter in the western Great Lakes. They simply could not bring in or collect enough food to feed themselves, while at the same time carrying on the fur business. At the same time, as described later in more detail, traders needed a variety of native-manufactured supplies. The multifaceted nature of this trade meant that native people interacted with traders in many ways.

The varied interactions of Ojibwa men and women with traders were manifested in the complex set of trade patterns that made up a complete trading year. In the eighteenth century, a trading year in a southwestern Ojibwa community would begin with the arrival in the fall of the trader with a new supply of goods. Once established in a fort or trading house, he gathered members of the community and gave and received ceremonial gifts. Goods such as clothing and utensils designed to help the Ojibwa survive the winter were then given out on credit, and customers went on their fall and winter hunts. The trader often purchased supplies of wild rice for his own survival and in some cases hired a hunter and his family to provide him with meat during the winter. Later, the trader or his men might visit native families to collect the furs they produced. Similarly, native people might revisit the trading post bringing in furs. In such circumstances, there could be further gifts and further credit. At the end of the trading year in the spring, before the trader's departure, certain goods were traded in direct exchanges and there might be concluding gifts and ceremonies.[11]

Gift, barter, and credit transactions were differentiated in a variety of ways. One means of differentiation was simply the way in which both parties spoke about them. Both traders and customers gave speeches in which they explained what they expected of their relationship as a whole and what they expected of any particular transaction. The temporal and seasonal context was also important. Gifts began the trading year, cemented other exchanges, and ended the year.[12] Credit was largely given in the fall. Direct exchanges of furs for merchandise took place in late winter or in the spring.

Another means of differentiating these various transactions was in the trade goods and native products. Evidence suggests the existence of spheres of exchange, or categories of trade goods subject to different rules and procedures.[13] For example, cloth goods and alcohol were defined and treated in strikingly different ways in the trade context. Alcohol, whether brandy, high wines, or rum, had some obvious culturally defined characteristics in the fur trade as well as native-European diplomacy.[14] Among traders in the Lake Superior region in the late eighteenth and early nineteenth centuries, alcohol in the form of rum or brandy was chiefly given to native people in two kinds of transactions: as gifts and in exchange for food. [. . .] The food on which the trader depended, such as wild rice, game, and maple sugar, was often obtained with liquor.[15] By contrast, cloth, clothing, and blankets were mainly exchanged in the context of credit/debt transactions or in direct exchange for furs and possibly for supplies. Thus, contrary to the usual picture of the fur trade, the bulk of furs received by traders were not actually obtained in barter. Rather, they were received as repayment for credit granted in the fall, in the form of cloth, tools, and utensils.

Trade transactions were not only differentiated by time and type of trade merchandise, but also by gender. The full extent of men's and women's participation in the trade among the Ojibwa is difficult to document. No complete sets of account books have been found that fully record all aspects of any trader's business. [. . .] Some traders say almost nothing about women. Others mention them in passing, referring to them in generic fashion, using terms such as "a widow" or simply "a woman," or by their relationship to male Ojibwa. Because of this, scholars may assume that, without contrary evidence, all named persons in traders' narratives are men. This may not always be a safe assumption.[16] Nor is it safe to assume that because a particular trader never mentions women, he never had dealings with them.

Despite these problems, some conclusions can be drawn about the role of women in the trade. Men appear to have been the most frequent participants in trade ceremonies, as they were in other kinds of non-trade-related diplomacy. Leading men in the community gave speeches and sometimes, especially at the beginning of the trading year, presented gifts of furs or food. In return, they were given gifts of liquor, which they appear to have shared with men and women alike. It was also on such occasions that leading

men were presented with chief's coats and other symbols of their role in the trade and in the community. Sometimes they were "made chiefs," that is, given status by the trader that they did not actually have in the community. It should be noted that the skillful leader—one who understood the need of leaders to give things away in order to increase their own status in the community—often gave away the clothing and other symbols of power given them by traders.[17] Such gifts may have gone to women as well as men. In any case, trade ceremonies also involved more general gifts to men and women in the community. Alexander Henry, the younger, a North West Company trader on the Red River in 1800, made this clear in his account of the transactions that took place on his arrival in the region of trade. On 21 August of that year, he presented several male community leaders with scarlet laced coats, laced hats, red feathers, white linen shirts, leggings, breech cloths and flags, as well as tobacco and alcohol. A few weeks later, in addition to unspecified goods on credit to the amount of twenty skins' worth each to a number of individuals, he also gave "an assortment of small articles gratis, such as one Scalper, two Folders, and four Flints [apiece to the men], [and to the] Women, two awls, three needles, one seine of net Thread, one fi[r]e steel, a little Vermilion, and a half f[atho]m of Tobacco."[18]

It is usually asserted that men were the primary traders of furs. This is hard to document, given the fact that few furs were actually traded directly. Instead they were exchanged in credit/debt transactions. Traders seldom listed the goods they gave out on credit or even to whom credit was given, though usually traders recorded debts in the names of men.[19] It is impossible to know whether women or men chose the goods given out in this fashion. It could be argued that even if the credit was granted to the hunters or trappers who were expected to produce the furs, this does not preclude the possibility that women were involved in the choice of goods or that men discussed with their wives what the wives or children needed for the winter. Given the documented concern of Ojibwa people for their families, it is hard to picture Ojibwa men who acted like mythical "economic men" in the theoretical sense, maximizing their own self-interest at the expense of their families.[20] This would, perhaps, have been productive for them in the short run, but would have lowered their status in the community.[21]

As for the repayment of the debts during the winter, a variety of people could be involved, including the hunter or trapper, his children, and his wives or female relations. Often the trader would be notified that a particular group of trappers had produced some furs.[22] He would then send off his men to pick them up. Subsequently, the hunter or other members of the family would be given a gift of alcohol in some form, which would, again, be shared among men and women.[23] It should also be noted that there were occasions when women traded furs directly.[24] While men were the primary hunters and trappers in Ojibwa communities, women processed the furs, a fact that would have given them greater authority in deciding what would happen to the furs, as well as the opportunity to trade them.

The occasional role of women in bartering furs was part of a larger role in bartering. Food was an important part of women's trade. They supplied wild rice and maple sugar, both of which were mainstays for the trader. The characteristic return for such items of food was liquor. However, there were exceptions to this pattern. Michel Curot, a young clerk trading along the St Croix River in 1803–4, for example, stated that because food supplies were scarce during the winter, traders were paying blankets for wild rice. In other years, this was an unusual transaction and after paying a two-and-a-half-point blanket to one woman in late February 1804, Curot felt obligated to explain: "I resolved to give the blanket, having only a single fawn of rice for provisions." Normally such a blanket was

worth three beaverskins or more. He went on to describe the failure of his men to obtain fish to feed them.[25]

Wild rice was important not only as a trade item to be consumed by traders while living in an Ojibwa village near the Great Lakes, but also as an important way to feed brigades travelling further west. One account of large-scale trading of wild rice suggests something of women's power in the trade and in the Ojibwa community. The British trader Alexander Henry, the elder, went west of Lake Superior for the first time in 1775. When he reached Lake of the Woods, he and his men received a warm welcome:

From this village we received ceremonious presents. The mode with the Indians is, first to collect all the provisions they can spare, and place them in a heap; after which they send for the trader, and address him in a formal speech. They tell him, that the Indians are happy in seeing him return into their country; that they have been long in expectation of his arrival; that their wives have deprived themselves of their provisions, in order to afford him a supply; that they are in great want, being destitute of every thing, and particularly of ammunition and clothing; and what they most long for, is a taste of his rum, which they uniformly denominate *milk*.

The present, in return, consisted in one keg of gunpowder, of sixty pounds weight; a bag of shot, and another of powder, of eighty pounds each; a few smaller articles, and a keg of rum. The last appeared to be the chief treasure, though on the former depended the greater part of their winter's subsistence.

In a short time, the men began to drink, while the women brought me a further and very valuable present, of twenty bags of rice. This I returned with goods and rum, and at the same time offered more, for an additional quantity of rice. A trade was opened, the women bartering rice, while the men were drinking. Before morning, I had purchased a hundred bags, of nearly a bushel measure each. Without a large quantity of rice, the voyage could not have been prosecuted to its completion. The canoes, as I have already observed, are not large enough to carry provisions.[26]

There was a great deal more going on in this encounter than is evident in Henry's description. In this trading encounter, men played their usual ceremonial role, describing what it was they sought from the traders. Their words, along with their "ceremonious presents," suggest that their aim was to establish a continuing relationship, one that would ensure them of a supply of merchandise, not just a one-time interaction. Unfortunately, Henry was only passing through. The ceremony did not initiate a full year's worth of credit, debt, trade, and gift.[27] Instead, the only native product to be traded was wild rice, a product largely harvested by women and, for trading purposes, under their control. Given the limited nature of the encounter and the need, and the pressing schedule of the trader, these women had the power to obtain not just alcohol, but, apparently, a full range of goods.

Canoes—the product of both men's and women's labour—were often traded by women and were a useful way to obtain a full range of trade goods. [. . .] Supplies for maintaining canoes were also produced by women. In early April 1804, Curot and his men left their Yellow River wintering post to camp out on the St Croix River. Curot's canoes were badly in need of repair and the trader sent off one of his men with rum and cloth "to hire the women to make gum that I absolutely need, since we cannot make use of any of our canoes without it filling immediately." It was not until 1 May that Curot was able to purchase gum from a woman named La Petite Riviere, or Little River, in return for a three-point

blanket, generally worth three or four beaverskins. Curot obtained birch bark and *wadab*, the spruce roots used for tying panels of bark, from an unidentified person—possibly from Little River—in return for some jewellery, and the next day his men were able to repair the canoes. They finally set off for Grand Portage the following day.[28] Little River, who was unusual in being identified by her own name, also tanned three deerskins in return for two pairs of wool leggings, which together were worth four beaverskins.[29]

Considering their role in trading a wide variety of food and supplies, it may be that women were more often involved in direct trade than men. Curot's journal provides some statistical evidence on this point. As suggested by the examples given here, Curot not only used his journal as a way of recording a narrative of trade activities, but also for recording specific trade transactions. While he was generally vague about the quantity of goods given on credit—usually recording only the name of the person given credit—he was more specific about direct trade. Throughout the pages of the journal, Curot recorded 64 separate transactions that were clearly examples of direct trade. Of these, 19 involved men and 22 involved women. In addition, there were 23 transactions in which the gender of the person trading was not evident. Given the frequency with which Curot named the male Ojibwa with whom he traded, and the fact that most of the men had received credit from him, it is very likely that most of the anonymous trade transactions were also examples of trade with women. This suggests that the vast majority of Curot's direct trade transactions were with women.[30]

Beyond these opportunities for women to trade their own products for a wide range of goods, some women took part in the ceremonial trading roles of giving and receiving gifts and getting credit, the more typical role of men. A prime example was Netnokwa, the Ottawa mother of the adopted white captive, John Tanner, who lived with her family among Ojibwa west of the Red River around 1800. On the occasion of trading with one trader, according to Tanner, Netnokwa "took ten fine beaver skins, and presented them to the trader. In return for this accustomed present, she was in the habit of receiving every year a chief's dress and ornaments, and a ten gallon keg of spirits."[31] Around the time described in the narrative, Charles Chaboillez, a North West Company trader, stated that on arriving in the region of the Red River, he exchanged presents with and gave credit to the "Old Courte Oreille [Ottawa] & Two Sons." This was clearly a reference to Netnokwa, Tanner, and Tanner's adopted brother. Later, Chaboillez stated that he gave her a present of rum and tobacco, "to encourage her to return" with furs and other products, a suggestion of her primary role in trading.[32] How typical Netnokwa was of other women in the community in which she lived is not clear. Laura Peers pointed out that "while Netnokwa was an exceptionally strong and charismatic woman . . . her influence was presumably neither unprecedented nor unparalleled."[33]

There were various explanations for Netnokwa's participation in trade rituals more frequently undertaken by men. For one thing, when she and her family were coming west several years before, Netnokwa's husband had died. Death or illness of a husband and other emergencies appear to have been important reasons for women to undertake activities that were normally the work of men, as it would have been for men to undertake the work of women on occasion. [. . .]

In the case of Netnokwa, however, her transcendence of usual gender roles was evident even before her husband's death. As an older woman who had been married to a younger husband with two other wives, Netnokwa was, according to Tanner, considered to be the head of the household, even before his adopted father's death. Tanner stated that Netnokwa was 17 years older than her husband, was an accomplished trader, and was owner of most of the family's wealth. Tanner

said, perhaps exaggerating, that she was "notwithstanding her sex, . . . regarded as principal chief of the Ottawwaws," and that "whenever she came to Mackinac, she was saluted by a gun from the fort." Perhaps most significant of all—in terms of Ojibwa and Ottawa culture—Netnokwa was, as described by Tanner, a person of strong spirituality, and she used her power to aid her sons in hunting.[34]

Dreams and visions were often cited as providing authorization for Ojibwa men and women to transcend the gendered division of labour. Despite the tendency of scholars to analyze gender roles based on material factors, including participation in the fur trade, power in an Ojibwa community was never purely material, and even material power was usually seen as having a non-material basis. [. . .] As recounted in the story of the woman who married the beaver, girls fasted at puberty, seeking to gain a continuing relationship with a being who could help them in their lives. Having this relationship—especially when it was renewed from time to time through ceremony and further visions and dreams—helped men in important activities like hunting and war. For women, such a relationship might aid them in activities usually described as women's work.[35] This may have been the case with Netnokwa, whose spirituality was evident in her actions, though her own puberty visions were never recorded.[36]

Thus, despite the existence of a well-understood division of labour, described as rigid in many generalized descriptions of the Ojibwa, the more recent ethnographic evidence suggests that the Ojibwa gave cultural acceptance to those who violated the usual gender roles, and who demonstrated competence brought about by spiritual aid.[37] Such cultural acceptance suggests that for many Ojibwa, creative, dynamic women forging a unique course were seen as having a beneficial effect on their communities. This is also evident in a major aspect of the role of women in the fur trade, their role as the wives of traders.

FUR TRADE MARRIAGES

[. . .] Among the Ojibwa, marriage was defined by the decision of two parties, sometimes through the intercession of parents or other relations, to sleep, live, and carry on their day-to-day lives together. Although the event was not marked by the ceremonies with which Europeans were familiar, it could involve ceremonial exchanges of gifts.[38] From the point of view of the native community, marriages between traders and native women could help achieve the important aim of ensuring a steady supply of merchandise. Ties of affection could increase the likelihood that a trader would return to the community in future years and that he might be more generous with gifts and in the rates exacted for direct exchange.

Historian Jacqueline Peterson wrote that "tribal people, throughout the fur trading era, saw intermarriage as a means of entangling strangers in a series of kinship obligations. Relatives by marriage were expected not only to deal fairly, but to provide protection, hospitality, and sustenance in time of famine."

Early accounts of encounters between Ojibwa women and traders did not always clarify the political, social, or economic implications of what took place, making it difficult to interpret the behaviour described. [. . .]

In the aforementioned account of trading rice with women at Lake of the Woods, Alexander Henry stated: "When morning arrived, all the village was inebriated; and the danger of misunderstanding was increased by the facility with which the women abandoned themselves to my Canadians. In consequence, I lost no time in leaving the place." Apparently, for Henry the sexual overtures of the women were a potential cause of jealousy and complication, due to his fear that the behaviour of these women would result in violence on the part of Ojibwa men. Henry does not make clear who these women were or even whether they were married. However, it is possible that their overtures were not, from the Ojibwa point of view, dangerous in that

sense, but were rather actions sanctioned by the community for the purpose of establishing long-term trade. In fact, it may have been that long-term entanglement, not sexual jealousy, was what Henry feared, since he hoped to travel much further west.

Whether or not the strategy succeeded in the case of the people described by Henry is not known. However, there were many cases of marriage between Ojibwa women that did accomplish this purpose and enabled long and peaceful trade. Benjamin G. Armstrong, a trader among the Ojibwa in the 1840s who was married to a daughter of Chief Buffalo of La Pointe, stated that when a trader came into an Ojibwa community to trade, people would at first have nothing to do with him, except in a small way, so that they could gauge his honesty. "If satisfied on these points, the chiefs would together take their marriageable girls to his trading house and he was given his choice of the lot." If the trader made a choice, trade would begin right away. If not, he was compelled to move on his way and trade elsewhere, because the band would not trade with him "unless he took one of their women for his wife." As Peterson stated, this description "seems overly rationalistic." However, she stated that in such cases Indian wives "served as the cement between a band and a trader with long-range expectations."[39]

For fur traders, their wives or the wives of their employees could prove to be useful socially and economically. The evidence suggests that leading traders often married the daughters of Ojibwa leaders, although it is sometimes hard to say which came first.[40] In marrying a leader's daughter, a trader gained a powerful ally among his Indian customers. Since the authority of a leader was in part the result of extended kin ties, the trader may have formed ties with a large number of people. The leader's influence over kin and non-kin alike depended also on his persuasive oratory.[41] Thus, through marriage, the trader gained an alliance with a man of demonstrated ability to influence his fellows. The father-in-law could become, in a sense, an economic agent for the trader, useful in persuading the people to be friends and clients.

[. . .]

A trader who benefitted from a connection to a prominent native family was Charles Oakes Ermatinger, who, from a base at Sault Ste Marie, shipped goods to trading posts south and west of Lake Superior from 1800 to the mid-1820s. Ermatinger married Charlotte, the daughter of Kadowaubeda, or Broken Tooth, a member of the Loon clan and a civil leader described by Henry R. Schoolcraft, an Indian agent and a noted writer on Ojibwa culture, as "patriarch" of the region around Sandy Lake and the upper Mississippi, the area of Ermatinger's trade. After her husband's retirement in the 1820S, Charlotte went to live with him and her children in Montreal, where she spent the rest of her life.[42]

Important traders like Ermatinger were not the only members of their companies married to native women. [. . .] When the North West Company wintering partner John Sayer was stationed on the St Croix River, his Ojibwa wife went to the sugar bush in 1803 and 1804 to process maple sugar for their food supply.[43] When food was scarce at the trading post, traders were sometimes fed by their wives' families. On 17 March 1804, George Nelson wrote: "Brunet with my permission goes with his family to his father in law's lodge, as we have nothing here to eat. I give him a little ammunition & a few silverworks to trade provisions— for we have now nothing else to trade. We subsiste [sic] upon indian Charity."[44]

Beyond providing food, native women and the trade kinship networks served as a source of information for traders as much as for Indian people. In 1804, Michel Curot learned that one Ojibwa family did not want to give their furs to the opposition North West trader because the man was out of rum. Curot said he had heard it from the wife of his man Savoyard, who had in turn heard

it from the wife of the North West trader's clerk.[45]

Some fur companies had economic reasons for encouraging such marriages. If the employee himself was responsible for the expense of a wife, he would take more of his wages in goods purchased from his employer, thus effectively discounting the company's wage burden. In August 1799, Alexander Mackenzie wrote to John Sayer, the head of the Fond du Lac department, giving him a reading on the financial health of Sayer's outfit: "Were it not that Men Spend their Wages and the extraordinarily high price of Bears and Beaver, it would be to us a losing business. With these advantages there will be very little profit this last year."[46]

A few years later, after leaving the North West Company to head the rival XY Company, Mackenzie took a different point of view, at least according to George Nelson. Nelson told in his journal and reminiscences of an incident that occurred in the fall of 1803 when he was a young man, working as Simon Chaurette's clerk for the XY Company in northern Wisconsin. Assigned to act as Nelson's guide was an Indian the traders called "le Commis" (the clerk) because "formerly traders would give him about a 9 gallon keg of rum & other things and send him trading among or with the other Indians. He was always sure to make good returns." The Commis had a teenage daughter. Very early in the fall the man decided that 18-year-old Nelson should marry her. Nelson suspected that Chaurette— or as he spells the man's name, Chorette—was behind it. "This old fellow either took a fancy for me, or Chorette took a fancy for my little wages. I believe both to be the case."[47]

[. . .]

The implication of some accounts of marriages arranged by traders and the parents of native women is that women were passive objects like the furs, food, and merchandise exchanged in the fur trade. But to be effective in achieving the purposes native communities might envision for such marriages, women could not be passive. They had to exert influence and be active communicators of information. Further, there is evidence that marriages were not simply arranged by male and female elders in communities. Rather they were embraced by many women themselves as a way of achieving useful purposes for themselves and for the communities in which they lived.

Marriages between traders and native women were based on a variety of factors, not just material motives. [. . .] One example was Oshahgushkodanaqua, a woman from the western end of Lake Superior who married the Sault Ste Marie trader John Johnston in the 1790s.[48] Oshahgushkodanaqua was the granddaughter of Mamongeseda (Big Foot or Big Feet), a La Pointe leader noted for his prowess in war and diplomacy. One of Mamongeseda's daughters—one source suggests her name was Obemaunoqua—was the wife of John Sayer, who was in charge of the entire Lake Superior area for the General Company of Lake Superior and the South in the 1780s and the North West Company from 1794 to 1805. One of Mamongeseda's sons, Waubojeeg (White Fisher), also based at La Pointe, was as renowned in war and diplomacy as his father. Waubojeeg was the father of Oshahgushkodanaqua.[49]

Oshahgushkodanaqua's marriage was preceded by a dream during the vision quest she undertook at puberty. She told the story many years later, after her husband's death, to a visiting British writer named Anna Jameson. The story of the dream has some interesting parallels to the story of the woman who married the beaver.

According to Jameson, Oshahgushkodanaqua fasted "according to the universal Indian custom, *for a guardian spirit.*" She went to a high hill and built a lodge of cedar boughs, painted herself black, and then began to fast:

She dreamed continually of a white man, who approached her with a cup in his hand, saying, "Poor thing! why are you punishing yourself? why do you fast? here is food for you!" He was always accompanied by a dog, which looked up in her face as though he knew her. Also she dreamed of being on a high hill, which was surrounded by water, and from which she beheld many canoes full of Indians, coming to her and paying her homage; after this, she felt as if she were carried up into the heavens, and as she looked down upon the earth, she perceived it was on fire, and said to herself, "All my relations will be burned!" but a voice answered and said, "No, they will not be destroyed, they will be saved"; and she *knew it was a spirit,* because the voice was not human. She fasted for ten days, during which time her grandmother brought her at intervals some water. When satisfied that she had obtained a guardian spirit in the white stranger who haunted her dreams, she returned to her father's lodge.[50]

Some time after this dream, John Johnston appeared at her parents' home at Chequamegon to trade for furs. He asked the woman's father, Waubojeeg, for her hand in marriage. Her father at first was scornful of Johnston because he did not believe the trader was seeking a long-term relationship. He told Johnston to return to Montreal in the spring and if he still wished to marry her, he could come back to Lake Superior and marry her, "according to the law of the white man *till death.*" Johnston returned to Lake Superior and the marriage was arranged.

The young woman, however, was not keen on the idea and took some persuasion to stay with her husband. Given the possibilities for dissolving marriage among the Ojibwa, this fear may have been due in part to Johnston's insistence on marriage until death. Once she consented, however, the couple remained married for 36 years.[51] All evidence suggests that she served an important and influential role in relations between her people and her husband, who was an important trader in the Lake Superior region from the

1790s to the 1820s. Oshahgushkodanaqua throughout her life carried on a variety of subsistence activities characteristic of Ojibwa women—activities that would have been advantageous for her husband's business. She sugared every year and fished.

Later in her life, Oshahgushkodanaqua also taught Ojibwa and Ojibwa culture to her children and to visitors to the region, including her son-in-law, Henry R. Schoolcraft. Her career transcended the fur trade, lasting into an era when Ojibwa people had need for intermediaries who would help them in dealings with the U.S. government. All in all, Oshahgushkodanaqua actively made use of the situation in which she found herself.[52]

It should be said that Oshahgushkodanaqua's interpretation of the experience may have evolved over the years. It may have been coloured by the death of her husband. It may have been shaped by her Christian conversion, as suggested by some of the imagery and wording in the story. On the other hand, her experience bears the clear imprint of Ojibwa culture. The vision quest, though an apparently solitary endeavour pursued by young people, was shaped in part by the Ojibwa educational process, including the telling of stories, some of which, in Oshahgushkodanaqua's case, may have resembled the story of the woman who married the beaver. The process of seeking a vision was also usually supervised by adults, who encouraged certain desirable results.[53]

It may be that in this way, Oshahgushkodanaqua's experience was shaped by community needs. Her story contains the suggestion that a marriage with an outsider could be of benefit to the woman's relations, that there was some social purpose in undertaking the marriage with such a person who could provide something useful to the community. She felt some fear about the risks involved to herself and her community, but in the long run, the marriage was a good one. In her life she achieved a great deal.

All of these elements were found, too, of course, in the story of the woman who married the beaver, a story which tells a great deal about how the Ojibwa community did honour to women who followed unique destinies. [. . .]

This story can serve as a guide to interpreting experiences and events, suggesting other ways of looking at them and providing Ojibwa alternatives to scholarly scenarios. Far from being beasts of burden, subsidiary to interactions with outsiders, Ojibwa women were central to the process, honoured for the role they played. The way in which these and other women used their relationships with outsiders for their own benefit, the benefit of the communities, or of their husbands—and in the process influenced the patterns of interaction with outsiders—must be evaluated based on all the available details, on a case-by-case basis. It would be wrong to see in any of the women described here a single set of motives or a single path for Ojibwa women.[54] Nonetheless, it is only by considering all the available Ojibwa models of women's roles as warriors, shamans, wives, suppliers of food, traders, intermediaries, brokers, and teachers, that one can hope to understand the role of Ojibwa women in the fur trade.

CONCLUSION

The fur trade is sometimes seen simply as an exchange that took place between men of European and native cultures. However, an examination of the trade among the Ojibwa of Lake Superior shows that women and men both participated in the trade. They also had different opportunities, different expectations, and different roles to play. As acknowledged by traders in their gift giving and trade, men and women sought a different assortment of trade goods. Women also played an important role in providing the resources that were their responsibility in native life: wild rice, maple sugar, and a variety of vital supplies necessary for the function of trade. While most women did not usually participate in trade ceremonies or receive credit from traders, they were able to trade the products of their labour for goods they needed. Finally, women also could serve as a vital link between their communities and European traders by marrying traders. Such marriages could ensure a steady supply of merchandise for a community by providing an incentive for traders to return to the communities from which their wives came and, possibly, by increasing their generosity toward their wives' relations. Although such marriages were encouraged and often arranged by men, women were not mere objects to be exchanged. The value of such marriages to a native community could only be achieved if women exercised influence on the trader and served to increase the flow of information and merchandise in both directions.

[. . .] The fur trade provided more than a few opportunities for Ojibwa women. While the fur trade was important to native communities, both men and women had distinct and powerful roles to play in relation to a trade that was never simply one of furs for merchandise. Women had many opportunities to trade food, supplies, and on occasion, furs, to obtain what they needed and wanted from traders.

This does not deny the possibility that there may have been particular situations in which women had fewer opportunities to trade the products of their work for the things that they needed. With the improvement of transportation methods and the growth of white population centres in the Great Lakes, traders may have been able to bring better supplies of food, allowing them to trade for furs more exclusively. It should be noted, however, that while later fur traders may have had less use for Ojibwa women's food and supplies, there was a contemporaneous growing market for maple sugar, wild rice, and berries among lumbermen, settlers, and city people, which may well have provided greater opportunities for women than before.

The extent to which Ojibwa women's power and status in their own communities may have changed since contact with Europeans remains to be demonstrated. A major problem with describing the course of changes in Ojibwa society in the last 400 years is the difficulty of reconstructing Ojibwa gender relations in the era prior to European contact using only documents that result from that contact. Analysis of the changes in Ojibwa society in the era of the fur trade also requires care, especially if it is based on documents that interpret Ojibwa gender from a European point of view of how men and women should live their lives. Scholars must take into account some of the Ojibwa beliefs about women's spiritual power and the accounts of individual women's lives and dreams discussed here. Though the Ojibwa did have a distinct division of labour, one that may have changed at various times in response to interaction with Europeans, women could make a distinct course for themselves through their spiritual power.

NOTES

1. William Jones, *Ojibwa Texts*, Truman Michelson, ed., *Publications of the American Ethnological Society*, vol. 7, part 2 (New York, 1919), 251–7.

2. Thomas W. Overholt and J. Baird Callicott, *Clothed-in-Fur and Other Tales: An Introduction to an Ojibwa World View* (Washington, DC, 1982), 26.

3. Overholt and Callicott use the stories to help explain Ojibwa world view in ibid., 24–9.

4. Henry M. Rideout, *William Jones: Indian, Cowboy, American Scholar, and Anthropologist in the Field* (New York, 1912), 98, 109–11. Notes entitled "Penessi goes hunting" are found in the William Jones Papers, American Philosophical Society, Philadelphia.

5. For a discussion of these beliefs and their bearing on the fur trade, see Bruce M. White, "'Give Us a Little Milk': The Social and

Cultural Meaning of Gift Giving in the Lake Superior Fur Trade," in *Rendezvous: Selected Papers of the Fourth North American Fur Trade Conference, 1981,* Thomas C. Buckley, ed. (St Paul, MN, 1984), 187–8.

6. Bruce M. White, "Encounters with Spirits: Ojibwa and Dakota Theories about the French and Their Merchandise," *Ethnohistory* 41 (summer 1994): 376–81; B. White, "'Give Us a Little Milk,'" 189–92; Richard White, *The Middle Ground: Indians, Empires, and Republics in the Great Lakes Region, 1650–1815* (Cambridge, 1991), 95, 112–14.

7. On Native American origin tales, see Stith Thompson, *The Folktale* (1946; reprint, Berkeley, CA, and Los Angeles, 1977), 303.

8. For a discussion of the varying themes covered in the study of gender among Native American groups, see Patricia Albers, "From Illusion to Illumination: Anthropological Studies of American Indian Women," in *Gender and Anthropology: Critical Reviews for Research and Teaching,* Sandra Morgen, ed. (Washington, DC, 1989), 132–48.

9. The argument here is in favour of a desire for and an interest in European merchandise, not necessarily a complete dependence upon it. For a longer discussion of the multiple nature of this interest in merchandise, see B. White, "Encounters with Spirits," 376–81. For one trader's account of Ojibwa interest in merchandise, see Alexander Henry, the elder, *Travels and Adventures in Canada and the Indian Territories* (1809; reprint edn, New York 1976), 196. For a discussion of "dependency" in relation to Great Lakes Indian groups, see R. White, *Middle Ground,* 482–6.

10. For accounts of expeditions to Montreal, see Nicolas Perrot's account in *Indian Tribes of the Upper Mississippi Valley and Region of the Great Lakes,* Emma H. Blair, ed. (Cleveland, OH, 1911), 1: 175, 210–20. In an earlier period, around 1609, Algonquin men and women from the upper Ottawa River, perhaps related to Great Lakes Algonquin peoples, did travel together to trade with the French in Montreal. See Bruce G. Trigger, *The Children of Aetaentsic: A History of the Huron People to 1660* (1976; reprint edn, Montreal, 1987), 249. See also a nineteenth-century account of a seventeenth-century Ojibwa husband and wife

travelling east to discover the French, cited in B. White "Encounters with Spirits," 373.

11. Bruce M. White, "A Skilled Game of Exchange: Ojibway Fur Trade Protocol," *Minnesota History* 50: 229–40.

12. Ibid., 231–34.

13. On the concept of spheres of exchange, see Frederick Barth, *The Role of the Entrepreneur in Social Change in Northern Norway* (Bergen, Norway, 1963), 10; Paul Bohannan and George Dalton, eds, *Markets in Africa* ([Evanston IL], 1962), 3.

14. B. White, "'Give Us a Little Milk,'" 191–2.

15. B. White, "A Skilled Game of Exchange," 235.

16. Ojibwa women's names often, though not always, have the suffix *-ikwe* at the end, which is the Ojibwa word for woman. See John D. Nichols and Earl Nyholm, *A Concise Dictionary of Minnesota Ojibwe* (Minneapolis, MN, and London, 1995), 64. English or French translations of such names may not always have included this portion of the name. On Ojibwa naming practices, see M. Inez Hilger, *Chippewa Child Life* (1951; reprint edn, St Paul, MN, 1992), 35–9.

17. On the generosity of Ojibwa leaders, see Kohl, *Kitchi-Gami: Life Among the Lake Superior Ojibwa* (1860; reprint edn, St Paul, MN, 1985), 66.

18. *The Journal of Alexander Henry the Younger, 1799–1814,* Barry M. Gough, ed., (Toronto, 1988), 1: 26, 53. These entries correspond to 48, 111, in the original journal transcript in Public Archives of Canada, Ottawa, ON.

19. Traders mentioned credit books or ledgers in their narrative journals, but none have been found for this period. Even credit books, however, do not make clear the role of the hunter's family in choosing the goods received on credit. For an analysis of a credit book from a later period, one kept using pictographic symbols, see George Fulford, "The Pictographic Account Book of an Ojibwa Fur Trader," *Papers of the Twenty-third Algonquian Conference,* (Ottawa, ON, 1992), 190–217.

20. Ivan Illich, *Gender* (New York and Toronto, 1982), 9–11; Lionel Robbins, *An Essay on the Nature and Significance of Economic Science* (1931; reprint edn, London, 1952), 94–9.

21. On Ojibwa attitudes toward generosity, see Kohl, *Kitchi-Gami*, 66.

22. For examples of women notifying the trader of available furs and other items, see Michel Curot's journal, 8 (22 September 1803), 19 (13 November 1803).

23. Curot journal, 10 (13 October 1803), (14 October 1803), 13 (24 October 1803), original in Masson Collection, Public Archives of Canada. A garbled translation of this narrative was published as "A Wisconsin Fur-Trader's Journal, 1803–4," *Collections of the State Historical Society of Wisconsin* 20 (1911): 396–471.

24. Some examples of direct trade of furs by women in Curot's journal include 23 (2 December 1803), 32 (9 February 1804).

25. Ibid., 3 (17 and 18 August 1803), 6 (12 September 1803), 9 (4 and 5 October 1803),13 (24 October 1803),18 (10 November 1803), 21 (22 and 23 November 1803), 23 (2 December 1803), 28 (17 December 1803), 29 (23 December 1803), 32 (9 February 1804), 33 (20 February 1804), 41 (18 March 1804), 47 (15 and 16 April 1804).

26. Henry, *Travels and Adventures*, 243–4.

27. There are many examples in trade literature of food gifts to initiate the trading year. See B. White, "'Give Us a Little Milk,'" 187, 193.

28. Curot did some trading and collecting furs during the period when he was camped on the St Croix River. Curot journal, 46 (7 April 1804), 47 (15 April 1804), 50 (8–10 May 1804). See also 5 (5 September 1803), in which it is noted that David can go nowhere because of a lack of gum for his canoe. On *wadab*, see Nichols and Nyholm, *Concise Dictionary*, 113; Frances Densmore, *Chippewa Customs* (1929; reprint edn, St Paul, MN, 1979), 150.

29. Curot journal, 47 (15 April 1804).

30. Figures on trade transactions were compiled from the Curot journal by the author.

31. John Tanner, *A Narrative of the Captivity and Adventures of John Tanner* (1830, reprint edn, New York, 1975), 64, 69, 70, 75, 78,101–2.

32. Harold Hickerson, ed., "Journal of Charles Jean Baptiste Chaboillez," *Ethnohistory* 6 (1959): 275, 299, 374.

33. Laura Peers, *The Ojibwa of Western Canada* (St. Paul, MN, 1994), 56–7.

34. Tanner, *Narrative*, 36, 37, 39, 40. Tanner demonstrates Netnokwa's ability as a trader in the transaction through which she obtained him from his original captors. On her dreams used to help her sons in hunting, see 52, 72.

35. Ruth Landes, *The Ojibwa Woman* (1938; reprint edn, New York, 1971), 20; Kohl, *Kitchi-Gami*, 126–8.

36. Such visions or dreams were not usually discussed casually. See Kohl, *Kitchi-Gami*, 203.

37. Landes *Ojibwa Woman*, 156–62, 165; Kohl, *Kitchi-Gami*, 125, 126, 128.

38. For descriptions of marriage customs, see Densmore, *Chippewa Customs*, 72–3; Hilger, *Chippewa Child Life*, 158–60; Peter Grant, "The Sauteux Indians about 1904," in *Les Bourgeois de la Compagnie du Nord Ouest*, Louis F.R. Masson, ed. (1890; reprint edn, New York, 1960), 320.

39. Benjamin G. Armstrong, *Early Life among the Indians: Reminiscences from the Life of Benjamin G. Armstrong* (Ashland, OR, 1892), 101–2; Jacqueline Peterson, "The People in Between: Indian-White Marriage and the Genesis of a Métis Society and Culture in the Great Lakes Region, 1680–1830" (PhD diss., University of Illinois at Chicago Circle, 1981), 89.

40. It is sometimes unclear whether the extensive influence of the Ojibwa leader made the trader successful, or whether traders backed with large capital helped increase the renown of Ojibwa leaders. This is an area that needs further research.

41. For a discussion of oratory and other leadership qualities, see James G.E. Smith, *Leadership among the Southwestern Ojibwa* (Ottawa, ON, 1973), 17.

42. B. White, *Fur Trade in Minnesota*, 41; Lawrence Taliaferro journal, 8 (9 October 1827): 92, Minnesota Historical Society; Thomas L. McKenney and James Hall, *The Indian Tribes of North America*, Frederick Webb Hodge and David I. Bushnell Jr., 2: 316–19 (Edinburgh, 1934); Kohl, *Kitchi-Gami*, 147–8; Henry R. Schoolcraft, *Personal Memoirs of a Residence of Thirty Years with the Indian Tribes on the American Frontiers* (Philadelphia: 1851), 293. Information on Charlotte, sometimes listed as Charlotte Kattawabide, after her father, is

found in Montreal Protestant church registers, compiled in MG19, A2, series 4, Public Archives of Canada, Ottawa, ON. Charlotte died on 9 July 1850 at the age of 75. See also the Ermatinger family history in MG25, G38, Public Archives of Canada.

43. On Sayer's wife making sugar, see Curot journal, 39 (8 March 1804); John Sayer journal, erroneously printed as that of Thomas Connor in Charles M. Gates, ed., *Five Fur Traders of the Northwest* (1933; reprint edn, St Paul, MN, 1965), 270 (1 March 1805); Nelson journal, 25. See also Douglas A. Birk, ed., *John Sayer's Journal, 1804–5* (Minneapolis, MN, 1989), 49.

44. Nelson journal, 25.

45. Curot journal, 51 (15 May 1804).

46. W. Kaye Lamb, ed., *The Journals and Letters of Sir Alexander Mackenzie* (Cambridge, 1970), 495.

47. Nelson journal, 3.

48. The Ojibwa name Oshahgushkodanaqua, spelled in various ways, was translated by the woman's son-in-law, Henry R. Schoolcraft, as "Woman of the Green Valley." See Schoolcraft, *Personal Memoirs of a Residence of Thirty Years with the Indian Tribes on the American Frontiers* (Philadelphia, 1851), 431, 662, 676. It may be that the name is a garbled misspelling of some combination of the Ojibwe words for green (*ozhawaawashko-*, the lexical prefix for green or blue, occurring on verbs and on some nouns and participles), prairie or plain (*mashkode*) and woman (*ikwe*). See Nichols and Nyholm, *Concise Dictionary*, xii, 64, 78, 111.

49. Charles H. Chapman, "The Historic Johnston Family of the 'Soo'," *Michigan Pioneer and Historical Collections* 32: (1903) 305–43. On 341, in letter six of a series of autobiographical

letters written by John Johnston, there is reference to Mamongeseda's daughter as being "a Mrs. Jayer." However, an examination of the original letter (filed with the first letter of the series, 14 January 1828) in the Henry R. Schoolcraft Papers, Library of Congress, Washington, DC, suggests that the name should really be read as Sayer. On John Sayer, see Douglas A. Birk, "John Sayer and the Fond du Lac Trade: The North West Company in Minnesota and Wisconsin," Buckley, ed., "Rendezvous," 51–61.

50. Anna Jameson, *Winter Studies and Summer Rambles in Canada* (London, 1838), 3: 211–14.

51. Jameson, *Winter Studies*, 210–11; Chapman, "The Historic Johnston Family," 308, 313.

52. Chapman, "The Historic Johnston Family," 308, 313; Philip Mason, ed., *The Literary Voyager or Muzzeniegun* ([Lansing, MI], 1963), xxv, xxiii.

53. On the cultural nature of dreams experienced during vision quests, see Radin, "Some Aspects of Puberty Fasting Among the Ojibwa," *Museum Bulletin* 2: 69–78; "Ojibwa and Ottawa Puberty Dreams," *Essays in Anthropology Presented to Alfred Kroeber* (Berkeley, CA, 1936), 233–64. Landes, *Ojibwa Woman*, 9–10.

54. As Ruth Landes noted in writing of women who tested the flexible boundaries of Ojibwa gender roles: "It cannot be assumed that one woman's motivations are similar to those of other women," Landes, *Ojibwa Woman*, 148. On 140, Landes also noted, "The important factor is that a girl grows up seeing these unconventional possibilities about her, and sees them easily accepted."

---

4   From Carolyn Podruchny, *Making the Voyageur World: Travellers and Traders in the North American Fur Trade* (Toronto: University of Toronto Press, 2006), 165–200, 337–44. © University of Toronto Press, 2006. Reprinted with permission of the publisher.

RENDEZVOUS: PARTIES, TRICKS, AND FRIENDSHIPS

Fort William is the great emporium for the interior. An extensive assortment of merchandise is annually brought hither from Montreal, by large canoes, or the Company's vessels on the lakes, which, in return, bring down the produce of the wintering posts to Canada, from whence it is shipped for England . . . Fort William may therefore be looked upon as the metropolitan post of the interior, and its fashionable season generally continues from the latter end of May to the latter end of August. During this period, good living and festivity predominate; and the luxuries of the dinner-table compensate in some degree for the long fasts and short commons experienced by those who are stationed in the remote posts. The voyageurs too enjoy their carnival, and between rum and baubles the hard-earned wages of years are often dissipated in a few weeks.[1]

The Montreal fur trade was a far-flung enterprise spanning thousands of miles. Central administrative posts were established in the interior of the pays d'en haut to facilitate the organization of trading and the transfer of goods. Ross Cox's description of Fort William quoted here, from his *Adventures on the Columbia River* (1831), conveys an image of a bustling and diverse centre of commerce and cavorting. At these administrative nodes fur traders and labourers congregated in midsummer to exchange furs for European trade goods. These gatherings, called rendezvous, became a time of celebration and feasting. Arriving voyageurs were relieved to have survived their gruelling journey, pleased to meet up with friends, and excited about fresh supplies of food and drink. In the 1770s trader Peter Pond described the rendezvous at Mackinac (at the junction of Lakes Michigan and Huron), where many "ware amuseing themselves in Good Cumpany at Billards Drinking fresh Punch Wine & Eney thing thay Please to Call for while the Mo[re] valgear Ware fiteing Each other feasting was Much atended to Dansing at Nite."[2] After 1803 the most famous rendezvous was at Fort William, at the western end of Lake Superior, which became a "great emporium," as Ross Cox aptly described it. Here pork eaters and northmen unloaded and loaded their ladings, the bourgeois held their annual meetings to plan business operations for the coming year, independent merchants set up shops to sell wares, and retired voyageurs who had settled in the area came to the fort

to hear about the past year's adventures.[3] In the midst of all this activity, voyageurs' celebrations dominated the scene. When clerk George Nelson arrived at Grand Portage for the first time in 1802, he observed high levels of "Gambling, feasting, dancing, drinking & fighting."[4]

Although voyageurs were hired for extremely difficult work, a large part of their lives was occupied with celebrations, festivity, and play. [. . .] Perhaps play came to comprise a significant part of voyageurs' lives because they worked in a liminal space, on the boundaries between French Canada and Aboriginal societies, constantly moving through the pays d'en haut. Scholars have argued that liminality encourages playfulness and trickery; in particular cultural anthropologist Victor Turner asserted that "liminality is particularly conducive to play. Play is not to be restricted to games and jokes; it extends to the introduction of new forms of symbolic action . . . parts of liminality may be given over to experimental behaviour."[5] Voyageurs regularly moved across the thresholds of new worlds, and the thrill and adventure of travelling into the unknown were expressed in their parties, tricks, and friendships.

Following Turner's lead, this article takes a broad view of the concept of play, not simply as an opposite to work, but rather as a comprehensive term for festivities, pastimes, relief from work, and trickery. Parties, singing, dancing, gaming, and joking made up the play of voyageurs when they were working as well as resting. Play offered them amusement and diversion, but it also became a means through which they could shape their world.

CARNIVAL ON CANOE JOURNEYS

Group celebrations were an especially revealing aspect of the play of voyageurs, and historians have developed lines of analysis to interpret the celebrations of lower orders of people, such as peasants and workers. In play Mikhail Bakhtin found a window to late medieval and early renaissance European folk culture. Bakhtin saw "carnival" as providing

[a] boundless world of humorous forms and manifestations opposed to the official and serious tone of medieval ecclesiastical and feudal culture. In spite of their variety, folk festivities of the carnival type, the comic rites and cults, the downs and fools, giants, dwarfs, and jugglers, the vast and manifold literature of parody—all these forms have one style in common: they belong to one culture of folk carnival humor. . . . All these forms of protocol and ritual based on laughter and consecrated by tradition existed in all the countries of medieval Europe; they were sharply distinct from the serious official, ecclesiastical, feudal, and political cult forms and ceremonials. They offered a completely different, nonofficial, extraecclesiastical and extrapolitical aspect of the world, of man, and of human relations; they built a second world and a second life outside officialdom, a world in which all medieval people participated more or less.[6]

In the fur trade the same applied to voyageurs, who constructed a world that differed dramatically from that of their masters. Voyageurs' distinctive identities and practices were not confined to specific celebrations, such as rendezvous, but permeated all their forms of play. [. . .]

As in other early modern folk settings, carnivals, and especially rendezvous, helped to shape the voyageurs' world. Literally translated as "meeting," rendezvous represented a time when fur traders came together to celebrate, encouraging camaraderie, competition, and social distinctions among everyone in the trade. Earlier we noted the omnipresent divisions between voyageurs and their

masters. During rendezvous, however, divisions among voyageurs themselves became more pronounced. Throughout the rest of the year, celebrations served the same functions: they unified men in camaraderie but also fostered social fissures.

In fur trade departures festivity pervaded the chaos of last-minute hirings, packing, and planning. This flurry of activity was most intense at the large annual leave-taking from the St Lawrence valley at the beginning of a season.[7] People gathered around the crews at Montreal and Lachine, the departure point just west of the rapids near Montreal, to send off the brigades.

Clerk George Nelson reminisced that the young men bade farewell to their relatives and friends "with tears in their eyes & singing as if going to a banquet!"[8] Large parties were held at Lachine the night before the brigades intended to set out, and most people became intoxicated. In his biography of the voyageur Jean-Baptiste Charbonneau, Georges Dugas described the parties that were held before crews set out: "During fifteen days, it was, for these old wolves of the North, a series of celebrations and amusements; they invited all their friends, and reveled; one had to say that they kept spending down to the last cent, and left their gusset [pocket] completely empty. The drink was flowing in torrents; in the evening they had a dance. . . . On the day of departure, a crowd of people went to Lachine to witness the spectacle."[9] [. . .]

The pageantry of departures and arrivals was heightened with "Indian war whoops" and firing muskets.[10] The yelling and musket fire were a form of salute to the brigades, a gesture of respect, and a wish of goodwill. "Indian war whoops" may have symbolized entry into a "savage world," unknown, exotic, and dangerous to voyageurs, and perhaps marked the beginning of the men's transition from French-Canadian habitants to voyageurs who lived among Aboriginal peoples. The war whoops probably reflected both a fear of Aboriginal peoples as well as admiration for them. Dugas described the desires of new voyageurs to imitate Aboriginal people: "The savage life appealed to them; it seemed to them that down there, that could be rid of all brakes, dressed like the Indian, sleeping with him the tent, and hunting like him for livelihood."[11] The most common of voyageur labour, canoeing, was a practice learned from Aboriginal peoples. The war whoops symbolized the extensive cultural borrowing of Canadians from Aboriginal peoples, but they also symbolized French colonists' view of Aboriginal peoples as an undifferentiated and exotic "other".[12] Philip Deloria has found similar cultural ambiguity in American appropriation of Aboriginal actions. He argues that "[t]he indeterminacy of American identities stems, in part, from the nation's inability to deal with Indian people. Americans wanted to feel a natural affinity with the continent, and it was Indians who could teach them such aboriginal closeness. Yet, in order to control the landscape they had to destroy the original inhabitants."[13] Voyageurs did not want to control the landscape to the same degree as American colonists, but they knew they were at the mercy of those who did. Thus voyageurs had to appease Aboriginal peoples, despite their fear. Imitating Aboriginal customs was a way in which voyageurs could familiarize themselves with these strange new people. Yet voyageurs' behaviour was similar to that of American colonists in other ways. Deloria asserts that in the context of carnivalesque holidays, such as in Tammany societies, when the "real" world was suspended in favour of a topsy-turvy world of unstable power, the figure of the Indian became central. The Indian became a means through which to articulate a revolutionary identity separate from Europe and attached to the North American continent.[14] Likewise, "Indianness" or "Aboriginality" was evoked in the formation of the voyageurs' distinct identity.

The pattern of celebrations at departures carried over into the interior. Alexander Henry the Younger described his men's party in the summer of 1800 after the first day on the route from Grand Portage to Lake Winnipeg: "All were merry over their favourite regale, which is always given on their departure, and generally enjoyed at this spot, where we have a delightful meadow to pitch our tents, and plenty of elbow-room for the men's antics."[15] This treat was especially appreciated after the arduous portage at that site.

Arrivals were marked with the same festivity and pageantry as departures. A sense of relief rather than excitement dominated the occasions, as men celebrated the completion of a safe and successful journey. Arriving back in Montreal was an especially momentous occasion, as it marked passage out of the fur trade world. When Ross Cox's crew a arrived at the Lake of Two Mountains, near Montreal, in September 1817, he presented his voyageurs with a keg of rum as a "valedictory allowance" and shook hands with each man.[16] At Fort William and Grand Portage men were treated with regales of bread, pork, butter, liquor, and tobacco, and usually held parties.[17] At smaller posts men were treated with drams when disembarked.[18] The fur trade arrivals were reminiscent of sailors reaching ports after long bouts at sea or lumbermen completing a river drive. Drunken merriment and unruly rioting were expressions of joy in finishing a round of gruelling labour. [. . .]

Incoming crews were usually met by the inhabitants of a post, including families that the men had left behind for the summer. Especially large crowds gathered at Grand Portage and Fort William.[19] Alexander Ross described the pageantry and pomp that could accompany the arrival of a crew: "On this joyful occasion, every person advances to the waterside, and great guns are fired to announce the bourgeois' arrival. A general shaking of hands takes place, as it often happens that people have not met for years: even the bourgeois goes through this mode of salutation with the meanest."[20] At smaller posts flags were raised and crews were saluted with musket shots.[21] Men were often sent out to meet expected canoes to help guide the crews into the posts.[22] Boisterous arrivals seemed to be a longstanding custom.[23] [. . .]

Parties at the start and the end of journeys were not unique to voyageurs or French Canada in the eighteenth century, but these celebrations became distinctive social markers of the voyageur's journey, underscoring the journey's importance to the trade, its danger, as well as its defining status for voyageurs. The pageantry and festivities helped to separate the voyageur social order from French Canada and marked the transition between the distinct social spaces and the emergence of a new voyageur world. The designated (though limited) space for revelry allowed voyageurs an opportunity to express their fear, anxiety, sadness, and excitement at travelling between these different worlds. By "letting go" or "going wild" at the parties, men were then better able to focus on the task of efficient travelling, so necessary to the effective functioning of the trade.

The rendezvous, on the other hand, was unique to the fur trade. It assumed great significance because it brought together most parts of the disparate trading operations and underscored the extreme division of times of plenty from times of want in the trade. Some rendezvous may have been modelled on Aboriginal trading fairs, such as those at Montreal in the second half of the seventeenth century.[24] In the continental interior many Aboriginal peoples met with one another in large groups on an annual basis.[25] Among the most significant of these gatherings on the plains were the annual summer trading fairs at the Mandan-Hidatsa villages, but smaller fairs also occurred among the Crees, the Ojibwes, the Assiniboines, the Shoshones, and the Blackfeet.[26] David Meyer and Paul Thistle contend that fur traders built their posts along the Saskatchewan River in the vicinity of annual religious gatherings of Cree people.[27] Ironically the fur trade rendezvous

could become a source of consternation for Aboriginal peoples. Victor Lytwyn has shown that Ojibwe hunters and trappers were intimidated by traders at Grand Portage, especially during the rendezvous, when revelry got out of hand.[28]

ANNUAL CYCLE OF CARNIVAL AT TRADING POSTS

Voyageurs had much more leisure time during the winter months spent at interior posts than they did during the canoe journeys of the summers. Yet here they also had more time to feel homesick and anxious in the midst of a foreign world. Much of their play was reminiscent of French Canada, such as celebrating annual holidays, drinking, and holding balls; these festivities helped voyageurs create a sense of home away from home. Voyageurs also had the time to create new connections, form new families, and solidify a distinctive society in the northwest. Their celebrations helped them create new memories and new traditions rooted in their new locations.

An annual schedule of holiday celebrations accompanied the yearly round of labour, which was especially important to the men living at isolated posts, away from their families and friends. Men often journeyed from outlying posts to congregate at larger central forts to celebrate the holidays and gladly risked the dangers and discomfort of winter travel, even a week of walking with snowshoes, to avoid spending a holiday alone.[29] Holidays helped mark the passage of time and provided structure during the long, dreary, and often lonely months at the interior posts. Coming together to celebrate at specific times helped to generate camaraderie and fellow feeling with one another, their masters, and Aboriginal peoples.

Christmas and New Year were the most popular holidays for the fur traders and were rarely forgotten or ignored. Other holidays that were sometimes celebrated included All Saints' Day on November 1, St Andrew's Day on November 30, and Easter in early April.[30] Similar celebrations occurred at HBC posts.[31] The occasional mention of celebrations occurred on Palm Sunday, the king's birthday (June 4, George III), and Epiphany, or "little Christmas" (January 6).[32] Men seemed willing to commemorate any day, regardless of its origins or significance to them, because it served as an excuse for a celebration and drams from the bourgeois. Commemorating St Andrew, the patron saint of Scotland, and observing the birthday of George III, king of Great Britain, were probably holidays introduced by the Scottish and English bourgeois and clerks, while Christmas, New Year's, All Saint's Day, and Easter would have been common celebrations in French Canada.[33] George Landmann noted that in late-eighteenth-century Montreal, New Year's Day was "a day of extraordinary festivity, which was extended to the two or three following days. Amongst the Canadians it was . . . the fashion for everybody to visit everybody during one of the three first, days of the year, when a glass of noyeau or other liquor was, with a piece of biscuit or cake, presented to the visitor, which, after a hard day's work in calling at some twenty or thirty houses, frequently terminated in sending a number of very respectable people home in a staggering condition toward the close of the day."[34] Feasting, drinking, and levees, or paying courtesy calls on masters (particularly on New Year's Day) were characteristic of celebrations in fur trade society.

The holiday celebrations seemed to follow a formula. Specific rituals and ceremonies, giving the day a sense of orderly formality and tradition, were followed by chaotic parties, where wild abandon and heavy drinking predominated. Alexander Henry the Younger complained on New Year's Day in 1803 that he was plagued with ceremonies and men and women drinking and fighting "pell mell".[35]

During most holiday celebrations at fur trade posts, men generally did not have to work.[36] During the Christmas and New Year's holidays, voyageurs and bourgeois frequently arranged to visit other posts or invited visitors to their post for the day or for the entire holiday season.[37] Many men tried to organize their work schedules so they would not miss any of the festivities. [. . .]

The day's festivities on Christmas and New Year's usually began early in the morning. Voyageurs ceremoniously called on their bourgeois or clerk to formally wish him well and pay their respects.[38] The early morning firing of muskets or cannons usually woke the masters.[39] In 1793 Alexander Mackenzie wrote: "On the first day of January, my people, in conformity to the usual custom, awoke me at the break of day with the discharge of firearms, with which they congratulated the appearance of the new year. In return, they were treated with plenty of spirits, and when there is any flour, cakes are always added to the regales, which was the case, on the present occasion."[40] Like the firing of muskets when a brigade arrived at a post, this salute was a symbolic welcome and a formal honouring of the holiday.

After the firing of muskets, all the residents of the fort gathered together in a general meeting where the bourgeois or clerk would provide regales to the voyageurs. Depending on the wealth of the post, regales as little as a single dram or as much as great quantities of alcohol, especially if there was a shortage of food.[41] At the beginning of 1802, Daniel Harmon gave his men a dram in the morning and then enough rum to drink throughout the course of the day, to help distract them from the scarcity of meat.[42] In an effort to secure more alcohol for the day's festivities, men would go to great lengths to salute their bourgeois or any passing visitor or dignitary, in hopes of gaining a treat.[43] Regales on New Year's seemed to be slightly more generous than those at Christmas, as men were frequently given tobacco in addition to drams.[44] At wealthier posts the men's regales included food, usually specialty items that were hard to procure, such as flour and sugar, though the regale could include meat and grease.[45]

Regardless of wealth most posts mustered some kind of feast on Christmas and New Year's as part of the day's ceremonies. Voyageurs took great pleasure in their food and in feasting, especially since survival could be so precarious in the pays d'en haut, and their victuals were often mundane and limited. In 1812 Gabriel Franchère commented: "The 25th of December, Christmas Day, was spent most pleasantly. We treated our men to the best that the post could offer, which delighted them as they had lived for nearly two months on fish dried by fire, which is very poor food."[46] Bourgeois were not always so generous. Alexander Henry the Younger wrote on 1 January 1814, that the bourgeois could scarcely collect liquor enough out of the kegs to give the men one dram each, so they provided them with rice, salt beef, and swans as well. The bourgeois, however, provided themselves with a great feast of rice soup, boiled swans, roast wild fowl, roast pork, potatoes, rice pudding, wild fruit pie, cranberry tarts, cheese and biscuits with porter, spirits, and two bottles of Madeira.[47] However, it seemed to be more usual for the bourgeois and the voyageurs to celebrate the day together.[48] This temporary lowering of class barriers probably stemmed from the loneliness of the bourgeois and the clerks who were isolated from other masters. [. . .] By providing voyageurs with a decent feast, masters could ensure goodwill from their men. Working together to create a celebratory feast fostered a feeling of fellowship among the men.

After the formal ceremonies of honouring the day, exchanging gifts, and feasting, the real party began: Men celebrated by drinking liberally.[49] Serious drinking could last for several days after the holiday.[50] Both Edith Burley and Anne Morton found that at HBC posts, Christmas and New Year's could be celebrated with almost a week of "incessant carousing".[51] Drinking heavily usually led to fighting among the men.[52] Duncan McGillivray commented that "the Holidays [had been] spent as usual in dissipation & enjoyment, intermixed with quarreling and fighting—the certain consequences of intoxication among the men."[53] Dancing, fiddle playing, and singing were also significant ingredients of the parties.[54] During this part of the day's festivities, disorder and subversion dominated. In the word of Mikhail Bakhtin, "[w]hile carnival lasts, there is no other life outside it. During carnival time life is subject only to its laws, that is, the laws of its own freedom."[55] Yet the chaotic mayhem was constrained and limited by its designated site and meaning. It was a socially sanctioned time where voyageurs as well as their masters were allowed to carouse to the extreme.

This style of celebrating holidays— starting with formal ceremonies then moving on to wild abandon—lasted well into the mid-nineteenth century at the interior fur trade posts. [. . .]

Many groups of all-male sojourners seemed to enjoy music and dances in their leisured moments. Nearly all shanty camps in northern Ontario had a fiddler, and singing and dancing were popular Saturday-night pastimes.[56] [. . .]

Holding a formal ball was an importation from French Canada, but the dancing and music were culturally distinctive. The "old fiddle and Indian drum" symbolized the mixing of European and Aboriginal forms.[57] Dancing was not restricted to holidays but continued throughout the seasons at fur trade posts. Having dances or "balls" was a fairly common occurrence both at the Great Lakes posts and in the interior.[58] Either fiddlers or singers provided the music. Fast and spirited dancing predominated. The descriptions of the "lively reels" of country dances reflected a rough and tumble joie de vivre that was characteristic of many voyageurs' activities. Balls at Grand Portage during the rendezvous, however, were genteel affairs for the benefit of the bourgeois, with music from the bagpipe, violin, and fife.[59] Yet even at these balls, "country music" combined musical from Canada, Scotland, England, and Aboriginal peoples. Dances were often held to celebrate specific events, such as the coalition of the XYC and the NWC in 1804, but the most common occasions were weddings and to honour visitors to the post.[60] Men from different companies frequently attended each others' dances.[61] Sometimes dances were held for no particular reasons other than to have fun and enliven the monotony of post life, especially during the long winters.[62]

ALCOHOL

In eighteenth-century European and colonial settings, most people drank a significant amount of alcohol.[63] Historian Craig Heron explains that "alcohol was regularly consumed in the home as a beverage and a tonic, and to a degree now unimaginable it also saturated almost all arenas of work and leisure. European settlers, especially men, drank often, though only occasionally to get drunk."[64] The voyageurs' use of alcohol or attitudes toward it probably did not differ from those of habitants or other groups of labouring men. A key difference, however, was that alcohol was restricted and controlled by the bourgeois, and voyageurs did not have habitual access to it as they would have had in French Canada. The bourgeois and the clerks controlled the rations of alcohol to save money and to exert control over their men. Although the bourgeois and the clerks probably drank as much as their men, they often disparaged voyageurs as useless drunks. They frequently reprimanded their men for drunkenness.[65] Bourgeois and clerks sometimes refused to sell alcohol to their men in an effort to curb their drinking practices, especially when the bourgeois wanted voyageurs to pay their debts.[66] Seeing themselves as distinct from their men in regard to drinking helped the bourgeois to distance themselves socially from their voyageurs, which helped them maintain authority. These attitudes are ironic when compared to the behaviour of the bourgeois at the Montreal Beaver Club and annual rendezvous, where the dinners were notorious for excessive drinking and revelry.[67] After the merger of the HBC and the NWC in 1821, the new governor, George Simpson, imposed stringent temperance regulations on posts but met with little success.[68]

Drinking also occupied a central place in seafaring culture. Unlike the Northwest, where cargoes had to be physically hauled over unending portages, deadly excesses of drinking were common. Drink offered respite from an often punishing life on ship. Marcus Rediker speculates that "[t]oo much plain dealing, with the elements and with the conditions of life at sea, led to a lot of plain old drinking."[69] Unfortunately for the voyageurs, they could not carry enough liquor to offer respite from their journeys. Yet, as for sailors, drinking served critical social functions for voyageurs, allowing the men to bond with one another and form enduring friendships.

The masters' control over supplies and the frequent shortage of alcohol on canoe voyages and in the interior probably encouraged voyageurs to develop a "feast-famine" attitude toward drinking. If they knew that the supply of alcohol was precarious, they would drink with abandon while it was available. Although these occasions were described in considerable detail in the journals of the bourgeois and the clerks, limited supplies of alcohol made them exceptional rather than routine.

In some extreme cases voyageurs were drunk when they worked.[70] Periodically a master mentioned that the drunkenness of the voyageurs had impeded their work. One bourgeois could not send off his goods as early as he wished because his men "were amusing themselves and not fit to travel."[71] Voyageurs sometimes began to drink their regales while paddling, and journeys had to be interrupted because the voyageurs were not fit to continue.[72] A few posts were known for general drunkenness, but more commonly heavy and raucous drinking had a designated time and form at all posts, such as during holiday celebrations.[73] On canoe journeys and at interior posts men usually confined their heavy drinking to the occasional evening.[74] The bourgeois and the clerks sometimes used alcohol as a means of maintaining good faith among their men on a particularly difficult journey. In the summer of 1793 while on an arduous mission to find an overland passage to the Pacific Ocean, Alexander Mackenzie described the end of one hard day of work: "At the close of the day we assembled round a blazing fire; and the whole party, being enlivened with the usual beverage which I supplied on these occasions, forgot their fatigues and apprehensions."[75]

Heavy drinking was reserved for special occasions, such as when supplies arrived and during parties and "balls," and especially the rendezvous, where voyageurs received generous *regales*.[76] Some instances of "wild excess" are to be found further in the interior. One small creek near the Red River earned the name "Drunken River" when a carousing group of voyageurs had a particularly memorable party.[77] At least one voyageur was nicknamed "the Drunkard," and this mark of notoriety made it into official correspondence.[78]

Often excessive drinking led to violence. A voyager named Voyer, between 40 and 50 years of age and described as "a great drunkard," went to Grand Portage to visit friends. When he became drunk, some of the clerks and bourgeois smeared his face with "caustie'" (encaustic?) and drew lewd figures on it. Voyer became enraged when he sobered and swore revenge on those who had marked him. The following summer, when the same bourgeois denied him alcohol and chided him for his drunkenness, he killed several of their horses and threatened them with a knife.[79] These exceptional cases of "drunkards" can be found in most early modern societies; they represent the edges of social acceptability rather than the norm.

Despite the outbreaks of violence, drunkenness was contained rather than excessive. Drinking did not seriously threaten the social order of the fur trade; rather it provided an outlet for debauchery and disorder. Michael found the same pattern at York Factory—although excessive drinking caused some social tensions, alcoholism was not widespread and fatalities resulting from drinking were limited.[80] The "boundaries of containment" were set by the availability of alcohol and the commonly accepted social sites for heavy drinking. Voyageurs became apprehensive when violence became excessive, when the functioning of the fur trade was disrupted for a great length of time, and when food was in short supply. In one extreme case a bourgeois named Duncan Campbell, charged with drunkenness by the NWC in 1809, had allowed his trading post to become a corrupt, filthy, and starving "heart of darkness". He lost all his trade goods, ran out of food, drank himself into oblivion, and neglected his paternal duties to his servants. He was court-martialled, and his voyageurs testified that they were disgusted by his behaviour.[81]

GAMES AND CONTESTS

The voyageurs' ethic of nonaccumulation derived in part from the fact that they could not carry many material goods while working in the fur trade. But for many money became less important the longer they worked in the trade and were away from their families in French Canada. Wealth became measured in different ways. Pierre Bourdieu's economic metaphor of "capital" provides a way to understand voyageurs' notions of wealth and how this connected to their play.[82] Bourdieu expands the notion of capital beyond its economic conception to the realm of the cultural, social, and symbolic. Different types of capital can be acquired, exchanged, and converted into other forms. Cultural capital refers to the value that can be found in family background, social class, education, and other factors that may lead to success. For voyageurs cultural capital would have included knowledge of skills such as making canoes and snowshoes. Cultural capital can be inherited, purchased, or earned. Bourdieu defines social capital as connections among people. Voyageurs could enhance their social capital through their relationships with Aboriginal people, with the bourgeois and clerks, and with each other. Symbolic capital represents prestige and honour, which voyageurs could earn by demonstrating their manliness. The masculine values of strength, courage, and risk taking became expressions of symbolic or masculine capital. Play, especially games and contests that demonstrated these qualities, became a means of accumulating masculine capital.

Because voyageurs had few possessions and could not carry many personal belongings with them into the interior, games could not involve elaborate equipment.[83] Playing cards and gambling were common pastimes.[84] Michael Payne also found small board games such cribbage and dominoes at York Factory.[85] Voyageurs played games from French Canada, such as those with a ball.[86] Other games or amusements, such as "pagessan" or "le jeu au plat" and body tattooing, were learned from Aboriginal peoples.[87] John Richardson, a surgeon in the Royal Navy and a travelling companion of John Franklin, described games played by Crees at Cumberland House. The game *puckesann* involved betting on the number of stones tossed out of a small wooden dish. In the "game of the mitten," one marked and three unmarked balls were placed under four mittens, and contenders had to guess under which mitten the marked ball lay. These games, along with lacrosse, required little equipment, which could be easily made from materials in the surrounding environment.[88]

Voyageurs gained symbolic currency both by enhancing their reputations for toughness and skill and by their own belief in their strength and ability. In reminiscing about his life, the elderly voyageur on Lake Winnipeg bragged to Alexander Ross: "I beat all Indians at the race, and no white man ever passed me in the chase."[89] The value of beating Aboriginal peoples implies that Aboriginal men were faster and stronger and thus more manly than European Canadians. The desire to excel at skills necessary for survival in the northwest, skills that were usually learned from Aboriginal peoples, was a clear example of shifting cultural values among voyageurs. Being more "Indian" than the "Indians" was a measure of manliness and success in adapting to new social and physical spaces.

Currency could also be earned in physical contests among voyageurs. In canoe races, a popular form of competition, crews would race against one another within a brigade or race against other brigades.[90] These contests built a sense of fellowship, trust, and co-operation among the crews. Masters encouraged their men to race, and they often set out to break one another's records for the fastest time between major posts. Recall George Landmann's record for the journey from St Joseph's Island, near Detroit, to Montreal, which his crew completed in seven and one-quarter days.[91] After the 1821 merger, Montreal canoes and York boats frequently raced at York Factory.[92]

Brawling was a common social activity and had a variety of meanings among the voyageurs. Fighting frequently accompanied parties and heavy drinking and in these contexts hostilities and maliciousness sometimes led to mayhem or riots.[93] However, brawling was often an organized event or competition in which men sought to demonstrate their prowess, boost their reputations, and amuse their mates.[94] They often "fought for a set," and a "drawn battle" could be decided with "fair boxing at head quarting."[95] Brawling could demonstrate strength and toughness, and it underscored the dimension of physicality in voyageur culture, which was encouraged by the nature of the job. One Métis voyageur, Paulet Paul, achieved fame as a fighter after the 1821 merger.[96]

Fur trade journals are filled with stories about the difficulty of fur trade work and the almost mythical strength, endurance, and joviality of the voyageurs. The literate in the fur trade frequently referred to voyageurs as "beasts of burden," which both reduced them to animals and elevated them to "hypermasculine" superheroes. Clerk George Nelson wrote: "[Voyageurs] seem to do more than ever was meant for human nature; . . . [they] rise at dusk in the morning and until near sunset, are either pulling on their paddles, or running with 180, or 200 lbs wt. on their backs, as if it were for life or death; never stop to take their meals peacably, but with a piece of pemmican in their hands eat under their load."[97] He went on to marvel that voyageurs seemed tougher, stronger, and swifter than dogs or horses. Voyageurs tried to outperform one another to demonstrate their masculine capital. Contests were not limited to physical prowess but extended to almost any area. Competing to see who could eat or drink the most functioned like gaming; voyageurs could gamble small amounts of their symbolic capital for entertainment's sake. In the spring of 1808 while journeying between interior posts, two of George Nelson's voyageurs, Leblanc and Larocque, decided to see who could eat the most during one of their meals. Both unfortunate men began to feel ill and shake, when lynx excrement was discovered at the bottom of the pot, which elicited "many coarse & filthy jokes."[98]

[. . .]

Although play became an area for the expression of new social practices that made voyageurs distinct from habitants and other early modern peasants, it did not threaten the paternalistic order of the fur trade or the masters' subordination of the voyageurs. Most of the play of voyageurs was highly structured and occurred within designated and contained contexts. It provided a safe space for voyageurs to express their anxiety and fear at the exotic pays d'en haut, their anger at unfair masters and unreliable colleagues, and their excitement at setting off on new adventures. Forms of play generally sanctioned by the bourgeois allowed voyageurs to frolic without threatening the pace or effectiveness of their work and encouraged values that were consistent with effective working skills, such as strength, bravery, risk taking, and perseverance.

Play and sociability were central to voyageurs' working lives. All forms of play, including carnivals, games, contests, tricks, and friendship, helped to create and support a distinctive voyageur world by both encouraging social bonding and facilitating the growth of social fissures and divisions. Three dominant themes emerged in the play of voyageurs. Contests provided men with "symbolic capital" in their efforts to bolster their reputations as strong men. The liminal space particularly encouraged jokes and trickery. Finally, voyageurs tried to form a unified and somewhat collective culture in the face of centrifugal forces caused by their transience and mobility of the job. These ideals and themes distinguished voyageurs from habitants in French Canada, fur trade bourgeois and clerks, and Aboriginal societies.

NOTES

1. Ross Cox, *Adventures on the Columbia River, including the Narrative of Residence of Six Years on the Western Side of the Rocky Mountains, among Various Tribes of Indians Hitherto Unknown: Together with a Journey across the American Continent.* 2 vols. London: Henry Colburn & Richard Bentley, 1831; 2:287.

2. Peter Pond, "The Narrative of Peter Pond," 47, in Charles M. Gates, *Five Fur Traders of the Northwest*. St Paul: Minnesota Historical Society, 1965, 9–59.

3. For the central position of Grand Portage and Fort William in the Montreal fur trade, see Carolyn Gilman, *The Grand Portage Story*. St Paul: Minnesota Historical Society, 1992; and Jean Morrison, *Superior Rendezvous-Place: Fort William in the Canadian Fur Trade*. Toronto: Belfords, Clarke, 1880.

4. Toronto Metropolitan Reference Library Baldwin Room (TBR), S13, George Nelson's journal "No. 1," 15–16. See also George Nelson, *My First Years in the Fur Trade: The Journals of 1802–1804*. Edited by Laura Peers and Theresa Schenck. St Paul: Minnesota Historical Society Press, 2002, 42.

5. Victor Turner, "Variations of a Theme of Liminality," 57, in Victor Turner, *Blazing the Trail: Way Marks in the Exploration of Symbols*. Tucson: University of Arizona Press, 1992, 48–65.

6. Mikhail Bakhtin, *Rabelais and His World*. Translated by Hélène Iswolsky. Bloomington: Indiana University Press, 1984, 4, 5–6.

7. Nelson, *My First Years*, 32–3.

8. Nelson, *My First Years*, 32–3; see also Library and Archives of Canada (LAC), MG19 A17, June 15, 1791, 15.

9. Georges Dugas, *Un Voyageur des pays d'En Haut*. (1890) St Boniface, MB: Éditions des Plaines, 1981, 25, 30 (my translation). Original French: "Pendant quinze jours, c'était, pour ces vieux loups du Nord, une suite de fête et de divertissements; ils invitaient tous leurs amis, et faisaient bombance; on aurait dit gu'ils tenaient à dépenser jusqu'à leur dernier sou, et à partir le gousset complètement vide. La boisson coulait à flots; le soir il y avait bal. . . . Le jour du depart, une foule de personnes se rendaient à Lachine pour être témoins du spectacle."

10. For one example of muskets being fired at departure, see Captain John Franklin, *Narrative of a Journey to the Shores of the Polar Sea in the Years 1819, 20, 21 and 22*. London: J.M. Dent, 1819, February 8, 1820, 109. Muskets were fired on both arrival and departure on February 16, 1820, 112–13.

11. Dugas, *Un Voyageur*, 27 (my translation). Original French: "La vie sauvage leur souriait; il leur semblait que là-bas, débarrassés de tout frein, vêtus comme l'Indien, couchant avec lui sous la tente, et chassant comme lui pour vivre."

12. For the influence of Aboriginal cultures on French Canada, see Denys Delâge, "L'influence des Amérindiens sur les Canadiens et les Français au temps de la Nouvelle France." *Lekton* 2, 2 (Autumn 1992): 103–91.

13. Philip J. Deloria, *Playing Indian*. New Haven: Yale University Press, 1998, 5.

14. Deloria, *Playing Indian*, 11–20.

15. Alexander Henry (the Younger), *New Light on the Early History of the Greater Northwest: The Manuscript Journals of Alexander Henry*. Edited by Elliott Coues. 2 vols. Minneapolis: Ross & Haines; New York: F. Harper, 1897, July 20, 1800, 1:8. Similarly, at York Factory, the main administration post of the HBC, the departure of ships for England was always marked by a celebration. Michael Payne, *The Most Respectable Place in the Territory: Everyday Life in Hudson's Bay Company Service, York Factory, 1788 to 1870*. Ottawa: Ministry of the Environment, Canadian Parks Service, 1989, 87.

16. Cox, *Adventures on the Columbia River*, September 19, 1817, 304–5.

17. Alexander Mackenzie, "A General History of the Fur Trade from Canada to the North-West," 52, in Mackenzie, *Voyages from Montreal on the River St. Laurence through the Continent of North America to the Frozen and Pacific Oceans in the Years 1789 and 1793 with a Preliminary Account of the Rise, Progress, and Present State of the Fur Trade of That Country*. London: R. Noble, Old Bailey, 1801; and Nelson, *My First Years*, 40–2.

18. Ontario Archives (OA), MU 2199, Edward Umfreville, July 24, 1784, 26; and Rare Books and Special Collections Division of the McGill University Libraries (MRB), MC, c.28, October 2 and 3, 1807, 8. See also Lloyd Keith, ed., *North of Athabasca: Slave Lake and Mackenzie River Documents of the North West Company, 1800–1821*. Montreal: McGill-Queen's University Press, 2001, 311–12.

19. TBR, S13, George Nelson's diary of events on a journey from Cumberland House to Fort William, June 19, 1822; and John McDonnell, "The Diary of John McDonnell," in Gates, *Five Fur Traders of the Northwest*, 92.

20. Alexander Ross, *Fur Hunters of the Far West: A Narrative of Adventures in the Oregon and Rocky Mountains*. 2 vols. London: Smith, Elder, 1855, 1: 303–4.

21. OA, MU 842, September 27, 1818, 3.

22. Nelson, *My First Years*, August 22, 1803, 103; and LAC, MG19 A9, Simon Fraser Collection, vol. 3, Fraser to Mr. McDougall, Sturgeon Lake, August 6, 1806, 15.

23. John Henry Lefroy, *In Search of the Magnetic North: A Soldier-Surveyor's Letters from the North-West, 1843–1844*. Edited by George F.G. Stanley. Toronto: Macmillan, 1955, Lefroy to his mother, Toronto, November 20, 1844, 136; and Robert M. Ballantyne, *Hudson Bay; or, Every-Day Life in the Wilds of North America during Six Years' Residence in the Territories of the Honourable Hudson's Bay Company*. London: William Blackwood & Sons, 1848. Reprint, Edmonton: Hurtig, 1972, 212.

24. Nicholas Perrot, *The Indian Tribes of the Upper Mississippi Valley and the Region of the Great Lakes*. Edited and translated by Emma Helen Blair. 2 vols. Cleveland: Arthur H. Clark, 1911, 1:174–5, 210–20; Louise Dechêne, *Habitants and Merchants in Seventeenth-Century Montreal*. Montreal: McGill-Queen's University Press, 1992 (first published as *Habitants et marchands de Montréal au XVIIe siècle* (Paris: Éditions Plon, 1974); and Allan Greer, *The People of New France*. Toronto: University of Toronto Press, 1997, chapter on "French and Others".

25. See Helen Hornbeck Tanner, ed., *The Settling of North America: The Atlas of the Great Migrations into North America from the Ice Age to the Present*. New York: Macmillan, 1995, 28–29.

26. John S. Milloy, *The Plains Cree: Trade, Diplomacy and War, 1790 to 1870*. Winnipeg: University of Manitoba Press, 1988, II, 17, 51–2, 54; and Laura Peers, *The Ojibwa of Western Canada, 1780 to 1879*. Winnipeg: University of Manitoba Press, 1994, 30.

27. David Meyer and Paul C. Thistle, "Saskatchewan River Rendezvous Centers and Trading Posts: Continuity in a Cree Social Geography." *Ethnohistory* 42, 3 (Summer 1995): 403–4.

28. Victor P. Lytwyn, "The Anishinabeg and the Fur Trade," 32, in *Lake Superior to Rainy Lake: Three Centuries of Fur Trade History*, edited by Jean Morrison. Thunder Bay: Thunder Bay Historical Museum Society, 2003, 27–45.

29. Lefroy, *In Search of the Magnetic North*, Lefroy to Isabella, Lake Athabasca, Christmas Day, 1843, 84.

30. For examples of All Saint's Day, see LAC, MG19 C1, vol. 12, November 1, 1804, 25; MRB, MC, c.28, November 1, 1807; and Keith, *North of Athabasca*, 316. For examples of St Andrew's Day, see OA, reel MS65, Donald McKay, Journal from January to December 1799, November 30, 1799, 43 (my pagination); and MRB, MC, c.24, Sunday, November 30, 1800, 6. For examples of celebrating Easter, see LAC, MG19 C1, vol. 1, April 8, 1798, 53; LAC, MG19 C1, vol. 14, April 12, 1800, 23; and, OA, MU 842, April 11, 1819, 43.

31. Anne Morton, "Chief Trader Joseph McGillivray." Paper presented at the Rupert's Land Colloquium 1998, Winnipeg and Norway House, June 1998; and Payne, *Most Respectable Place*, 65, 87–92.

32. For an example of celebrating Palm Sunday, see OA, MU 842, April 4, 1819, 42. For examples of celebrating the King's birthday, see TBR, S13, George Nelson's journal, April 1, 1810–May 1, 1811, June 4, 1810, 11 (my pagination); and George Landmann, *Adventures and Recollections of Colonel Landmann, Late of the Corps of Royal Engineers*. 2 vols. London: Colburn, 1852, 2:167–8. For an example of celebrating Epiphany, see Henry (the Younger), *New Light*, January 6, 1801, 1:165.

33. For comments on New Year's celebrations as a French Canadian custom, see Daniel W. Harmon, *Sixteen Years in Indian Country: The Journal of Daniel Williams Harmon, 1800–1816*. Edited by W. Kaye Lamb. Toronto: Macmillan, 1957, January 2, 1801, 41; see also Hector Grenon, *Us et coutumes du Québec*. Montreal: La Presse, 1974, 153–68; Sophie-Laurence Lamontagne, *L'hiver dans la culture québécoise (xviie–xixe siècles)*. Quebec: Institut québécois de recherche sur la culture, 1983, 101–3; and Jean Provencher, *Les Quatre Saisons dans la vallée du Saint-Laurent*. Montreal: Boréal, 1988, 499–57, 463–70.

34. Landmann, *Adventures and Recollection*, 1:239–40.

35. Henry (the Younger), *New Light*, January 1, 1803, 1:207.

36. OA, reel MS65, Donald McKay, Journal from January 1805 to June 1806, December 25, 1805, 47 (my pagination); TBR, S13, George Nelson's journal, November 3, 1807–August 31, 1808, December 25, 1807, 14; November 1, 1807, 7; and Henry (the Younger), *New Light*, November 1, 1810, 2:660.

37. OA, reel MS65, Donald McKay, journal from January to December 1799, December 24, 1799, 46 (my pagination); TBR, S13, George Nelson's journal, November 3, 1807–August 31, 1808, December 25, 1807, 14; George Nelson's journal, April 1, 1810–May 1, 1811, December 23, 1810, 39 (my pagination).

38. LAC, MG19 C1, vol. 14, January 1, 1800, 9; Hugh Faries, "The Diary of Hugh Faries," in Gates, *Five Fur Traders of the Northwest*, January 1, 1805, 244; LAC, MG19 C1, vol. 8, January 1, 1805, 37; and Keith, *North of Athabasca*, 197.

39. MRB, MC, C.13, January 1, 1800, 11 (my pagination); Henry (the Younger), *New Light*, January 1, 1801 and 1802, 1:162, 192; TBR, S13, George Nelson's journal, November 30, 1815–January 13, 1816, Monday, December 25, 1815, 91; George Nelson's journal and reminiscences, 84; and Gabriel Franchère, *Journal of a Voyage on the North West Coast of North America during the Years 1811, 1812, 1813 and 1814*. Toronto: Champlain Society, 1969, 107–8.

40. Mackenzie, *Voyages from Montreal*, January 1, 1793, 252. On other comments of the long-standing custom, see MRB, MC, C.28, January 1, 1808, 20; Keith, *North of Athabasca*, 326; and Franklin, *Narrative of a Journey*, January 1, 1802, 53.

41. For drams, see LAC, MG19 C1, vol. 1, November 1 and December 25, 1797, 17, 27; MRB, MC, C.24, December 25, 1800, 13; LAC, MG19 C1, vol. 6, December 25, 1800, 72; vol. 8, December 25, 1804, 34; and MRB, MC, C.28, December 25, 1807, 20; see also Keith, *North of Athabasca*, 122, 196, 325. For large quantities of alcohol, see LAC, MG19 C1, vol. 7, December 25, 1798, 23; MRB, MC, C.13, December 25, 1799, 10 (my pagination); Harmon, *Sixteen Years*, December 25, 1801, 52; and LAC, MG19 C1, vol. 12, November 1 and December 25, 1804, 25, 34.

42. Harmon, *Sixteen Years*, January 1, 1802, 53.

43. TBR, S13, George Nelson's journal, November 30, 1815–January 13, 1816, December 25, 1815, 91.

44. MRB, MC, C.7, January 1, 1794 and 1795, 6, 23; OA, MG19, C1, vol. 1, January 1, 1798, 29; LAC, MG19, C1, vol. 7, January 1, 1799, 24; and vol. 12, January 1, 1805, 35.

45. Mackenzie, *Voyages from Montreal*, January 1, 1793, 252; Henry (the Younger), *New Light*, December 25, 1800, 1:161; LAC, MG19 C1, vol. 9, January 1, 1806, 21; Cox, *Adventures on the Columbia River*, 305–6; and MRB, MC, c.8, January 1, 1806, 10.

46. Franchère, *Journal of a Voyage*, 107. See also LAC, MG19 A14, January 1, 1806, 6.

47. Henry (the Younger), *New Light*, 2:781.

48. OA, reel MS65, Donald McKay, journal from August 1800 to April 1801, December 25, 1800, 17; and TBR, S13, George Nelson's journal, September 1, 1801–March 31, 1810, January 1, 1809, 14 (my pagination).

49. OA, MG19, C1, vol. 1, January 1, 1798, 29; Harmon, *Sixteen Years*, January 2, 1801, 40; and Montreal, McCord Museum, M-22074, James Keith, Fort Chipewyan to McVicar, January 31, 1825, 2.

50. Faries, "Diary," December 25–27, 1804, 223.

51. Morton, "Chief Trader Joseph McGillivray"; and Edith I. Burley, *Servants of the Honourable Company: Work, Discipline, and Conflict in the Hudson's Bay Company, 1770–1879*. Toronto: Oxford University Press, 1997, 133.

52. Henry (the Younger), *New Light*, January 1, 1802 and 1803, 1:192, 207; Harmon, *Sixteen Years*, January 1, 1811, 136; and Faries, "Diary," January 1, 1805, 224.

53. Duncan McGillivray, *The Journal of Duncan McGillivray of the North West Company at Fort George on the Saskatchewan, 1794–5*. Edited by Arthur S. Morton. Toronto: MAcmillan, 1929, Fort George, January 26, 1795, 51.

54. Harmon, *Sixteen Years*, January 2, 1801, December 25, 1805, 40, 99; TBR, S13, George Nelson's journal, April 1, 1810–May 1, 1811, December 1810 to January 1811, 39 (my pagination); and George Nelson's journal, September 1, 1808–March 31, 1810, January 1, 1809, 14 (my pagination).

55. Bahktin, *Rabelais and His World*, 7.

56. Ian Radforth, "The Shantymen," in *Labouring Lives: Work and Worker in Nineteenth-Century Ontario*, edited by Paul Craven, 204–76. Toronto: University of Toronto Press, 1995, 231–2.

57. See also Sylvia Van Kirk, *"Many Tender Ties": Women in Fur-Trading Society, 1670–1870*. Winnipeg: Watson & Dwyer, 1980, 126–9.

58. For examples of balls at Great Lakes posts, see Pond, "Narrative," Mackinaw, 47; and OA, MU 1146, Frederick Goedike, Batchiwenon, to Geroge Gordon, Michipicoten, February 11, 1812, 1–3. For examples of balls at interior posts, see TBR, S13, George Nelson's journal, November 3, 1807–August 31, 1808, Fort Alexandria, June 18, 1808, 42; and Alexander Ross, *Adventures of the First Settlers on the Oregon or Columbia River: Being a Narrative of the Expedition Fitted Out by John Jacob Astor, to Establish the "Pacific Fur Company" with an Account of Some Indian Tribes on the Coast of the Pacific*. Ann Arbor: University Microfilms, 1966 (first published in 1849 by Smith, Elder, London), Spokane House, summer 1812, 212.

59. Harmon, *Sixteen Years*, Grand Portage, July 4, 1800, 22.

60. TBR, S13, George Nelson's coded journal, June 28, 1821, 29; Henry (the Younger), *New Light*, September 6, 1810, 2:626; and Faries, "Diary," December 16, 1804, February 24, March 31, April 28, May 12 and 17, 1805, 222, 230, 234–5, 238, 240–1.

61. For an example of NWC and HBC men dancing together at Fort George, see McGillivray, *Journal*, March 22, 1795, 66. For an example of NWC, XYC, and HBC men dancing together, see Faries, "Diary," January 11, 1805, 244–25. For an example of NWC, XYC, and HBC men dancing together at Rivière Souris, Fort Assiniboine, see Harmon, *Sixteen Years*, May 27, 1805, 89–90.

62. Henry (the Younger), *New Light*, January 27, 1810, 2:584.

63. Thomas Brennan, *Public Drinking and Popular Culture in Eighteenth-Century Paris*. Princeton: Princeton University Press, 1988. For a discussion of how drinking can be understood as part of the social order, see Mary Douglas, ed., *Constructive Drinking: Perspectives on Drink from Anthropology*. Cambridge: Cambridge University Press, 1987.

64. Craig Heron, *Booze: A Distilled History*. Toronto: Between the Lines, 2003, 17.

65. For one of many examples of bourgeois drunkenness and brawling, see TBR, S13, George Nelson's journal and reminiscences, 57.

66. MRB, MC, C.24, January 2, 1801, 15; and OA, MU 842, March 3, 1819, 34–35.

67. See Carolyn Podruchny, "Festivities, Fortitude and Fraternalism: Fur Trade Masculinity and the Beaver Club, 1785–1827," in *New Faces in the Fur Trade: Selected Papers of the Seventh North American Fur Trade Conference*. Edited by William C. Wicken, Jo-Anne Fiske, Susan Sleeper-Smith, 31–52. East Lansing: Michigan State University Press, 1998.

68. Burley, *Servants of the Honourable Company*, 134–5; and Jan Noel, *Canada Dry: Temperance Crusades before Confederation*. Toronto: University of Toronto Press, 1995, 189–93.

69. Marcus Rediker, *Between the Devil and the Deep Blue Sea: Merchant Seamen, Pirates, and the Anglo-American Maritime World, 1700–1750*. Cambridge: Cambridge University Press, 1987, 192.

70. For two examples see Cox, *Adventures on the Columbia River*, June 29, 1812, and July 30, 1817, 74, 280. However, Alexander Mackenzie characterized it as a regular occurrence, in his "General History," 17–18.

71. LAC, MG19 B1, A. McKenzie to John Layer [Sayer?], Grand Portage, August 9, 1799, 87. For another example of drunk voyageurs preventing a departure, see LAC, MG C1, vol. 12, September 20, 1804.

72. Nelson, *My First Years*, 100–1, August 5, 1803.

73. Regarding posts known for heavy drinking, see MRB, MC, C.7, October 27, 1793, 2.

74. MRB, MC, C.7, December 14, 1794, 22; LAC, MG19, C1, vol. 14, November 11–12, 1799, 3a; MRB, MC, C.26, October 10, 1800, 9; and Keith, *North of Athabasca*, 133.

75. Mackenzie, *Voyages from Montreal*, June 15, 1793, 329.

76. For an example of drinking when supplies arrived, see Henry (the Younger), *New Light*, March 7, 1814, 2:851. For examples of drunkenness during parties, see McGillivray, *Journal*, March 22, 1795, 66; Faries, "Diary,"

January 11–12, 1805, 224–5; and Harmon, *Sixteen Years*, May 27, 1805, 89–90. For examples of heavy drinking at a rendezvous, see Nelson, *My First Years*, 42–3; and Mackenzie, "General History," 1789, 52.

77. Ross, *Fur Hunters*, 2:249–50.

78. LAC, MG19 B1, Alexander Mackenzie to the proprietors of the NWC, Grand Portage, June 16, 1799, 71.

79. TBR, S13, George Nelson's journal and reminiscences, 57.

80. Payne, *Most Respectable Place*, 83.

81. TBR, S13, George Nelson's journal "No. 5," June 1807–October 1809, 20–1 (my sequential pagination), 204–5 (Nelson's pagination).

82. Pierre Bourdieu, "The Forms of Capital," in *Handbook of Theory and Research for the Sociology of Education*, edited by John G. Richardson, 242, Westport, CT: Greenwood Publishing Group, Inc., 1986. See also Pierre Bourdieu, *The Logic of Practice*. Translated by Richard Nice. Stanford: Stanford University Press, 1980, 112–21; and Pierre Bourdieu and Loïc J.D. Wacquant, *Invitation to Reflexive Sociology*. Chicago: University of Chicago Press, 1992, 119.

83. In his discussion of the cargoes carried in canots du maître, Bruce M. White notes only the basic necessities of food, clothing, and alcohol as equipment for voyageurs, in his "Montreal Canoes and their Cargoes," 185–7, in *Le Castor Fait Tout: Selected Papers of the Fifth North American Fur Trade Conference, 1985*. Edited by Bruce Trigger et. al., 164–92. Montreal: St Louis Historical Society, 1987.

84. For an example of playing cards, see Harmon, *Sixteen Years*, November 16, 1800, 37. For an example of playing a game called "La Mouche" with cards and chips, see TBR, S13, George Nelson's journal and reminiscences, 63. On gambling as a widespread practice, see Cox, *Adventures on the Columbia River*, 306.

85. Payne, *Most Respectable Place*, 69.

86. OA, reel MS65, Donald McKay, Journal from August 1800 to April 1801, Sunday, December 28, 1800, 17.

87. For an example of voyageurs playing Aboriginal games, see Johann Georg Kohl, *Ktichi-Gami: Life among the Lake Superior Ojibway*. Translated by Lascelles Wraxall. St Paul: Minnesota Historical Society Press, 1985 (first published in Germany in 1859), 82. On voyageurs tattooing themselves, see MRB, MC, C.24, January 22–23, 1801, 19. On Cree tattooing, see Dr. Richardson's account in Franklin, *Narrative of a Journey*, 67.

88. Franklin, *Narrative of a Journey*, 63, 68.

89. Ross, *Fur Hunters*, 2:236–7.

90. Henry (the Younger), *New Light*, August 11, 1800, 1:30–1; McGillivray, *Journal*, August 18, 1794, 11–12; and TBR, S13, George Nelson's diary of events, July 9, 1822, July 21–August 22, 1822, August 19, 1822.

91. Landmann, *Adventures and Recollections*, 1:167–9.

92. Payne, *Most Respectable Place*, 68–9.

93. Henry (the Younger), *New Light*, May 6, 1804, 1:243; and MRB, MC, C.24, April 10, 1801, 31.

94. LAC, MG, C1, vo. 14, April 11, 1800, 23. For another example of brawling referred to as a sport or competition, see TBR, S13, George Nelson's journal, April 1, 1810–May 1, 1811, May 13, 1810, 7 (my pagination), which mentions two voyageurs fighting "rough and tumble" and a "pitch battle".

95. OA, MU 1146, Athabasca River, May 3, 1819, 69.

96. Payne, *Most Respectable Place*, 69; and John E. Foster, "Paulet Paul: Métis or 'House Indian' Folk Hero?" *Manitoba History*, 9 (Spring 1985): 2–7.

97. TBR, S13, George Nelson's diary of events, June 21, 1822. For other examples see diary entries for July 4 and 9, and August 6, 1822; Mackenzie, *Voyages from Montreal*, 251–52; Ross, *Fur Hunters*, 1:303 and 2:179, 186; George Heriot, *Travels through the Canadas, containing a Description of the Picturesque Scenery on Some of the Rivers and Lakes*. London: Richard Phillips, 1807, 246–47; and Extracts from a Letter of Andrew Graham, master at York Fort, to the Governor and Committee of the HBC, dated York Fort, August 26, 1772, in W. Stewart Wallace, ed. *Documents Relating to the Northwest Company*. Toronto: Champlain Society, 1934, 43.

98. TBR, S13, George Nelson's journal, "No. 5," 28–9 (my sequential pagination)/212–13 (Nelson's pagination).

Chapter 8

Immigration in the Early to Mid-Nineteenth Century

READINGS

Primary Documents

Historical Interpretations

INTRODUCTION

One method of successful colonization is to increase the population of residents within the colonial space—but not just anyone will do. Residents who are likely to be so absorbed in their own livelihoods that they offer little opposition to the colonial administration are good candidates, as are residents likely to view the move to the colony as a step forward. In the early part of the nineteenth century, British North America had the capacity to accept such migrants, and the elites in the colonies were eager to settle newcomers on their lands. One of the ways this project moved forward was to offer subsidized ship transport and settlement assistance to willing Irish and Scottish people. Earlier in the eighteenth century, thousands from these groups had come to the territory that became the United States, so the promoters of migration to British North America were not treading entirely new ground. However, these later migrations were state-sponsored, and began to affect the demographic profiles of the receiving colonies almost immediately.

The primary documents here address all phases of the project to settle new people in the Canadas. First, an inquiry into the conditions on the ships bringing the migrants across the Atlantic conveys the sense that these passengers were considered only a notch or two above cargo. The second primary document is directed to the prospective migrants themselves, and advises them to bring certain goods along, while leaving others behind—a clear ranking of the strengths of industrial Britain and the North American frontier, as well as a commentary on the voyage.

Of course, the trip and the early prospects facing migrants were not the only considerations. Elizabeth Jane Errington's reading focuses on Upper Canada, and how connected migrants were to the kin and communities they had left behind. Correspondence maintained this connection, informing potential migrants of what they might expect and helping those who had already relocated to feel like they were still part of a family, even though the possibility of daily contact had vanished. Scott See's reading on the Irish famine migration reflects on another aspect of the immigrant experience: the hostility with which many immigrants were received in British North America. Anti-Catholic prejudice was widespread among the Protestants of British North America and it was exacerbated by the large number of destitute Irish who arrived in the colonies in the mid-nineteenth century.

QUESTIONS FOR CONSIDERATION

1. What does Buchanan tell us about the experiences of these immigrants? Are officials holding to the spirit or the letter of regulations regarding passage?
2. Why might passengers be suspicious of assisted immigration schemes?
3. If you were a potential immigrant to the Canadas, how might you find Dunlop's information helpful?
4. Do you think that some of the letter writers that Errington discusses were really the best candidates for immigration after all? Why or why not?
5. How did anti-Irish nativism express itself in British North America? What factors explain the surge in nativism in the mid-nineteenth century?

SUGGESTIONS FOR FURTHER READING

Wendy Cameron and Mary McDougall Maude, *Assisting Emigration to Upper Canada: The Petworth Project, 1832–1837* (Montreal and Kingston: McGill-Queen's University Press, 2000).

Wendy Cameron, Sheila Haines, and Mary McDougall Maude, eds, *English Emigrant Voices: Labourers' Letters from Upper Canada in the 1830s* (Montreal and Kingston: McGill-Queen's University Press, 2000).

Lucille H. Campey, *Atlantic Canada's Irish Immigrants: A Fish and Timber Story* (Toronto: Dundurn, 2016).

———, *Seeking a Better Future: The English Pioneers of Ontario and Quebec* (Toronto: Dundurn, 2012).

Bruce S. Elliott, *Irish Migrants in the Canadas: A New Approach* (Montreal and Kingston: McGill-Queen's University Press, 2004).

Elizabeth Jane Errington, *Emigrant Worlds and Transatlantic Communities: Migration to Upper Canada in the First Half of the Nineteenth Century* (Montreal and Kingston: McGill-Queen's University Press, 2007).

Sharon A. Roger Hepburn, *Crossing the Border: A Free Black Community in Canada* (Urbana, IL: University of Illinois Press, 2007).

Cecil Houston and W.J. Smyth, *Irish Emigration and Canadian Settlement: Patterns, Links, and Letters* (Toronto: University of Toronto Press, 1990).

Mark McGowan, *Creating Canadian Historical Memory: The Case of the Famine Migration of 1847* (Ottawa: The Canadian Historical Association, 2006).

Michael E. Vance, *Imperial Immigrants: Scottish Settlers in the Upper Ottawa Valley, 1815–1840* (Toronto: Dundurn Press, 2012).

Catharine Anne Wilson, *A New Lease on Life: Landlords, Tenants and Immigrants in Ireland and Canada* (Montreal and Kingston: McGill-Queen's University Press, 1994).

Primary Documents

1 From "Testimony of Alexander Buchanan," *Third Report of the Select Committee on Emigration from the United Kingdom* (London, 1827), 106–13.

Sabbati, 3° die Martii, 1827.
Alexander Carlisle Buchanan, Esq. called in; and Examined.

815. YOU are generally acquainted with the circumstances of the trade in the carrying of passengers between this country and the United States, as well as between this country and Canada?—From Ireland I am perfectly.

816. Have you made any comparison between the expense that will be occasioned by the restraints proposed in this Act, which has been laid before the Committee as a substitution for a former Act, and the expense occasioned by the Act of the year 1825?—I have.

817. What would be the difference of expense between the two Acts?—About 12 s. 6 d. for each passenger.

818. What do you consider would be the expense at present?—It is now perhaps 40 s. for an adult, or 3 l.

819. From what port to what port?—From Londonderry and Belfast, which are the great ports of emigration to our colonies; to the United States it is about 5 l. or 6 l.

820. What would be the expense of the poorest class of passengers from Belfast to Quebec?—About 50 s., finding their own provisions.

821. By this Act, a certain quantity of provisions is necessary?—They are; but the representations were so numerous from the poor people, that the provisions prescribed by the Act were so expensive, that the officers of His Majesty's Customs saw that it would in effect almost prohibit emigration if it were enforced, and they took upon themselves, I believe, to wave that part of the Act.

822. Do you consider that in point of fact, with respect to emigrants going from Ireland

generally, the provisions of that Act have virtually been waved?—Not generally; the restriction as to numbers, and a proper supply of water, surgeon, &c. was particularly attended to by the officers of Customs, and although they waved that clause respecting a certain description of provisions, they generally made inquiry into the supply the passengers had.

823. Have you an opportunity of knowing that to be the case with respect to the south of Ireland as well as the north?— I have not.

824. Is it your impression that it has been so in the south?—I should think it has been. I dare say I have accompanied 6,000 emigrants to America myself, within the last ten years.

825. In those cases, the provisions of that Act were not enforced?—Not to any great extent; it has been the custom, for the last six or seven years, for the passengers to find their own provisions; formerly the ships found them.

826. Then in point of fact, the passengers themselves took that quantity of provisions which they thought necessary?—They did.

827. Do you imagine that the amount of provisions proposed to be required by this new Act, is greater than what is taken by the poorest of the emigrants who provide for themselves?—I do not think it is near so much.

828. The question applies to the quality as well as the quantity?—I understand it so.

829. Do the emigrants take pork or meat, for instance?—Very seldom; they take a little bacon.

830. Have the provisions which the Act prescribed with respect to tonnage, been actually observed?—They have.

831. The Custom-house officers have uniformly taken care, although they have relaxed with respect to provisions, to have the proportions of passengers to tonnage preserved?—They examine the list of passengers going out, to see that it corresponds with the licence; the licence is granted in proportion to the registered tonnage.

832. Is it the custom after the Customhouse-officer has examined the list, that passengers are taken off the coast?—I do not think it is; I have heard of trifling instances of the kind; the price paid for passage to our own colonies is so trifling, that a captain of a ship would hardly take the trouble.

833. Did you ever know it to happen in any vessel which you yourself were on board?—Never; I have repeatedly seen some relanded that have hid away on board; on the captain examining on leaving port, if he found he had any above his number, he would hove to, and put them on shore.

834. What practical inconvenience do you anticipate from allowing passengers to take with them such provisions as they may think fit, without any legislative enactment on the subject?—I think that the description of emigrants from Ireland particularly are very ignorant, and they have latterly got such an idea of the quick dispatch to America, that they would take a very short supply; they hear of packets coming over from New York to Liverpool in twenty or twenty-five days, and many of them come into Derry, calculating upon a twenty days passage, and without a quantity of oatmeal and other necessaries in proportion, and they are obliged to provide themselves with a larger quantity before they go on board.

835. Have you ever known any inconvenience actually to arise in consequence of a deficiency of provisions?—I have not known any myself, but formerly I have understood there were very great privations suffered, and a great many lives lost, before the Passengers Act passed.

836. Is that an opinion which you have heard from so many quarters as to leave no doubt in your mind of it being the fact?—I am perfectly satisfied of it.

837. Have you not stated that these legislative regulations have, in point of fact, not been adhered to?—They have not, as regards provisions.

838. But although they were not adhered to, they were not so entirely evaded as not to leave them in considerable operation?—Decidedly not.

839. Supposing a passenger, under the expectation of a quick passage, had brought only half the food which this new Act contemplates, what would have taken place in that instance; is any inquiry made by the captain of the passenger, as to the quantity of provision he has?—Always.

840. If the quantity of provisions he had brought was manifestly under what was necessary for an average voyage, would not the captain insist on his taking more?—Decidedly, he would not receive him without.

841. With respect to the tonnage, will you state to the Committee the reason why you are of opinion that there is a necessity for requiring the height of five feet six inches between the decks, and for prohibiting all stores from being placed between the decks?—I consider it indispensable in a ship carrying at the rate of one passenger to every two tons, to reserve the entire space between decks for their accommodation, and the deck of the ship not being at least five feet and a half, it would not be proper to have it double birthed; and a ship carrying at the rate of one passenger to every two tons, will require to be double birthed, and to have six persons in each birth.

842. Are the double-decked merchant vessels usually of that height between the decks?—Generally more; there are very few that are not.

843. Then have you any reason to anticipate that ships would be built for the express purpose of carrying out emigrants, which would be of a less height between decks than the ordinary merchant vessels, or that the vessels that would be used for that purpose would probably be old merchant vessels?—Not at all; there are very few ships that trade to America that are not five feet and a half high between decks, and over.

844. Then do you conceive that there is any necessity for any regulation enforcing that which actually exists without any regulation?—The reason of that clause is, that ships carrying one to every five tons would be saved the necessity of any delay in making an application for a licence; they could take their one to five tons, and proceed on their voyage in the ordinary way; whereas if they take in a greater number than that, some restriction should be imposed.

845. Do you imagine that there will be any practical inconvenience in these regulations being enforced, either at the Custom-house at the port from which they go in England, or at the Custom-house at the port at which they land in the colony?—None whatever.

846. Do you consider that any expense would be incurred in consequence of those regulations, which would of necessity add to the expense of the passage?—None whatever.

847. Then you are of opinion, that if those regulations were considered to be necessary, there would be no objection against them upon the ground of any real inconvenience being sustained by the trade in consequence of them?—None whatever; I am satisfied they would be approved of, both by the emigrants and the shipowners.

848. Do you entertain the opinion, that the parties going out would rather be protected by legislation to the extent proposed, than to have no legislation upon the subject?—I am perfectly satisfied they would.

849. Are the Committee to understand that they object very much to those extreme

regulations, which make the expense of the passage beyond their means?—They have a great objection to being obliged to have a particular description of provisions, but that has been latterly dispensed with.

850. Then, in point of fact, has emigration from Ireland been prevented, in consequence of that part of the Act which relates to provisions?—I do not think it has.

851. As you have stated that the restrictions of this Act with respect to provisions have been virtually superseded in practice, it is presumed that emigration from Ireland cannot have been prevented by the operation of this Act?—To a very small extent; perhaps to the amount of 100 a year or 200 a year more at the outside might have gone; the difference can only be about 10 or 12 shillings in the expense. I have heard a great many statements made about the Passengers Act; as to the Act increasing the expense of passage to the United States, and amounting to a prohibition of emigration, I am satisfied that if the Act were repealed the price would not be diminished one farthing, as the American law imposes a greater limitation as to number than the British and other local regulations.

852. Supposing this Act were not to be passed, requiring the emigrant to take with him a certain specified quantity of food for 75 days, do you imagine that the emigrant could in prudence take a less quantity?—I do not think he could, for I have known instances of very fast sailing ships from Liverpool being 75, 80 or 90 days going out to New York, and frequent instances occur of ships being 60, 70 and 80 days going to Quebec.

853. You say, that you think the emigrants would not take a less quantity of provisions than that which is prescribed by the Act?—I do not think they would; they generally consult the captain; they tell the captain of the ship what quantity

they have got, and if he thinks they have not got enough, they put on board more.

854. That Act provides for a certain quantity of bread, meal and flour; is that the species of provision upon which the lower Classes in Ireland live, either entirely or in a great measure?—It is generally their chief support.

855. You are not much acquainted with the south of Ireland?—Not particularly; I consider that oatmeal and potatoes form the principal food of the Irish peasantry generally; I include potatoes when in proper season, say in the spring of the year, very necessary, but in case of bad weather or other casualty, oatmeal, flour or biscuit can only be depended on.

856. You are not aware that in the south of Ireland the peasantry never taste bread from one year's end to another?—I am not aware that they never taste bread, they chiefly live on potatoes; but this Act merely says, that there shall be that quantity of that or any other wholesome food equivalent thereto; I only submit that there should be a certain quantity of something on board, enough to keep them in life for 75 days.

857. If there were no restriction whatever by law as to the food to be taken by the passengers, do not you think that the captain of every ship carrying out passengers would for his own sake take care that no person should be taken on board who had not a proper quantity of provisions?—I think he would, or ought to do.

858. Have not you stated that that is the habit?—They generally inquire what quantity of provisions the passengers have brought; the ship is under a very heavy responsibility; I have known instances where the ship has taken on board a quantity of meal to guard against the possibility of the passengers falling short; I have done so myself, I have taken in a few tons of oatmeal, at the expense of the ship, to prevent any accident.

859. In case of a passenger falling short of provisions, would not the captain have to supply that deficiency?—Perhaps the captain might not have any to spare.

860. Does the captain generally go to sea so short of provisions?—A ship going to sea in the North American trade, if she victuals at home, may take in three or four months provisions, but what would a redundancy of a barrel of biscuit or a barrel of meal be among 300 emigrants.

861. What is the general burthen of those ships that carry 300 persons?—From 300 to 400 tons.

862. How many emigrants, according to the regulations of this Act, would be shipped on board a vessel of 350 tons?—I have put on paper a few observations with respect to the points of difference between the proposed Act and the former Act, which I will read to the Committee. In the first place, the proposed Act permits the ship to carry her full number, say one to two tons register, children in proportion, exclusive of the crew; the former Act included the crew. Secondly, it dispenses with carrying a doctor; the former Act imposed that necessity. Thirdly, it permits the ship carrying cargo, reserving a sufficiency of space, with the whole of the between-decks, for passengers, provisions, water, &c.; the former Act prohibited carrying cargo, or it was so construed by the Irish Board of Customs. Fourthly, it relieves the shipowner and captain from obnoxious and frivolous clauses and expenses that never perhaps would be resorted to, but operated in the calculation of a conscientious shipowner, not to permit his ship to embark in such trade. Fifthly, it permits the passenger or emigrant to lay in his own provisions, or to make any contract they think fit with the captain for that purpose, the captain being responsible that a sufficiency of wholesome food

for 75 days of some kind is on board for each adult passenger; the former Act obliged the ship to have on board a particular description of provisions, not suited to the habits of emigrants, and of increased expense. And the proposed amended Act gives every protection to the emigrant, at the same time removing many absurd difficulties to the ship, and permits as many passengers to be put on board as could possibly be justified with any due regard to their health and lives. I shall state in my humble opinion how it operates in a pecuniary way: first, a ship 400 tons by the former Act could only carry, deducting crew, about 180 adults; now 200; difference 20, at 40 s. per head, deducting expense of water, &c. 40 l.: secondly, free from expense of doctor, at least 50 l.: thirdly, giving liberty to carry cargo, is at least worth equal to 25 l.: fourthly, I consider that dispensing with the obligation that many ships are under, to put salt provisions on board to conform to old Act, although not used equal with other matters, to 25 l.; making a total of 140 l., which on two hundred emigrants would be equal to 12 s. or 14 s. per adult; and supposing that a ship was taking in emigrants, and that plenty were offering, it would enable the ship to carry them for so much less than under the former Act, and form as much actual gain on the passage as charging so much higher, so that in fact the emigrant gets his passage for so much less, and without any loss to the ship. A ship of four hundred tons has about seventy-five feet in length of space, and twenty-six feet wide between decks; so, to have her doubled birthed, would give you about twenty-six births aside, or fifty-two in all; and allowing six persons to each birth, would accommodate three hundred and twelve persons, which a ship of four hundred tons is permitted to carry; say two hundred adults, with average proportion of children, would at least make (if not more) the number stated, and with twenty of crew, would give on board altogether 332 persons in a space about 95 feet long, 25 to 26 feet wide, and $5\frac{1}{2}$ or 6 feet high.

863. If there were no responsibility imposed upon the captains of vessels, either with respect to provisions or with respect to tonnage, are you apprehensive that captains might be found who would be willing to incur risks from which great evils might occur to the passengers?—I am afraid many instances might occur, and unless some legislative regulation existed, I fear captains and shipbrokers would be found that would cram them into any extent, and great hardship would be likely to follow.

864. Do you know of any serious consequences that did arise previous to the passing of the Passengers Act?—I know instances where passengers were carried a thousand miles from the place they contracted for.

2 From William Dunlop, *Statistical Sketches of Upper Canada, for the Use of Emigrants: by a Backwoodsman* (London: John Murray, 1832), 14–20.

PREPARATIONS FOR EMIGRATION

When a man has determined to quit home, and settle himself in a foreign land, and he should not do so on slight grounds, much trouble and vexation may be saved by his taking a little good advice, and that we are about to give in this chapter, in so far as emigration to Canada is concerned.

It cannot be too strongly impressed upon emigrants the inexpediency of carrying to the woods of Upper Canada heavy lumbering articles of wooden furniture. All these can be procured here for far less than the cost of transport from Quebec and Montreal. The only exception to this rule is, when a person has valuable furniture for which he cannot get any thing like a reasonable price at home; and in that case, it may be cheaper to carry it to Canada than to sacrifice it in England. [. . .] Clothes, more particularly coarse clothing, such as slops and shooting jackets, bedding, shirts, (made, for making is expensive here,) cooking utensils, a clock or time-piece, books packed in barrels, hosiery, and, above all, boots and shoes, (for what they call leather in this continent is much more closely allied to hide than leather, and one pair of English shoes will easily outlast three such as we have here,) are among the articles that will be found most useful. As a general rule also, every thing that is made of metal, (for ironmongery is very dear,) as well as gardening and the iron parts of farming tools, and a few of the most common carpenters' tools, can never come amiss; for, though a man may not be artist enough to make money as a carpenter for other people, he may save a great deal himself by having the means within his reach of driving a nail or putting in a pane of glass. A few medicines ought to be taken for the voyage, and those chiefly of the purgative kind, as ships are very frequently but indifferently furnished with a medicine chest. Among these I would recommend Anderson's, or any other of the aloetic and colocynth pills, Epsom salts, magnesia and emetics, made up in doses. If you take Seidlitz powders, or soda powders, or any of that tribe of acids and alkalies, let them be made up in phials, well stopped, not, as usual, in papers, for in that case they will get melted, or (as the learned express it) deliquate, before the passage is half over. With these phials will of course be required measures, to take out the proper proportions of each powder. Fishing and shooting tackle ought, also to be taken; but of these I shall come to speak more at large when I treat, as I mean to do in a separate chapter, of the field-sports of Upper Canada.

In the choice of a ship, steerage passengers should look out for one high, roomy, and airy between decks; and there can be no great difficulty in finding one of that description, as a very great number of the timber ships are so constructed. A fast sailer also should be preferred; for the difference of a fortnight or three weeks in arriving at your destination may make the difference of nearly a year's subsistence to the emigrant. If he arrive in time to put in a small crop of potatoes, turnips, oats, Indian corn, and a little garden stuff, it will go a great way towards the maintenance of a family for the first year, as it will enable them to feed pigs and keep a cow, which they could not otherwise accomplish. For a similar reason, it will be to the obvious advantage of all settlers to come out in the earliest ships that sail.

To all passengers, but more especially to those of the cabin, a civil, good-tempered captain ought to be a very great inducement to sail in his ship,—as much of the comfort or discomfort of a voyage depends upon him. There are many of the regular traders between Montreal and Greenock and Liverpool who answer this description, as well as on the London and Liverpool lines to New York. And to any person who goes by the latter route, I would strongly recommend my worthy, though diminutive friend, Captain Holridge of the Silas Richards. Above all, passengers of every description should ascertain, that the captain with whom they sail is a sober man; for the most fatal accidents may occur, and have occurred, from drunkenness on the part of the officers of the ship. I prefer coming to Canada *via* Montreal, as it saves money, time, and transhipment of baggage.

It is a question often asked, how should money be taken to Canada? I reply, in any way except in goods. Not that I have not often known that mode of bringing it prove highly profitable; but it is a risk; few who come out being good judges of the price of goods at home, and none of them knowing what kind of goods will suit the Canada markets. British silver or gold make a very good investment; as the former is bought up by merchants and tradesmen, and used to purchase bills on the Treasury through the Commissariat, and the latter is remitted by the same classes to meet their engagements in England. A Sovereign generally fetches 23*s*. or 24*s*. currency, that is 5*s*. to the dollar;—1*s*. sterling passes for 1*s*. 2*d*. currency;—so that either description of bullion gives a good remittance. One great objection, however, to bringing out money, is the liability there is of losing or being robbed of it: so that, upon the whole, the better way perhaps may be, to lodge it with T. Wilson and Co. of Austin Friars, Agents for the Bank of Upper Canada, or at the Canada Company's Office in St. Helen's Place, taking an acknowledgment; and then you can draw upon the fund from Canada, receiving the premium of the day on the exchange.

People who find themselves on the outward voyage, should lay in a very considerable quantity of potatoes and oatmeal, not only because these articles are cheap, but because they have a tendency to correct the scorbutic qualities of salt meat. A few onions and leeks likewise will be found a great comfort on a long voyage, as also a good supply of vinegar and pickles.

Emigrants would find their account in bringing out small quantities of seeds, particularly those of the rarer grasses, as lucern, trefoil, &c.; for if they did not need such articles themselves, they would find plenty who would buy them at a high price. To these may be added some small parcels of potato oats, and of the large black oat of the south of Ireland for seed, as that grain, if not renewed, degenerates into something little better than chaff in the course of time.

All kinds of good stock are wanted here, and those who can afford it will always find their account in bringing such. Pigs are valuable, in many parts of this country, according to the size to which they can be fatted. Thus, supposing a hog which weighs 2 cwt. fetched twopence halfpenny per lb., one weighing 3 cwt. would fetch threepence, and so on, adding a halfpenny per lb. for each cwt. of the weight. A good bull would also be of great value; and it is my firm belief, that we have not a first-rate draught stallion in the province. I have no doubt, moreover, that a Clydesdale cart-horse, a Suffolk punch, or even a moderate-sized Flanders stallion, would be a good speculation. The best description of working cattle we have is the Lower Canadian horse, which has many of the properties and much the appearance of the Scotch galloway: he is strong, active, and indefatigable in harness, but makes a bad saddle horse, as he is often not sure-footed. A breed between this and the American horse makes a good, useful farm-horse; and it is possible that a cross between the Canadian mare and the Flanders horse would make something like the Clydesdale,—tradition asserting, that the ancestors of the Carnwath breed sprang from a cross of some Flanders mares brought to Scotland by the Duke of Hamilton with the galloway stallions of the country.

As to dogs for household use, the English sheepdog or Scotch colley, or the lurcher, would be highly valuable, particularly if trained to bring home the cattle, which often stray in the woods and get injured by not being regularly milked. With careless settlers, indeed, one half the day is often spent in hunting up and driving home the oxen.

It has often struck me, that much time and trouble might be saved in collecting and bringing home the cattle, by taking out a few hundred weight of rock salt from Liverpool. In Cheshire they used to prepare lumps, for the purpose of putting in sheepwalks, by cutting them in the form of a ball, so that the rain ran off them without melting them. These might be put in certain places of the woods, and the cattle would not stray far from them; and they might be removed from time to time, as the pasture became scarce. Wherever there is a salt spring, or a salt "lick," as salt earth is called in this country, the deer and cattle flock to it from all quarters. A friend of mine had one on his farm, and no fence could keep off these intruders; till at last he was obliged to come to a compromise with the four-footed congress, and fairly fenced in a road to the spring, and by this species of Whig conciliation, by a sacrifice of part of his rights, saved the rest of his property.

When you arrive in the St. Lawrence, having been on shortish allowance of water, you will be for swallowing the river water by the bucket full. Now, if you have any bowels of compassion for your intestinal canal, you will abstain from so doing;—for to people not accustomed to it, the lime that forms a considerable constituent part of the water of this country, acts pretty much in the same manner as would a solution of Glauber's salts, and often generates dysentery and diarrhoea; and though I have an unbounded veneration for the principles of the Temperance societies, I would, with all deference, recommend, that the pure fluid be drank in very small quantities at first, and even these tempered with the most impalpable infusion possible of Jamaica or Cognac.

Historical Interpretations

3 From Elizabeth Jane Errington, "Transatlantic Webs of Kin and Community," in *Emigrant Worlds and Transatlantic Communities: Migration to Upper Canada in the First Half of the Nineteenth Century* (Montreal: McGill-Queen's University Press, 2007), 136–58.

When young Harriet Pengelly finally arrived in Upper Canada, she was exhausted, bewildered, and miserable. The difficult voyage from Plymouth to New York had been followed by a slow and disagreeable journey by way of Albany and Oswego to Toronto and then west to Flamborough. "Alas! What am I come to! My heart is breaking with grief," she wrote at the end of May 1835.[1] She was almost overwhelmed by "the dirt and misery"[2] of their new lodgings; and while Robert travelled about looking for land, she was desperately lonely. "I feel very low in spirits, would I were home," she cryptically reported after a week in the colony.[3] The arrival of the first letters from home was bittersweet: "I am still very low. Wept when I read Sophy's and Uncle Irving's kind letters, such prayers for my happiness, dear friends may God bless you all."[4] To help her assuage her sense of alienation and, when Robert was away, her feeling of being "all alone in this second Siberia,"[5] Harriet reached across the Atlantic. She frequently wrote to sister Sophy and to other friends and relations in Guernsey. When not writing, she was thinking of her "absent friends";[6] and when letters arrived from home, she "felt happier than [she] had done for some time."[7]

Harriet's correspondence with home provided an emotional lifeline. It is clear from her journal that, from the beginning, she had been hesitant about emigrating to the colonies. Married in September 1834, in the space of six months she had had to adjust to life as a newlywed and to leaving her "happy home" and "dear Guernsey friends," along with all she loved "so dearly," for a foreign land.[8] Letters home were a way of maintaining contact with the familiar world of her youth. They also reaffirmed the emotional, if not physical, proximity of friends and family. On the very day the couple boarded the packet at Plymouth and also on the day they landed in New York, Harriet sent letters home.[9] Especially in the early months of her journal, Harriet's notations that she had written home often appeared in entries that recounted some disappointment, whether it was the abrupt decision of her maid Emily not to accompany the couple to America or the failure of the luggage to arrive; or, once they were in the colony, the realization that their original choice of land "was mistaken".[10]

Even after the Pengellys had bought a farm and built a home on Rice Lake and had begun to settle into the rhythms of their new lives, Harriet maintained an active correspondence across the Atlantic. She was "truly miserable" when anticipated letters from home did not arrive.[11] One "disagreeable" day in August 1835, for example, she recorded, "No letters from home, could eat no dinner—very, very unhappy."[12] Even after the couple had decided to return to Guernsey for a visit after two years and Harriet's sense of exile began to abate, letters from home remained a vital part of her daily life, something to be cherished and read "over and over".[13] As she read of the comings and goings of kith and kin in Guernsey and England, she was able to maintain a sense of belonging to a community that was far removed from her daily round of housekeeping and visiting neighbours, and at times "the awful silence of the woods of Canada".[14] [. . .]

Until her death a little more than a year after she arrived in the colony, Harriet remained emotionally rooted in a world that lay more than three thousand miles away. Although she had "the smiles and love of a very dear husband," on New Year's Day 1836 she longed for her mother's smile and "a kind mother to wish me many happy returns of the day."[15] Letters provided Harriet with the means of participating, at least vicariously, in the community of family and friends "at home" even while she was forging new friendships and becoming part of a new community at Rice Lake. For Harriet, letters were also tangible evidence that she had not been forgotten and had not lost her place in the family circle. As was the case for many around her, letters from home were a touchstone, an affirmation of who one was and, for a time at least, where one continued to belong.

Certainly, not all or even most emigrant settlers maintained such an active transatlantic correspondence. Like her husband Robert, a former British officer and a gentleman of some means, Harriet was a member of the "letter writing classes".[16] The couple could afford to travel in a cabin on a packetship, and Robert had the capital to buy land and hire neighbours to help build his house and clear his fields. And when they arrived in the colony with their letters of introduction to the lieutenant-governor, they became part of a society that was directly tied to London and the Colonial Office. Harriet was determined "to do without" a servant after she had sacked, for insolence, the one they had brought from Guernsey; she hoped, she said, that work would keep her "alive in this dull disagreeable country." But the young wife obviously had considerable time on her hands.[17] She had no children to attend to and was often alone when Robert worked in the fields.

Most new arrivals had not the time, the means, or perhaps the inclination to write home so often or at such length. As George Pashley recorded in his diary, his first letters home—one to his father, a second to a friend, and the third to his "dear partner's" father—were not sent until three months after he landed in British America: "I could not get Money to Pay the Postage till then."[18] Of course, some emigrants may have chosen not to write. They wanted to sever ties with home—whether because they were fleeing from particular responsibilities (as in the case of absconding husbands) or from the court, or because they were determined to grasp the new opportunities of America and, in the process, re-invent themselves. However, it is clear that for many, re-establishing contact with home was an integral part of the process of making a new life away from home. As the new arrivals joined kin, former neighbours, and even just acquaintances who were already settled in Upper Canada and were integrated into or helped to create new families and communities and gradually become residents, the desire to maintain contact with those at home persisted. Frequently, the responsibilities attendant on kinship—coping with the needs of an elderly parent, providing aid to a young sibling or cousin, or settling disputes over parents' estates—continued to tie emigrant settlers

to those they had left behind. Letters were also a means of integrating the Old World and the New, of tying the familiar domestic landscapes, people, and relationships of home into the new and increasingly familiar world of a face-to-face colonial community. On both sides of the Atlantic, receiving or sending even one brief letter reaffirmed who one was and where one fitted into the world.

The transatlantic community sustained by correspondence was for many intensely personal, and despite distance in time and space, remained surprisingly immediate. Letters became an integral part of the ongoing cycle of British emigration and were one of the central pillars of the emigrants' world. Throughout Great Britain and Ireland, they frequently became the centrepiece of discussions in family parlours, churches, and taverns about the viability of "going to America". Letters from Upper Canada that included personal accounts of the journey and life in the New World helped to make the imagined world of emigration more real and tangible; at the same time, letters that arrived in the backwoods of the colony nourished the imagination of emigrant settlers with images of familiar landscapes and faces. The arrival of family members or friends of former neighbours, sometimes years later, reinforced these rather ethereal transatlantic communities. The receipt of letters, parcels, and even newspapers—even the appearance of a complete stranger with an introduction from a former acquaintance—was enough to sustain this world, both in its tangible form and in its participants' imagination.

[. . .]

Each year, hundreds if not thousands of emigrants of all social classes and occupations wrote home to announce their arrival and to report on the state of their health and that of their companions.[19] Sometimes these first letters were sent almost as soon as the family or the individual landed at Montreal or Quebec (or, in the case of Harriet Pengelly and Anne Langton, New York). A number included a journal or an account of the voyage and a promise to write again when settled.[20] Many emigrants waited and wrote their first letters weeks or even months after they had landed, and they included some "account of Canada" or a commentary about "the state of the country" (as they had apparently promised their readers before they left home), in addition to information about their own circumstances. As William Knox's first letter home to his uncle explained, "I would have written you before this time to have acquainted you of our safe arrival in this country. But knowing that Mr George Gounlock had written to Greenhill shortly after we arrived here I told him to let you know that we were all well and I would write you as soon as we got a settlement."[21]

Not surprisingly, emigrants' first letters home varied widely in tone and content. Some had to report the death of a companion or child on the voyage or how ague, scarlet fever, cholera, or other diseases had devastated family and friends.[22] Others noted that the country was "discouraging at first" or that because of injury or ill health, they had initially had problems finding work.[23] But most letters, particularly those written after emigrants had found work or taken up land, expressed satisfaction with the country and the writer's situation; and implicitly, and often explicitly, they included assurances that they "did not repent [their] journey."[24] George Hill's mother and father must have received some comfort when their son concluded his letter, "We left you almost broken-hearted, but you may be satisfied that we have bettered our condition by coming here."[25] Perhaps most importantly, the arrival of George's letter was concrete proof that he was still alive.

For most newly arrived emigrants, the purpose of their first letter was to make contact and to renew what they obviously hoped would be an ongoing relationship with those at home. Many expected that not only would the initial recipient read their letter but that its contents and often the letter itself would be passed among "Dear Friends And Relations".[26] Mary and Arthur Stokes explicitly asked that their brothers and sisters write and they added, "Please pass this letter to others."[27] William Upton's letter to his mother asked that she give his love to all his brothers and sisters, and said, "Tell them that can write to write to me soon."[28] [. . .] Others sent salutations to specific neighbours, former employers, or members of the extended family.

[. . .]

Sending news, information, and messages to family and friends was clearly only one purpose of an emigrant's first letter home. Just as important was to urge the readers to reply as soon as possible. Almost without exception, the letters included such statements as, "I long to hear from them all"[29] or pleaded, "Please to let us hear from you as soon as convenient after receiving this; and acquaint us with all particulars, and how you all are."[30] John Luff, an apprentice and one of the Petworth emigrants, wrote to his aunt saying, "Whether we shall have the pleasure of seeing each other in this world again, lord only knows; if we should not, I wish you would join me in writing, it seems to be the only satisfaction we can truly have here."[31]

It was clearly important to those who had newly arrived in Upper Canada to know that they had not been forgotten and, indeed, that they remained part of their communities at home. For the first few weeks or months, many must have felt betwixt and between. They were no longer residents of a particular village or neighbourhood in Great Britain or Ireland; at the same time, they had few connections or commitments to new communities in America. First letters were a way of asserting their continuing relationship with communities at home; and the responses to these letters reassured them that they still had a place in the world, an identity that was firmly rooted in place and time—one which they had taken with them to America and on which they could forge new relationships. Many new arrivals therefore waited anxiously for some acknowledgement from those they had left behind.[32]

Not all (and perhaps not even most) emigrants wrote to reassure the family of their safe arrival. As many of the "information wanted" notices suggest, some men had emigrated to escape family or financial responsibilities. Even those with the best of intentions may have found that once they were in America, it was easy to disappear, leaving wives and children at home unknowingly deserted.[33] Many more new arrivals probably did not have the ability or the means to write. Most were nonetheless determined to let those at home know that they had arrived safely and, later, to tell them how they were settling in.

Those who arrived in Upper Canada as part of a group, like John Gemmill or members of the Petworth expeditions 10 years later, or those who joined family or former neighbours already established in the colony, could always find someone to write on their behalf or, at the very least, could send greetings that would be expected to reach those at home. In the 1820s John Gemmill frequently sent messages from former shipmates and current neighbours in Lanark County, through his son Andrew, to friends and relatives in the old neighbourhood. In the summer of 1823, for example, he asked Andrew to "acquaint all Enquiring friends that Dr. Gemell John McFarline Walter Stirline James Cohune's family are all well."[34] Three years later, in a postscript to a letter, he wrote, "James Colquhoun wishes us to mention to you if you could hear anything of his brother Robert to let him know that he is well & is surprised that he has not heard from him for more than two years."[35] Andrew tracked down James Colquhoun's brother and reported back to his father. Unfortunately, the situation in Upper Canada had changed. "In your letter you desired me to let James Colquhoun know that you [had heard] from his brother," John wrote Andrew the

following August, 1827. But now John had to ask Andrew to break the news to the brother that James was "no more": "He was killed in April last while at work upon his own land."[36] More often, Andrew was given a happier commission. A year after John reported James's death, he asked his son, "Give James Wrights Compliments to Mr David Strachan and Wife" and "if David Strachan be writing to his sister he may let James Wrights Relations know that he is in good health."[37]

Various members of the Petworth parties also regularly wrote home on behalf of their companions and neighbours. [. . .] James Rapson, another member of the first Petworth group, not only wrote letters on behalf of other emigrants[38] but also regularly sent his family news about his companions (some of whom were now near neighbours, and others he had heard about second or third hand), knowing that this information would be passed on.[39] For both John Gemmill and James Rapson and their friends, the world of emigration was a small world and continued to be characterized by face-to-face communication even when such conversations spanned the Atlantic. The intimacy of this world was also apparent to other Petworth emigrants who arrived in subsequent years and sought out James Rapson for advice and assistance.

In many ways, emigrant correspondence recreated and was an extension of the familiar relationships of village life. What is striking is that even with only intermittent correspondence, or with news received second or third hand and months if not years out of date, the assumption of a shared community persisted. So, too, did the apparent immediacy of the relationships. This was undoubtedly one of the factors that encouraged some family members or friends who emigrated years later to assume that a face-to-face relationship could be resumed and that they could call on those in the New World for emotional and physical support when they arrived in the colony.

Not all, of course, participated in or maintained their connections with this dynamic transatlantic community. Many new arrivals to British North America were restless and moved frequently to look for work or for better opportunities. Friends and family in Great Britain and Ireland too might move in response to local circumstances. Many on both sides of the Atlantic refused to give up hope that some lost family member or friend could be found, however. In addition to the hundreds of "information wanted" notices placed by emigrants and settlers looking for a particular individual or family, colonial newspapers sometimes printed cards of family members or friends "at home" who were hoping to get in touch with "lost" relatives abroad. In 1835, for example, English friends offered a reward to anyone who had information about Ann Hall. "A native of London," Ann had come to Canada three years earlier with a Chelsea pensioner and his wife, who had subsequently died. No one had heard from Ann since she had written in July 1832.[40] [. . .]

Often the problem for those in the British Isles was finding the beneficiary of an estate. In some instances, executors used a local agent to conduct the search. In 1829, for example, "A.B." began to look for George Long, "a Tailor by trade" who had left England 10 years earlier with his wife and four children. It was thought that he now lived "somewhere near Philadelphia" and was a farmer. His wife's family, who lived near Knightsbridge, London, were trying to contact him, for he would "hear something to his advantage."[41] In 1829 Catherine Evans of Colham, Shrewsbury, Shropshire, contacted the *Herald* office in Kingston for help finding her brother Spencer Evans, who had been discharged from the Queen's Rangers some 25 years earlier and was, she thought, now living in Upper Canada.[42] At other times, the family or its agent in Great Britain or Ireland made a direct appeal.[43] Infrequently, an anxious parent or sibling would write directly to the postmaster of the relative's last known address in America to try to track the person down.

Many emigrants and their families were determined not to lose touch. A sense of familial obligation, ongoing business affairs, or just the need to maintain the image of familiar faces and places promoted an extensive correspondence which, in a few instances, continued into the second generation. Maintaining such a correspondence had significant difficulties. Paper was often scarce, and postage, which was paid in part by the recipient, was relatively expensive and beyond the means of many.[44] Moreover mail "service" was haphazard at best. Although the larger centres in Upper Canada had postal service that linked Halifax, Quebec, and Montreal to the interior, for much of the period the most economic and quickest route for mail was through New York.[45] [. . .] Even so, to the frustration of correspondents on both sides of the Atlantic, letters were often misdirected or lost in transit.

Almost a year after arriving in Lanark, John Gemmill grew increasingly concerned that he had heard nothing from his wife Ann. He had already written twice and "had got no answer." Ironically, even this third letter, which included detailed instructions about the family's reunion, took almost nine months to reach Glasgow and arrived long after Ann had already left home.[46] The frustration with mail to Scotland persisted. In one of his first letters to son Andrew, John noted, "We are sorry to here that you have only received one letter in the course of two years. We have not been neglectfull of writting to you neither is the Country as poor but it can produce plenty of Paper but it is the post offices that must be neglectfull of not forwarding them."[47] [. . .]

In Upper Canada, some letters from home arrived at their destination only to languish because the intended recipient did not know they were there or, as often seemed to happen, because the emigrant had left the area altogether. Local newspapers regularly published lists of letters waiting to be picked up. Isaac Wilson, the pre–War of 1812 emigrant living just outside York, discovered to his dismay in 1821 that "they now have a regulation at the post office . . . to send all letters remaining unclaimed after three months down to the General Post Office at Quebec." He had not been to York for some time, and the new clerk did not know him; as a result, he explained to his brother Jonathan his letter "was sent with a raft."[48] Harriet Pengelly, on the other hand, ever anxious to receive news from home, made a point of checking the post regularly and was always sorely disappointed when there was "none from home."[49] Mary Gapper, after deciding to marry Edward O'Brien and remain in the colony, remarked that mail sent by way of York in 1836 was delivered by "an Indian . . . who now calls regularly at very irregular times."[50]

To avoid expensive postage and problems with the mail service, letter writers on both sides of the Atlantic frequently relied on friends, acquaintances, or agents who were travelling overseas to carry their mail. It appears that a few Lanark residents returned home to visit, to fetch their family, or to go to college. Each time they left, they carried letters from John Gemmill to his son.[51] [. . .]

Personally delivered letters were a double benefit to the recipient. When the son of the Reverend William Bell from Lanark went "home" to college and delivered John Gemmill's letter, Andrew also received a first-hand account of his father and the family and could get detailed answers to the myriad questions that could not be answered by post.[52] Isaac Wilson was "pleased to inform" his brother Jonathan in the summer of 1821 "that John Barnes and his wife [had] arrived at York" and he had received Jonathan's note. "I am much obliged to you for your kindness," he wrote, "as they will afford me much information and entertainment." As Barnes had arrived with a letter from Jonathan asking Isaac to assist the bearer in any way he could, Isaac ruefully concluded that they would also afford him "some vexation, no doubt."[53] [. . .]

Entrusting acquaintances, friends, or family members with letters did not guarantee their speedy or safe arrival. Before Allanason delivered the letter, he had already spent some time travelling around America. Even so, for much of the period, "private conveyance" was less expensive and could be more reliable than the "regular" post.[54] However, sometimes the traveller or acquaintance forgot to put the letter in the post on the other side of the Atlantic or found it too much trouble to deliver it. George Pashley was disconcerted to find that his letters had not been delivered as promised. "This week I was informed that our Letters we had sent to Eng were within 2 miles of our own house because the man we expected to take them had fallen sick so they did not set off till the end of Jan."[55] Nonetheless, the imminent departure of a friend, or a visitor returning home, or the sailing of a particular ship presented an opportunity to write and make contact. [. . .]

Whether letters were mailed or sent with a traveller on the day they were written, they usually took months to reach their destinations. Correspondence between family and friends often crossed each other. News and information might be repeated in a subsequent letter when the writer realized, or feared, that the first had not arrived. This may help explain, in part at least, why some correspondents waited weeks if not months to reply to a letter; or if one arrived particularly late, saw no need to reply at all.[56] And there was, of course, the perpetual problem that writing took time and considerable thought and effort, all of which were at a premium in most new settlers' lives. What is so startling, therefore, is the sense of immediacy and often the conversational tone of many letters.

[. . .]

Of prime and increasing importance, however, was news about the health and welfare of various family members, and the primary focus of most of the transatlantic conversations revolved around family affairs. Each letter from Upper Canada began with an almost formulaic greeting. In June 1823, for example, John [Gemmill] began, "Dear son, We received your letter darted the 26TH of March on the 26 of May and the other Dated the 29 of March which Gave us Great Pleasure to hear of your Well fare and they find us all in good health at Preasant thank God for it."[57] Such almost ritualized openings were not empty rote; they were a crucial affirmation of the intimacy that existed between the writer and the recipient and a clear declaration of what was of greatest concern to both. Each of John and Ann Gemmill's letters included references to their and their children's health; they also specifically alluded to the power of the Almighty. In November 1825, Ann and John told Andrew, "This at present leaves us in the full enjoyment of that valuable Blessing for which we have great reason to praise God."[58] The letters also always asked after family members still in Scotland, and they admonished Andrew when he did not include information concerning his sisters' welfare. "We were very much Surprised," the couple wrote in May 1823, "that you never Mention nothing about your two Sisters Margeret and Jane."[59] A month later, they asked Andrew to "be so good as to lett them know of our Welfare."[60] The Gemmills' letters presumed that the ongoing relationship between Lanark, Upper Canada, and Glasgow rested on far more than passive interaction. John expected Andrew to pass on information and to assume some responsibility for the welfare of his sisters.

At the same time, John and Ann were ensuring that Andrew remained part of the family circle in Upper Canada. Their letters reported major family events. Andrew vicariously followed his sisters as they went "out to service" and watched as the little ones, including David, who had been an infant when he left home, go to school. In 1826 Andrew heard of the marriages of sisters Ann and Mary, and in turn he related his own marriage in 1827. To John, this was an opportunity to extend the family network, and thereafter his letters included greetings to "all

your [Andrew's] relations in Scotland." Two years later, while rejoicing with Andrew over the birth of his first child, John wrote, "We think that you forgot to mention her name and hope you will have a better memory when you write next."[61]

Especially in the early years, when all the children were living in the parental household, Andrew was drawn farther into life in Lanark when John's letters included notes of specific greetings from other members of the family. Sometimes, it was a brief "Jennet sends her best respects to you"[62] or, somewhat later, "Your Brothers & Sisters all join in love to you & your Family, David [the youngest son] has some recollection of you . . . but says he would know you better if you would send him the suit of cloaths."[63] Through her father's letters, Jennet, who was two years younger than Andrew, teased him about being a bachelor: "She thinks that if you do not bring a wife with you that you will remain an Old Batchelor that you would not get a Negor or Indian Squaw in the Country they will think so little of you."[64] In one of the few letters from Andrew that have survived, he replied, "Tell Janet to belief herself besides those black Ghosts of Indians."[65]

The occasion of Jennet's engagement to be married about six months later best illustrates the texture of this imagined familiar fireside. At the end of April 1824, a postscript cryptically noted, "Janet will be married before you come here so you put on spurs."[66] There may have been some hope that Andrew would arrive in time to be the best man. But John reported in November, "Since you did not come forward to be the best man, they made as merry as they could without you." And later in the same letter he passed on a message from Jennet: "As soon as you send intimation of your comming they [Jennet and her new husband] will Joyfully saddle the Tea Kettle and have everything ready to make you comfortable but they dare not put it on yet lest the bottom boil out of it before you come."[67] A year later, as John continued to hope that Andrew and his sisters would arrive, he bemoaned, "If you don't come soon, the Bottom will be out of the kettle."[68] One of Andrew's brothers, John, reintroduced the teapot to the transatlantic conversation many years later: "But my Mother says that if you don't come soon she is afraid that you have to take your tea out of the pot for the botem is out of the old tea ketel and she has got A new one and she is afraid that it will go the same way before you reach this place."[69]

The references to the familiar and domestic tea kettle—which in many Scottish homes was the symbol of welcome—helped create the illusion of a continuing and face-to-face relationship within a family divided by the Atlantic. By 1832, it must have been clear to all that Andrew and his new young family were unlikely to emigrate. Three years earlier, John had told Andrew that he "had almost despair[ed] of the realization of your wishes of our meeting again with the rest of my family around my fireside." He turned to his faith to help sustain him. The Gemmills shared an unshakable belief that "Kind Providence . . . provided all things liberally."[70] All their trials and tribulations, including family separations, were "from the Supreme Disposer of Events," John observed, and were "generally for our good."[71] Thus, he took solace that "though that [the family's reunion] may not take place upon earth, let us with the Divine assistance conduct ourselves in such a manner that we look forward to our meeting together in another and better world."[72]

In the meantime, the Gemmills created their own world—one with a tea kettle on the hob—in which, through their imagination, they shared their concerns, their triumphs, and their sorrows. And the whole family took part in the conversation that lasted for more than 10 years. After the birth of the first of Jennet's children, John told Andrew that she was "living in great hopes of her son being heir to your inheritance . . . You made this promise & she will make you keep it."[73] At the age of eight, young David was proud of the gold piece that Andrew had sent from home.[74] And when Andrew's brother, young John, wrote his first letter (and apologized for his spelling), it was sent to Andrew with the hope, wrote John, "that you are intending to pay us a visit sure that would be a hapy meting."[75] This was a world that offered all its participants emotional support—and a continuing sense of security. And for John Gemmill and his family, it provided a means of remaining part of the larger community of the extended family and friends at home in Scotland while they helped to create a new community abroad.

Frances Stewart, Mary Gapper O'Brien, and such women as Catharine Parr Traill and Susanna Moodie too maintained a regular transatlantic correspondence with family and friends in Britain. For Mary, like a young Harriet Pengelly, the arrival of letters and packages from home were a delightful treat, particularly after she had decided to marry Edward O'Brien and remain in the colony.[76] As she explained to her sister Lucy in England in 1832, "The real event of importance which glads the day is the arrival of letters."[77] [. . .] Even letters with bad news were welcomed. Mary "fretted" when letters did not arrive, and when they did they were cherished and often reread time and again.[78] In the summer of 1836, just after the birth of her third child, she wrote in her journal, "A letter from Lucy arrived a few hours after my baby & I am not very sure which was the more welcome."[79]

For women and men, both the newly arrived in the colony and those who had become well settled, letters were part of a sustained transatlantic conversation. As the Peterborough area resident Isabelle Brownlie wrote to her brother at home in a lengthy letter, "But I will tire you with my talk for I think I am talking to you but I dought I will never have the pleasure to do but if we never meet in this world I hope we will meet in the happier one."[80] Until that day, the very act of writing allowed one to enter the familiar world of family and friends. Although one might be replying to news that was months old or renewing contact after a lengthy silence, the transatlantic correspondence nearly always had a sense of immediacy. For Isabelle, as for Mary O'Brien and thousands of others, this imaginary world was as real and present as the physical world in which they now lived.

For many, the continuing connection to home was reinforced by unfinished business or family obligations. John Gemmill seems to have expected Andrew, as the eldest son, to assume some responsibilities for the two sisters who were still in Scotland.[81] John also gave Andrew authority to deal with various financial matters on his behalf. In October 1824, for example, he gave his son power of attorney to settle Ann's father's estate on the family's behalf. [. . .] Three years later, Andrew was again given authority, this time to settle a debt claimed by a former neighbour.[82] Throughout the years, John offered Andrew advice on how he might proceed, but it is clear that he had confidence in his son. Five years after the affair of the will had begun, he told Andrew, "You have at least got the better of your Uncle," and expressed his satisfaction that the estate was finally settled.[83]

Isaac Wilson, a settler in Upper Canada, too relied on his younger brother Jonathan to represent his interests at home. Isaac and Jonathan maintained a regular correspondence from the time of Isaac's arrival in the colony in 1811 until his death in 1838.[84] Like many other emigrant settlers, Isaac does not seem to have written letters per se, although Jonathan apparently did. Instead, Isaac sent home an annual or semi-annual journal that was filled with details about the landscape and local politics and described his health, his work establishing his farm, and gave news of his neighbours; and, after his sister and family arrived in 1819, their news too. In 1811 Isaac was not sure that he intended to remain in the colony. The coming of war in 1812 "confounded" his plans to travel and

see something of America; it also permanently interrupted Jonathan's plan to join him in Upper Canada.[85] Isaac made a brief visit home in 1814 to settle some affairs after his father's death in 1812 and undoubtedly to see his mother. He was restless, however, and he returned to his farm outside York a year later, explaining to his brother, "I have fixed myself here for some time to come if not for life."[86] Even so, for the next 20 years, Isaac still considered himself very much part of the old household and community. He kept up to date with "the state of affairs at home"[87] from Jonathan's letters, from newspapers Jonathan sent him, and from the first-hand reports of newly arrived emigrants or travellers who occasionally appeared with letters or packages. He also periodically offered advice to his brother about how to manage various family affairs.[88]

[. . .]

The tangible bonds of family obligations and entitlements bound many emigrants to Britain long after they had begun to settle into their new homes. Only a relative few, however, would have had an inheritance to collect or were entitled to the proceeds from an ongoing business interest. Yet sons and daughters, sisters and brothers, parents and children often continued to feel a sense of responsibility for kin—especially for their parents—on the other side of the Atlantic. Shortly after Isaac Wilson returned from his visit home, he wrote to his brother saying, "I hope my mother and you are living agreeably together in the way I left you. You must indulge her as much as you can to preserve peace among you."[89] Mother and son obviously did not live together for long. In 1824 Mrs Wilson's house was broken into. After expressing his sorrow at the damage, Isaac wrote, "It is gratifying to me to hear that things are taken care of," and he thanked his brother for his efforts.[90] Three years later, Isaac commented, "I am sorry to hear my Mother has not her health so well as usual. I think it would be better for her to try to live along with Ann or somebody than to live any longer by herself, so that she could be taken care of in case of sickness."[91] Divided by the Atlantic, there was little that Isaac could do directly for his mother, however, except provide advice and encouragement to her and his brother.

When all the children had left home, the situation could become even more complicated and worrying. For some, the problem was resolved when their parents decided to join them in America. A number of letters from Upper Canada urged parents to come, offering to send them "some assistance" for the passage.[92] Others asked friends or relations still in Britain to ensure that Mother or Father was settled and healthy. Two Petworth emigrants, for example, George and Mary Boxall, asked friends to "pray leave" their "poor mother at Henly, a sovereign" before they left.[93]

Emotional and financial support flowed both ways. John Scott's first letter to his uncle Andrew Redford was prompted by the loan of 50 pounds received from Andrew and "other kind friends."[94] Mary O'Brien periodically received monetary gifts from Aunt Sophie, for which she was always most grateful.[95] And for the first few years in the Belleville area, Fanny and William Hutton relied on funds they received from his parents to offset their growing debts. Although Fanny was a hesitant and apparently infrequent correspondent, she explained in a lengthy letter to "Dear Mrs Hutton" (as the letter began) the specific circumstances that had given rise to one particular request for assistance in this "time of trouble".[96] The details of the problems concluded with a plea for help: "The present exigency of our circumstances had prompted me to through ourselves on your kindness." If the immediate family could not lend them the "sum asked by William," she said, or "if you take a different view of our affairs from us," then she and William "would be glad" of "any suggestions which may at any time strike any of you as useful or necessary to us."[97]

Although most new arrivals could not expect financial assistance, a number did look forward to receiving parcels from family and friends at home. Isaac Wilson was "much obliged" to his brother for sending local newspapers, and he offered, "If you would like to have a newspaper from York, I could send you one."[98] Isaac also often received parcels from his brother that had been brought by recently arrived emigrants. "I believe I received everything safe," he wrote to Jonathan in 1822. "Both newspapers, one pair of good stockings, and the spectacles I find very useful."[99] Fanny Hutton, John and Anne Langton, and Mary O'Brien were delighted when packages arrived containing cloth, books, and clothing that were often difficult to find in Upper Canada. Often as important were small tokens or presents from family and friends at home. David Gemmill's new watch, Anne Langton's pictures drawn by her brother, and other mementos became treasured possessions. They were physical representations that the recipient was not forgotten;[100] they reinforced the emotional ties to home, and they helped keep alive the images of family and friends and the landscape of their youth.

Six years after he left home, John Scott wrote to his cousin, "My heart still warms when I think on many localities in my native land I used to frequent and the friends and acquaintances I have left behind—tho' I have forgotten the names of many persons and many places, with the Poet I can still exclaim—'yet he behold her with the eyes of spirit—He sees the form which he no more shall meet—She like a passionate thought is come and gone—while at his feet the bright well bubbles on.'"[101] John Scott was certainly not the only emigrant who wrote home with vivid images in his mind. As one of his brothers wrote, "You can scarcely form any idea of a person's feeling and Emotion who has been absent from his native country so long as I have been." He explained, "Time and distance gives a sort of enchantment, a melancholy pleasure which words are quite unable to express."[102] For the two brothers, even after years away, the landscape of Scotland continued to capture their imagination and give them a connection to home. In his letters, Archibald Scott remembered walking to school with friends past local landmarks and wondered what had happened to his old schoolmaster. This was the place, he wrote, where he was born and spent his childhood: "It seems as I was then completely happy."[103]

Such racking homesickness was not shared by all in the family. John explained to his cousin in 1844 that most of his brothers and sisters, who were all younger than he, did not "care much about seeing Scotland again." Of course, his parents could "never forget old friends, old faces and bygone times in Scotland," but after 10 years in the colony he and his siblings were "all naturalized now". John continued, "I am now become part Dutchman, part Canadian and part everything else for I live among all kinds of people and feel at home with them all."[104] A year later, he commented that he understood when many of his acquaintances who had gone home for a visit had thankfully returned "home" to Upper Canada. "They could nor remain in the Old Country" he explained, because they were "so accustomed to American habits." John felt the same and declared, "We are now, of course, all Canadians."[105]

[. . .]

Even after years away, for the Scott children and cousins living in Upper Canada, letters and newspapers from home were tangible evidence that they had not been forgotten. As William Knox wrote to his cousin in 1843, "I was beginning to think you had forgotten me altogether as it was such a very long time since I had received a Letter from Hermiston [the home farm]. I can assure you nothing for this long time gave me more pleasure than your Letter which I received last Month."[106] Letters and newspapers evoked images of home. Emigrant settlers knew that

this was often an imaginary world. But they maintained the sense of a shared landscape and a shared past with those they had left behind. Although relationships were often idealized and landscapes unchanging, this increasingly imaginary world was very real in many emigrant settlers' minds. As they wrote home, they could see the faces and places of those they wrote to; they could smell the teapot brewing on the hearth and could hear the sounds of cattle or sheep, or the marketplace. This provided much of the foundation for the conversational nature of emigrant letters and the immediacy of their tone. Many, like John Scott, "fondly yet wish again to see my old Fetherlaw and my friends there."[107] In the meantime, letters would have to suffice.

[. . .]

For those who remained behind, maintaining the transatlantic community may well have been more difficult, particularly if emigrant settlers did not have the means or desire to return for a visit. But maintain it many did, and in the process they vicariously became part of the emigrants' world. For those waiting for letters from home and then responding often months and sometimes years later, the post was a vital part of their new lives. Maintaining contact over a great distance was not easy. The vagaries of the mail complicated the problems created by mobile populations and accidents, illness, or even death that abruptly ended such connections. Many emigrants, either by choice or by chance, lost touch with family at home. Many others were determined not to. Even those who did not write sent and received "reports" to and from family and friends at home. The arrival of visitors from the other side of the Atlantic certainly strengthened these long-distance relationships; for most, however, their continuing ties to home depended on the vital links of letters.

Transatlantic correspondence was an integral part of the emigrants' world. In the early years, it provided a sense of place and reassurance as they negotiated their way through a strange land. Many wrote home, either regularly or after years of silence, to renew bonds of affection. Sending and receiving letters also affirmed their identity as fathers, mothers, sisters, brothers, and cousins—in short, as part of a familial network that was rooted not in time and place but in relationships of affection and obligation. In many ways, this part of the emigrants world rested on imagined landscapes, faces, and relationships. For the Gemmills, the Scotts, the Wilson brothers, and the thousands of others both at home and away, this transatlantic web of kin and community was central to their lives.

NOTES

1. Pengelly Family Papers, Harriet Pengelly Diary, 27 May 1835, Trent University Archives (TUA), 70–001/1/4.
2. Ibid., 26 May 1835.
3. Ibid., 29 May 1835.
4. Ibid., 5 June 1835.
5. Ibid., 8 June 1835.
6. Ibid., 10 June 1835.
7. Ibid., 14 July 1835. See also 26 August 1835, when Harriet wrote: "Received a nice long letter from Sophy . . . very, very happy."
8. Ibid., 14 March, 12 April 1835.
9. Ibid., 6 April, 8 May 1835.
10. Ibid., 26 March, 28 May 1835; also 3 March 1836, when she noted "a very disagreeable day" and that she had written three letters.
11. Harriet Pengelly Diary, 20 August 1835; also 14 August; 5, 10, 12 and 22 September, 1 October 1835.
12. Ibid., 21 August 1835. See also 27 February, 5 March 1836.
13. Ibid., 4 October 1835. See also reference to returning home, 21 July 1835.
14. Ibid., 3 January 1836. See also 16 December and 29 November 1835.
15. Ibid., 1 January 1836.
16. Charlotte Erickson, *Invisible Immigrants* (Ithaca & London: Cornell University Press, 1972) was one of the first historians to gather and analyze nineteenth-century immigrant letters. Not surprisingly, she discovered that most surviving letters were from immigrants of the literate, "middling" ranks of British society. David Fitzpatrick's ground-breaking study, *Oceans of Consolation: Personal Accounts of Irish Migration to Australia* (Ithaca & London: Cornell University Press, 1994), gathers and rests on letters from those who travelled steerage.
17. Harriet Pengelly Diary, 3 August 1835.
18. Journals of George Pashley, 2 or 3 December, Archives of Ontario (AO) MU843.
19. Jane Harrison, *Until Next Year: Letter Writing and the Mails in the Canadas, 1640–1830* (Ottawa: Canadian Postal Museum and the Canadian Museum of Civilization, 1997), 2, notes that in a somewhat earlier period, literacy, at least in Lower Canada, was relatively high. The collection of letters in Wendy Cameron, Mary McDougall Maude, and Sheila Haines, eds., *English Immigrant Voices* (Montreal and Kingston: McGill-Queen's University Press, 2000), attests to this in the Upper Canadian situation; Cameron notes that among the Petworth emigrants, about one-third were literate (ibid., xxvii–ix).
20. In addition to those in *Voices*, see letter of John Connel, 12 July 1845, National Library of Scotland (NLS), ACC7021. See also journal of George Forbes from Canada to Aberdeenshire, included in letter of 18 July 1845; Forbes's first letter was sent to "Dear Parents" on 23 May 1845 (Forbes Letters, Scottish Record Office [SRO], RH4/80).
21. William Knox to Andrew Redford, 28 October 1838, Redford Papers, SRO, GD1/815/15.
22. See, for example, the letter of Rebecca Longhurst to Mrs Weller (mother), 4 October 1832, no. 31, *Voices*, 61.
23. See letter of Simeon Titmouse to — Jackson, 11 September 1832, no. 23, *Voices*, 47.
24. William Hewitt to father and mother, William and Elizabeth Hewitt, 6 July 1836, no. 108, *Voices*, 206. See also Henry Smart to James Napper, 5 November 1832, no. 44, *Voices*, 77.
25. 5 August 1832, no. 16, *Voices*, 33.
26. This is the salutation for the letter of Richard Neal, 20 July 1832, no. 5, *Voices*, 16.

27. Letter to John Colquhoun, 10 December 1823, "Emigrant Letters," SRO, GD1/814/5. See also John Barnes to his father, 1 January 1837, no. 126, *Voices*, 246–50, which included specific directions on how and to whom it was to be distributed; also letter of Jesse Penfeld to Mr and Mrs Hill, 1 January 1833, no. 50, *Voices*, 94.

28. Upton to mother, 19 September 1832, no. 27, *Voices*, 52–3.

29. William Phillips to Mrs Newall, 5 August 1832, no. 13, *Voices*, 30.

30. Simeon Titmouse to — Jackson, 11 September 1832, no. 23, *Voices*, 48.

31. John Luff to Aunt Foster, 29 July 1832, no. 11, *Voices*, 25–6.

32. References to this appear in almost all letters or journals. See, for example, letter of Richard Neal to William and Abigail Neal, 18 November 1832, no. 46, *Voices*, 79, which stated, "I have sent you a letter in July; but I have not had any answer yet: but Hope you will send me one soon." See also Edward and Hannah Bristow letter to brother, 20 July 1833, no. 82, *Voices*, 138.

33. See chapters 1 and 4 above and Elizabeth Jane Errington, *Wives and Mothers, School Mistresses and Scullery Maids* (Kingston & Montreal: McGill-Queen's University Press, 1995), chap. 3, for discussion of desertion within the colony.

34. Gemmill Family Papers, John Gemmill to Andrew Gemmill, 25 June 1823, SRO, TD293.

35. Ibid., 6 December 1826. See also a later letter, 2 May 1828, asking Andrew to find the brother of William Miller, who wanted him to write because he was "anxious".

36. John Gemmill to Andrew Gemmill, 6 August 1827.

37. Ibid., 17 September 1828.

38. See Thomas Adsett to his father, 25 June 1833, no. 71, *Voices*, 123, which ended: "Wrote by James Rapson: his wife and family are all well." Also Elizabeth Wackford to Mrs Sarah Green, 25 June 1833, no. 71, Voices, 124–5. See discussion in *Voices*, xix. The problems of literacy went both ways. For example, Charles Johnston wrote to his former employer, Thomas Tryon, Esq., announcing his arrival and asking Tryon to pass on news to family members; he also asked Tryon to

let him know how his wife's parents were, since they could not write; and he sent on a message to his brother that if he intended to emigrate, he should write and Johnston would "remain here till he comes" (Tryon of Bulwick Collection, Northamptonshire Record Office [NRO], TB869).

39. For example, his August 1836 letter concluded, "John Heather from Petworth wishes you to call at Botting's, to know how his sister is at Redhill: he is well" (James Rapson letter, 30 August 1836, no. 115, *Voices*, 214). See also Rapson letters nos. 2, 12, 38, 76, in *Voices*, and letters of his in-laws, the Tribes, Henry and Charlotte Tribe (12 February 1833, no. 54, *Voices*, 102). The annotations in the published letters of the Sussex emigrants suggest that sometimes letters were communal undertakings, with two or three people writing individual notes to different recipients, well aware that all would read their news (*Letters from Sussex Emigrants* [Chichester, 1837], 37–41).

40. *Chronicle and Gazette*, 11 July 1835. A reward was also offered for information about James Honey, a tailor—either his current place of residence or a certificate attesting to his death (ibid., 19 August 1835).

41. *Farmer's Journal*, 13 May 1829. See also *Kingston Gazette*, 25 August 1818, looking for Alexander Langton, who had last been heard of in 1799 or 1800; *Kingston Chronicle*, 3 August 1819, looking for John Spence; *Kingston Chronicle*, 13 April 1821, looking for Donald Campbell, originally of Argyleshire, by agent in York.

42. *Kingston Chronicle*, 13 June 1829. See also *Cobourg Star*, 30 August 1843, Thomas Eyre of Cobourg and Richard Dingley, Esq., of Launceston, England, were looking for Edmund Turner Colwell, from Devon, who would learn something to his advantage.

43. See, for example, *Kingston Chronicle*, 4 July 1823, looking for William Holliday, native of Yorkshire; *Christian Guardian*, 19 April 1837, looking for "Edward, the son of Anthony and Sarah Brown" of London, who was entitled to £2000 from the estate of his maternal uncle: the solicitors were looking for him. Also *Cobourg Star*, 2 October 1844, Messrs Trehern & White, solicitors, in London were

looking for John Blomfield, who had left home nine years before.

44. See discussion in *Voices*, xxxiii–xxxv.

45. See Harrison, *Until Next Year*, 125–7. David Gerber notes in *Authors of Their Lives* (New York: New York University Press, 2006) that sending letters overseas could be expensive and required planning and some knowledge of the postal system. For an intriguing discussion of "Using the Postal Service," see ibid., chap. 4.

46. John Gemmill to "Dear Wife and Family," 2 March 1822, with annotations that it was received on 23 November 1822, SRO, TD293.

47. Ibid., John to Andrew, 19 September 1823.

48. Isaac Wilson, Dear brother, 24 June 1821, Isaac Wilson Diaries.

49. Harriet Pengelly Diary, 5 September 1835, Pengelly Family Papers. In this particular sequence, Harriet became increasingly anxious, because she continued to check the mails (10 September, 12 September, 22 September, 1 October), but the long-awaited letters did not arrive until 3 October 1835. She noted similar delays and frustrations in later months.

50. Mary O'Brien Journals, 1 January 1836, AO.

51. See, for example, letters to Andrew of 1 June and 17 September 1823, SRO, TD293/1.

52. John Gemmill to Andrew, 21 June 1823.

53. Dear Brother, 24 June 1821, Isaac Wilson Diaries.

54. Wilson noted in a letter to his brother, 13 December 1834, Isaac Wilson Diaries, that he intended to send deeds home by private conveyance for exactly this reason.

55. Journals of George Pashley, February 1834, 16.

56. See Wilson letter to his brother, 26 April 1832, Isaac Wilson Diaries.

57. John Gemmill to Andrew, 21 June 1823.

58. Ibid., 21 November 1825.

59. Ibid., 21 May 1823.

60. Ibid., 21 June 1823.

61. Ibid., 8 June 1829.

62. Ibid., 17 September 1823.

63. Ibid., 6 December 1826.

64. In a remarkable passage, John passed on remarks from Jennet: "She has not got the imitation of that Black Man you sent her yet," ibid.

65. Andrew to Mother and Father, 2 October 1824, ibid.

66. Ibid., John to Andrew, 30 April 1824.

67. Ibid., 8 November 1824.

68. Ibid., 21 November 1825. This image of the kettle was also invoked by John and Caroline Dearling to Brothers and Sisters (15 July 1838, no. 134, *Voices*, 276–7).

69. Ibid., John Gemmill to Andrew Gemmill, 25 September 1832.

70. Ibid., 8 November 1824.

71. Ibid., 24 November 1829. Five years earlier, John had replied to what appears to have been a thoughtful letter from Andrew: "I take you kind advice . . . and I hope you will daily and hourly take to yourself the uncertainty of time and the precarious nature of all its enjoyments ought never to be forgot and our preparation for our eternal state ought to be our daily or hourly our constant study and employ as the basis of our Eternal felicity" (4 October 1824).

72. Ibid., 24 November 1829.

73. Ibid., 6 December 1826.

74. Ibid., 6 August 1827.

75. Ibid., 25 September 1832.

76. See Errington, *Wives and Mothers*, chap. 1, for an account of Mary making her decision.

77. Mary O'Brien Journals, AO, 13 February 1832.

78. Ibid., 15 April 1830, 14 February 1832, 13 July 1836.

79. Ibid., 25 July 1836.

80. The Miller Letters, TUA, B–70–1001, 24 March 1845.

81. See, among others, John Gemmill to Andrew, letters of 11 May and 21 June 1823, John Gemmill Family Papers, SRO.

82. Ibid., 6 August 1827.

83. Ibid., 8 June 1829.

84. Isaac Wilson Diaries. Isaac and his father had arrived in the colony in mid-1811. His father apparently returned home and John stayed. See 21 June and 19 November 1811.

85. Ibid., mentioned in letter of 24 May 1815.

86. Ibid., 30 August 1815. The letters/journal included considerable detail about the War of 1812, Wilson's sympathy with the Reformers in the 1830s, and a host of other political, social, and economic events in the colony.

87. See Isaac Wilson Diaries, 24 June 1817, 7 September 1819, and 15 November 1830.

88. See ibid., 24 June 1817 and 13 July 1822.

89. Isaac Wilson Diaries, 20 August 1815.

90. Ibid., 27 April 1824.

91. Ibid., 31 March 1827.

92. See, for example, letter of William Upton to his mother, 16 September 1832, no. 27, *Voices*, 53. See also Ann Thomas to Father, 15 October 1832, no. 37, *Voices*, 68–9; Thomas Adsett to Rev. Robert Bidsall, 21 December 1832, no. 49, *Voices*, 87–8. Charles Moore, on the other hand, in a letter to his father (c June 1833, no. 69, 110–11), told his father not to come: "It is not fit for old people."

93. George and Mary Boxall and William Tilly to family, 16 September 1832, no. 25, *Voices*, 50. See also George and Anna Hills to Father, Mother, Brother, and Sister, 8 March 1833, no. 63, *Voices*, 108–9, who "hoped" that family members would "ever be kind" to mother and father now living with them. John and Caroline Dearling to brother and sister, 15 July 1838, no. 134, ibid., 276–7.

94. Redford Papers, John Scott to Andrew Redford, 29 September 1835.

95. Mary O'Brien Journal, 20 June 1830 and 24 September 1835.

96. *Hutton of Hastings*, ed. Boyce, 2 July 1837, 57.

97. Ibid., 61.

98. Isaac Wilson Diaries, 28 October 1828. Newspapers were sent on 26 July 1830. In the early 1820s there were apparently problems having newspapers forwarded from Montreal (9 September 1820).

99. Ibid., 13 July 1822. See also 24 June 1821 and package that arrived with emigrant William Brown, 26 July 1830.

100. See, for example, Redford Papers, letter of Isabel Scott to her aunt Mrs Redford, 16 April 1840.

101. Ibid., John Scott to George Redford, 18 September 1840.

102. Ibid., undated letter, Archibald to his cousin.

103. Ibid.

104. Ibid., John Scott to cousin, October 1844.

105. Ibid., John Scott to Uncle Andrew Redford, 12 November 1845.

106. Ibid., William Knox to cousin, John Redford, 24 April 1843.

107. Ibid., John Scott to uncle Andrew Redford, 12 November 1845.

4 From Scott See, "'An Unprecedented Influx': Nativism and Irish Famine Immigration to Canada," *American Review of Canadian Studies* 30, 4 (2000): 429–53. © ACSUS, reprinted by permission of Taylor & Francis Ltd, www.tandfonline.com on behalf of ACSUS.

During the dreadful famine summer of 1847, as thousands of indigent Irish streamed from floating "coffin ships" to meet their fate in the cities and countryside of British North America, a growing number of people vociferously expressed fears that had been simmering for well over a decade. Disquieted members of Canada's House of Assembly, for example, unanimously agreed to address Queen Victoria with their "apprehensions" concerning the "unprecedented influx of Emigrants from Great Britain and Ireland in a state of destitution, starvation, and disease, unparalleled in the history of this province."[1] Genuine concern for the condition of the immigrants was swiftly tempered, and then virtually disappeared, as native-born and immigrant Protestants considered the possible ramifications that the accelerated introduction of large numbers of Irish Catholics would have on British North American society. Within a decade, the same Toronto newspaper that had once greeted the famine migration with humanitarian appeals for aid had hardened its opinion into a nativist resolve to bar further Irish-Catholic emigration entirely. In response to news from the United States that thousands of "unenlightened and bigoted Romanists" might slip northward across the border, the *Globe* predicted "a great calamity, dangerous to our civil and religious liberty, a calamity which every true patriot, Protestant as well as Roman Catholic, should endeavour, by all means in his power, to avert."[2]

The first clear episode of nativism—the emphatic rejection of immigrants because of their foreign identification—in pre-Confederation Canadian history was triggered by the events of the late 1840s. Strikingly, this response to the famine Irish, which was fuelled by a mixture of Protestant anxiety over the global spread of Roman Catholicism and an antipathy to Celtic peoples, has to date received little historiographical attention.[3] Yet the Canadian experience coincided with nativism in the United States, a more widely recognized phenomenon that became an integral component of nationalism and political-party formation. Canada's nativism may even have matched America's in fervour during the mid-nineteenth century, although its manifestations were certainly different.

This study seeks to identify and explain the nativist response to the famine Irish who made their way to Canada. British North American nativism was complex and varied, depending on economic, demographic, and social themes in various provinces, yet its disparate elements may be characterized by several interrelated themes. The first might be understood as a critical mass dynamic, which suggests that a dramatic number of Irish-Catholic immigrants rapidly surpassed an acceptable "threshold" when they settled among or near native-born and immigrant Protestants. The international context of anti-Catholicism, a pervasive impulse in the Western world of the nineteenth century, represents another basic principle at work. The third addresses chronology, suggesting a confluence of events as this immigrant cohort altered and was in turn shaped by British North America's political, economic, and social landscapes. Nativism was one of the tremors that rippled across North America as powerful ethnoreligious plates collided in the mid-nineteenth century.

Nativism has been a recurrent social and political force in the last two centuries of American history. John Higham, who concentrated his energies on American movements, defined nativism as the "intense opposition to an internal minority on the ground of its foreign . . . connections," or a "defensive type of nationalism." Though Higham cautioned that the word "nativism," of nineteenth-century derivation, over time assumed

pejorative connotations, his definition provides a durable intellectual device for analyzing a host population's reaction to immigrants.[4] [. . .]

In Canada, nativism is found in Indigenous organizations, such as the Protestant Protective Association, and imported ones, such as Ireland's ultraloyal and zealously Protestant Orange Order. Loyalty to the British Empire constituted a core element of Canadian nativism. The following argument challenges the notion that Canadian nativism was dramatically weaker than the American version in the nineteenth century.[5]

With some notable exceptions, including Native peoples, blacks, and pockets of European immigrants, the British North American colonies were relatively homogeneous well into the nineteenth century. Anglo-Saxon and Gallic influences predominated, reflecting the classic British and French "European charter groups" of colonial Canadian history. While revisionist scholars have convincingly demonstrated that a significant number of Irish Catholics were present in Canada before the years of the potato blight, most agree that the Irish famine migrants had a profound and lasting influence, especially in the principal ports of embarkation.[6] In 1847 alone, Canada absorbed approximately 100 000 arrivals, of whom roughly 90 per cent were Roman Catholics. By the time the famine abated and Irish-Catholic immigration dropped precipitously in the early 1850s, tens of thousands of newcomers had landed, ensconced themselves in urban enclaves, and moved into hinterland communities in search of farmland and work.[7]

The Maritime colonies, and New Brunswick in particular, received thousands of famine migrants. The stream of Irish peoples, which had coursed steadily during the 1840s, became floodwaters during the famine years. The 15 000 who arrived in New Brunswick during the peak year of 1847 indicated a seventeen-fold gain over 1843's figure. Immigration rates decreased dramatically after 1848, and by 1855 numbers would once again be on a par with 1843.[8] Saint John, the province's leading port, was poorly prepared to cope with the overwhelming number of immigrants. As was typical of coastal North American cities, a quarantine station in the harbour—Partridge Island—was constructed to serve as a primitive buffer between passengers with communicable diseases and local residents.[9]

Although many Irish used New Brunswick as a temporary depot on their way to the United States, approximately half of those who arrived settled in the ports or hinterland. During the late 1840s, Irish flocked to enclaves in the Saint John region; while those areas already contained some native-born and more established Irish-Protestant immigrants, contemporaries rapidly identified them as bastions of Irish Catholicism.[10] Famine immigrants also sought out towns and larger agrarian communities; many were prompted by an established provincial policy to encourage the interior settlement of badly needed farm labourers and servants who would work for "moderate wages."[11] Their migration patterns can be traced along the major river systems of the St John, the Miramichi, and later the St Croix. Large numbers of immigrants located in Fredericton, the provincial capital, where in 1851 an impressive 45 per cent of the heads of households claimed Irish birth.[12] Along the Miramichi, they settled close to established communities on the tributaries and poorer land that had been passed over by original settlers. The Irish took jobs as wage labourers in lumber mills, they set up tailor shops and clerked, and many pursued their old occupations of farming and agrarian labour.[13]

Nova Scotia's experience with famine immigrants differed in significant ways from its neighbour's. A province born of North American skirmishes in larger French and British imperial conflicts, Nova Scotia had by the nineteenth century a population

that included prominent clusters of Roman Catholics. By 1827 they numbered just over 20 000 of a total population of 95 083, or 21 per cent; by the census of 1851 provincial Roman Catholics had grown to 69 634 of a total population of 257 675, or 27 per cent. While the percentage of Roman Catholics declined by the census of 1871, for the critical years around mid-century the infusion of famine Irish galvanized an anti-Catholic response in the colony.[14] This was particularly true in Halifax, Nova Scotia's major port, which had been recognized since the late eighteenth century as a city with a substantial number of Irish-Catholic residents. By 1837 fully 35 per cent of its population was Catholic; in 1851 the figure had grown to over 42 per cent. About 1200 famine immigrants arrived in 1847, a modest number by North American standards, but the increasing percentage of the city's Catholic population helped to account for growing Protestant intolerance.[15] As the provincial figures did not reflect such a dramatic immigrant surge, Halifax with its commanding Irish-Catholic population became the focal point for nativism in the colony.

Prince Edward Island's population mixture facilitated the introduction of nativist elements in the mid-nineteenth century as well. [. . .] Throughout the 1840s and 1850s, the Island experienced a population growth that surpassed any comparable period in its history. In 1841 the population stood at over 47 000; by 1861 it reached 80 857. The number of foreign-born as a percentage of the Island's total population, for example 30 per cent in 1848, was also substantial during this period. Second only to Scots immigrants, most of whom were Protestants, Irish Catholics migrated to the province around mid-century. Subsequently the Island's rate of growth began a decline that would linger into the next century.[16] Thus the nativist reaction became entrenched when immigrants, notably Irish Catholics, comprised a considerable proportion of Prince Edward Island's population.

The famine immigration's impact on Quebec rivalled or surpassed the drama found in the Maritime colonies, primarily because the St Lawrence River provided direct access to Quebec City and Montreal. Of the roughly 80 000 migrants who arrived in 1847, virtually all were channelled through the two cities.[17] While many of the immigrants pushed inland to Ontario or south to the United States, thousands located in the province. The Irish accounted for almost 44 000 of Quebec's population in 1844; by 1851–52 they had grown to 51 499.

Perhaps most importantly, they settled in great numbers in port communities where their predecessors had established a modest presence before the famine. The bulk of Irish-Catholic males gravitated to unskilled positions in the workforce; for example they comprised a key labour component in the construction of canals from the late 1820s through the 1840s.[18] Quebec City experienced an 800 per cent growth of Irish between 1821 and 1851, but probably the legacy of the famine migration was felt most acutely in Montreal. Irish Catholics represented over 20 per cent of its total population by the early 1860s and, much to the alarm of many Quebeckers, they outnumbered the Protestant Irish, Scots, and English combined.[19] The Irish eked out an existence in squalid areas that became identified with their cultural and religious traditions, such as Griffintown in the city's southwestern section along the riverbanks.[20] While Montreal housed nearly 40 per cent of Quebec's Irish by the early 1860s, substantial numbers were also drawn to smaller cities such as Sherbrooke and Trois-Rivières. Rural settlements attracted the Irish Catholics as well; individuals and families made their way along the river systems to marginal lands in the interior, including the Laurentian valley, the eastern reaches of the Ottawa River, and the Eastern Townships near the American border.[21] While some Irish Catholics undeniably became rural residents, their concentrated and explosive growth in urban locations such as Montreal contributed most to the colony's nativist reaction.

[. . .] Ontario's Irish-Catholic numbers rose dramatically in the 1830s. By 1851, Toronto's Irish Catholics comprised one-quarter of the city's population of 30 775, an increase from one-sixth in 1841; moreover they had grown at a faster rate than the other ethnoreligious groups in the prior decade. The city initially absorbed over 38 000 Irish Catholics in 1847 alone, and in that year over 1000 died in the hastily erected fever sheds along the waterfront in the poorer quarters, one of which was dubbed Cabbagetown.[22] Yet one historian estimates that 35 650 abandoned the area almost immediately. The movement of peoples into the interior was kinetic and unstable; thousands of famine migrants attempted to settle on farms or find rural labour, but a significant proportion of this group returned to cities such as Toronto after they failed to procure land or employment.[23] While Irish Protestants routinely outnumbered Irish Catholics in the city that was known as the "Belfast of North America," the rapid introduction of considerable numbers of destitute Irish Catholics in the late 1840s directly contributed to a nativist response in Ontario that easily matched the fervour that other colonies witnessed.

This process essentially guaranteed that the transformation of Irish Catholics to British North America would be a doubly traumatic experience. In addition to the degradation of poverty and ever-present threat of disease, thrusting agrarian Celtic Catholics into Protestant strongholds led to massive culture shock for the immigrants and kindled a nativist reaction amongst the native-born majority. Irish-Catholic famine immigrants had dispersed throughout British North America in the late 1840s, but most had concentrated in a few urban areas close to native-born residents and more established Protestant immigrants. The combination of their decidedly "foreign" Celtic culture and Roman Catholic beliefs fuelled Canada's first significant nativist response, a phenomenon that will be brought into sharper focus by considering international patterns of anti-Catholic behaviour.

Religion placed a heavy stamp on nineteenth-century peoples; it often proved a more compelling determinant of an individual's social, economic, and political status than did secular considerations. In Canada, as was the case in Europe and the United States, religious ardour cannot be understated as an important cultural and social backdrop for the Victorian age.[24] Religious beliefs often became intensified in the rigorous urban and backwoods environments of the Canadas and the Maritime colonies, where they provided a comforting refuge.[25] Religious orientation served as a keystone for both self and community identification; for the Catholic and Protestant immigrants in North America, arguably it comprised the most conspicuous piece of "cultural baggage" that people transported to the new world.[26] The sheer intensity of religious convictions created a fertile ground for denominational conflict between Protestants and Catholics. Countless "No Popery" tracts, to cite only one example, issued forth from busy Protestant-owned presses. As the century progressed, these diatribes against the Roman Catholic Church and its adherents became intricately interwoven with racially based attacks on the Celtic Irish—the famine migration's legacy.[27]

The combination spawned one of the most powerful incentives for the nativist response in British North America, as the Irish diaspora did in Britain, the United States, and various British colonies.[28] While anti-Catholicism in Canada clearly exhibited a "derivative character," drawing sustenance from European doctrines and an international literature, it also found nourishment in local stimuli. The news of raging Papal controversies across the Atlantic, carried by the mail boats and transcribed by a robust press, touched British North America with an unmistakable poignancy. These included the "Papal Aggression" controversy, triggered by a strengthening of England's Catholic hierarchy, the authoritarian nature of the Roman Catholic church, in particular the Pope's purported authority in dictating temporal matters such as politics, pseudo-theoretical arguments about the numerous theological flaws of Catholic practices, and the perception that Catholic adherents were credulous servants who performed the bidding of priests, bishops, and ultimately the Pope.[29] Closer to home, alarmed Protestants thought of Irish Catholics as a fifth column of zealous warriors who were bent on destroying the very tenets of British North American self-identity: loyalty to the Empire and Protestantism.[30]

[. . .]

By the advent of famine migration, Canadian anti-Catholicism coursed through well-established channels. Nativism crystallized as Irish Catholics poured into the British North American colonies, giving Protestant defenders a sense of urgency that had been missing before mid-century. For example, the prolific Thomas Chandler Haliburton pointedly targeted the Irish Catholics, who were "emigrating in masses," in a classic nativist statement: Romanism "thought that if it could break down the civil power, reduce all ranks to a common level, and gradually weaken any constitutional connection between the several governments and Protestantism, it would recruit its forces from the population of its adversaries, overthrow them in succession, or perhaps overwhelm them all together."[31] Myriad editors, politicians, and Protestant votaries echoed Haliburton's points about Romanism and its purported assault on democracy.[32]

Perhaps the nativist response achieved its greatest clarity in the Maritime colonies and

Ontario, where Protestant denominations enjoyed majority status. Inflated rhetoric flourished, often couched in the apocalyptic language of Papal conspiracies. One author succinctly captured the drama of the moment: "It is high time, my fellow Protestants, for us to assume in our own defence, and in behalf of our Catholic fellow subjects, a position of firm and fearless antagonism to the encroachments of the Papacy."[33] A New Brunswick newspaper noted, "perhaps a final conflict is at hand between Protestant truth and Popery leagued with Infidelity."[34] According to nativists, Catholics lied, cheated, and even murdered without remorse, secure in the knowledge that they would receive temporal forgiveness from corrupt priests. Ultimately, the conspiratorial theme became the dominant characteristic of nativist dogma in mid-nineteenth-century Canada. Fear of "the very worst kind of [Popery], *Irish* Popery," the visible spread of Catholic churches, and a general paranoia that the famine immigration signalled Catholic ascendancy, all contributed to the nativists' arsenal.[35]

Racial dogma underpinned the nativist response to the famine immigrants as well. Irish Catholics were variously characterized as the "ignorant masses" and "untameable barbarians." They comprised the quintessential "lower orders," their civility suspect because they appeared "unrestrained by any code of morals."[36] Catholics were consistently portrayed as easily duped, whereby the church hierarchy might perpetuate its "gross superstitions" or "old wives tales," and poison the minds of the "poor simple, priest-ridden" Catholic parishioners.[37] Moreover, some Protestants linked intemperance to Irish-Catholic behaviour.[38] Variations of that contention, often presented in editorials, characterized Irish Catholics as being woefully enamoured with intoxicating beverages.[39] The anti-Catholic barrage touched the minds and hearts of many individuals who naturally sought out organizations, such as the Orange Order, that would most effectively muster the Protestant vote and construct formidable defensive barriers.

Evidence abounds of the Protestants' stiffening resolve. The editorial content of Joseph Howe's *Nova Scotian* changed dramatically in the wake of the famine migration and increased confrontations between Catholics and Protestants. Whereas Howe had actively sought the readership and political support of Catholics in the years before mid-century, by the 1850s his editorials took on decidedly nativist overtones. In a characteristic attempt to draw connections between the corporate powers of the Catholic Church and Celtic proclivities, he observed: "Of the Irish Nation, or of the Irishmen in Nova Scotia, no man ever heard me breathe an ungenerous sentiment. But I am not blind to the national characteristics and foibles. I know that no people on the face of the earth have suffered more from gross misleading. Irish history teems with proofs of this assertion, and there is scarcely a City on this continent where men with some fluency, and little judgment, have not embroiled the emigrant with the resident population."[40]

[. . .]

While nativists chose from a seemingly inexhaustible supply of illustrations to rationalize their fears of Irish-Catholic encroachment, the fact that the famine immigrants settled for a time amongst the Protestant host society provided an essential rationale for Canadian nativism. A prime seed for its genesis sprouted in this atmosphere of alarm, created by the perception that destitute Irish Catholics were inundating the colonies in mid-century. The anti-Catholic reaction was most virulent in those areas that, with the possible exception of Quebec, received the greatest number of immigrants. Tensions between natives and immigrants in Quebec were tempered by the fact that virtually all of the province's French Canadians were practising Catholics. As one nineteenth-century historian observed, the "Catholic city" of Montreal was perhaps the most attractive location in Quebec for Irish Catholics to settle.[41] Quebec's case was somewhat unique, for as a general rule anti-Catholic diatribes and discord were spawned most frequently by the propinquity of Irish famine immigrants and Protestants.

Nativism was also indelibly shaped by events that coincided around mid-century. The entrenchment of anti-Catholics in the political arena, the tensions associated with struggling colonial economies, and the emergence of social institutions designed to channel and articulate Protestant goals, all provided form and substance to nativist forces. Perhaps these dynamics were most clearly signalled by the gradual removal of official anti-Catholic measures before mid-century. By 1830, in the wake of Britain's Roman Catholic emancipation measures, all of the British North American colonies had opened the franchise to adult Roman Catholic males.[42] While political tensions existed between Protestants and Catholics before the famine, they would become more widespread and varied after the 1840s.[43]

In all the colonies, the spectre of large numbers of potential Irish-Catholic voters strengthened the bonds between Protestants and political parties, especially the Conservatives, while fraternal organizations such as the Orange Order often erected the bridge-work between the two. To many British North Americans, the choice between Protestant political unity and Catholic tyranny was starkly clear. Even some Liberals and Reformers shared this belief, including one politician who succinctly warned, "so long as the Protestants of this country are divided, it must be ruled by a Catholic minority."[44]

Substantial political tensions between Protestants and Catholics, for example, were clearly etched in Nova Scotia's developing political system. The tenuous coalition that had been struck between Protestant Reformers and Catholics during the 1830s all but disintegrated during the 1850s, as religious issues thoroughly infused provincial politics

with an intensity that has probably not been equalled since. The Catholic political base was varied, shaped by the settlement patterns of Acadians, Irish, and Scots. Protestants, who clearly held majority status, often suppressed their denominational quarrels in order to concentrate their energies on confronting the greater Irish-Catholic peril.[45] Conservative elements, in order to undermine the alliance between Reformers and Catholics, promulgated the notion that Irish famine immigrants would have a deleterious social and economic impact on Halifax in particular and the province in general. Many asserted that Irish Catholics were incapable of behaving as loyal citizens of the British Empire.[46] The nascent Protestant Association of Nova Scotia, with ideals quite similar to those long espoused by the Orange Order, and the bitter House of Assembly Debates of 1859 epitomized the political chasm that separated Catholics, especially those of Irish ancestry, from Protestants.[47] In addition, violent episodes, the most important of which was the Gourlay Shanty riot between Scots Presbyterians and Irish Catholics in 1856, magnified political tensions.[48]

Fears of an apparent alliance between Roman Catholics and the Reform Party in Prince Edward Island, under the rubric of tenant reform, provided a touchstone for Protestants who suspected Papal interference. For example, the *Islander*'s editor characterized his pro-Catholic counterparts of the *Vindicator* and *Examiner* as follows: "the proprietors of those papers have a common object, of far greater importance than the settlement of the land question—the attainment by the Roman Catholic Hierarchy of the supreme governing power in this island."[49] Editors encouraged Protestants to take up the "ominous war-cry," and stand "shoulder to shoulder" in a Protestant defence against supposed Roman Catholic incursions. With the party divisions increasingly being defined according to religious affiliation, and with the Catholics abandoning the Conservatives in favour of the Liberals, Protestants were drawn to the Conservatives almost by default. Dire threats of what might happen with the escalating Irish presence at the polls, evidence of the Catholics' "Godless system demanded by their Bishop," and spurious comparisons with Newfoundland's government were promulgated to convince Protestants to defend their interests in political settings.[50] A popular nativist rationale for this course of action was the 1847 election riot in Belfast, the Island's most dramatic nineteenth-century illustration of ethnic and religious confrontation.[51] In the critical year of famine immigration, it fanned the fears of Protestants who dreaded the thought of politicized Irish Catholics determining the outcome of future elections.[52]

[. . .]

New Brunswick's anti-Catholic experiences mirrored those of the other Maritime provinces. In the wake of the famine migration Orangemen and other fervent Protestants enjoyed an overwhelming political edge over the Irish Catholics, who found themselves contending with innumerable legislative and social obstacles that effectively barred them from provincial and community service.[53] The Orange Order, consisting of both native-born and Irish immigrant Protestants, garnered support to ward off the perceived encroachments of the Irish Catholics during the 1840s.[54] Another impulse to attract Protestant voters to the Tory party yielded a remarkable marriage of interests in provincial assignments, as well as in community-level positions such as magistrates, councillors, bureaucrats, mayors, constables, sheriffs, policemen, judges, and juries.[55]

Another bedrock apprehension for anti-Catholic forces in New Brunswick, as was the case elsewhere, involved the pressing economic competition between native-born and Irish immigrants. The 1840s brought a series of depressions to New Brunswick's crucial timber industry. Irish famine immigrants, arriving during the worst years of economic distress, willingly laboured for wages far below those of the average native-born workers. Patterns of economic nativism, established before the famine, were heightened. As large numbers of Irish Catholics filtered into the colony's depressed cities and towns, unskilled native-born labourers, fearing for their jobs, greeted the penniless immigrants as anathema. The stevedores of Saint John and Portland, the day labourers in Fredericton, and the lumbermen of Carleton County and the Miramichi, all demonstrated antipathy toward the hungry Irish immigrants. This competition played an important role in the growth of nativism. Protestants called for economic segregation; merchants and employers should do business with members of their own religion, they argued. Ultimately, they hoped that ostracism would curtail Irish-Catholic immigration.[56] Thus nativists exploited a traditional fear in labour's rank and file and fashioned it into a devastating salvo in the campaign against Irish Catholics.

In Quebec, the famine immigration created similar impulses among Protestants to concentrate their modest political forces and use economic measures to ward off the perceived onslaught of Irish Catholics. The diaphanous alliance that had existed between French Canadians and Irish Catholics during the 1820s rapidly shredded during the 1830s as greater numbers of Irish caused both the French Canadians and the Protestant minority to feel socially and politically threatened. As "resentment of the Irish gradually replaced the bond of Catholicism," hostile diatribes appeared more regularly in newspapers.[57]

Tensions were perhaps most palpable in urban settings. In the ethnically concentrated environments of Montreal and Quebec City, the major point of contention between Irish Catholics and French Canadians was the establishment of separate Irish parishes. For example, by 1847 St Patrick's Church had opened its doors in Montreal, an emphatic illustration of the growing prominence of Irish Catholics. The expanding number of Irish in the workforce created another nativist fault line. As was the case in other colonies, Irish Catholics often took the most menial, lowest paying, and dangerous jobs. They toiled on canals such as the Lachine and Beauharnois, sweated as stevedores along the docks of Quebec City and Montreal, and laboured in the shipyards that dotted the St Lawrence River.[58] The infusion of large numbers of Irish Catholics exacerbated competition for employment in Quebec, but it clearly did not engender the wide-scale nativism exhibited by its western neighbour. Perhaps, as some historians have argued, the tensions between Irish Catholics and French Canadians were mitigated by the common bonds of religious identification, in spite of the rivalries noted above.[59]

Ontario's political and economic landscapes were also fundamentally transformed by the arrival of the famine Irish, and the province experienced a nativist reaction that more closely mirrored the Maritime colonies. Native responses varied according to the location of Irish-Catholic settlement and socio-political conditions; they ranged from a fear of the spread of communicable diseases to a criticism of the British government's apparently deliberate policy of depositing an unwanted human cargo in the colony.[60] Some of the nativists' concerns were anything but fanciful. For example, the famine Irish all but destroyed the Protestant consensus in several areas, the most conspicuous location being Toronto. As more and more immigrants flooded into the province, a powerful coalition of Protestants—both native-born and immigrant—sought the political and economic means to isolate the Irish Catholics and somehow contain the spread of their religion and culture.[61] One newspaper suggested that the immigrants be transported to the interior as rapidly as possible to avoid "moral contamination" in the cities.[62]

In the hostile climate of nativism, manifested in political, economic, and social assaults, Irish Catholics struggled to survive. They were regularly vilified in the Ontario press, and through the use of tactics that were similar to those employed by their New Brunswick compatriots, Protestants assiduously worked to shut Irish Catholics out of the power structure for most of the century.[63] The Orange Order, an effective vehicle for this process, found its influence burgeoning in the decades around mid-century, its growth coinciding with the famine immigration. As one historian pointed out, despite the fact that the organization was roundly condemned by various British governors because of its vitriolic stance against Irish Catholics, it successfully forged linkages with Tory elements. As late as 1897, Irish Catholics held few municipal, police, and judicial positions in Ontario. These remained overwhelmingly the preserve of Protestants, Conservatives, and Orangemen.[64]

[. . .] Other Ontario skirmishes materialized over a host of socio-political issues. The fronts included election campaigns, the development of Sunday Schools, the use of the Bible in public education, temporal variations on the theme of "No Popery," and a rejection of famine immigrants as being unworthy and unproductive members of society.[65] Throughout all these struggles, Ontario's alarmed Protestants effectively used nativist techniques to protect themselves against the encroachment of "Irish Papists".[66]

Many Canadians believed that their future should be designed according to exacting Protestant, Tory, and British standards in the nineteenth century, and the famine Irish appeared as interlopers of the first magnitude. Political and social organizations sought to corral disparate Protestant elements in an effort to deflect the deleterious effects of Irish-Catholic immigration after the late 1840s; they formalized and legitimized nativism. The Orange Order, especially in Ontario and New Brunswick, the Protestant Alliance in Nova Scotia during the late 1850s, and the Protestant Protective Association of the 1890s, all represented societies that rose to confront the challenge of spreading Irish-Catholic interests.[67] In general, although the process was riddled with imperfections and never achieved complete success, these groups and others sought a lasting coalition between Canada's evolving Conservative parties and Protestants. Anti-Papal rhetoric, evident before the arrival of the famine immigrants, continued for the remainder of the century as "Liberal Catholics" made modest political inroads.[68] It was periodically revitalized by events such as the Red River and North-West rebellions, the separate schools controversy, the Jesuits' Estates Act, and episodes of collective violence, such as those generated by the fiery and charismatic apostate Charles Chiniquy, whose lectures left a trail of disturbances in the post-Confederation years.[69]

British North America experienced a nativist reaction to famine migrants in the mid-nineteenth century that rivalled the better-known American saga. Irish-Catholic males certainly had the opportunity to engage in the political process throughout most of the century, and they aggressively competed for positions in the provincial assemblies and municipalities. Still, it would be decades before they achieved a representational cohort that provided an effective counterweight to their nativist opponents. Linkages clearly took place between Conservative, Protestant, and fraternal forces to impede the perceived encroachments of Catholics in general, and the famine Irish in particular. In light of the various religious struggles in the political sphere, the intense economic competition between native-born and immigrants, the racially charged language that was bandied about in provincial assemblies, pamphlets, and newspaper editorials, the obvious attraction of nativist organizations, and the many confrontations between Protestants and Irish Catholics, Canada's history of nativism deserves closer scrutiny.

NOTES

1. *Globe* (3 July 1847).
2. *Globe* (9 February 1856).
3. Scott W. See, *Riots in New Brunswick: Orange Nativism and Social Violence in the 1840s* (Toronto: University of Toronto Press, 1993); A.J.B. Johnston, "Nativism in Nova Scotia: Anti-Irish Ideology in a Mid-Nineteenth-Century British Colony," in Thomas P. Power, ed., *The Irish in Atlantic Canada 1780–1900* (Fredericton, NB: New Ireland Press, 1991), 23–9.
4. John Higham, *Strangers in the Land: Patterns of American Nativism, 1860–1925*, rev. edn (New Brunswick, NJ: Rutgers University Press, 1988). Higham subjected his own work to a rigorous scrutiny in "Another Look at Nativism," *Catholic Historical Review* 44 (1958): 148–50; and "The Strange Career of Strangers in the Land," *American Jewish History* 76 (1986): 214–26.
5. For examples of the argument that Canada's anti-immigrant reaction was tepid by North American standards, see John White, *Sketches from America* (London: Sampson Low, Son and Marston, 1870), 355; Donald H. Akenson, *Small Differences: Irish Catholics and Irish Protestants, 1815–1922* (Montreal: McGill-Queen's University Press, 1988), 88; and Kerby A. Miller, *Emigrants and Exiles: Ireland and the Irish Exodus to North America* (New York: Oxford University Press, 1985), 276, 323.
6. Donald H. Akenson, "The Historiography of the Irish in the United States of America," in Patrick O'Sullivan, ed., *The Irish World Wide: The Irish in the New Communities* (Leicester: Leicester University Press, 1992), 99–127; Akenson, *Small Differences*; Peter Toner, "The Irish of New Brunswick at Mid Century: The 1851 Census," in Peter Toner, ed., *New Ireland*

Remembered: Historical Essays on the Irish in New Brunswick (Fredericton: New Ireland Press, 1988), 106–32.

7. Cecil J. Houston and William J. Smyth, *Irish Emigration and Canadian Settlement: Patterns, Links, and Letters* (Toronto: University of Toronto Press, 1990), 3; Donald MacKay, *Flight from Famine: The Coming of the Irish to Canada* (Toronto: McClelland and Stewart, 1990), 290–91.

8. Immigration Returns, New Brunswick Blue Books, 1840–1855, National Archives of Canada (NAC); "Report on Trade and Navigation," New Brunswick, *Journal of the House of Assembly*, 1866, Public Archives of New Brunswick (PANB).

9. Note James M. Whalen's description of the general trauma endured by immigrants in "'Allmost as Bad as Ireland': The Experience of the Irish Famine Immigrant in Canada, Saint John, 1847," in Robert O'Driscoll and Lorna Reynolds, eds, *Untold Story: The Irish in Canada*, 2 vols (Toronto: Celtic Arts of Canada, 1988), 155–6. See also W.A. Spray, "'The Difficulties Came Upon Us Like a Thunderbolt': Immigrants and Fever in New Brunswick in 1847," in Power, ed., *Irish in Atlantic Canada*, 101–26.

10. See, *Riots in New Brunswick,* 43–70; T.W. Acheson, *Saint John: The Making of a Colonial Urban Community* (Toronto: University of Toronto Press, 1985), 92–114.

11. Perley to Saunders, 22 April 1846, Correspondence, Immigration Papers, PANB.

12. William A. Spray, "Reception of the Irish in New Brunswick," in Toner, ed., *New Ireland Remembered*, 231.

13. John J. Mannion, *Irish Settlement in Eastern Canada: A Study of Cultural Transfer and Adaptation* (Toronto: University of Toronto Press, 1974), 17–27; William F. Ganong, *A Monograph of the Origins of Settlements in the Province of New Brunswick* (Ottawa: Royal Society of Canada, 1904), 73–9.

14. Census of Nova Scotia, 1851, 1861, 1871; Alexander Monro, *New Brunswick; with a Brief Outline of Nova Scotia, and Prince Edward Island* (Halifax: Richard Nugent, 1855), 319–20; Duncan Campbell, *Nova Scotia in Its Historical, Mercantile and Industrial Relations* (Montreal: John Lovell, 1873), 505; John B. Calkin, *A History and Geography of Nova Scotia* (Halifax: A. & W. Mackinlay, 1878), 88.

15. *Nova Scotian* (19 July 1852); Johnston, "Nativism in Nova Scotia," 26–27; A.J.B. Johnston, "Popery and Progress: Anti-Catholicism in Mid-Nineteenth-Century Nova Scotia," *Dalhousie Review* 64, 1 (1984): 147; Terrence M. Punch, "Irish Halifax: The Immigration Generation, 1815–1859," *Canadian Ethnic Heritage Series* 5 (1981): 6–7.

16. For dramatic evidence of Roman Catholic growth by 1861, see the detailed denominational breakdown by lots, counties, and electoral districts in the *Islander* (5 July 1861). Also note Andrew Hill Clark, *Three Centuries and the Island: A Historical Geography of Settlement and Agriculture in Prince Edward Island, Canada* (Toronto: University of Toronto Press, 1959), 83, 121. Ian Ross Robertson provided a compelling challenge to Clark's figures in "Reform, Literacy, and the Lease: The Prince Edward Island Free Education Act of 1852," *Acadiensis* 20 (1990): 55. Robertson argued that by the 1850s the Island's foreign-born population was in significant decline. Nonetheless, the compressed bulge of Irish-Catholic immigrants during the late 1840s created a population cohort that concerned Protestant elements in the following decades.

17. G.R.C. Keep, "The Irish Adjustment in Montreal," *Canadian Historical Review* 31 (1950): 39–40.

18. Ronald Rudin, *The Forgotten Quebecers: A History of English-Speaking Quebec, 1759–1980* (Quebec: Institute québécois de recherche sur la culture, 1985), 83–7; James M. O'Leary, *History of the Irish Catholics of Quebec: Saint Patrick's Church to the Death of Rev. P. McMnhon* (Quebec: Daily Telegraph, 1895), 9.

19. MacKay, *Flight from Famine,* 321.

20. Robert J. Grace, *The Irish in Quebec: An Introduction to the Historiography* (Quebec: Institute québécois de recherche sur la culture, 1993), 60–70; Herbert B. Ames, *The City Below the Hill* (1897; reprinted, Toronto: University of Toronto Press, 1972).

21. MacKay, *Flight from Famine,* 313–21; Keep, "Irish Adjustment in Montreal," 40–4.

22. Brian P. Clarke, *Piety and Nationalism: Lay Voluntary Associations and the Creation of an Irish-Catholic Community in Toronto, 1850–1895* (Montreal: McGill-Queen's University Press, 1993), 15–17; Michael Cottrell, "St. Patrick's Day Parades in Nineteenth-Century Toronto: A Study of Immigrant Adjustment and Elite Control," *Histoire sociale/Social History* 25 (1992): 61.

23. Kenneth Duncan, "Irish Famine Immigration and the Social Structure of Canada West," *Canadian Review of Sociology and Anthropology* 2 (1965): 23.

24. W.L. Morton, "Victorian Canada," in W.L. Morton, ed., *The Shield of Achilles: Aspects of Canada in the Victorian Age* (Toronto: McClelland and Stewart, 1968), 314–16; Arthur R.M. Lower, *Canadians in the Making: A Social History of Canada* (Toronto: Longmans, Green and Co., 1958), 202; William Baker, "The Irish Connection," *Acadiensis* 12 (1983): 128.

25. William H. Elgee, *The Social Teachings of the Canadian Churches* (Toronto: Ryerson Press, 1964).

26. Carl Wittke, *The Irish in America* (Baton Rouge: Louisiana State University Press, 1956), 10.

27. For useful assessments of this dynamic in Britain, see E.R. Norman, ed., *Anti-Catholicism in Victorian England* (London: George Allen and Unwin, 1968); and L.P. Curtis, *Anglo-Saxons and Celts, a Study of Anti-Irish Prejudice in Victorian England* (Bridgeport, CT: Conference on British Studies, 1968).

28. The literature on the migration of Irish in the nineteenth century is extensive. For useful collections of essays on this subject, see *The Irish World Wide* series edited by Patrick O'Sullivan, especially *The Meaning of the Famine* (London: Leicester University Press, 1997). See also Donald H. Akenson, *The Irish Diaspora: A Primer* (Streetsville, ON: P.D. Meany, 1993). The American experience is explored in Lawrence J. McCaffrey, *The Irish Catholic Diaspora in America* (Washington, DC: The Catholic University of America Press, 1997); and Arthur Gribben, ed., *The Great Famine and the Irish Diaspora in America* (Amherst: University of Massachusetts Press, 1999). For works on the Irish in the British Empire, see Patrick O'Farrell, *The Irish in Australia* (Sydney: New South Wales University Press, 1993); Donald H. Kenson, *Half the World From Home: Perspectives on the Irish in New Zealand, 1860–1950* (Wellington: Victoria University Press, 1990); and Donald H. Akenson, *Occasional Papers on the Irish in South Africa* (Gananoque, ON: Langdale Press, 1991).

29. Succinct discussions of these dynamics are found in two works by J.R. Miller: "Anti-Catholicism in Canada: From the British Conquest to the Great War," in Terrence Murphy and Gerald Stortz, eds, *Creed and Culture: The Place of English-Speaking Catholics in Canadian Society, 1750–1930* (Montreal: McGill-Queen's University Press, 1993); and "Bigotry in the North Atlantic Triangle: Irish, British and American Influences on Canadian Anti-Catholicism, 1850–1900," *Studies in Religion* 16 (1987): 289–301.

30. See, *Riots in New Brunswick*, 53–5; Johnston, "Popery and Progress," 146; Duncan, "Irish Famine Immigration," 26–7; Terrence Murphy, "The Emergence of Maritime Catholicism, 1781–1830," *Acadiensis* 13 (1984): 44.

31. *Rule and Misrule of the English in America* (London: Colburn & Co., 1851) 2: 319–21.

32. For a selection of anti-Catholic diatribes, see Rev. Robert Sedgwick, *The Papacy: The Idolatry of Rome* (Halifax: Wesleyan Conference Steam Press, 1859); Rev. Andrew King, *The Papacy: A Conspiracy against Civil and Religious Liberty* (Halifax: Wesleyan Conference Steam Press, 1859); Rev. J.L. Murdoch, *The Causes which since the Reformation Have Led to the Revival and Increase of Popery* (Halifax: Wesleyan Conference Steam Press, 1859).

33. H.M. Richey, *The Spirit of Popery, and the Duty of Protestants in Regard to Public Education* (Halifax: Wesleyan Conference Steam Press, 1859), 36.

34. *Weekly Chronicle* (18 July 1851).

35. Murdoch, *Revival and Increase of Popery*, 22 [italics in the original]; *Loyalist* (24 September 1847); *Church Witness* (6 July 1853).

36. John Earle's address, House of Assembly, 13 April 1850, in *Reporter* (10 May 1850); editorials, *Loyalist* (16 July, 17 September, 15 October 1847).

37. *Protestant and Evangelical Witness* (4 April 1863).

38. *Protestant and Evangelical Witness* (6 June 1863).

39. *Prince Edward Islander* (22 July 1864).

40. *Now Scotian* (16 June 1856).

41. John Francis Maguire, *The Irish in America* (New York: D. & J. Sadlier, 1868), 96.

42. All the other colonies had granted Roman Catholics the vote by 1810. See John Gamer, *The Franchise and Politics in British North America, 1755–1867* (Toronto: University of Toronto Press, 1969), 138–40.

43. Two notable pre-famine events that were shaped by tensions between religious and ethnic groups included the 1832 election in Montreal and a series of socio-political struggles in Bytown [Ottawa] during the 1830s. See France Galarneau, "Election partielle du quartier-ouest de Montréal en 1832: analyse politico-sociale," *Revue d'histoire de l'Amérique française* (1979): 565–84; and Michael S. Cross, "The Shiners' War: Social Violence in the Ottawa Valley in the 1830s; *Canadian Historical Review* 54 (1973): 1–26.

44. Joseph Howe, *To the People of Nova Scotia* (Halifax: n.p., 1857), 6.

45. D. Campbell and R.A. MacLean, *Beyond the Atlantic Roar: A Study of the Nova Scotia Scots* (Toronto: McClelland & Stewart, 1975), 20–3, 51–2, 55–60, 69–70,74, 221–2.

46. Punch, "Irish Halifax," 38–9, 46.

47. For descriptions of Howe and the political struggles of the 1850s, see J. Murray Beck's various works: *Politics of Nova Scotia* (Tantallon, NS: Four East, 1985), 1: 143–6, 154; *Joseph Howe: Conservative Reformer* (Montreal: McGill-Queen's University Press, 1982), 144–5; *Joseph Howe: The Briton Becomes Canadian* (Montreal: McGill-Queen's University Press, 1983), 119–21; "The Nova Scotia 'Disputed Election' of 1859 and Its Aftermath," *Canadian Historical Review* 36 (1955): 310. The Protestant Association is addressed in *British Colonist* (18 and 25 March 1858); and Nicholas Meagher, *The Religious Warfare in Nova Scotia 1855–60* (Halifax: n.p, 1927), 191–3.

48. A description of the riots is found in *Nova Scotian* (2, 16, and 23 June 1856). The trial proceedings are included in *Nova Scotian* (22 December 1856).

49. *Prince Edward Islander* (4 March 1864).

50. *Prince Edward Islander* (17 July 1857, 12 and 19 July 1861, 6 February 1863).

51. For assessments of the clash, see *Journal of the House of Assembly of Prince Edward Island*, Appendix 1, 1847, Public Archives of Prince Edward Island (PAPEI); H.T. Holman, "The Belfast Riot," *The Island Magazine* 14 (1983): 3–7; and Ian Ross Robertson, "Highlanders, Irishmen and the Land Question in Nineteenth-Century Prince Edward Island," in L.M. Cullen and T.C. Smout, eds, *Comparative Aspects of Scottish and Irish Economic and Social History 1600–1900* (Edinburgh: John Donald, 1977), 234–5.

52. Ultimately the riot became an Island legend, as evidenced by one verse that lionized the Protestants and disparaged the Irish: "Belfast Riot," in Randall Dibblee and Dorothy Dibblee, eds, *Folksongs from Prince Edward Island* (Charlottetown: Williams and Crue, 1973), 74–8. See also *The Burning Bush and British Family Visitor* (23 June 1866).

53. House of Assembly Records, 1840–1860, PANB.

54. See, *Riots in New Brunswick*, 71–111.

55. *Carleton Sentinel* (16 and 23 July 1850, 22 July 1851, 17 July 1852, 9 July 1853); Circular from Amaranth Office, 14 January 1850, Hill to Lenentine, 31 August 1853, Resolutions from York County Lodge, 6 February 1854, Circular from James S. Beek, 17 March 1854, in Campbell Papers, PANB.

56. Saint John Common Council Report, 13 May 1840, in *Courier* (16 May 1840); Perley's Report on 1846 Emigration, in Colebrooke to Grey, 29 December 1846, Colonial Office Papers, vol. 188; *Royal Gazette* (17 March and 7 July 1847); Graeme Wynn, *Timber Colony: A Historical Geography of Early Nineteenth Century New Brunswick* (Toronto: University of Toronto Press, 1981), 155–6.

57. Mary Finnegan, "Irish-French Relations in Lower Canada," *The Canadian Catholic Historical Association, Historical Studies* (1985): 36.

58. Rudin, *Forgotten Quebecers*, 83–7, 111–13.

59. Allan Greer, *The Patriots and the People: The Rebellion of 1837 in Rural Lower Canada* (Toronto: University of Toronto Press, 1993), 158–9; Keep, "Irish Adjustment in Montreal," 45–6.

60. Pauline Ryan, "A Study of Irish Immigration to North Hastings County," *Ontario History* 83 (1991): 25.

61. One tactic employed by the Irish Catholics to cope with nativist pressure was to gather regularly in holiday celebrations. See Cottrell, "St. Patrick's Day Parades." 57–73.

62. *Packet* (24 April 1847), quoted in G.J. Parr, "The Welcome and the Wake, Attitudes in Canada West toward the Irish Famine Migration," *Ontario History* 66 (1974): 104.

63. Issues of the *Globe* throughout this period provide the mast compelling evidence in support of this point.

64. J.L.P. O'Hanly, *The Political Standing of Irish Catholics in Canada; a Critical Analysis of its Causes, with Suggestions for its Amelioration* (Ottawa: n.p., 1872), 31–3; Murray Nicholson, "The Irish Experience in Ontario: Rural or Urban?" *Urban History Review* 14 (1985): 42.

65. William Westfall, *Two Worlds: The Protestant Culture of Nineteenth-Century Ontario* (Montreal: McGill-Queen's University Press, 1989), 22, 122–3.

66. *Globe* (11 February 1856).

67. *British Colonist* (18 and 25 March 1858); James T. Watt, "Anti-Catholic Nativism in Canada: The Protestant Protective Association," *Canadian Historical Review* 48 (1967): 45–58.

68. Charles Lindsey, *Rome in Canada: The Ultramontane Struggle for Supremacy over the Civil Authority* (Toronto: Lovell Brothers, 1877), 397.

69. Pastor Chiniquy, *Fifty Years in the Church of Rome: A Record of the Life of Pastor Chiniquy* (London: The Protestant Literature Depository, 1886); Rev. Archibald Gillies, *Popery Dissected: Its Absurd, Inhuman, Unscriptural, Idolatrous and Anti-Christian Assumptions, Principles and Practices Exposed From its Own Standard Works; Being a Series of Unanswered Letters Addressed to the R.C. Bishop of Arichat, N.S.* (Pictou, NS: William Harris, 1874).

Chapter 9

Rebellions in Lower and Upper Canada

READINGS

Primary Documents

1   From Ninety-Two Resolutions, in *Journals of the House of Assembly of Lower Canada*, 4th session of the 14th Provincial Parliament (7 January–8 March 1834)

2   From "The Seventh Report on Grievances (April 18, 1835)," in *Appendix of the Journal of the House of Assembly of Upper Canada*

Historical Interpretations

3   From "Closing the Last Chapter of the Atlantic Revolution: The 1837–38 Rebellions in Upper and Lower Canada," Michel Ducharme

4   From "From Folklore to Revolution: Charivaris and the Lower Canadian Rebellion of 1837," Allan Greer

INTRODUCTION

Like the seigneurial regime we addressed in Chapter 3, the 1837 and 1838 rebellions in Lower and Upper Canada are a touchstone in the history of the colonial period. They mark the culmination of two processes: the growth of a reform movement in Lower Canada that resented its limited influence in the colony's political life, and the growth of an alternative to unquestioned Loyalism in Upper Canada. In the case of Lower Canada, the colonial administration (especially Governors Craig and Dalhousie) had made it difficult for French speakers to exercise real power in the colony, even though they formed the majority of the population. Although the Lower Canadian reformers conceived all their demands within the British constitutional framework, until 1828 they achieved nothing. Their failure encouraged them to adopt more radical demands (inspired by republicanism) which were embodied in the Ninety-Two Resolutions in 1834. This radicalization oriented the reformers (who were called *patriotes* in the 1830s) toward rebellion. In Upper Canada, the desire among the governing group and their wealthy allies to fulfill the vision of the colony as a kind of miniature Britain led to a society that was more stratified than many citizens (reformers and radicals alike) would have preferred, and contrasted sharply with the egalitarian aura that citizens of the neighbouring United States cast about themselves. Led by William Lyon Mackenzie, the radicals also developed a republican rhetoric in favour of reform in the 1830s. "The Seventh Report on Grievances" is one document illustrating this discourse.

In his article, Michel Ducharme discusses the nature of the patriotes' and radicals' intellectual discourse and political program in the 1830s and argues that the Canadian rebellions were part of a broader movement that shook the foundation of the Atlantic world at the end of the eighteenth and beginning of the nineteenth centuries. Privileging a social approach, Allan Greer studies the politicization of the charivaris in Lower Canada in 1837. He shows that republican values and principles were not simply imposed on the local population by the patriote leadership, but that a popular brand of republicanism appeared in the countryside on the eve of the rebellions.

QUESTIONS FOR CONSIDERATION

1. Which of the 92 Resolutions do you find most radical or confrontational?
2. How different or similar were the demands made by the patriotes and radicals in the 1830s?
3. Why did the patriotes and radicals focus on the reform of the legislative institutions in the 1830s? Why didn't they ask for the advent of a local cabinet (responsible government)?
4. How similar and dissimilar were the charivaris held in Lower Canada before and in 1837?
5. Would there have been a way to prevent the rebellions?

SUGGESTIONS FOR FURTHER READING

Phillip A. Buckner, *Transition to Responsible Government: British Policy in British North America 1815–1850* (Westport: Greenwood Press, 1985).

Colin Coates, "The Rebellions of 1837–38, and Other Bourgeois Revolutions in Quebec Historiography," *International Journal of Canadian Studies* 20 (1999): 29–34.

Donald G. Creighton, *The Empire of the St. Lawrence* (Toronto: MacMillan of Canada, 1956).

Michel Ducharme, *The Idea of Liberty in Canada during the Age of Atlantic Revolutions, 1776–1838* (Montreal and Kingston: McGill-Queen's University Press, 2014).

F. Murray Greenwood and Barry Wright, eds, *Canadian State Trials, vol. 2: Rebellion and Invasion in the Canadas, 1837–1839* (Toronto: University of Toronto Press, 2002).

Allan Greer, *The Patriots and the People* (Toronto: University of Toronto Press, 1993).

Benjamin Jones, *Republicanism and Responsible Government: The Shaping of Democracy in Australia and Canada* (Montreal and Kingston: McGill-Queen's University Press, 2014).

Fernand Ouellet, *Economic and Social History of Quebec, 1760–1850: Structures and Conjunctures* (Toronto: MacMillan of Canada, 1980).

Colin Read, *The Rebellion of 1837 in Upper Canada* (Ottawa: Canadian Historical Association, 1988).

Carol Wilton, *Popular Politics and Political Culture in Upper Canada 1800–1850* (Montreal and Kingston: McGill-Queen's University Press, 2000).

Primary Documents

1 From Ninety-Two Resolutions, in *Journals of the House of Assembly of Lower Canada,* 4th session of the 14th Provincial Parliament (7 January–18 March 1834).

1. Resolved, That His Majesty's loyal subjects, the people of this province of Lower Canada, have shown the strongest attachment to the British Empire, of which they are a portion; that they have repeatedly defended it with courage in time of war; that at the period which preceded the Independence of the late British Colonies on this continent, they resisted the appeal made to them by those colonies to join their confederation.
   [. . .]

9. Resolved, That the most serious defect in the Constitutional Act, its radical fault, the most active principle of evil and discontent in the province; the most powerful and most frequent cause of abuses of power; of the infraction of the laws; of the waste of the public revenue and property, accompanied by impunity to the governing party, and the oppression and consequent resentment of the governed, is that injudicious enactment, [. . .] which invests the Crown with that exorbitant power (incompatible with any government duly balanced, and founded on law and justice, and not on force and coercion) of selecting and composing without any rule or limitation, or any predetermined qualification, an entire branch of the legislature, supposed from the nature of its attributes to be independent, but inevitably the servile tool of the authority which creates, composes and decomposes it, and can on any day modify it to suit the interests or the passions of the moment.
   [. . .]

17. Resolved, That [. . .] the principal Agent of His Majesty's Government in this Province [. . .] has destroyed the hope which His Majesty's faithful subjects had conceived of seeing the Legislative Council reformed and ameliorated, and has confirmed them in the opinion that the only possible mode of giving to that body the weight and respectability which it ought to possess, is to introduce into it the principle of election.
   [. . .]

41. Resolved, [. . .] that the neighbouring States have a form of government very fit to prevent abuses of power, and very effective in repressing them; that the reverse of this order of things has always prevailed in Canada under the present form of government; that there exists in the neighbouring States a stronger and more general attachment to the national institutions than in any other country, and that there exists also in those States a guarantee for the progressive advance of their political institutions towards perfection, in the revision of the same at short and determinate intervals, by conventions of the people, in order that they may without any shock or violence be adapted to the actual state of things.
   [. . .]

44. Resolved, That the unanimous consent with which all the American States have adopted and extended the elective system, shows that it is adapted to the wishes, manners and social state of the inhabitants of this continent; [. . .] and that we do not hesitate to ask from a Prince of the House of Brunswick, and a reformed Parliament, all the freedom and political powers which the Princes of the House of Stuart and their Parliaments granted to the most favoured of

the plantations formed at a period when such grants must have been less favourably regarded than they would now be. [. . .]

49. Resolved, That this House and the people whom it represents do not wish or intend to convey any threat; but that, relying as they do upon the principles of law and justice, they are and ought to be politically strong enough not to be exposed to receive insult from any man whomsoever, or bound to suffer it in silence; that the style of the said extracts from the despatches of the Colonial Secretary, as communicated to this House, is insulting and inconsiderate to such a degree that no legally constituted body, although its functions were infinitely subordinate to those of legislation, could or ought to tolerate them; [. . .]
[. . .]

52. Resolved, [. . .] That the majority of the inhabitants of this country are in nowise disposed to repudiate any one of the advantages they derive from their origin and from their descent from the French nation, which, with regard to the progress of which it has been the cause in civilization, in the sciences, in letters, and the arts, has never been behind the British nation, and is now the worthy rival of the latter in the advancement of the cause of liberty and of the science of Government; from which this country derives the greater portion of its civil and ecclesiastical law, and of its scholastic and charitable institutions, and of the religion, language, habits, manners and customs of the great majority of its inhabitants. [. . .]

64. Resolved, That the claims which have for many years been set up by the Executive Government to that control over and power of appropriating a great portion of the revenues levied in this province, which belong of right to this House, are contrary to the rights and to the constitution of the country; and that with regard

to the said claims, this House persists in the declarations it has heretofore made. [. . .]

73. Resolved, That it was anciently the practice of the House of Commons to withhold supplies until grievances were redressed; and that in following this course in the present conjuncture, we are warranted in our proceeding, as well by the most approved precedents, as by the spirit of the constitution itself. [. . .]

75. Resolved, That the number of the inhabitants of the country being about 600,000, those of French origin are about 525,000, and those of British or other origin 75,000; and that the establishment of the civil government of Lower Canada for the year 1832, according to the yearly returns made by the Provincial Administration, for the information of the British Parliament, contained the names of 157 officers and others receiving salaries, who are apparently of British or foreign origin, and the names of 47 who are apparently natives of the country, of French origin: that this statement does not exhibit the whole disproportion which exists in the distribution of the public money and power, the latter class being for the most part appointed to the inferior and less lucrative offices, and most frequently only obtaining even these by becoming the dependents of those who hold the higher and more lucrative offices; [. . .]
[. . .]

79. Resolved, That this House, as representing the people of this province, possesses of right, and has exercised within this province when occasion has required it, all the powers, privileges and immunities claimed and possessed by the Commons House of Parliament in the kingdom of Great Britain and Ireland.
[. . .]

84. Resolved, That besides the grievances and abuses before mentioned, there exist in this province a great number of

others (a part of which existed before the commencement of the present administration, which has maintained them, and is the author of a portion of them), with regard to which this House reserves to itself the right of complaining and demanding reparation, and the number of which is too great to allow of their being enumerated here: that this House points out, as among that number,

lstly. The vicious composition and the irresponsibility of the Executive Council, [. . .] and the secrecy with which not only the functions, but even the names of the members of that body have been kept from the knowledge of this House, [. . .]

2dly. The exorbitant fees illegally exacted in certain of the public offices, and in others connected with the judicial department, under regulations made by the Executive Council, by the judges, and by other functionaries usurping the powers of the legislature.
[. . .]

4thly. The cumulation of public places and offices in the same persons, and the efforts made by a number of families connected with the administration, to perpetuate this state of things for their own advantage, [. . .]

5thly. The intermeddling of members of the Legislative Councils in the election of the representatives of the people, for the purpose of influencing and controlling them by force, and the selection frequently made of returning officers for the purpose of securing the same partial and corrupt ends; the interference of the present Governor-in-chief himself in the said elections; his approval of the intermeddling of the said legislative councillors in the said elections; [. . .]

6thly. The interference of the armed military force at such elections, through which three peaceable citizens, whose exertions were necessary to the support of their families, and who were strangers to the agitation of the election, were shot dead in the streets, [. . .]

7thly. The various faulty and partial systems which have been followed ever since the passing of the Constitutional Act, with regard to the management of the waste lands in this province, and have rendered it impossible for the great majority of the people of the country to settle on the said lands; the fraudulent and illegal manner in which, contrary to His Majesty's instructions, Governors, Legislative and Executive Councillors, Judges and subordinate officers have appropriated to themselves large tracts of the said lands; [. . .]
[. . .]

85. Resolved, [. . .] that this House expects from the honour, patriotism and justice of the reformed Parliament of the United Kingdom, that the Commons of the said Parliament will bring impeachments, and will support such impeachments before the House of Lords against the said Matthew Lord Aylmer, for his illegal, unjust and unconstitutional administration of the government of this province; and against such of the wicked and perverse advisers who have misled him, as this House may hereafter accuse, [. . .]

86. Resolved, That this House hopes and believes, that the independent members of both Houses of the Parliament of the United Kingdom will be disposed, both

from inclination and from a sense of duty, to support the accusations brought by this House, to watch over the preservation of its rights and privileges which have been so frequently and violently attacked, more especially by the present administration; and so to act, that the people of this province may not be forced by oppression to regret their dependence on the British Empire, and to seek elsewhere a remedy for their afflictions.
[. . .]

2 From "The Seventh Report on Grievances (April 18, 1835)," *Appendix of the Journal of the House of Assembly of Upper Canada*, 1835, vol. 1, A21-1–A21-15.

To the Honorable the Commons House of Assembly,
[. . .]

Your Committee respectfully submit the results of their enquiry, together with the evidence. If it shall appear to the House that there is just cause of complaint, and that the government has not exerted its Constitutional powers to remedy the evils from which the people desire relief, the course to be pursued is to address the Throne, stating their grievances and praying redress. If, on the other hand, the House shall be of opinion that the government is administered impartially, with sound discretion and a single eye to the general welfare; that its officers and ministers enjoy the public confidence and worthily discharge their various duties, there can be no doubt but that the Representatives of the people will mark their approbation of their conduct by cheerfully placing in their hands the small Annual Grant, which in name, more than reality, indicates a popular influence in the government.

The almost unlimited extent of the patronage of the Crown, or rather of the Colonial Minister for the time being and his advisers here, together with the abuse of that patronage, are the chief sources of Colonial discontent. Such is the patronage of the Colonial Office that the granting or withholding of supplies is of no political importance unless as an indication of the opinion of the country concerning the character of the government, which is conducted upon a system that admits its officers to take and apply the funds of the Colonists without any legislative vote whatever.
[. . .]

The patronage of the Crown, as now exercised in this Province, includes the payments of gifts, salaries, pensions, and retired allowances to the Clergy of the Methodist, Presbyterian, Protestant Episcopal & Roman Catholic orders, and to nearly the whole of the civil officers of the government, including Sheriffs, Collectors of Excise and Customs Revenue, Coroners, Justices of the Peace, Commissioners of the Court of Requests, the heads of the several departments and all in the subordinate stations under them; to Judges of the District and Surrogate Courts, Registrars of Conveyances, Wills, &c., Commissioners of Customs, Clerks of the Peace, &c. &c. These officers hold their several situations only during the pleasure of the Crown. The Royal patronage also embraces the judicial establishment, many pensions, the nomination of the Legislative Council, and the appointment of its speaker and other officers,—the selection of the officers of the House of Assembly—the control of the Indian Department, of King's College, and of Upper Canada College—the appointment of the twelve District Boards of Education, and the direction of the expenditure of public monies in aid of Emigration—the selection of the Executive Council—the uncontrolled management of millions of Acres of public Lands—the appointment of 1500 commissioned Militia Officers—the sole control of the Military and Naval Forces— and (subject to the votes of the House of Commons in this case) the regulation of the whole Military and Naval expenditure.

The Crown also controls the expenditure of a large annual amount of local taxation by its power of appointing the District Magistracy during its pleasure—the justices thus appointed select the District Treasurers and a large number of subordinate officers, and exercise varied and extensive civil and criminal jurisdiction. The refusal of the bench of Magistrates of the Eastern District during the present Session, to render to the House an account of the receipt and expenditure of the local taxes and revenues raised from the people, and entrusted to the charge of these functionaries, under the authority of several acts of the Legislature, affords another proof that the system under which they are appointed requires instant revision; more especially as the complaints of the people of that District against magisterial peculation, as recorded on the journals, are of long standing.

The Crown appoints the members of the Court of King's Bench, and the Judges of that Court regulate at their discretion the tariff of fees to be paid therein by suitors. These judges are dependent on the Crown for such retiring pensions as it may see fit to award them, if any, and enabled to look forward with hope and expectation to the enjoyment of other offices and situations within its gift, by themselves and their families.

The Canada Company, the several incorporated establishments for Banking, Canalling and other purposes, and the Harbour, Dock & Wharf Companies, in nearly all cases, unite their patronage with that of the local government, and steadily strive to increase the influences of the Crown.

The Post Office Department, with about a hundred Deputy Post Masters, is under the solo control of the Crown—contracts are made, and all appointments held during its pleasure; the surplus revenue is transmitted to England. No detailed accounts of receipts and expenditure, have ever been laid before the Colonial Legislature. The rates of letter postage between the different places in the Colony, between this Colony & the others—and between Upper Canada and England, are very extravagant. The correspondence with Europe is chiefly carried on via: New York, which is at once the cheapest and most expeditious route.

[. . .]

THE LEGISLATIVE COUNCIL

This body forms a part of the patronage of the British Government; they are the nominees of the Minister of the colonies; who can add to their numbers at his discretion. In continually rejecting the many valuable measures earnestly prayed for by the people, they may be fairly presumed to act in obedience to the power from whence their appointments were derived. Your committee examined some of the members of the council holding offices of emolument under the government, and from their answers it will readily be seen whether they are or are not under the influence of the Lieutenant Governors for the time being.

[. . .]

A RESPONSIBLE GOVERNMENT

The Governors of colonies, like other men, are individually liable to all the infirmities of human nature, and in their political capacity, when left to act without restraint, they, no doubt, sacrifice occasionally the interests and happiness of the people, to the gratification of their own passions and caprices. One great excellence of the English constitution consists in the limits it imposes on the will of a King, by requiring responsible men to give effect to it. In Upper Canada no such responsibility can exist. The Lieutenant Governor and the British Ministry hold in their hands the whole patronage of the Province; they hold the sole dominion of the country, and leave the representative branch of the Legislature powerless and dependent.

[. . .]

In Upper Canada the efforts of the Legislature have been directed towards improving the Executive Council; yet it appears on enquiry that that body affects to have done neither good nor harm—some of its individual members may, (as is asserted by Bishop Macdonell) have acquired influence near the Lieutenant Governors and misled them, but the body has few if any definite attributes, other than in the Land Granting Department, and, there, nothing but ministerial acts to perform. It is shewn in evidence by Colonel Rowan and others that the Lieutenant Governor may or may not shew the Executive Council his despatches, and may or may not ask their advice, and may or may not follow that advice after having asked it, except there be an instruction from Europe to the contrary. They are occasionally called on to report on special matters for the information of the government at home, which is often seriously and intentionally misled by them.

In the appointment to offices, and concerning the accepting or rejecting Legislative Bills, it does not appear that they have ever been consulted. Their power in the Land Granting Department has been done away in this Province by the appointment of Mr. Peter Robinson, and in Lower Canada by that of Mr. Felton, with whom the respective Governors (alone) are supposed to consult and determine on all applications for land. The Canada Land Company monopoly too, necessarily, renders applications for grants to the government less frequent. It appears to Your Committee that the Executive Council is a nondescript with which it is folly further to contend.

There have been three classes of persons examined before Your Committee—the first, of whom Venerable Dr. Strachan is one, are of opinion that the Government is well enough as it is, and that as to responsibility it is as responsible as other Governments.

The second class desire a responsibly Ministry—some heads of departments well paid, to direct the government, to prepare bills and most of the business of the session, and to hold office or lose it according as they may happen to be in the minority or majority in the House of Assembly. This system was never attempted in any of the old colonies, but Your Committee have asked many questions with a view of ascertaining what is the public opinion concerning its practicability here; and it appears that Mr. Mackenzie, in his letters to Lord Goderich, expressed a belief that with some modifications it might be productive of a greater share of good government and public prosperity than is at present enjoyed by the people.

A third class contend for elective institutions, and affirm that while Governors come from without, and Judges are commissioned from without, favoritism towards their connexions will prevail to an extent that would destroy the influence of any set of "Ministers," constituted upon the principles desired by the second class; that the influence of Downing Street will continue to prevail as hitherto; and that the favourites of the Secretary of State will, as at present, be placed in important offices to the exclusion of better qualified men.

[. . .]

The class of persons who are in favor of elective institutions contend, that they were found to work well in the old North American colonies while in a colonial state—that the people of Upper Canada are entitled to the enjoyment of institutions equally free with those enjoyed by the old colonists during the time they were colonial, and under British protection—that few politicians are now found contending that these continental colonies, capable of containing a large population, will for a long series of years be required to submit to the inconveniences resulting from perpetual interference by the Home Government in their internal concerns—that in the House of Assembly many useful bills are proposed and carried for many successive sessions which are continually thrown out in the Legislative Council, of which the return moved for in the House of Commons by Mr. Hume and appended hereto gives particulars up to the year 1832—that it is the wisdom of the aristocracy to try to make the people fearful of themselves, by raising idle cries about loyalty, republicanism, Jacobinism, and revolution—that birth, office, or peculiar privileges ought not to give to a few superiority over the many—that the legislative council neglect and despise the wishes of the country on many important matters which a council elected by the freeholders would not—that the people, if united in claiming their privileges to constitute the second branch of the legislature, would obtain it, and that it is weakness and wavering among their representatives which alone can make them timid as to claiming the enlargement of their liberties—that the prejudices of early education, borrowed from books written by or under the authority of pensioners and salaried lawyers who have with one voice endeavoured to lull the people into the very erroneous belief that the union of church and state and the wisdom of former ages in devising great privileges for the peerage are the causes of the greatness of England, while in truth it is owing to what she has saved of popular institutions—that elective institutions are the only safeguards to prevent the Canadas from forming disadvantageous comparisons between the condition of the colonists and the adjoining country—and that the crown of England, by its ministers, exercised no patronage in Connecticut and Rhode Island; none in the other New England States, save the appointment of a Governor; none in the proprietary governments; and that hence there is no disloyalty in freely and calmly discussing which of these modes of government that have been

granted to British subjects and countries will best suit Canada.

[. . .]

The dependence of the legislative council is strikingly manifested by the facts stated in the evidence of the Honorable Colonel Clark, and the Honorable William Dickson, members of that body, before a select committee of the house of assembly during a late parliament. It appears that several legislative councillors had objected to a measure strongly urged by the executive, and its failure was inevitable. To ensure its passing, coercive means were adopted, and those members who were dependent on the government were told either to vote directly contrary to the opinions they had thus publicly expressed, or be dismissed from their offices. After this disgraceful attempt to coerce men to disingenuous and inconsistent conduct, those unacquainted with the threats which had been used were astonished at the sudden, unexpected, and unexplained change in the conduct of several members: and when this surprise was expressed to the late Honorable James Baby, (who was also an executive councillor, and the senior member) he shed tears at his humiliation, and only exclaimed "my children!" "my children!" and the late Honorable Chief Justice Powell replied to a similar enquiry of surprise, "I have received a new light within the last ten minutes."

[. . .]

We have already adverted to the circumstance of the Chief Justice being introduced into the Legislative Council, of which he is Speaker; and altho' the House of Assembly have repeatedly pointed out to His Majesty's Government, the inexpediency, in a limited community like this, of blending the judicial and political duties together, yet the same injurious system is continued. Its impropriety has been lately manifested by the result of a pecuniary negociation likely seriously to impair the independence of the judiciary and increase the distrust of the people.

[. . .]

It appears therefore that the Legislative Council, as at present constituted, has utterly failed, and never can be made to answer the ends for which it was created; and the restoration of legislative harmony and good government requires its re-construction and the elective principle.

The opinions of Mr. Fox, Mr. Stanley, Earl Grey, Lord Erskine, Mr. Ellice, Mr. Hume, Sir James Mackintosh, Mr. O'Connell, Mr. Warburton, and many other eminent British Statesmen, have been expressed in favour of elective and it appears to Your Committee that Mr. Stanley correctly describes the Legislative Council as being "at the root of all the evils complained of in both Provinces."

[. . .]

It appears to your Committee that it is more important than legislation, rendered fruitless as it is by the Legislative Council, to adopt such measures as are likely to ensure such an alteration in the system of our public affairs as seems indispensable for the peace, welfare, and good government of this important part of His Majesty's dominions. The history of all colonies shew that there has been too much inattention in the British government in the selection of Governors, it being considered a matter merely of patronage with the colonial minister, in Downing Street. Men, from the too long possession of lucrative power, whatever at first might be their relative stations soon acquire a community of interests, and thus identified in the purpose of sustaining each other in office, they have in this province made common cause against that redress of our grievances, and that conciliation of the public mind, and that economy of the public wealth, which are equally dictated by justice and wisdom.

Although the members of the Executive Council seem from their own account to render no benefit to the country, receiving however a salary from it, yet a very different duty is imposed upon them by the 31st Geo. 3rd, chap. 31, called the constitutional act,

from which it appears they are appointed expressly to advice His Excellency upon the affairs of the Province. This they have never done satisfactorily. As far back as the first Session of the 10th Provincial Parliament, the House of Assembly expressed their dissatisfaction to His Excellency Sir John Colborne, in the most constitutional mode of doing so, at the opening of the Session of the Legislature; and in the following year the same sentiments were again frankly conveyed to His Excellency in the answer to His Speech from the Throne, by a solemn declaration that the Executive had long and deservedly lost the confidence of the country. In the hope of their just and constitutional wishes being attended to, the people patiently waited for relief, but the relaxation of their vigilance, which some remaining confidence in His Excellency unhappily produced, has only served to bring disappointment, and to afford a farther opportunity for the accumulation of the abuses which pervade all our institutions.

The growing condition of this part of the Empire, in population, wealth and commerce, requires there should be an entire confidence between the Executive and the Commons House of Assembly; and this confidence cannot exist while those who have long and deservedly lost the esteem of the country are continued in the public offices and councils. Under such a state of things, distrust is unavoidable, however much it is to be deplored as incompatible with the satisfactory discharge of the public business.

[. . .]

This is a state of things which, the British nation, it is presumed, cannot desire to perpetuate against us. After the right was conceded to the present United States, at the close of the Revolution, to form a constitution for themselves, the loyalists took refuge in this Province; and, by an act passed in 31st year of Geo. 3. they received the charter of their liberties, conferring upon them a constitution for their peace, welfare, and good government. His Excellency, Governor Simcoe, was entrusted with the duty of putting it into operation, and in the first speech delivered by him from the throne, he made the following memorable declaration:—"I have summoned you together under the authority of an Act of the Parliament of Great Britain, passed last year, which has established the British Constitution, and all the forms which secure and maintain it, in this distant colony." And upon closing the same session he said "I particularly recommend to you to explain that this Province is singularly blest, not with a mutilated constitution; but with a constitution which has stood the test of experience, and is the very image and transcript of that of Great Britain."

It is reasonable for the people to desire to see these declarations from the throne, recorded on our Journals, faithfully observed by those in the confidence of His Majesty, and that these institutions may be made such as will secure to them their civil and religious liberties to their just extent. This country is now principally inhabited by loyalists and their descendants, and by an accession of population from the mother country, where is now enjoyed the principles of a free and responsible government; and we feel the practical enjoyment of the same system in this part of the empire to be equally our right; without which it is in vain to assume that we do or can possess in reality or in effect "the very image and transcript of the British Constitution."

The House of Assembly has, at all times, made satisfactory provision for the civil government, out of the revenues raised from the people by taxation, and while there is cherished an unimpaired an continued disposition to do so, it is a reasonable request that His Majesty's adviser in the province and those about him should possess and be entitled to the confidence of the people and their representatives, and that all their reasonable wishes respecting their domestic institutions and affairs should be attended to and complied with.

[. . .]

W. L. MACKENZIE
    CHAIRMAN.
T. D. MORRISON,
DAVID GIBSON,
CHARLES WATERS.

Committee Room, House of Assembly,
10th April 1835.

Historical Interpretations

3 From Michel Ducharme, "Closing the Last Chapter of the Atlantic Revolution: The 1837–38 Rebellions in Upper and Lower Canada," *Proceedings of the American Antiquarian Society* 116, 2 (2007): 411–28.

Half a century ago, two historians, Robert Palmer and Jacques Godechot, proposed that the late-eighteenth-century revolutions of the Atlantic World be integrated into one analytical framework. They argued that the American Revolution of 1776, the Dutch uprising of the 1780s, the unrest in the Austrian Low Countries after 1787, the French Revolution of 1789, and all of the European revolutions of the 1790s were, in fact, a single phenomenon. It was, in their view, as if one single, great revolution had shaken the Atlantic world between 1776 and 1800.[1]

Even if we can appreciate the transnational ambition of their analysis, we must recognize that this description of the so-called "Atlantic Revolution" was really quite limited in scope, as it focused only on the United States and Europe.[2] Not a single word was said about Saint Domingue, although its unrest and revolts of the 1790s eventually led to the creation of Haiti in 1804. In fact, if we exempt the United States, it was as if the entire New World had gone missing from this Atlantic Revolution. In recent decades, historians have tried to correct this deficiency. They successfully integrated the nineteenth-century Central and South American revolutions by exploring Spanish and Portuguese colonial histories.[3] Finally, it can be said that the historical analysis of the Atlantic Revolution covers all Europe and America, between 1776 and 1840. Or can it? There is, in fact, one country's history that continues to be left out of the Atlantic framework: Canada's.

When Canadian historians have studied Canadian history at the time of the American and French revolutions, very few have tried to integrate it into an Atlantic framework. [. . .] It is true that the British North American colonies that eventually became Canada did not join the Thirteen Colonies in their revolution. It is also true that these same colonies did not take the opportunity to declare their independence during the French Revolution, or during the subsequent French Revolutionary War. This is not to say that the American and French revolutionary and republican ideals did not spread throughout the colonies during the 1780s and '90s. This is especially so in the portion of the province of Quebec that became Lower Canada in 1791. Fleury Mesplet, for instance, a French printer who had come from Philadelphia to Montreal in 1776, remained in the city after the withdrawal of American troops in May 1776.[4] Between 1785 and his death in 1794, he indirectly promoted republican ideals through his bilingual newspaper, La Gazette de Montréal/The Montreal Gazette. The promotion of republican and revolutionary principles was not only the work of people within the colony. In June 1793, Edmond-Charles Genêt, the French minister in Philadelphia, strongly urged Canadians to join the French struggle for freedom in an appeal entitled, Les Français libres à leurs frères les Canadiens.[5] His appeal failed to rouse his "brothers" in the colony.

So it appears that republicanism, the main ideology behind the Atlantic Revolution, did not represent a serious threat in the northern British colonies at the end of the eighteenth and beginning of the nineteenth centuries. The question arising is thus: Did republicanism or any of the key principles that inspired the Atlantic revolutionaries have any impact on Upper and Lower Canada—now Ontario and Quebec? Some distinguished scholars have argued over the years that it had a "negative" impact, Canadian history being the result of a counterrevolutionary experiment.[6] It would be interesting to discuss this question, but I will confine my paper to exploring the direct or "positive" influences of republicanism in Lower and Upper Canadian history between 1776 and 1838. I will argue that republicanism did indeed have a major "positive" impact on these colonies, although much later than in other countries around the Atlantic.

CANADA DURING THE ATLANTIC REVOLUTION (1776–1828)

In 1791, a few years after the British acknowledged American independence in the Versailles Treaty, the British government granted a new constitution to the province of Quebec. It was called the Constitutional Act in Canada, but known as the Canada Act everywhere else. One of the conscious goals of the British government in adopting the Constitutional Act was to stop the dissemination of republican principles in the province. To achieve this, the British parliament split the province into two distinct colonies: Upper Canada (now Ontario), which was mainly settled by refugees from the United States or, as we know them, "Loyalists," and Lower Canada (now the province of Quebec), comprised of French Canadians with a vocal English-speaking minority. Thus, the Crown made sure that the Upper Canadian Loyalists could no longer complain that they were living in a French colony, while French Canadians in Lower Canada could feel less afraid of being outnumbered in their colony, could continue to live under their own civil laws, and could have free exercise of their Roman Catholic faith. This division also allowed for the granting of rudimentary parliamentary institutions to the two new colonies. The British government organized these colonial governments along the principles of "mixed" government—a system in which the king (represented by the governor or the lieutenant-governor) had the executive power and in which provincial legislatures (composed of the governor, an appointed legislative council, and an elected legislative assembly) had the legislative power. The system of government conferred on Canadians in 1791 followed the usual British political system and practices, as far as colonial status would allow.

Since one of the objectives of the British government was to prevent republicanism from becoming a real threat in the province of Quebec—and thereby preventing the colony from falling into an American-style revolution—the Constitutional Act can be seen to have been a great success. It effectively prevented the spread of republican practices into the colonies. Looking at their new legislative assemblies, Canadians thought they were enjoying an excellent form of government. The fact that the assembly shared the legislative power with a British governor and an appointed legislative council did not seem to bother anyone at first.[7] On the one hand, French-speaking Lower Canadians were too busy trying to exercise their new rights in the parliamentary system to pay attention to such "details". On the other hand, Upper Canadians were too busy trying to wrestle a life out of the Ontario forests to really criticize their constitution.

If the last decades of the eighteenth century were more or less quiet in Upper and Lower Canada, things changed during the first decade of the nineteenth century. In both colonies, reform movements appeared in 1805–6, although the Lower Canadian movement was better organized, more coherent, and more efficient than its Upper Canadian counterparts. While these movements were created at the same time as the Central and South American colonies were fighting for their independence, their objectives were very different. On the whole, Canadians did not fight to obtain independence or articulate republican demands, though there were a few exceptions in Upper Canada.

Most of these reformers did not question their belonging to the British Empire or the legitimacy and form of their government. Until 1828, their demands, inspired by their reading of Locke, Blackstone, and De Lolme, aimed at gaining, for the assembly, genuine control over the executive power through a kind of ministerial responsibility, through impeachment trials, or through budgetary management, all three of which were political mechanisms that had allowed the eighteenth-century members of the British House of Commons to exercise power over the government.[8] In the end, we can say that republicanism did not have a direct or positive impact in the colonies before 1828.

REPUBLICANISM IN UPPER AND LOWER CANADA (1828–38)

Until 1828, Upper and Lower Canadian reformers, as their label implies, were not demanding revolution. But results count, and after more than 20 years of political struggles in both colonies, they had achieved nothing.

By 1828, the reformers understood that they needed tougher vocabulary if they were to convince the British to reform the Canadian system. And this is how colonial reformers rediscovered the power of the republican discourse. Republican rhetoric not only gave them stronger arguments against the status quo, but it also encouraged them to question the legitimacy and the organization of the colonial political structure. After 1828, republicanism as discourse and ideology became the main source of inspiration for Lower Canadian Patriots and Upper Canadian radicals. From that moment until 1838, Canadian colonies went through a political process that corresponded to the criteria of the Atlantic Revolution. The Upper and Lower Canadian unrest of the 1830s, and its culmination in the 1837–38 rebellions in both colonies, must be considered, in my view, as the last chapter of the Atlantic Revolution, a chapter that did not end happily for Canadian republicans.

During the 1830s, all colonial republicans invoked the ideas, examples, and authority of well-known Atlantic republicans. By making these references, they were trying to gain respectability, credibility, and legitimacy. It is interesting to note that they did not often refer directly to Greek or Roman republicanism. Unlike the American patriots, the Canadian republicans did not try to connect their movement to ancient times. They were instead consciously trying to connect it to the Atlantic republican tradition that had developed during the eighteenth century. During the 1820s, their inspiration came mainly from the United Kingdom and, during the 1830s, from the United States and, to a lesser extent, from Ireland. Canadian republicans sometimes mentioned and celebrated Central and South American revolutions in their newspapers, but they were not particularly inspired by these events. Rousseauian-style rhetoric about the social contract was widely used, especially in Lower Canada, but its author was rarely mentioned or quoted extensively, nor were other

French republicans. The painful memory of the Terror and the ultimate failure of the Revolution, heralded by the Restoration, led the Lower and Upper Canadian republicans to turn to Anglo-American references.

The American example was seen as useful, during the 1830s, for at least two reasons. Firstly, the American Revolution was a success and its republic an emerging power. Secondly, the Canadian republicans hoped that, by presenting their cause in a distinctly American manner, the Americans would eventually side with them, should a conflict arise between them and the British.

In 1835 Louis-Joseph Papineau, the Lower Canadian French-speaking Patriot leader, argued that if the British parliament tried to dominate Lower Canada as it had tried to dominate the thirteen colonies during the 1770s, many a new Jefferson or Washington would rise in Lower Canada.[9] In Upper Canada, William Lyon Mackenzie, an important radical leader, sometimes referred to Scottish heroes, such as William Wallace, Archibald Campbell (the first Marquess of Argyle), and William Russell to promote Canadian autonomy.[10] But, as in Lower Canada, it was the American Revolution and the American republic that was his real source of inspiration. In his *Sketches of Canada and the United States* (1833), Mackenzie did not hide his admiration for America's independence and institutions.

In 1836–37, the American Revolution was clearly used to encourage Canadians to fight for their rights. It had by then become "the" example to follow. In Lower Canada, the Patriots organized a boycott of British products during the summer of 1837, just as the American patriots had done during the 1770s. In October 1837, they organized a "militia" called *Les Fils de la Liberté* (the Sons of Liberty).[11] A most important public assembly was held in October 1837, a few weeks before the rebellion, which saw the adoption of many resolutions. Interestingly, the first of these was to translate the second paragraph of the American Declaration of Independence, beginning with "We hold these truths to be self-evident, that all men are created equal."[12] At this same public assembly, a few of the Patriots urged violent actions against the state, although Papineau, their leader, was not in favour of it. He fled the colony a few weeks later, just before the rebellion. In Upper Canada, Mackenzie defended the right of Canadians to choose their form of government as a "right [that] was conceded to the present United States at the close of a successful revolution."[13] He went as far as to reprint, in the summer of 1837, in his newspaper the *Constitution,* Thomas Paine's pamphlet, *Common Sense,* first published in 1776 to promote American independence.[14] Mackenzie also wrote in his newspaper, in July 1837: "Canadians! It has been said that we are on the verge of a revolution. We are in the midst of one; a bloodless one, I hope, but a revolution to which all those which have been will be counted mere child's play."[15] By November, he published a short text entitled *INDEPENDENCE* in which he openly promoted rebellion.

The desire of Canadian republicans to connect their movement to the Atlantic Revolution, especially in its American incarnation, was clearly apparent during the 1830s.

REPUBLICANISM IN THE CANADAS: THE IDEOLOGY

Lower Canadian Patriots and Upper Canadian radicals not only appealed to the example of the republican thinkers of the Atlantic world but also adopted their ideals and principles. Therefore, they were Atlantic revolutionaries.

For Lower Canadian Patriots and the Upper Canadian radicals, as for all other republicans, freedom and equality were very closely linked. For them, individuals needed to be equal in order to be free. When republicans talked about equality, they were not talking only about equality under the law

or equality of rights; they were also talking about moral equality and a certain amount of material equality. This is why both Papineau in 1823 and Mackenzie in 1833–34 were shocked by the inequalities they saw in the United Kingdom during their visit in the metropolis.[16] Not that the Canadian republicans were social levellers; they never intended to level fortunes. But they thought that it was impossible for individuals to be free (to participate equally in political life) if there was too great a disparity between citizens, because the rich could bribe the poor and establish a form of clientelism. Amury Girod, a Swiss immigrant who came to Lower Canada in 1831, took the side of the Patriots during the 1830s, and fought as a "general" in Saint Eustache in 1837, considered that "Property is the cause of all good and all evil in society. If it is equally distributed, knowledge and power will be also . . . Liberty will sooner or later be the inevitable result."[17] Mackenzie thought much the same, and he quoted Abbé Raynald: "People of America! [. . .] Be afraid of too unequal a distribution of riches, which shows a small number of citizens in wealth, and a great number in misery—whence arises the insolence of the one and the disgrace of the other."[18]

In order to ensure the economic and social equality of citizens, these republicans envisioned a society of small landowners, all independent of one another. Mackenzie himself said: "Agriculture, the most innocent, happy and important of all human pursuits, is your chief employment—your farms are your own—you have obtained a competence, seek therewith to be content."[19] This economic independence would ensure political independence. For most Canadian republicans, life in Canada was already characterized by social equality. Their main goal was to reform political institutions to fit this social reality. In this context, colonial republicans were very suspicious of accumulation of wealth, of capitalism, of primogeniture, and of bank monopoly, which they considered detrimental to equality among citizens and might allow corruption to destroy freedom.

Canadian republicans incorporated these principles into a sophisticated set of political proposals. Considering the importance that they were giving to equality, they structured their political institutions around the idea of political equality. For them, the right of the citizens to participate in the political process was their first and most important right. The importance given to political participation implied that citizens should have the right to elect their representatives. These representatives were the only ones who could legitimately adopt laws for the well-being of all. In this context, the Patriots and the radicals concentrated their claims around the constitution of legislative power during the 1830s. Their efforts had two objectives. The first was to improve the representativeness of the Legislative Assembly in Upper Canada. In this colony, unlike Lower Canada, the radicals could not gain control of the Assembly, except between 1834 and 1836. It was clear to them that if they could not obtain a majority of the seats in the Assembly, the problem lay not in themselves but in the way that representation was framed.[20] In both colonies the efforts of colonial reformers aimed at making the legislative councils of the colonies elective, not composed of appointed members of the elite. During the 1830s, colonial republicans did not concede any legitimacy to the appointed legislative councils, the upper houses of the Upper and Lower Canadian legislatures. While a few demanded outright abolition of these bodies, most wanted to make them elective. This was the Lower Canadian Patriots' main demand. Thirty-four of the "Ninety-Two Resolutions" (the charter of Lower Canadian republicanism) adopted by their Assembly in February 1834 concerned this reform (resolutions 9–40, 51, 54).[21] Upper Canadian republicans also fought for this reform, though not with the same energy as the Lower Canadians. In its *Seventh Report* *on Grievances* of 1835 (the charter of Upper Canadian republicanism), a committee of the House of Assembly, chaired by Mackenzie, presented the "elective institutions [as] the only safeguards to prevent the Canadas from forming disadvantageous comparisons between the condition of the colonists and the adjoining country."[22]

By contesting the authority of the legislative councils, the colonial republicans were contesting the existing constitutional order of the two colonies, based on the British principle of mixed government. They were demanding the reconfiguration of power relations in both Canadas according to a model of state legitimacy drawn from republican principles. They were asking the British government to acknowledge the sovereignty of the people rather than the sovereignty of parliament.

In this context, though, as in the past, Canadian republicans were loath to criticize the legitimacy of the British monarchy or the governor's presence in the colony. If they did not do so, it was because they thought that once the legislative power was made to really represent the "people," the legislature could then impose its will on the governor. The governor would then be transformed into the first of all civil servants, with no independent voice. The People would become, effectively, the Crown.

The republican discourse in both Canadas during the 1830s focused primarily on the concept of political liberty, not on those of individual rights or civil liberties. In a larger sense, Canadian republicans wanted to impose virtue. In Canada, as elsewhere in the Atlantic, virtue was one of the key words in republican rhetoric. This word had at least three meanings. First, a virtuous citizen was a citizen who was independent socially and economically: this independence was the best guarantee that he could not be corrupted and that he would be independent politically. Secondly, to be virtuous implied an ethic of simplicity and frugality. Thirdly, virtue meant the willingness of a citizen to defend the common good instead of his own personal interests; in this sense, virtue meant patriotism. Because the Canadian rebels adopted this vision of a virtuous society, they cannot be seen as classical liberals, as some have argued. They were not demanding more civil freedom, nor autonomy from the State. They aimed instead to control the state.

THE REBELLIONS AND THEIR FAILURE

The republican discourse in the Canadas during the 1830s echoed the discourses that American, Central American, Caribbean, French, and British republicans had articulated earlier in the Atlantic Revolution. The political struggles of the 1830s in the two Canadas and the rebellions of 1837–38 can be best explained by the challenge that republicanism represented for the colonial constitution. Republicans were contesting the premises upon which the authority of the colonial state rested.

In Lower Canada, for instance, by 1836–37, it had become clear to the Patriots— who controlled the Assembly—as it was also to their opponents—who controlled the Legislative Council—that their struggle could only be settled outside the framework of existing colonial institutions. The Patriots did not recognize the legitimacy of the Legislative Council, and their opponents rejected most of the reforms proposed or adopted by the Patriot Assembly. By 1837, under such conditions, neither camp could negotiate with the other. Paralysis of legislative power was the result.

Lower Canada's Patriots launched an attack on the state in November 1837. Three battles ensued. After an initial victory at Saint Denis, the British won at Saint Charles and Saint Eustache. In December 1837, Upper Canada's radicals then began their drive to overthrow the colonial government. The two rebellions were crushed, as was a second Lower Canadian uprising in November 1838 and the unrest at the Upper Canadian border with the United States. In 1837–38, superior British military might decided that the Canadas would not be republics. Just as the 1776 Declaration of Independence and the subsequent British military defeat heralded the beginning of the Atlantic Revolution, the failure of the Canadian rebellions and the victory of British forces and Canadian volunteers, 62 years later heralded its true end.

CONCLUSION

Political life in Upper and Lower Canada became very difficult from 1828 onwards, especially in Lower Canada, where the Patriots controlled the Legislative Assembly for a decade—something the Upper Canadian radicals were never able to do. By the fall of 1837, the Patriots of Lower Canada and the radicals of Upper Canada had launched an assault on the legitimacy of the colonial state in British North America. These two groups were not simply seeking to overthrow the existing government. At a more fundamental level, they were trying to refashion the existing constitutional order of the colonies and to reconfigure power relations in both Canadas, according to a model of state legitimacy drawn from republican principles. In accordance with their republican ideals, the Patriots and the radicals fought for, among other things, the ultimate sovereignty of the people, primacy of legislative power over executive power and the economic and political independence of all citizens. In this way, the Canadian rebellions participated in the larger revolutionary movement that was fundamentally reshaping the Atlantic World at the end of the eighteenth and the beginning of the nineteenth centuries. Although Canadian uprisings occurred much later, they were not ideologically different from the upheavals that preceded them.

Had they succeeded, they would have been known as the Canadian Revolution.

It is because these movements failed to overthrow the state—their leaders being better at articulating speeches and making constitutional claims than at organizing a rebellion—that the Patriots and the radicals are not often connected to the wider political and intellectual currents that were reshaping the Atlantic World at the time, even though they were clearly inspired by them and aimed to create republics in Canada. The 1837–38 rebellions may have been a failure, but they were very closely related to the complex story of the Atlantic Revolution at the end of the eighteenth and the beginning of the nineteenth centuries. They are best understood as its last chapter.

NOTES

1. Robert R. Palmer and Jacques Godechot's proposal first appeared in "Le problème de l'Atlantique du XVIIIème au XXème siècle," in *Storia Contemporanea, Relazioni del X Congresso Intenazionale di Scienze Storiche*, 6 vols (Florence: G.C. Sansoni Editore, 1955), 5: 219–39. Each wrote a history of the Atlantic Revolution: Robert R. Palmer, *The Age of the Democratic Revolution. A Political History of Europe and America, 1760–1800*, 2 vols (Princeton: Princeton University Press, 1959); Jacques Godechot, *Les Révolutions (1770–1799)* (1963; reprint, Paris: Presses Universitaires de France, 1986), 99–177.

2. Many American and European scholars have followed the path opened by Palmer and Godechot. See, among others, Bernard Bailyn, *The Ideological Origins of the American Revolution* (Cambridge: Belknap Press of the Harvard University Press, 1967); Gordon Wood, *The Creation of the American Republic, 1776–1789* (1969; reprint, Chapel Hill: University of North Carolina Press, 1998); J.G.A. Pocock, *The Machiavellian Moment* (Princeton: Princeton University Press, 1975), 333–552; J.G.A. Pocock, "The Dutch Republican Tradition,"' in *The Dutch Republic in the Eighteenth Century: Decline, Enlightenment and Revolution*, Margaret Jacobs and Wijnand W. Mijnhardt, eds (Ithaca: Cornell University Press, 1992), 188–93; Stephen Small, *Political Thought in Ireland, 1776–1798: Republicanism, Patriotism and Racialism* (Oxford: Oxford University Press, 2002); Annie Jourdan, *La Révolution, une exception française* (Paris: Flammarion, 2004).

3. See, among others, David Patrick Geggus, *Haitian Revolutionary Studies* (Bloomington: Indiana University Press, 2002); Jaime E. Rodríguez O., ed., *Mexico in the Age of Democratic Revolutions: 1750–1850* (Boulder: Lynne Rienner, 1994).

4. For the biography of Mesplet, see Jean-Paul de Lagrave, *Fleury Mesplet, 1734–1794: Diffuseur des Lumières au Québec* (Montreal: Patenaude, 1985); and Patricia Lockhart Fleming, "Cultural Crossroads: Print and Reading in Eighteenth- and Nineteenth-Century English-Speaking Montreal," *Proceedings of the American Antiquarian Society* 112 (2003): 23–48.

5. Genêt's text is reproduced in Michel Brunet, "La Révolution française sur les rives du St-Laurent," *Revue d'histoire de l'Amérique française* II (1957):158–62.

6. Seymour Martin Lipset, *Revolution and Counterrevolution: Change and Persistence in Social Structures* (New York: Basic Books, Inc., 1968), 31–63; and from the same author, *Continental Divide: The Values and Institutions of the United States and Canada* (New York: Routledge, 1990), 1–56, 59–60; Jerry Bannister, "Canada as Counter-Revolution: The Loyalist Order Framework in Canadian History, 1750–1840," lecture, The Liberal Order in Canadian History Conference, McGill Institute for the Study of Canada, 3 March 2006.

7. Samuel Neilson, a Whig reformer, and Fleury Mesplet, a republican, welcomed the Constitutional Act by publishing the same text promoting the new constitution in their respective newspapers: *La Gazette de Québec/ The Quebec Gazette* (23 February, 1, 8, and

15 March 1792) and *La Gazette de Montréal/ The Montreal Gazette* (15 and 22 March 1792). Its author, Solon, was Jonathan Sewell, the future chief justice of Lower Canada (1808–38): John Hare, *Aux origines du parlementarisme québécois 1791–1793* (Sillery, QC: Septentrion, 1993), 46, 131.

8. In Lower Canada, Pierre Bédard was the first to ask for the introduction of a kind of ministerial responsibility in the colony in his newspaper *Le Canadien* between 1806 and 1810. In Upper Canada, this claim was first articulated by William Baldwin in 1828–29 in a petition to the king and then in a letter to the Duke of Wellington: "Petition To the King's Most Excellent Majesty," reproduced in *Appendix to Journal of the House of Assembly of Upper Canada*, 1835, 1st session of the 12th Provincial Parliament (15 January–16 April 1835), I: 51; "William Warren Baldwin to the Duke of Wellington, January 3rd, 1829," in *Documents Relating to the Constitutional History of Canada 1819–1828*, A. Doughty and Norah Story, eds (Ottawa: J.O. Patenaude, 1935),482. Lower Canadian reformers asked for the creation of a system of impeachment trials against judges and civil servants during the 1810s. In Upper Canada, Baldwin mentioned the installation of such a system in his 1828 petition to the king. During the 1800s, in Upper Canada, and the 1820s, in Lower Canada, reformers saw the vote on supplies as their only means to influence the executive power. The confrontation between the Lower Canadian House of Assembly, on the one hand, and the governor and the upper house of the Legislature, on the other, on this issue during the 1830s paralyzed the political life in Lower Canada.

9. Papineau, "Nécessité de nommer un délégué de la Chambre d'Assemblée a Londres" (House of Assembly, 17 November 1835), in *Un demi-siècle de combats: Interventions publiques,* Yvan Lamonde and Claude Larin, eds (Montreal: Fides, 1998), 367.

10. *Constitution,* 19 October 1836.

11. See the "Adresse des Fils de la liberté de Montréal aux jeunes gens des colonies de l'Amérique du Nord," 4 October 1837, reproduced in *Assemblées publiques, révolutions et déclarations de 1837–1838,* Jean-Paul Bernard, ed. (Ville St-Laurent, QC: VLB éditeur, 1988), 216.

12. This resolution was reprinted in *La Minerve,* 30 October 1837.

13. *Constitution,* 2 August 1837.

14. *Constitution,* 19 and 26 July; 2 and 9 August 1837.

15. *Constitution,* 26 July 1837.

16. Even if Papineau was not a republican in 1823, he was shocked by what he saw in Britain. See the letters he wrote to his wife between 5 April and 22 September 1823: Louis-Joseph Papineau, *Lettres à Julie,* Georges Aubin and Renee Blanchet, eds (Sillery, QC: Septentrion, 2000), 72–91. For Mackenzie, see *Colonial Advocate,* 27 June 1833.

17. Amury Girod, *Notes diverses sur le Bas-Canada* (Village Debartzch: J.P. de Boucherville, 1835), 63.

18. Mackenzie, *Sketches of Canada and the United States* (London, E. Wilson, 1833), 60.

19. *Colonial Advocate,* 9 September 1830.

20. Mackenzie began to contest the state of representation in Upper Canada in 1831. A committee of inquiry was created the same year with Mackenzie as its chair. Its report was introduced in the House on 16 March 1831. Its conclusions were predictable: "the imperfect state of the representation in the House of Assembly is and has been the cause of much evil to the Community." (*First Report on the State of the Representation of the People of Upper Canada in the Legislature of that Province* [York: Toronto Office of the Colonial Advocate, 1831, 4]). Major reforms were necessary, but this report notwithstanding, no major changes were brought to the representation in Upper Canada before the 1837 rebellion.

21. *Journals of the House of Assembly of Lower Canada,* Fourteenth Provincial Parliament, Fourth session (7 January–18 March 1834), 311–35.

22. "Seventh Report on Grievances," *Appendix to Journal of the House of Assembly of Upper Canada,* Twelfth Provincial Parliament, First Session (15 January–16 April 1835), 1:11.

4 From Allan Greer, "From Folklore to Revolution: Charivaris and the Lower Canadian Rebellion of 1837," *Histoire sociale/Social History* 15, 1 (1990): 25–43. Reprinted by permission of Taylor & Francis Ltd. (www.tandfonline.com).

For those interested in the connections between politics and popular culture, the charivari holds a peculiar fascination. Originally an aggressive ritual directed against marital deviants, the charivari came in France to be used for overtly political purposes. "The charivari," Charles Tilly has observed, "deserves special attention because it illustrates the displacement of an established form of collective action from its home territory to new ground; during the first half of the nineteenth century French people often used the charivari and related routines to state positions on national politics."[1] But the French were not the only people who deployed the charivari form for political purposes in the first half of the nineteenth century; a broadly similar development occurred at about the same time in the former French colony of Canada. Indeed, the transition was much more abrupt in North America than in Europe. The French-Canadian charivari had long been notable for its traditionalism as to form, object, and occasion, but suddenly in 1837, when Lower Canada (now the province of Quebec) was rocked by a revolutionary upheaval, this folkloric ritual made a dramatic appearance as an important vehicle for mobilizing the population against the colonial government. Enlisted not simply to "state positions" or register "protests," the charivari form was actually used to destroy elements of the existing state structure and even to prefigure a new regime. This was displacement with a vengeance!

On the surface, there was little in the Canadian charivari custom in the years before the Rebellion of 1837 that foreshadowed its future political role. To British visitors of the early nineteenth century, it seemed a picturesque but essentially harmless practice, something that could be written up in travel books to enliven the standard account of vast forests and magnificent waterfalls. The following description was based on a charivari that occurred at Quebec City in 1817:

> Here is a curious custom, which is common through the provinces, of paying a visit to any old gentleman, who marries a young wife. The young men assemble at some friends house, and disguise themselves as satyrs, negroes, sailors, old men, Catholic priests, etc., etc. Having provided a coffin, and large paper lanthorns, in the evening they sally out. The coffin is placed on the shoulder of four of the men, and the lanthorns are lighted and placed at the top of poles; followed by a motley group, they proceed towards the dwelling of the new married couple, *performing* discordantly on drums, fifes, horns, and tin pots, amidst the shouts of the populace. When they arrive at the house of the offender against, and hardy invader of, the laws of love and nature, the coffin is placed down, and a mock service is begun to be said over the supposed body. In this stage of the affair, if Benedict invites them into his house and entertains them, he hears no more of it. If he keeps his doors shut, they return night after night, every time with a fresh ludicrous composition, as *his courtship*, or *will*, which is read over with emphasis, by one of the frolicking party, who frequently pauses, whilst they salute the ears of the persecuted mortal with their music and shouting. This course is generally repeated till they tire him out, and he commutes with them by giving, perhaps, five pounds towards the frolic, and five pounds for the poor.[2]

Though this all seemed "curious" to an Englishman, a charivari along these lines would not have looked strange to a tourist from France. The mocking, carnivalesque tone of the proceedings, the nocturnal setting, the loud and raucous noise, the masks and costumes of the participants and the elaborate, insistently public, street procession all recall French practices dating back to the Middle Ages.[3] Similarly the occasion of charivaris, following a wedding, particularly that of an ill-assorted couple, matches the customs of Canada's original mother country. There were differences, however. French customs, in this as in other matters, varied greatly from region to region. Moreover, practices seem to have evolved over the years so that, even before the emergence of the fully political charivari in the nineteenth century, charivari-type harassment, sometimes associated with other customs, was often directed against all kinds of unpopular figures such as corrupt officials, submissive husbands, or promiscuous women. The colonial ritual, by contrast, seems quite uniform and consistent, from the seventeenth century to the nineteenth and from one end of Lower Canada to the other. More faithful than their European cousins to early modern models, the French of Canada always directed charivaris at newly married couples only. This seems to be one of those areas in which a European overseas settlement functioned as a sort of "cultural museum" in which customs were distilled, purified, and preserved, even as they changed drastically or disappeared in the old country. Such resolute orthodoxy prior to the rebellion makes the politicization of the charivari in 1837 all the more surprising. What was there about this "curious custom"—annoying but hardly subversive in appearance—that lent itself to a situation of acute political strife?

Although the charivari was a custom characteristic of a pre-industrial society, it would be a mistake, in my view, to regard it as simply a throwback, an expression of a "primal ethic," hostile to market relations and punitive in its reaction to nonconformist behaviour.[4] In its Canadian guise, at least, the ritual was not part of any larger pattern of collective regulation of marriage and domestic life through public demonstrations. There was no French-Canadian equivalent of the azouade ("donkey-ride") or "skimmington," humiliating punishments inflicted in early modern France and England on submissive husbands, scolding wives, and other deviants.[5] Neither did drunks and women accused of pre-marital sex have reason to fear a charivari, as was the case in some areas of Germany and the US South. Here it was the marital match itself that was at issue, not the content of domestic life. Prior to 1837, Canadian charivaris always followed a wedding and, in every case I have examined, the marriage was a "mismatch": either the groom was much older than the bride or vice versa, or else one of the partners had been previously married. Several accounts also mention a social mismatch accompanying the disparity in age or marital status. There was, for example, Monsieur Bellet, the target of the Quebec City charivari described above. A prominent merchant of the town, this 67-year-old widower had married his young servant girl. Just as typical was the charivari directed against a "widow lady of considerable fortune" who wed "a young gentleman of the Commissariat Department."[6]

Widowers marrying again were never the exclusive, or even the primary target of Canadian charivaris. Indeed, weddings joining widows and bachelors were far more likely to trigger a demonstration than the remarriage of men. Moreover, people of all ages and both sexes took part in the festivities, though men appropriated the starring roles. [. . .]

As far as the church was concerned, the wedding ceremony was a sacrament and therefore it could only be approached in a special spiritual state. The *Rituel* of the diocese of Quebec, a sort of priests' manual published in 1703 but still widely used more than a century later, insisted that prospective brides and grooms must "have a genuinely pure intent, looking to marriage only for the glory of God and their own sanctification, and not for the satisfaction of their cupidity, their ambition, their greed and their shameful passions." The fiancés, of course, had to take confession before the nuptials and curés were expected to impress upon them the true nature of marriage:

> Curés will inform the faithful that the purpose of this sacrament is to give to married persons the grace which they require to help and comfort one another, to live together in sanctity, and to contribute to the edification of the Church, not only by bringing forth legitimate children, but also by taking care to provide for their spiritual regeneration and a truly Christian education. *They will above all point out to those who wish to marry that persons who wed out of sensuality, seeking in marriage only sensual pleasure, or out of avarice, endeavouring only to establish a temporal fortune, commit a great sin, because they profane this sacrament*, and, in using something holy to satisfy their passions, they offend against the grace that Our Lord has attached to it.[7]

To marry for money or out of mere sexual appetite was not just morally reprehensible then, it was a serious sin for it defiled the holy sacrament of marriage.

This was all very well at the theoretical level, but how was a priest to detect such impure motives and prevent them from profaning the wedding rite? Unless candidates for matrimony made a direct confession of greed or lust, he could never be sure about their spiritual state. To refuse to marry anyone about whom he harboured suspicions would be to court disasters of all sorts (lay hostility, unsanctioned cohabitation, recourse to Protestant ministers . . .); furthermore, secular law would not allow refusal without good cause. In practice, then, the effort to ensure the purity of marriage consisted mainly of general exhortations to this effect and personal discussions, in the confessional and elsewhere, with candidates for wedlock. [. . .]

A priest had to marry an "ill-assorted" couple even if he harboured doubts about the purity of their intentions, but the crowd in the street might react differently to the outward signals of impurity, giving loud and dramatic voice to widely held suspicions.[8] The charivari might then be seen as a symbolic accusation of defiling a sacred rite. This surely is why a wink-and-nudge sexual jocularity, not to say downright obscenity, formed a central theme of most charivaris. Admittedly, sexual allusions were a feature of other carnival-type festivities but it seems to me that, beyond the general cheekiness, there was a specific and personal charge of illicit lust implied in the charivari. It is important to emphasize, however, that it was not "immorality" as such that was being chastised. Recall that, in French Canada, charivaris were not directed against adulterers, spouse beaters, and the like. Nor, as far as I can tell, were couples of roughly the same age ever persecuted by crowds who cited other grounds for believing they were marrying out of sensuality or avarice. The immediate purpose of charivari was not to correct immorality or even to guard the sanctity of marriage against "real" impurity. It amounted, rather, to a ritualistic response to the *signs* of desecration, a public rebuke filled with accusations of lasciviousness, that aired suspicions shared by clergy and laity alike.

But more was involved than a simple clearing of the air; charivari was also, as many commentators have pointed out, a punitive procedure. Victims were punished through both humiliation and monetary exaction, two penal techniques favoured by the church and the criminal courts of the period. Public shaming was, of course, a central feature of any charivari, inseparable from the noisy charge of desecration. It recalled the *amende honorable*, a practice common under the French regime when criminals had to go through the town wearing only a shirt and stopping occasionally to beg God's forgiveness.[9] The ecclesiastical version of the *amende honorable*, much milder than that prescribed by the judiciary, involved a public confession of sin, for example by couples who had engaged in pre-marital sex.[10] Like these practices of church and state, charivari penalized people by making a public spectacle of their faults. The *amende honorable* was more than simply a penal technique, however. In the forms deployed by both priests and judges the wayward subject had to become a penitent, confessing his sin and participating in his own correction. The charivari, too, as I shall argue below, involved an important penitential element. But, before leaving the subject of the punitive aspects of charivari, let us look at the monetary penalties that, along with public shaming, were designed to make the ceremony an unpleasant experience for its victims.

Considerable emphasis was placed, by Lower Canadian crowds at least, on the payment of what amounted to a charivari fine. The sums involved were often quite substantial—50 pounds, to take one example from Montreal[11]—though the exact amount varied from case to case, depending, it seems, on the subject's ability to pay. The level of the fine was indeed the subject of elaborate and prolonged negotiation. Usually some respected local figure was employed as a mediator during the daytime intervals between the raucous visitations and he would try to establish the terms of peace and then, later, he might see that the funds were disposed of according to the agreed-upon arrangement. Meanwhile, as negotiations proceeded by day, at night the air still rang with increasingly annoying demonstrations calculated to break down the resistance and loosen the purse-strings of the unfortunate victims. The proceeds of a charivari were normally divided fifty-fifty, with half the fine going to the participants to pay for their "expenses" (i.e., celebratory drinks in the

tavern) while the other half was contributed to an organized charity or distributed directly to the local poor.

[. . .]

Besides functioning as a penalty and as a means of soaking the rich, the charivari fine played a third and equally important role. It acted as a token of agreement signifying the re-establishment of peace between the targets and the perpetrators of ritual attack. In offering money, the newly married couple signified, however reluctantly, their submission to the judgement of their neighbours. Moreover, this forced gift implied a recognition—purely at the level of outward acts, of course—of the legitimacy of the charivari itself. The subjects were needled, nagged, annoyed, and threatened until they made a gesture signifying acceptance of the charivari, until they themselves became participants in the proceedings. When victims treated the ceremony with disdain, when they refused to sue for peace or, worse still, when they called on the "forces of order" to stop the demonstration, the invariable result was that the charivari intensified. From the crowd's point of view, the offence was then compounded for, in addition to soiling the wedding rites, the subjects had also challenged its own authority to right the wrong. This is why charivaris could go on and on—sometimes for three weeks or a month—and with escalating intensity; when couples were stubborn in their refusal to pay, the custom itself became the issue and the struggle therefore raged all the more fiercely.

As soon as a fine had changed hands, however, the harassment stopped. The money served then as a token for the crowd as well as for the victim and it placed the former under an obligation to drop hostilities. [. . .] There may have been some hard feelings in the wake of a charivari, but there is no indication that, under normal circumstances, they would have been lasting. We hear, on the contrary, of a young man of Montreal who married a widow in 1833; exactly a year after his charivari he was elected for the first time as local representative to the colonial assembly.[12] Certainly there is no reason to think that Canadian charivari victims were "permanently marked" as were, according to E.P. Thompson, the targets of the less restrained sort of "rough music" dished up in the English-speaking world.[13] But then, accusation and punishment were only part of the ritual of charivari; these were but preliminaries to the treaty of peace and reconciliation, marked by the presentation of expiatory coin.

We have moved, in discussing the charivari fine, from the area of punishment to the realm of reconciliation. Except where the crowd was defeated or thwarted in its aims, the thrust of its actions seems to have been to bring about, willy-nilly, the reintegration into the community of wayward members suspected of desecration. Nowhere in the French-Canadian record prior to 1837 does one find relentless persecution, or any apparent desire to expel or eliminate a "cancerous element" by means of charivari. [. . .]

The pre-1837 charivari was not in any clear sense oppositional. Whereas themes of social and political criticism were very much a part of charivari and carnivalesque entertainments in Renaissance Europe, in French Canada, despite the presence of anti-clerical overtones and such "ritual inversion" symbolism as cross-dressing, subversive messages were quite muted. Indeed, one might well consider the charivari a "conservative" ceremony (in so far as the vocabulary of political doctrine has any meaning in this context). Not only did it ape the procedures of priests and magistrates, it functioned as a complementary form of social control, helping to chasten deviants of a very particular sort in strictly limited circumstances. Its ultimate point of reference, moreover, was the orthodox teachings of Catholicism. Intervening when the purity of the marital sacrament was in jeopardy, the charivari crowd acted so as to restore harmony and equilibrium, in the relationship between individuals and the

community as well as in that linking God and humanity.

[. . .]

Charivari presumed a sort of "people power" of the street as one of the constituents of the larger political-ecclesiastical order. It was, then, "democratic" in a literal sense. This was a combative democracy, one which had to be defended against the repressive measures of officialdom. It was nevertheless a subordinate democracy, an exercise of popular power which assumed the existence of non-popular authority in a well-regulated community. But what if the community was not well regulated and the government no longer legitimate? This was the situation during the revolutionary crisis of 1837 when the colonial regime lost the capacity to rule with the consent of the governed. At that juncture, when attempts were made to base authority on popular sovereignty, the charivari form came to serve as a very useful vehicle for pressing the claims of the embryonic new order. This instrument of popular governance within the state (and church) became a weapon of revolt against the state.

The Lower Canadian crisis of 1837, which culminated in armed insurrection in November and December of that year, grew out of the campaign for colonial autonomy and democratic reform led by the middle-class radicals of the "Patriot party". Thanks mainly to the consistent electoral support of the bulk of the French-Canadian population, these liberal politicians managed to control the provincial legislative assembly. Opposed to the Patriots was a coalition of merchants, government officials, and settlers from the British Isles who tended to dominate all the other branches of the colonial state, including the executive, the judiciary, and the non-elective legislative chamber. Acute political conflict had brought the machinery of representative government to a grinding halt by 1836. Finally, the imperial government intervened in the following spring, hoping to end the impasse by issuing a clear refusal to Patriot demands for constitutional reform and depriving the assembly of its financial powers. The result was a storm of protest that lasted through the summer of 1837, with great public rallies, calls for a boycott of British imports and vague talk by Patriot leaders about a re-enactment of the American Revolution at some point in the future. The constant theme of radical rhetoric was that the British measures against the assembly had made colonial rule in Lower Canada illegal and illegitimate. Apart from stirring up popular indignation, however, the Patriots made no serious efforts to prepare for a war which they still believed to be many years away. Events moved toward a showdown more quickly than predicted, though, as the mobilization of the populace, particularly the inhabitants of the Montreal District, provoked repressive counter-measures which in turn led to further resistance.

As the conflict intensified in June and July, noisy demonstrations, often carried out at night by disguised bands, became common. In August newspapers began to report ritual attacks against government partisans that they did not hesitate to call "charivaris" (victims and attackers also used this term) and that did indeed seem to be closely modelled on the popular custom. This was the first appearance of political charivaris in Lower Canada and it came in two quite distinct phases. The first phase, from August to mid-October, seems to have been rather more spontaneous and popular in origin whereas, during the second phase (late October–early November 1837), the coordinating role of the Patriot bourgeois leadership became more apparent and charivaris were used for more clearly strategic purposes.

In the late summer and early fall of 1837 there were reports from several villages that a masked party gathered by night outside the home of a prominent Tory and "gave him a serenade whose chords were scarcely soothing to the ears."[14] These demonstrations resemble the politicized charivaris that became common in France under the July monarchy; indeed, they may have been inspired by European models, although I have no evidence of a direct connection. Certainly the negative serenades fit into established Canadian charivari traditions that were, of course, a French import of an earlier century; the link with native custom appears particularly in the choice of specific targets during this first phase of political charivaris. Masked revellers did not attack such obvious objects as officials or soldiers.[15] Nor did they direct their serenades against members of the English-speaking minority, even though many of the latter manifested a paranoid counter-nationalism that made them violent defenders of the British Empire. Anti-Patriot anglophones might be ostracized by their neighbours or they might find the tails and manes of their horses cut off. (This last form of harassment could certainly be placed under the broad heading of the carnivalesque, for it was a kind of symbolic castration designed to make the animal's owner a laughing stock when he rode it in public.)[16] However, attacks modelled much more closely on the charivari were reserved, in the early fall of 1837, for French-Canadian partisans of the government, and particularly for individuals who had until recently taken part in the Patriot movement but had "deserted the cause of the nation" when revolution loomed on the horizon. Members of the group—whether defined linguistically or in terms of political allegiance—who had broken ranks during an emergency when petty differences had to be forgotten, these "turncoats," were perfect targets for a treatment, the charivari, which had always served, not to attack "outsiders," but to reprove and punish the familiar deviant. Essentially expressions of hostility, these early political charivaris did not demand anything in particular of their victims, but they did probably have the effect of curbing the activities of influential French Canadians who might have been inclined to speak out in favour of the government.

Political charivaris of a special sort came to play a much more important role at a later stage of the confrontation—that is, in the two months preceding the military denouement of late November 1837. The central development of this period—one which led inexorably to the armed clash—was the breakdown of local administration in the countryside of western Lower Canada. While it awaited the arrival of additional troops from neighbouring colonies in the summer of 1837, the government had tried to stem the tide of agitation by banning "seditious assemblies," but it found that proclamations to this effect were simply ignored. Particularly in the heavily populated Montreal District, long a Patriot hotbed, giant rallies succeeded one another and often it was the justices of the peace and militia captains, upon whom the colonial authorities depended to enforce their writ, who were organizing them. The governor reacted to this flagrant defiance by dismissing "disloyal" magistrates and officers. Denouncing this move as further proof of British tyranny, Patriots who held the Queen's commission but who had been overlooked in the purge made a great show of resigning. Beginning in October, meetings were held in many parishes to set up new local administrations and, in the ensuing elections, the "martyred" officers were usually reinstated. A parallel local government, based on popular sovereignty and completely divorced from the colonial regime, was then taking shape. On 23–24 October a great public meeting held at the village of St Charles to establish a federation of six counties south of Montreal gave official Patriot approval to these uncoordinated local initiatives and urged all good citizens to imitate them.

Local government in Canada had always been rather rudimentary and subordinate to the central authorities in Quebec City. (The child of absolutism, Canada was ruled by colonial regimes—first the French, later the British—whose preoccupations were largely military and who dispensed with direct taxation and therefore with the communal institutions that could be so troublesome to western European monarchies.) By the time of the rebellion, justices of the peace and militia captains, whose responsibilities were more of a police than of a military nature, were the only important public authorities, apart from priests, in the rural parishes of Lower Canada. They were all appointed by the governor but they were definitely members of the communities they administered. Indeed, the inhabitants found various ways of "domesticating" officials who appeared in theory to be the agents of an external power. Each captain, for example, was presented with a "maypole," a tall tree trunk decorated with flags and banners and planted in the ground in front of his house, in an elaborate ceremony that implied popular ratification of the governor's choice. In the fall of 1837 many maypoles became "liberty poles" and, to mark the transformation, a sign reading "elected by the people" was attached to a captain's mast.[17]

But what about officers and magistrates who declined to resign? There were many loyalists who tried to maintain their positions, even in areas where the population was overwhelmingly hostile to the government. From the Patriot point of view, these holdouts were the willing agents of despotism and rebels against the emergent local regimes. At a more practical level, they appeared as potentially dangerous spies and fifth-columnists at a time when war with Great Britain looked less and less remote. The issue of the Queen's commissions therefore served to personalize the struggle by identifying important enemies and bringing great constitutional conflicts down to the local level. Accordingly, loyalist officers and magistrates in massively Patriot communities came under great pressure to resign. Some suffered the fate of Captain Louis Bessette, a prosperous inhabitant whose evening meal was disturbed by the sound of axes biting into wood. Going out to investigate, he found a band of men with blackened faces in the process of chopping down his maypole. The mast crashed to the ground and a great cheer went up from the party; the house was then besieged by the noisy, stone-throwing crowd until Bessette agreed to turn over his commission.[18] The cutting down of captains' maypoles was a favourite gesture in 1837 and one rich in symbolic meaning. If the mast had originally been planted as a phallic token of respect for a patriarchal figure, Bessette's experience was, then, one of symbolic castration. At another level, however, this action should be seen as revoking the popular ratification of the captain's appointment that the maypole embodied. "You are no longer our captain," was the clear message addressed to Louis Bessette.

Whether accompanied by the severing of maypoles or not (and, of course, many of the magistrates and officers who held commissions were not militia captains), the charivari form was the preferred mechanism in the countryside south of Montreal for forcing refractory office holders to resign. National origin and previous political commitments were now (October–November) no longer a consideration. Anyone who continued to hold office was subject to attack. Dudley Flowers of St Valentin was the victim of one typical charivari, which he described two weeks later in a judicial deposition:

> I am a Lieutenant in the Militia. On the twenty seventh day of October last in the afternoon the following persons viz. C.H.O. Côté, Olivier Hébert, L.M. Decoigne, Julien Gagnon, Amable Lamoureux and Jacob Bouchard, came to my house and demanded my commission as such Lieutenant to which I made answer that I would give it up to none but the governor of the Province. Doctor Côté said that if I did not give up my commission I would be sorry for it—to which Gagnon added, "Si vous ne voulez pas vivre en haine avec nous autres rendez votre commission." Upon this they

went away. About eleven o'clock in the night of the same day the same persons returned—at least I have every reason to believe that they were the same persons. . . . They began yelling in the most frightful manner. They threw stones at my house and broke the greatest part of my windows. A large stone passed very near one of my children and would have killed him if it had struck him. Julien Gagnon who had seen my barn full of oats when he came in the day time told me that I should not have to thresh them unless I gave up my commission and also said that my grain, my house and outhouses would be burnt. I saw one of the mob go with a firebrand to my barn with the intention as I verily believe of setting fire to it. But it was in a damp state from the recent rain and the fire would not take.

> On the night of the following day (28th October last) it might be about ten o'clock a masked mob, composed of about thirty or forty persons attacked my house in a similar manner . . .

> On the following day (Sunday) about seven in the evening, some sixty or seventy individuals attacked my house a third time in the same manner and with the same threats as on the former occasions but if possible with much more violence, beating kettles and pans, blowing horns, calling me a rebel, saying it would be the last time they would come as they would finish me in half an hour. They had in a short time with stones and other missiles broken in part of the roof of my house and boasted that it would soon be demolished. Fearing that such must inevitably be the case, I opened the door and told them that if four or five of their party would come in and give their names I would give them up my commission. Four or five of them did come in, disguised in the most hideous manner but refused to give their names.

Finding that my life was actually in danger if I refused to comply with their requests, I handed them my commission. There were about fifteen of the last mentioned mob masked . . .

The same persons have declared in my presence that they were determined to compel in the same manner all persons holding commissions from her Majesty to surrender them. One of these individuals told me boastingly that they had obtained no less than sixty-two commissions in one day. I firmly believe that if Doctor Côté and some of the ringleaders were taken up and punished it would have the effect of alarming the others and keeping them quiet.[19]

Many of the features of the "traditional" charivari were present in this episode: the nocturnal setting, the "hideous" disguises, the raucous serenade of blaring horns, banging pots and shouted insults. Even the lieutenant's initial encounter with the Patriot delegation recalled the negotiating process by which charivari fines were normally set: the talks were businesslike, superficially friendly but with an undertone of menace, and they were held in daylight, in an atmosphere that contrasted sharply with that of the charivari itself. Flowers resisted for some time the summons to resign but, following the example of an ordinary charivari crowd faced with a stubborn old widower, his attackers simply intensified their efforts, bringing more supporters and threatening ever more ferocious punishment on each successive evening. There were differences too, of course, notably in the stone-throwing and the overt threats of serious violence.

That the Patriots should have had recourse to the charivari custom at this juncture is not surprising. A coercive practice in which the aggressors' identities were concealed had obvious attractions at a time when arrest was still a real danger. This anonymity probably also served an equally important psychological purpose for the participants, that of overcoming inhibitions against aggressive behaviour. Indeed, the entire ritualistic package of charivari surely had this function. After all, Dudley Flowers was apparently a long-time resident of the community and he knew his attackers personally; even though he was a political enemy, the lieutenant was also a neighbour and therefore someone with whom it was important to maintain peaceful, though not necessarily cordial, relations. To turn on him with overt hostility would be to go against ingrained habits; masks and a familiar ritual may have made easier the transformation of neighbourly Jekylls into frightening Hydes.

The charivari custom offered more than simply an antidote to fears and uncertainties, however. The turning over of a sum of money was the central event of a traditional charivari and much of the pageantry was designed to extort this gift from an unwilling giver. What a perfect vehicle for forcing loyalists to resign or, more precisely, to "turn over their commissions" as the Patriot mobs usually put it. The political charivaris of this second stage of the drama of 1837 were rather blunt in declaring their intention to overcome opposition to their demands, and low-level violence, consisting mainly of stone-throwing, was common. Men like Dudley Flowers, who resisted the initial attack, were likely to have their windows broken. Captain Bessette suffered more damage than any of the other charivari victims; after chopping down his maypole, the attacking party forced its way into his house and, calling for his resignation with a deafening roar, the intruders pounded out a rhythm with sticks and clubs until his table, windows, and stovepipe had been smashed to bits. Now this toll of broken glass and damaged roofs, though severe by the standards of ordinary pre-rebellion charivaris, seems quite light considering the context of serious political crisis. Even more striking is the complete absence of personal injuries. When one places this record against the cracked heads and burned houses that resulted from, for example, the anti-Irish riots of contemporary New England and New Brunswick—not to mention the destruction wrought by crowd action in revolutionary episodes comparable to 1837—the restraining influence of the charivari form becomes all the more apparent.[20]

Of course Dudley Flowers was not impressed by the relative mildness of the treatment he received: he truly thought his life and his property were in real and immediate peril and, though he was no coward, he was frightened enough to abandon his home and flee with his family to the city shortly after the events reported in his deposition. This is because the charivari, "political" or otherwise, was designed to be frightening, particularly in the eyes of those who resisted its edicts. Before 1837, coffins and skull-and-crossbones designs hinted at deadly intentions but, during the rebellion, the threats were much more explicit. Crowds attacked stubborn magistrates and officers with talk of arson and murder. Who could be sure they were simply bluffing when, as was often the case, masked revellers were seen carrying guns as well as firebrands? Lieutenant Flowers felt he had had a lucky escape and that only the damp weather had saved his barnful of grain from the Patriot torches. He might have been less worried had he known how many other loyalists had been similarly threatened, without one single building ever being fired. The fact that he did believe himself to be in serious danger shows just how well the charivari served its theatrical purposes in the fall of 1837, when dozens of local officials capitulated to the Patriot mobs.

So far I have been discussing the way in which the charivari form was applied during the campaign of late October–early November for wholly novel political purposes. Yet, beyond the surface resemblances, there were also elements of continuity with the past in the basic functions of the ritual. For example, the extortion of royal commissions seems to have been more than simply a means of destroying the government presence in the countryside; it also had meaning in the context of the specific relationship between an individual and the community of which he was a member. In other words, this forced gift played a role analogous to that of the ordinary charivari fine in signifying the giver's submission to the authority of the collectivity. But now the community as a whole and the Patriot cause were identified. Accordingly, some charivari victims were forced to shout "*Vive la liberté!*" or to cheer for Papineau, the Patriot chief, as further proof of recognition of the incipient new regime. In accepting the victim's commission, the crowd gave its implicit assurance (sometimes it was clearly stated) that the charivari was at an end.

There was a sense, then, in which a non-resigning officer such as Dudley Flowers was treated as a sinner, a contaminating influence in a community otherwise true to new civic ideals. The charivari worked so as to force him into the position of a penitent who had to purchase his reintegration into the fold at the price of a militia commission. Thus the admonition addressed to Lieutenant Flowers by Julien Gagnon during the preliminary visit to his home: resign your position, "if you do not wish to live in a state of hatred with us." No one expected him to become a militant Patriot overnight, but he was being offered an opportunity to make peace with his offended neighbours. It is important to emphasize that, just as conventional charivaris were aimed not against general immorality but against a specific affront to the wedding ceremony, so Flowers was targeted for a specific offence rather than some general nonconformity. Though government supporters at the time, not to mention later historians, saw the Rebellion of 1837 as stemming from a xenophobic French-Canadian hostility to English-speaking fellow-citizens, no one reproached Dudley on national or religious grounds. His "crime" was not in professing Protestantism, in speaking English, or even in believing in the Queen's majesty, but simply in retaining a commission at a time when all good citizens had a duty to resign. The atonement required of this wayward soul was just as specific and limited as the "sin" itself. He had merely to make a gesture—that of turning over his commission—that signified a renunciation of former "treason" and an acceptance of the authority of the Patriot crowd. The emphasis was on the outward act indicating a transfer of allegiance without any further surrender of personal autonomy. This was made clear to another loyalist militia officer, who proclaimed to the 50 blackened faces shouting for his resignation "that if they compelled him to give up his commissions they could not change his principles"; that is all right, came the sarcastic reply, we do not wish to alter your religion.[21]

The boast reported by Dudley Flowers of 62 political charivaris in his region alone may have been exaggerated but the basic point that, within a few weeks, dozens of resignations had been secured by this means is undeniable. By the second week of November there was, to all intents and purposes, no official government presence in most of the populous rural parishes of the District of Montreal, and an elective magistracy and militia were beginning to operate in its place. In such a situation the government naturally had recourse to its now reinforced military forces to enforce its own claim to sovereignty. The British expeditions that ventured out from Montreal were surprised at the resistance offered by the inhabitants, hastily organized through the revolutionized militia companies. The initial armed encounter at St Denis (23 November) was, in fact, a Patriot victory but, since the insurgent military effort was localized, fragmented, and defensive, the troops soon crushed their amateur opponents. What followed, in many localities, was a series of very unritualistic punitive actions; loyalists then had the satisfaction of watching flames race through the homes of neighbours who had so recently issued empty threats of arson. Turmoil continued for over a year, in Upper Canada (Ontario) as well as Lower Canada, while Patriot refugees in the northern states tried to enlist American support. But, by the end of the decade, the republican movement had been effectively destroyed.

[. . .]

For such an orthodox and mild-mannered custom, the traditional French-Canadian charivari had proved remarkably effective as a vehicle of revolt. Of course the Patriots were soundly beaten. This is hardly surprising, given the relative strength of the parties in conflict: a small colony with no external allies faced the premier imperial power on earth at a time when the latter was not distracted by serious difficulties at home or abroad. The wonder is that the inhabitants of Lower Canada were able to cripple colonial rule to the extent that they did in the fall of 1837. This is where the politicized charivari form made a crucial contribution. Serving at first, as in contemporary France, as a medium of complaint and protest, it was soon deployed as the central element in a campaign to destroy government power in the countryside and to assert a practical sort of popular sovereignty. This was a truly revolutionary role for a venerable ritual, even if the ensuing debacle did expose the military and diplomatic weaknesses of the Patriot movement.

The charivari was well suited for its insurrectional mission in a number of practical ways. The very fact, first of all, that it was a custom of collective action made it an important cultural resource when groups of people had to be assembled and organized. Since collective institutions and traditions were rather weak in French Canada, recourse to the charivari was all the more natural. Additionally, and more specifically, charivari was a more useful device under the circumstances because of the way it concealed the identity of aggressors. Above all, the traditional focus on extortion lent itself to Patriot strategies in the fall of 1837, as did the larger drama of forcing wayward individuals to make a gesture of renunciation and submission. Charivari had always been coercive, but only in a very discriminating way. Its techniques were therefore well adapted to the delicate task of exacting a particular type of obedience from certain recalcitrant individuals, all without bloodshed.

In addition to its strictly tactical role, the charivari form functioned as a framework within which the villagers of Lower Canada grappled with the moral and philosophical problems of revolt. Linked to widely held and longstanding beliefs concerning relations between the individual, the community and the cosmic order, the custom was deeply rooted in dominant political and religious ideologies. At the same time, it embodied an implicit assertion of popular rights to a share of public authority. Here was a democratic germ, and one whose claims to legitimacy were formidable. Thus, when the crisis of colonial rule came, a law-abiding peasantry that brought out its charivari masks and noise-makers in order to depose local officials could feel it was doing the right thing in the right way.

NOTES

1. Charles Tilly, *The Contentious French* (Cambridge, MA, 1986), 30.
2. John Palmer, *Journal of Travels in the United States of North America and in Lower Canada performed in the year 1817* (1818), 227–8.
3. Among the works dealing with the charivaris of early modern France, see Arnold Van Gennep, *Manuel de folklore français contemporain*, 4 vols (Paris, 1937–49), II, 614–28; Roger Vaultier, *Le folklore pendant la guerre de Cent Ans d'après les lettres de rémission du trésor des chartes* (Paris, 1965); Natalie Z. Davis, "The Reasons of Misrule" in *Society and Culture in Early Modern France* (Stanford, 1975), 97–123; Claude Gauvard and Altan Gokalp, "Les conduites de bruit et leur signification a la fin du Moyen Age: le charivari," AESC, 29e année (May–June 1974), 693–704; Jacques LeGoff and Jean-Claude Schmitt (eds), *Le Charivari* (Paris, 1981).
4. This phrase comes from Bertram Wyatt-Brown, *Southern Honor: Ethics and Behavior in the Old South* (New York, 1982), 435–6.
5. In addition to the work cited in the previous note, see E.P. Thompson, "'Rough Music': le charivari anglais," AESC 27e année (March–April 1972), 285–3; Martin Ingram, "Ridings, Rough Music and the 'Reform of Popular Culture' in early modern England," *Past and Present*, cv (Nov. 1984), 79–113; Christian Desplat, *Charivaris en Gascogne: la "morale des peuples" du XVIe au XXe siecle* (Paris, 1982).
6. Edward Allen Talbot, *Five Years' Residence in the Canadas: including a Tour through part of the United States of America, in the year 1823* (1824), 300.
7. *Rituel du diocèse de Québec, publié par l'ordre de Monseigneur l'évêque de Québec* (Paris, 1703), 347, 329 (my translation and my emphasis). Cf. Jean-Louis Flandrin, *Families in Former Times: Kinship, Household and Sexuality*, trans. Richard Southern (Cambridge, 1979), 161–4.
8. Serge Gagnon, "Amours interdites et misères conjugales dans le Québec rural de la fin du XVIIIe siècle jusque vers 1830 (l'arbitrage des prêtres)" in François Lebrun and Normand Séguin (eds), *Sociétés villageoises et rapports villes-campagnes au Québec et dans la France de l'ouest, XVIIe–XXe siècles* (Trois-Rivières, 1987), 323 (my translation). This case occurred in 1810.
9. André Lachance, *La justice criminelle du roi au Canada au XVIIIe siècle: tribunaux et officiers* (Quebec, 1978), 113–15.
10. Gagnon, op. cit., 324.
11. Talbot, op. cit., 303.
12. Robert-Lionel Séguin, *Les divertissements en Nouvelle-France* (Ottawa, 1968), 73.
13. Thompson, op. cit., 290.
14. *La Minerve* (Montreal), 10 Aug. 1837 (my translation). See also *Le Populaire* (Montreal), 27 Sept. 1837; 2, 9, and 16 Oct. 1837; *Montreal Gazette*, 30 Sept. 1837.

15. There was one exception to this pattern. A crowd that had turned out to greet the Patriot leader Louis-Joseph Papineau at St Hyacinthe, learning that the commander of British forces happened also to be staying in the town, gathered round the house where the latter was staying for a noisy vigil punctuated by catcalls and anti-government slogans.

16. Archives nationales du Québec, documents relatifs aux événements de 1837–1838 (hereafter ANQ, 1837), deposition of Robert Hall, 15 July 1837.

17. Robert Christie, *A History of the Late Province of Lower Canada, Parliamentary and Political, from the Commencement to the Close of its Existence as a Separate Province*, 6 vols (Montreal, 1866), V, 32–3.

18. ANQ, 1837, no. 257, deposition of Louis Bessette, 5 Nov. 1837.

19. ANQ, 1837, no. 146, deposition of Dudley Flowers, 3 Nov. 1837.

20. Ray Billington, *The Protestant Crusade 1800–1860: A Study of the Origins of American Nativism* (New York, 1938); Scott W. See, "The Orange Order and Social Violence in Mid-Nineteenth Century Saint John," *Acadiensis* XIII (Autumn 1983): 68–92. See also Sean Wilentz, *Chants Democratic: New York City and the Rise of the American Working Class, 1788–1850* (New York, 1984), 264–5.

21. PAC, RG4, AI, vol. 524, no. 11, deposition of Loop Odell, 17 Nov. 1837.

Chapter 10

Women in British North America

READINGS

Primary Documents

1   "To the Electors of Quebec County," *Le Canadien*, 21 May 1808

2   From *The Proper Sphere and Influence of Woman in Christian Society: Being a Lecture Delivered by Rev. Robert Sedgewick before the Young Men's Christian Association, Halifax, N.S., November 1856*, Robert Sedgewick

Historical Interpretations

3   From "Women and the Escheat Movement," in *Separate Spheres: Women's Worlds in the 19th-Century Maritimes*, Rusty Bitterman

4   From "Women's Agency in Upper Canada: Prescott's Board of Police Record, 1834–1850," Katherine McKenna

INTRODUCTION

Converging political, economic, and social forces fundamentally reshaped British North America in the nineteenth century. From small, isolated, and weak colonies dependent on the metropolitan state, Lower and Upper Canada, New Brunswick, Nova Scotia, and eventually Prince Edward Island (to say nothing of Rupert's Land and the west coast) came to form a new entity called the Dominion of Canada. As important and noteworthy as this evolution was, it was hardly the only one. Another fundamental change was the transition from a pre-industrial to an industrial society. The advent of a new social order had huge economic and social consequences. One of these concerned the roles, rights, privileges, and expectations ascribed to men and women, both at home and in the community. It promoted the separation of the private and public spheres as the proper way to organize society. According to this discourse, women were expected to participate only in those areas of life that touched upon womanly or family welfare. But the rise of this cult of domesticity in the 1850s should not hide the fact that the place of women in the social and political life of the colonies had been more extensive in the first half of the century.

The primary documents chosen for this topic reflect the evolution of attitudes toward women in public and private life from 1808 to 1856. The first document reminds us that gender did not automatically disqualify women from voting in early-nineteenth-century British North America, even if admittedly very few women met the property qualification to be enfranchised. The property laws in Lower Canada, inherited in part from France, granted more property rights to women, and most female voters in British North America were from this colony. Though the letter to voters from Quebec County was probably intended to harm the election campaign of the candidate named, it tells us a lot about contemporary morality and expectations surrounding male–female relationships. The second primary document illustrates the emergence of the cult of domesticity in British North America. Rev. Sedgewick's lecture, a recitation of the existing boundaries between men and women and a declaration that women were to *complement* men, is notable as well because it was pitched at young men who were supposed to be forming their own systems of belief and ethics.

In his article, Rusty Bitterman discusses the violence in Prince Edward Island in the context of the Escheat movement. He demonstrates that women did not shy away from violence in the 1830s as they enthusiastically participated in defending their lands from landlords' claims, and joined larger community resistance. His article shows that women's lives in Prince Edward Island during the first half of the nineteenth century were different from the ideal promoted by Sedgewick. For her part, Katherine McKenna discusses how women dealt with the Prescott's Board of Police Record in Upper Canada. She shows how this institution progressively adopted and imposed new gendered principles when dealing with women.

QUESTIONS FOR CONSIDERATION

1. What does the letter from "The Unfortunate Jeannette" suggest about attitudes toward women's participation or non-participation in political life during the early part of the nineteenth century?
2. How does Rev. Sedgewick justify not extending various rights and privileges to women, even though he seems to be in favour of all of these benefits for men?
3. Without thinking about questions of fairness or justice, were there any practical purposes for women and men maintaining these semi-exclusive existences?
4. What sources can historians use to study women's participation in colonial societies? What are these sources' limitations?
5. What kinds of violent behaviours do Bitterman and McKenna highlight in their respective articles? What would account for the difference between the violence experienced by women in Prince Edward Island and Upper Canada?

SUGGESTIONS FOR FURTHER READING

Constance Backhouse, *Petticoats and Prejudice: Women and Law in Nineteenth-Century Canada* (Toronto: Women's Press, for the Osgoode Society, 1991).

Bettina Bradbury, *Wife to Widow: Lives, Laws, and Politics in Nineteenth-Century Montreal* (Vancouver: UBC Press, 2012).

Lori Chambers, *Married Women and Property Law in Victorian Ontario* (Toronto: University of Toronto Press, 1997).

Lara Campbell, Tamara Myers, and Adele Perry, eds, *Rethinking Canada: The Promise of Women's History* (Toronto: Oxford University Press, 2016).

Janet Guildford and Suzanne Morton, eds, *Separate Spheres: Women's Worlds in the 19th-Century Maritimes* (Fredericton: Acadiensis Press, 1994).

Willeen Keough, *The Slender Thread: Irish Women on the Southern Avalon Peninsula of Newfoundland, 1750–1860* (New York: Columbia University Press, 2006).

Cecilia Morgan, *Public Men and Virtuous Women: The Gendered Languages of Religion and Politics in Upper Canada 1791–1850* (Toronto: University of Toronto Press, 1996).

Carmen J. Nielson, *Private Women and the Public Good: Charity and State Formation in Hamilton, Ontario, 1846–93* (Vancouver: UBC Press, 2015).

Françoise Noël, *Family Life and Sociability in Upper and Lower Canada, 1780–1870: A View from Diaries and Family Correspondence* (Montreal and Kingston: McGill-Queen's University Press, 2003).

Jan Noel, *Along a River: The First French-Canadian Women* (Toronto: University of Toronto Press, 2013).

Mary Anne Poutanen, *Beyond Brutal Passions: Prostitution in Early Nineteenth-Century Montreal* (Montreal and Kingston: McGill-Queen's University Press, 2015).

Primary Documents

1   "To the Electors of Quebec County," *Le Canadien*, 21 May 1808

TO THE ELECTORS OF QUEBEC COUNTY

Gentlemen,

Although it is not customary for women to address you at election time, I hope you will forgive the liberty of an unfortunate soul who has no other resource than to appeal to your sense of justice. To whom else could I appeal? The ungrateful wretch I complain of is the Judge himself.

You know well enough, Gentlemen, the trouble I went to in working for him during the election campaign at Charlesbourg four years ago; he had suffered badly in the election in the Upper Town; and out of pity, as many of you did, I worked as hard as I could to assure his triumph. Gentlemen, you witnessed this triumph of which he boasted so much. Yet, no sooner had he won than he forgot all I had done for him, and, coward that he is, abandoned me. He had the insolence to tell me that it was I who was harming his reputation among you. Gentlemen, will you let this kind of treachery go unpunished? Will your votes in his favour reward his betrayal? Will you elect him for having broken faith with me?

The ingrate even got married, and began to frequent the Church; this was to obtain your votes. He is inconstant I assure you; I know him, he will use any means to achieve his end.

He makes promises to you, but how many promises did he make to me? He will deceive you as he deceived me. He will deceive you as he deceived the Lower Town. How many promises did he not make to the voters on the day of his triumph four years ago?

This false man has never been able to win an election except in Three Rivers. . . . What honour will you gain in electing him? The Upper Town scorned him four years ago, Deschambault had driven him out, Nicolet had driven him out. Will it be that Charlesbourg will join Three Rivers in electing him!

What will be said of Charlesbourg? What will be said of Beauport, where he is so well known? People will say that it was because he was a Judge, that it was out of fear of losing their cases in court that voters elected him. Did the Upper Town succomb to such fears? Did Deschambault and Nicolet? What now! Canadiens who never feared enemy fire in battle will become cowards for fear of losing a court case!

What an honour for Canadiens to see *their judge* running for election, to see him profane the image of the King whom he represents so unworthily? Do English judges run in elections? . . . Only Canadiens so dishonour themselves. I am a Canadienne, Gentlemen, and I would die rather than consent to such dishonour.

The Unfortunate Jeannette

2 From Robert Sedgewick, *The Proper Sphere and Influence of Woman in Christian Society: Being a Lecture Delivered by Rev. Robert Sedgewick before the Young Men's Christian Association, Halifax, N.S., November 1856* (Halifax: J. Barnes, 1856), 3–30.

LECTURE

The errors and blunders which are interwoven with the subject of woman's rights and woman's place in modern society are, as these points now engage public attention, to be traced either to the ignoring of the fact or the omission of the fact that in the economy of nature or rather in the design of God, *woman is the complement of man*. In defining her sphere and describing her influence, this fact is fundamental. Unless this fact be admitted as an axiom in every way self-evident, no reasoning on this subject is sound, and no conclusion legitimate, and the whole theme becomes little better than a mass of mere assumption, alike illogical in its progress and unsatisfactory in its conclusions. [. . .]

If it be thus clear that woman is the complement of man, it must follow that the sphere of the one is different from that of the other. The spheres in which they severally move are concentric indeed, and thus there must be a very great similarity between them; but there is a vast difference between diversity and opposition, and hence when it is asserted that the sphere of woman is different from that of man, it is not to be understood as if it were opposed or contrary to that of man. [. . .]

It may be worth while, therefore, to enquire what, after all, is the sphere of woman; and here it may be as well to adopt the good old way of showing what it is not, and then of showing what it is, looking at the subject negatively and then positively. [. . .]

It would never do, however, from these premises, to draw the conclusion that woman behoves and is bound to exert her powers in the same direction and for the same ends as man. This were to usurp the place of man— this were to forget her position as the complement of man, and assume a place she is incompetent to fill, or rather was not designed to fill. [. . .]

Were it not that so much is said about it in the neighboring States, it would seem utterly preposterous to assert that Parliament was the proper sphere of woman, and that she is just where she ought to be when sitting on the red benches, and is engaged as she ought to be in drawing out Bills—in explaining and defending them—in standing in the arena of angry debate, and condemning and counter-working one course of policy by justifying and furthering another, and as is thought a better. Now first of all it might be asked how are women to get there? Are they to set up as candidates for the representation and come out on the hard-shell ticket or the soft-shell ticket, on the red or the blue; and are they to appear on the hustings on the day of nomination, and, unless unanimously elected, to demand a poll? One thing is certain—he would be a sheriff indeed who succeeded in keeping the peace, on the day of election, provided the contest lay between a male and a female candidate, and much more if it lay between two female candidates. And then is it to be a mixed Assembly, are the honorable man-members and woman-members to meet together and unite their wisdom in legislating for their country, [. . .] or are the women to have a separate house and to manage the public business themselves, untrammelled by the presence, unawed by the criticism of their fellow male-members? This would be a Parliament with a vengeance. This if ever would be a speaking Assembly. And what are the powers with which such a House is to be invested? Are they to be subordinate to the other House? That would never do.

Or are they to be co-ordinate with them? That would be as unsatisfactory. Or, as probably the ladies would wish it, are they to be superordinate? Why, the claim would be resented as a most presumptuous invasion of the rights of men, and as utterly intolerable as fairly beyond the limits of the Constitution. [. . .]

But seriously, that the question of investing woman with similar political rights with man, and demanding of her the discharge of similar political duties, should have arisen at this time of day, after such a world-wide and a world-long experience, is indeed one of the wonders of the age.

There is a passage in one of the Lectures of Horace Mann on the powers and duties of woman, which is every way so appropriate and withal so clear and convincing and eloquent as illustrating this point, that it deserves an acquaintanceship as extensive as possible:—[. . .]

Nothing, as it seems to be, can account for the present clamour in behalf of women voters and women office-holders but the amazingly false notions which prevail respecting the intrinsic dignity and enduring importance of education, as compared with the ephemeral tinsel of political distinctions. Respecting the clean and beautiful work of the teacher, training up characters to empyrean height and purity, as compared with the noisome and bloody work of the politician, sometimes flaying and cauterizing, and sometimes amputating and beheading, to cure or cut away from the body politic those frightful gangrenes whose very existence would have been prevented by the intelligent and faithful performance of woman's earlier and holier service. As to the idea that woman has a self evident and inalienable right to assist in the government of the race, I reply she does assist in that government now, and would to heaven she would exercise a still larger share in its administration. But this great work, like all others, is naturally divided between the sexes, the nobler government of children belonging to women, the less noble government of adults to man.

But, if the Halls of Legislature and of Congress were opened to women, they would purify them it is said. The answer to this must recognize both hypotheses respecting the sexes. First, if woman is like man, why should she not do as man has done, only aggravating and multiplying his evil works, because then the competitors would be doubled and all restraints withdrawn. But secondly, as I contend, woman is unlike man, better when she is good and worse when she is bad. Then, at least, in the present state of society, I believe that her participation in political strifes, ambitions and cupidities, would rouse to tempestuous fury all the passions that ever swept her to swiftest perdition—Men and women are yet drawn together by too many passional affinities to allow us even to hope that husbands could leave their wives, and wives their husbands, and pass for months and months, by day and by night, through all the enforced intimacies and juxtapositions of legislative life without something more than pure platonic emotions, and she who wishes her sex to encounter these perils has forgotten the wisest prayer that was ever made, "Lead us not into temptation." [. . .]

In justice, however, to the other side of this question, perhaps I ought not to omit certain collateral and incidental benefits which may be claimed to accrue should woman strip off her sex and rough it with man in the turbulence and riot of the political arena. What a beautiful school for domestic debate; prolonged not merely from morn to dewy eve, but from eve to early morn, should the father be a whig, the mother a democrat, and the daughter a third party man. On the stump, at the hustings or other bear-garden, the intimate relation of husband and wife would furnish admirable facilities for mutual impeachment and recrimination, which to bachelors and marriage haters would be intensely edifying. If husband and wife were rivals for the same office, then, no matter which party might prevail, the honour and emoluments would still come into the family, or, if both were elected to Senate or House, they might pelt each other from the opposition benches, which would be a great relief from closer quarters. [. . .] As to the parents' equal right to inculcate hostile political doctrines on the minds of their children they might make a compromise, each devoting alternate lessons on alternate days to the exposure of the other's iniquities, so that the children in the end would have a good opportunity to know the weakness of them both. [. . .]

It is now time that woman's sphere in Christian society be defined and described. [. . .] The sphere of woman is home and whatever is co-relative with home in the social economy. [. . .]

It is only at home and its co-relative situations that man finds woman to be his complement. In no other situation she can fill, in no other sphere in which she can move, will she so answer the end of her being, so far as this point goes, but at home; and this fact also, for fact it is, settles the question—what is the sphere of woman? In the camp she must either be the superior or the subordinate or the equal of man; she cannot be his complement, or, at least, she is so with multitudinous drawbacks. [. . .]

It is not the design of this lecture to treat on female education. It would seem that this point was taken for granted in the subject, and that it was admitted that, whatever the sphere, woman was qualified rightly to move in it, still the unity of the theme could not have been preserved unless some slight reference were had to this matter.

Now, there can be no doubt that the three r's, as the Irishman said, are important parts of female education, reading, writing and arithmetic. These lie at the foundation of all useful knowledge, indeed, without them the main instrumentality of acquiring knowledge is awanting, and there can be as little doubt also that the elegant accomplishments, when they can be acquired, may add very much to the usefulness of woman at home. Music and drawing, and painting and embroidery, and a smattering of French and Italian, of heavy German and clumsy Dutch, are all so many acquirements which, if once obtained, may serve to enliven a drawing room conversation and amuse and please for the nonce a drawing room party, and then they are easily retained, other things being equal, and may be exceedingly useful in various situations in life; nor can any body refuse to admit, who is willing to do woman justice, that it is quite competent and that it may be advantageous for her to dabble among the 'ologies and dive deep down into their dark regions. There is geology and ethnology and conchology and entomology, then biology and phrenology and astrology, if you will, all of them in their place somewhat instructive, all of them in their place somewhat profitable, even for a woman to know. Indeed, in certain circles of society, where these and cognate themes may happen to be the subject of conversation, a woman looks exceedingly small, if, by her silence or the irrelevancy of her remarks, she betrays her entire ignorance and the defective nature of her education; and hence the necessity and the propriety of introducing these departments of knowledge into the curriculum of our female academies and boarding-schools. But there are other 'ologies as well of which no woman, if she is to move in her sphere as she ought to, can afford to remain ignorant. There is the sublime science of washology and its sister bakeology. There is darnology and scrubology. There is mendology, and cookology in its wide comprehensiveness and its untellable utility, a science this the more profoundly it is studied it becomes the more palatable, and the more skilfully its principles are applied its professors acquire the greater popularity and are regarded with a proportionate degree of interest and complacency. Now, all this knowledge must be embraced in any system of female education that pretends to prepare woman for the duties of life.—The knowledge of housekeeping is not only not beneath her notice and regard, but is essentially necessary if she is to be at home what home expects her to be, if, in a word, she is at all to fill her place with credit to herself and comfort to those with whom she may be associated, as daughter or sister, as wife or mother, as instructress or friend, or any other relationship she may sustain to general society. And, in order that these several departments of her education may be kept in their due place and pursued according to their relative importance—that they may be purified and elevated and chastened, and thus that by their union they may subserve to the grand end of manifesting in all its varied and attractive loveliness the female character, they must be baptized, nay, permeated with the spirit and power of true religion. It has been said that man, with all his irreligion, is a religious being. The paradox, if true at all, is eminently true of woman. There is a special unnaturalness existing and manifest between the doctrines and duties and delights of evangelical Christianity and the intellectual and spiritual process of her inner nature, and hence her aptitude for piety in its principles and practices and pleasures, hence too her attainments, and hence the vast influence which godliness exerts on herself and which it enables her to exert on others. Now, to complete her education, religion must come in—not to subsidize, but to regulate and control—not as subordinate, but as principal—not as mere *addenda* to what may be regarded as otherwise complete in itself, but as that without which nothing else is or can be complete—in short, the end of true religion, the glory of God as connected with the source of true religion; the sacrifice of Christ, must be exhibited everyday as the grand object that is to be sought by all the essential and ornamental departments of her physical and mental and moral training, according as it is written. [. . .]

Having thus ascertained the sphere of woman, and adverted to the qualifications which she behoves to possess, that she may be and do what her situation demands, the way is now prepared for the consideration of the influence she exerts in Christian society.

Now, first of all the things—the qualifications just indicated being granted—this influence is extensive, nay, universal.—Where woman is she makes herself felt, but where woman is enlightened by education, and elevated and purified by piety, she makes herself felt for good through every ramification of the body-social. Like the light and heat of the sun, which diffuse themselves everywhere, so everywhere are there indications of her presence and her spirit. From the cellar to the attic there are marks of her tidy hand and her thoughtful heart. The well ordered kitchen owns her sway. The bedroom and parlour and drawing-room confess her authority. The table, and the chimney itself, are fairly within the reach of her pervasive power and must yield to the decisions of her judgement. Children smile in her approval or grieve under her frown.—Old men regard her as a ministering spirit commissioned to cheer and comfort when every other source of enjoyment has gone. She is the light of the dwelling when the dark cloud of adversity envelopes it, and when death crosses the threshold and with ruthless hand snatches away from it the valued and the dear, it is her hand which wipes away the tear, even when her own eyes are streaming—it is her meek and quiet demeanour and calm submission which soothes and tranquillizes the bereaved mourner.

And, as has been asserted, this influence extends beyond her own proper sphere. If it be chiefly felt at home, it is nevertheless felt and acknowledged abroad. It reaches the school-room and college-hall. It finds its way into the workshop and the busy store. It is realized on 'Change, and even, as some of you well know, in the sweating room of the Bank. And though woman herself, as has been demonstrated, would be altogether out of her place on the red benches of the Parliament House, yet, who will deny that she makes herself felt, even in these high places of the land, and helps to modify the actings of our representatives and rulers?

And then this influence is powerful, extensive. It is mighty. It may be resisted indeed, even as the pleasant light may be excluded from some dirty room lest its filth and its disorder be made manifest. It may be resisted indeed, as the genial heat may be prevented from

radiating, and thus warming all within its scope. But, let it have fair play and full action, and just as light and heat, unchecked in their operation, reveal and revive all within their reach, so will this influence affect and subdue, and enlighten and raise, and purify and etherialize and sublimate, all and every one whose nature is capable of feeling this influence, all and every thing that, as an enchantress, she touches with her wonder working wand. [. . .]

One more general statement. This influence is refining and polishing. It rubs down the hirsute coarseness of men. It frowns vulgarity into a corner, and abashes the impudent forwardness of the pert and assuming. Where it is unknown or trodden under foot, why there is savageism untamed, there is license unbridled, there is heartless cruelty and beastly debasement; but, where it is known and felt, the savage is a savage no more, licence and libertinism tremble and flee, kindness supplants cruelty and manly dignity beastly degradation. A well educated and godly woman can make, and has made, the bully quiet and the boor mannerly, and the brawler meek and gentle as a lamb. In the presence of such a woman the lips of the profane are sealed and the tongue of the obscene is locked in his jaws. Ribaldry and scurrility are frightened into propriety, and, in spite of all that is said to the contrary, it is nevertheless true that slander herself is reft of her weapons, and, if not, yet what is as good, she is shorn of her power to use them as she chooses. [. . .]

Historical Interpretations

3 Rusty Bitterman, "Women and the Escheat Movement," in Janet Guildford and Suzanne Morton, eds, *Separate Spheres: Women's Worlds in the 19th-Century Maritimes* (Fredericton: Acadiensis Press, 1994), 23–38.

In September of 1833, Constable Donald McVarish, acting on behalf of Flora Townshend,

the resident owner of an estate in eastern Prince Edward Island, made his way to her property with a bundle of papers in hand. These were warrants of distress, legal documents which permitted Townshend to seize the goods of her tenants for back rents which she claimed were due. It was not to be a pleasant day for McVarish. Rents were going unpaid, as always, because tenants found it difficult to meet these costs, but growing military resistance to the entire structure of landlordism made rent resistance a political act, too. In the wake of political initiatives begun earlier in the decade, the dream of an escheat was the talk of the countryside. Members of the House of Assembly and the rural population alike were discussing the legitimacy of proprietorial claims to the colony's land and arguing that because landlords had never fulfilled the settlement obligations of the Original grants of 1767, they did not in fact have valid deeds; their grants had reverted to the Crown by default. Establishment of a court of escheat, it was contended, would expose the fraudulence of landlords' claims on the Island's tenantry and permit them to gain title to the farms they had made productive. McVarish, acting for the landlords, could no longer count on deference to law officers in the rural regions in the fall of 1833. Believing that the existing land system, was fundamentally flawed because the titles that supported it were invalid, rural residents balked at complying with the laws pertaining to rents.

McVarish's mission to the Naufrage region of northern Kings County took him into a region that was known for the strength of its anti-landlord sentiments—arguably, the heartland of agrarian radicalism on the Island. William Cooper, the leading advocate of the idea of an escheat, had pronounced his ideas on the flaws of proprietorial title and the rights of tenants in Kings County during the general election of 1830 and then again in a by-election in 1831. The support he received ultimately permitted him to promote these ideas from the House of Assembly. The enthusiastic response from country people in Kings County and elsewhere, expressed in public meetings, petitions, and rent resistance, marked the beginning of what came to be known as the Escheat movement. The loaded pistol that McVarish had tucked in his pocket before leaving home probably reflected his understanding of rural sentiments in the region, as did his attempts to hide his mission from those he met and his decision to sometimes travel through fields rather than on the road. McVarish's precautions notwithstanding, he was seen and confronted by a cluster of the tenants for whom his warrants were intended. Hard words were spoken and McVarish drew his pistol. He was, nonetheless, knocked to the ground, disarmed, and conveyed to the main road. Having promised he would never return, he was released and helped on his way with a blow from a board.[1]

The person wielding the board was Isabella MacDonald, then well advanced in a pregnancy. Judging from testimony from a subsequent trial, Isabella was the most vociferous party in the altercation. McVarish claimed that the three male and two female tenants who confronted him "were all alike active and threatening," but when he pulled his pistol he aimed it at Isabella. It would seem that he perceived her as the most violent of the group. This move allowed men who were not receiving McVarish's primary attention to pull him down from behind and disarm him, in turn exposing him to Isabella's wrath. Her blow with the board was the only gratuitous violence McVarish received. Perhaps she was settling scores for his aiming his pistol at her, perhaps fulfilling the promise of violence which had prompted McVarish's move in the first place.

McVarish's discomfiture at the hands of Isabella and her companions was not an isolated incident. It cannot be explained simply as the act of a particularly forceful female tenant, a matter of personality. Again and again over the course of the Escheat movement, women assumed prominent roles in physically resisting the enforcement of landlords' claims in the countryside. This paper examines these women's behaviour and argues that the modes of resistance they employed had roots in, and were extensions of, the conditions of their daily lives. To discern this, however, it is necessary to move away from the image of rural women most commonly found in North American literature on the preindustrial countryside. The conception of the rural woman's sphere that dominates this literature draws too heavily from middle-class experiences and sentiments and does not provide an appropriate starting place for understanding the actions of women such as Isabella MacDonald. Attentiveness to the early-nineteenth-century perceptions that gave birth to these pervasive images may, however, help us to better understand the roles rural women assumed in violent confrontations. Upper-class beliefs concerning women's sphere shaped the context in which Escheat activism unfolded. Being perceived as the weaker sex and the guardians of domesticity may have permitted women more latitude than men in their use of violence.

While it is important to recognize the significant part that women played in direct action, their participation in this form of popular politics needs to be set in the broader context of the Escheat struggle in the 1830s and early 1840s and the political changes which were occurring during this period, direct action was not Escheat's main focus. The Escheat challenge was primarily grounded in the development of a new mass politics in the formal political arena. Formal politics, unlike community-level direct action, excluded women. To examine the role of women in the Escheat movement is to be reminded that the changes associated with the rise of bourgeois democracy included the decline of an older popular politics which once afforded women a substantial place.

Direct resistance to the claims of landlords, the area of Escheat activism in which women were most prominent, occurred in two forms. There were household-level defences, such as that Isabella MacDonald engaged in,

and there was larger community-organized resistance. Women were active at both levels. In the first, the members of a single household, or perhaps adjoining households, responded defensively to the arrival of law officers. When officials attempted to serve legal papers, remove possessions, or arrest members of the household, those directly involved resisted. Women took part in such protective actions on their own and in the company of men. Catherine Renahau and her husband, John, acted together to resist the enforcement of their landlord's claims against their premises in southern Kings County in the spring of 1834. In this case, the wife and the husband were both indicted and found guilty of assaulting and wounding the constable who had arrived at their door.[2] The actions of Mrs MacLeod and her husband, Hugh, fit the same pattern. When a constable and a sheriff's bailiff came to seize their cattle in the summer of 1839, Mrs MacLeod took up a pike and Hugh an axe. Together they rebuffed the law officers. When a posse was subsequently sent to arrest the two, the entire family took a hand in attempting to prevent the high sheriff and his deputies from invading their house.[3] Charges laid against Mary and Margaret Campbell for assaulting constable William Duncan in 1834 provide some evidence that women also acted without men in farm-level defences.[4]

In addition to these sorts of spontaneous farm-level defences, tenants were involved in more broadly organized actions aimed at securing entire communities or regions from the enforcement of landlords' claims. Women figured prominently in many of these actions. Attempts to arrest the five tenants charged with repelling McVarish provoked two major community-level confrontations. In the spring of 1834, a posse was dispatched from Charlottetown to Naufrage to arrest the miscreants. They were turned back at the Naufrage bridge by a crowd, said to include "a large number of women," which had assembled in anticipation of their arrival.[5] Armed with muskets, pikes, and pitchforks, the assembly informed the deputy sheriff that they were prepared to fight and die before they would permit him to arrest the five tenants he sought. When yet another posse led by the sheriff himself attempted a similar mission the following year, women were said to make up more than one-third of the armed crowd that waited for the posse in the pre-dawn darkness and again blocked the sheriff.[6]

Women were active as well in a series of major community-level confrontations in the fall and winter of 1837–8 that, with the mass meetings being held in support of Escheat, prompted some observers to believe that the Island, like the Canadas, was on the verge of civil war. The first of these confrontations concerning land title was on Thomas Sorell's estate in northern Kings County. In September 1837, when the sheriff and his deputies attempted to enforce court orders Sorell had obtained against John Robertson, a long-time resident on the estate, they were repulsed by a crowd wielding sticks and throwing stones. As well, one ear was removed from each of the law officers' horses, which had been left at a distance from the farm.[7] Women were part of the crowd that blocked the sheriff, and they were reputed to be the primary actors in the violence.[8] Later that winter, women made up part of an armed party which assembled near Wood Islands to repel people whom they believed to be law officers initiating rent actions in that district. In a case of mistaken identity, shots were fired over the head of the rector of Charlottetown and his elite friends, who were on a baptismal mission on behalf of a spiritual lord rather than a rental mission on behalf of a secular one.[9] While the actions of the tenant group were misdirected, they nonetheless served notice that those who might attempt to enforce rent collection in the region were not welcome. On the Selkirk estate the following month, women again were active in coordinated crowd actions which blocked the enforcement of rental claims. In several locales, bailiffs attempting to seize farm goods were confronted by tenants armed with pitchforks and sticks. Men and women alike took a hand in resisting the seizure of goods and driving law officers from the communities they had attempted to enter.[10] The cumulative effect of these actions was, for a time, to bring the enforcement of rental payments to a halt across much of the Island and to force the government to consider whether it was willing to hazard deploying troops—then in short supply due to the demands made by the risings in the Canadas—in order to uphold the claims of the Island's landlords.

That rural women would be active in household defences and collective action of this sort would come as no surprise to the student of Old World popular protest. In locations on the eastern side of the Atlantic, a rich array of research has pointed to the importance of women in protest actions and has suggested ways of understanding this activity in terms of their everyday lives.[11] The evidence of female involvement in the popular resistance associated with the Escheat movement fits less easily within North American historiography and its portrayal of rural women. To be sure, the literature is broad and varied, and blanket descriptions are misleading. Nonetheless, what emerges again and again in North American descriptions of women in northern pre-industrial rural settings is the image of the farm woman as nurturing caretaker of the domestic sphere. Though her work was tiring and she was often incessantly busy, hers was an existence bounded by walls and sheltered from the coarser aspects of life. Women looked after the household and, perhaps, the adjacent garden and barns, while the men tended to rough work and public affairs.

In his late-nineteenth-century reminiscences on rural life in Ontario in the first half of the century, Canniff Haight drew the common distinctions: "The farmer was a strong, hardy man, the wife a ruddy cheerful body, careful of the comforts of her household."[12]

Male muscularity was applied to the exterior world, female gentleness and diligence to the interior: "While the work was being pushed outside with vigour, it did not stand still inside. The thrifty housewife was always busy."[13] "The work" was of course male. The division is clear as well in Robert Leslie Jones's characterization of farm life on the Upper Canadian frontier. While the man of the house "split rails, built worm fences, and erected his log cabin," his wife attended to "various household industries, ranging from spinning and sometimes weaving, to the preservation of fruits by drying, and the making of butter and cheese."[14] Or, in a recent version of the theme as played out in Lower Canada: Féllicité tended to "feeding, washing, and cleaning the family, its clothes, and its house" as well as "milking the cows, making butter, and feeding the fowls." Théophile ploughed, "erected fences around the fields," and saw to "repairs to house, barn and equipment."[15] "Women's work," Christopher Clark has argued in the case of pre-industrial rural New England, "remained separate, functionally distinct from men's": "In addition to cooking, cleaning, and looking after children, women undertook the myriad tasks associated with preserving food, making and mending clothing, and keeping up their houses."[16] Or, as a classic textbook of Canadian women's history has it, farm women "scrubbed clothes on scrub boards (if they were lucky enough to have one), hauled water from the creek or the well, cooked on wood stoves, and made most of the family clothes. In addition they grew vegetables, gathered fruit, preserved and baked, and looked after their children."[17]

No doubt many "ruddy" farm women did spend their days tending to berries, butter, bread, and babies in eighteenth- and nineteenth-century North America and, no doubt, there were many households where prosperity and culture blended to create the domestic feminine sphere that is described in so much of the literature.[18] The scholarship that has given rise to this image is not

incorrect. But in the absence of more nuanced studies of the experiences of women in rural settings, it has sustained misleading impressions. A vision of country life rooted in the experiences of relatively prosperous, well-established households and heavily grounded in mid-nineteenth-century circumstances has, often enough, come to stand as a general portrait of the pre-industrial rural world. Thus, our view of the rural past tends to be too uniform and too rosy.[19] One might profitably explore the reasons for the dominance of this image and its significance to broader myths concerning rural life and North American exceptionalism. For comprehending the actions of women within the Escheat movement, the immediate problem is finding a more appropriate starting place for explaining how Mrs Macleod came to pick up a pike and Isabella MacDonald a board, and how other country women came to join in the armed groups organized to repulse law officers in Naufrage, Wood Islands, and elsewhere about Prince Edward Island in the 1830s. While some of these women no doubt tended to the domestic duties that have been assigned to the feminine sphere of rural life, there is much that these sorts of descriptions leave out, matters that go a long way toward helping us to understand how women came to participate as they did in the Escheat movement.

For most country women in Prince Edward Island in the early nineteenth century, life was much rougher and the bounds, of work much broader than the prevailing images suggest. Indeed, for the rural poor, of whom there were many, the notion of a distinct feminine sphere could not have had much meaning. While there was work that was exclusively female, even in poorer households—having babies, early childcare, and so on—it is less clear that there was much work about the farm that women could avoid because it was securely outside their domain. In many rural households, particularly the poorer ones, the men were away for extensive periods earning wages in the woods, shipyards, and other sites where farm income might be supplemented.[20] Of necessity, then, women's work expanded beyond the women's sphere that is described in much of the literature. In such households, women often assumed the dominant role in maintaining the farm.[21] In farm households where life was lived on the margin, even when men were present, women often participated in heavy tasks such as clearing, planting, and harvesting. In his early-nineteenth-century observations on life in Prince Edward Island, Walter Johnstone spoke disparagingly of rural women from comfortable backgrounds who were "unable and unwilling to take the hoe, and assist their husbands in planting the seed, and raising the crop."[22] To make a go of it in the New World, immigrant women needed to apply themselves to the hard outdoor tasks of farm-making. Land-clearing work, which Johnstone described as being "the most dirty and disagreeable" and "tiresome as any I have seen in America," was shared by the entire family, women and men alike.[23] Similar observations of women's roles in the hard task of farm-making are found in the works of John MacGregor and George Patterson, who commented as well on women's part in the subsequent tasks of planting and harvesting.[24] Women, MacGregor observed, "assist in the labours of the farm during seed-time, hay-making, and harvest."[25] Getting the crops in, Johnstone noted, was the work of the entire household—"man, wife, children, and all that can handle a hoe, must work, as the season is short"—and disaster loomed for the poor if the crops were not successful.[26] It is not surprising then that Island evidence from the 1832 murder trial of Martin Doyle indicates that Martin and his wife were working side by side among the charred stumps of their field on the day that Martin was said to have shot his brother.[27] From the scattered evidence that is available concerning women's work, such was a common pattern of rural life.

The dominant image of the daily lives of rural women is inadequate not only because women's work could be much broader than it depicts, but also because the domestic sphere of work was often much narrower, too. Again and again the existing literature emphasizes the long hours that women spent, cleaning house, washing clothes, preparing meals, and spinning and weaving, No doubt long hours were spent in this work by those who possessed frame houses and ample wardrobes, ate a varied diet, kept sheep, and had spinning wheels and looms. We need to recognize, though, that many did not. In the Maritimes of the early nineteenth century, this picture of the woman's sphere pertains to the rural middle class and does not reflect the circumstances of the whole of the rural population. Indeed, for many, the physical requirements for the woman's separate sphere—multi-roomed house, kitchen and pantry, area for textile manufacture, adjoining dairy, and poultry shelters—quite simply did not exist. It did not take long to clean a one-room dwelling, assuming that this was even an objective, nor did cooking and washing absorb a day's labour when household members ate boiled potatoes and oatmeal and possessed little clothing beyond what they were wearing. We need not paint the picture this starkly, however, no matter how real it was for many, to point out that much, of the existing view of the rural women's sphere assumes material circumstances that were far more comfortable than those of much of the rural population.

As well, we must re-examine the notions of domesticity and of lives sheltered from the rough and tumble of the public world, which are commonly associated with characterizations of the pre-industrial North American farm woman, if we are to understand the behaviour of the women who were involved in direct action during the Escheat movement. In part because many Island women did engage in outdoor farm labour, they, like men, became involved in physical disputes over resources and household relations. Margaret Taylor and Jane Maclachlan fought it out with fence pickets and fists in the spring of 1830 when they differed over ownership of a piece of ground.[28] A similar physical dispute over land and fencing brought Catherine McCormack and Alexander Macdonald before a court later that year.[29] The same court session that heard the Taylor/Maclachlan case also heard the case of Elizabeth Cahill and Margaret Shea, whose personal differences had moved to the level of heaving stones.[30] As with women's work, evidence bearing on women's use of violence, or the threat of violence, in the public realm is fugitive.[31]

Certainly what emerges in the court record is but a fraction of a broader phenomenon. What percentage of the disputes where women picked up a stick or a stone or brandished their fists ultimately ended up before a judge or a justice of the peace? And what percentage of these disputes is preserved in the incomplete legal record?

In addition to engaging in direct violence, Island women were also repeatedly cited for resorting to maiming animals.[32] In this traditional form of rural retribution, livestock received the violence directed toward their owners. Vengeance was taken, or a threat communicated, by hamstringing, slashing, or otherwise mutilating the animals of an enemy.[33] There was nothing unusual in the methods used against the horses of law officers who came to Robertson's farm in the fall of 1837; they were employed against the mounts of law officers on many other occasions. Animal-maiming, by women and men, was not uncommon in intra-household disputes.

Women's participation in violent actions was not an unusual feature of the Escheat movement, nor was the targeting of law officers. Consider, for instance, the 1836 rescue of Rose Hughes from a constable's custody. Arrested near Fort Augustus in the late fall of 1836 for obtaining goods under false pretenses, she was forcibly released when the arresting constable, Angus MacPhee, was attacked by a group who had pursued him beyond the community. Though there were four men present in the rescue party, they remained in the background. The assault itself was said to be the work of nine women.[34]

We need, then, to broaden our notion of female lives and experiences if we are to make sense of women's participation in direct action during the Escheat movement. Isabella, used to hard physical labour, is unlikely to have thought it peculiar, or inappropriate, for women to use physical means to uphold their interests. When we examine the role of women in the Escheat movement, we see in part an extension of the normal patterns of work and life to meet the challenges thrown up by the land war of the 1830s. Women familiar with the rough and tumble of outdoor rural life dealt with the law officers who came to their farms as they would any other threat to their household. Accustomed to the heft of an axe and the swing of a fence picket, they applied their strengths, skills, and inclinations to the problems at hand.

Those like McVarish who were on the receiving end of these responses were caught in an unenviable dilemma. On the one hand they were, often enough, dealing with women who possessed strength, endurance, physical tenacity, and the urge to cause considerable physical harm. McVarish's choice of targets when he levelled his pistol probably showed his appreciation of women's abilities. On the other hand, he and the other law officers on the front lines of the land war were, in one fashion or another, linked to a culture which saw women differently. According to increasingly dominant middle-class and upper-class views, women were revered as submissive nurturers of the domestic sphere.[35] Historians studying women's roles in collective action in other nineteenth-century contexts have suggested that plebeian protesters may have sought to exploit such perceptions when they challenged the status quo. Women, the argument goes, enjoyed some degree of immunity in violent confrontations, or at least believed that they did, and scattered evidence does suggest they were less likely than men to suffer harm or be prosecuted for their actions. This fact may help explain their prominence in illegal protest.[36] Might this have been the case with women's participation in the direct action associated with the Escheat movement?

The evidence bearing on this question is limited, but it supports an affirmative answer. Interestingly, despite the prominent role played by women in resisting the enforcement of landlords' claims in Kings and Queens Counties in the tense fall and winter of 1837–8, none was named in the law officers' reports nor were any indicted for their actions. Only men were tried. Such preliminary screening raises questions concerning how adequately indictments and court cases document women's participation in direct action or, indeed, in other sorts of activities of this type. Were law officers uncomfortable with admitting that their lumps and bruises were the work of women or that they had been chased or intimidated by women? And, other things being equal, did law enforcement take place in a cultural context where charges against males were preferable, if an example was to be made of a few members of a larger riotous assembly? Women, it would appear, were more likely to be indicted in household-level confrontations where the numbers involved were quite small. Even when charged, however, they sometimes fared better than men. Although two women were indicted for the assault on Donald McVarish, neither served a prison term or paid a fine. The charges were dropped against Nancy MacDonald, and Isabella MacDonald, though found guilty, was pardoned by the Island's governor, Aretas Young, on account of her "being far advanced in pregnancy and having six young children."[37] All three men involved were committed to prison.

The ways in which contemporaries referred to gender when assigning meaning to incidents of Escheat-related collective action provided another window on these issues. In the wake of the resistance to the sheriff at Robertson's farm in the fall of 1836, pressure was brought on the new governor, Charles FitzRoy, to send troops into the region to sustain the civil forces in their enforcement of landlords' claims. FitzRoy sent Charlottetown's mayor, Ambrose Lane, to the region as his personal emissary to inquire into the current state of the countryside and to conspicuously make arrangements for billeting soldiers. Seeking to downplay the seriousness of the incidents that had brought Lane to the region, Robertson and his family told him that the sheriff and his assistants had never been in any real danger as "all the violence offered was by women and boys." The law officers who had beaten a hasty retreat from the mob assembled at the farm had been "unnecessarily alarmed."[38] Similarly, a dispute over the significance of the Wood Islands incident of January 1838 came, in part, to revolve around the composition of the crowd which pad assembled and fired shots over the heads of the rector's party. Those seeking to downplay the confrontation insisted that it had, in large part, been staged by women and boys. Those intent on seeing it as an indication of a broader spirit of rebellion threatening the status quo on the Island were equally insistent that the crowd had been "composed chiefly of able-bodied men."[39] What the disputants in these battles of words shared, or claimed to share, was the notion that females could not figure as real threats in violent confrontations. It is not clear whether exploitation of these perceptions of women figured into the strategic planning of household- and community-level rent resistance prior to confrontations or whether they were invoked only after the violence. Cases such as the rescue of Rose Hughes, where men were present but remained at a distance while women assaulted the constable, or the resistance at Robertson's farm, in which, according to reports, men were present but not active in the physical confrontation with law officers, suggest a conscious gendered strategy that made use of upper-class assumptions concerning women's behaviour.

[. . .] Charles Tilly has argued that [patterns of rural protest such as those on Prince Edward Island] fit within a broader category of "reactive" collective action, locally focused efforts to protect existing rights or to uphold popular notions of justice.[40] John Bohstedt's term "common people's politics" aptly captures another facet of this type of collective action. In contexts where ordinary people were excluded from participation in formal politics, direct action provided a means for articulating plebeian sentiments; it permitted them to act as "proto-citizens."[41] As Bohstedt and others have noted, women often participated extensively in this sort of political action. "Common people's politics" tended to be an extension of plebeian life, and in locales where women "worked shoulder to shoulder with men" they also "marched shoulder to shoulder with men" in defence of their households and communities.[42] Such was the case with women's participation in the direct action associated with the Escheat movement. Local-level politics of this type was a matter for women and men alike.

This was not the case in the formal political arena. There the rules and norms that governed participation were extensions of elite and middle-class ways of life. In these circles, other notions of womanhood, held sway. This would be of no small significance for the majority of women when, beginning in the late eighteenth century and extending across the nineteenth century and beyond, ordinary people about the Atlantic rim increasingly pushed themselves into, or were incorporated within, the field of formal politics. Lower-class entry into the sphere of political life was gained by compromise and by the acceptance of many of the modes of procedure that had been established by the upper classes. On the Island one thinks even of simple matters such as dress. When the Escheat leader John LeLecheur went off to Quebec to discuss the land question with Lord Durham, a fundraising campaign was necessary in order to buy him a new set of clothes. Such props were unnecessary for engaging in political debate in Murray Harbour, but they were a part of the basic entry requirements for being taken seriously in the governor general's circles.[43] Certainly, involvement in formal politics did lead to fundamental changes in the nature of plebeian politics. As historians have noted in other contexts, one of the many prices popular forces paid for entrance into the formal political arena in the nineteenth century was the relegation of women to a sphere outside direct participation in political life. A new mass politics was emerging at the time of the Escheat movement, but as it embraced larger numbers of previously excluded lower-class elements, it also denied political expression to women.[44] On the Island, women were legally disenfranchised on the eve of Escheat's electoral victory of 1838.[45]

The involvement of women in the local politics of direct action needs to be set in this larger context. While recognizing women's participation in the "common people's politics" of the 1830s, it is important to note the transitional nature of the period and the immediate and long-term significance of the zone of political life in which women had a prominent place. Rural protest in Prince Edward Island had by the 1830s largely shifted away from direct action. A relatively broad franchise allowed many male tenants to vote; some even possessed sufficient wealth to meet the property requirements necessary for assuming a seat in the House of Assembly. The energy of the Escheat movement was directed toward exploiting the political possibilities these openings permitted. Escheat leaders sought to make agrarian voices heard in the formulation of state policy by achieving power in the legislature. This pursuit drew rural protest into an exclusively masculine sphere. The activities in which women had a substantial presence were not at the forefront of the Escheat movement, nor would they be central to the new politics that developed in the years which followed.

NOTES

1. Minutes of Naufrage Trial, Colonial Office Records [CO] 226, vol. 52, 91–4, Public Record Office, Great Britain [microfilm copies in Harriet Irving library, University of New Brunswick]. I would like to gratefully acknowledge the assistance of the Social Sciences and Humanities Research Council of Canada, whose financial support aided this research. Many thanks are due as well to Margaret McCallum for her comments on an earlier version of this paper.

2. *Royal Gazette* (Charlottetown), 24 June 1834, 3; Supreme Court Minutes, 25 June 1834; Indictments, 1834, RG 6, Public Archives of Prince Edward Island [PAPEI].

3. *Royal Gazette,* 23 July 1839, 3.

4. *Royal Gazette,* 16 Dec. 1834, 3.

5. *Royal Gazette,* 17 June 1834, 3.

6. *Royal Gazette,* 6 Jan. 1835, 3; "Council Minutes," 7 Jan. 1835, CO 226, vol. 52, 330–2.

7. Executive Council Minutes, 5 Sept. 1837, RG 5, PAPEI; *Royal Gazette,* 5 Sept. 1837, 3.

8. Hodgson to Owen, 30 Sept. 1837, MS 3744, vol. 26, PAPEI.

9. George R. Young, *A Statement of the "Escheat Question" in the Island of Prince Edward: Together with the Causes of the Late Agitation and the Remedies Proposed* (London, R. and W. Swale, 1838), 2; "One of the Party" to the editor, *Colonial Herald* (Charlottetown), 27 June 1838, 3; "O.P.Q." to the editor, *Colonial Herald,* 23 Jan. 1841, 3; "Plain Common Sense" to the editor, *Colonial Herald,* 6 Feb. 1841, 2–3; John Myrie Hall to the editor, *Colonial Herald,* 20 Feb. 1841, 2; "The Only Clergyman Resident Within the Bounds of the District" to the editor, *Colonial Herald,* 20 Mar. 1841, 3; Charles Stewart and W.P. Grossard to the editor, *Colonial Herald,* 27 Mar. 1841, 3.

10. Statement of-Angus McPhee, George Farmer, and Robert Bell, 27 Feb. 1838, CO 226, vol. 55, 176–80.

11. John Bohstedt, "Gender, Household, and Community Politics, Women in English Riots, 1790–1810," *Past and Present* 120 (Aug. 1988), 88–122; Rudolf Dekker, "Women in Revolt: Collective Protest and Its Social Setting in Holland in the Seventeenth and Eighteenth Centuries," *Theory and Society* 16 (1987): 337–62; E.P. Thompson, "The Moral Economy of the English Crowd in the Eighteenth Century," *Past and Present* 50 (1971): 76–136; George Rudé, *The Crowd in the French Revolution* (Oxford: Galaxy Books, 1959); George Rudé, *The Crowd in History, A Study of Popular Disturbances in France and England, 1730–1848* (London, Serif Publishing, 1964); Olwen Hufton, "Women in Revolution," *Past and Present* 53 (1971): 90–108; John Stevenson and Roland Quinault, eds, "Food Riots. in England, 1792–1818," in *Popular Protest and Public Order: Six Studies in British History, 1790–1920* (London, St Martin's Press, 1974), 33–74; Natalie Zemon Davis, *Society and Culture in Early Modern France* (Stanford: Stanford University Press, 1975), 124–87; Kenneth J. Logue, *Popular Disturbances in Scotland, 1780–1815* (Edinburgh: Birlinn Publishers, 1979); Malcolm I. Thomas and Jennifer Grimmet, *Women in Protest 1800–1850* (London: St Martin's Press, 1982). A useful Canadian extension of this rich literature is Terence Crowley, "'Thunder Gusts': Popular Disturbances in Early French Canada," in Michael Cross and Gregory Kealey, eds, *Readings in Canadian Social History,* vol. 1, *Economy and Society during the French Regime* (Toronto: McClelland and Stewart, 1983), 122–51.

12. Canniff Haight, *Country Life in Canada Fifty Years Ago: Personal Recollections and Reminiscences of a Sexagenarian* (1885; rpt, Belleville, ON, 1971), 86.

13. Haight, *Country Life in Canada,* 46.

14. Robert Leslie Jones, *History of Agriculture in Ontario, 1613–1880* (1946; rpt, Toronto, 1977), 20–1.

15. Graeme Wynn, "On the Margins of Empire," in Craig Brown, ed., *The Illustrated History of Canada* (Toronto: Lester Publishing, 1987), 247.

16. Christopher Clark, *The Roots of Rural Capitalism, Western Massachusetts, 1780–1860* (Ithaca, NY: Cornell University Press, 1990), 274.

17. Alison Prentice et al., *Canadian Women: A History* (Toronto: Harcourt, 1988), 116. See also 76, 79, 83.

18. Hal Barron's call for the study of the extent, and timing, of the spread of the bourgeois ideals of the cult of domesticity among "the less affluent and less 'enlightened' strata of rural society" usefully indicates a single facet of a broader challenge, that of disaggregating and more closely examining rural experiences and rural change. John Faragher's critique of stereotypes in the writing of rural women's history, and call for moving beyond these, is to the point as well. Hal Barron, "Listening to the Silent Majority: Change and Continuity in the Nineteenth-Century Rural North," in Lou Ferleger, ed., *Agriculture and National Development: Views on the Nineteenth Century* (Ames: Iowa State University Press, 1990), 16; John Mack Faragher, "History from the Inside-out: Writing the History of Women in Rural America," *American Quarterly* 33 (1981): 537–57.

19. There are, of course, exceptions to this characterization. Marjorie Griffin Cohen, for instance, notes that farm women in early-nineteenth-century Ontario frequently performed "men's work," though she tends to treat this as a temporary frontier phenomenon. *Women's Work, Markets, and Economic Development in Nineteenth-Century Ontario* (Toronto: University of Toronto Press, 1988), 69–71. As well, it is not unusual for contradictory evidence to be integrated with a more idyllic picture of the countrywoman's sphere. See, for instance, The Clio Collective, Roger Gannon and Rosalind Gill, trans., *Quebec Women: A History* (Toronto: The Women's Press, 1987), 89.

20. Rusty Bittermann, "Farm Households and Wage Labour in the Northeastern Maritimes in the Early Nineteenth Century," *Labour/Le travail* 31 (Spring 1993): 13–45.

21. When a Cape Breton farmer noted in the coal boom of 1871 that "farmers and their sons by hundreds, nay, thousands, [were] leaving their farms to the women, and seeking employment at the collieries and railways," he was describing the efflorescence of an older pattern. *Journal of Agriculture for Nova Scotia* (July 1871): 652.

22. Walter Johnstone, *A Series of Letters, Descriptive of Prince Edward Island* (1822) reprinted in *Journeys to the Island of St John*, D.C. Harvey, ed. (Toronto: Macmillan, 1955), 143.

23. Johnstone, *A Series of Letters,* 108.

24. John MacGregor, *British America* (Edinburgh: Blackwood, 1832), 329; George Patterson, *A History of the County of Pictou Nova Scotia* (1877; rpt, Belleville, ON, 1972), 223.

25. MacGregor, *British America,* 346.

26. Johnstone, *A Series of Letters,* 109.

27. *Royal Gazette,* 28 Feb. 1832, 1.

28. *Prince Edward Island Register* (Charlottetown), 15 June 1830, 3.

29. *Royal Gazette,* 13 July 1830, 3.

30. *Prince Edward Island Register,* 15 June 1830, 3.

31. See also the case of Mary Prendergast v. Ellen Prendergast, *Royal Gazette,* 3 Jan. 1837, 3; and Isabella Stewart v. Edward Wilson, *Royal Gazette,* 13 July 1830, 3.

32. *Royal Gazette,* 21 Jan. 1834, 3; 22 Sept. 1835, 3; 7 July 1840, 3.

33. For a good discussion of the tactic see John E. Archer, "'A Fiendish Outrage'?: A Study of Animal Maiming in East Anglia, 1830–70," *Agricultural History Review* 33, 2 (1985): 147–57.

34. *Royal Gazette,* 20 Dec. 1836, 3.

35. Barbara Leslie Epstein, *The Politics of Domesticity: Women, Evangelism, and Temperance in Nineteenth Century America* (Middletown, CT: Wesleyan University Press, 1981), 67–87; Nancy F. Cott, *The Bonds of Womanhood: "Women's Sphere" in New England, 1780–1835* (New Haven, CT, Yale University Press, 1977).

36. Malcolm I. Thomas and Jennifer Grimmet, *Women in Protest 1800–1850* (London: St Martin's Press, 1982), 54; Logue, *Popular Disturbances in Scotland,* 199–203.

37. Young to Hay, 20 Mar. 1835, CO 226, vol. 52, 89.

38. Hodgson to Owen, 30 Sept. 1837, MS 3744, vol. 26, PAPEI.

39. "One of the Party" to the editor, *Colonial Herald,* 27 June 1838, 3.

40. Charles Tilly, *From Mobilization to Resolution* (Reading, MA: Rowman and Littlefield, 1978), 143–71.

41. John Bohstedt, "The Myth of the Feminine Food Riot: Women as Proto-Citizens in English Community Politics, 1790–1810," in Harriet B. Applewhite and Darline G. Levy,

eds, *Women and Politics in the Age of the Demo-cratic Revolution* (Ann Arbor, MI: University of Michigan Press, 1990), 21–60.

42. Bohstedt, "The Myth of the Feminine Food Riot," 21. See also Thomas and Grimmet, *Women in Protest,* 54–5.

43. Rusty Bittermann, "Escheat!: Rural Protest on Prince Edward Island, 1832–42" (PhD diss., University of New Brunswick, 1992), 321–8.

44. Useful views of the process are provided In Wayne Ph. te Brake, Rudolf M. Dekker, and Lotte C. van de Pol, "Women and Po-litical Culture in the Dutch Revolutions," in

Applewhite and Levy, eds, *Women and Politics in the Age of Democratic Revolution,* 109–46; Joan B. Landes, *Women and the Public Sphere in the Age of the French Revolution* (Ithaca, NY: Cornell University Press, 1988); Allan Greer, "La république des hommes: les patriotes de 1837 face aux femmes," *Revue d'histoire de l'Amérique française* 44, 4 (Spring 1991): 507–28; Bohstedt, "The Myth of the Feminine Food Riot."

45. They were disenfranchised by statute in 1836. John Garner, *The Franchise and Politics in British North America, 1755–1867* (Toronto: Univer-sity of Toronto Press, 1969), 155.

 4 From Katherine McKenna, "Women's Agency in Upper Canada: Prescott's Board of Police Record, 1834–1850," *Histoire sociale/Social History* 36, 72 (2003): 347–70. (Modified/shortened)

Just before midnight on a dark, chilly November night in 1837 in Prescott, Upper Canada, Mary Greneau was startled out of her sleep by the sound of a mob outside her house. Male voices shouted, "Kill her" and "By God I'll fix her!" Her attackers pounded on her door, heaving against it until the hinges burst and her home was broken open. Spilling inside were six horrifying figures, dressed in grotesque imitation of Native Indians. Their faces were blackened and streaked with red and they wore blanket coats. As they whooped and hollered, they went on a destructive rampage, smashing her windows, breaking her furniture, and throwing her possessions out into the street. Mary and the two women living with her, Jane Craig and Elizabeth Brady, felt entirely defenceless and in real terror for their lives. Only when a neighbour threatened to shoot them if they did not desist did the six marauders depart.[1]

Although this incident bears some resem-blance to the classic charivari, there are im-portant differences. Mary Greneau was, it is true, a well-known local figure. She was a con-stant nuisance to those living near her, and in particular had an ongoing feud with her neigh-bours across the street, John and Catharine

Kelleaugher. They were fed up with her run-ning what was then called a "disorderly house," a place of entertainment operating at all hours and outside the law. She sold liquor, employed a fiddler, and entertained drunken men with "dancing and indecent conduct."[2] Women of doubtful reputation were living there and going in and out at all hours, on at least one occasion fighting in the street. Catharine Kelleaugher later testified that, on one May evening, Bridget Savage and Margaret Doneghan disturbed the peace as they were coming out of Mary Gre-neau's house by engaging in a shouting match, calling each other "bitch," "whore," and "bas-tard" for all to hear.[3] The Kelleaughers took to displaying their displeasure in a non-violent but pointed manner. Crossing to the drainage ditch in front of their disruptive neighbour's house, they emptied their slops and chamber pots there. When she complained to them, they replied with very "insolent answers."[4]

Earlier that November, Mary had clashed with some of her patrons as well. Late one Saturday night, she brought back three men to her home in a state of intoxication, gig-gling and laughing. One, William Glazier, called for four glasses of liquor, one for him, one for her, and one each for James Campbell and John Honeywell. The latter whispered to her, perhaps in jest, that because Glazier was a newcomer to Prescott from Glengarry "that she might skin him." When Mary tried to cheat William out of his change, he declared "he would have the change or the worth of it before he left the house." They scuffled, falling against the stovepipes with such violence that they were knocked over. She finally chased the men out of the house at gunpoint, firing a warning shot into the street in the wee hours of the morning.[5] This was too great an insult to the pride of John Honeywell, who promptly went to the authorities and charged her with firing the gun, and on the Sabbath, too, a double bylaw violation. Mary Greneau was duly fined, but was not prepared to take this passively. She countercharged Campbell and Honeywell, perhaps angry with them for not defending her against Glazier, for having "abused her in her own house." The public testimony that resulted was not to her advantage. One witness asserted that "for some weeks past" she had "kept a very noisy house, after hours, Sunday evenings not excepted." The whole story about the evening's doings became a matter of public record. Samuel Indicott, who had been employed by Mary as "waiter and fiddler," tried to put a good face on it, testifying that he only "saw drunken people there occasionally, saw some dancing and indecent conduct sometimes, heard singing frequently." Pandering to racist sentiment, he asserted in her defence that he "never saw the coloured people use her familiarly." As for the accusation of carrying on such activities on Sunday, he assured his listeners that he had in fact seen "some say grace before drinking."[6] This did not persuade local authorities of the justice of her case. The charges against Campbell and Honeywell were dismissed, and Greneau assessed steep costs of £1.3.6.[7]

This victory did not appease John Honeywell. A few days later, he and some others launched the attack on her house, wreaking revenge on a woman who they thought needed to be put in her place. Their intentions were well known locally. One witness had "heard it frequently said that she ought to be rid on a rail." Others had been invited to join the raiding party but had declined. Honeywell's band hatched their plot at the store of Alexander Thomas, where they met to put on their costumes. A passerby heard them say, "damn the old devil, she'll not know us." They carried the charade to the point that they "spoke in imitation of the Indians" when spoken to on the street, responding "Chip, Chip, Chuck" in a crude mimicking of Native dialect. After the raid was over, they conveniently left their disguises at Thomas's store, where they were easily found and later presented as evidence. The men then repaired to Beale the barber's for a drink to celebrate their triumph over Mary Greneau.[8]

Charivaris were a not uncommon form of "rough justice" in Upper Canada.[9] This one deviated from the norm because it was not a political protest and was less an expression of community censure than the settling of a personal quarrel. Even though it is clear that there were many in the Prescott community who objected to the behaviour of Mary Greneau, the raid on her premises was not accepted by her neighbours as "rough justice." After some initial delay in recognizing that the attack was something more than just the usual carousing heard from her home, they turned out in her defence. Surprisingly, it was the short-changed Glazier who finally drove the rioters off with the threat of shooting. Other members of the community, Mr Deneau and Mr Cavalier, had not only refused to join the party, but testified against Honeywell's band. Mary Greneau herself, as we have seen, was not one to accept attack passively, and she quickly sought her own revenge through legal means, successfully prosecuting Alexander Thomas, Thomas Meredith, and John Honeywell for disturbing the peace. As an expression of community censure, they were handed exceptionally punitive fines of £2.10 with costs of 17 shillings, 3 pence each.

Such a remarkable story about a woman of the popular class is rare in Upper Canadian history. That it has survived is due to the existence of an equally remarkable document—the Minute Book of the Board of Police for Prescott, Ontario. For almost 150 years this record has sat virtually untouched in the vault of the municipal offices of Prescott. What it reveals is an unparalleled source of social history on many aspects of Upper Canadian life. Standards for acceptable community behaviour on everything from control of livestock, health regulations, road maintenance, keeping the sabbath, licensing alcohol and entertainment, and even what language was permissible to use in public space are recorded in the 400 densely written pages of this Minute Book. Of particular interest are the cases brought to the Board of Police that involved woman as prosecutors or plaintiffs or were brought on their behalf by men during the 16 years it presided over Prescott life, from 1834 to 1850.

In the 1830s and 1840s Prescott was at the peak of its success, a rapidly growing small town of more than 2,000 persons.[10] Situated just above a section of the St Lawrence River made unnavigable by rapids and with a natural, deep harbour, it was an important transfer point for goods and people arriving overland from Montreal en route to Ogdensburg to the south and points west such as Kingston and Toronto. This forwarding trade meant that merchants prospered, and associated activities such as shipbuilding and marine insurance developed.[11] During the 1837–1838 Rebellion, the decrepit Fort Wellington was rebuilt, and from 1843 to 1854 it was garrisoned with a company of men from the Royal Canadian Rifle Regiment.[12] After the Montreal–Toronto railway was built in the 1850s, Prescott subsided in importance. The time covered by the Board of Police Record, then, coincided with the town's height of prosperity and activity.[13]

[. . .]

By 1834 Prescott had grown to the extent that it was incorporated as a town, and at that time the Board of Police was established. Within the town limits, it replaced the Court of Quarter Sessions as the governing body of civic life. From 1793 the Court had been presided over by magistrates appointed by the Parliament of Upper Canada and handled everything to do with local government. Although this may seem to have been an autocratic system, as Donald Akenson has observed for the neighbouring counties of Leeds and Landsdowne, "it worked, chiefly because . . . [it] was a system of mixed social control . . . a combination of local civic management and the control of anti-social behaviour."[14] [. . .]

As the Upper Canadian population grew, however, the burden of work proved too great for the local magistrates. Thus in the 1830s a new governing model was implemented in eight rapidly developing communities across Upper Canada, incorporating them as towns and establishing local Boards of Police to take over the comprehensive duties of the Quarter Sessions. If the Quarter Sessions was flexible and well suited to frontier needs, so too were the Boards of Police. They were also more democratic and more closely tied to their communities. In Prescott, presiding Board members were chosen from among local male property holders of at least £60 assessed value and elected by men who were British subjects owning a dwelling house and a plot of land or paying rent of at least £5 per annum within the boundaries of the corporation. The town was divided into east and west wards, each of which elected two members. The four chosen then nominated a fifth board member. All officers of the town, such as the Surveyor of the Streets, Clerk, Tax Assessors, Treasurer, Bailiff, and Constable were then chosen. The Board was responsible for enacting and enforcing the town bylaws, written by the Board members and renewed on an annual basis. This system held sway until a new Municipal Act in 1849 called for the establishment of a mayor and council, with a separate Police Court. The records of Prescott's Board of Police cover the period from its establishment in 1834 up to and including 1850, when the first mayor presided over the court.

As Paul Craven points out, "[L]ittle is known about these inferior tribunals which constituted the broad base of the judicial pyramid."[15] [. . .] In Prescott in the earlier part of the century, there was only a bailiff or constable who would act upon the complaints of ordinary citizens. The Board of Police, as did the Quarter Sessions, judged on matters brought to it by individuals, who, along a British model, were considered the prosecutors rather than the Crown. All court costs were paid by either the plaintiff or the defendant, not the corporation. Even charges brought to the court by the bailiff or constable were represented as private charges brought by him. As Allan Greer has observed, early Upper Canadian justice was a "ramshackle affair" which "could not function as the instrument of an external and superior state power to anything like the degree that modern police forces later would."[16] Only after the change in government in 1850 do we see a few charges brought to trial on behalf of the Board as a corporate body, despite the fact that the Board often asked town officials to perform bylaw enforcement duties.

In keeping with this personalized model of justice, cases were summarily dealt with, often the same or the next day. There were no judges, lawyers, prosecutors, or police witnesses, only the members of the Board, sometimes the bailiff or constable, the plaintiff, defendant, and the witnesses whom they had brought. The Board members themselves were not remote from those who appeared before them. Although some professionals such as lawyers and physicians served, for the most part the members were practical men of business, local merchants and manufacturers.[17] In their daily affairs they rubbed shoulders with those brought before them, even if they did have the authority to impose taxes and fines

and to imprison defaulters for up to 30 days. Despite the fact that many of the individuals who appeared in front of this informal tribunal were not able to elect its members, it was nonetheless a community-responsive and immediate form of justice.

As a record of the public activities of ordinary women, the Board record provides us with rare insight into their transgressive behaviour, as well as the gender-based and class-linked sanctions increasingly brought to bear on them by the Prescott town fathers throughout this period. There was a rough total of 139 cases involving women between 1834 and 1850. Only 12 of these were brought on behalf of women by men. Of the 139, more than half (about 76) were independently initiated by the women themselves as prosecutors. Overwhelmingly, these were ordinary labouring women of the popular class, most of whom did not skirt the boundaries of the law in their daily lives like Mary Greneau. More often, they appeared at the court to settle everyday disputes that arose in their community. To a greater extent than the more formal Court of Quarter Sessions or the Police Courts established after 1850, the Board of Police was a practical means of dealing with community problems. [. . .] It was not costly; it was informal and conveniently located in the town. Nor, especially initially, was it mainly an instrument of institutional control, like the Upper Canadian church tribunals. More often, it was a tool used by the local populace for their convenience, as a strategy for negotiating dissent within their neighbourhoods. [. . .]

On the other hand, it is worth underlining that the Board of Police was a coercive institution, ultimately representing the interests of the wealthier male members of the Prescott community. It was no idealized, democratic, grass-roots body. Yet, since it did not always control the charges brought before it, but only sat in judgement, it was easily used by common citizens as a tool in negotiating social difficulties. [. . .] Those who appeared before the court were not criminals, but were using the courts for their own private purposes.

Public records such as the Prescott Board of Police Minute Book, it has been argued, reveal at least as much about the institutions that created them as they show about the subjects whose histories are recorded in their pages. All too often the entries followed a prescribed script that undermines their value as authentic sources of information about people's lives.[18] Although this problem can never be totally removed, the Board of Police for Prescott is perhaps less prone to it, due to the Board's informality and the fact that in 1834 it was a new Upper Canadian institution with little in the way of established practice to follow. Although not totally unmediated, the Board record appears to provide a summary of actual testimony recorded by the Clerk, taken verbatim from the lips of those who testified, complete with grammatical mistakes and colloquialisms. It is likely to be as close as one is going to get to hearing the real voices of women of plebeian origin for this early-nineteenth-century period. This is a record, then, that can provide us with rare insight into the public roles of ordinary Upper Canadian women.

Many of the women of Prescott who brought charges before the Board were married with their spouses still living, despite the fact that, according to British law, they were not supposed to act as legal entities apart from their husbands. Constance Backhouse's path-breaking work on women and the law in early Canada indicates that, in particular, married woman were legally subjected to patriarchal control.[19] Law and custom do not always coincide, however. Women in Prescott could and did take the law into their own hands, acting as full citizens in the eyes of the Board of Police, if not in any other capacity in Upper Canadian society. Rusty Bitterman has observed similar behaviour among rural women in the 1830s in Prince Edward Island, in what he calls

"the politics of direct action," which could include violent public behaviour.[20] [. . .] Perhaps this characteristic was shared by Prescott in this period. Women of Prescott of the popular class, the record shows, were publicly vocal not only on the street, but also in front of the Board. There is even at least one recorded instance of a woman successfully charging her own husband with disturbing the public peace by striking her.[21] Married as well as single women in Prescott could and did have their day in court, acting independently of their husbands despite the fact that law might dictate otherwise.

In this public role, women of the popular class of Prescott differed from their bourgeois sisters. Throughout the nineteenth century in Upper Canada, a new consensus was emerging about middle-class gendered social and moral values.[22] "The Cult of True Womanhood" prescribed that women's role was in the private domestic sphere. Purity, chastity, delicacy, and retirement from the male world of politics, law, and business were requisite to this ideal of femininity.[23]

The chasm that separated the classes in Upper Canada is dramatically revealed in the pages of the Board of Police record. Middle-class ladies were not to appear in public unescorted and were never to raise their voices. Compare this to the behaviour of Mrs Hannah Ahern and Mrs Catharine Murphy, screaming insults at each other in the street in a dispute over a pig. This fracas was concluded by Hannah's employment of a favourite contemporary insult, placing, as the record shows, "her hand upon her hind parts" and inviting her neighbour to kiss her there.[24] Contrast the ideal of the "domestic angel" with the behaviour of Mrs Thursbay and Mrs Chamber toward Mr Reynolds, Mrs Chamber's former landlord. Mrs Chamber had departed without paying her rent, so Reynolds was holding as security a box of her possessions. The two women arrived at his door one day, in the company of "one or two" soldiers, to reclaim her property. According to the court record,

"Chamber pretended to offer him 3/—being the balance due . . . but would not let him see the money. He refused to give up the box without the same." The two women then left the house and "commenced breaking his Windows" with their umbrellas. "Both then made great confusion in the street cheering as they broke the glass crying out whores thiefs and villains." Not many women behaved as outrageously as these two, and the stiff fines of 25 shillings each with costs of 2 shillings, 6 pence ensured that they would most likely have been sent to jail for 30 days in default of payment.[25] Still, their case and those of other women in the Board of Police record of Prescott show the striking differences between the genteel ideal to which the colony's social leaders aspired and the rough and ready nature of small-town street life. It is rare to locate such information about women of the popular class for this early period of Canada's history.

The records of the Board of Police may have been dominated by the lower-class citizens of Prescott, but it was not a criminal court. It merely tried bylaw infractions, however broadly defined. [. . .] Although the behaviour that brought individuals to the Board of Police was deviant, it was not deviant enough to lead to exclusion from society. There are even accounts of prominent male citizens who appeared before the Board without seriously damaging their social position.

Butcher Joseph Cowan's wife Jane, for example, was charged in connection with a former servant, Margaret Fitzgerald. Margaret had returned to the Cowans' house to pick up some of her belongings, perhaps hoping that her former mistress would not be at home. Fellow servant Peggy Wilson testified that, when Jane Cowan saw Margaret, she "took up a Broomstick and beat her with it striking her over the head and arms." Jane was found guilty and given the usual fine of 5 shillings plus costs of 8 shillings, 3 pence. Jane was furious and accused Margaret in the open court of being a whore. Thus, three days later,

Margaret had Jane before the Board again, this time defending her reputation. Witnesses asserted that Jane Cowan had told them that she had found a man in bed with Margaret and had caught her stealing, but something had happened between the first and second trials to change Jane's opinion. Perhaps the violence of Jane's attack on Margaret had been caused by Jane's belief that the sexual transgressions of the former servant had been committed with Jane's husband. Possibly to prevent this information from becoming public, Jane now did a complete about-face, saying that Margaret was a good girl, that Jane had never had cause to complain of her, and that she was honest. This still did not prevent Jane from being fined £1.3.3 including costs.[26] Nor was this the only time that the Cowans had been accused of violent offences. Three years earlier, Joseph had been charged but not convicted of assaulting Catherine Collins, and in 1840 Jane was also unsuccessfully charged with treating a small girl roughly.[27] None of this prevented Joseph from being elected three times to the Board, in 1841, 1842, and 1848.

[. . .]

The illustrious Jessup family, staunch Loyalists and founders of Prescott, were represented locally by two male descendants in the 1830s and 1840s. One, Hamilton D. Jessup, was a local physician who was a respectable pillar of his community and elected to the Board in 1837, 1843–1845, and 1848. The other headed a decaying branch of the family tree. Henry James Jessup came up before the Board on many occasions, caused by either his hot temper or by his predilection for frequenting houses of "disorder". In 1844 Jessup was rumoured to be "keeping a bad woman" at the house of Mrs Black, by the name of Mary Delany.[28] Two years later he had tired of her, but Mary was not taking his abandonment without protest. She took to following him around, accosting him in public barrooms, and calling him a "damned whoremaster". This got to be too much for him, and he charged her with "annoying, insulting and abusing" him. The members of the Board were all too aware of the pair's former relationship, and they sought to mediate the dispute. The matter was finally concluded when "defendant agreed with Prosecutor that if he would give two pounds ten shillings and give up her cloths and she to give up his they were to part. He gave up her cloths, gave her the money. She gave up his cloths, they appeared to be satisfied at parting." This settlement did not prevent the Board from fining Mary Delany 15 shillings plus court costs, however, which made a substantial dent in her £2 from Jessup.[29]

Henry Jessup may have already taken up with a new woman by this time, by the name of Marian or Mary Lang or Lane. She was living in Mrs McLean's house, which earlier that summer of 1846 had been such a nuisance to the neighbourhood. Jane McLean, Mary Lane, Mary Keating, and Bridget Wood were "brought before the Board for a violation of the Bylaws" by their neighbour and later Board member, merchant Robert Headlam, for a "Breach of Public Decency and good order and for intoxication." Witnesses testified that they had been "annoyed by these prisoners for a long time," but, on one particular night, "a large party of drunken men [were] in and about the house creating a riot and disturbance in the door of the house where the prisoners live." One "saw men passing and repassing with Bottles in their hands, drunk . . . , saw one man pulling Mrs Lane by the arm outside the house."[30] This may have been the same woman who, like Mary Delany, began shouting abusive names at Jessup in the street a year later. The first time Jessup charged her, the case was dismissed, but a month later, when she added threats to throw stones through his window to her insults, she was fined 5 shillings plus costs.[31] The comparatively light fine that she received may have been an acknowledgement by the Board of Jessup's role in provoking such behaviour from two different women.

[. . .]

In the earlier years of the Board of Police records, even if disorderly houses were not appreciated, neither were they were especially condemned. The line between them and houses of prostitution was not sharply delineated. Katz, Doucet, and Stern note this later in the century as well. "In fact," they observe, "little distinction was made between houses in which prostitution took place and ones where loud, uninhibited behaviour annoyed the neighbours or attracted the attention of the police."[32] Selling a little bit of sex on the side was rarely a speciality for most popular-class woman, who adopted a number of strategies of survival, which in Prescott included, as Bettina Bradbury has noted for Montreal, keeping pigs and other livestock and taking in boarders.[33] Selling liquor and providing entertainment, as did Mrs Greneau, was an easy way of augmenting one's income. Certainly a ready clientele would be found among the soldiers at Fort Wellington and the sailors and traders who passed through Prescott. Such women did not consider themselves to be prostitutes and might even have had other occupations such as needlework or laundering that did not pay them enough to survive.[34] Catherine Curry, for example, who appeared before the Board on three occasions on charges related to keeping a disorderly house, was listed on the 1851 census as a dressmaker, with two female "servants" living with her.[35] Mary Keating, Mary Lane, Bridget Wood, and Jane McLean, when charged with public drunkenness, were all women on their own who had combined their households to stretch their limited means. Although they may very well have been providing sexual services to their patrons, they were not charged with prostitution.

In fact, there was no bylaw that specifically referred to prostitution, only a vaguely worded general ordinance that called for penalties for any breach of public decency or order, which included, among other things, breaking the sabbath, cutting down shade trees, and defacing buildings.[36] Most of the charges against disorderly houses came under this bylaw. Although in testimony it was often mentioned that the defendants were keeping disorderly houses, on only three occasions before 1848 were women actually charged with this offence, and one of these charges was dismissed. In 1841, perhaps alarmed by the military presence of British soldiers at Fort Wellington after the Upper Canadian Rebellion, the Board for the first time brought in two bylaws dealing specifically with keeping bawdy houses and "vagrant public Prostitutes loitering about the streets."[37] No charges were ever brought under these new bylaws, however, and they were not renewed the following year.

Indeed, although almost all of the charges involving women included some element of public disorder, most were not for offences related to providing entertainment. A significant number—about 32 cases of the 139 involving women—were related to violence against women committed by men, in particular between husbands and wives. A much smaller number—about nine—involved violence against women committed by women. Often alcohol abuse was implicated, as when Henry Hughes disturbed the public peace by striking Mrs Anne Crowthers in the street outside the Dog and Duck tavern.[38] When labourer Jonathan Houlihan was charged by Constable Cavalier "for being drunk on Sunday night and for abusing his wife" Teresa, he admitted his guilt, but blamed it on the drink.[39] [. . .]

Sometimes violent cases involved some element of sexual coercion, as when Charles Gray and Joseph Webb were charged in 1848 "for disturbing the public peace, and abusing Mrs Webb this day and previously and for keeping a house of ill fame."[40] One particularly disturbing case involved William Lee, who had been charged before for public intoxication and using profane language, and the young daughter of Mrs Keating. Lee was charged by Alexander MacMillan, a well-off farmer who had been a Board member for 10 years, "for committing a breach of public decency." Witnesses testified that, although "Mrs Keating's daughter desired Lee to leave her Mother's residence," he refused. Passersby heard the "child cry murder" and call Lee "a blackguard." The record implies that perhaps she had resisted Lee's sexual advances. Apparently he beat her severely; others heard "screeches from Mrs K's child, went there and saw the child almost breathless and in a state of suffocation from the ill treatment of Lee, and her face was covered with blood." Lee was given a heavier fine than normal, 15 shillings, but it was still nothing close to what Lewis Beale had been fined for biting a white man's thumb.[41]

Popular-class women were not simply passive victims as these cases of assault have implied. More typical was the behaviour of Dorothy Erringy toward her husband Thomas, a local hotelkeeper. Their marriage was in crisis in the summer of 1850. Thomas had moved into the home of Minerva Coons (alias Finley, according to the record), who was considered to be keeping a house of ill fame. Rather than accept this abandonment, Dorothy went to the house, broke the windows, and "called Mrs Finley a whore." She then publicly berated her husband, calling him a "whoremaster," and ended up in a violent argument which ended with him hitting her. Even though Dorothy had started the altercation, the neighbours charged Thomas and Minerva with disturbing the peace, and they were fined 25 and 20 shillings respectively. Thomas launched his own complaint against his wife for her role in disturbing the peace, but such was the community censure of his behaviour that, when the Board convened, he did not show up and was charged costs. In the 1851 census, Dorothy and Thomas were listed as occupying the same premises and Minerva Coons/Finley had evidently moved out of town, so it appears that Dorothy's aggressive action had reclaimed her husband.[42]

Such violent cases were not typical of the charges brought to the Board, however. By far the greatest number, about 78 of the 139 cases involving women, had to do with name-calling. In any public dispute involving women, such as with Minerva and Dorothy, far and away the favourite insult was some variant of whore. Men, in contrast, were called a variety of names such as scoundrel, thief, villain, or blackguard, which more generally reflected on their character or integrity rather than their sexual behaviour.[43] Ethnic insults were relatively rare, according to the Board record. Cases of name-calling often involved women from the "respectable" part of the popular classes, as well as the obvious easy targets of such insults. [. . .]

Insults which called into question a woman's moral honour could be used to put her in her place, as when Mr Desordie responded to Hannah Ahern's attempt to collect payment for bread by calling her a "drunken woman."[44] They could also be a way in which a woman whose reputation had been maligned might counterattack, by discrediting her critics. When William Dove accused Christina Brogan of keeping a disorderly house, she replied by calling his wife a whore and a bitch.[45] Another noteworthy case involved Mrs Elizabeth Gillard, who found some letters "as she supposed very suspicious" between her husband and Mrs Girnash, the wife of a local bar owner. Mrs Gillard went to the bar to confront the other woman, who, as soon as she realized who Gillard was, called Gillard "a streetwalker" and pushed her out of the room and outside, where she fell on some bushes. Clearly Mrs Girnash was trying to keep her husband from finding out about her and Mr Gillard, and at least for the moment it worked. John Girnash joined in the abuse, yelling at Mrs Gillard that "if one man was not enough he had two more in the barroom."[46] Both Girnashes received hefty fines, perhaps out of sympathy with the injured wife. Most often insults to a woman's reputation took place in the context of disputes over other issues. A number of these were provoked by irritations caused by town life. Pigs running at large were a particular problem. A whole neighbourhood erupted on one June day when a particularly vicious pig owned by Mrs Ahern tried to bite the child of Mr and Mrs Parsons. They threw hot water on the pig to chase it away and apparently scalded it. When Mrs Ahern came over to complain, the dispute escalated with the result that the two women accused each other of a number of things, including being whores, being drunkards, and stealing the cloak of Mrs Spiller, a local schoolteacher.[47]

It is important to note that these cases were not defamation charges, but usually complaints brought under the bylaws for disturbing the peace. It was a matter of utmost indifference to the Board whether the charges were justified or not, simply whether or not the breach to the public peace had occurred. Just calling a woman a whore in public was considered inappropriate, whether or not she actually was one. It was very likely that the size of the fines given reflected the Board's opinion of the woman's respectability, but only in exceptional circumstances was more than 5 shillings assessed for public insults. Although the many women who brought charges for name-calling obviously must have felt they were defending their honour, they did not have to prove it. Thus Catherine Curry was able, for example, immediately following a conviction for keeping a house of ill fame, to charge Henry James Jessup successfully with using insulting and improper language to her.[48]

Since it was so easy to obtain convictions, and the consequences for being found guilty were usually so minor, the women of Prescott came to use the Board more and more for settling personal disputes. This peaked in 1840–41, when about twice as many cases involving insults against a woman's reputation were heard by the Board than in the previous five years; this number was about the same as that of similar cases heard over the next eight years. Anxiety about the increased complaints may have been another reason that motivated the Board to enact the bylaws concerning streetwalking and keeping bawdy houses in 1841. It may have also been behind a stern warning issued in June 1840 reminding citizens "that anyone after the date hereof entering complaint" should be aware that "the Board will not hold themselves responsible for whatever costs the said complaint may incur to the Clerk or constable for said complaint."[49] Although after this the frequency of charges dropped, the use of the Board had become part of an individual's personal arsenal in disputes between women in Prescott. [. . .]

Particularly after 1848, however, the use of the Board changed. The steady drop in charges brought to it by women may have had to do with a growing sense that such public displays were damaging to female reputation. From a peak of 25 cases involving women in 1840, the number steadily dropped to only three by 1844. Then the numbers slowly began to rise, hitting a smaller peak of 13 by 1850. The cause of the second rise, however, was not more women themselves bringing charges, but rather more aggressive action by the town fathers, particularly aimed at reducing the incidence of disorderly houses.

In the mid-nineteenth century, a wave of Evangelical reform was sweeping over North America as well as Britain. [. . .] In Prescott, this may have also been fuelled by concern over the number of destitute Irish immigrants who were arriving after 1847. In the summer of that year, the Board had been ordered by the Governor General to take steps to prepare to deal with an expected onslaught of the ill and the desperate.[50] Nonetheless, although such steps were taken, in 1849 the Board responded to complaints about "the occupation of a dilapidated house in the main street by emigrants, that said house being in a filthy state." Orders were given to "abate the aforesaid nuisance by ejecting the parties living in said premises and cleaning and securing the same from further annoyance to the Neighbourhood."[51]

The same urge to clean up was directed toward alcohol consumption and public morality. After 1848 there are cases of applications for liquor permits being turned down, something that was unheard of before this time. [. . .]

The Board was equally concerned about the "crying evil" of female immorality and the public disorder it caused. In 1848 a new bylaw specifically prohibited prostitution and houses of ill fame occupied by "loose" women.[52] The first three charges brought under this bylaw, however, were dismissed for lack of evidence. It is not clear who brought the charges, but obviously people were not willing to testify against their neighbours under the new law.[53] The local authorities then became increasingly involved in pressing charges, as when Constable Benjamin Cavalier charged Bridget Agar with "riotous conduct," "scolding," and keeping a "bad house." He actually entered her home and, when he "saw part of a man's pantaloon stuck out of a hole," he pulled out the half-undressed Patrick Griffin. Fines also became stiffer, and thus imprisonment more likely. Bridget Agar was fined 20 shillings and sent to Brockville jail in default of payment for 21 days, although Griffin was not charged.[54] A local lock-up was also built, so that miscreants such as Mary Hutton could be imprisoned locally while they awaited trial. Both she and her husband were found drunk and arguing in the street, but only Mary was locked up until the Board assembled on Monday.[55] Obviously this would send a strong message to women who were fond of drinking. Increasingly, women of the popular class stopped laying charges, and several charges before the court were delayed and then quietly died. Accordingly, the Board stepped up its role in prosecution. In late 1849 the Corporation took it upon itself to charge William Sanders with keeping a bawdy house. Even though he confessed, he was fined

10 shillings and had his liquor licence revoked.[56] Half a dozen other successful charges were brought after 1848 against women for keeping disorderly houses, the most notable of which was that against Catherine Curry, brought by none other than Henry James Jessup. Her neighbours turned out in force to defend her, asserting that they never saw men there, that the house was always quiet by 9:00 PM, and that she did not allow gambling. Jessup, they said, was having a quarrel with her and had said publicly that "he would perjure himself to have Mrs Curry turned out of town." Jessup alone testified against her, and on that basis she was convicted. This was quite a departure from the judgments of earlier boards.[57] Still, as we have already noted, Catherine Curry successfully countercharged Jessup the following day and was not run out of town. She was still in Prescott the next year and shows up on the census as a dressmaker.

[...]

Although women could still have their day in court, by 1850 the Board of Police was playing a very different role in the Prescott community than it had in 1834. From a peak of cases brought by women in 1841, women's use of the Board declined as it became increasingly the instrument for a gendered and class-based agenda of social control and moral reform, led by professional men of the bourgeois class. The character of the record changes as well, and we no longer hear as much from the voices of the women themselves as we do from their accusers. From 1850, municipal enforcement bodies such as the police and police courts were established, which were much more effective in asserting the power of local authorities. Throughout the latter part of the nineteenth century, the process of establishing the hegemony of gendered middle-class values of appropriate female behaviour was well advanced. By the late nineteenth and early twentieth century, if a woman was raped or assaulted, she was the one on trial, and her male attacker's crime was mitigated by any failure on her part to live up to the domestic and moral ideal of "True Womanhood".[58] We still struggle with this legacy today. [...]

NOTES

1. Board of Police Records, Prescott, Ontario, November 28, 1937 [hereafter referred to by date].
2. November 6, 1837.
3. May 15, 1836.
4. November 2, 1835.
5. November 6, 1837.
6. November 1837.
7. November 20, 1837.
8. November 28, 1837.
9. On charivaris, see Allan Greer, "From Folklore to Revolution: Charivaris and the Lower Canadian Rebellion of 1837," *Social History* 15 (January 1990): 25–43; Bryan Palmer, "Discordant Music: Charivaris and Whitecapping in Nineteenth-Century North America," *Labour/Le Travailleur* 3 (1978): 5–62; and *Working Class Experience: The Rise and Reconstruction of Canadian Labour,* *1800–1980* (Toronto: McClelland & Stewart, 1992), 66–9.
10. Toronto, Archives of Ontario, 1851 Prescott Census.
11. Douglas McCalla, *Planting the Province: The Economic History of Upper Canada,* *1784–1870* (Toronto: University of Toronto Press, 1993), 118–121, 158.
12. Katherine M.J. McKenna, *Family Life in a Military Garrison: History of the Routines and Activities of the Royal Canadian Rifle Regiment at Fort Wellington, Prescott, 1843–1854* (Ottawa: Canadian Heritage Parks Canada, Microfiche Report Series No. 533, 1995).
13. Ruth McKenzie, *Leeds and Grenville: Their First Two Hundred Years* (Toronto: McClelland & Stewart, 1967), 188.
14. Donald Harmon Akenson, *The Irish in Ontario: A Study in Rural History* (Montreal and

Kingston: McGill-Queen's University Press, 1984), 91.

15. Paul Craven, "Law and Ideology: The Toronto Police Court," in David H. Flaherty, ed., *Essays in the History of Canadian Law,* vol. II (Toronto: University of Toronto Press, 1983), 249.

16. Allan Greer, "The Birth of the Police in Canada." in Allan Greer and Ian Radforth, eds, *Colonial Leviathan: State Formation in Mid-Nineteenth-Century Canada* (Toronto: University of Toronto Press, 1992), 19.

17. Information on the occupations of Board members and of citizens who appeared before the Board has been obtained by checking names against the 1848 and 1851 Prescott censuses.

18. Karen Dubinsky, "Afterward: Telling Stories about Dead People," in Franca Iacovetta and Wendy Mitchinson, eds, *On the Case: Explorations in Social History* (Toronto: University of Toronto Press, 1998), 359–66; Franca Iacovetta and Wendy Mitchinson, "Introduction: Social History and Case Files Research," in *On the Case,* 3–21; Annalee Golz, "Uncovering and Reconstructing Family Violence: Ontario Criminal Case Files," in Iacovetta and Mitchinson, eds, *On the Case,* 289–311.

19. Constance Backhouse, *Petticoats and Prejudice: Women and the Law in Nineteenth-Century Canada* (Toronto: Osgoode Society, 1991); and "Pure Patriarchy: Nineteenth-Century Canadian Marriage," *McGill Law Journal* 31 (1984): 264–312.

20. Rusty Bitterman, "Women and the Escheat Movement: The Politics of Everyday Life on Prince Edward Island," in Janet Guildford and Suzanne Morton, eds, *Separate Spheres: Women's Worlds in the Nineteenth-Century Maritimes* (Fredericton: Acadiensis Press, 1994), 38.

21. September 7, 1841.

22. In the development of these new ideas about the gendered public and private spheres propagated by the middle class, see Andrew C. Holman, *A Sense of Their Duty: Middle-Class Formation in Victorian Ontario Towns* (Montreal and Kingston: McGill-Queen's University Press, 2000); Lynne Marks, *Revivals and Roller Rinks: Religion, Leisure, and Identity in Late-Nineteenth-Century Small-Town Ontario* (Toronto: University of Toronto Press, 1996); Katherine M.J.

McKenna, *A Life of Propriety: Anne Murray Powell and Her Family, 1755–1849* (Montreal and Kingston: McGill-Queen's University Press, 1994); Cecilia Morgan, *Public Men and Virtuous Women: The Gendered Languages of Religion and Politics in Upper Canada, 1791–1850* (Toronto: University of Toronto Press, 1996).

23. On the genesis of the new ideal of middle-class womanhood in eighteenth- and early-nineteenth-century England, see Leonore Davidoff and Catherine Hall, *Family Fortunes: Men and Women of the English Middle Class, 1780–1850* (London: Croom Helm, 1987). For similar developments in the United States, see Mary P. Ryan, *Cradle of the Middle Class: The Family in Oneida County, New York, 1790–1865* (Cambridge, MA: Cambridge University Press, 1981); Christine Stansell, *City of Women: Sex and Class in New York, 1789–1860* (Urbana and Chicago: University of Illinois Press, 1986).

24. June 12, 1840.
25. February 8, 1841.
26. May 8 and 11, 1838.
27. September 22, 1835; December 7, 1840.
28. April 29, 1844.
29. August 4, 1846.
30. May 26, 1846.
31. June 30 and July 6, 1847.
32. Michael Katz, Michael J. Doucet, and Mark J. Stern, *The Social Organization of Early Industrial Capitalism* (Cambridge, MA: Harvard University Press, 1982), 231.
33. Bettina Bradbury, "Pigs, Cows and Boarders: Non-Wage Forms of Survival among Montreal Families, 1861–91," *Labour/Le travail* 14 (1984): 9–46.
34. Judith Fingard has also seen this type of practice of prostitution in Halifax; see *The Dark Side of Life in Victorian Halifax* (Porter's Lake, NS: Pottersfield Press, 1991), 95–113.
35. February 24, 1848; January 29, 1849; May 8, 1850.
36. See bylaws for April 1834.
37. June 7, 1841.
38. July 26, 1839.
39. July 1, 1850.
40. September 15, 1848.
41. September 5, 1844.
42. July 1, 1850.

43. S.M. Waddams observes the same gendered pattern in name-calling in English ecclesiastical courts in his book, *Sexual Slander in Nineteenth-Century England: Defamation in the Ecclesiastical Courts, 1815–1855* (Toronto: University of Toronto Press, 2000). Cecilia Morgan looks at another aspect of honour for men of the upper classes during this period in her article, "'In Search of the Phantom Misnamed Honour': Dueling in Upper Canada," *Canadian Historical Review* 76 (1995): 529–62.

44. July 12, 1837.

45. August 26, 1850.

46. June 12, 1840.

47. August 24, 1840.

48. May 9, 1850.

49. June 15, 1840.

50. June 7, 1847.

51. June 4, 1849.

52. Mary Anne Poutanen also sees a sharp rise in the number of women arrested for prostitution in the 1840s in Montreal ("'To Indulge Their Carnal Appetites': Prostitution in Early Nineteenth-Century Montreal, 1810–1842" [PhD diss. Université de Montréal, 1996], 233).

53. February 28, 1848.

54. July 13, 1850.

55. April 28, 1849.

56. December 3, 1849.

57. May 8, 1850.

58. On women's supposed responsibility for crimes committed against them, see especially Karen Dubinsky, *Improper Advances: Rape and Heterosexual Conflict in Ontario, 1880–1929* (Chicago: University of Chicago Press, 1993); Golz, "Uncovering and Reconstructing Family Violence."

Chapter 11

Indigenous People in British North America

READINGS

Primary Documents

1   From "Report on the Affairs of the Indians in Canada," (1842–44), in *Appendix to the Fourth Volume of the Journals of the Legislative Assembly of the Province of Canada 1844–45*

2   "The Robinson-Superior Treaty," in *The Treaties of Canada with the Indians of Manitoba and the North-West Territories, Including the Negotiations on which They Were Based, and Other Information Relating Thereto*, Alexander Morris

Historical Interpretations

3   From "Empire, the Maritime Colonies, and the Supplanting of Mi'kma'ki/Wulstukwik, 1780–1820," John G. Reid

4   From "'An Equitable Right to Be Compensated': The Dispossession of the Aboriginal Peoples of Quebec and the Emergence of a New Legal Rationale (1760–1860)," Alain Beaulieu

INTRODUCTION

The period comprising the late eighteenth and early nineteenth centuries was one in which treaties between Indigenous peoples and colonial authorities began to institutionalize relations and to more sharply segregate the two groups. In return for certain territories, Indigenous people were to stay away from settlers who were taking up land for agricultural purposes. The nullification of Indigenous title happened along lines set out by the Colonial Office. This dictation or shaping of the terms was the prerogative of the stronger force—a pattern that continued after Confederation.

The report from the early 1840s illustrates clearly that the British colonial authorities believed that they had continually treated an Indigenous population that was prone to temptation with "forbearance and kindness". The second primary document is a treaty known as the Robinson-Superior

Treaty. Signed in 1850, it offered lump-sum and yearly compensation to the affected bands for the loss of their lands, and granted reserves, presumably in places that the bands wanted to continue living. John Reid's reading discusses this process (which occurred earlier in the Maritimes than in central Canada) by using the term "supplanting," which is especially appropriate because it conveys a sense that one way of life was elbowed out of the way to make room for another. His view is a bit more hopeful in that he notes that Maritime Indigenous people experienced some success in having their grievances remedied. Perhaps this was because colonization required things to happen quickly and authorities did not want to delay the process. Alain Beaulieu's account shows that the British authorities followed a different pattern in dispossessing Indigenous peoples in the St Lawrence Valley than in other parts of British North America. Following a tradition established under the French regime, the British did not conclude treaties with Indigenous people in Quebec, but instead proceeded unilaterally with the appropriation of their land.

QUESTIONS FOR CONSIDERATION

1. What goal did the British colonial administration seem to be moving toward? In other words, what changes did they hope to bring about in the relationship between Indigenous people and immigrants/settlers?
2. What did the Robinson-Superior Treaty ask of those who signed it?
3. From the perspective of Indigenous peoples in British North America, what were the possible advantages and disadvantages of being treated as individual nations?
4. What were the strategies that Maritime Indigenous people used to "negotiate" with colonial authorities?
5. How did the British dispossess Indigenous people of their land in Quebec? Why did they not conclude Indigenous treaties in the colony?

SUGGESTIONS FOR FURTHER READING

Ted Binnema, and Susan Neylan, eds, *New Histories for Old: Changing Perspectives on Canada's Native Pasts* (Vancouver: UBC Press, 2007).
Sarah Carter, *Aboriginal People and Colonizers of Western Canada to 1900* (Toronto: University of Toronto Press, 1999).
Olive Patricia Dickason, with David T. McNab, *Canada's First Nations: A History of Founding Peoples from Earliest Times* (Don Mills: Oxford University Press, 2009).
Margery Fee, *Literary Land Claims: The "Indian Land Question" from Pontiac's War to Attawapiskat* (Waterloo, ON: Wilfrid Laurier University Press, 2015).
Celia Haig-Brown and David Nock, eds, *With Good Intentions: Euro-Canadian and Aboriginal Relations in Colonial Canada* (Vancouver: UBC Press, 2006).
J.R. Miller, *Compact, Contract, Covenant: Aboriginal Treaty-Making in Canada* (Toronto: University of Toronto Press, 2009).
———, ed., *Sweet Promises: A Reader on Indian-White Relations in Canada* (Toronto: University of Toronto Press, 1991).
L.F.S. Upton, *Micmacs and Colonists: Indian-White Relations in the Maritimes, 1713–1867* (Vancouver: University of British Columbia Press, 1979).

Primary Documents

1 From "Report on the Affairs of the Indians in Canada," (1842–44), in *Appendix to the Fourth Volume of the Journals of the Legislative Assembly of the Province of Canada 1844–45* (Montreal: R. Campbell, 1845), Appendix EEE.

SECTION I. HISTORY OF THE RELATIONS BETWEEN THE GOVERNMENT AND THE INDIANS.

The spirit of the British Government towards the Aborigines of this Continent, was at an early date characterized by the same forbearance and kindness which still continues to be extended to them. [. . .]

Since 1763 the Government, adhering to the Royal Proclamation of that year, have not considered themselves entitled to dispossess the Indians of their lands, without entering into an agreement with them, and rendering them some compensation. For a considerable time after the conquest of Canada, the whole of the western part of the Upper Province, with the exception of a few military posts on the frontier, and a great extent of the eastern part, was in their occupation. As the settlement of the country advanced, and the land was required for new occupants, or the predatory and revengeful habits of the Indians rendered their removal desirable, the British Government made successive agreements with them for the surrender of portions of their lands. The compensation was sometimes made in the shape of presents, consisting of clothing, ammunition, and objects adapted to gratify a savage taste; but more frequently in the shape of permanent annuities, payable to the tribe concerned, and their descendants forever, either in goods at the current price, or in money at the rate of ten dollars (£2 10s.) for each member of the tribe at the time of the arrangement. [. . .]

It has been alleged that these agreements were unjust, as dispossessing the natives of their ancient territories, and extortionate, as rendering a very inadequate compensation for the lands surrendered.

If, however, the Government had not made arrangements for the voluntary surrender of the lands, the white settlers would gradually have taken possession of them, without offering any compensation whatsoever; it would, at that time, have been as impossible to resist the natural laws of society, and to guard the Indian Territory against the encroachments of the whites, as it would have been impolitic to have attempted to check the tide of immigration. The Government, therefore, adopted the most humane and the most just course, in inducing the Indians, by offers of compensation, to remove quietly to more distant hunting grounds, or to confine themselves within more limited reserves, instead of leaving them and the white settlers exposed to the horrors of a protracted struggle for ownership. The wisdom and justice of this course is most strongly recommended by Vattel, in his Law of Nations, from which the following passage is an extract:—

There is another celebrated question to which the discovery of the new world has principally given rise. It is asked whether a nation may lawfully take possession of some part of a vast country in which there are none but erratic nations, whose scanty population is incapable of occupying the whole? We have already observed, in establishing the obligation to cultivate the earth, that these nations cannot exclusively appropriate to themselves more land than they have occasion for, or more than they are able to settle and cultivate. Their unsettled habitation in those immense regions, cannot be accounted a true and legal possession, and the people of Europe, too closely pent up at home, finding land, of which the Savages stood in no particular need, and of which they made no actual and constant use, were lawfully entitled to take possession of it and to settle it with Colonies. The earth, as we have already observed, belongs to mankind in general, and was designed to furnish them with subsistence. If each nation had from the beginning resolved to appropriate to itself a vast country, that the people might live only by hunting, fishing and wild fruits, our globe would not be sufficient to maintain a tenth part of its present inhabitants. We do not, therefore, deviate from the views of nature, in confining the Indians within narrower limits. However, we cannot help praising the moderation of the English Puritans, who first settled in New England, who, notwithstanding their being furnished with a charter from their Sovereign, purchased of the Indians the lands of which they intended to take possession. This laudable example was followed by William Penn, and the Colony of Quakers that he conducted to Pennsylvania.

Nor can the friend of the Indian claim for him a monetary compensation based on the present value of the land, which has been created solely by the presence and industry of the white settlers. Its only value to the denizen of the forest, was as a hunting ground, as the source of his supply of game and furs. Of the cultivation of the soil, he then knew nothing. The progress of settlement, and the consequent destruction of the forests, with the operations of the lumberer, and fur trader, was shortly about to destroy this value; in every case the Indians had either the opportunity of retreating to more distant hunting grounds, or they were left on part of their old possessions, with a reserve

supposed at the time to be adequate to all their wants, and greatly exceeding their requirements as cultivators of the soil at the present day, to which were added the ranges of their old haunts, until they became actually occupied by settlers, and in many cases, an annuity to themselves and their descendents forever, which was equivalent at least to any benefit they derived from the possession of the lands.

If subsequent events have greatly enhanced the value of their lands, it has been in consequence of the speedy and peaceable settlement of the country, by means, chiefly, of the agreements in question, and the Indians are now in possession of advantages which far exceed those of the surrounding white population, and which afford them the means, under a proper system of mental improvement, of obtaining independence, and even opulence.

These agreements have been faithfully observed by both parties. The Indians have not disputed the title of the Crown to the lands, which they have surrendered; and the annuities have always been the first charge upon the revenue derived from the sale of Crown Lands, and have been *punctually paid up to the present time*.

From the earliest period of the connexion between the Indians and the British Government it has been customary to distribute annually certain presents, consisting chiefly of clothing and ammunition. [. . .]

The practice has continued to the present time, partly owing to a renewal of the occasions which first led to it; partly to repeated, but apparently unauthorised, declarations of officers of the Government, that the system should for ever be maintained; and partly to the apprehension that its sudden discontinuance would cause inconvenience and hardships to a large portion of the race within the Province.

The British Government have always considered the Indians to be under their special charge. In the Lower Province the tribes were early converted and collected in settlements by the Jesuits, who received large grants of land from the French Crown for this service. Upon the Conquest, the Crown took possession of these estates, and thus cut off any further benefit which the Indians might have derived from them. In the Upper Province, however, Christianity and civilization had, until a recent period, made little progress among them. They were an untaught, unwary race, among a population ready and able to take every advantage of them. Their lands, their presents and annuities, the produce of the chase, their guns and clothing, whatever they possessed of value, were objects of temptation to the needy settlers and the unprincipled trader, to whom their ignorance of commerce and of the English language, and their remarkable fondness for spirits, yielded them an easy prey. Hence it became necessary for the Government to interfere. Laws were passed to prevent or limit trading with them—to hinder the sale of spirits to them—to exclude whites from their settlements—and to restrain encroachments upon their lands. Officers were appointed at the principal Indian settlements, to enforce these laws, and to communicate between the tribes and the Government; to attend to the distribution of their presents and annuities; to prevent discussion; and, generally, to maintain the authority of the Government among the tribes.

The system of dealing with them was essentially military. For a long time they were under the head of the military department, and were considered and treated as military allies or stipendiaries.

Little was done by the Government to raise their mental and moral condition. In Lower Canada the Roman Catholic Missionaries, originally appointed by the Jesuits, were maintained. In Upper Canada, until a very late period, neither Missionary nor Schoolmaster was appointed. The omission was in later years supplied by various religious Societies, whose efforts have in many instances met with signal success, and within a still more recent period the Government has directed its attention to the same object.

As the Indian Lands were held in common, and the title to them was vested in the Crown, as their Guardian, the Indians were excluded from all political rights, the tenure of which depended upon an extent of interest, not conferred upon them by the Crown.

Their inability also to complete with their white brethren debarred them, in a great measure, from the enjoyment of civil rights, while the policy of the Government led to the belief that they did not in fact possess them.*

They were thus left in a state of tutelage, which although devised for their protection and benefit, has in the event proved very detrimental to their interests, by encouraging them to rely wholly upon the support and advice of the Government, and to neglect the opportunities which they have possessed of raising themselves from the state of dependence to the level of the surrounding population.

It is easy, at the present day, on looking back, to trace the error of the Government, and its evil consequences; but it is only just to observe that the system was in accordance with the legislation of the times. The regenerative power of religion and education was not then as now appreciated. The effects of

---

*The records of the Courts of Justice furnish undoubted evidence that the Indians are amenable to, and enjoy the protection of, both the civil and criminal laws of the Province. That they may share in, and are entitled to, all the political privileges of the whites when individually possessed of the necessary qualifications may be inferred from the fact, that John Brant, an Indian Chief of the six nations, was elected a Member of the Legislative Assembly of Upper Canada. The subsequent loss of his seat in that body, was occasioned in consequence of his not possessing sufficient Freehold property, and not on account of his origin. Mr. Justice Macaulay's, and Mr. Attorney General Ogden's opinions on this subject are given in the Appendix, No. 98.

civilization, and the necessities arising out of it, were not foreseen. The information of the Imperial Government was very imperfect. It was not easy nor safe rashly to change a mode of treatment to which the Indians had become accustomed, and thus the system has been allowed to continue up to the present time, long after the Government has become aware of its imperfections and inconveniences.

It must also be acknowledged that the system was never fully carried out. The protection which the Government intended to throw over the Indians was not and could not be sufficiently maintained. No supervision was adequate to guard so many detached and distant bands from the evils inflicted on them by their white neighbours, aided by their own cupidity and love of spirits. Their lands were encroached upon, frequently with their own consent, bought with a bribe to the Chief. Their complaints were often adjudicated upon by parties interested in despoiling them, or prejudiced against them; and thus a system, erroneous in itself, became more hurtful from its necessarily imperfect development. Of late years, however, the government has become sensible of the necessity for introducing some change in this policy.

2 "The Robinson-Superior Treaty," in Alexander Morris, *The Treaties of Canada with the Indians of Manitoba and the North-West Territories, Including the Negotiations on which They Were Based, and Other Information Relating Thereto* (Toronto: Belfords, Clarke, 1880), 302–4.

This Agreement, made and entered into on the seventh day of September, in the year of Our Lord one thousand eight hundred and fifty, at Sault Ste. Marie, in the Province of Canada, between the Honorable William Benjamin Robinson, of the one part, on behalf of Her Majesty the Queen, and Joseph Peandechat, John Iuinway, Mishe-Muckqua, Totomencie, Chiefs, and Jacob Warpela, Ahmutchiwagabou, Michel Shelageshick, Manitoshainse, and Chiginans, principal men of the Ojibewa Indians inhabiting the Northern Shore of Lake Superior, in the said Province of Canada, from Batchewananng Bay to Pigeon River, at the western extremity of said lake, and inland throughout the extent to the height of land which separates the territory covered by the charter of the Honorable the Hudson's Bay Company from the said tract, and also the islands in the said lake within the boundaries of the British possessions therein, of the other part, witnesseth:

That for and in consideration of the sum of two thousand pounds of good and lawful money of Upper Canada, to them in hand paid, and for the further perpetual annuity of five hundred pounds, the same to be paid and delivered to the said Chiefs and their tribes at a convenient season of each summer, not later than the first day of August at the Honorable the Hudson's Bay Company's Posts of Michipicoton and Fort William, they the said Chiefs and principal men do freely, fully and voluntarily surrender, cede, grant and convey unto Her Majesty, Her heirs and successors forever, all their right, title and interest in the whole of the territory above described, save and except the reservations set forth in the schedule hereunto annexed, which reservations shall be held and occupied by the said Chiefs and their tribes in common, for the purposes of residence and cultivation,—and should the said Chiefs and their respective tribes at any time desire to dispose of any mineral or other valuable productions upon the said reservations, the same will be at their request sold by order of the Superintendent-General of the Indian Department for the time being, for their sole use and benefit, and to the best advantage.

And the said William Benjamin Robinson of the first part, on behalf of Her Majesty and the Government of this Province, hereby promises and agrees to make the payments as before mentioned; and further to allow the said Chiefs and their tribes the full and free privilege to hunt over the territory now ceded by them, and to fish in the waters thereof as they have heretofore been in the habit of doing, saving and excepting only such portions of the said territory as may from time to time be sold or leased to individuals, or companies of individuals, and occupied by them with the consent of the Provincial Government. The parties of the second part further promise and agree that they will not sell, lease, or otherwise dispose of any portion of their reservations without the consent of the Superintendent-General of Indian Affairs being first had and obtained; nor will they at any time hinder or prevent persons from exploring or searching for minerals or other valuable productions in any part of the territory hereby ceded to Her Majesty as before mentioned. The parties of the second part also agree that in case the Government of this Province should before the date of this agreement have sold, or bargained to sell, any mining locations or other property on the portions of the territory hereby reserved for their use and benefit, then and in that case such sale, or promise of sale, shall be perfected, if the parties interested desire it, by the Government, and the amount accruing therefrom shall be paid to the tribe to whom the reservation belongs. The said William Benjamin Robinson on behalf of Her Majesty, who desires to deal liberally and justly with all her subjects, further promises and agrees that in case the territory hereby ceded by the parties of the second part shall at any future period produce an amount which will enable the Government of this Province without incurring loss to increase the annuity hereby secured to them, then, and in that case, the same shall be augmented from time to time, provided that the amount paid to each individual shall not exceed the sum of one pound provincial currency in any one year, or such further sum as Her Majesty may be graciously pleased to order; and provided further that the number of Indians entitled to the benefit of this treaty shall amount to two-thirds of their present numbers (which is twelve hundred and forty) to entitle them to claim the full benefit thereof, and should their numbers at any future period not amount to two-thirds of twelve hundred and forty, the annuity shall be diminished in proportion to their actual numbers.

_____

Schedule of Reservations made by the above named and subscribing Chiefs and principal men.

First—Joseph Pean-de-chat and his tribe, the reserve to commence about two miles from Fort William (inland), on the right bank of the River Kiministiquia; thence westerly six miles, parallel to the shores of the lake; thence northerly five miles, thence easterly to the right bank of the said river, so as not to interfere with any acquired rights of the Honorable Hudson's Bay Company.

Second—Four miles square at Gros Cap, being a valley near the Honorable Hudson's Bay Company's post of Michipicoton, for Totominai and tribe.

Third—Four miles square on Gull River, near Lake Nipigon, on both sides of said river, for the Chief Mishimuckqua and tribe.

(Signed)   W. B. Robinson.

Joseph Pean-de-chat.	His x mark.	[L.S.]
John Minway.	" x "	[L.S.]
Mishe-Muckqua.	" x "	[L.S.]
Totominai.	" x "	[L.S.]
Jacob Wapela.	" x "	[L.S.]
Ah-mutchinagalon.	" x "	[L.S.]
Michel Shelageshick.	" x "	[L.S.]
Manitou Shainse.	" x "	[L.S.]
Chiginans.	" x "	[L.S.]

Signed, sealed and delivered at Sault Ste. Marie, the day and year first above written, in presence of—

(Signed)   George Ironside, S. I. Affairs.
            Astley P. Cooper, Capt. Com. Rifle Brig.

H. M. Balfour, 2nd Lieut. Rifle Brig.
John Swanston, C. F. Hon. Hud. Bay Co.
George Johnston, Interpreter.
F. W. Keating.

Historical Interpretations

3 From John G. Reid, "Empire, the Maritime Colonies, and the Supplanting of Mi'kma'ki/ Wulstukwik, 1780–1820," *Acadiensis* 38, 2 (2009): 78–97.

It has become a historical truism that the effects of the Loyalist migration to the Maritime colonies, reinforced by other substantial migrations including those of the Scots, were intensely destructive for the Native populations of the territories involved. L.F.S. Upton wrote in 1979 that "the arrival of the Loyalists completed Britain's conquest of Acadia"; the occasional "flicker of independence" notwithstanding, wholesale dispossession followed. For Upton, it quickly became clear that, "the Indians were no longer of account as allies, enemies, or people."[1] In another important and influential study, Harald E.L. Prins argued in 1996 that the Loyalist influx "overwhelmed" the Native economy, and the resulting destitution—along with the absence of support from potential diplomatic allies in France and the United States— ensured that by the 1790s, "the Mi'kmaq and other tribal nations on the Atlantic seaboard were painfully aware that the old times were over."[2] Depictions such as these are consistent with the more general historical narrative of an ongoing, far advanced dispossession of Native peoples in eastern North America as a whole. [. . .]

This article will suggest, however, that the supplanting of Mi'kma'ki and Wulstukwik by the Maritime colonies, while certainly entering a critical phase during the waning years of the "long" eighteenth century, was characterized by a complex and distinctive pattern.[3]

In this substantial portion of northeastern North America there were discrete though intertwined lines of development in, on the one hand, environmental and territorial matters and, on the other hand, in those connected with military and diplomatic history. That dispossession was widespread is beyond doubt, even though a review of the evidence also suggests significant spatial variations in the scale and implications of environmental change. Yet this damaging process co-existed with the continuing Native ability to represent complaints and demands based on longstanding treaty obligations, and to extract conciliatory responses from reluctant imperial officials. Owed in part to the tensions prevailing during a period of recurrent conflicts embroiling Great Britain, France, and the United States, this persistent diplomatic capacity waned after 1815. While it lasted, it had not only carried through to a later era the practice of discussing treaty-based assertions with representatives of the Crown, but it also had continued an extended narrative of Native-imperial relations through a period that had seen a profound discontinuity in the form of greatly intensified pressure imposed by colonial settlement.

In important respects, the Mi'kmaq and Wulstukwiuk shared common or analogous histories. Interaction and intermittent military co-operation with French imperial officials characterized the late seventeenth and early eighteenth centuries for both, and reached further into the eighteenth century for Mi'kmaq who maintained a relationship with Louisbourg. The Mi'kmaw experience, and to a lesser degree that of the Wulstukwiuk, also included a relationship of general though not uninterrupted peaceful co-existence with Acadian colonists while the disruptions created by the Planter migrations of the 1760s had also proved to have limited environmental consequences.[4] When it came to the history of diplomatic relations with the British, the Mi'kmaq, along with the Wulstukwiuk and Passamaquoddy, shared a process of evolution that from 1725 onwards diverged markedly from the experience of Wabanaki neighbours. It was characterized, in particular, by the negotiation of similar and closely linked treaties in 1760–1, which marked the last major phase of treaty-making even though further negotiations and more localized treaties followed during the era of the American Revolution.[5] The Mi'kmaq and Wulstukwiuk also shared an ability to meet the pressures that arose during the 1780–1820 period by drawing on two centuries of experience not only with intercultural trade relations but also with diplomatic engagements, including citation of treaty obligations to protect essential resource harvests and the containment of agricultural settlement. The stresses imposed by colonization during this crucial transitional era were unprecedented, with the settlement of non-Native populations characterized by land hunger and a profound sense of entitlement. The results were intensely destructive, and yet there was no military defeat, no formal land surrender, and the principle of a treaty relationship that enshrined Native-imperial peace and friendship was one that—far from weakening—continued in Native political cultures to evolve and gain strength. These are the elements that demonstrate, in this geographical and cultural context as in other areas of history, that general narratives have their place but must ultimately be disciplined according to the particularities of experience.

As Upton showed many years ago, the late eighteenth century—especially the era following the closing stages of the American Revolution—saw not only profound changes in the non-Native demographics of the Maritime colonies but also an acceleration of territorial colonization and environmental change that exerted damaging and long-lasting pressures on Mi'kmaw society and economy. Subsequent studies have elaborated and re-emphasized this characteristic of the era for the Mi'kmaq, and the evidence yields little suggestion that the Wulstukwiuk experience differed significantly.[6] For all that, within a general pattern of encroachment by Loyalist refugees, Scottish rural settlers, and others there were variations. The greatest concentration of environmental pressures came with the peninsula of mainland Mi'kma'ki, where land configuration combined with encroachment and resource depletion to create by the mid-1790s a critical juncture. In early 1794, the Nova Scotia Indian Commissioner George Henry Monk wrote from Windsor to Governor John Wentworth, enclosing a petition in the name of "the Mickmack Indians". Monk had been reluctant to have the Mi'kmaw concerns addressed to Wentworth, for "their remarks and representations were such that I wished rather to discourage then [sic] to communicate them," but following a contentious meeting with Mi'kmaq from Pictou and Cape Sable and a threat that Natives would converge on Halifax to confront Wentworth directly, he finally "reduced their Representations into the form of a Petition . . . , adhering strictly to their own Observations and remarks."[7]

Despite the possibility that Monk may have sanitized the content as well as shaping the form of the petition, its language was uncompromising even though polite. Contrasting Nova Scotia with New Brunswick, where "there are Countries back [i.e., back countries] for the Indians," the petitioners declared that "all Nova Scotia is Coast and Rivers, and that the English have taken all the Coast and Rivers, and make Roads and Settlements through the Woods every where, and leave no place for the Indians to hunt in." As a result, they continued, "a great many Mickmacks have died for want of Victuals and Cloaths."[8] As the petitioners were undoubtedly aware, there was more to the dispossession of the Mi'kmaq than simply the loss of hunting territory. Fishing was another source of repeated tension. As early as in August 1784, Charles Baker of Cumberland wrote of a conversation with the Mi'kmaw leader François Argamo, who "expressed his fears of the [Loyalist] Refugees and complained of the hardship of being drove from their hunting Grounds and fisheries."[9] Among subsequent complaints was one directed to Wentworth from the Cape Sable Mi'kmaq in 1802, that "white people set Nets intirely across the Brooks and small rivers, which intirely prevent any Fish running up the streams," while a correspondent of the Pictou *Colonial Patriot* recalled in 1828 that "we have heard . . . of a white man taking a fish from the river, and an Indian taking it from him, saying it was not his."[10] Epidemic disease was a further danger, whether smallpox and dysentery brought directly by settlers— as at Pictou in 1801—or measles, as reported at Remsheg in 1803.[11] Nevertheless, the relatively confined dimensions of the peninsula ensured that loss of territory in itself quickly became a prime threat to the Native economy and to subsistence. [. . .]

The problems in Cape Breton and on the Island of St John—later known as Prince Edward Island—were distinct although related. Settlement in Cape Breton during the Loyalist era was initially sparse, with Sydney and surrounding communities remaining small in numbers.[12] Samuel Holland's celebrated map of Cape Breton preceded the American Revolution, but in the early years of Loyalist settlement there was little territorial encroachment that would have altered his designation of the entire northern peninsula and everything directly south of it (to a point only slightly north of the Canso Strait) as "the Savage Country or Principal Hunting District."[13] Change, however, was soon precipitated through overhunting by non-Natives, although initially many of these non-Natives were not colonial residents of Cape Breton itself. While Mi'kmaw hunters responded to the earliest Loyalist settlement by selling and trading moose meat in Sydney, by March 1790 the Cape Breton Council was debating how to prevent catastrophic levels of moose kills by visiting hunters who sought hides to export to other colonies. In 1789, for instance, the council heard "near 9,000 Moose were killed in this Island . . . merely for the sake of their Skins."[14] A hastily mounted military expedition reached Cape North some weeks later and apprehended a few hunters, but by that time serious damage had been done to the stock. "The Indians . . . " reported the colony's provost-marshal, the Loyalist David Tait, in late 1792, "complain much of the whites having destroyed their Game, which is rely [sic] the case, the skin and fur trade having dwindled to very Little."[15] Less than four years later, the blame for overhunting was being put squarely on the Cape Breton settlers themselves. The colony's administrator, David Mathews, noted in the summery of 1796 that "the Native Indians were last Winter in a most deplorable situation, the Moose Deer which were their sole dependence for a Subsistence having been almost extirpated by the new Settlers."[16]

Worse was to come as Scottish settlement began. Increasing territorial encroachment eroded Native resource harvesting as well as raising related issues such as the desecration of sacred sites and the non-Native occupation of areas that even by colonial authorities had been designated formally or informally for Native use. By 1821 the Surveyor-General Thomas Crawley was taking aim specifically at Highland settlers as exemplifying "those who regardless of every principle of Justice, would deprive these inoffensive Savages of their Property."[17] In Prince Edward Island, meanwhile, the inroads made by other Scottish settlers from such tenantries as those of the former Lord Advocate for Scotland, Sir James

Montgomery, led Montgomery's factor James Douglas to record in 1802 that "the Indians complain they have not a spot of ground on all these, their ancestors and their Native Coasts to make a residence upon."[18] In a previous letter, Douglas had obliquely revealed that overhunting was an issue there as elsewhere, commenting that "the White people . . . alledge in times of Scarcity which is pretty frequent with them, the Indians do not scruple to kill their Cattle slyly now and then to satisfy their hunger."[19] The heart of the matter was approached more closely in 1806, however, by the French emigré priest Jacques-Ladislas-Joseph de Calonne, who linked dispossession of the Mi'kmaq directly to the proprietary division of the Island. For "these unhappy aborigines," Calonne informed Governor Edmund Fanning, "the English government having divided up the entire Island among various proprietors, the result is that they cannot situate themselves anywhere without being quickly expelled."[20] [. . .]

In New Brunswick, which represented the imperial claim to an important portion of Mi'kma'ki as well as to Wulstukwik, patterns of dispossession were similar in many respects, though again with distinct elements stemming from both historical and geographical factors. Here, Loyalist settlement assumed prime importance, as the 15 000 or so Loyalist refugees almost instantly outnumbered the pre-existing population—Native and settler combined—by a factor of perhaps three to one.[21] Dislocation of entire Native communities resulted, among the most conspicuous being the southward migration of many Passamaquoddy following the establishment of the town of St Andrews and other encroachments.[22] By 1787, Governor Thomas Carleton felt able to offer the assurance that the Wulstukwiuk, as "a wandering tribe," had been treated with "civility and kindness" and that "the plenty of fish in summer and Moose in winter has hitherto prevented the settlement of the Whites in their neighbourhood from occasioning any

inconvenience."[23] Less sanguine was the New Brunswick committee of the British-based missionary organization known as the New England Company, which in 1793 took note of a report originating in Maugerville regarding "the great decrease of their [Natives'] hunting grounds by the Settlement of the Country."[24] Some years later, Major-General Martin Hunter likewise informed London from Fredericton that, to the cost of Native inhabitants, "the wild animals of the Country are become so few as to be no longer an adequate resource." Hunter's interest, unsurprisingly, was based on military considerations, as he emphasized that the Wulstukwiuk—and, presumably, the Mi'kmaq elsewhere in New Brunswick—should be offered "some occasional relief" because their enmity would be a severe threat "in a Country where the settlements are made fronting on the Rivers, with a wilderness every where close upon the Rear."[25]

Thus, in New Brunswick and in Cape Breton, unlike in Prince Edward Island and peninsular Nova Scotia, there was a back country—even though its value for subsistence was suffering continuous erosion through resource depletion and the expansion of settlement as immigration proceeded. While in New Brunswick rivers long continued to attract settlement, thus cutting off Native transportation routes as well as providing points of departure for the inland spread of settlement, elsewhere the building of roads represented a powerful thrust at the environmental integrity of Native economies. Among the earliest advocates of extensive road construction in Nova Scotia was Michael Francklin, an acting governor on a number of occasions during the 1760s and 1770s who had some command of the Mi'kmaw language and who served later in his career as the colony's superintendent of Indian affairs.[26] For Francklin, writing as early as 1766, roads would be the means by which "the Country will become fully explored, and the most valuable of the interior parts will be soon settled . . . ; this once accomplished . . . will render abortive every effort the Indians can make, should they here-after be inclined to give us trouble."[27] While Francklin framed the matter in terms of pro-jecting military force as well as economic de-velopment, a later advocate of road-building, Governor John Wentworth, was frank about its environmental consequences. "The ex-tended roads and Settlements," Wentworth commented of the Mi'kmaq in 1793, "have been the means of destroying and driving off the wild beasts which formerly Supplied them with food and rayment." Two successive mild winters, he added, had made hunting even more difficult, "and I fear some of them per-ished."[28] While this represented, in one sense, an element of the particular process by which peninsular Nova Scotia increasingly became a settler space, it also represented the more general principle that road construction could lead to rapid environmental degradation with deadly consequences.

Not that these developments went un-challenged. Remonstrances directed at Of-ficials such as George Henry Monk were frequent. One examples was a group of main-land Mi'kmaq confronting Monk; they ended a tense conversation when "they Instantly took up their Packs and went away without the usual acknowledgments," and Monk re-ported with some concern in 1794 that "some of the more Intelligent of them make Circu-itous visits to the different Tribes, and give false reasons for such long and unusual Ex-cursions."[29] Beyond such responses, Native strategies for offsetting the effects of settle-ment and environmental change included, where possible, the addition of agricultural cultivation to other sources of subsistence as well as deliberate migration. Cultivation, however, gave no protection from encroach-ment, as the philanthropist and would-be centralizer of Native communities Walter Bromley stated forcefully in 1822: "You will scarcely meet an Indian, but who will tell you that he has cleared and cultivated land some time or other, but that the white men have taken it from him."[30] Migration away from settlement sites and environmentally affected areas was reported by, among others, the surveyor and naturalist Titus Smith, who ob-served following a tour of northern Nova Sco-tia in 1801: "I think a considerable number of them [Mi'kmaq] have left the Province, as I have been informed at many different settle-ments, that there are not half so many Indians about them as there was some years ago."[31]

As a way of turning long-established and customary mobility to advantage in the con-text of drastically altered environmental cir-cumstances, migration over shorter or longer distances could enable a semblance of the tra-ditional economy to survive in places—much to the chagrin of colonial officials such as the Nova Scotia governor the Earl of Dalhousie in 1817, who deplored in the Mi'kmaq the tenacity of "their natural habits and inclination for a wandering life."[32] Even in the context of the increasing creation of reserves—systematic in Nova Scotia from 1819, more haphazard elsewhere—mobility, as Natasha Simon has pointed out, was not surrendered.[33] Yet the pressures that had characterized the preced-ing quarter-century had taken a heavy toll and continued to do so. Unlike previous colonizing thrusts in Mi'kma'ki and Wulstukwik, the im-migration of the late eighteenth and early nine-teenth centuries was too strong and persistent to be decisively turned aside or accommodated by Native populations now drastically out-numbered. It had also been rapid. Although cultural and environmental pressures had not begun in 1782, but had a more extended past, retrospectives on the era of Loyalist and then Scottish immigration contrasted strikingly the previous availability of resources with the sub-sequent prevalence of poverty and ill-health.

[. . .]

Yet the rapid change in the relationship be-tween colonization and the Native population did not necessarily extend to Native-imperial relations. Neither the Mi'kmaq nor the Wuls-tukwiuk experienced military defeat or made a formal surrender of territory. And both had ex-tended experience of diplomatic relations with French and British imperial officials based on the principle of reciprocity. In these areas, there were important elements of continuity rather than discontinuity and thus a more elongated historical narrative. It is true, of course, that the overlay of colonial settlement on Mi'kma'ki and Wulstukwik during the late eighteenth and early nineteenth centuries had its own far-reaching effect on the entire process of British–Native interaction, especially in matters affecting land use and occupancy. Most noticeably at first in those areas where back countries ceased to exist, Mi'kmaw and Wulstukwiuk access to land was narrowed and Native economies hollowed out accordingly. Varying by locality, special arrangements might be made to safeguard Native use of particular areas. These included the issuing of a series of licences of occupation in Nova Scotia in late 1783 for eight tracts of land, such as the 2500 acres on the Stewiacke River that also carried for local Mi'kmaq the guarantee of "Hunting and fishing as Customary".[34] Grants of land were made to individuals such as "Benwa the Indian," who in 1810 received 140 acres on Boularderie Island in Cape Breton, while some grants to non-Natives contained survey references to lands designated—as at Pugwash—as "Indian land" or—as at Chester—as "Land Claimed by the Indians."[35] In Cape Breton, a number of land documents referred without explanation to "the Indian Line" or "the Indian Boundary," or in other cases made grants that were qualified by such statements as "if it do not interfere in the Indians Settlement."[36] More formal was the setting aside of Chapel Island for Mi'kmaw use by the Cape Breton Council in 1792 and the 10 reserves of varying size created by the Nova Scotia Council in 1820.[37] A report of the New Brunswick surveyor-general in 1803 referred to a total of some 116 000 acres "allotted to the different Indian Tribes Throughout the Province."[38] What all of these arrangements, formal or less formal, had in common was that they offered no immunity from further encroachment.

At a more general level, however, the legitimacy of the entire settlement project was frequently brought into question in Native–imperial dialogue, either explicitly or through diplomatic demands for reciprocity. The most direct statements were reported by imperial officials in Cape Breton. Lieutenant-Governor William Macarmick reported to London in 1790 that the Cape Breton Mi'kmaq were "a fierce, restless and uncontrollable Tribe continually claiming an exclusive right to the possession of the whole Island," and the Cape Breton Council supported Macarmick's assessment some weeks later in declaring that "it is well known that the native Indians have ever held up the Idea of an intrusion being made on their property by the many Settlements forming on the Island."[39] The newspaper correspondent "Philo Antiquarius" recalled that early settlers at Pictou "were constrained to submit to numerous indignities from the aborigines, who viewed their operations with no very friendly eye: these considered the settlers as usurpers of their national rights, who had encroached on their undoubted property," while the Cumberland settler Edward Barron informed George Henry Monk with some dismay in 1784 that his Mi'kmaw informants had told him that colonization could in any event extend no further than the tidal limits of the rivers. "In that case," Barron added, "the interior of the Country can never be settled."[40] The Native demand for reciprocity, meanwhile, raised the question of legitimacy by connecting the non-Native presence with the fulfilment of promises made in return—most often, though not exclusively, in terms of the presents that underpinned diplomatic activity.[41] From the period immediately following the 1760–61 treaties, imperial officials found this connection inescapable and directly tied to the treaties. John Cunningham declared in 1767 that the purpose of his capacity as agent in Nova Scotia for distributing presents was "to supply the Tribes of Indians with Provisions and the Usual Presents in Virtue of Treaties of Peace," and a few months later the acting governor, Michael Francklin, wrote of the need to find a Roman Catholic priest to minister to Native groups "Conformable to the promises made them at their first making Peace."[42]

By the 1780s and beyond, such issues had lost none of their potency. In 1780 Lieutenant-Governor Richard Hughes of Nova Scotia noted that "the expediency of preserving the Indians in their present Sentiments of Allegiance and Tranquility (which can only be done by these Supplies) remains still in its full Force."[43] That Hughes chose to couch his observation in terms of "allegiance" during a time of warfare, and to make it explicitly contingent on the supply of presents, made his statement all the more striking. Francklin, meanwhile, who was now superintendent of Indian Affairs for Nova Scotia, confirmed that presents were essential to diplomacy. "It has ever been the Custom," Francklin reported later in 1780, "even in times of the most Profound Peace, to Assist the Indians Occasionally with Provisions from the Kings Stores, but now it is indispensably necessary, for it is totally impossible to see, or be seen by the Indians, or can a Messenger be sent to, or from them, without an Expence of Provisions."[44] And so it continued. The later superintendent, George Henry Monk, recorded early in 1794 a conversation with the Mi'kmaw Francis Emable, who had recently found the hunt disappointing in the Canso-Antigonish region and demanded to know what measures the Nova Scotia governor proposed to take in order to ensure a living for the Native population.[45] Cape Breton Mi'kmaq, meanwhile, exerted another form of pressure. Cape Breton's acting governor, David Mathews, complained to London in 1796 that outside of the presents more readily covered by provincial funds, "they have cost me Privately double that sum; many families of them, during the last Winter, remained at my House for Weeks." A year later, Mathews again reported that Mi'kmaw visitors considered his house "a rightful home" for the leaner months of the year, or whenever they wished to visit Sydney.[46] Governor John Wentworth of Nova Scotia later reinforced the importance of reciprocity by again linking it with mutual fidelity in wartime: "The

Micmacs . . . had formerly exhibited by me some assistance for their support, from His Majesty which they considered as an obligation of Loyalty. This Gratuity I discontinued toward the close of the late war and they, according to their savage customs, would not refuse presents form the French."[47]

As Wentworth implied, betrayal of reciprocity—in the view of his Mi'kmaw contacts—would jeopardize any legitimacy in the British colonial presence, which existed without a formal surrender of territory and so created a reciprocal obligation. Loss of legitimacy in turn would—for them—deserve an armed response, bringing into play the absence of any military defeat inflicted on either Mi'kmaq or Wulstukwiuk. The ability of Native forces to police the relationship affirmed in the treaties of 1760–61 had thus become evident in the era immediately following the treaties.[48] In subsequent years, and notably as Scottish and Loyalist migrations gathered force, the independent military capacity of Native groups inevitably declined. Population levels, although reliable numbers are unavailable, were clearly being affected by environmental degradation and resource depletion. Poor health and the struggle for subsistence further eroded the potential for sustaining hostilities. Governor Wentworth, in 1804, was skeptical of rumours that 2000 warriors were assembling to travel west to confront Iroquoian adversaries, "in which case they [the Mi'kmaq] must be joined by the Marisite indians of New Brunswick, and Penobscots who inhabit in the eastern districts of Massachusetts, near to Passamaquoddy. All of these cannot, I think, send more than twelve hundred Men, of which the Micmacs cannot exceed, three hundred, very inferior Warriors, badly armed in quantity and quality—almost naked—with little ammunition."[49] Whether or not Wentworth's estimation was accurate in its details—non-Native enumerations of a highly mobile population were notoriously arbitrary—the deterioration identified and its connection with colonial settlement were realities that could not be discounted. [. . .] Nevertheless, the later years of the "long" eighteenth century were characterized by extended periods of imperial warfare and almost continuous tensions between, on the one hand, Great Britain and, on the other, France and the United States. For imperial officials operating in Mi'kma'ki and Wulstukwik, who had increasing numbers of vulnerable settlements to defend as immigration accelerated, it was impossible to ignore either the localized inroads of which Native forces were capable or the potentially wider significance of such disruptions in the context of other enmities. The Cape Breton councillor and former military officer Ingram Ball, for example, worried in 1794 that in the event of war with the United States, Cape Breton might quickly find itself "in the midst of three [fires], a French one, an American one, and an Indian one."[50]

Such considerations figured consistently in imperial approaches to Mi'kmaw and Wulstukwiuk diplomatic representations and to demands for reciprocity. Of the four colonies, Prince Edward Island was the one in which these issues surfaced the least. The Island's acting governor Phillips Callbeck reported to London during the American Revolutionary War that "the Indians avowed Dispositions to Rebellion in these parts" had meant that "I am obliged to give provisions and presents."[51] [. . .] Cape Breton, not surprisingly in view of the limited extent of initial settlement, saw much more urgently phrased assessments of the extent and the implications of shows of force by the Mi'kmaq. Macarmick, in 1790, complained of their "frequently assembling in Bodies if four or five hundred and Boasting of the Force they could procure" and remarked on "the impossibility in such case of enforcing the power of the civil authority and the Laws."[52] Some two years later, the provost-marshall David Tait declared bluntly that "the Indians talk very high" and that, in the absence of presents and the ministry of a British-supplied priest, "at present they have in their Power to destroy the whole Colony."[53]

It was within this context, later in the 1790s, that the acting governor David Mathews—a Loyalist and a former mayor of the city of New York—found it necessary to submit to Mi'kmaw demands that they should stay at his house while in Sydney. [. . .]

In Nova Scotia, concerns on the part of Monk, Wentworth, and others regarding Mi'kmaw unrest arose frequently, and were consistently bracketed with a sense of urgency in offering presents. Late in 1793, for example, Wentworth directed Monk to the Windsor area, where a Mi'kmaw assembly had led to sheep seizures and, in Wentworth's view, "audacious intentions". Monk's instruction was to try to seize Mi'kmaw hostages—men, women, children—or "on the other hand and which I should prefer, if you can attach them to our cause in such a manner that the peace of our scattered inhabitants may not be disturbed by them, and also that they will join us, in case of an invasion you may promise they shall have some provisions and cloathing for their women and children." Monk, in turn, despatched an officer who downplayed the threat of "any immediate hostilities," but who also confirmed that "supplies" represented the key to resolving the situation.[54] During the ensuing winter, Monk had a series of further confrontations with Mi'kmaq who asserted, as did one group in March 1794, "that the Governor gave [sic] the Indians Blankets, Guns, Powder and everything as much as they pleased to take."[55] Although Monk was at a loss to satisfy the immediate demand, over the next two years Wentworth launched an increased distribution of supplies that he justified not only on humanitarian grounds but also on the ground that "these People would probably otherwise have been disaffected and required Coercion."[56] [. . .]

Thus, although it would be entirely wrong to portray Mi'kmaw leaders as negotiating with Nova Scotian officials from a position of strength at the turn of the eighteenth century, it remained true that they had enough remaining strengths to be able to negotiate. Recurrent periods of tension had similar results. Late in 1807 Wentworth reported that Monk had set off in an attempt to "collect and secure the obedience of these People [Mi'kmaq], and their aid in case of necessity. Otherwise, they might prove very mischievous upon the scattering unprotected settlements." Some weeks later, he commented again in the context of a possible United States invasion that "the Indians having observed there are preparations making for defence, manifested a disposition to be considered of some importance" and that immediate provision of supplies "will tend to relieve the scattering settlers from apprehensions of mischief, that might retard the Levies of Militia."[57] Even so, by April 1808, Monk was warning that Mi'kmaq from Cape Breton and Nova Scotia were coordinating their response to the likely invasion, opting to remain neutral until they had decided who was the stronger side. Citing the threat of some to devastate Pictou, Monk cited with approval the intention of Mi'kmaq in the Cumberland area to remain neutral and perhaps even to take the British side if pressed. Since the real difficulty, in his view, lay in the undermining of the traditional economy by "the Improvements of their Conquerors," the solution lay not only in "management and relief" but ultimately in restricting the Native population to sedentary agricultural settlement. A byproduct of Monk's report, however, was to make it clear—even though Native démarches were not necessarily united or consistent, as the Cumberland example revealed—that the "Conquerors" still had some way to go before making "orderly subjects" of the Indigenous population.[58]

Governor Thomas Carleton of New Brunswick, meanwhile, was initially dismissive of both the Wulstukwiuk and the Mi'kmaq. Although 1786 saw a hostile Wulstukwiuk presence at Fredericton (during the trial of two Loyalist settlers for the murder of a Wulstukwiuk man) as well as the apprehensions of upriver settlers later that year "of being reduced to the necessity of quitting their settlement" because of Native threats,

Carleton was confident of the success of forceful measures to be taken the next year "for the removal of all future apprehensions of danger, from either the insolence or any more serious unfriendliness of the Savages."[59] But the Loyalist and half-pay officer Daniel Lyman was not so sure: "On the subject of the Indians, although they are not so formidable as to threaten any ruin or imminent danger to the province, yet they are sufficiently numerous to be very troublesome, particularly if they are encouraged by our enemies. . . . I would here suggest the idea, of cultivating their friendship, by the usual mode of gaining indians."[60] Although no system of gift-giving comparable to that of Nova Scotia emerged in New Brunswick, the ensuing years saw a series of intermittent tensions that yielded equally intermittent negotiations. Carleton, finding that Wulstukwiuk interventions were capable of making communications between New Brunswick and Lower Canada "precarious and unsafe," persuaded London to authorize an additional regiment to maintain key outposts. Yet by 1794 he was warning that, in the context of tensions with the United States that might bring about an active Wabanaki alliance, "it is certainly requisite to guard against their disaffection." Carleton's chosen course was to employ a French emigré priest as a missionary, although with results that were just as unreliable as those deriving from the Protestant schools and missions maintained by the New England Company.[61] Efforts by such prominent New Brunswick figures as Robert Pagan and Ward Chipman to draw on Native expertise on the geography of the disputed border with the United States yielded respectful exchanges, notably with Passamaquoddy elders, but in 1808 Major-General Martin Hunter observed "the Indian Natives of New Brunswick," in the event of war, "would be formidable as Enemies," and that distribution of presents was needed.[62] All in all, when the War of 1812 finally began, it seemed to be a matter for profound relief to Hunter's successor as military commander in New Brunswick,

Major-General George Stracey Smyth, that not only was an agreement reached "with the Indians in the neighbourhood of the County of Charlotte, for the purpose of securing their Neutrality," but also that—as Smyth had "the satisfaction to state"—similar agreements had been concluded with "the Indians of the River Saint John, Miramichi, and other parts of the Province."[63] That the negotiation of Native neutrality was cause for celebration was an eloquent comment on the persistence of an armed capacity that was residual but still significant.

When the wars ended, changes followed. As non-Native immigration continued and accelerated, the pace of dispossession quickened with it. Walter Bromley, whose primary goal was to induce "transient Indians" to "become settlers" by cultivating the land, was blunt in public statements regarding the violence with which force of numbers enabled non-Natives to take control of essential Native territories. As a part of the "gross barbarities" committed by the settlers, he reported that even a burial ground had been "lately ploughed up."[64] At the same time, the significance for imperial officials of any armed threat presented by Native warriors receded with the ending of any immediate external danger. [. . .]

From the early 1780s until 1815, a military and diplomatic continuity had been preserved that co-existed with the territorial and environmental discontinuity of that era. That Native leaders could readily capture the attention of imperial officials and make demands for reciprocity with conviction was a longstanding state of affairs that had persisted through many vicissitudes of both British and French assertions in both Mi'kma'ki and Wulstukwik. These demands had long depended on the threat, and sometimes the reality, that territory would be defended or reclaimed by force. Since the onset of Loyalist and other large-scale migrations, the threat of force had come to depend increasingly both on localized potential to disrupt settlements and on imperial apprehensions of invasion by French or US forces, following which Native

intervention—local or more general—might prove crucial one way or the other. At the same time, as demands for reciprocity—or what might be seen on the non-Native side as "relief"—necessarily became more urgent and insistent, officials such as Wentworth saw no alternative but to comply even at the risk of disputes with London over budgetary excesses. As a result, the distinctive tenor of Native-imperial exchanges, far from being eroded by territorial encroachment and environmental change, was extended and entrenched. Some forms of leadership were new in style if not in substance, as in the case of the Bear River chief Andrew Meus, who spoke successfully to the Nova Scotia House of Assembly in 1821 in defence of the Mi'kmaw porpoise fishery in the Digby Gut, and subsequently journeyed to London in a less fruitful effort, according to the *Halifax Journal*, "to solicit permanent grants of land to the Indians, in order that they may become cultivators of the soil."[65] Other methods were tried and true, as when Joseph Howe complained in 1843 while he was Indian commissioner for Nova Scotia that his home was "besieged, at all hours, by Indians, who had been taught to believe that unbounded wealth was at my disposal, and that they were to be fed and clothed hereafter at the expense of the Government."[66] Rather than more general appeals to the principle of reciprocity, officials such as Howe and his successor Abraham Gesner reported more explicit references to the treaties as embodiments of the Native-imperial relationship. Gesner noted that treaty principles were "stamped upon the minds of each succeeding generation," as he had frequently been reminded by the Mi'kmaq with whom he dealt.[67]

The era from 1780 to 1820, therefore, saw the interplay of two important though distinct processes. In a territorial and environmental sense, the Mi'kmaq and Wulstukwiuk experienced rapid, unprecedented damage and constraint. Even allowing for geographical particularities, the process was abrupt and the effects long-lasting. In terms of the ability to make diplomatic use of armed capacity, however, another process drew upon a long-established pattern of Native-imperial relations in Mi'kma'ki and Wulstukwik that extended backwards in time through the treaty-making years and beyond. The two processes were not disconnected. Although colonization would ultimately erode the threat of force that underpinned Native demands for reciprocity, the wider warfare of the era joined with the vulnerability of proliferating settlements to lend strength to these demands while the critical results of dispossession gave them added urgency. As a result, the narratives to which the two processes gave rise did not conform to any over-arching narrative of Mi'kmaw or Wulstukwiuk decline in Native–imperial affairs. Even the members of a group of Nova Scotia commissioners, which included George Henry Monk, were willing to admit in 1800 that there were moral obligations toward "the aboriginal proprietors of this country,"[68] but the claims on the Crown that were advanced from the Native side went far beyond moral obligation and with time they became more insistent and more explicitly focused on the treaties. While the realities of the nineteenth century would prove inhospitable to the realization of such claims—at least in any form that could effectively offset the depredations of land loss, economic struggle, and the social and health-related dislocations that came with them—the long version of this narrative nevertheless stretched forward into the legal evolutions of the twentieth century that would bring these issues before the Supreme Court of Canada.

That the narrative persisted was also owed in part to historical circumstances that distinguished Mi'kma'ki and Wulstukwik from other portions of North America. In particular, in contrast to most of the Aboriginal groups of eastern North America, the Mi'kmaq and the Wulstukwiuk experienced the aftermath of the American Revolution without either a forced migration or the need to deal with an entirely new imperial regime. Although the disruptions associated with colonial settlement in Mi'kma'ki and Wulstukwik were far from unusual in themselves, the long and evolutionary diplomatic response to the same Crown on the same territory was distinctive. Earlier in the eighteenth century, imperial and colonial interventions had been more complex and yet highly manageable, with both French and British regimes exerting significant but localized influences while the largely coastal and compartmentalized colonial populations of the Acadian and Planter eras had proved generally able to co-exist with Native neighbours.[69] The influx of settlers that marked the closing years of the American Revolution, an influx that only accelerated, was not manageable in the same sense. Yet the skills of those whom Wentworth referred to as "the old men," or of younger leaders such as Andrew Meus, remained relevant. Even when, after 1815, the attention of imperial officials was harder to gain and the damage wreaked by colonization was unavoidable, the demand for reciprocity was too strongly entrenched to do otherwise than persist. That it did so spoke of a narrative of Native-imperial relations that had originated long before the period from 1780 to 1820 and would extend into a future far beyond—a narrative that this limited, 40-year era confirmed rather than muted. The colonial inroads of these years had irrevocably moved the Maritime colonies away from preceding territorial and environmental characteristics and in the direction of being colonies of settlement, with all the damage to Mi'kmaq and Wulstukwiuk subsistence that these developments implied. Yet this was no simple extension of an ineluctable, continent-wide process. In this place and in an elongated span of time, there were continuities that, for whatever they might prove to be worth, accompanied the more immediate and ruinous discontinuity.

NOTES

1. L.F.S. Upton, *Micmacs and Colonists: Indian-White Relations in the Maritimes, 1713–1867* (Vancouver: University of British Columbia Press, 1979), 78, 80, 84. An earlier version of this article was presented at the Atlantic Canada Studies Conference at the University of Prince Edward Island in May 2009. The research was funded by the Social Sciences and Humanities Research Council of Canada. I thank my research assistants Emily Burton and Kelly Chaves as well as the three anonymous readers for *Acadiensis*.

2. Harald E.L. Prins, *The Mi'kmaq: Resistance, Accommodation, and Survival* (Fort Worth: Harcourt Brace, 1996), 161–3. Other authors who have put forward similar arguments include Daniel N. Paul, *We Were Not the Savages: A Mi'kmaq Perspective on the Collision Between European and Native American Civilizations*, 2nd edn (Halifax: Fernwood, 2000) and, though attributing continuous dispossession to a more extended timespan rather than identifying specific turning points, Jennifer Reid, *Myth, Symbol, and Colonial Encounter: British and Mi'kmaq in Acadia, 1700–1867* (Ottawa, ON: University of Ottawa Press, 1995).

3. In this article, I have used the terms Mi'kma'ki and Wulstukwik to refer respectively to the territories of the Mi'kmaq and Wulstukwiuk (Maliseet). Following the scheme initially set out in Emerson W. Baker and John G. Reid, *The New England Knight: Sir William Phips, 1651–1695* (Toronto: University of Toronto Press, 1998), xxii. I refer separately to the Wabanaki as a broad definition of ethnicity in the portion of the later State of Maine, extending approximately from the Saco River to the Penobscot River. Also separately identified are the Passamaquoddy who, while closely related to the Wulstukwiuk in cultural terms, occupied a territory that came to straddle the Canada–United States border, and whose population centre shifted south-westwards during the 1780s following pressure from the Loyalist migration into New Brunswick. For a thorough discussion, see William Wicken, "Passamaquoddy Identity and the Marshall Decision," in *New England and the Maritime Provinces: Connections and Comparisons*, ed. Stephen J. Hornsby and John G. Reid (Montreal and Kingston: McGill-Queen's University Press, 2005), 53–7. [. . .]

   Thus, to summarize, this article will take Mi'kma'ki as extending throughout the present-day Maritime Provinces (as well as to the Gaspé and Gulf islands) with the exception of the Wulstukw Valley and territories surrounding it and to the west, while Wulstukwik is defined as including the entire Wulstukw Valley—but with the proviso in both cases that the area surrounding the mouth of that river and its lower tributaries was a borderland frequented by both Mi'kmaq and Wulstukwiuk in the relevant period. The Passamaquoddy continued to occupy territory southwest of the Wulstukwiuk, but with the primary population base now on the US side of where the still-contested boundary with British North America would eventually be drawn.

4. See John G. Reid, "*Pax Britannica or Pax Indigena?* Planter, Nova Scotia (1760–1782) and Competing Strategies of Pacification," *Canadian Historical Review* 85, 4 (December 2004): 669–92 (esp. 687–8).

5. William C. Wicken, *Mi'kmaq Treaties on Trial: History, Land, and Donald Marshall Junior* (Toronto: University of Toronto Press, 2002); Rosalie M. Francis, "The Mi'kmaq Nation and the Embodiment of Political Ideologies: Ni'kmaq, Protocol and Treaty Negotiations of the Eighteenth Century" (Masters thesis, Saint Mary's University, 2003).

6. Upton, *Micmacs and Colonists*; Paul, *We Were Not the Savages*, 165–80; Prins, *The Mi'kmaq*, 153–66; Reid, *Myth, Symbol, and Colonial Encounter*, 31–45. Wulstukwik still awaits a detailed study of this era, but see Ann Gorman Condon, "1783–1800: Loyalist Arrival, Acadian Return, Imperial Reform," in *The Atlantic Region to Confederation: A History*, ed. Phillip A. Buckner and John G. Reid (Toronto and Fredericton: University of Toronto Press and Acadiensis Press, 1994), 201–4.

7. George Henry Monk to John Wentworth, 24 January 1794, CO 217/65/150, United Kingdom National Archives (UKNA); on the

meeting, see Report of George Monk, 12 January 1794, Monk Papers, MG 23, Letterbook, Indian Affairs, 1783–1797, pp. 1047–51. Library and Archives Canada (LAC).

8. "Petition of the Mickmack Indians," [24 January 1794] CO 217/65/148, UKNA. See also, on Mi'kmaw exclusion from fur trapping, Julian Gwyn, "The Mi'kmaq, Poor Settlers, and the Nova Scotia Fur Trade, 1783–1853," *Journal of the Canadian Historical Association*, new ser., 14 (2003): 65–91.

9. Charles Baker to Edward Barron, 7 August 1784. Monk Papers, MG 23, Letterbook. Indian Affairs, 1783–1797, p. 1032. LAC.

10. John Wentworth to Commissioners for Relief of Indians, 28 September 1802, RG 1, vol. 430, no. 117, Nova Scotia Archives and Records Management (NSARM); Letter of "Philo Antiquarius," *Colonial Patriot* (Pictou), 11 January 1828.

11. William Nixon to Sir John Wentworth, 20 November 1801, RG 1, vol. 430, no. 88. NSARM; G. Oxley to Charles Morris and Michael Wallace, 4 February 1803, RG 1, vol. 430, no. 127, NSARM; see also Nova Scotia Council Minutes, 29 August 1801, RG 1, vol. 191, p. 80. NSARM.

12. See Robert J. Morgan, *Rise Again! The Story of Cape Breton Island*, Book One (Wreck Cove: Breton Books, 2008), 74–5; and Stephen J. Hornsby, *Nineteenth-Century Cape Breton: A Historical Geography* (Montreal and Kingston: McGill-Queen's University Press, 1992), 3–4, 25–8.

13. Samuel Holland, "A Plan of the Island of Cape Breton," [1767], Additional MSS. vol. 57,701, no. 7. British Library; see also Hornsby, *Nineteenth-Century Cape Breton*, 19–25.

14. Minutes of Cape Breton Council, 9 March 1790, CO 217/107/138–42. UKNA; also found at RG 1, vol. 319, pp. 313–5, NSARM.

15. David Tait to Evan Nepean, 4 December 1792, CO 217/109/173, UKNA.

16. David Mathews to the Earl of Portland, 7 July 1796, CO 217/112/93, UKNA.

17. Crawley to Rupert George, 5 November 1821, RG 1, vol. 430, no. 158, NSARM. For a more focused treatment of the impact of Scottish settlement, see John G. Reid, "Scots in Mi'kma'ki, 1760–1820," *The Nashwaak Review* 22/23, no. 1 (Spring/Summer 2009): 527–57.

18. James Douglas to Sir James Montgomery, 26 August 1802, Blackwood and Smith Papers, GD 293/2/20/4, National Archives of Scotland (NAS); see also J.M. Bumsted, "Sir James Montgomery and Prince Edward Island, 1767–1803," *Acadiensis* VII, 2 (Spring 1978): 76–102.

19. Douglas to Montgomery, 24 November 1800, Blackwood and Smith Papers, GD 293/2/20/2, NAS.

20. Calonne to Fanning, 16 July 1806, CO 226/21/192, UKNA (author's translation). The original French reads as follows: "ces malheureux aborigines"; "le gouvernement anglois ayant distribué toute l'Isle entre divers propriétaires, il en resulte qu'ils ne peuvent se placer nulle part sans en etre bientot chassé." See also Claude Galarneau, "Jacques-Ladislas-Joseph de Calonne," in *Dictionary of Canadian Biography (DCB)*, ed. George W. Brown et al. (15 vols to date; Toronto: University of Toronto Press, 1966–), VI: 105–7.

21. See J.M. Bumsted, *Understanding the Loyalists* (Sackville, NB: Centre for Canadian Studies, Mount Allison University, 1986), 23–35; Condon, "1783–1800: Loyalist Arrival, Acadian Return, Imperial Reform," in *The Atlantic Region to Confederation*, 184–93; and John G. Reid, *Six Crucial Decades: Times of Change in the History of the Maritimes* (Halifax: Nimbus, 1987), 61–84.

22. Wicken, "Passamaquoddy Identity and the Marshall Decision," 53; Vincent O. Erickson, "Maliseet-Passamaquoddy," in *Handbook of North American Indians*: Volume 15, Northeast, ed. Bruce G. Trigger (Washington: Smithsonian Institution, 1978): 124–5.

23. Carleton to Earl of Dorchester, 31 January 1787, RS 330, A7b, Letterbook of Thomas Carleton, vol. VII, 1786–1808, no. 2, Provincial Archives of New Brunswick (PANB).

24. Minutes of New Brunswick Commissioners, 5 March 1793, New England Company MSS, vol. 07954, Guildhall Library.

25. Martin Hunter to Viscount Castlereagh, 25 May 1808, CO 188/14/27, UKNA.

26. See L.R. Fischer, "Michael Francklin," *DCB*, IV: 272–6.

27. Francklin to Board of Trade, 30 September 1766, CO 217/21/357–8, UKNA.

28. Wentworth to [Henry Dundas?], 3 May 1793, CO 217/64/171–2, UKNA; see also John Parr to Viscount Sydney, 8 September 1787, CO 217/60/50–1, UKNA.

29. Report of George Monk, 12 January 1794, Monk Papers, Letterbook, Indian Affairs, 1783–1797, p. 1050, LAC.

30. Walter Bromley, *An Account of the Aborigines of Nova Scotia called the Micmac Indians* (London: Luke Hansard, 1822), 10; see also Judith Fingard, "Walter Bromley," *DCB*, VII, 107–10.

31. Titus Smith, "General Observations on the Northern Tour," 1801, RG 1, vol. 380, pp. 113–4, NSARM. For another example, see Minutes of New Brunswick Commissioners, 5 March 1793, New England Company MSS, vol. 07954, Guildhall Library.

32. Draft letter of Dalhousie, 8 March 1817, Dalhousie Papers, sect. 1, pp. 26–9, NAS.

33. Natasha Simon, "Towards a Just Relationship: The Role of Treaty Negotiations in Mi'kmaq Reserve Formation in New Brunswick" (paper presented to Canadian Historical Association Annual Meeting, Saskatoon, SK, 2007), 1–2.

34. Licenses of Occupation, 17–18 December 1783, RG 1, vol. 430, no. 23½, NSARM.

35. Grant to Benwa the Indian, 22 January 1810, RG 20, ser. B, vol. 3, no. 550, NSARM; Pugwash Survey, n.d., RG 20, ser. C, vol. 86, no. 236, NSARM; "Survey of the Indians Claims at Chester by William Nelson," 25 April 1791, RG 20, ser. C, vol. 90a, no. 60, NSARM.

36. See, for example, Petition of Angus MacDonald, [1806], RG 20, ser. B, vol. 2, no. 245, NSARM; Petition of Alexander and Norman MacLeod, [1822], RG 20, ser. B, vol. 13, no. 2864, NSARM; Petition of William Mathewson, 1814, and Council endorsement, 3 October 1814, RG 20, ser. B, vol. 5, no. 1067, NSARM.

37. Minutes of Cape Breton Council, 28 November 1792, CO 217/109/20–1, UKNA; Minutes of Nova Scotia Council, 8 May 1820, RG 1, vol. 193, pp. 450–6, NSARM. On equivalent measures in New Brunswick and Prince Edward Island, see Upton, *Micmacs and Colonists*, 99–101, 114–5.

38. "State of His Majesty's Lands in the Province of New Brunswick taken from the Records in the Surveyor Generals and Auditors Office, Fredericton," 12 July 1803, CO 188/12/56, UKNA.

39. Macarmick to Lord Grenville, 30 April 1790, CO 217/107/118, UKNA; Minutes of Cape Breton Council 31 May 1790, CO 217/107/120, UKNA.

40. Letter of "Philo Antiquarius," *Colonial Patriot* (Pictou), 11 January 1828; Edward Barron to Monk, 12 August 1784, Monk Papers, Letterbook, Indian Affairs, 1783–1797, pp. 1030–1, LAC.

41. On reciprocity as a principle, see Katherine Hermes, "'Justice Will be Done Us': Algonquian Demands for Reciprocity in the Courts of the European Settlers," in *The Many Legalities of Early America*, ed. Christopher L. Tomlins and Bruce H. Mann (Chapel Hill: University of North Carolina Press, 2001), 123–49; see also John G. Reid, "Imperial-Aboriginal Friendship in Eastern British America, 1775–1815" (paper presented to conference on "Loyalism and the Revolutionary Atlantic World," University of Maine, Orono, ME, 5 June 2009).

42. Memorial of John Cunningham, 14 December 1767, CO 217/45/3, UKNA; Francklin to Lord Hillsborough, 20 July 1768, CO 217/45/165–6, UKNA.

43. Richard Hughes to Lord George Germain, March 1780, CO 217/55/33–4, UKNA. For an example of the continuing significance of providing Crown-subsidized Roman Catholic clergy, see the comments of Governor Thomas Carleton of New Brunswick in Carleton to Dundas, 14 June 1794, CO 188/5/184, UKNA.

44. Francklin to Germain, 4 May 1780, CO 217/55/37, UKNA.

45. Report of George Henry Monk, 26 February 1794, Monk Papers, Letterbook, Indian Affairs, 1783–1797, pp. 1067–8, LAC.

46. David Mathews to the Earl of Portland, 7 July 1796, CO 217/112/93, UKNA; Mathews to Portland, 2 August 1797, CO 217/113/211, UKNA.

47. John Wentworth to Lord Hobart, 3 May 1804, CO 217/79/16, UKNA.

48. See Reid, "*Pax Britannica or Pax Indigena?*"; for alternative interpretations, see those cited on pages 671–2 of that article as well as the more recent John Grenier, *The Far Reaches of Empire: War in Nova Scotia, 1710–1760* (Norman, OK: University of Oklahoma Press, 2008), esp. 207–15.

49. Wentworth to Hobart, 3 May 1804, CO 217/79/15, UKNA.

50. Minutes of Cape Breton Council, 30 April 1794, CO 217/110/180, UKNA. On Ball, see R.J. Morgan, "Ingram Ball," *DCB*, V: 53–4. I thank Jim Phillips for making the point to me

regarding the increasing vulnerability of proliferating settlements.

51. Callbeck to Germain, 2 September 1777, CO
    226/6/188, UKNA.

52. Macarmick to Grenville, 30 April 1790, CO
    217/107/118, UKNA.

53. Tait to Evan Nepean, 4 December 1792, CO
    217/109/173, UKNA.

54. Wentworth to Monk, 18 October 1793, Let-
    terbook of Wentworth, 1792–3, RG 1, vol. 50,
    NSARM; George Deschamps to Monk, 4 No-
    vember 1793, Monk Papers, Letterbook, In-
    dian Affairs, 1783–1797, p. 1040, LAC.

55. Report of George Monk, 7 March 1794, Monk
    Papers, Letterbook, Indian Affairs, 1783–1797,
    p. 1072, LAC.

56. Wentworth to Portland, 8 October 1796, Let-
    terbook of Wentworth, 1793–6, RG 1, vol. 51,
    NSARM.

57. Wentworth to Castlereagh, 26 October 1807,
    Letterbook of Wentworth, 1805–7, RG 1,
    vol. 54, NSARM; Wentworth to Castlereagh,
    3 January 1808, CO 217/82/19–20, UKNA.

58. Report of George Monk, 23 April 1808, CO
    217/82/202–5, UKNA.

59. Carleton to Dorchester, 5 December 1786,
    RS 330, A7b, Letterbook of Thomas Carleton,
    vol. VII, 1786–1808, no. 1, PANB. On the
    Fredericton incident, see W.S. MacNutt, New
    Brunswick: A History, 1784–1867 (Toronto:
    Macmillan, 1963), 78.

60. Memorial of Daniel Lyman, c. 1790, CO
    188/4/391, UKNA; on Lyman's background,
    see List of MLAs, CO 188/6/141, UKNA.

61. Carleton to Dundas, 20 November 1792, RS
    330 A3b, Letterbook of Thomas Carleton,

vol. III, 1791–5, no. 16, PANB; Carleton to
    Dundas, 14 June 1794, CO 188/5/184–5,
    UKNA; Missionary List, 29 June 1807, CO
    188/13/289, UKNA. See also Judith Fingard,
    "The New England Company and the New
    Brunswick Indians, 1786–1826: A Comment
    on the Colonial Perversion of British Benev-
    olence," Acadiensis I, 2 (Spring 1972): 29–42.

62. Chipman to Carleton, 12 August 1796, CO
    188/7/211–15, UKNA; Pagan to Chipman, CO
    188/10/289, UKNA; Hunter to Castlereagh, 25
    May 1808, CO 188/14/27–8, UKNA.

63. Smyth to Bathurst, 31 August 1812, CO
    188/18/70, UKNA. On Smyth, see D.M. Young,
    "George Stracey Smyth," DCB, VI: 723–8; on
    Hunter, see D.M. Young, "Sir Martin Hunter,"
    DCB, VII: 428–30.

64. Bromley, An Account of the Aborigines of Nova
    Scotia, 7–8 (and passim).

65. Halifax Journal, 27 December 1824; Petition of
    Andrew Meus, 16 January 1821, Journal and
    Proceedings of the House of Assembly of the prov-
    ince of Nova Scotia, 1821, p. 36; Upton, Mic-
    macs and Colonists, 88.

66. Joseph Howe, "Report on Indian Affairs," 25
    January 1843, Journal and Proceedings of the
    House of Assembly of the province of Nova Scotia,
    1843, Appendix 1, p. 4.

67. Abraham Gesner, "Report on Indian Affairs,"
    29 September 1847, Journal and Proceedings of
    the House of Assembly of the province of Nova Sco-
    tia, 1847, Appendix 24, p. 117.

68. "Report of Commissioners," 15 April 1800,
    RG 1, vol. 430, no. 33½, NSARM.

69. See Reid, "Pax Britannica or Pax Indigena?"
    687.

4 From Alain Beaulieu, "'An Equitable Right to Be Compensated': The Dispossession of the Aboriginal Peoples of Quebec and the Emergence of a New Legal Rationale (1760–1860)," *Canadian Historical Review* 94, 1 (March 2013): 1–27. Reprinted with permission from University of Toronto Press (www.utpjournals.com).

When the British seized control of New France in 1760, they had already built a long tradition of purchasing Aboriginal land.[1] By the second half of the eighteenth century, this approach had become central to British colonial thought. Made official in the Royal Proclamation of 1763, this policy was implemented in an extensive portion of the Canadian territory.

Starting in the 1780s, the British concluded land-cession treaties with the Aboriginal people living west of the Ottawa River, in what would become the colony of Upper Canada in 1791 (and then the province of Ontario in 1867). In the mid-nineteenth century, this colony's entire territory had been covered by cession treaties, some of which addressed only small portions of land while others involved immense expanses. Following Canadian Confederation, this system was extended to encompass western Canada, where Canada proceeded to carry out, over a few short decades, the largest operation of Aboriginal land purchases in its history.

The policy stipulated by the royal proclamation, however, was not applied to the Saint Lawrence Valley or to what is now the province of Quebec. Concerning these lands, the British, followed by the Canadian government, adopted a policy of unilateral appropriation, dispossessing the Aboriginal peoples without reliance on a treaty system. Long overlooked by researchers, this particularity in the British land policy has been garnering increased attention since the 1970s as a direct consequence of the growing number of land claims by Quebec First Nations. For some, the explanation lies in the French colonial past: since the French never recognized the specific land rights of Aboriginal peoples, such rights could not have survived the French regime.[2] Others have attempted to establish that the French never denied the existence of Aboriginal land rights, but were merely deterred from formally recognizing them in treaties by situational factors.[3] The Royal Proclamation of 1763 has also been invoked both by researchers defending the thesis that the British were not required to make land-cession treaties in Quebec and by those supporting the contrary view.[4]

[. . .] The aim of this article is not to identify a standard to explain why the British did not conclude treaties—in short, to decode the past according to law—but rather to follow legal standardization in which colonial practice is inscribed through trial and error, detours, shifts in meaning, and improvisations, into a legitimizing framework. In this analysis of British legal rationales, the law is not considered in its causal dimension, as a leading factor that would explain (by creating obligations) the past or enable the identification of how things should

have taken place. Instead, it is examined in its instrumental role, as a flexible tool of colonialism, which lends itself to the mutations required to justify the dispossession process.

[. . .]

The idea underlying this article is that the refusal to conclude land treaties with the Aboriginal peoples of Quebec was not the result of a pre-existing policy, but the outcome of a succession of tinkerings, in which elements of the French colonial past and British tradition were embedded. The British policy concerning Aboriginal lands in Quebec was thereby set out and implemented in a series of specific contexts, which gave rise to a new legal imaginary. The amalgamation stemmed more from fiction than from history, but it did provide the basis of a system that emerged in the 1830s, in which the creation of reserves appeared as a means of compensating Aboriginal peoples for the loss of their lands.[5]

The Royal Proclamation of 1763 holds a special place in the history of Aboriginal land dispossession in Canada. Published in the context of the Pontiac's War,[6] the proclamation established the limits of three new colonies (Quebec and the two Floridas) and also created an expansive territory, temporarily reserved "for the use of the . . . Indians." This "Indian country" included the land beyond the source of the rivers that flowed to the Atlantic Ocean and the land outside the new colonies and Rupert's Land (see Map 1). The proclamation also stipulated that governors could not grant land within the boundaries of their respective colonies, which had not yet been ceded by the Aboriginal peoples. Thenceforth, the "Lands reserved to the . . . Indians" could be purchased in the name of the British Crown only "at some public Meeting or Assembly" of the Aboriginal people in question.

The proclamation resulted in the implementation of a new legal logic throughout the former territory of New France, a logic that formally recognized Native land rights.

Map 1 The Royal Proclamation of 1763

In Quebec, the document quickly acquired significant symbolic value. Aboriginal people living in the Saint Lawrence River Valley who had received copies of it regularly invoked its premise to support their land claims at the end of the eighteenth century and during the nineteenth century.[7] Did that mean that the provisions concerning Aboriginals in the royal proclamation were applicable within the province of Quebec in 1763? The formulation of the text leaves some doubt on the subject. The passage forbidding concessions to be granted "upon any Lands whatever, which, not having been ceded to or purchased by Us as aforesaid, are reserved to the said Indians, or any of them" seems to apply only to the governors of the former colonies and not to those in the "Province of Quebec" or in the two Floridas.[8]

Some scholars interpreted this passage as revealing the inclination of the British authorities to continue the French policy of not recognizing Native rights in Quebec. However, evidence of this conclusion is very weak and in fact is practically non-existent. The historical context provides no proof to sustain the idea that Britain intended to exclude Quebec lands from the provisions of the royal proclamation. Rather, the documents elucidating the development of the British policy on this subject indicate a willingness to implement a global policy, which would apply to all North American land in its possession.[9]

If the intention of the British authorities had been to exclude Quebec from the protections afforded to Aboriginal lands, it was certainly not reflected in the instructions prepared in December 1763 for James Murray, governor of Quebec. These instructions indeed contained clear provisions on applying the royal proclamation.[10] In the colony of Quebec, the proclamation was invoked several times to refuse granting land concessions. A revealing example concerns the 1766 refusal of Governor Murray to allow merchants to settle and build in Chicoutimi, as this land was "reserved by his Maj[esty]'s

Proclamation to the savages within the Province."[11] On two other occasions, the British authorities, taking support from the restrictions imposed by the royal proclamation, refused to allocate grants for lands on the northern banks of the Restigouche River. The first was presented in 1766 by merchant Joseph Philibot, who attempted, in vain, to execute an order from the King granting him 20 000 acres of land within the limits of the new colony.[12] The Executive Council of Quebec reminded him that according to the proclamation of 1763, the lands in question belonged to the Mi'kmaq.[13] In 1767, the same council rejected a similar request from Hugh Finlay, Scottish merchant and land owner, who was claiming lands near the mouth of the Restigouche River for the Acadians.[14]

However limited, these interventions suggest that, from the perspective of colonial authorities, the policy on the protection and purchase of Native land was applicable to 1763 Quebec. Other examples, however, indicate that the British were not inclined to extend this reasoning to all Aboriginal peoples in this colony. The groups affected by the above-mentioned claim grants, namely the Innu (Montagnais) and Mi'kmaq, lived outside the centres of colonization; the British therefore had no reason to question the ancestral basis for their presence on these lands. But this was not the case for the communities living in the Saint Lawrence Valley. The Huron-Wendat had moved into the Quebec area after the Iroquois' destruction of Huronia in 1650. In the 1660s, they were followed by the Iroquois, who settled in three villages: Kahnawake, Kanesatake, and Akwesasne. The Abenakis began migrating to the Saint Lawrence Valley in the mid-1670s and settled on the southern shore of the river at the beginning of the eighteenth century, in the villages of Odanak and Wolinak. At the end of the French Regime, these villages were grouped into the Seven Nations confederacy, which also included the village of Oswegatchie (see Map 2).[15]

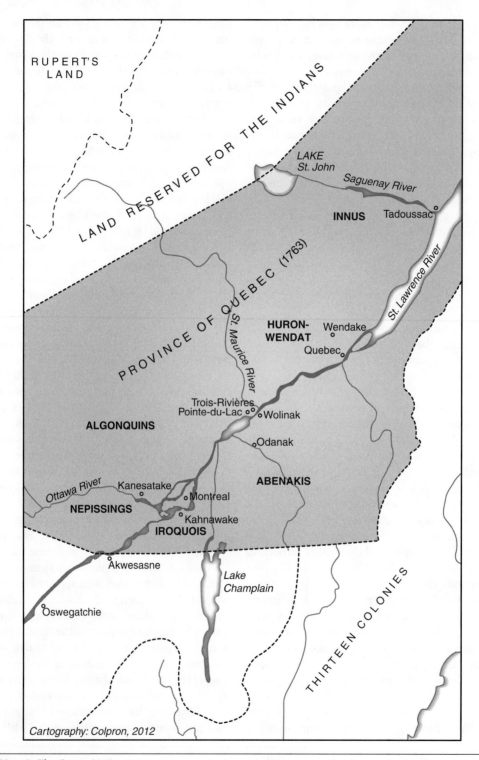

RUPERT'S
LAND

LAND RESERVED FOR THE INDIANS

LAKE
St. John

Saguenay River

INNUS   Tadoussac

PROVINCE OF QUEBEC (1763)

St. Lawrence River

HURON-
WENDAT   Wendake

Quebec

St. Maurice River

Trois-Rivières
Pointe-du-Lac   Wolinak

ALGONQUINS   Odanak

ABENAKIS

Ottawa River   Kanesatake

NEPISSINGS   Montreal

Kahnawake

IROQUOIS

Akwesasne   Lake
                     Champlain

Oswegatchie

THIRTEEN COLONIES

Cartography: Colpron, 2012

Map 2 The Seven Nations

Familiar with the history of these communities, the British knew that their presence was the result of relatively recent migration flows. This influenced their legal interpretation: if these Aboriginals were not the original occupants, they could not hope to be indemnified for any land in that location that was opened up for colonization, even if they used that land regularly. Their rights were limited to land granted to them by the French beginning in the second half of the seventeenth century. The British rapidly began to draw a distinction between Aboriginal people who, they presumed, lived on their ancestral lands, and those who had migrated to new territories relatively recently. This idea was apparently asserted for the first time in 1764 by William Johnson, who wrote to Thomas Gage that the guarantees of the 1763 Royal Proclamation regarding hunting grounds did not apply to the Iroquois and Abenakis of the Saint Lawrence Valley because they had left their traditional lands in order to settle near the French.[16] Gage, who had also been the governor of Trois-Rivières, shared Johnson's views,[17] as Guy Carleton would do a few years later in the context of a claim presented by the Iroquois of Akwesasne.[18]

In the first years after the conquest of New France, the colonial authorities had therefore outlined a territorial policy that incorporated the idea that some Aboriginal peoples in the province of Quebec had rights over their land by virtue of the royal proclamation. The French colonial past influenced this system in an incidental way, through the history of the migration of some Aboriginal people in the Saint Lawrence Valley, but not as a structuring legacy that would have determined a precise policy to follow. In this first legal framework, the concept of prior rights played a key role, as it made it possible to differentiate between two categories of rights: the rights of original land occupants, and those of the others. For a few years, this filtering mechanism led the British to consider that some Aboriginals living in the Saint Lawrence Valley did not have any specific rights over their land, aside from those that had been formally granted to them by the French.

[. . .] The first true test of British territorial policy came after the American War of Independence, when thousands of American Loyalists went north to seek refuge in the province of Quebec. As a result of the 1774 Quebec Act, the provincial boundaries had been extended considerably and thenceforward encompassed a large portion of the territories that had been reserved in 1763.

The Quebec Act, which abrogated the royal proclamation within the borders of the province of Quebec, contained no provisions on what procedures should be followed to purchase land from Aboriginal peoples.[19] In theory, the formal requirement to conclude treaties had disappeared. In practice however, the British authorities did not expect to change their policy on this matter. This is clearly indicated in the instructions given to Governor Guy Carleton in 1775. Article 31, which concerns portions of former Indian territory that were now within the province of Quebec, instructs the governor to ensure that the limits of any outposts in the "interior Country" be well-established and that no colonization be allowed beyond that, "seeing that such Settlements must have the consequence to disgust the Savages" and "to excite their Enmity."[20]

At any rate, the political and strategic climate did not lend itself to making significant changes on this matter. The Treaty of Paris of 1783, which put an end to the American War of Independence, had resulted in a widespread movement of discontent among the Aboriginal peoples of the interior of the continent, who could not understand how the British could have ceded their land to the Americans.[21] At one point, the British even feared that their allies would turn against them, and they launched an extensive diplomatic offensive in an attempt to decrease tensions. Caution, particularly in territorial matters, was called for to prevent the alliance from breaking up. This was particularly the case west of the Ottawa River, where a large group of Loyalists had taken refuge. To ensure that the establishment of their settlement in this sector would go smoothly, the British rapidly concluded a few land-cession treaties, notably with the Mississauga nation.[22]

Colonial authorities apparently did not question the length of time that the Mississaugas had been in the sector; they simply assumed that they were the original inhabitants of the land and benefitted from the rights associated with ancestral occupation. But the British were not ready to follow this way of reasoning for every Aboriginal nation, as was borne out by their reaction to the protests of the Akwesasne Iroquois, who opposed the surveying of their land for the benefit of Loyalists. In support of their territorial claims, this time, the Iroquois invoked a deed given to them by the French that had been lost in a church fire.[23] While he refused to admit the legitimacy of the Iroquois claim, Governor Haldimand, "being desirous to avoid all difficulties with the Indians," chose a conciliatory course of action. In his mind, the deed being invoked by the Iroquois did not exist, but they had considered themselves "the Proprietors of that Land" for so many years that it was wiser to offer to compensate them than to insist "upon the right of the Crown."[24] The Iroquois, however, refused to give up their land in exchange for financial compensation; instead, they insisted upon preserving a specific tract of land. Haldimand would have preferred a different solution, but given the political and military tensions and the upcoming conference between Aboriginal peoples and the United States Congress, he reluctantly agreed to the Iroquois request, expressing his frustration in a letter to the British negotiator: "They must be made fully to understand and consider this as an Indulgence during the King's pleasure, no part of it ever having been granted to them."[25]

The pragmatic decision of Haldimand was a good illustration of the problem arising from the implementation of a rigid legal rationale in a context where the British still needed the military help of the Aboriginal peoples. By complying with the Iroquois request, the governor avoided creating strong dissatisfaction among useful allies. But his decision would also have an enduring (and involuntary) consequence. Paradoxically, the apparent recognition of the Iroquois' rights to the land would indeed become, in the nineteenth century, the basis for a rationale legitimizing dispossession without treaties.

This new legal logic would, however, take a few decades to fully emerge. Meanwhile, looking for a new way to justify their refusal to conclude land-cession treaties in the province of Quebec, the British would temporarily borrow certain aspects of the French legal conception. This borrowing was incited by a claim raised in the Gaspé Peninsula, as the Chaleur Bay had become an area of refuge for hundreds of Loyalists. As we have seen, in the 1760s the colonial authorities had considered this region, or at least the Restigouche River area, to be Mi'kmaq territory (or land protected by the royal proclamation) and had refused to grant some land concessions. In the 1775 instructions to Governor Carleton, London had apparently confirmed this impression by associating the Gaspé region with the "Interior Country" in which the progression of settlements should be closely monitored to avoid vexing the Aboriginal people.[26]

In the ensuing years, the colonial authorities showed some willingness to protect the rights of the Mi'kmaq in this area. For example, in 1780, Governor Haldimand wrote to Governor Nicholas Cox that the hunting privileges of the Mi'kmaq along the Restigouche River should be protected, so long as this did not interfere with commerce.[27] Two years later, Haldimand repeated that he did not want the Mi'kmaq to be treated unfairly, and he asked that steps be taken to prevent their land from being encroached upon.[28] In

1784, Nicholas Cox recommended drawing a boundary between "the hunting ground and fisheries belonging to the Savages" and the land belonging to colonists.[29] In an ordinance published the same year, he established that the colonists should pay one dollar to the Mi'kmaq to obtain the right to cut hay in the grasslands and marshes of the Restigouche River.[30] Reiterating the fact that the King wanted to protect the Indians throughout the province, Cox also confirmed that the Mi'kmaq had exclusive hunting and fishing rights along the Restigouche River.[31]

The political climate here, as in the area west of the Ottawa River, seemed to lend itself to the drawing up of a treaty with the Mi'kmaq, and in 1786, Nicholas Cox was given the responsibility, along with surveyor John Collins, of negotiating an arrangement with them. Negotiations took place over three days (29 June–1 July) in Listuguj and resulted in an agreement-in-principle. The Mi'kmaq would give up part of their land but preserve the land along the Restigouche River as well as exclusive fishing rights there. The British negotiators also promised them presents in exchange for their lands.[32] These negotiations were clearly in line with those carried out with the Mississauga[33] a few years before, and they demonstrated the will of the British authorities to continue, within the boundaries of this colony, a policy based on the recognition of the Aboriginal peoples' rights as "original occupants."

The two British negotiators showed great optimism about the agreement's chances of being confirmed by the colonial government. However, they had underestimated the importance of the economic stakes related to salmon fishing in the Restigouche River. The review of the agreement's terms in Quebec City gave rise to serious reservations, especially about the fishing rights.[34] In addition, there was pressure from an influential London merchant named John Shoolbred, who had received a concession from the King for 10 000 acres to be taken in the Chaleur Bay

area.[35] After several months of dickering, the colonial authorities finally decided not to ratify the agreement negotiated in 1786.

An Executive Council committee that had been set up to look into the rights of the Mi'kmaq along the Restigouche River had concluded that it was not necessary to approve the agreement. The committee members had consulted lawyer François-Joseph Cugnet, an influential legal expert, whose opinion on the colony's early laws was in great demand at the time. Cugnet, who also occupied the positions of secretary and translator for the Executive Council,[36] convinced them that the government could allocate the land on the northern shore of the Restigouche, without concern for any potential Mi'kmaq rights, given that the French practice had consisted of allocating land "with a perfect disregard of any supposed prior title in the Indians."[37]

This was the first time that an argument based on the French judicial practice was used to reject the necessity of concluding treaties with the Aboriginal peoples in order to abolish their rights. The argument was not specific to some areas of the former French colony, but general in its formulation. If it was applicable for the Chaleur Bay area, it would also have been valid for all the territory conquered by the British in 1760. But the colonial authorities in Quebec clearly had no intention of extending this logic west of the Ottawa River, in the Upper Countries. There, the political and strategic situation prevented the implementation of a policy that, even if founded on coherent legal reasoning, would have created serious problems with the Aboriginal nations.

East of the Ottawa River, the strategic role of the Aboriginal people was less important yet not completely negligible. The bulk of the British defence was located there and, until the early decades of the nineteenth century, the Saint Lawrence Valley remained the most densely populated sector in British North America. This situation offered the colonial rulers greater latitude but did not abolish the problems stemming from reliance on French legal reasoning that denied Native land rights. This is evident in the 1787 Executive Council decision: after having refused to ratify the terms of the agreement negotiated with the Mi'kmaq the previous year, the council still decided to offer them presents in exchange for the portion of land they seemed ready to cede in 1786.[38]

It is likely that there was some conceptual discomfort added to the specific difficulties of implementing such a legal rationale. Predicating unilateral Aboriginal dispossession on a French colonial heritage seemed particularly incongruous in the British system, which, until then, had been used to legitimize its appropriation of Native lands. Such a policy actually went against the official positions taken by the British before and after New France was conquered, positions based on the idea of negotiation and voluntary cession sealed by compensation. The Britons' self-legitimizing discourse usually played on the protective, just, and generous role of the British sovereign. This image was at the essence of the terminology regarding Aboriginal peoples in the royal proclamation, and it infused most of the official declarations concerning the protection of Aboriginal rights. Such a position was difficult to reconcile with the idea that the British need not be concerned with any rights Aboriginal peoples may have had on their land, since the French never were.

The aborted negotiations with the Mi'kmaq did not serve as a springboard for the integration of French legal logic; however, they nevertheless marked a significant step in the implementation of a Quebec-specific territorial policy. This event intensified a trend emerging in the Saint Lawrence Valley of refusing to negotiate for the purchase of Native land. Admittedly, the reasons invoked to deny the Aboriginal peoples their rights differed by area: in one case, they referred to prior migrations and in another, to the French practice of not recognizing Indian deeds. However the result remained the same.

The non-ratification of the treaty with the Mi'kmaq emphasized the lack of a consistent territorial policy within the boundaries of the province of Quebec. The same colonial power could decide, in some circumstances, to conclude treaties with Indigenous people for the purchase of their land, and in others, to proceed unilaterally, without supporting these different approaches with a coherent legal logic. This problem was resolved in part in 1791, when the province of Quebec was separated into two colonies: Upper and Lower Canada. This division did not entirely eradicate the British policy's lack of cohesion but it did dissimulate it in part, by overlaying it with a political structure that restored a consistency of practice within each of the colonies.

Nevertheless, the fickleness of British policy remained noticeable, and the Indigenous people of Lower Canada at times highlighted it to try to soften the colonial stance. This happened, for instance, in the 1790s, during a land claim in the Upper Saint Lawrence area. While the claim was submitted on behalf of the Seven Nations of Canada, in reality, it involved only the Saint Lawrence Iroquois. At that time, as perceived by an Indian affairs agent, the Iroquois were worried by the rapid reduction of their hunting grounds, due to the arrival of the Loyalists and to the expansion of colonization in the US territory.[39]

A first request was submitted in 1794[40] and it elicited a very careful reply from the colonial government. The governor emphasized that the British policy was not to seize Native land without due consideration. He stated that if the Seven Nations were unjustly dispossessed of their land, the situation was sure to be corrected because the King "administers justice to all his children and never takes anything from them without paying the price" [translation]. Without committing formally, Dorchester nevertheless opened the door to the recognition of the Seven Nations' territorial rights. [. . .]

This response seems even more surprising when we consider that its author, Lord Dorchester, also governed the province of Quebec in 1787, when the decision to not ratify the treaty with the Mi'kmaq was made. It was also Dorchester who, in the late 1760s, clearly rejected the idea that the Akwesasne Iroquois could have a right to the lands in the vicinity of the Saint Lawrence.[41] This radical change of perspective clearly illustrates the difficulty the British had with the instrumentalization of the French colonial past in their negotiations with the Aboriginal peoples, especially during times of crisis. Such a crisis occurred in the 1790s, when it appeared that a new conflict with the United States was on the horizon. Indeed, the Seven Nations were fully aware that this created a favourable situation for them and chose to initiate treaty negotiations with the state of New York at that time, regarding the cession of their hunting grounds south of the Canadian border.

In 1795, Dorchester had given Agent Alexander McKee the responsibility of carrying out a first inquiry into the Seven Nations' claims.[42] In July, the Kahnawake chiefs had submitted a document expounding the basis for their claims to land between the Longueuil and Kingston seigniories, "according to the partition" made by their ancestors.[43] In support of their rights, the Iroquois made reference to their immemorial occupation of the location, since "God" had "created them on these lands," and they presented their version of colonial history, in which they had welcomed the French, not vice versa. They had "never been conquered" by them, and when the "King of France" established himself on their land, he did it peacefully because the ancestors of the Iroquois shared with them the "land that the master of life" had reserved them.[44]

They were no doubt conscious of the fact that their ancestral-occupation argument had not hitherto been successful at convincing the colonial powers; therefore, the Iroquois also reminded the British that, in the past, they had purchased land from Aboriginal people who were not its original owners; these included the Mississaugas and Hurons. The Iroquois wondered why they should not benefit from the same treatment and why Governor Haldimand had not wanted to pay for their land before settling Loyalists on it. In order to put a little more pressure on the British, the Iroquois asserted that the Americans, against whom they had fought in war, were prepared to pay them for their territory on the other side of the border.[45]

The claim was submitted to John Sewell, attorney general of Lower Canada. He deemed it to be valid on certain points, but not on the extent of the land being claimed. To his knowledge, nothing would support "a pretension so unlimited." The land being claimed was within the borders of Upper Canada, but Sewell called to mind that, prior to the division of the province of Quebec, a portion of the land had been set aside for use by the Seven Nations—a reference to the 1784 negotiation between the Akwesasne Iroquois and Haldimand. John Johnson, the superintendent general of Indian affairs, knew full well the limits of that reserve, for which the Iroquois had yet to receive a formal concession. According to Sewell, a duly executed concession for this portion of land "will satisfy the seven villages, and silence their pretensions to the residue of the tract, claimed by their address and speeches."[46]

On 23 February 1797, James Green, the governor's military secretary, informed John Johnson of the opinion prepared by Sewell. He asked him to consult the attorney general on the subject and to prepare a speech in response that was to be submitted to the governor for approval.[47] The response, which was presented in June of the same year on behalf of the governor, focused on negotiations that were supposed to have taken place in 1784. In exchange for the reserve created for them, the Akwesasne Iroquois would have abandoned all their territorial claims over land in the area of the Saint Lawrence. The governor was committing to taking the necessary steps to ensure that the Akwesasne Iroquois would obtain a formal concession for that reserve, but he wanted that to put an end to all claims or representations by the Seven Nations.[48]

Despite the favourable political context, the Iroquois' argument, which clearly illustrated their capacity to force the colonial authorities to face their own contradictions, did not lead to a treaty negotiation. It did, however, trigger the first significant vacillation in the British method of analyzing Aboriginal land rights. In effect, Dorchester's response reinterpreted Haldimand's action in 1784, within the fictional framework of a negotiation, which impelled the Iroquois to renounce their rights to land in the vicinity of the Upper Saint Lawrence in exchange for the creation of a reserve. The French colonial past was not completely removed from the British discourse, which alluded to "assigned or promised" lands for the Iroquois. But this formulation remained sufficiently ambiguous to avoid aggravating the Iroquois' political sensitivity, while they continued to refer to their ancestors' sharing of the land.

The Iroquois reaction to Dorchester's response is unknown, but the lack of further claims for the land in the vicinity of the Upper Saint Lawrence intimates that the new British rationale was more acceptable, particularly because it recognized their rights, albeit only implicitly, and placed the extinguishment of those rights within a context of negotiation and renunciation. In this case, the British fiction was significantly more advantageous than the reality, since it partially reconciled both Iroquois and British conceptions, without requiring any change in practice. The idea of compensation by granting reserved land was also built on a useful illusion because, while the British affirmed that they indemnified the Iroquois for lost territories, they did so by reserving a portion of land that already belonged to them. But this fiction, which had the advantage of costing

nothing, was more consistent with traditional British legal ideas, since it focused on compensation, a key concept in the ongoing process of legitimizing the dispossession of land from Quebec's Aboriginal peoples.

In the same time period, compensatory logic was apparently also applied to another area: the policy of annual gift distribution to the Aboriginal peoples. The practice, which went back to the French rule, had been taken up by the British after 1763 to ensure that they would receive the support of Aboriginal nations who had previously been allied to the French. The presents—a tangible manifestation of the alliance linking them to the British Crown—held particular symbolic meaning for the Aboriginal peoples. At the end of the eighteenth century, the colonial power was tempted to modify the primary meaning of this distribution to make it an expression of a fictional negotiation, in which the Aboriginal peoples renounced their land rights.

The argument was seemingly invoked for the first time early in the nineteenth century with the Algonquins and Nepissings, who were protesting against the arrival of lumberjacks on their hunting grounds along the Ottawa River. Philemon Wright, the merchant who had hired the lumberjacks, defended his position by repeating what he had been told in Quebec City: the Algonquins and Nepissings "have no positive rights to these lands"; by receiving "yearly gifts from the government," they had relinquished "their claims on the lands" [translation].[49] It is not known whether his interpretation corresponded to an official government position, but the idea continued to circulate and even became partly integrated by certain Aboriginal peoples in the Saint Lawrence River Valley. As evidence of this integration, in 1837, the Seven Nations of Canada described these presents in a petition as a "sacred debt" that the "Kings of France" had promised their ancestors they would respect, as "compensation for the lands" that were "given up" to them. This debt had been "confirmed by the Kings of England since the country was ceded, and paid and carried out in a timely manner since then" [translation].[50]

If the British had played a role in disseminating this interpretation, they were no longer disposed to use it in the 1830s, as a result of the high cost of the yearly gift distributions. For several years, the authorities in London had insisted on the need to radically cut these expenses. Their requests came as part of an overall review of the Indian policy, which abandoned the idea of alliances to promote the civilization of the Aboriginal peoples.[51] The decline of the Aboriginal peoples' military importance after 1815 played a role in this redefinition of the Indian policy, while the rapid progression of colonization provided a new legitimization for projects to integrate Indigenous people into the colonial world. For the British administrators, the Aboriginal people did not have much choice: if they wanted to avoid being completely marginalized, or even disappearing altogether, they had to profoundly alter their way of life and take up agriculture and sedentary life.

The position of Britain's new Indian policy helped define the outlines of a new framework to legitimize the dispossession of Aboriginal peoples in Lower Canada. The review of the Algonquin and Nepissing claim played a key role in this process. Their protests against encroachment onto their hunting grounds had begun in the 1790s and continued into the early decades of the nineteenth century, during which time they addressed a series of petitions to the colonial authorities. In particular, the Algonquins and the Nepissings were asking for the creation of a territory reserved for their use and for the payment of compensation similar to that received by the Aboriginal peoples of Upper Canada.[52]

In 1836, after several years of haggling, the colonial government finally decided to assign a Lower Canada Executive Council committee to examine the numerous requests received from the Alonquins and Nepissings. In its 1837 report,[53] the committee concluded that their claim was valid and that they were entitled to compensation. This was essentially based on the Royal Proclamation of 1763, which the Alonquins and Nepissings had cited persistently in their different petitions. In previous years, the idea that this document entitled them to compensation for their hunting grounds had received solid support from officers of the Department of Indian Affairs. However, in its use of the document for its analysis, the Executive Council committee excluded one fundamental component, namely, the obligation of using treaties to buy Native lands, and they retained only the idea of compensation through reserving land.

To support its reasoning, the committee used the precedent of the land reserved for the Akwesasne Iroquois. Whether or not they deliberately omitted the circumstances leading up to the creation of that reserve in 1784 and 1797, the committee members gave the event new meaning: that of land reserved by virtue of the royal proclamation.[54] The notion that the Saint Lawrence Iroquois were not the original occupants had totally disappeared, and so had the idea of a concession promised by the French and confirmed by the British within the framework of an indulgent policy (1784), and that of a negotiation that would have led the Iroquois to renounce their rights in exchange for their reserve (1797). All that remained was the basis on which the reserved area had been created: the royal document of 1763. The 1837 report stated that, since the Alonquins and Nepissings also cited the proclamation, it would be unjust to treat them differently: "As that Act of State has been considered sufficient to guarantee to the Iroquois of St Regis [Akwesasne] the Possession of their present Reservation, to which it is stated that they had no other Right than as Part of their ancient Hunting Grounds, the Algonquin and Nipissing tribes may have some Ground to complain if they are deprived of the Benefit of the same Protection for their Claims."[55]

The 1837 report invested the royal proclamation with new meaning, in particular, that of royal protection exercised within the context of an Aboriginal subsistence economy. At the time of the Conquest, the Crown would have indeed showed its desire "to secure to the Indians their ordinary Means of Subsistence,"[56] by placing under its control the lands that the Aboriginal peoples owned or claimed. Invested with this new meaning, the royal proclamation enabled the development of a theory of just compensation that eliminated the obligation to negotiate. For the committee, this just compensation had to be based on the adoption of measures that would maintain living conditions for Aboriginal people that were similar to those they had had before they were subjected to the impact of colonial expansion.

[. . .]

This general principle indicated a road to follow to compensate the Alonquins and Nepissings: to reserve for them "a sufficient Tract of Land . . . in the Rear of the present Range of Townships on the Ottawa River" and to promote their settlement there by offering "such Support, Encouragement, and Assistance" required to lead them "to a State of Independence of further Aid."[57]

The Executive Council committee had skillfully managed to base a unilateral policy of territorial dispossession on the Royal Proclamation of 1763. The political dimension of this document, which had been expressed in the obligation of obtaining Aboriginal consent before taking possession of their land, had vanished and been replaced by the idea of just compensation, whose measure was the creation of a reserve and the granting of government assistance to help in the transition to a sedentary and agricultural way of life. It is doubtless not a coincidence that these two elements occupied a central place in Britain's new Indian policy, which was focused on civilization.

It would seem that this reinterpretation was grounded in the fear of seeing other Aboriginal nations from Lower Canada make similar claims if the committee consented to negotiating a land-cession treaty with the

Alonquins and the Nepissings. In February 1837, Duncan C. Napier, superintendent of Indian affairs, was already anticipating such demands from other Aboriginal nations if the request of the Alonquins and Nepissings received a positive response from the Executive Council committee.

[. . .]

While he did not identify the nations that might ultimately make such demands, Napier still observed that the "Hunting Grounds claimed by the Indians of Lower Canada comprise nearly the whole of the Waste Lands within the Limits of the Province."[58] The Executive Council committee was probably conscious of the broader reach that its recommendations on the Algonquin-Nepissing issue would have, and doubtless had in mind the possibility of future territorial requests coming from other nations. This would explain the effort it made to provide the basis for the principle of just compensation, which could be transposable to other claims.

The principle of just compensation set out in 1837 was approved by London two years later[59] and would become the core of the new legitimization for the territorial dispossession of Aboriginal peoples. In 1858, another commission responsible for investigating the administration of Indian Affairs fully reiterated this argument,[60] which in 1851 was indirectly expressed in a law setting aside 230 000 acres of land for the Aboriginal peoples of the former Lower Canada.[61] This law was the legal tool used to create a series of new reserves, which would, for a time, be associated to the idea of compensation for the loss of the larger hunting territories.[62]

The idea of just compensation also served as a framework for rethinking French territorial practices within a new fiction that emerged in the Bagot Commission's report. This commission of inquiry had been established in 1842 to look into the problem of the administration of Indian Affairs. [. . .] The "settlements had advanced rapidly before the conquest," wrote the commissioners, and the Aboriginal "territorial possessions . . . were therefore confined within fixed boundaries and, in several cases, were owned by virtue of letters of patent from the French Crown or from specific seigneurs" [translation]. In all of Lower Canada, according to the commission, there was only "one single place" where Aboriginal peoples "were dispossessed without compensation of their former hunting grounds" [translation][63] and that one place was the Ottawa Valley, in the territory claimed by the Algonquins and the Nepissings.

Despite their brevity, these comments suggest that, for the members of this commission, the actions taken by the French, that is, the granting of land to the Aboriginal communities, had resulted in limiting their territorial possessions to defined spaces. These observations also indicate that, in the Bagot Commission's reinterpretation of French colonial history, the lands granted by the French Crown had had the effect of compensating Aboriginal peoples for the loss of their hunting grounds. In fact, saying that there was only one area in which the Indigenous people had been dispossessed without compensation of their former territory was equivalent to saying that the other nations had been compensated by receiving land from the French authorities.

In a way, the Bagot Commission's analysis marks the endpoint of a long process of legitimization, which used history to justify a specific way of appropriating Native land. This rereading of the French colonial past was without any real historical foundations but it provided a specific meaning for the creation of new reserves in the mid-nineteenth century. It maintained an illusion, which was all the more powerful because it could be inscribed within a historical continuity, that the reserves, whose limited boundaries express the magnitude of Aboriginal dispossession, were, in fact, compensation.

Reconstituting the convoluted path that led the British to define a specific policy regarding Native lands in the province of Quebec indicates that the French colonial past did play a role in the process. But this role had little or nothing to do with the legal interpretations put forth in the closing decades of the twentieth century that rejected the idea that there was an "Indian title" on the land in Quebec at the time of the Conquest. Although the British did flirt, in the late 1780s, with the French notion that the Aboriginal peoples' title to their lands was worthless, this temporary deviation left no significant mark on their method of legitimizing the dispossession process for Aboriginal land.

Above all, the British retained from the French a way of doing things, which consisted of appropriating Native lands without reaching treaties with them. This borrowed method established itself fairly quickly, although it is impossible to identify a specific date in the early British regime, when the decision to act in this way was formally made. This practice did not at first rest on an overall strategy. Rather, it developed from a series of specific cases where each decision reinforced the trend, creating a sort of habit, which conditioned later decisions. As they accumulated, the precedents laid out a path from which the British surely could have deviated at any time; however, the risk of such a deviation opening the door to a series of claims created a highly effective guardrail.

[. . .]

One conclusion stands out in terms of this path: that practice determined the standard and not the reverse, at least until a new standard framework took its final shape with the theory of just compensation. Well established after 1837, this framework made it possible to reintegrate the French past into a new schema. The French colonial practice, based on the non-recognition of Aboriginal land rights, and the Royal Proclamation of 1763, the symbol par excellence of the recognition of those rights, fused into a syncretic model that coated dispossession without treaties with the varnish of compensation.

NOTES

1. For an overview of British policy related to Indigenous lands, see Stuart Banner, *How the Indians Lost Their Land: Law and Power on the Frontier* (Cambridge: Harvard University Press, 2005), 1–111.

2. This interpretation was the basis of the legal positions defended by Quebec and Canadian government prosecutors until the early 1990s. The Supreme Court of Canada rejected this interpretation in 1995. See Renée Dupuis, *Tribus, peuples et nations. Les nouveaux enjeux des revendications autochtones au Canada* (Montreal: Boréal, 1997), 59–63.

3. See, for example, W.J. Eccles, "Sovereignty-Association, 1500–1783," *Canadian Historical Review* 65, 4 (1984): 475–510.

4. For an overview of different points of view on this question, see Brian Slattery, *The Land Rights of Indigenous Canadian Peoples as Affected by the Crown's Acquisition of the Territories* (PhD diss., Oxford University, 1979); Jacqueline Beaulieu, Christiane Cantin, and Maurice Ratelle, "La Proclamation royale de 1763: le droit refait l'histoire," *La revue du Barreau* 49, 3 (1989): 317–40; Paul Dionne, "Les postulats de la Commission Dorion et le titre aborigène au Québec: vingt ans après," *La revue du Barreau* 51, 1 (1991): 128–71; Richard Boivin, "Pour en finir avec la Proclamation royale: la décision Côté," *Revue générale de droit* 25, 1 (1994): 136–42; David Schulze, "L'application de la Proclamation royale de 1763 dans les frontières originales de la province de Québec: la décision du Conseil privé dans l'affaire Allsopp," *Revue juridique Thémis* 31 (1997): 511–74; Michel Morin, *L'usurpation de la souveraineté autochtone. Les peuples de la Nouvelle-France et des colonies anglaises de l'Amérique du Nord* (Montreal: Boréal, 1997), 133–61.

5. The situation in Quebec was not uncommon in the British Empire. A similar policy of unilateral appropriation of Aboriginal lands was also in effect in the Maritime provinces, British Columbia, and Australia. These cases clearly show that the British approaches to the land rights of the Aboriginal peoples were more complex than is usually thought, the land-cessions treaties being only one method among others to legitimize dispossession. However, these cases should not be considered in a chronological perspective with an aim to locating explanatory precedents. It is clear, for example, that for the period studied here, the case of Nova Scotia does not occur as an example that justifies the decisions made in Quebec, just as Quebec and the Maritimes are not references that legitimate or explain the decisions made in British Columbia. The same method of land dispossession can be based on different factors and legal justifications, without it being necessary to identify a precedent that serves as an explanation, except when the documentation provides support for it, which is not the case in this situation. For the Maritime provinces, see L.F.S. Upton, *Micmacs and Colonists: Indian–White Relations in the Maritimes, 1713–1867* (Vancouver: University of British Columbia Press, 1979), 37; Olive P. Dickason, "Amerindians between French and English in Nova Scotia, 1713–1763," in James R. Miller, ed., *Sweet Promises: A Reader on Indian–White Relations in Canada* (Toronto: University of Toronto Press, 1991), 48. For British Columbia, see Paul Tennant, *Aboriginal Peoples and Politics: The Indian Land Question in British Columbia, 1849–1989* (Vancouver: University of British Columbia Press, 1990). For Australia, see Stuart Banner, *Possessing the Pacific: Land, Settlers, and Indigenous People from Australia to Alaska* (Cambridge: Harvard University Press, 2007).

6. See Gregory E. Dowd, *War under Heaven: Pontiac, the Indian Nations, & the British Empire* (Baltimore: Johns Hopkins University Press, 2002).

7. For example, see Denys Delâge and Jean-Pierre Sawaya, *Les traités des Sept-Feux avec les Britanniques. Droits et pièges d'un héritage colonial au Québec* (Quebec: Septentrion, 2001).

8. Royal Proclamation, 7 Oct. 1763, in Adam Shortt and Arthur G. Doughty, eds, *Documents Relating to the Constitutional History of Canada, 1759–1791* (Ottawa: J. de L. Taché, 1918), pt I, 166–7.

9. Ibid., 27–155.

10. Ibid., see articles 60 and 62, in 199.

11. Schulze, "L'application de la Proclamation royale," 526–7.
12. King's concession to Joseph Philibot, 18 June 1766, 76977–9, vol. 157, RG1-L3L, Library and Archives Canada (LAC).
13. Slattery, *Land Rights*, 266–7.
14. Ibid., 267.
15. Jean-Pierre Sawaya, *La féderation des Sept Feux de la vallée du Saint-Laurent, xviiᵉ–xixᵉ siècle* (Sillery: Septentrion, 1998).
16. Johnson to Gage, 27 Jan. 1764, *The Papers of Sir William Johnson* (Albany: University of the State of New York, 1925), 4: 307–8.
17. Gage to Johnson, 6 Feb. 1764, ibid., 318.
18. The claim was presented in 1769. See Claus to Johnson, ibid., 7: 127.
19. The Quebec Act, s. 4, in Shortt and Doughty, *Documents*, pt I, 571–2.
20. Instructions to Governor Carleton, 3 Jan. 1775, in *Report concerning Canadian Archives for the Year 1904* (Ottawa: S.B. Dawson, 1905), 237. A "Plan for Imperial Control of Indian Affairs" was attached to the instructions to the governor. This plan, dated 10 July 1764, had been drafted by the Lords of the Board of Trade in the months following the adoption of the royal proclamation. It contained numerous provisions concerning trade with Indigenous people, and three articles (nos 41, 42, and 43) spelling out the procedures to follow when buying their lands. These articles were clearly a reworking of the provisions of the royal proclamation. The plan was also attached to instructions to Haldimand in 1778 and to those of Carleton, who had become Lord Dorchester, in 1786. See Bruce Clark, *Native Liberty, Crown Sovereignty: The Existing Aboriginal Right of Self-Government in Canada* (Montreal and Kingston: McGill-Queen's University Press, 1990), 79.
21. On the reactions of the Indians to the Treaty of 1783, see Alan Taylor, *The Divided Ground: Indians, Settlers, and the Northern Borderland of the American Revolution* (New York: Alfred A. Knopf, 2006), 111–13.
22. On the land-cessions treaties west of the Ottawa River, in what would become the colony of Upper Canada in 1791 (and then the province of Ontario in 1867), see Robert J. Surtees, "Canadian Indian Treaties," in William C. Sturtevant, ed., *Handbook of North American Indians*, vol. 4, *History of Indian–White Relations* (Washington: Smithsonian Institution, 1988), 202–7; Jim R. Miller, *Compact, Contract, Covenant: Aboriginal Treaty Making in Canada* (Toronto: University of Toronto Press, 2009), 66–122.
23. Johnson to Haldimand, 11 Mar. 1784, 260, add. mss 21775, Haldimand Papers, British Museum. This strategy suggests that they were now familiar with the distinction, made by the British, between those who could claim the rights of "original inhabitants" and those who could not.
24. Haldimand to Campbell, 22 Mar. 1784, 1412, vol. 3, reel C-10997, RG10, LAC.
25. Haldimand to Campbell, 15 Apr. 1784, 154–5, vol. 14, reel C-1223, RG10, LAC; see also Haldimand to John Johnson, 15 Apr. 1784, 150–1, reel C-1223, RG10, LAC.
26. *Report concerning Canadian Archives for the Year 1904*, 237. At that time, the expression "Interior Country" generally designated the region situated west of the Ottawa River, but was also applied less frequently to other regions not yet opened to colonization.
27. Haldimand to Cox, 16 Aug. 1780, 70, mss 21862, Haldimand Papers.
28. Haldimand to O'Hara, 27 May 1783, 100v, mss 21862, Haldimand Papers.
29. Cox to Haldimand, 16 Aug. 1784, 133, mss 21862, Haldimand Papers.
30. Cox to Haldimand, 7 Aug. 1784, 132, mss 21862, Haldimand Papers.
31. Ibid.
32. 1785–1871, série Indiens, 1784–1900, SD8 Conseil exécutif, Provincial Archives of New Brunswick.
33. The two men invoked the treaties concluded west of the Ottawa River to convince the Mi'kmaq to cede part of their territory to the British Crown.
34. "General Observations upon the North of the Restigouche being granted to the Indians, read in Council the 2nd of March 1797," 54053–68, vol. 110, reel C-2535, series L-3-L, RG1, LAC.
35. "His Majesty Mandamus in favour of Mr John Shoolbred for lands in Chaleur Bay, June 29, 1785," 87197–202, vol. 181, RG1-L3L, LAC.
36. "Cugnet, François-Joseph," *Dictionary of Canadian Biography Online* (www.biographi.ca).

37. Minute Books on Land Matters, 13 Aug. 1787, 22, vol. A, RG1 L1, LAC.

38. Minute Books on Land Matters, 14 Aug. 1787, 8, col. A, RG1 L1, LAC.

39. "Remarques de J.B. De Lorimier sur les affaires sauvages," 22 Oct. 1793, 42–4, vol. 247, reel C-2848, RG8, LAC.

40. "Extract from minutes of an Indian Council held at Quebec 6th. February 1794," 433, pt 2, vol. 250, reel C-2849, RG8, LAC.

41. Guy Carleton was governor of the province of Quebec for a first term (between 1768 and 1778); he received the title of Lord Dorchester in 1786, at the beginning of his second term in Canada (1786–96).

42. "At a council held at Lachine with the Chiefs of the Caughnawaga's and of the Lake of the two Mountains," 26 July 1795, 222–4, vol. 248, reel C-2848, RG8, LAC.

43. "Paroles des Sauvages des Sept villages du Bas Canada . . . ," 28 July 1795, 230, vol. 248, reel C-2848, RG8, LAC.

44. Ibid., 230–1.

45. Ibid., 232.

46. Sewell to Prescott, 17 Feb. 1797, 210–12, reel H-2533, 1796–1797, Military Secretary's Entry Book, #1, vol. 17, series 1, Robert Prescott Papers, G II 17, MG23, LAC.

47. Green to Johnson, 23 Feb. 1797, 200, ibid.

48. "Lord Dorchester to the Indians, Quebec, June 5, 1797," 9238–9, vol. 10, reel C-11000, RG10, LAC.

49. "Témoignage de P. Wright," 4 Feb. 1824, in Journal de la Chambre d'Assemblee du Bas-Canada, 1824, Appendix R.

50. The chiefs of the Seven Nations to Governor Gosford, 3 Feb. 1837, Copies or Extracts of Correspondence since 1st April 1835, between the Secretary of State for the Colonies and the Governors of the British North American Provinces Respecting the Indians in those Provinces, 62, House of Commons, 1839.

51. On the new orientation of British Indian policy after the War of 1812, see John L. Tobias, "Protection, Civilization, Assimilation: An Outline History of Canada's Indian Policy," in Miller, Sweet Promises, 127–44.

52. See, for example, The Algonquins and Nipissings to John Johnson, 29 July 1824, 12692–3, vol. 3, reel C-11003, RG10, LAC; Speech of Algonquins and Nipissings, 31 May 1831, 32287–8, vol. 83, reel C-11030, RG10, LAC; The Algonquins and Nipissings to Mathew Lord Aylmer, July 1833, 34427–8, vol. 87, reel C-11466, RG10, LAC.

53. "Report of a Committee of the Executive Council," 13 June 1837, in Copies or Extracts of Correspondence, 27.

54. Ibid.

55. Ibid., 32.

56. Ibid., 27.

57. Ibid., 32.

58. Napier, "Answers to the Queries . . . ," 29 May 1837, in Copies or Extracts of Correspondence, 22.

59. "Copy of a Despatch from Lord Glenelg to the Earl of Durham," 22 Aug. 1839, in Copies or Extracts of Correspondence, 6–7.

60. Canada, Report of the Special Commissioners Appointed . . . to Investigate Indian Affairs in Canada (Toronto: Stewart Derbishire & George Desbarats, 1858), pt III.

61. An Act to authorise the setting apart of lands for the use of certain Indian tribes in Lower Canada, 14–15 Vict., 1851, ch. 106.

62. This was the perspective taken by the report of the commission in 1858 (Canada, Report of the Special Commissioners, pt II). See also Pennefather to Edmund Head, 4 May 1860, in "Copies or Extracts of Correspondence between the Secretary of State for the Colonies and the Governor General of Canada respecting Alterations on the Organization of the Indian Department in Canada," Ordered, by the House of Commons, to be printed, 25 Aug. 1860, Irish University Press Series of British Parliamentary Papers, Colonies, Canada, 23, 31; Hector L. Langevin, "On the Petition of the Algonquin Indians," Ottawa, 26 Oct. 1868, 1–3, vol. 723, reel C-13412, RG10, LAC.

63. "Rapport sur les affaires des Sauvages en Canada, 1845," s. iii, in Journaux de l'Assemblée législative de la Province du Canada, 1847, Appendice (T.), 3. Terres; 1. Titres aux terres.

Chapter 12

"Rushing" the Empire Westward

READINGS

Primary Documents

Historical Interpretations

INTRODUCTION

Even before Canada East, Canada West, New Brunswick, and Nova Scotia signed on to Confederation, the other parts of North America further west, controlled as colonies or trading territories by the British or British North Americans, were attracting notice. The potential riches in British Columbia's gold fields and the expansion of the rural settlement frontier into bison range and fur trade territory captured the imaginations of British North American colonists and colonial administrators alike. Understanding what was in these territories, and understanding how these territories and their inhabitants were defined for people who would probably never visit, is central to understanding why Great Britain (and the colonies themselves) sought to expand the imperial footprint, especially when it seemed that maintaining the Empire and international alliances was becoming increasingly troublesome. (Britain had just been at war against Russia in the Black Sea region, and a rebellion was unfolding in India in 1857).

Our primary documents here represent two different kinds of reporting on the state of two separate "frontier" areas. The letter from Charles Major paints a forbidding picture of British Columbia and is especially pessimistic about the possibility of earning a decent living in the colony. He describes a chaotic gold rush scene, one in which the authority of the Empire seems restricted to Victoria and is otherwise hardly noticeable. Though it does not deal with the rush for gold, John Palliser's commentary on the vast centre of the continent captures the same sort of expansionist spirit. He mentions deserts, but raises hopes for the regions north of the 49th parallel (the border between the United States and British/Hudson's Bay Company territory) by noting that it supported trees and grasses.

The historical interpretations urge us to think about British Columbia's colonial history, which is marked by desires to settle the land and to extract wealth from it. Adele Perry reminds us that the colonization project in British Columbia implied both the dispossession of Indigenous people and the establishment and reproduction of a settler society that was defined in racial, class, and gender terms. It is in this context that the "hardy backwoodsmen, wholesome women, and steady families" came to be seen as the ideal immigrants to Vancouver Island and British Columbia by colonial promoters. Tina Loo turns her attention to the establishment of the rule of law in the region. She reasons that even in places where it had a short history and colonial authorities desired strict enforcement, newcomers to the territory had a basic respect for the law.

QUESTIONS FOR CONSIDERATION

1. Compare Charles Major's letter to some of the correspondence that Elizabeth Jane Errington writes about in Chapter 8. Is Major trying to create the same sort of connections?
2. Judging from his report, how *scientific* do you think Palliser's expedition was?
3. How British were the inhabitants of British North America and associated territories in the late 1850s? What made them so?
4. Do you consider the informal model of miners' justice to be more suitable to areas like the BC gold fields, or were people like Governor Douglas right to push for more formal institutions?
5. How did the specific British Columbian economic and social context impact the ways in which "colonial promoters" conceptualized the kind of immigrants needed in the colony?

SUGGESTIONS FOR FURTHER READING

Jean Barman, *French Canadians, Furs, and Indigenous Women in the Making of the Pacific Northwest* (Vancouver : UBC Press, 2015).

———, *The West beyond the West: A History of British Columbia* (Toronto: University of Toronto Press, 2007).

Robin Fisher, *Contact and Conflict: Indian–European Relations in British Columbia, 1774–1890* (Vancouver: University of British Columbia Press, 1977).

Tina Loo, *Making Law, Order and Authority in British Columbia, 1821–1871* (Toronto: University of Toronto Press, 1994).

Doug Owram, *Promise of Eden: The Canadian Expansionist Movement and the Idea of the West, 1856–1900* (Toronto: University of Toronto Press, 1980).

Adele Perry, *Colonial Relations: The Douglas-Connolly Family and the Nineteenth-Century Imperial World* (Cambridge: Cambridge University Press, 2015).

———, *On the Edge of Empire: Gender, Race, and the Making of British Columbia, 1849–1871* (Toronto: University of Toronto Press, 2001).

Ruth Sandwell, ed., *Beyond the City Limits: Rural History in British Columbia* (Vancouver: UBC Press, 1999).

Primary Documents

1   "Letter of Charles Major, 20 September 1859," in *Daily Globe*, Toronto, 2 January 1860, reprinted in Robie L. Reid, "Two Narratives of the British Gold Rush," *British Columbia Historical Quarterly* 5, 3 (July 1941): 224–7.

[From *The Daily Globe*, Toronto, Canada West, January 2, 1860.]

NEWS FROM BRITISH COLUMBIA. (From the Sarnia *Observer*.)

The following letter recently received by a person in this neighborhood, from the writer who is at present in British Columbia, was handed to us for perusal. As it contains much valuable and reliable information in reference to the country, we requested permission to publish it, which was at once granted. We therefore lay the most important portions of the letter before our readers, without further apology, satisfied that it will be read with interest by all:—

Fort Hope, Frazer River
Sept. 20th, 1859

Dear Sir:—I am afraid you will think I had forgot my promise,—but I wanted to know something about the country before writing to you. In the first place, do not think that I have taken a dislike to the country because I am not making money; the dislike is general all over the country. To give you anything like a correct idea of it would take more paper than I have small change to purchase, and more time than I could spare, and then it would only be commenced.

The country is not what it was represented to be. There is no farming land in British Columbia, as far as I can learn, except a very small portion joining Washington Territory, and on Vancouver's Island, where there is one valley of 20,000 acres; but that cannot be sold until Col. Moody's friends come out from the old country, and get what they want.

It never can be a *place*, because there is nothing to support it, except the mines, and just as soon as they are done the place goes down completely, for there is absolutely nothing to keep it up; and I tell you the truth the mines are falling off very fast. There is nothing in this country but mines—and very small pay for that; they are you may say, used up. We have been making two, three and four dollars per day, but it would not last more than two or three days; and so you would spend that before you would find more. There has been great excitement about Fort Alexander, three hundred miles above this, and also about Queen Charlotte's Island. They have both turned out another humbug like this place. A party arrived here yesterday from Alexander, and they are a pitiful looking lot. They are what the Yankees call *dead broke*. They have been six hundred miles up the river. When they got down here they had no shoes to their feet. Some had pieces of shirt and trowsers, but even these were pinned together with small sharp sticks; and some had the rim of an old hat, and some the crown. They had nothing to eat for one week, and not one cent in money. This is gold mining for you!

I expect the Frazer River fever has cooled down by this time, at least I hope so; for I do pity the poor wretches that come out here to beg. They can do that at home; as for making money, that is out of the question. Since we came here (to use the miners' term,) we have been making grub; and those who can do that, think they are doing well. If there are any making arrangements to come to this place, let them take a fool's advice *and stay at home*. I would just about as soon hear that anyone belonging to me was dead, as to hear they had started to come here. They say it wants a man with capital to make money here; but a man with money in Canada will double it quicker than he will here. And if I, or any other, was to work as hard and leave [live] as meanly, I could make more money in Canada than I can here. Since we have been on the River we have worked from half-past two and three o'clock in the morning till nine and ten o'clock at night, (you can see the sun twenty hours out of the twenty-four in the summer season.)—and lived on beans! If that is not working, I don't know what it is. Besides this you go home to your shanty at night, tired and wet, and have to cook your beans before you can eat them. And what is this all for? For *gold* of course; but when you wash up at night, you may realize 50 cents, perhaps $1.

There have been some rich spots struck on this river, but they were very scarce, and they are all worked out; and the miners are leaving the river every day, satisfied there is nothing to be made. But now that I am in the country I will remain for a year or so, and if nothing better turns up by that time, I think I will be perfectly satisfied. I have met with some that I was acquainted with, and it is amusing to see those who felt themselves a little better than their neighbors at home, come here and get out of money, and have to take the pick and shovel, perhaps to drag firewood out of the woods and sell it, or make pack-mules of themselves to get a living. I do not mean to say that it is so all over the Colony, but it is from one end of Fraser River to the other. I dare anyone to contradict what I say; and I have good reason to believe it is as bad all over the country. I saw a patch of oats here the other day. They were out in head, only four inches in height, yellow as ochre, and *not thick enough on the ground to be neighbours*. Vegetables and other things are as poor in the proportion; and as for the climate, it is just as changeable as in Canada, if not more so. I can't say much about the climate on Vancouver's Island, but I think it is rather better.

I met T.G., the carpenter, from Sarnia, who left there about a year ago. He went round the Horn, and he was ten months and fifteen days in coming here. He is cutting saw logs making a little over grub. He says he is going to write to the Sarnia *Observer*, and give this place a cutting up! There are a great many Canadians here, and they would be glad to work for their board. A man could not hire out to work a day if he was starving. I have seen some parties from California; they say times are very hard there. There are just three in our party now, H.H., J.R., and myself. There were two of the H's; one was taken sick and had to leave the river; he is in Victoria, and is quite recovered again; has been there two months, and has not got a day's work yet. I was very sick myself when I just came here, but am quite healthy now, and so fat I can hardly see to write. The rest are quite well.

The Indians are not very troublesome at the mines; they are kept down pretty well. They are very numerous here and on the Island, the lowest degraded set of creatures I ever saw.

It is estimated that the number of miners who make over wages, is one in five hundred; and the number that do well in the mines is one in a thousand. So you see it is a very small proportion. If you know anyone that wants to spend money, why, this is just the place. Anyone bringing a family here would require a small fortune to support them in this horrible place, hemmed in by mountains on all sides, and these covered with snow all the year.

I have lived in a tent since I came up the river, and I have to lie on the ground before the fire and write; it gives a very poor light, so excuse the writing. It has been raining here steady one week, and the mountains are all covered with snow; for when it rains here it is snowing upon the mountains. It is a wild looking place. You will please tell our folks you hear from me, and that we are all well. I will write to some of them in about two weeks or so. I have wrote five letters already, but I have not heard from any of them; so many letters go astray in coming here and going from this place, that perhaps they do not get them at all. Give my respects to old friends, and tell them to be contented and stay at home.

I remain, yours truly
CHARLES MAJOR.

---

2 From John Palliser, *Journals, Detailed Reports and Observations Relative to the Exploration, by Captain Palliser* (London: Eyre & Spottiswood, 1863), 7, 10–11, 16–18.

The existence of a general law regulating the distribution of the woods in this portion of the continent suggested itself to us during our first summer's explorations, and subsequent experience during the seasons of 1858–9 fully confirmed it.

The fertile savannahs and valuable woodlands of the Atlantic United States are succeeded, as has been previously alluded to, on the west by a more or less arid desert, occupying a region on both sides of the Rocky Mountains, which presents a barrier to the continuous growth of settlements between the Mississippi Valley and the States on the Pacific coast. This central desert extends, however, but a short way into the British territory, forming a triangle, having for its base the 49th parallel from longitude 100° to 114° W., with its apex reaching to the 52nd parallel of latitude.

The northern forests, which in former times descended more nearly to the frontier of this central desert, have been greatly encroached upon and, as it were, pushed backwards to the north through the effect of frequent fires.

Thus a large portion of fertile country, denuded of timber, separates the arid region from the forest lands to the north, and the habit which the Indian tribes have of burning the vegetation has, in fact, gradually improved the country for the purpose of settlement by clearing off the heavy timber, to remove which is generally the first and most arduous labour of the colonist.

The richness of the natural pasture in many places on the prairies of the second level along the North Saskatchewan and its tributary, Battle River, can hardly be exaggerated. Its value does not consist in its being rank or in great quantity, but from its fine quality, comprising nutritious species of grasses and carices, along with natural vetches in great variety, which remain throughout the winter sound, juicy, and fit for the nourishment of stock.

Almost everywhere along the course of the North Saskatchewan are to be found simply, it would be natural to infer their existence along the whole line where the Rocky Mountains run parallel and retain their altitude; but the dry areas are evidently due to other causes primarily, and they are not found above the 47th parallel in fact. It is decisive of the general question of sufficiency of rain to find the entire surface of the upper plains either well grassed or well wooded, and recent information on these points almost warrants the assertion that there are no barren tracts of consequence after we pass the Bad Lands, and the *Coteaus* of the Missouri. Many portions of these plains are known to be peculiarly rich in grasses, and probably the finest tracts lie along the eastern base of the mountains, in positions corresponding to the most desert-like of the plains at the south. The higher latitudes certainly differ widely from the plains which stretch from the Platte southward to the Llano Estacado of Texas, and none of the references made to them by residents or travellers indicate desert characteristics. Buffalo are far more abundant on the northern plains, and they remain through the winter at their extreme border, taking shelter in the belts of woodland on the upper Athabasca and Peace rivers. Grassy savannas like these necessarily imply an adequate supply of rain, and there can be no doubt that the correspondence with the European plains in like geographical position—those of eastern Germany and Russia—is quite complete in this respect. If a difference exists it is in favor of the American plains, which have a greater proportion of surface waters, both as lakes and rivers.

Historical Interpretations

3   From Adele Perry, "Hardy Backwoodsmen, Wholesome Women, and Steady Families: Immigration and the Construction of a White Society in Colonial British Columbia, 1849–1871," *Histoire sociale/Social History* 33, 66 (2000): 343–60. (Modified/shortened)

Who was in and who was out? One of the primary ways in which mid-nineteenth-century British Columbians negotiated inclusions and exclusions was through the practice and discourse of immigration. Immigration derived its social and political significance from its double ability to dispossess local peoples and establish a settler-society in their stead. The settler society this process sought to build was explicitly racialized and deeply gendered. In seeking "hardy backwoodsmen," colonial promoters encouraged men committed to hard work, steadiness, and rural life; in demanding "wholesome women," they sought women who would simultaneously serve as beacons of imperial society and constrain the excesses of white men; in courting "steady families," they pursued stable units that would exemplify the virtues of the same-race, nuclear family. Together, "hardy backwoodsmen, wholesome women and steady families" were constructed as the immigrants able to transform British Columbia into the stable settler society of imperialists' dreams.

Studies of the flow of people between Europe and the Americas in the "Great Migration Era" have tended to leave a blind spot, namely their disinterest in interrogating the politicized character of nineteenth-century "new world" migration.[1] When people left Europe for the Americas or Australia, they did not simply move into large, empty spaces. Instead, they participated in a process of colonization in which Aboriginal dispossession and settler migration were irreparably linked. As Daiva Staisulis and Nira Yuval-Davis argue, migration is one of the chief ways in which settler societies constitute themselves.[2] For individuals and families, migration was probably motivated primarily by straightforward social and economic needs, but the overarching structure of imperialism transformed these needs into imperial acts.[3] Immigration sometimes troubled and sometimes nourished the politics of empire. In either case, it cannot be separated from them.

[. . .]

Acknowledging these ties is crucial to understanding white settler colonies like British Columbia. The significance of immigration in colonial contexts derives from its central position in the very business of imperialism. Settler societies aim simultaneously to dispossess Aboriginal peoples and to replace them with relatively homogeneous settler populations, and immigration is one of the tools that has allowed them to do so. Colonies of settlement are distinguished from other kinds of colonies chiefly by their reproductive and gendered character. That colonizers *settle* implies more than residence. It denotes a reproductive regime dependent on the presence of settler women who literally reproduce the colony. Immigration must therefore provide more than non-Aboriginal bodies. Ideally, it must provide the right kind of bodies, those suited to building a white settler colony.

These connections between immigration, empire, and gender came together in mid-nineteenth-century British Columbia in an especially revealing way. Its society was the product of three sometimes conflicting imperial intentions: the fur trade, the gold rush, and the British tradition of settler colonies. North America's northern Pacific coast and the Columbia Plateau were densely populated by linguistically, culturally, and politically diverse First Nations people reliant on foraging, hunting, and fishing. The Hudson's Bay Company (HBC) began trading with local peoples in the late eighteenth century, and formal colonial authority was established in 1849 when Vancouver Island was made a British colony.

The discovery of gold on the mainland's Fraser River in 1858 precipitated the creation of a mainland colony called British Columbia. It was, according to imperial opinion, destined to be a major colony of settlement.

"[N]ever did a colony in its infancy present a more satisfactory appearance," remarked one Anglican cleric. By 1866 and 1867, however, "those who once entertained most extravagant expectations began to despond."[4] Imperial downsizing followed despondency. In 1866 the two colonies were merged, retaining the name of British Columbia, and in July 1871 British Columbia joined Canada as a province, bringing the colonial period to a close.

These shifts in political form reflected widespread disappointment in British Columbia's performance as a settler colony. "The high tide of immigration expected never reached the Colony," explained Governor Frederick Seymour, "and the ebb proved much stronger than anticipated."[5] To be sure, the population expanded: there were fewer than 1000 settlers in 1855 and over 10 000 in 1871. But the settler population never rivalled the Aboriginal one, which, despite massive depopulation wrought by smallpox, likely hovered around the 45 000 mark in the early 1870s.[6]

Settler British Columbia did not grow as quickly as imperial observers hoped it would, nor did it grow in the way they had hoped. The periphery, like the metropole, defied pretences of ethnic and racial homogeneity.[7] For a supposed white settler colony, British Columbia was not very white: Chinese, African-American, Latino, and Kanaka (Hawaiian) settlers were a significant presence. Jews and continental Europeans pressed operative definitions of whiteness, and Americans unsettled the colony's claims to Britishness. In 1861 the local official for Douglas, a small gold-rush town on the mainland, enumerated 97 Chinese, 40 Americans, 20 Mexicans, 17 Europeans, and 6 "coloured" people. They dwelled amongst "About 700 Natives."[8] "It would have been difficult to find in one place a greater mixture of different nationalities," wrote German mathematician Carl Friesach after visiting Yale, another small mining town. "Americans were undoubtably [sic] in the majority—California, especially had sent a large contingent. Then followed Germans, French, and Chinese. Next came Italians, Spaniards, Poles, etc," he noted.[9]

[. . .] The diversity fostered by the gold rushes of the early colonial days diminished but never disappeared. When British Columbia entered Canadian confederation in 1871, its settler society was constituted, according to one probably conservative count, by 8576 whites, 1548 Chinese, and 462 Africans.[10]

That British Columbia's settlers were overwhelmingly male further suggested its failure to fit the norms of a white settler colony. While the female proportion ebbed and flowed over the colonial period, it never exceeded a high of 35 per cent of the white society and reached lows of 5 per cent.[11] Imperial discourse that accorded white women a special role as harbingers of empire rendered this demographic problem a political one. A popular emigration guide by "A Returned Digger," like so many others, despaired of what to do with a society so lacking in women. "The great curse of the colony," he explained, is the absence of women. I doubt if there was one woman to a hundred men twelve months ago. I am quite sure that now, when I am writing, there must be at least two hundred men to every woman."[12] In colonial discourse, the continuing demographic dominance of First Nations people, the plurality of settler society, and its prevailing masculinity became irreparably intertwined, a three-part symbol of British Columbia's departure from dominant social norms and expectations.

Colonial promoters—a term I apply to a loose collection of journalists, politicians, officials, missionaries, and self-appointed do-gooders—looked to immigration to address the smallness, diversity, and masculinity of settler British Columbia and to render it a prosperous and respectable settler colony. They attributed the colony's lamentable imperial performance to the sparseness of its settler society. The *British Columbian* newspaper argued that the colony's poor showing stemmed from its under-population, "because we have only a mere handful of population, a few thousand people living upon one another."[13] The colony lacked white population of nearly every description. The Victoria press noted,

> If we enter our churches, they want worshippers; our school houses want scholars; our streets and highways want pedestrians and vehicles; our merchants want trade; our traders want customers; our steamboats want passengers and freight; our workshops want workmen; our fertile valleys want farmers; our gold and silver mines want miners; in short, the two Colonies want population.[14]

While the colony had resources, wrote the *Cariboo Sentinel*, "without a population a country may remain forever a barren wilderness, dotted here and there with a few fisherman's huts and a few miners' and lumberman's cabins, and known only to the world as an inhospitable and poverty-stricken place."[15]

If colonial promoters suggested that British Columbia's ills stemmed from the sparseness of the white population, they had a related and almost boundless faith in the political potential of white bodies to make it a successful colonial enterprise. Even the most shameless boosters, however, recognized that British Columbia's distance from centres of white population meant that active state intervention was required for mass immigration to occur. If they wanted a white population, they would have to work for it, bidding it to come hither, assisting its passage, and supporting it on arrival. "To have our country filled up we must not only assist people to reach our shores, but we must show them the way to earn a living after they get here," wrote the *Colonist* in 1866.[16] The intervention of both the local and colonial state was required. "What right has the most remote of the British Colonies to expect immigration without even *asking for it*," agreed the New Westminster press, "to say nothing of *assisting* it?"[17]

Colonial promoters' demands for immigration were part and parcel of a program of asserting white supremacy in British Columbia. Himani Bannerji has recently dubbed immigration a "euphemistic expression for racist labour and citizenship policies."[18] In colonial British Columbia the process worked to exclude First Nations migrants and to minimize non-white settlers. It was difficult, although hardly impossible, to argue for the removal of First Nations with local and obvious territorial claims. Those from distant territories were easy targets for settlers committed to visions of racial segregation. The city of Victoria worked hard to control and limit the presence of the so-called Northern Tribes—people from the coastal societies of the Nisga'a, Hieltsuk, Nexalk, Kwakwaka'wakw, Tlingit, and especially the wealthy and politically powerful Haida and Tsimshian—who made annual spring visits to Victoria for trade, wage work, and festivity. In 1859 a police constable found 2235 Northern peoples, the bulk of them probably Haida and Tsimshian, living on the outskirts of Victoria.[19] As annually as they arrived, local burghers demanded their eviction. The language they used to stigmatize Northern peoples invoked the overlapping discourses of morality, criminality, and gender that have often been used to identify and marginalize immigrant groups. "Vagrancy, filth, disease, drunkenness, larceny, maiming, murder, prostitution, in a multiplied form, are the invariable results of an annual visit from the Northern Tribes," raged the *Colonist*. "We unhesitantly declare for stopping the immigration."[20]

Those who defended the rights of Northern peoples to visit Victoria—and, by implication, their status as legitimate immigrants and thus colonial citizens—relied on another staple of immigration discourse, namely the argument that the Northern peoples' presence, however unpalatable, was sweetened by their cheap labour. When settlers demanded that Northern peoples be forcibly evicted, missionary William Duncan argued that "the driving-away policy is contrary to the interests of our Colony, which needs at least the labor of the Indians." He referred those who doubted the local need for Aboriginal labour to "the kitchens and nurseries, the fields and gardens around Victoria."[21] Governor James Douglas proposed schemes of moral and social regulation as an alternative to eviction, arguing that Northern peoples' willingness to serve as a colonial labour force made them valuable to whites. "[I]t is hardly creditable to the civilization of the nineteenth century, that so especial an element of health, as labour of the cheapest description, should be, in a manner, banished from the Colony," he explained.[22]

The sweat and toil of the Northern peoples ultimately failed to buy them a legitimate role in settler Victoria. Those who wanted racial segregation of colonial space were bolstered and legitimated by the apocalyptic smallpox epidemic of 1862, when Northern peoples were repeatedly and forcibly evicted from Victoria, a process later condoned and organized by public health legislation.[23] A brand of settler imperialism premised on the removal and containment of local peoples ultimately won out over the version that positioned them as subservient labourers for the ruling minority. [. . .]

That this process worked to include whites and exclude others is confirmed by the experience of settlers of Asian and African extraction. Douglas—himself an archetypal hybrid figure, hailing from a "creole" mother and a Scottish father and having married the half-Cree Amelia Connolly—encouraged the migration of mainly middle-class African-Americans associated with the Pioneer Society of San Francisco in 1858. Other settlers did not share his enthusiasm. Despite the African-Americans' apparent fit with the colony's putative values of hard work, Protestantism, and respectability, their sizable presence in Victoria was regarded by many white people as a problem. Whether Victoria would replicate or challenge American-style segregation in her churches, theatres, and saloons was a significant item of debate until the black population began to disperse in the mid-1860s.[24]

It was Chinese immigration that created the most ambivalence among British Columbia's white commentators. Representations of Chinese men celebrated industriousness and sometimes located them on the colonists' side of the local imperial divide. The Grand Jury of Cayoosh (later Lillooet) told the governor in 1860 that Chinese settlers were a benefit to white traders and the government alike. The jury further requested that the state acknowledge the Chinese as settlers, asking that they "afford them every due protection to prevent their being driven away, wither by attacks from Indians or otherwise."[25]

More often Chinese men were positioned as undesirable immigrants who would imperil rather than bolster colonialism. The *Cariboo Sentinel* argued that Chinese men should not be colonists for a variety of reasons, all indicating their fundamental difference and many invoking explicitly gendered images. The Chinese, the newspaper argued, were "aliens not merely in nationality, but in habits, religion"; they never became "good citizens" or served on juries or fire companies; they never married or settled outside China and were "more apt to create immorality than otherwise"; they dealt "entirely with their own countrymen"; they hoarded their money and evaded taxes; and, lastly, they were, ironically for immigrants, "inimical to immigration."[26] No restrictions were imposed on Chinese immigration, although colonists debated ways—prominent among them being a miner's licence fee levied on Chinese men alone—designed to regulate their place within settler society.[27] Such discussions anticipated the highly organized, pervasive, and vociferous attacks on Chinese people

that began later in the nineteenth century and continue to shape contemporary life and politics.[28]

The role of immigration to colonial British Columbia was thus an explicitly racial one. The "'bone, muscle, and intellect,' that is required here," explained the Victoria press plainly, "differs materially from the Indian or the African. It is Caucasian—Anglo-Saxon bone, muscle, and intellect we want."[29] Class, and the politics of respectability that so often went with it, also helped determine who would be included and who excluded. Not all white people were created equal. British Columbia's colonial promoters did not want convicts, although one, tellingly, was willing to tolerate juvenile offenders as long as they were placed on First Nations settlements.[30] When the Colonial Office inquired about the emigration of distressed Lancashire mill operatives, local officials were similarly unreceptive. Douglas replied that "this Colony offers but a poor field for destitute immigrants," warning that "instead of improving their condition, it is to be feared, that by emigrating in great numbers to this Colony, they would only be involved in a more hopeless state of distress and poverty."[31] British Columbia's officials were ultimately as fearful of organized immigration's class implications—of the shovelling out of paupers—as were others in British North America.

Immigration to this settler colony was an issue of race and class, and also very much one of gender. British Columbia's colonial failure was linked, in critics' minds, not only to the smallness and diversity of the settler society but also to the failure of increasingly hegemonic gender norms to take root there. British Columbia was home to a small, highly mobile handful of settler men living amongst a large Aboriginal society. This particular demography fostered a rough, vibrant homosocial culture created by and for young men and the widespread practice of white-Aboriginal domestic and conjugal relationships. Immigration was sought as a corrective for both.

When promoters called for immigration, they called for a process that would address the society's perceived gendered deficiencies as well as its racial peculiarities.

Three gendered images dominated discussions of immigration. First, the hardy backwoodsman—a steady, hard-working man willing to meet the difficulties of colonial life and permanently settle in British Columbia—shaped discussions of men and migration. The hypothetical hardy backwoodsman was constructed in contrast to the rough gold miners who so pervaded the colony. British Columbia had two major gold rushes—the Fraser River Gold Rush of 1858 and the Cariboo Gold Rush of 1862–1863—and a host of smaller ones. Waves of young, footloose men disillusioned with the false promises of capitalist, industrial society were attracted by each strike of gold. Prevailing discourse understood these men as wandering, immoral, and anti-social. [. . .]

Miners' inadequacies as colonists became axiomatic in popular colonial discourse. [. . .] For British Columbia to fulfill its imperial potential, hardy backwoodsmen would have to replace the wandering miners. In 1859 Douglas told the Colonial Office, "The mining population are proverbially migratory and unsettled in their habits, seldom engaging in any other than their own absorbing pursuits, and therefore, it is he who tills the soil, the industrious farmer, who must clear the forest, bring the land into cultivation, and build up the permanent interests and prosperity of the Colony."[32]

The hardy backwoodsman stood in contrast not only to the wandering miner, but to another masculine drain on the colonial enterprise, the "croaker." This term, along with grumbler, was applied to men deemed unable to weather the difficulties of colonial life. Whether an erstwhile son of wealth or an urban loafer, the croaker was flummoxed by the realities of pioneering and proceeded to complain instead of work. Gilbert Malcolm Sproat, a sawmill owner, magistrate, amateur anthropologist, and promoter of immigration, described the croakers:

[C]ertain persons came into the country who had a strong desire to make a living without taking off their coats—a desire which could not be gratified. The friends of these persons at home sent them money, which they put into silly investments. They rode to the diggings, and road [sic] back again. They hung, like mendicants, round the doors of the Government offices. They croaked in the streets, spent their time idly in bar-rooms, and finally disappeared.[33]

Here, the language of class is put to work in the service of gender and race: the croaker is idle and delicate, bearing the mark of both femininity and bourgeois laxity. [. . .]

Just as they repelled the weak, colonies were thought to attract the most manly of British men who stood in contrast not only to their less rugged fellows, but to the Indigenous men they alternately feminized or feared.[34] "As a rule," commented the local press, "it is the most energetic, hardy, manly, self-reliant of her sons who first people her Colonies."[35] Ideal male immigrants were hard-working, disciplined, and predisposed to rural life. The new colony, argued a supporter in 1860, "does not want the idle, the profligate, and sickly."[36] The hardy backwoodsman embraced diligent labour, especially agricultural labour, just as the gold miner rejected it. His single state meant that he was able to devote himself fully to labour, to define himself as an entirely economic being. One much-reprinted emigration guide advised, "A family is a burden till a man is established."[37] [. . .]

Yet single men, hardy or otherwise, constituted an ambivalent force for colonial promoters. Sproat thought that their tendency to wander made them a waste of public funds.[38] More fundamentally, imperial regimes were consistently troubled by the large numbers of working-class men assigned responsibility for practically enforcing them.[39] White soldiers, miners, and farmers frequently failed to meet standards of racial distance and superiority set by imperial masters. Racial concerns about young, footloose men in colonial contexts were also gendered concerns. Colonial promoters were disturbed by how regularly white men formed relationships and families with local women. Settler men who opted to remain single were also a worry. Increasingly in the mid-nineteenth century the domestic family was constructed as a necessary component of adult life. To be rendered a responsible colonial citizen who was appropriately distanced from local peoples, the hardy backwoodsman needed a wholesome woman.

The scarcity of white women in British Columbia became, along with the smallness of the settler population, axiomatic for the colony's condition. As I have argued elsewhere, white women were constructed as "fair ones of a purer caste"[40] with three related roles in the local colonial project. White women would first compel white men to reject the rough homosocial culture of the backwoods in favour of normative standards of masculinity, respectability, and permanence. "Women! women! women! are the great want," wrote aristocrat Harry Verney from London. "The normal state is man with a help meet for him, and if something is not soon done, either by the Imperial or Colonial Government, or by some philanthropists at home, I know not what will become of us. Poor man goes sadly down hill if he remains long without the supporting influence of women."[41] White women were considered to be men's collective better half, as the only force capable of ensuring their proper behaviour. Such a discourse accorded them a role, albeit a limited one, as agents in both imperialism and immigration.

White women would secondly address shortages in the local labour market and relieve overpopulation in Britain. That the supposed need for domestic servants and wives in British Columbia neatly matched fears of "surplus women" in Britain gave calls for female immigration a special efficacy. A female immigration to British Columbia, wrote one observer, "would be as great a boon to the colony as I am sure it would be to many of the underpaid, under-fed, and over-worked women who drag out a weary existence in the dismal back streets and alleys of the metropolis."[42] Immigration was thus invoked as a mechanism for simultaneously resolving the different crises of gender that troubled the metropole and the periphery.

White women's third service to the colonial project was the explicitly racial one of discouraging mixed-race sexual, domestic, and conjugal relationships. As white men's "natural" objects of desire, they would draw men away from the temptations of Aboriginal women and, in doing so, shore up the colonial project as a whole. "That many of the native women are cleanly, industrious, and faithful, we do not pretend to deny," wrote New Westminster's *Mainland Guardian*, "but, we regret to to [sic] say, they are the exceptions. With the increase of our white female population, we look for new life in our agricultural pursuits and we hope that every inducement will be offered to healthy industrious women, who are desirous of finding good husbands and comfortable homes, in this province, to come out to us."[43] This discourse was premised on the construction of white women as uplifting and on the representation of First Nations women as base and threatening that circulated throughout colonial British Columbia.

In these ways, the discourse of wholesome women emphasized the political utility of ordinary, working-class women above those who held an official role in the colonial project like missionaries' or officials' wives. Their contribution lay not in independent action, but rather in their ability to transform plebeian men. Such a discourse imbued women migrants with an agency less often acknowledged in historiography. At any rate, the sheer ideological weight of the conviction that a society lacking white women could not be a moral or even adequate one provided the motivation necessary to orchestrate immigration schemes in 1862, 1863, and 1870. Organized as joint efforts of the local elite, missionaries, and British feminists, these immigration campaigns are remembered in popular lore as the "brideships," as colony-(and, later, nation-) building enterprises. Together, the *Tynemouth*, *Robert Lowe*, and *Alpha* carried roughly a hundred women, largely teenagers from working-class and sometimes indigent backgrounds. They were putatively destined to be domestic servants, but popular discourse ensured that their real destiny lay in the marriage market. As wives of miners and farmers, colonial promoters hoped, these wholesome women would render British Columbia's fragile colonial project a stable one.[44]

The young working-class women produced by these female immigration schemes ultimately unsettled the colonial project rather than securing it. Instead of behaving as beacons of imperial rectitude, the immigrants acted like the young, working-class women that they were. Colonial promoters were deeply disappointed. By the close of the colonial period, their faith in the political usefulness of white female migration was profoundly shaken. In 1872 Sproat looked back on his experience with three separate female immigration efforts, commenting, "How to send single women to Victoria safely across the continent, and through San Francisco, is a problem which I cheerfully hand over for solution to those who are more experienced in the management of that sex than I am."[45] The fundamental problem with white female migration, he argued, was that *single* women were necessarily a moral problem. "The very delicate and difficult question of introducing single unmarried women into British Columbia might be partly solved by sending out a few, in charge of the heads of families—the women being from the same district as the families, and thus having an addition[al] guard for their self-respect," he argued.[46]

Wholesome women, much like hardy backwoodsmen, challenged the colonial project at the same time as they bolstered it. The enthusiasm for white female migration was always tempered and eventually overwhelmed by the conviction that single women, like men, were a dangerous population that could only be properly contained by families. After the disasters of the assisted female migration efforts of 1862 and 1863, the "steady family" gained a special cachet in pro-immigration discourse that would only increase after the 20 servant-women transported on the *Alpha* in 1870 proved, like their predecessors, a disappointment to those who so sought their importation. The Female Immigration Board that oversaw this scheme recommended that the colonial government abandon the project of female immigration and shift its monies and attentions to the "assisted passages of Families, and relatives of Farmers, Mechanics, and others settled in this Colony."[47] In pledging their support for the importation of families, and not single women, members of the board endorsed the stable family as the best kind of immigration for the colony.

They were not alone in suggesting that same-race domestic families would be the best base for a settler society and thus the best immigrants. Families simultaneously constrained young women and encouraged men to be permanent and diligent settlers. The *Victoria Press* argued, "The very class which we want above all others is the married agriculturist—the man whose social circumstances will bring him to the soil, and make him a permanent as well as productive inhabitant."[48] Sproat agreed, writing that "the married farmer with modest means, and accustomed to work in the fields, is the best kind of immigrant for British Columbia."[49] The HBC supported family migration when it imported 36 married colliers to work Nanaimo's coalfields.[50] That the Colonial Office shared this familial ideal is suggested by its willingness to pay for the passage of the wives and families of the Royal Engineers, the soldier-settlers sent to enforce British claims to the mainland.[51] On rare occasions the colonial government subsidized the migration of individual families,[52] but more often used land law to buttress domestic family formation. In Vancouver Island, nuclear family formation was encouraged by laws that gave white men an additional 50 acres of free land if they were married and 10 more acres for each child under the age of 10.[53]

The overlap between immigration discourse and immigration practice was usually indirect. These demands for hardy backwoodsmen, wholesome women, and steady families were rarely parlayed into concrete action. Immigration was what colonial pundits always wanted and never got. In referring to immigrants as "mythical beings," politician John Sebastian Helmcken astutely recognized the somewhat hypnotic role immigration played in colonial discourse.[54] The mythic rather than actual character of immigration to colonial British Columbia was not for lack of heated rhetoric or wild scheming. Colonial promoters held mass meetings, struck committees, wrote passionate letters, and developed plans for using immigration to secure their imperial fortunes.[55] With the exception of the 20 servant women carried on the *Alpha* in 1870, however, the colonial government's immigration efforts were largely confined to the cheap and discursive: they subsidized mail, explored territory, printed essays, and hired lecturers to regale the masses of various urban centres. In 1861, for instance, British Columbia created an exhibit for the World's Fair designed to prove to "struggling, hard worked Englishmen how easily a livelihood may be earned here."[56]

The modesty of these efforts deeply disappointed those who considered immigration key to imperial success. They complained bitterly about the local government's apparent inability to organize immigration. In 1864 the mainland press commented that, excepting "fifty pounds paid to a parson at Lillooet for an Essay," the colony had "not yet expended a single dollar" on immigration.[57] Five years later, the same newspaper despaired that there was not one person responsible for immigration "[a]mongst the army of officials who absorb the revenue of the Colony."[58]

If British Columbia's local government was unable, its imperial masters were unwilling. The Colonial Office argued that, given its location, British Columbia could only reasonably expect emigrants from the Australasian colonies, not from Britain, and repeatedly announced that it had no intention of ever assisting emigration to the colony.[59] When pestered to subsidize steam communication, Colonial Office staff made it clear that they lacked the requisite political will. "When this Country was supposed to be over-peopled, there was the appearance of a domestic object in schemes for using the proceeds of English taxes to encourage emigration. But that state of things has long ceased to exist," one noted.[60] Domestic issues like overpopulation fuelled the various assisted emigration schemes of the 1830s and 1840s and would again motivate major emigration schemes in the *fin de siècle*. These efforts ground to a near halt when popular economic fortunes bettered and events like New Zealand's Maori Wars and the Indian Rebellion of 1857 challenged British faith in the imperial project.

Whether in London, Victoria, or New Westminster, many doubted British Columbia's ability to attract settlers, but only a few challenged its need for a large white population. [. . .] Ultimately, British Columbia's apparent inability to attract white and especially British immigrants served not as a reason for challenging the viability of colonialism, but rather as a rationale for the colony's entry into Canadian confederation.[61] If British Columbia could not use immigration to become a stable settler colony in its own right, it would try to do so as a Canadian province. That British Columbia finally registered a white majority in the first census taken after Confederation suggests that this strategy was effective. With continuing depopulation of First Nations and the arrival of the transcontinental railroad in 1886—that tangible technology of both capital and nation and conveyor of migrants *par excellence*—British Columbia would begin to look increasingly like a textbook white settler colony, but it would continue to be haunted by a spectre of hybridity that was, in the final analysis, more nurtured by immigration than vanquished by it.

[. . .]

NOTES

1. See, for instance, Bernard Bailyn, *The Peopling of British North America: An Introduction* (New York: Knopf, 1986). For a revealing example, see the explicit definition of Ontario's Leeds and Landsdowne townships as "empty" in Donald Harman Akenson, *The Irish in Ontario: A Study in Rural History* (Montreal and Kingston: McGill-Queen's University Press, 1984), 55.

2. Daiva Staisulis and Nira Yuval-Davis, "Introduction: Beyond Dichotomies . Gender, Race, Ethnicity and Class in Settler Societies," in Staisulis and Yuval-Davis, eds, *Unsettling Settler Societies: Articulations of Gender, Race, Ethnicity and Class* (London: Sage, 1995).

3. On this point in a later period, see Stephen Constantine, "Introduction: Empire Migration and Imperial Harmony," in Constantine, ed., *Emigrants and Empire: British Settlement in the Dominions Between the Wars* (Manchester: Manchester University Press, 1990). See also Rita S. Kranidis, ed., *Imperial Objects: Essays on Victorian Women's Emigration and the Unauthorized Imperial Experience* (New York: Twayne, 1998).

4. Henry Wright, *Nineteenth Annual Report of the Missions of the Church of England in British Columbia for the Year 1877* (London: Rivingtons, 1878), 16–17.

5. British Columbia Archives (hereafter BCA), GR 1486, mflm B–1442, Great Britain, Colonial Office, British Columbia Original Correspondence (hereafter CO 60), CO 60/32, Frederick Seymour to Duke of Buckingham and Chandos, 17 March 1868.

6. All population figures from colonial British Columbia are at best guesses. These are from British Columbia, *Report of the Hon. H. L. Langevin, C.B., Minister of Public Works* (Ottawa: I.B. Taylor, 1872), 22; and Edward Mallandaine, *First Victoria Directory, Third [Fourth] Issues, and British Columbia Guide* (Victoria: Mallandaine,

1871), 94–5. Also see R. Cole Harris and John Warkentin, *Canada before Confederation: A Study in Historical Geography* (Ottawa: Carleton University Press, 1991), chap. 7.

7. Antoinette Burton, *At the Heart of Empire: Indians and the Colonial Encounter in Late-Victorian Britain* (Berkeley: University of California Press, 1998).

8. BCA, "Colonial Correspondence," GR 1372, mflm B–1330, file 620/16, John Bowles Gaggin to W.A.G. Young, 3 April 1861.

9. Carl Friesach, "Extracts from *Ein Ausflug nach Britisch-Columbien im Jahre 1858*," in E.E. Delavault and Isabel McInnes, trans., "Two Narratives of the Fraser River Gold Rush," *British Columbia Historical Quarterly* 1 (July 1941): 227.

10. British Columbia, *Report of the Hon. H. L. Langevin*, p. 22.

11. On this, see Adele Perry, *On the Edge of Empire: Gender, Race, and the Making of British Columbia, 1849–1871* (Toronto: University of Toronto Press, 2000), chap. 1.

12. A Returned Digger, *The Newly Discovered Gold Fields of British Columbia* (London: Darton and Hodge, 1862, 8th edn), 7.

13. "Our Great Want," *British Columbian*, 9 January 1869.

14. "Our Wants," *British Colonist*, 5 June 1861.

15. "Emigration," *Cariboo Sentinel*, 18 June 1868.

16. "Assisted Immigration," *British Colonist*, 11 December 1866.

17. "Population, Population," *British Columbian*, 29 May 1869.

18. Himani Bannerji, *On the Dark Side of the Nation: Essays on Multiculturalism, Nationalism and Gender* (Toronto: Canadian Scholars. Press, 2000), 4.

19. "Our Indian Population," *Weekly Victoria Gazette*, 28 April 1859.

20. "Invasion of the Northern Indians," *British Colonist*, 18 April 1861.

21. Wm. Duncan, "The Indian Question," *British Colonist*, 4 July 1861. On Aboriginal wage labour, see John Lutz, "After the Fur Trade: Aboriginal Wage Labour in Nineteenth-Century British Columbia," *Journal of the Canadian Historical Association* (1992): 69–94.

22. National Archives of Canada (hereafter NAC), Great Britain, Colonial Office Correspondence, Vancouver Island (hereafter CO 305), CO 305/10, mflm B–238, James Douglas to Sir Edward Bulwer Lytton, 25 May 1859.

23. See Perry, *On the Edge*, chap. 5.

24. For an argument for black migration to Vancouver Island, see Mary A. Shadd, *A Plea for Emigration; or, Notes of Canada West, in its Moral, Social, and Political Aspect With Suggestions Respecting Mexico, West Indies, and Vancouver's Island, for the Information of Colored Emigrants* (Detroit: George W. Pattison, 1842), pp. 43–44. On black people in Victorian society, see Irene Genevieve Marie Zaffaroni, The Great Chain of Being: Racism and Imperialism in Colonial Victoria, 1858–1871. (MA thesis, University of Victoria, 1987), chap. 4; Crawford Killian, *Go Do Some Great Thing: The Black Pioneers of British Columbia* (Vancouver: Douglas and McIntyre, 1978).

25. NAC, CO 60/8, MG 11, mflm B–83, "Address of the Grand Jury at Cayoosh to Governor Douglas," in James Douglas to Duke of Newcastle, 9 October 1860.

26. "Our Chinese Population," *Cariboo Sentinel*, 16 May 1867.

27. See, for an explanation of why they were impracticable, NAC, CO 63/3, mflm B–1489, "Speech of His Honor the Officer Administering the Government at the Opening of the Legislative Council," *British Columbia Government Gazette*.

28. On this, see Kay Anderson, *Vancouver's Chinatown: Racial Discourse in Canada, 1875–1980* (Montreal and Kingston: McGill-Queen's University Press, 1991); Patricia E. Roy, *A White Man's Province: British Columbia Politicians and Chinese and Japanese Immigrants, 1858–1914* (Vancouver: University of British Columbia Press, 1989).

29. "Indian vs. White Labor," *British Colonist*, 19 February 1861.

30. "Convict Labor," *British Columbian*, 11 January 1865; "Juvenile Offenders—Colonization," *British Columbian*, 30 May 1869.

31. NAC, CO 305/20, MG 11, mflm B–244, and CO 60/16, MG 11, mflm B–89, James Douglas to the Duke of Newcastle, 14 July 1863.

32. NAC, CO 60/4, MG 11, mflm B–80, James Douglas to Edward Bulwer Lytton, 11 July 1859.

33. Gilbert Malcolm Sproat, *British Columbia: Information for Emigrants* (London: Agent General for the Province, 1873), 4.

34. On masculinity and colonization, see Mrinalini Sinha, *Colonial Masculinity: The "Manly Englishman" and the "Effeminate Bengali" in the Late Nineteenth Century* (Manchester: Manchester University Press, 1995); Elizabeth Vibert, *Traders' Tales: Narratives of Cultural Encounters on the Plateau, 1807–1846* (Norman: University of Oklahoma Press, 1997).

35. "The Colonial Policy of Great Britain," *British Colonist*, 2 May 1863.

36. "Testimonial to D. G. F. MacDonald, Esq., C.E.," *Weekly Victoria Gazette*, 30 January 1860.

37. A Returned Digger, *The Newly Discovered Gold Fields*, p. 8.

38. BCA, Add Mss 257, file 3, Gilbert Malcolm Sproat to Lieutenant Governor, "Memo re European Immigration into B.C.," 3 November 1871.

39. See, for instance, Kenneth Ballhatchet, *Race, Sex and Class under the Raj: Imperial Attitudes and Policies and their Critics, 1783–1905* (London: Werdenfeld and Nicholson, 1980), chap. 5.

40. One of the Disappointed, untitled piece in the *British Columbian*, 7 June 1862; Adele Perry, "'Fair Ones of a Purer Caste': White Women and Colonialism in Nineteenth-Century British Columbia," *Feminist Studies* 23, 3 (Fall 1997): 501–24.

41. "Sir Harry Verney Upon British Columbia," *British Columbian*, 20 August 1862.

42. A.D.G., "British Columbia: To the Editor of the Times," *London Times*, 1 January 1862.

43. "Immigration," *Mainland Guardian*, 9 February 1871.

44. See Perry, *On the Edge*, chaps. 6–7, for an analysis of female immigration to British Columbia.

45. BCA, GR 419, box 10, file 1872/1, British Columbia, Attorney General, "Documents," G.M.S., "Memorandum on Immigration, Oct 1972," pp. 95–6.

46. BCA, GR 419, box 10, file 1872/1, "Attorney General Documents," G.M. Sproat, "Memorandum of a few Suggestions for opening the business of emigration to British Columbia, referred to as Memo C, in a letter of G.M. Sproat to the Honourable the Provincial Secretary, dated 29th August 1972," pp. 4–5.

47. BCA, GR 1372, mflm B–1314, file 955/23, "Colonial Correspondence," Wm. Pearse, John Robson, W.J. MacDonald to Colonial Secretary, 12 July 1870; E.G.A., "The Immigration Board," British Colonist, 24 June 1870.

48. "The Overland Route," Victoria Press, 16 March 1862.

49. BCA, GR 419, box 10, file 1872/1, British Columbia, "Papers Related to Immigration, 1972," G.M.S., "Memorandum on Immigration, Oct 1872."

50. BCA, Add mss E/B/M91A, Andrew Muir, "Private Diary," 9 November 1848–5 August 1850 [transcript]; Add Mss A/C/20.1/N15, James Douglas—Joseph William McKay, "Nanaimo Correspondence, August 1852–September 1853" [transcript].

51. NAC, MG 11, CO 60/9, mflm B–83, G.C. Lewis to James Douglas, 11 August 1860, draft reply, in James Douglas to the Duke of Newcastle, 12 May 1860.

52. See, for instance, James E. Hendrickson, ed., Journals of the Colonial Legislatures of the Colonies of Vancouver Island and British Columbia, 1851–1871, vol. 1: Journals of the Council, Executive Council, and Legislative Council of Vancouver Island, 1851–1866 (Victoria: Provincial Archives of British Columbia, 1980), 133–4.

53. "The New Land Proclamation for Vancouver Island," British Colonist, 8 March 1861; "Salt Spring Island," Victoria Press, 10 November 1861; Matthew Macfie, Vancouver Island and British Columbia: Their History, Resources and Prospects (London: Longman, Green, Longman, Roberts & Green, 1865), p. 205.

54. "Legislative Council," British Colonist, 4 February 1869.

55. See examples in Hendrickson, ed., Journals of the Colonial Legislatures, vol. 2: Journals of the House of Assembly, Vancouver Island, 1856–1863, vol. 3: Journals of the House of Assembly, Vancouver Island, 1863–1866, and vol. 4: Journals of the Executive Council, 1864–1871, and of the Legislative Council, 1864–1866, of British Columbia.

56. "Industrial Exhibition Circular," British Columbian, 30 May 1861.

57. "Emigration," British Columbian, 15 June 1864.

58. "What Shall We Do With Them?," British Columbian, 4 June 1869.

59. NAC, MG 11, CO 60/5, mflm B–81, T.W.C. Murdoch and Frederic Rogers to Herman Merivale, April 28, 1859; mflm 69.303, Great Britain, House of Commons, Parliamentary Papers, vol. 38 (1863), no. 430, "Emigration: Number of Emigrants who left the United Kingdom for the United States, British North America, the several colonies of Australasia, South Africa, and other Places respectively; distinguishing, as far as practicable, the Native Country of the Emigrants, 1860–1863," mflm 69-303, p. 7.

60. NAC, MG 11, CO 60/14, mflm B–87, H.M. [Herman Merivale], April 8, note en verso in T.W.C. Murdoch to Frederic Rogers, 31 March 1862.

61. BCA, GR 1486, CO 60/29, mflm B–1440, Frederick Seymour to Duke of Buckingham and Chandos, 24 September 1867.

4

From Tina Loo, "'A Delicate Game': The Meaning of Law on Grouse Creek," *BC Studies* 96 (Winter 1992–93): 41–65. Reprinted with permission from BC Studies.

At the end of June in 1862, 100 miners returning from the Cariboo boarded the steamer *Henrietta* in Douglas for the trip to New Westminster. They refused to pay for their passage, claiming that their misadventures in the upper country gold fields had left them "starving and broken," as well as broke. Despite the obvious illegality of the miners' actions, Douglas magistrate John Boles Gaggin advised the master of *Henrietta* to "take the men on, and on arrival at New Westminster, apply to the proper authorities for redress." Gaggin took this course of action believing, as he told the Colonial Secretary, that

> to attempt coercion with a force unable to command it would have weakened the apparent power of the Law; . . . [and] that the getting of these men out of Douglas was in every way desirable, . . . any attempt to arrest would have provoked a riot, perhaps bloodshed, and I believe I acted prudently in avoiding the least risk of this.[1]

In an effort to further justify his actions, Gaggin closed his report on a defiant note with this telling observation:

> Magistrates in these up country towns have a delicate game to play, and I believe we are all of opinion that to avoid provoking resistance to the Law is the manner in which we best serve the interests of His Excellency, the Governor. . . . [A]s it is the matter passed off without riot and without defiance of the Magistrate, though the Master of the steamer . . . was somewhat annoyed—I shall be very sorry if the cautious way I acted, with such quiet results, does not meet His Excellency's approval, but I acted for the best.[2]

The colonial government chastised the magistrate for his "want of nerve and judgment" in allowing "the occurrence of so lawless a proceeding."[3] "It appears," noted Colonial Secretary W.A.G. Young,

> that you consider yourself vested with discretionary power to temporize with your duties, and that you are unaware that, while rigidly dispensing the laws for the protection of life and property, a

Magistrate may act with perfect temper and discretion.[4]

This brief episode raises questions about the social meaning of the law which I am concerned to address. Gaggin considered law to be the preservation of order—"quiet results"—and told his superiors so. From his vantage point in Victoria, Governor James Douglas saw things rather differently. The law, through its rigid application, served a more particular end by securing life and property. There was yet another perspective. Both Gaggin and Douglas considered the miners' actions "lawless," but those who boarded *Henrietta* likely did not feel the same way. Different people attached different meanings to the law, and when they used the courts to resolve their disputes these differences became apparent. As legal anthropologists argue, courts are forums in which people "bargain for reality;" not only do they dispute the "facts"—what happened—but they also dispute what constitutes legal and just action.[5]

From their arrival, British Columbia's miners possessed a reputation as a self-conscious and vocal interest group with a penchant for self-government which they learned in California's gold fields. Despite their impermanent character, California's gold mining camps developed an elaborate system of informal regulation centred on the Miners' Meetings.[6] These were elected tribunals of local miners who drafted the rules which governed behaviour in a specific locale. Their regulations covered a wide range of activities, from claim size, the technicalities of ditch widths and water rights to the use of alcohol and firearms in the camps.[7] This experience instilled the miners with a taste for local government and a certain degree of independence.[8] It was this independence that made those who streamed northward to British Columbia in 1858 to try their luck in the Fraser and Cariboo rushes so dangerous in the eyes of British colonial administrators like James Douglas and Supreme Court Judge Matthew Baillie

Begbie.[9] These men considered the miners a lawless bunch and took steps to prevent local government from gaining a foothold on the banks of the Fraser River.

In September 1858, just a month after the mainland colony was formed, James Douglas issued the first Gold Fields Act.[10] It and subsequent acts created and elaborated formal government institutions and regulations specifically designed to regulate gold mining.[11] An Assistant Gold Commissioner presided over locally based Gold Commissioner's or Mining Courts. He had jurisdiction to hear all mining or mining-related disputes and to dispose of them summarily. By doing so, the Gold Commissioner's Court allowed suitors to avoid the costly delays associated with Supreme Court actions and jury trials. A locally elected Mining Board replaced the Californian Miners' Meetings, drafting bylaws which governed behaviour. Unlike the American institution they replaced, however, the decisions of the Mining Board could be overturned by the Assistant Gold Commissioner, who also possessed the power to dissolve the board at his pleasure.

Despite the early intrusion of this formal regulatory institution into the gold fields, British Columbia's miners retained a sense of themselves and their enterprise as distinct and crucial to the development of the colony. Despite their impermanent character, gold rush communities were localistic, regardless—paradoxically—of their location.[12] Miners were particularly interested in the administration of the law, watching Mining Court decisions with an eye to their own fortunes. Though the law and the courts brought British Columbia's diverse and far-flung miners together in a common process of dispute settlement, they also were the cause of much division, for they resolved differences by creating other ones. The law defined plaintiffs and defendants, assessed guilt and innocence, and ultimately, in the eyes of those involved, determined right and wrong. The potential for conflict was thus inherent in the process of dispute settlement. As will be seen, different concepts of law stood in bold relief against this structured background of formal dispute resolution.

British Columbians understood and measured their laws with a standard that was rooted in a particular geographic, social, and cultural milieu and that was not always shared by those charged with its administration. Conflicting understandings of what constituted law underlay the disputes which culminated in the Grouse Creek War (1867) and which form the focus of the following narrative.

* * *

The three cases that lay at the centre of the controversy over the colony's judicial administration were all disputes over the ownership of mining claims.[13] Each is rather unremarkable in terms of the issues of fact involved, which consisted of the recording and re-recording of claims and the placement of stakes.[14] Once the cases were appealed to the Supreme Court, however, the issues of fact in these cases became secondary to Supreme Court Judge Matthew Baillie Begbie's actions. The judge's behaviour in the three cases and public reaction to them neatly illustrate the problems associated with administering the law in British Columbia, and adumbrate the limits of formal, institutional dispute settlement.

The first of these, launched in 1865, pitted the Borealis Company against the Watson Company. After the Assistant Gold Commissioner's decision awarding a disputed claim to the Watson Company was upheld by Begbie, the Borealis Company took the case to the Court of Chancery.[15] There, sitting this time as Chancery Court judge, Begbie reversed his earlier decision, and awarded the disputed ground to the Borealis Company! By all accounts, the mining community of the Cariboo was incredulous, and the colony's three main opposition newspapers wasted no time in adding their voices to the growing cries of indignation over Begbie's ruling emanating from the gold fields. Most distressing to British Columbians was the use of the Chancery Court as a court of appeal, a process that was not only expensive and protracted, but was also capricious, because decisions appeared to be unfettered by any reference to statute law. "The late decision in the Borealis & Watson case strikes me as being the most flagrant and arbitrary stretches of power that has even been committed by an individual occupying the position of Judge," wrote "Miner" to the *Cariboo Sentinel* in 1866:

> . . . we have mining laws containing explicit provisions as to the manner in which claims should be taken up and held, but at the same time that any parties having money enough to stand the costs of a Chancery suit may omit to comply with these provisions and set the law at defiance; it tends to create a feeling of insecurity as the value of every title, no man is secure if he strikes a good claim, as after strictly complying with the law which he supposed to be protection and spending his last dollar in prospecting, he may find when he thinks he has reached the long hoped for goal of his ambition, that some more favoured individual had intended in taking up the same ground long previously, but had neglected . . . staking it off or recording it, a grave error certainly, but one which can be expiated by filing a bill in Equity, making a score or two of affidavits, and paying his own costs in a Chancery suit, and this is what is called "Equity".[16]

Less measured was the commentary of the Victoria-based *British Colonist*, which contended that the "endless round of litigation" in British Columbia's mining districts was "ruining claimholders, shutting up the country's wealth and causing disasters in communities hundreds of miles away from the scene of the dispute." "The risks of mining are a mere bagatelle," the newspaper concluded, "it

is the risks of Begbie's Chancery Court that terrify the miner."[17]

Public indignation over Begbie's actions in the Borealis case scarcely subsided when his handling of another mining dispute again drew the attention and the wrath of British Columbians. After issuing an injunction ordering the Davis Company to cease work on disputed ground, Begbie discovered that the Supreme Court seals necessary to validate the injunction were unavailable—detained, with the rest of his luggage, on a wagon that had broken down en route to Bridge Creek. Undeterred, the judge sent a messenger to Richfield with the injunction and orders for William Cox, the Stipendiary Magistrate and Assistant Gold Commissioner there, to attach seals to the injunction in his capacity as Deputy Registrar of the Supreme Court. Cox, whose decision Begbie had overturned in issuing the injunction, declined to act as ordered, claiming that while he "entertain[ed] high respect for Mr. Begbie as Mr. Begbie and also as Supreme Court Judge," he held no commission as Deputy Registrar. Moreover, continued the magistrate,

> Finding now that it is attempted to drag me into this disagreeable quarrel, and act contrary to my own conscience, I would if I actually did hold a commission as Deputy Registrar of the Supreme Court resign the post at once.[18]

Although delayed by Cox's "decisive stand," *Aurora v. Davis* came to trial before Matthew Baillie Begbie and a special jury on 18 June.[19] After deliberating until midnight, the jury awarded half of the disputed ground to each side, because "the Aurora and Davis Companies have expended both time and money on said ground in dispute."[20] According to the *Sentinel*, the jury's decision met with the general approval of the entire mining community.

There is probably no instance on record where trial by jury has been so fully appreciated. . . . We are convinced that there is not a single miner on the creek that would not gladly submit his grievances to the decision of seven disinterested fellow citizens, and thus avoid the expensive and vexatious proceedings in Chancery.[21]

Despite the satisfaction with the jury's verdict evinced by the *Sentinel*, Begbie insisted that a decision by his court "would not end the litigation, and the expense of actions in one or two other branches of this Court would be heavy on both parties." Instead of accepting the jury's verdict, the judge suggested "that the whole matter be referred to me, not in my capacity as Judge, but as an arbitrator and friend, and that whatever decision I may arrive at will be final and absolute."[22] The two sides agreed, and the following day—19 June—Begbie rendered his decision to an "anxious" courtroom. Perhaps hoping to forestall any criticism, the judge made it a point to downplay the irregularity of his actions and to praise the jury as an institution. "I have always had every reason to be satisfied with the findings of juries during the whole period of my own official experience in this colony," Begbie remarked; but if "a jury finds a verdict contrary to the evidence, resulting from ignorance, fear, or any other cause it is [the judge's] privilege to set aside their verdict." Noting that "when men go to jump ground they do not see their enemies' stakes," Begbie ruled against the Davis Company and awarded all of the disputed ground to the appellant.[23]

Reaction was immediate. Five or six hundred miners and residents of Cariboo gathered in front of the Richfield Court house on a rainy Saturday night six days after Begbie's decision to discuss the administration of the colony's mining laws.[24] Amid a great many speeches lasting well into the night, the participants passed three resolutions:

RESOLVED, "That in the opinion of this meeting the administration of the Mining Laws by Mr. Justice Begbie in the Supreme Court is partial, dictatorial, and arbitrary, in setting aside the verdict of juries, and calculated to create a feeling of distrust in those who have to seek redress through a Court of Justice."

RESOLVED, "That the meeting pledges itself to support the Government in carrying out the Laws in their integrity, and beg for an impartial administration of justice. To this end we desire the establishment of a Court of Appeal, or the immediate removal of Judge Begbie, whose acts in setting aside the Law has destroyed confidence and is driving labor, capital and enterprise out of the Colony."

RESOLVED, "That a Committee of two persons be appointed to wait upon His Excellency the Administrator of the Government [Arthur Birch] with the foregoing resolutions, and earnestly impress upon him the immediate necessity of carrying out the wishes of the people."

With three cheers for "Judge" Cox, the *British Colonist*, the *Cariboo Sentinel* and the Queen (in that order), and three groans for Judge Begbie, the meeting adjourned.[25]

As a result of the mounting public pressure for reform, the colonial government amended the Gold Fields Act in April 1867, limiting appeals from the Mining Court to questions of law only.[26] [. . .]

The *Borealis v. Watson* and *Aurora v. Davis* cases set the stage for the final and, according to one magistrate, most "humiliating" part of this mining trilogy: the Grouse Creek War.[27] Having found Chancery and arbitration wanting, and his government colleagues sensitive to public pressure, in 1867 Matthew Baillie Begbie found only one option remaining: to adhere to the newly amended Gold Fields Act and refuse to hear appeals from the Mining Courts. This course was not successful in restoring British Columbians' faith in the administration of the law. The fault was not Begbie's, however. A less outspoken Supreme Court judge might have succeeded in blunting the sharpest barbs, but no one could have bridged the gulf between the different meanings of law created by the colony's geography.

In late April 1864, the Grouse Creek Bedrock Flume Company, a Victoria-based joint stock company, applied to Peter O'Reilly, Richfield's Assistant Gold Commissioner, for the rights to a certain portion of land on Grouse Creek. O'Reilly granted the company title for ten years provided they fulfilled the usual conditions of occupation, licensing, and recording of the claim as outlined in the Gold Fields Act. During 1864 and all of 1865 the "Flumites," as they came to be known, developed their claim, investing $20 000 to $30 000; but in late 1866 the company ran out of money, and their claim was left unoccupied from September to November. During this time—on 8 October—the Canadian Company, a locally based association of free miners, entered the Flume Company's claim, and finding it apparently abandoned, applied for rights to it. Warner Spalding, who had replaced Peter O'Reilly as interim Assistant Gold Commissioner, duly recorded the ground in the Canadian Company's name. At the beginning of the next mining season, in March, the Flumites renegotiated their lease to the Grouse Creek claim with the Crown, managing to extricate themselves from all previous conditions regulating their occupation of the ground. Inexplicably, Spalding, who had just six months earlier granted the same piece of land to the Canadian Company, presided over this renegotiation on behalf of the Crown! It was only a matter of weeks before the two companies clashed, and the dispute was taken to the district's Mining Court, again to be heard before Spalding.[28] There Spalding ruled in favour of the plaintiffs, and ordered the Canadians off the disputed ground.[29] The Canadians gave notice of appeal, but obeyed the Commissioner's order.

Though the Canadians left quietly, they were back on Grouse Creek in a month. At the end of May, Anthony Melloday and three other Canadian Company members commenced work on the Grouse Creek Flume Company's claim. This time, however, the Flumites took their complaint to the Magistrate's Court, laying criminal charges of trespass against the Canadians. The foreman, Melloday, received the heaviest sentence: one month's imprisonment The others were sentenced to 7 and 14 days.[30] [. . .]

At the beginning of July Begbie informed the two companies that he would not, in keeping with the newly amended Gold Fields Act, hear the appeal. [. . .] Undeterred, the Canadians regrouped, and now 30 or 40 strong, they again returned to Grouse Creek. Three constables and one surveyor were dispatched to eject the Canadians, but were prevented from doing so when the company's men "surrounded [them] . . . without showing any hostile disposition, or making any threats of violence, but simply claiming that as they all acted as one man, if any one was liable to arrest they all were. . . . "[31] The constables left.

Local sentiment seemed to be very much on the side of the Canadians, particularly in light of Begbie's refusal to hear their appeal— a situation that was doubly ironic, given that local sentiment, and notably the pressure of the Canadian Company's principals, John MacLaren and Cornelius Booth, had led to the 1867 amendment! Writing on behalf of the members of the Canadian Company, Booth insisted they were not "acting in opposition to the law of the land." Since they could not appeal, they were more than willing to force a new case.[32] [. . .] Booth told the same thing to a public meeting of 500 people gathered to hear "a full and truthful statement of the grievances and position of the Canadian Company." The sympathetic crowd passed a resolution recording their sympathy with the Canadians and their commitment to aid the company "by all lawful means to obtain their rights."[33]

The good will manifested toward the Canadians made itself apparent the next day, when the district's magistrate proceeded to Grouse Creek, backed this time by 25 or 30 of "the most prominent businessmen, and respectable citizens of this town" who had answered court summonses to act as special constables. Once there, the "posse comitatus" exchanged "the most friendly greetings" with the Canadians and the nearly 400 eager onlookers who had "splashed through mud and mire, knee-deep, in haste to reach the rendezvous." All settled in for a long and what must have been anti-climactic afternoon of negotiation by letter between the two companies. In the end, with no hope of settlement, the magistrate read a writ of injunction to the Canadian Company and asked them to leave the claim. "[A] unanimous NO was returned, whereupon Mr. Ball, along with his constables, left Williams Creek, and the crowd dispersed."[34] The magistrate immediately telegraphed the governor, requesting that a detachment of marines be sent to assist him.[35] The Royal Navy refused to intervene, and Seymour, "at very considerable inconvenience to myself proceeded . . . to Cariboo."[36]

It was this stalemate that greeted the governor when he arrived in Richfield a few weeks later, on 7 August. Seymour, along with the rest of the colony, had been treated to a series of alarmist reports of "mob law" on Williams Creek from the *British Colonist* and the *British Columbian*, and no doubt expected the worst. "In our most important gold field the arm of justice hangs powerlessly by her side, while a company of men, under the most hollow and hypocritical professions of a desire to respect the law are wantonly and openly trampling it underfoot," screamed the *Columbian*:

It is simply a question of British Law vs. Lynch Law. . . . [with reference to Governor Seymour's visit] To go to the scene of strife unarmed with a force to *compel* submission will simply to be to toy

with outlawry while the coveted treasure is being grabbed up.[37]

Calling for the imposition of "martial law," the *Colonist* noted that "by offering armed resistance to the mandate of a court" the Canadians were "criminals" who "went into court determined to obey the law if it was *with* them; [and] to break it if it was *against* them."[38] The *Cariboo Sentinel* took issue with its competitors' treatment of the Grouse Creek "War". "Victorians," the *Sentinel* speculated, "no doubt wrought up to the highest pitch of excitement by the graphic descriptions of the warlike attitude of the Canadians, would be surprised if they were here."

Canadians and Flumites may be seen daily in the streets of Barkerville, habited in the usual miners' garb, saluting each other without the slightest appearance of hostility.[39]

The *Sentinel's* attempts to emphasize the peacefulness of the Cariboo were not aided by the events which followed, however.

A few days after Governor Seymour's arrival, the Canadian Company strode into Richfield, not, noted one anonymous writer "in obedience to any order or summons," but at the suggestion of their leader, Cornelius Booth. Though Booth—the "Talleyrand of the band"—assured his compatriots they would not be arrested, seven of their number were. Conveyed immediately to the courthouse, the seven received three-month sentences for resisting arrest (stemming from Magistrate Ball's earlier attempt to eject the Canadians from Grouse Creek); however, with the exception of one man, all refused to go to jail. Instead, they "warned the constables not to touch any of them, and abused and blackguarded the Commissioner on the Bench!"[40] The seven told the court "that if they had treated the Commissioner to more champagne &c. they would have won their case."[41] Ball left the courtroom, and the governor requested a parley with Booth. After extracting a promise from Seymour to commute the sentences to 48 hours' imprisonment, Booth "*persuaded* his comrades to walk towards the gaol, promising them that they would not be confined three days!"[42] This concession to the form of law was continued once the redoubtable Canadians arrived at the Richfield jail. There, wrote "Crimea," "they would not allow the doors of the jail to be locked upon them and had free access to all the Court house grounds during the term of their imprisonment."[43] [. . .]

When Seymour left Richfield, he left behind conflicting impressions of what he accomplished. The Canadian Company believed they had secured a promise for a new trial, while the *Colonist* and the *Columbian* were convinced that Seymour had merely offered the services of Joseph Trutch, the Chief Commissioner of Lands and Works, as arbitrator. Added to this confusion was yet another round of vitriolic newspaper reports from Victoria, condemning the governor's actions. Claiming that Governor Seymour's negotiation legitimized the actions of the Canadian "mob," the *Colonist* predicted an end to the "security of life and property in the country."[44] The Canadians rejected arbitration, insisting that they would "accept nothing less than the law allows them": a new trial.[45] [. . .]

Seymour then appointed Joseph Needham, Vancouver Island's Supreme Court judge, as arbitrator. Needham arrived in Richfield in mid-September, prepared to try the Grouse Creek case (as well as other mining appeals) *de novo*.[46] Noting that every court had the power to suspend its rules if "any technicality arises that might tend to defeat the ends of justice," the judge began hearing evidence in the *Canadian Company v. the Grouse Creek Flume Company* on 17 September. After two weeks of testimony, Needham awarded all of the disputed ground to the Flumites. "I cannot be blind to the fact

that much public excitement has existed with regard to this case," he told the court,

but I do hope and believe that all will acquiesce in the decision of this court; I can only say that it has been arrived at after anxious consideration, and a simple desire to administer justice according to the law. I hope, and firmly believe, that armed alone with the authority of the law, a child may execute this judgment, and that no one will here be found whose wish is not to uphold and obey the judicial tribunals of this country—tribunals which have always been regarded by Englishmen as the fountain of justice, and the bulwark of freedom.[47]

With this plea for peace, Needham ended one of the most protracted disputes in the colony's short history, and one which was noted for the bitterness engendered between island and mainland as much as for that between the rival mining factions. It also ended Begbie's stormy tenure as mining appeal court judge. After 1867 the "tyrant Judge" heard few mining cases, leaving them to his less controversial colleagues.[48]

* * *

These three cases have been discussed before by David Williams, who called them "*causes célèbres*."[49] They were certainly that, and more, for *Aurora, Borealis,* and *Grouse Creek* illustrate the difficulty of, in Joseph Needham's words, "administering justice according to the law." The Supreme Court judge's distinction is an important one. While the Canadians and the Flumites were of one voice as to the ends of the law and the process of dispute resolution, they disagreed on how best to secure justice through the law. This was because of the variety of meanings the law in a colony as loosely organized as British Columbia. Their various definitions of the law revealed the importance of geography in determining its contours, as well as showing the limits of authority.

Despite their differences, Flumites and Canadians used the same language of laissez-faire capitalism, which linked liberty to the security of property, to frame criticisms and to justify their actions. The New Westminster *Columbian* and the Victoria *Colonist* contrasted "British Law" with the Canadians' "mob rule," and predicted an end to "that security of life and property in the country which has ever been our proud boast."

> Capital, finding its tenure insecure, will fly to countries where people are made to respect the laws, and where possession of property rests upon a more stable and secure foundation.[50]

At the same time, the Canadian Company, that "mob" of "footpads" and "filibusters," used the very same language of law and property to predict the same ends if *its* demands were not met. "There are three things the most despotic governments claim," Cornelius Booth told a crowd of 500 gathered at Fulton's saloon, "namely the right to take property, liberty and life."

> The first of these have already been taken from the Canadian Co., and there is but one step to the last. I repeat that these men do not wish to be looked upon as outlaws; they consider they have been unjustly shut out from having a hearing; and would be perfectly satisfied in obtaining one, even if a decision was given against them.[51]

The crowd agreed, as they had done in the wake of the *Borealis v. Watson* and the *Aurora v. Davis* cases, when they informed the colonial government that its laws and Begbie's administration of them were driving "labor, capital and enterprise out of the Colony."[52] To British Columbians on both sides of the Grouse Creek War, as well as the mining disputes that preceded it, just laws and legitimate authority were defined by their positive effect on economic development. Begbie's Chancery Court was viewed with contempt not only because the laws of chancery appeared capricious, but also, and perhaps more importantly, because of the costly delays associated with its proceedings. Jury trials could not guarantee satisfaction either, as *Aurora v. Davis* showed. Recourse to a jury trial was a poor alternative to Chancery because verdicts could be set aside by an "arbitrary" judge. The "tyranny" of Begbie's court lay in its unpredictability and inefficiency—the two enemies of capitalist enterprise.

Just as they used the same language and agreed on the ends that the law served, British Columbians on both sides of the Grouse Creek war recognized the same process of dispute resolution. The ends sought by those who opposed the government's administration were always to be achieved with the existing structures of formal dispute settlement. In *Borealis v. Watson*, Caribooites criticized the use of the Court of Chancery to resolve mining appeals because its ponderous proceedings were singularly unsuited to mining activity. But what did the miners propose as a solution? The establishment of a Court of Appeal! Similarly, in *Aurora v. Davis* arbitration was rejected in favour of trial by jury. And in the Grouse Creek war, the Canadian Company did not ask for public sanction of extralegal action (in fact, it did not consider that it was acting in an illegal manner), but for "*nothing less than the law allows us*": a full hearing of its case.[53] Indeed, as David Williams noted, both Cornelius Booth and John MacLaren visited Begbie in early July 1867 to ask for his intervention—surely an indication they had not lost faith in the legal options available.[54] Even after seven company members were arrested in August, the Canadians still demanded that the "tyrant Judge" or his island counterpart replace Joseph Trutch as arbitrator.[55] Clearly, those who took issue with British Columbia's legal administration

did not reject the structures of dispute resolution; rather it was to the official framework
of English institutions that they looked for relief. In fact, the law might be seen as a kind of
social cement holding colonists together.

If Caribooites agreed about the ends of
the law and the institutional means of executing it, they took issue with what the law
was and how to achieve justice through that
law. British Columbians in other parts of
the colony considered that a body of rules
applied evenly and predictably ensured justice. Reflecting on the *Borealis* and *Aurora*
cases, the *Colonist* pointed to Begbie's lack
of legal experience as the cause of the trouble. "Unlike Judge Needham," the newspaper
reported, Begbie "had no legal experience
to recommend him, and it is by no means
a matter of surprise that his decisions instead of partaking of that judicial clearness
and point which are the universal characteristics of the decisions of English judges,
should be generally rambling, disconnected
and irrelevant."[56] Nevertheless, both the *Sentinel* and the Canadians dismissed the Chief
Commissioner of Lands and Works, Joseph
Trutch, as a suitable adjudicator for the same
reasons and called for the intervention of the
Supreme Court: "He [Trutch] lacks the legal
acumen which is necessary to unravel those
knotted points of law that are inseparably
involved in the settlement of the dispute in
question." [. . .][57] "Legal acumen" was not
necessarily specialized knowledge, however.
The valued acumen was a knowledge of community standards and local circumstance:
what Caribooites wanted was law that was
self-evident.

In the wake of *Aurora* and *Borealis*, Caribooites let it be known that "common sense"
was the chief hallmark of just laws and just
administration. The *Cariboo Sentinel* published a telling editorial emphasizing just
this point by contrasting the conduct of Peter
O'Reilly (the previous magistrate) with that of
his predecessors and his successor, William
Cox. Prior to O'Reilly's arrival, the mining

court "was virtually, if not nominally, a Court
of Conscience."

Then the mining laws consisted of
only a few proclamations issued from
time to time by the Governor, and the
Commissioner supplemented these with
his own judgment. Since then extensive
mining laws have been passed and
partially consolidated. It was not until
the administration of Mr. O'Reilly that
this Court, by his false pretensions to
legal ability, declared itself to be a Court
of Equity or Law, or both combined . . . .
The policy of Mr. Cox, on the other
hand, was quite different: he made no
pretensions to legal ability, yet his policy
was at once most agreeable to the miners;
he converted this Court back once again
almost wholly into a Court of Conscience,
and presided in it with no little success.

Cox's success, the *Sentinel* concluded, was
due to the fact he was guided by "common
sense rather than a smattering of law."[58]

As the *Sentinel's* editorial revealed,
common sense was an important yardstick
of the law's legitimacy. Sociologists argue
that common sense occupies an important
place in human interaction.[59] The strength
and influence of common sense lies in its
"taken-for-granted" nature. Common sense
is common knowledge; it is a body of truths
that does not need explanation (and probably
cannot be explained) for it is instantly recognized as self-evident.[60] According to sociolo-
gist Siegwart Lindenberg, common sense is
a "general baseline for human interaction."[61]
It is a frame of reference against which humans gauge events and understand the world
as well as a "court of appeal".[62] "Common
sense," argue van Holthoon and Olson, "provided the basis of appeal . . . to criticize and
overthrow a more specialized and restrictive
world view."[63] By appealing to a body of self-
evident truths, critics attempt to show that
the status quo is unnatural and illogical. But

the concept could just as easily be used to buttress the existing order of things. Just as often, notes philosopher Herman Parret, "'Use your common sense,' 'Behave commonsensically' —these mean 'Be conventional,' 'Be conservative.' . . . It is used to stop argument, fantasy and originality, and it is often a *deus ex machina*, a rhetorical device to express power."[64] Given the ambiguous nature of common sense, literary critics argue that it is a powerful rhetorical device, "part of 'the formal language of ideological dispute.'"[65]

Although common sense implied a commonality of experience that cut across political, social, and economic divisions—indeed, this is part of its strength—it was rooted in a cultural and social matrix particular to a time and place. Concepts of common sense were tied to particular locales; they were, as anthropologist Clifford Geertz contended, part of "local knowledge".[66] As such, "the law . . . is not a bounded set of norms, rules, principles and values . . . but part of a distinctive manner of imagining the real."[67] Thus, when Caribooites appealed to common sense in criticizing the colonial legal administration, their meaning was clear only within their frame of reference. They wanted the law to be self-evident; however, what was common knowledge varied from place to place. Common sense dictated what was just, but because it was bounded by space and by local experience with the law, the concept had different meanings for different people. British Columbia's great distances, thin population, and poor systems of communication accentuated the localism of the colony's mining population. The mainland lacked an internal coherence that would have narrowed the variations in common sense. Its communities were uncoupled from each other, as well as the administrative centres of New Westminster and Victoria.[68] In such a geographical context a variety of concepts of law proliferated; the historian's task is to recreate that milieu so that others can appreciate it as "commonsensical".

The *Caribou Sentinel's* opposition of common sense and conscience on one hand, and law and equity on the other is important. A Court of Equity was another name for a Court of Chancery—not the miners' favourite legal institution, as Borealis showed. Initially, cases tried by equity courts had been resolved by applying the "standards of what seems naturally just or right, as contrasted with the application . . . of a rule of law, which might not provide for such circumstances or provide for what seems unreasonable."[69] By the early nineteenth century, however, the principles of equity had become a body of settled law rather than a personal and arbitrary assessment of fairness.[70] Ironically, though equitable jurisdiction evolved as a corrective to the inflexibility of the law, the Court of Chancery acquired a reputation as a morass of legal complexity and delay into which unwitting suitors could fall and never gain a settlement. When Caribooites equated Peter O'Reilly's tenure as Magistrate and Assistant Gold Commissioner with a "Court of Equity or Law," and contrasted it with Cox's "common sense," they revealed that they considered the two kinds of knowledge to be antithetical. The complexities of equity and statute law were far from self-evident truths; in fact, they were "pretensions" that caused unnecessary delays and thwarted justice. Cox's common sense cut through all this. He circumvented legal technicalities by letting "conscience" guide his decisions. In the eyes of Caribooites, Cox's "court of conscience" was the surest route to justice. Yet courts of conscience were, in legal parlance, merely another name for courts of equity or chancery![71] Why was Cox's "conscience"—his ability to apply "standards of what seems naturally just or right"— superior to Begbie's? Why, in short, was the magistrate's common sense superior to that of the Supreme Court judge?

Caribooites recognized the magistrate's decisions and actions as expressions of common sense because he was part of their community. Common sense was bounded by locale and rooted in specific constellations of social relations. Keith Wrightson shows that magistrates, constables, and jurymen were caught between "different kinds of order" in which the execution of the law had to be balanced against the more tangible pressures of familiarity in the face-to-face communities of seventeenth-century England.[72] Nineteenth-century British Columbia demonstrates the same pattern. Because the colony's magistrates were a part of the communities they administered, they quickly became enmeshed in the politics of familiarity, a situation that both aided and limited their ability to execute the law. William Cox's knowledge of miners and mining won him the admiration and support of 490 of his neighbours, who petitioned against his removal in 1866. "From the very long acquaintance we have had with Mr. Cox, and the intimate knowledge he has acquired of mining in Cariboo, we consider him much better qualified for the office than any other gentleman in this Colony"; they wrote. "Mr. Cox's conduct . . . has been such as to inspire the public with the utmost confidence in his integrity, . . . while his judicial decisions have had the effect of checking litigation."[73] These judicial decisions were often unconventional: on one occasion the magistrate settled a mining court claim by making the opposing parties race from the steps of the Richfield Court House to the disputed ground—winner take all. On another occasion Cox swore in Chinese witnesses by decapitating a chicken instead of administering the usual and less spectacular oath.[74]

Cox's "intimate knowledge" consisted of a proper understanding of community morals, and it was this empathy that underlay justice in the Cariboo. Community sentiment about what was right and wrong made it impossible to keep the Canadian Company under lock and key. Henry Maynard Ball, whose misfortune it was to preside over the Grouse Creek dispute, failed because "he had but little experience in the mining districts."[75] Familiarity also limited the ineffectiveness of enforcement. For the most part, policing was done by special constables, sworn in from the local population as the need arose. In the Grouse Creek case the special constables, who as men of capital and business presumably stood to lose from the unrest, were of no use in ejecting their neighbours; nor could the district's jailer incarcerate the Canadians. "The public feeling was rather in favour of the Canadians," complained Frederick Seymour. "At all events no one would come forward to assist the Government in an emergency."[76]

Despite the constraints of familiarity on the execution of the law, British Columbians would have it no other way. The interventions of outsiders in their affairs were considered despotic, even when that intervention was done by a figure as magisterial as a Supreme Court judge. In this context, juries became an important bridge between law and justice. "[T]his community," reported the Richfield Grand Jury,

> owing to its isolated position, the peculiarity of its interests, and especially its national origin, has a decided preference for local trial by jury, and is extremely jealous of all verdicts by its peers. . . .[77]

The *Cariboo Sentinel* was even more direct, asserting that "a man is wrong when almost every person in the community thinks and says he is wrong."[78] When Begbie overturned the jury verdict in *Aurora v. Davis*, he not only breached what Caribooites perceived to be established practice, he also burned the only bridge between the law as a set of overarching rules and as a set of social and locally constructed norms. The judge's cavalier treatment of the jury in this and other cases led many colonists to conclude that Begbie did not consider them qualified to pass judgement on their peers. What these British Columbians objected to was not so much Begbie's failure to adhere to statute law and common law practice as the fact that he was not guided by the same self-evident truths as they were. He could not have been. The Supreme Court judge was outside their community: he resided in Victoria, visiting the colony's far-flung communities only once a year. His circuits were metaphors for his status as an outsider. Begbie's actions and decisions appeared arbitrary, particularly in a colony that lacked the social organization that would support the arbitrariness of paternal authority. Because his decisions were not necessarily commonsensical and because of the important role the law played in establishing some cohesion in the colony, Begbie's actions and decisions not only threatened the colonists' economic security but also eroded one of the few bonds tying them together.

Caribooites also considered the Grouse Creek Flume Company an outsider. Not only were the Flumites based in Victoria, headed by one of the city's largest merchants, but they also represented "big capital'" in a region where small, independent entrepreneurs were the norm.[79] The Canadians styled themselves a "company," but their Victoria opponents were the real thing. The Grouse Creek Flume Company was a joint stock venture, capitalized to the tune of $50 000. The Flumites were harbingers of a different kind of resource entrepreneur in British Columbia. By the late 1860s, most of the easily accessible surface gold in the Cariboo was gone. Continued success on the upper country creeks depended on a hydraulic process which required a substantial capital investment to construct the necessary flumes. Such an investment was beyond the means of most independent miners. Part of the support for the Canadians and the wrath directed at Begbie likely stemmed from an antipathy toward this form of large corporate enterprise that would eventually dominate resource exploitation and push out the smaller upper country operations.

Conflicting concepts of law were central to the controversies surrounding the administration of British Columbia's mining laws in the colonial period. While recent writing in Canadian legal history has cast a critical eye on the law, revealing its normative nature, few studies deal with the variety of meanings the law could take on.[80] As I have discussed, despite its detached nature, the law gained much of its meaning through the very local experiences people had with it. [. . .]

The Grouse Creek War and the events leading to it demonstrate the importance of geography in creating "local frames of awareness" that shape social meaning.[81] The law Caribooites wanted had to be self-evident; it had to be commonsensical. Because common sense was *local* knowledge, however, its meaning was spatially limited. This localism was accentuated by the colony's geography, which effectively precluded the integration of the archipelago of small settlements that was British Columbia. Geographers and sociologists have recognized that space is deeply implicated in social life.[82] Because human relations and the extension of authority are spatially as well as socially constructed, understanding what the law means involves more than contextualizing behaviour in time. Distant places like the Cariboo were uncoupled from New Westminster and Victoria, the colony's centres of authority.[83] In this spatial context, law and authority were rooted in specific and local constellations of social relations. For Caribooites, the law was more a collection of community norms than a set of hard-and-fast rules. Face-to-face relations, the politics of the personal and personality loomed large in determining authority. Being recognized as an authority conveyed more power in these localized settings than being *in* authority by virtue of some extra-community sanction.[84]

Although I have put local knowledge at the crux of understanding behaviour, local frames of reference were not the only ones that influenced the meaning of law.

On Grouse Creek, common sense may have gone a long way to shape what the law meant to British Columbians, but clearly the larger framework provided by the structure, institutions, and traditions of the common law itself also played an important role.[85] Magistrate William Cox's decisions may have been commonsensical, but he and those who came before him still operated within a set of rules and procedures that at least nominally constrained action and provided a standard for measuring legality. As I discussed, British Columbians on both sides of the Grouse Creek War and the disputes that led to it never challenged the authority of the law and its institutions; instead, they took issue with their administration and looked to the existing forms of law for redress. Perhaps more important in shaping the social meaning of the law than its forms were its traditions and the expectations they created. The "rule of law" promised freedom from the dictates of arbitrary sovereigns for all, no matter their condition. The idea of the rule of law became intimately tied to the security of life and property, and became the keystone of English liberty. For British colonists, the law was an important source of unity, particularly in the years immediately following settlement. Though differences brought them before a magistrate, the British Columbians who resorted to the law were tied together in a common adversarial process that imposed a degree of structure, organization, and predictability on social relationships in a colony where such characteristics were rare commodities. More broadly, both for those directly involved in litigation and for those who perhaps afterwards discussed and criticized its administration, the law was a link to and a symbol of a common, storied, and secure past that stood in marked contrast to the new and alien environment they found themselves in. The common law conferred citizenship to colonists whose sense of place had been eroded by the experience of migration.

Much of the social meaning of the law, then, was provided by the forms and traditions of the law itself—forms and traditions which had their genesis outside the locale that has been the focus of my analysis.

Although they were physically distant from the main centres of population, as well as from the rest of British North America, Caribooites were tied to another frame of reference through extensive webs of credit: the wider world of commercial capitalism. So dominant was economic activity in the collective experience of the colony that the language of laissez-faire infused British Columbians' discussions of the law and provided the standard with which they measured political authority. Begbie's actions and decisions provoked the reactions they did because they were the antithesis of what commercial capitalist enterprise demanded and defined as the criteria for legitimate action: efficiency, predictability, and standardization.

Though British Columbians on both sides of the mining disputes demanded these characteristics of the law and conceived of it as an instrument of economic development, there was room for a diversity of opinion because of the spatial context in which the law was administered. Divergent concepts of law became apparent only when the localism of the colony was penetrated by the annual circuits of British Columbia's Supreme Court. Begbie and the Supreme Court represented a different level of law and a different level of social interaction. To Caribooites, the Supreme Court judge was an outsider; his reasoning and decisions were not self-evident because he operated in a world outside the community of local interaction. To be effective, Begbie and his fellow magistrates had to balance the demands of colonial administration with local sentiment. With these conflicting demands, "administering justice according to the law" was a difficult, and sometimes impossible, task. This was Gaggin's "delicate game," and it was one that would be played over and over again amid the western mountains.

NOTES

1. Gaggin to the Colonial Secretary, Douglas, BC, 2 July 1862. British Columbia Archives and Records Services (hereafter BCARS), Colonial Correspondence, GR 1372, reel B-1330, file 621/14. For more on this episode and Gaggin, see Dorothy Blakey Smith, "'Poor Gaggin': Irish Misfit in the Colonial Service," *BC Studies* 32 (Winter 1976–7): 41–63.

2. Ibid.

3. Cited in Smith, "Poor Gaggin,'" 45.

4. Ibid., 47.

5. For instance, see Clifford Geertz, "Local Knowledge: Fact and Law in Comparative Perspective," in his *Local Knowledge: Further Essays in Interpretive Anthropology* (New York, 1983); John L. Comaroff and Simon Roberts, *Rules and Processes: The Cultural Logic of Dispute in an African Context* (Chicago, 1981); Lawrence Rosen, *Bargaining for Reality: The Construction of Social Relations in a Muslim Community* (Chicago, 1984), and his "Islamic 'Case Law' and the Logic of Consequence," in June Starr and Jane F. Collier, eds, *History and Power in the Study of Law: New Directions in Legal Anthropology* (Ithaca, N.Y., 1989), 302–19. In the latter essay, Rosen notes "Law is . . . one domain in which a culture may reveal itself. But like politics, marriage, and exchange, it is an arena in which people must act, and in doing so they must draw on their assumptions, connections, and beliefs to make their acts effective and comprehensible. In the Islamic world, as in many other places, the world of formal courts offers a stage—as intense as ritual, as demonstrative as war—through which a society reveals itself to its own people as much as to the outside world" [318]. This essay shares Rosen's assumptions about the law and what it can reveal about society.

6. See Hubert Howe Bancroft, *Popular Tribunals* (San Francisco, 1887), v. 1, Chapter Ten; Charles Shinn, *Mining Camps: A Study in American Frontier Government (New York: 1885)*; and on California and British Columbia, David Ricardo Williams, "The Administration of Civil and Criminal Justice in the Mining Camps and Frontier Communities of British Columbia," in Louis Knafla, ed., *Law and Justice in a New Land: Essays in Western Canadian Legal History* (Calgary, 1986).

7. Williams, 217–9.

8. See Shinn, Introduction.

9. Morley Arthur Underwood, "Governor Douglas and the Miners, 1858–1859," University of British Columbia, BA Essay, 1974.

10. *The Gold Fields Act, 1859* [31 August 1859]; William J. Trimble, *The Mining Advance into the Inland Empire* (Madison, Wisconsin, 1914), 187–214, 336–7.

11. Rules and Regulations for the Working of Gold Mines under the "Gold Fields Act 1859" [7 September 1859]; Rules and Regulations for the Working of Gold Mines, issued in conformity with the "Gold Fields Act, 1859" (Bench Diggings) [6 January 1860]; Rules and Regulations under the "Gold Fields Act, 1859" (Ditches) [29 September 1862]; Further Rules and Regulations under the "Gold Fields Act, 1859" [24 February 1863]; Proclamation amending the "Gold Fields Act, 1859" [25 March 1863]; The Mining District Act, 1863 [27 May 1863]; The Mining Drains Act, 1864 [1 February 1864]; An Ordinance to extend and improve the Laws relating to Gold Mining [26 February 1864] and An Ordinance to amend and consolidate the Gold Mining Laws [28 March 1865]; An Ordinance to amend the Laws relating to Gold Mining, 2 April 1867.

12. On this theme, and more generally, the idea that mining society was not as disorganized as traditionally thought, see Thomas Stone, *Miners' Justice: Migration, Law and Order on the Alaska-Yukon Frontier, 1873–1902* (New York, 1988).

13. Williams discusses them in " . . . *The Man for a New Country": Sir Matthew Baillie Begbie* (Sidney, BC, 1977), 68–80.

14. Ibid.

15. A Court of Chancery is a court that has jurisdiction in equity; that is, it resolves disputes according to the rules and procedures of equity rather than the rules and procedures of common law. Though the principles of equity

initially reflected the chancellor's own arbitrary and sometimes idiosyncratic ideas of justice (the Tudor Court of Star Chamber was the repository and dispensary of equity, for instance), over the seventeenth, eighteenth, and early nineteenth centuries the principles of equity evolved into a more settled body of rules. Chancery never lost its negative reputation for arbitrary, protracted, and unnecessarily complex proceedings, however (see Charles Dickens' *Bleak House* [1859], for instance). Until 1870, Matthew Baillie Begbie was British Columbia's only Supreme Court judge. This meant that the division of labour in the colony's superior court was one in name only. Begbie acted as judge in assize, nisi prius, appeal, chancery, bankruptcy, probate, and admiralty cases, often in the same session.

16. Letter from "Miner," *Cariboo Sentinel*, 31 May 1866.
17. "The British Columbia Judiciary," *British Colonist,* reprinted in *Cariboo Sentinel*, 2 July 1866.
18. "Irresponsible Deputies," *Cariboo Sentinel*, 31 May 1866.
19. Ibid.
20. "Supreme Court," *Cariboo Sentinel*, 18 June 1866.
21. Ibid.
22. *Cariboo Sentinel*, 21 June 1866.
23. Ibid.
24. "Mass Meeting," *Cariboo Sentinel*, 25 June 1866.
25. Ibid. Also see "The Tyrant Judge," *British Colonist,* 28 June 1866; "Another Verdict Set Aside," and "From Cariboo," *British Columbian*, 27 June and 4 July 1866.
26. An Ordinance to amend the Laws relating to Gold Mining [2 April 1867].
27. Nind to O'Reilly, Yahwalpa, Pimpama, Brisbane, Queensland, 11 April 1868. O'Reilly Family Papers. BCARS. Add. MSS. 412, v. 1, file 6a.
28. *Canadian Company v. Grouse Creek Flume Co., Ltd.*, 27 September 1867. Archer Martin, *Reports of Mining Cases decided by the Courts of British Columbia and the Courts of Appeal therefrom to the 1st of October, 1902. . . .* (Toronto, 1903), 3–8.
29. "Magistrate's Court," *Cariboo Sentinel*, 3 June 1867. Spalding heard the case on 22 April

1867, and the order ejecting the Canadian Company was issued on 24 April.
30. Ibid.
31. "Grouse Creek Difficulty," *Cariboo Sentinel,* 15 July 1867.
32. Letter to the Editor from C. Booth, dated 13 July 1867. *Cariboo Sentinel*, 15 July 1867.
33. "Public Meeting," Cariboo Sentinel, 15 July 1989.
34. "Grouse Creek Troubles—Great Excitement," *Cariboo Sentinel*, 18 July 1867.
35. Seymour to Buckingham and Chandos, New Westminster, 16 August 1867. CO 60/28. National Archives of Canada (hereafter NAC). MG 11, reel B-97, 333.
36. Ibid.
37. "The Situation," *British Columbian*, 27 July 1867.
38. "The Grouse Greek Difficulty," *British Colonist,* 24 July 1867.
39. "The Governor and the Grouse Creek Difficulty," *Cariboo Sentinel*, 12 August 1867.
40. Anonymous letter to the Editor, dated Williams Creek, 21 August 1867, *British Colonist*, 2 September 1867.
41. Letter to the Editor from "Crimea," dated Richfield, 20 August 1867, *British Colonist*, 9 September 1867.
42. Anonymous letter to the Editor, dated Williams Creek, 21 August 1867, *British Colonist*, 2 September 1867.
43. Letter to the Editor from "Crimea," dated Richfield, 20 August 1867, *British Colonist*, 9 September 1867.
44. "The Grouse Creek War," *British Colonist,* 29 July 1867; also see "The Grouse Creek Imbroglio," 19 August 1867, and "The Patched Up Peace on Grouse Creek," 23 August 1867.
45. Resolution passed by the Canadian Company, at Booth's Saloon, Grouse Creek, 30 August 1867. Reprinted in "Grouse Creek Dispute Again," *Cariboo Sentinel*, 2 September 1867.
46. *Cariboo Sentinel*, 16 September 1867.
47. *Canadian Company v. Grouse Creek Flume Co., Ltd.*, 27 September 1867. Martin, *Reports of Mining Cases. . . . ,* 8.
48. "Tyrant Judge" from "The Tyrant Judge," *British Colonist*, 28 June 1866. For Begbie and mining cases after 1867, see Williams, " . . . *The Man for a New Country,"* 80.

49. Williams, ". . . *The Man for a New Country*," 68.

50. "The Grouse Creek 'War,'" *British Colonist*, 29 July 1867.

51. "Public Meeting," *Cariboo Sentinel*, 15 July 1867.

52. "Mass Meeting," *Cariboo Sentinel*, 25 June 1866.

53. Emphasis added. Resolution passed at a meeting of the members of the Canadian Mining Company, convened at Booth's Saloon, Grouse Greek, on the evening of the 30th August 1867. "Grouse Creek Dispute Again," *Cariboo Sentinel*, 2 September 1867.

54. Williams, ". . . *The Man for a New Country*," 76.

55. Letter to the Editor from Cornelius Booth, dated 31 August 1867, *Cariboo Sentinel*, 2 September 1867.

56. "British Columbia's Judiciary," *British Colonist*, reprinted in the *Cariboo Sentinel*, 2 July 1866.

57. "The Grouse Creek Dispute Again," *Cariboo Sentinel*, 2 September 1867.

58. "The Administration of the Mining Laws," *Cariboo Sentinel*, 15 December 1866.

59. Frits van Holthoon and David R. Olson, eds, "Introduction," *Common Sense: The Foundations for Social Sciences* (Lanham, MD, 1987); Thomas Luckmann, "Some Thoughts on Common Sense and Science," in van Holthoon and Olson, eds, 179–98; Siegwart Lindenberg, "Common Sense and Social Structure: A Sociological View," in van Holthoon and Olson, eds, 199–216.

60. Van Holthoon and Olson, "Introduction," 3–4.

61. Lindenberg, "Common Sense and Social Structure," 202–3.

62. Ibid.; "court of appeal" from van Holthoon and Olson, "Introduction," 3.

63. Van Holthoon and Olson, "Introduction," 3.

64. Herman Parret, "Common Sense: From Certainty to Happiness," in van Holthoon and Olson, eds, 19.

65. Van Holthoon and Olson, eds, "Introduction," 8.

66. Clifford Geertz, "Local Knowledge."

67. Ibid., 173.

68. Anthony Giddens discusses the influence of space on the integration of societies. The key to integration is the extension or the "stretching" of experience over time and space (something he calls "time–space distanciation"). When people do not share common understandings of time and space the communities they live in become "uncoupled" from each other and from the central administrative state, thus posing problems for the exercise of power (i.e., the regulation of behaviour by the state). See his *A Contemporary Critique of Historical Materialism* (Oxford, 1981), 65–7.

69. David M. Walker, "Equity," *The Oxford Companion to the Law* (Oxford, 1980), 424.

70. Ibid., "Chancery," 204.

71. On courts of chancery and conscience, David Walker notes, "The Court of Chancery was sometimes referred to as a court of conscience because its jurisdiction was originally founded on relief granted by the Chancellor, as Keeper of the King's Conscience, in circumstances where equity and justice demanded it." See his *Oxford Companion to the Law*, 272.

72. Wrightson, "Two Concepts of Order: justices, constables, and jurymen in seventeenth-century England," in John Brewer and John Styles, eds, *An Ungovernable People: the English and their Law in the Seventeenth and Eighteenth Centuries* (London, 1980).

73. Petition dated Williams Creek, BC, 3 November 1866. Colonial Correspondence. BCARS. GR 1372, reel B-1355, f 1352.

74. Both examples from Margaret Ormsby, *British Columbia: A History* (Toronto, 1958), 181.

75. Seymour to Buckingham and Chandos, New Westminster, 12 May 1868. CO 60/32. NAC. MG 11, reel B-100, 368.

76. Seymour to Buckingham and Chandos, Victoria, 4 September 1867. CO 60/29. NAC. MG 11, reel B-97, 5.

77. "From Cariboo," *British Colonist*, 4 July 1866.

78. "The Administration of Justice," *Cariboo Sentinel*, 30 November 866.

79. Selim Franklin was the president of the Grouse Creek Flume Company, and J.P. Cranford was its treasurer.

80. On gender bias, see Constance Backhouse's work, including "Shifting Patterns of Nineteenth Century Canadian Custody Law," in D.H. Flaherty, ed., *Essays in the History of Canadian Law* (Toronto, 1981), v. 1, 212–48; and "Nineteenth Century Canadian Rape Law, 1800–1892," in Flaherty, ed., *Essays in the History of Canadian Law* (Toronto, 1984), v. 2, 200–47; on class

bias in enforcement, see Michael Katz *et. al.*, *The Social Organization of Early Industrial Capitalism* (Cambridge, MA, 1982), Chapter Six; and Nancy Kay Parker, "The Capillary Level of Power: Methods and Hypotheses for the Study of Law and Society in Late-Nineteenth Century Victoria, British Columbia," University of Victoria MA thesis (history), 1987.

81. Geertz, *Local Knowledge*, 61; cited in Aletta Biersack, "Local Knowledge, Local History: Geertz and Beyond," in Lynn Hunt, ed., *The New Cultural History* (Berkeley, 1988), 82.

82. According to geographers Jennifer Wolch and Michael Dear, space impinges on social practices in three generalized ways: first, social relations are *constituted* through space; they are *constrained* by space; and they are *mediated* by space. For instance, to understand law and authority we must look at how geography influences the construction of legal institutions (the constitutive role of space); how distance hinders or facilitates the imposition and articulation of law and legal institutions (the constraining role of space); and finally how space facilitates the construction of the social meanings of the law (the mediating role of space). See Michael Dear and Jennifer Wolch, "How Territory Shapes Social Life," in Wolch and Dear, eds, *The Power of Geography: How Territory Shapes Social Life* (Boston, 1989), 9.

83. Giddens, *A Contemporary Critique of Historical Materialism*, 65–6.

84. Stephen Lukes, "Power and Authority," in Tom Bottomore and Robert Nisbet, eds., *A History of Sociological Thought* (New York, 1978).

85. On this theme see Greg Marquis, "Doing Justice to 'British Justice': Law, Ideology and Canadian Historiography," in W. Wesley Pue and Barry Wright, eds., *Canadian Perspectives on Law and Society: Issues in Legal History* (Ottawa, 1988), 43–69.

Chapter 13

The Emergence of Métis Identity

READINGS

Primary Documents

1   From "J. Halkett to Earl Bathurst, 3 June 1818," in *Correspondence in the Years 1817, 1818, and 1819, between Earl Bathurst and J. Halkett, Esq. on the Subject of Lord Selkirk's Settlement at the Red River, in North America*

2   From "Declaration of the People of Rupert's Land and the North West," Fort Garry, December 8, 1869, in *The Collected Writings of Louis Riel*, vol. 1, Raymond Huel, ed.

Historical Interpretations

3   From "Scuttling along a Spider's Web: Mobility and Kinship in Métis Ethnogenesis," Nicole St-Onge and Carolyn Podruchny

4   From "Prologue to the Red River Resistance: Pre-liminal Politics and the Triumph of Riel," Gerhard Ens

INTRODUCTION

The Métis in western Canada were, initially at least, the offspring of relationships between fur trade workers and Indigenous women. The dominant characteristic of the earliest of these relationships was that the men tended to be French-speaking, thanks to employment practices in the trade. Over time, however, this early pattern became less dominant—English-speaking men also fathered children, Métis entered into relationships with Indigenous, European, or other Métis people—to the point that there are several possible paths to being Métis today. Ancestry may have assisted in the creation of this distinctive group, but it is not the only element constitutive of this new ethnic identity. After all, many people in the St Lawrence Valley who had Indigenous ancestors never considered themselves or were considered Métis. Kinship networks, economic activities, and cultural factors also played a role in the advent of what came to be known as the "New Nation" in the 1860s.

At various times in Canadian history, especially on the prairies, "mixed-blood" people and their interests have driven events. They found themselves between First Nations and European-origin societies, connected to each but not belonging wholly to either. To the extent that their presence served the dominant order, they were tolerated, but they tended to be most comfortable in communities of their own, pursuing jobs that could take advantage of their "between-ness". The fur trade had been their genesis, and until the middle of the nineteenth century, it had much to do with the trajectory of Métis life. Halkett's strong denunciation of the Métis as the hired thugs of the North-West Company and opponents of Lord Selkirk's colonization scheme at Red River during the later 1810s shows how easily racial animosity and commercial competition could bleed together. The "Declaration of the People of Rupert's Land and the North West" shows how Métis reacted to the Hudson's Bay Company's surrender of Rupert's Land to the Dominion of Canada in 1869. They strongly contested the transfer of what they considered their land and asked to be treated as a "sovereign" people. In their historical interpretation, Nicole St-Onge and Carolyn Podruchny offer an analysis concerning the processes that led to the emergence and development of this ethnic group with its own distinct identity in the northwest. Finally, Gerhard Ens provides background to the 1869–70 Resistance, showing how divisions and doubts existed within the Métis community—divisions that were directly related to questions of identity.

QUESTIONS FOR CONSIDERATION

1. What is Halkett's attitude toward the Métis in the Red River region? Why does he hold this attitude?
2. Why did the Métis resent the ways in which their territory was transferred from the Hudson's Bay Company to the Dominion of Canada?
3. Why do you think people were and are so fascinated by racial or ethnic origins?
4. How do St-Onge and Podruchny define the Métis? What do you think about their definition?
5. Ens presents us with a picture of Red River society on the eve of the resistance there. Compare and contrast the competing ideals of community that Ens describes.

SUGGESTIONS FOR FURTHER READING

Christopher Adams, Gregg Dahl, and Ian Peach, eds, *Métis in Canada: History, Identity, Law and Politics* (Edmonton: University of Alberta Press, 2013).

Chris Andersen, *"Métis": Race, Recognition, and the Struggle for Indigenous Peoplehood* (Vancouver: UBC Press, 2015).

Heather Devine, *The People Who Own Themselves: Aboriginal Ethnogenesis in a Canadian Family 1660–1900* (Calgary: University of Calgary Press, 2004).

Gerhard J. Ens, *Homeland to Hinterland: The Changing Worlds of the Red River Métis in the Nineteenth Century* (Toronto: University of Toronto Press, 1996).

——— and Joe Sawchuk, eds, *From New Peoples to New Nations: Aspects of Metis History and Identity from the Eighteenth to the Twenty-first Centuries* (Toronto: University of Toronto Press, 2015).

Michel Hogue, *Métis and the Medicine Line: Creating a Border and Dividing a People* (Regina: University of Regina Press, 2015).

Brenda Macdougall, *One of the Family: Métis Culture in Nineteenth-Century Northwestern Saskatchewan* (Vancouver: UBC Press, 2010).

Nicole St-Onge, Carolyn Podruchny, and Brenda Macdougall, *Contours of a People: Métis Family, Mobility, and History* (Norman: University of Oklahoma Press, 2014).

W. Brian Stewart, *The Ermatingers: A 19th Century Ojibwa-Canadian Family* (Vancouver: UBC Press, 2008).

Primary Documents

1 From J. Halkett to Earl Bathurst, 3 June 1818, in *Correspondence in the Years 1817, 1818, and 1819, between Earl Bathurst and J. Halkett, Esq. on the Subject of Lord Selkirk's Settlement at the Red River, in North America* (London: J. Brettell, 1819), 34–45.

Seymour Place, January 3, 1818.

MY LORD,

I take the liberty of again addressing your Lordship on the subject of the British Colonists at the Red River, in consequence of intelligence recently received from that quarter. The last accounts from the interior of North America communicate the satisfactory information that Lord Selkirk has succeeded in re-establishing the settlers upon the lands from which they had been twice driven by the North-West Company of Montreal.

Having left Fort William as early in the last summer as the state of the river navigation would admit, Lord Selkirk proceeded into the interior, and arrived at the Red River in the month of June. In the preceding winter he had taken measures to enable a small party of the settlers, who had been driven away in the summer before, to return in safety to the Settlement; and, upon his arrival there, he found that they had again begun to re-establish themselves, and to cultivate the lands which had been assigned to them. Under the circumstances in which they were placed, their agricultural operations were, of course, much circumscribed; and the horses of the Settlement having been carried away, or

destroyed, by their opponents, they were prevented from putting so much land into tillage as they otherwise would have done. They had sowed, however, above sixty acres of grain. The crops of the former year had been destroyed by the persons employed by the North-West Company, who, after Mr. Semple and twenty of his people were killed,—the surviving settlers driven away,—and their habitations reduced to ashes—turned their horses loose into the fields of wheat, and other grain, for the purpose of laying them waste. The malicious satisfaction which the Company's adherents felt in thus destroying the promising crops of the Settlement, was, however, somewhat damped by the circumstance of nearly fifty of their horses having died in consequence of the surfeit. The European cattle and sheep, which had been sent to the Settlement, as a breed, were also destroyed by the persons employed by the North-West Company, whose brutality, throughout the whole of these transactions, was such as scarcely to be credited.

A few days after the 19th of June, the day when Mr. Semple and his followers were put to death without quarter by their opponents, Mr. Archibald Norman McLeod the magistrate, one of the Company's principal agents, together with several of his partners, accompanied by a considerable number of the half-breeds who had been engaged in the slaughter of the 19th, rode to the spot, and, having assured these half-breeds that they had done well, the party, with loud shouts and laughter, began to exult over, and even to kick the dead bodies which had remained upon the ground. On the side of the North-West Company, only one person, a half-breed, had fallen. His body was buried, and a paling placed round his grave; but the bodies of the settlers, (with the exception of a few who had been brought away and interred by some native Indians), were all left unburied on the spot, and were afterwards devoured by dogs. In the following spring their bones were collected, and interred by Captain D'Orsonnens, who, at Lord Selkirk's request, had proceeded to the Red River with a party of the new colonists in the preceding winter.

Shortly after Lord Selkirk had arrived at the Settlement, he was joined by a large portion of the remaining settlers who had been driven away in the summer before. Contrary to the expectations of the North-West Company (who had exulted in the idea that these colonists must have been all compelled to go back to Hudson's Bay for the purpose of returning to Europe), they had passed the autumn and winter towards the north end of Lake Winnipic, and at the Saskatchawan. Having heard that Lord Selkirk had arrived in North America, and was proceeding into the interior, they trusted that now they would not be entirely forsaken, and that means would be found to enable them to return with safety to the Red River.

By the latest accounts from that place it appears, that these settlers, together with the new ones who had recently arrived from Canada, (including the discharged men of the De Meuron and Watteville

regiments), were establishing themselves, with every reasonable prospect of success. During their route, they had invariably experienced the friendly offices of the Indian population; and the native tribes in the immediate neighbourhood of the Red River, have formally and solemnly declared their intention to support them. With respect to the miserable race termed Metifs, Half-breeds, or Bois-brulés, a band neither in the slightest degree formidable from their numbers, nor their courage, even a large portion of these have now declared that they mean to support the Red River Colony. It cannot, indeed, be expected that such banditti are to be trusted, while within the sphere of the influence and bribes of those who originally hired them to commit acts of aggression against the colony, and afterwards remunerated them for their hostility. But if the North-West Company, by whom they were so employed, can be restrained, by the interference of Government, from again instigating these ignorant and deluded people to renew the outrages against their fellow-subjects, there can be no doubt of the Settlement remaining henceforward secure and undisturbed. Without some adequate interference, however, it can scarcely be expected that the Company's partners in the interior, will be induced to relinquish their endeavours to cause it final destruction. Their rancour towards the colony has, in all probability, increased in proportion to their disappointment, in being twice baffled in their hopes to effect a permanent dispersion of the colonists.

A sufficiency of documents, I should suppose, has been submitted to your Lordship in the course of the last two or three years, fully to satisfy His Majesty's Government, that, from the commencement of the Red River Colony, there existed, on the part of the North-West Company, a determined resolution to destroy it. If that fact be admitted,—and I do not hesitate in asserting, that it is impossible for any person who will investigate the matter with attention, to entertain the slightest doubt on the subject,—every thing which ensued must appear a natural consequence of such determination. If the Company, in following up their resolution, happened not to succeed in their attempts to destroy the Settlement in one way, they were ready to try it in another. They began by endeavouring to instigate the native Indians against the colonists; but in this they completely failed. Their next proceeding—in addition to bribing and seducing a considerable portion of the settlers to desert from the colony, and break their contracts—was to hire, arm, and array their half-breed dependents, and make them,

under the personal direction of partners and clerks of the Company, attack the colonists, burn their houses, and drive them by force from the Settlement. And, at the very time they were planning and executing these measures, their agents and principal partners were addressing memorials to Government, in which they boasted of their humanity and kindness towards these people, whom they were thus shamefully oppressing.

I have the honour to be,
My Lord,
Your Lordship's obedient
And humble Servant,
J. HALKETT.

Earl Bathurst,
&c. &c. &c.

---

2 From "Declaration of the People of Rupert's Land and the North West," Fort Garry, 8 December 1869, in Raymond Huel, ed., *The Collected Writings of Louis Riel, vol. 1: 1861–1875* (Edmonton: The University of Alberta Press, 1985), 42–4.

DECLARATION

Of the People of Rupert's Land and the North West

WHEREAS, it is admitted by all men, as a fundamental principle that the public authority commands the obedience and respect of its subjects. It is also admitted that a people when it has no Government is free to adopt one form of Government in preference to another to give or to refuse aliegance [sic] to that which is proposed. In accordance with the first principle the people of this Country had obeyed and respected that authority to which the circumstances surrounding its infancy compelled it to be subject.

A company of adventurers known as the "Hudson's Bay Company" and invested with certain powers granted by His Majesty (Charles II.) established itself in Rupert's Land, AND IN THE NORTH-WEST TERRITORY for trading purposes only. This Company, consisting of many persons, required a

certain constitution. But as there was a question of commerce only, their constitution was framed in reference thereto. Yet, since there was at that time no government to see to the interests of a people already existing in the country, it became necessary for judicial affairs to have recourse to the officers of the Hudson's Bay Company. Thus inaugurated that species of government, which, slightly modified by subsequent circumstances, ruled this country up to a recent date.

WHEREAS, this government thus accepted was far from answering the wants of the people, and became more and more so as the population increased in numbers, and as the country was developed, and commerce extended, until the present day, when it commands a place amongst the Colonies; and this people ever actuated by the above mentioned principles, had generously supported the aforesaid government, and gave to it a faithful allegiance; when, contrary to the law of nations, in March, 1869, that said Government surrendered and transferred to Canada all the rights which it had or pretended to have in this territory, by transactions with which the people were considered unworthy to be made acquainted.

AND WHEREAS, it is also generally admitted that a people is at liberty to establish any form of government it may consider suitable to its wants, as soon as the power to which it was subject abandons it, or attemps [sic], to subjugate it without its consent, to a foreign power; and maintain that no right can be transferred to such foreign power. Now, therefore,

1st. We, the Representatives of the people in Council assembled at Upper Fort Garry, on the 24th day of November, 1869, after having invoked the God of nations, relying on these fundamental moral principles solemnly declare in the name of our constituents and in our own names, before God and man, that from the day on which the Government we had always respected, abandoned us by transferring to a strange power the sacred authority confided to it, the people of Rupert's Land and the North-West became free and exempt from all allegiance to the said Government.

2d. That we refuse to recognise the authority of Canada, which pretends to have a right to coerce us and impose upon us a despotic form of government still more contrary to our rights and interests as British subjects than was that Government to which we had subjected ourselves through necessity up to a recent date.

3rd. That by sending an expedition on the 1st of November charged to drive back Mr William McDougall and his companions coming in the name of Canada to rule us with the rod of despotism without a previous notification to that effect, we have but acted conformably to that sacred right which commands every Citizen to offer energetic opposition to prevent his country being enslaved.

4th. That we continue and shall continue to oppose with all our strength the establishing of the Canadian authority in our country under the announced form. And in case of persistence on the part of the Canadian Government to enforce its obnoxious policy upon us, by force of arms, we protest before hand against such an unjust and unlawful course, and we declare the said Canadian Government responsible before God and men for the innumerable evils which may be caused by so unwarrantable a course.

Be it known, therefore, to the world in general and to the Canadian Government in particular, that as we have always heretofore successfully defended our country in frequent wars with the neighbouring tribes of Indians, who are now on friendly relations with us, we are firmly resolved in future not less than in the past, to repel all invasions from whatsoever quarter they may come.

And furthermore, we do declare and proclaim in the name of the people of Rupert's Land and the North-West that we have on the same 24th day of November, 1869, above mentioned, established a Provisional Government, and hold it to be the only and lawful authority now in existence in Rupert's Land and the North-West, which claim the obedience and respect of the people.

That meanwhile we hold ourselves in readiness to enter into such negotiations with the Canadian Government, which may be favorable for the good government and prosperity of this people.

In support of this declaration, relying on the protection of Divine Providence, we mutually pledge ourselves on oath, our lives, our fortunes, and our sacred honor to each other.

Issued at Fort Garry this 8th day of December in the year of our Lord one thousand eight hundred and sixty-nine.

(Signed,) JOHN BRUCE, President.
LOUIS RIEL, Secretary.

Historical Interpretations

3 From Nicole St-Onge and Carolyn Podruchny, "Scuttling along a Spider's Web: Mobility and Kinship in Métis Ethnogenesis," in Nicole St-Onge, Carolyn Podruchny, and Brenda Macdougall, eds, *Contours of a People: Métis Family, Mobility, and History* (Norman: University of Oklahoma Press, 2012), 59–92.

Métis ethnogenesis is an ill-defined process of cultural creation for those who study it, just as it was for those who lived through it. Accessing the process is hard because those who experienced it often did not do so deliberately or consciously, and few recorded the process for historians to discover. Ancestors of the Métis, both European and Indigenous, did not have categories of ethnic and cultural identity that match with those in use today. Indigenous ancestors in particular organized their worlds through relationships with people, landscapes, and the spirits they called on for assistance and guidance to survive and flourish.[1] When scholars write about men in the fur trade, it is often difficult to distinguish who was French Canadian, Métis, Cree, or Ojibwe. We can try to discover where someone grew up, who their parents were, what languages they spoke, those with whom they traded, and where they chose to live and work. But are these things the actual ingredients of a cultural identity? Do they suffice in defining a particular identity? Moreover, why do historians care about defining a Métis identity and understanding its formation? Why attempt to describe the process of Métis ethnogenesis if it was meaningless or murky for the people who supposedly initiated it, performed it, and lived it?

We do so for three reasons. First, Métis communities across the northwest of North America have for generations celebrated their distinct culture, played Métis fiddle music, woven Métis sashes, spoken Michif, and waved the Métis flag, both literally and conceptually.[2] For these people and for their families, friends, neighbours, and fellow citizens, it is important to discern the beginnings of historical processes that, no matter how murky, later became defined, entrenched, and lived meanings of Métis-ness. The next two closely related reasons are that Métis people are politically recognized and their Aboriginal rights affirmed in the Canadian Constitution Act of 1982 and the Supreme Court of Canada's 2003 decision to recognize the traditional harvesting rights of the Métis community of Sault Sainte Marie.[3] Neither the government nor the courts have yet worked out who is legally considered part of "the people." We believe that scholars of Métis history have an obligation to contribute to this process of defining Métis historical roots. Today's land and comprehensive claims processes, with their need to clearly define territories, do not accurately reflect eighteenth- and nineteenth-century mindsets of fur trade communities and their inhabitants. Echoing jurist Jean Teillet, we argue that court decisions such as *R. v. Powley*, which advance definitions of the Métis as a rights-bearing group as long as they can show that they are a "group of people living together in a stable and continuous community in the same geographic area" distort the lived reality and historical experience of the Métis within the fur trade.[4] We caution researchers and jurists against focusing too closely on territorial delineations and worry that current notions of nation, rooted to state and with clear concepts of territoriality, may come to dominate definitions of a Métis Nation. [. . .]

In our attempt to describe Métis ethnogenesis, we consider those who worked in the fur trade in what became Canada's northwest. They came from the St Lawrence valley, the British Isles, and the plains and boreal forests and have been identified as having French Canadian, Orcadian, Scottish, Cree, Ojibwe, Oji-Cree, Assiniboine, Blackfoot, Dene, Iroquoian, and Salish backgrounds. When European and Euro-Canadian men encountered Indigenous societies, they traded with them and formed friendships and alliances with them, and sometimes children, ensued from sexual unions. In some cases, the European and Euro-Canadian men and Indigenous women formed long-lasting, stable unions, marrying *à la façon du pays* (in the custom of the country); their children married each other to form, new and distinct communities and kin networks.[5] In this reading, we attempt to put brackets around this murky process without pinning down individuals in one fixed and bounded category, instead tracing the movement of individual lives, loyalties, friendships, and kin ties. We argue that understandings of Métis-ness are distinct from other groups in the northwestern part of North America because the category of Métis was created from such a large variety of other ethnic groups and because, for the greater part of its history, it was not rooted to any particular place. The Métis carved economic niches within the fur trade as voyageurs and servants, as suppliers of pemmican, as freighters and trip men, as small traders and freemen, and as interpreters, guides, and go-betweens.[6] Métis probably thought of themselves as part of a far-flung network of commerce, and they probably had a distinct view of the world as a vast, mobile, and interconnected territory, as opposed to being long-term farmers with clear-cut quarter sections or river lots, held for generations within a bounded community. Most Métis social locations (including those that featured farming in addition to work as trip men and buffalo hunters) were rooted to a mode of life

that happened to be mobile—the mercantile world of the fur trade and its contact points in the continental interior. The ever-expanding fur trade's water and land routes became the geographic architecture for Métis ethnogenesis because Métis communities emerged around the constantly opening and closing fur trade posts. In addition, during the eighteenth and nineteenth centuries Métis people generally moved westward to access new resources of fur, meat, fish, and fertile land to cultivate. In the midst of their migrations, both seasonal and permanent, they came to rely on kin and define themselves through kin networks.

Our metaphor for conceptualizing Métis ethnogenesis is a spider web, with finely spun connections of family, kin, and friendship obligations. Like spider webs, these connections were woven in surprising and complex patterns and multiple dimensions, could be hard to see, could be easily broken and re-spun, and yet were strong and durable. [. . .]

In this reading, we likewise emphasize the multiple processes of initiation of Métis ethnogenesis, rather than a main centre in the Red River settlement and a periphery of the West; we also emphasize that the traffic along the web of Métis kin networks moved in all directions. Connections formed among many of the small communities and extended families along the fur trade routes, and new regional centres such as Fort St Joseph, Île à la Crosse, Lac la Biche, Batoche, Wood Mountain, and St-Laurent, were constantly emerging. The dynamics of the fur trade, the plains-provisioning economy, and the freighting business all informed the webs of kinship and loyalty being constantly forged, broken, and remade.

SCUTTLING AROUND THE WEB

Many studies of Métis have focused on fixed communities, such as the Red River settlement; St-Laurent, Manitoba; Batoche,

Saskatchewan; and Prairie du Chien, Wisconsin.[7] But some scholars have started to recognize the centrality of extensive migrations to Métis culture and history. The Métis demonstrated their mobility repeatedly, in multiple ways, beginning with voyageurs moving westward from the St Lawrence valley to work in the trade and continuing both with the migration of individuals and families from the Great Lakes region to the Red River valley in the late eighteenth century and with the slow westward movement across the plains from the Red River settlement that accelerated after the 1870s, when it was clear that Métis were losing out on the rights to land and compensation that they had won in the Red River Resistance of 1869–70.[8] [. . .]

The people from mixed origins who coalesced into these far-flung, mobile fur trade communities descended from kin-based (and often clan-based) societies that were also experiencing an accelerating history of mobility. From the eighteenth century on, more and more Scots were forced to emigrate by changing economic and social circumstances. Many of these migrants from the Scottish Highlands entered the fur trade and brought their clan alliances with them.[9] [. . .]

In both groups [Highlanders and Indigenous people], clan leaders were expected to act for the good of their people. The similarities between Highlands and many Indian groups extended beyond clans: "They lived in tribal societies with a strong warrior tradition, they inhabited rugged homelands, and they were accustomed to deprivation and inured to hardship." Both Highlanders and Indians also lived as tribal people on the edge of an empire that spanned the Atlantic, and their identities were forged by often-bitter experiences with British colonialism and English cultural imperialism.[10]

Of course the parallels between Highlanders and Indians can only go so far. Whereas the Highland Scots constituted a single ethnic group with a common culture and language who inhabited a relatively small homeland, Indian societies were numerous, possessed tremendous cultural and linguistic diversity, and inhabited a vast continent. Highland clans were feudally organized, clan chiefs had considerable control over members of their clan, and clans organized land distribution and defence, whereas Native American leaders rarely wielded the power, paraphernalia, or economic leverage of Highland clan chiefs.[11] And yet these similarities were strong enough that they shaped Highlander and Indian encounters and encouraged cultural mixing and intermarriages.[12]

[. . .]

Christian Morissoneau observed that French Canadians from the St Lawrence valley held family ties, even across vast continental distances, to be the most important characteristic of their consciousness. He explained that theirs "is a homeland writ small, a movable homeland, and it provides a basis for solidarity . . . and negates geography. Thus the people preserve their identity through their very instability."[13] French Canadians, like their Scottish counterparts, went into the interior in search of work and money and, sometimes, the quest for a better life. Between the 1700s and the early 1830s, over 34 000 fur trade contracts were signed before Montreal notaries by men eager to work in the "upper country" writ large.[14] Some might remain only one season, others a handful of years, and still others spent the balance of their lives in the North American interior.[15] Over the decades, a mercantile network was constructed and maintained across a broad crescent of interconnected waterways from Montreal to Michilimackinac, to the Red River settlement, to the Fort Des Prairies along the Saskatchewan River, farther north to the subarctic, to St Louis, and finally to New Orleans. United by language, religion, and diffuse but very real webs of actual and fictive reciprocal kin obligations, this French River World endured and prospered into the nineteenth century.[16] Métis kin networks grew out of these Scottish and French-Canadian familial and clan traditions, and the networks also incorporated indigenous kin and clan networks to adapt and create a unique web well suited to life in the Great Lakes, the Great Plains, and the northwestern boreal forest.[17]

Although kinship has not received the attention it deserves in the writing of North American Indigenous history, Raymond J. DeMallie asserted that kinship is of central importance to understanding Indigenous peoples, explaining, "Kin terminologies, descent and inheritance systems, marriage and residence patterns all combine in the family to shape the texture and dynamics of daily life, and serve as the foundations for Native American societies." He proposed that kinship is not simply a model for understanding social relations among families and tribal members but extends "to include the relationship of human beings to all other forms of existence in a vast web of cosmic interrelationship."[18] Robert Alexander Innes took up DeMallie's challenge to place kinship front and centre by infusing kinship into our understanding of the Indigenous people living in what became the northwest of Canada. In his work on the Cowessess First Nation in southeastern Saskatchewan, Innes found that kinship practices explain how this community came to be composed of Plains Cree, Saulteaux (western Ojibwe), Assiniboine, and Métis.[19]

Traders, both European and Indigenous, were born into a fluid and mobile fur trade world where the smallest hunting camps and outposts were connected to global systems of trade and alliances over vast geographic expanses through extended webs of kin as well as economic, social, and cultural activities that bound people together. Bethel Saler and Carolyn Podruchny recently used the metaphor of a Russian nesting doll to envision the interconnectedness of the many spatial scopes of the fur trade, ranging from the macro views of global and hemispheric trade networks to discrete company geographies and regional and local trading realms.[20] In the nineteenth century, this fur trade

world was both widening and shifting westward in geographic and demographic terms. Montreal and Michilimackinac were slowly declining centres, whereas Fort Chipewyan and York Factory (especially after 1821) were ascending.[21] Given these kin or tribal structures' roots in a mercantile economy based on cross-cultural linkages and exchanges across vast swaths of the North American continent, it would be an error to see them as anachronistic. They were adaptive to the social, cultural, and geographic challenges faced in the North American interior. In the same vein, the mode of life necessitated by successful Métis economic pursuits of freighting, plains provisioning, and trading in the North American interior encouraged the preservation and adaptation of kin-based networks inherited from both the maternal and paternal sides. In her examination of Indian men and French women in the western Great Lakes, Susan Sleeper-Smith found that the French Catholic kin ties, often expressed through godparenting, combined with the kin structures of Indigenous people to produce a widespread kin network and collective identity that subsumed individuality, incorporated mixed-ancestry offspring, and facilitated the expansion of the fur trade.[22] [. . .] The need for these ties may have been reinforced by the increased mobility and greater horizons of the eighteenth and nineteenth centuries in the North American interior. The Métis were born into a world where a degree of reciprocity and group cohesion was necessary. Beyond the logistics of bridging the sheer distances involved and the logistics of the economic endeavours pursued, there were competitions among fur trade companies, clashes with competing Indian bands, epidemics, famines, and struggles for access to bison herds, fishing grounds, and wintering sites. Métis cohesion within the fur trade was necessitated by the internal dictates of trading and plains provisioning and by the ever-present possibility of external competing interests and potential threats.

So, how should we view the contours of this emerging people? In the eighteenth and nineteenth century, Métis people were defined by their links to the fur trade; by networks of connectedness formed while working in the fur trade; by commonalities and relatedness formed in families; by inherited appreciation of family, kin, and clan structures; and by their mobility. Certainly some appearances of stability, in the form of fixed places, appeared in the northwest. Mackinac, Fort William, Red River, La Loche, Lac la Biche, and French Prairie were examples of geographical rootedness to a site, and many of these endure to this day. But these examples of geographical rootedness can give a false impression of physical stability. People within these communities moved within and between these and myriad other places, from large farming settlements to mobile hunting camps to temporary winter camps. Both their economy and culture encouraged this mobility, which became one of their prime societal markers. Such societal markers certainly could exist within neighboring ethnic and occupational groups, such as Cree middlemen and Iroquoian voyageurs, but what made the Métis distinct were the particular combinations of occupational ranges and patterns of mobility.

One could characterize the Métis as a variety of groups that drew on mixed heritage in different ways in a wide range of circumstances. But among this range of communities and families emerged a sense of commonality and eventually a sense of collectivity to survive, produce, and reproduce in an environment of immense human, physical, and socio-economic flux. They came from (to use Calloway's words) tribal peoples both on the European and the Indian side. They recreated vast networks real or fictive kinships that they could call on for help and support while maintaining the high degree of mobility required by the fur trade economy. Places like the Red River settlement provided stability to support the movements and chain migration within the Red River families and

kin networks. Even those who were born and died at Red River were mobile. This mobility becomes obvious when life histories and family genealogies are reconstructed. Children were often born away from the Red River settlement in wintering sites, at other trading posts, or on the buffalo hunt. While working in the fur trade, Métis servants were left alone or in groups to winter, hunt, fish, or work in families or clans like the Delorme, Desjarlais, or, Parenteau. These kin groups maintain to this day and enduring presence in communities such as the Red River settlement, but a great number of their members moved along the fur trade links to Batoche, La Loche, English River, and Fort Chipewyan. To understand the eighteenth- and nineteenth-century Métis, locale is less important than webs of kinship.

[MÉTIS] AND THEIR KIN

In addition to seasonal migrations to follow resources and progressive westward migrations in search of new opportunities, a third type of migration pattern further complicates the tracing of Métis ethnogenesis: the movement of individuals in and out of different social and economic situations and in and out of different identifications, categories, and lifestyles. [. . .]

Our first example is an eighteenth-century Great Lakes woman who used kin connections to construct elaborate, powerful, and far-flung fur trade networks but remained rooted to a single place. Marie Madeleine Réaume L'archevêque Chevalier was the daughter of an Ilini woman, Simphorose Ouaouagoukoue, and a French-Canadian father, Jean-Baptisete Réaume, who worked as an interpreter for the French Crown at Fort St Joseph on the southeastern shore of Lake Michigan and Green Bay on the west side of the lake. [. . .] At 24, Chevalier married Augustin L'archevêque, an Illinois Country fur trader. Over the next 15 years, she gave birth to at least four daughters, all of whom survived to maturity, and a son who probably did not reach adulthood. Her first husband died when Chevalier was in her thirties, and at 41 she married Michilimackinac trader Louis Thérèse Chevalier.[23] Chevalier spent most of her life at Fort St Joseph, a life fully shaped by the fur trade: she was the daughter of a fur trader and married two fur traders, and her five daughters also married fur traders. Mobility characterized her life not through migration or livelihood but rather, through kin networks.

Marie Madeleine Réaume L'archevêque Chevalier's adult identity was defined by the ever-expanding Catholic kin network of the fur trade, which extended north of Michilimackinac, west to Green Bay, east to Montreal, and south to Cahokia and St Louis.[24] She expanded and solidified kin networks by choosing godparents for her children. She chose Iliniwik women or her own daughters to serve as godmothers to her children. Each godfather, however, was French: the fort commandant, his sons, and an interpreter. Only for her last child did she select a godfather of mixed ancestry.[25] She dramatically increased her kin connections when she married Louis Thérèse Chevalier. One of her daughters married one of Louis's brothers, whereas another daughter married Louis's Montreal business partner. Other members of Louis's family married Winnebago women, and the merger of these two families integrated and extended their kin connections in many directions.[26]

By the mid-eighteenth century, as the French population at Fort St Joseph dramatically declined, the Pottawatomi, her kin, and her trading partners increasingly came to define Chevalier's world. About 1200 Potawatomi lived near or at the post, and several hundred Miami lived in an adjacent village.[27] By 1760, all but one of her children had moved to larger fur trade communities, but they all frequently returned to Fort St Joseph to have their own children baptized or to serve as godparents. Chevalier

expanded and adjusted her kin networks as her circumstances and environment changed. Sleeper-Smith explained, "Marriage served as a planned extension of kin networks, Catholicism further extended those linkages through fictive kinship, and mobility ex-tended that kin network throughout the western Great Lakes."[28] Although Chevalier stayed in a single place, she manipulated her kin connections to move among different communities to trade.

In later times and places, she might readily have identified as Métis. But a crucial question is, What made her Métis? Can we know whether she thought of herself and her family as Métis, or as distinct from the Indian and French people living around her? It is clear that she operated successfully in multiple worlds, which included Illinois, Pottawatomi, Miami, and French.

[. . .]

The quintessential French-Canadian freeman (and one of the most famous) was Charles Racette, who called himself the Lord of Lake Winnipeg.[29] Although he was not descended from Indian and European parents, Racette's life closely resembled those of Métis. He and his children lived in the Lake Winnipeg and Lake Manitoba area, moving in and out of economic and social situations in search of prosperity. Racette was born in 1765 or 1773 in the parish of St Augustin, just west of Quebec City along the St Lawrence River. He entered the fur trade by at least 1790, joining a Michilimackinac-based group of Nipigon traders. We can be certain Racette's parents had managed to provide him with an education because he entered the service as a youthful clerk rather than a paddler. His start as a clerk probably explained his disdain for "common labourers," but he shared their language and probably suffered discrimination from Scottish and English bourgeois, especially when Racette worked on short-term labour contracts as a guide and interpreter. In the late 1790s, the HBC hired Racette to establish a post on the upper Red River. This venture failed because the Orcadian English-speaking servants, who could not understand the French-speaking Racette, refused to work under his authority. Some years later, Racette tried again to work within the confines of a large company, this time for the NWC, whose workforce was primarily francophone. He procured several hundred pounds to establish a post near Grand Portage, but this venture failed as well. Disillusioned with working for companies, he began to trade on his own in the 1790s. By 1807, he was living as a freeman with his family on the west side of Lake Manitoba, near Fort Dauphin, while continuing to work informally for the NWC.

Racette began a family in the northwest in the last years of the eighteenth century, when he would have been either 25 or 32. He married a woman of Ojibwe descent—referred to in the records as Josephte Sauteux, who would have been about 20—and had at least five children with her between 1787 and 1824. Josephte, or "Mother" Racette, is regularly mentioned in sources as an active part of the family enterprise. She traded regularly with fur trade companies and probably trapped with her husband.[30] After this time, Racette began to refer to himself as the "lord of Lake Winnipeg."[31] Racette moved in and out of a variety of circumstances to find the best economic opportunities for his family, and he eventually settled on living as a freeman.

Some scholars, particularly John Foster and Heather Devine, consider the category of freeman as a part of Métis ethnogenesis, specifically the proto-generation of Métis. In his classic article "Wintering, the Outsider Adult Male and Ethnogenesis of the Western Plains Métis," Foster argued that the ethnogenesis of the Métis required a two-step process. The first was the wintering of an outside (European) male with an Indian band, which led to the outsider's marriage to a prominent Indian woman and the formation of close bond with adult Indian males, while

still maintaining close bonds with the male outsider (European) fur traders. The second step involved the outsider male leaving the fur trade service, or "going free"—living apart from both the fur trade post and the wife's Indian band—and establishing bands of freemen and their families. The freeman relied on kin ties with Indian people and economic ties to fur trade companies to exploit economic niches in the fur trade. The social milieu of these freeman bands, which drew on but were distinct from European trading posts and Indian bands, created the circumstances for new cultural forms to emerge, and these were reinforced when the children of freemen married one another.[32]

[. . .]

Johnny Grant, our [third] example of an individual Métis negotiating an identity in a variety of places throughout his life, was born in 1833 at Fort Edmonton. His grandfather William Grant was a Scottish-born Montreal and Trois-Rivières merchant. The community of Trois-Rivières was located in the St Lawrence valley, a region with very deep roots to employment in the fur trade economy. William Grant "of Three River," as the grandfather became known, was part of a large and active fur trading family focused on the Michilimackinac Great Lakes trade. William's wife, Marguerite Fafard Laframboise, was the daughter of a prosperous Trois-Rivières merchant named Jean Baptiste Fafard Laframboise. William's son, and Johnny Grant's father, Richard Grant, was a HBC trader raised in Trois-Rivières. Johnny Grant was therefore born on his father's side to the dual French and British fur-trading elite of Lower Canada. These ties were reinforced after the death of Johnny's mother, when Richard Grant took him back to Trois-Rivières to be raised by his paternal grandmother until the age of 17.[33] Johnny's mother was a Métis woman, Marie Anne Breland, the daughter of Pierre Breland and Louise Umfreville. Here again the ties into the Métis world ran deep, especially in the vicinity of the Red River settlement and Fort Edmonton. Pierre Breland was a hunter and free trader along the Saskatchewan River who eventually moved with his family to the Red River settlement.[34] By 1832, Maria Anne's siblings resided in Grantown (St Francois-Xavier), continuing the tradition of freighting, trading, farming, and bison hunting. They were considered one of the well-to-do and well-connected families of Red River.[35] Marie Anne was also partially raised by her stepfather, John Rowand, who was chief factor of Fort Edmonton from 1823 to 1854.[36] Several of John Rowand's sons and his daughter married into prominent Métis families and became active in the northwest fur trade. Johnny Grant considered all these relations and their descendants to be part of his kin network.

If the vertical webs of kin ran deep, Johnny Grant also ensured that horizontal lines of kinship and mutual obligations were quickly in place. In the 1850s, a few years after his return to the northwestern Great Plains, Johnny Grant struck out on his own and became a free trader in the vicinity of Fort Hall, Idaho, where his father was stationed. There, he married his first wife, a Shoshone woman, who helped cement his trading ties to her band. As Gerhard Ens noted, this was the beginning of a recurring theme for Johnny Grant. He had relationships with at least four different Native women who bore him at least a dozen children in the Montana/Idaho region. These kinship connections ensured good relations with the various Indian groups and enhanced his trading relations.[37] After making and losing several fortunes, he sold his ranch in Deer Lodge, Montana, and relocated to the Red River settlement. Prior to leaving, he sent a letter to John Rowand, Jr, his mother's half-brother, and asked whether he could bring his family to the Red River settlement to live near them. Rowand was dead by that time, and so the reply came from the Hon. John McKay, who was married to Margaret Rowand, Grant's mother's half-sister.

It was McKay who told him to come up with his family.[38]

There is no evidence that Grant was in Red River prior to his initial scouting mission in the late 1860s, when he spent three months visiting with different kin and acquaintances, renewing friendships, and making new ones. He also organized the move of his large family and entourage, returning to Montana to fetch them.[39] When Grant finally set out for Red River, he led 62 wagons, 12 carts, and 500 horses, 200 of which were his. There were 106 men plus numerous women and children. Some of these people were heading "to the States," but many followed Grant to Red River settlement.[40] He used his tried-and-true strategy for securing a place in a community by immediately marrying Clotilde Bruneau, the Métis daughter of a judge in the Red River Colony.[41]

Grant lived in the Red River settlement from 1867 to 1892, standing apart from those Métis who opposed Canadian annexation and participated in the 1869 resistance. Grant instead supported Canadian officials and amassed another fortune in land speculation following the exodus of many Métis families further west after Manitoba's entry into Canadian Confederation. By 1882, Grant owned 13 000 acres of land, a substantial two-story house, and a large herd of cattle at Rivière aux Ilets des Bois (today the site of Carman, Manitoba).[42] Although Grant worked hard to become a member of the new commercial elite in Manitoba, he was not successful. He eventually lost his land, his home, and his cattle through unpaid debts and changing herding laws. Grant moved west to Alberta to start over as a homesteader and fur trader but with little success. He died in 1907 with little to his name.[43] Even if Grant was primarily a rancher throughout most of his life, his extended family illustrates the centrality of fur trade networks in creating patterns of economic opportunities and mobility, and these patterns were very easily adapted to an open-range ranching lifestyle.

Gerhard Ens described Johnny Grant as representative of many Métis traders and merchants in the last half of the nineteenth century: men who were able to amass wealth and property working as intermediaries between Native economies and incoming European-based capitalism. Success depended on their ability to move easily between Indian worlds and European settlement, using interpersonal and intercultural skills in the trade of furs and cattle. However, as Indians became dispossessed and their economies plummeted after the rapid demise of the buffalo, many Métis entrepreneurs could not adapt to the new capitalist environments, which required standardized management, accounting, planning, and knowledge of contracts and corporations. Furthermore, they lacked financial connections and access to capital in central Canada.[44] Throughout his life, Grant fluctuated among a variety of identifications, including Euro-Canadian, Métis, and Indian, depending on which was most economically and socially advantageous.[45]

Some of the examples discussed above show that the development of Métis identifications and communities could be grounded in a region with core foci. Marie Madeleine Réaume L'archevêque Chevalier rooted her life and extensive kin network at Fort St Joseph, though the family ties ranged throughout the Great Lakes basin. The family of Charles Racette gained prominence in the Interlake region of present-day Manitoba. [. . .] But even these regions may not have been particularly fixed, for they expanded, shifted, and contracted over time, depending on economic resources and possibilities. The nuclear unit may or may not have been especially mobile, but the larger web of kinship was diffuse and shifting, responding to new opportunities or socio-economic pressures.

Mobility came in many guises. Although it could mean individuals and families moving around a great deal over varying distances, it also meant mobility in alliances and family connections as well as socio-economic

mobility and the constant search for new sources of livelihood. More often than not, the Métis themselves viewed it as a combination of all three. Yet, in whatever guise, this mobility was both anchored in and defined by expansive kinship networks rooted in the fur trade's innumerable trails and waterways. The multiple webs, both tangible and obscure, were made manifest by those who came to be called Métis. Although the people themselves may only have used collective terms such as Métis or La Nation in the nineteenth century when forced to deal with external and often hostile entities, they understood their unique position within multifaceted geographic, economic, social, and ideological networks. They lived a Métis life even if they did not have the need, time, or inclination to articulate it out loud or brand it with a label.

GATHERING THE STRANDS

The stories in the previous section lead one to wonder what was particularly Métis about the extended webs of kin and relatedness and the multiple guises of mobility. [. . .] We argue that a generalized vision of Métis-ness can be derived from the myriad of specific examples of Métis community and individual histories that have been published in the last 25 years. Métis are distinct from neighbouring communities because of the sheer size of the area over which they travelled, lived, and worked; their emergence out of the fur trade; their close economic relationship to mercantile capital; their reliance on fur trade networks in the eighteenth and nineteenth centuries; and cultural practices passed down over generations. All these factors combine to give shape and coherence to their kin-structured communities.

Evidence suggests that Métis ethnogenesis in the eighteenth and nineteenth centuries in the northwest of North America was a singularly adaptive manifestation with a particular twist—the Métis used webs of kinship to succeed in an ever-expanding mercantile economy. The Métis represent not only an enduring form of organizing one's larger social, economic, and political world through webs of real and imagined kin, but one that could be fashioned and refashioned to meet eighteenth- and nineteenth-century realities. In these centuries, imperial trans-Atlantic economies consolidated and expanded, requiring ever-lengthening lines of secure communications and exchanges. Concurrently, emerging nation-states carved out territories, hardened their borders, and introduced national "state" categories of identification. Yet, all the while, groups variously termed classes,[46] tribes, peoples, and nations endured and adapted by transcending these national and state identifications. French Canadians, Scots, Métis, and the interior Indian tribes all survived, at least for a time, by proactively adapting older forms of social organizations, which allowed for stability through long-term and far-flung webs of reciprocity. These forms of social organization could endure even in situations of frequent mobility. As with other multicultural bands, the Métis web allowed for the incorporation of outsider—including new Indian bands or incoming fur trade employees—via marriage and fictive kin practices such as godparenting and adoption. The fur trade world certainly lent itself to such "stable mobility" with the regular back-and-forth movements of goods and people along its river routes and cart trails. The very emergence of fur trade mercantilism allowed old, forms of tribalism or clanship to adapt and serve as a means of prospering and eventually creating a new people. The Métis were unique among other multicultural tribes because they embraced the opportunities that the expanding capitalist system provided. The rise of capitalism did not obliterate old forms of social organization but, rather, allowed the Métis to survive and refine themselves. In turn, the fur trade business needed the Métis

as experienced suppliers, entrepreneurs, labourers, and middlemen in order to function effectively.

The concept of the fur trade world as constituted of webs and nodes, with people deriving from it their self-understandings and social locations through kinship ties, is a compelling one. Places like Red River or Mackinac are important nodes in part because of their undeniable physical attraction in terms of geographic location and economic nexus, but also because of the webs of kinship that ran thick through them. Johnny Grant, after finally deciding to leave Montana, took his kin and entourage to the Red River settlement, a place he had never been, because he knew that the settlement offered both economic opportunity and a network of kin. Although he had never met his Red River settlement relatives, he knew that they would help him settle and take up his usual economic pursuits of ranching and trading. Webs as mental spaces and physical realities could be resilient and robust. On the ground, the "Northwest" was continuously being redefined. Western geographic centres, such as Red River, Fort Edmonton, Fort Chipewyan, Rocky Mountain House, and Fort Astoria, eclipsed eastern geographic centres, like Mackinac, Grand Portage, and Fort William. Equivalent social centres, like the forged ties of kin, alliance, and friendship between and within Métis communities, were also being continuously renegotiated as new Indian tribes were incorporated into the fur trade, populations moved farther west to follow bison herds, and old routes were abandoned and new ones opened, with attendant new trading posts. Continuous influxes of people were brought into the fur trade kin network not only from European arrivals and the interior Indian tribes, but also from eastern Indians who moved west to take advantage of trading opportunities. [. . .]

Identifications based on expansive and extensive webs of kinship enabled Métis people to endure, survive, adapt, and prosper in changing, fluid, and sometimes hostile environments. This form of social adaptation and societal arrangement was a viable mechanism to maintain necessary social and economic cohesion over vast distances, in a milieu of merchant capitalism, and mingling with multiple cultures, societies, and economies. It was an effective basis for a group identification that could transcend local and regional ties and allow for economic pursuits predicated on mobility to flourish and, in turn, reinforce the far-flung kin-based structures. Being Métis and being part of a Métis world—whether one formally labelled oneself

as such or not—was an intrinsically adaptive social construct given the conditions prevalent in the nineteenth-century fur trade world. Obviously the contours of this identification ebbed and flowed given specific conditions in specific moments and places. In some cases, internal and especially external pressures hardened Métis identification into a national militant category that used a clear us-them discourse. As Gerhard Ens suggests, it occurred in Red River at specific times for specific reasons, but, for the *longue duree,* Métis identification was an embedded and adaptive category that incorporated or co-opted individuals rather than pushed them out.[47]

NOTES

1. For a discussion on the instability of the term "identity," see Rogers Brubaker and Frederick Cooper, "Beyond 'Identity,'" *Theory and Society* 29 (February 2000): 1–47.

2. For examples, see the Gabriel Dumont Institute at http://wvvw.gdins.org, and especially their Virtual Museum of Métis History and Culture at http://www.métismuseurn.ca (accessed 13 October 2009).

3. On the *Powley* decision of 2003, see "*Powley* Case: Fulfilling Canada's Promise, Métis Nation of Ontario," at http://www.métisnation.org/harvesting/Powley_Case/legalol.html (13 October 2009); and Gwen Reimer and Jean-Philippe Chartrand, "Documenting Historic Métis in Ontario," *Ethnohistory* 51, 3 (Summer 2004): 567–607.

4. Jean Teillet, "The Métis of the Northwest Towards a Definition of a Rights-Bearing Community for a Mobile People." Master's thesis. University of Toronto, ON, 2008. 1–8.

5. For the classic works on the relations between male fur traders and Indigenous women, see Jennifer S.H. Brown, *Strangers in Blood: Fur Trade Company Families in Indian Country* (Vancouver: University of British Columbia Press, 1980); and Sylvia Van Kirk, "*Many Tender Ties*": *Women in Fur-Trade Society, 1670–1870* (Winnipeg, MB: Watson and Dwyer, 1980).

6. For examples of the range of Métis economic activities, see Gerhard J. Ens, "Dispossession or Adaptation?: Migration and Persistence of the Red River Métis," *Historical Communications/ Communications Historiques* (1988): 120–44; Nicole St-Onge, "Variations in Red River: The Traders and Freemen Métis of Saint-Laurent,Manitoba," *Canadian Ethnic Studies* 2 (1992): 2–21; Heather Devine, *The People Who Own Themselves: Aboriginal Ethnogenesis in a Canadian Family 1660–1900* (Calgary, AB: University of Calgary Press, 2004); and John E. Foster, "The Plains Métis," in R. Bruce Morrison and C. Roderick Wilson, eds, *Native Peoples: The Canadian Experience* (Toronto, ON: McClelland and Stewart, 1986), 375–404.

7. Gerhard J. Ens, *Homeland to Hinterland: The Changing World of the Red River Métis in the Nineteenth Century* (Toronto: University of Toronto Press, 1996); Diane P. Payment, *The Free People-Les Gens Libres: A History of the Community of Batoche, Saskatchewan* (Calgary: University of Calgary Press, 2009); Nicole St-Onge, *Saint-Laurent, Manitoba: Evolving Métis Identities, 1850–1914* (Regina: Canadian Plains Research Center, University of Regina, 2004); Lucy Eldersveld Murphy, *A Gathering of Rivers: Indian, Métis, and Mining in the Western Great Lakes, 1737–1832* (Lincoln: University of Nebraska Press, 2000).

8. On voyageurs and their extensive travels, see Carolyn Podruchny, *Making the Voyageur World* (Lincoln: University of Nebraska Press, Toronto: University of Toronto Press, 2006). On the westward migrations of the Métis, see Ens, *From Homeland to Hinterland,* 14–15, 73, 77, 80, 92, 111–12, 114, 117–22, 139, 154, 170–2.

9. On the Highland traders and their clans, see Colin Calloway, *White People, Indians, and Highlanders: Tribal Peoples and Colonial Encounters in Scotland and America* (Oxford: Oxford University Press, 2008), 23–8, 118–46.

10. Ibid., 8–10; quote from p. 9.

11. Ibid., 8–10.

12. On Highland Scots becoming dominant in both the HBC and the Montreal-based companies, as well as in the upper echelons of the HBC after its merger with the North West Company (NWC), see ibid., 120–1. As for Highlander fur traders marrying Indian women and having mixed-blood children, see ibid., 156–74.

13. Christian Morissonneau, "The 'Ungovernable' People: French-Canadian Mobility and Identity," in D.R. Louder and E. Waddell, eds, *French America: Mobility, Identity and Minority Experience across the Continent,* (Baton Rouge, LA, and London, UK: Louisiana State University Press, 1993), 15–32; at p. 28.

14. Nicole St-Onge, "Tracing the Voyageurs: Understanding the Background to the Métis Nation and Métis Homeland-Voyageur Contract Database Project," University of Ottawa and the Saint-Boniface Historical Society, 2002–2009.

15. Nicole St-Onge, "Early Forefathers to the Athabasca Métis: Long-term North West Company Employees," in David McNab and Ute Lischke, eds, *The Long Journey of a Forgotten People: Métis Identities and Family Histories* (Waterloo, ON: Wilfrid Laurier University Press, 2007), 109–61.

16. Robert Englebert, "Beyond Borders: Mental Mapping and the French River World." PhD diss., University of Ottawa, ON, 2010.

17. Susan Sleeper-Smith, "Women, Kin and Catholicism: New Perspectives on the Fur Trade," *Ethnohistory* 47, 2 (Spring 2000): 423–52.

18. Raymond J. DeMallie, "Kinship: The Foundation for Native American Society," in Russell Thornton, ed., *Studying Native America: Problems and Prospects* (Madison: University of Wisconsin Press, 1998), 306–56, at p. 306.

19. Robert Alexander Innes, "Elder Brother, the Law of the People and Contemporary Kinship Practices of Cowessess First Nation Members: Reconceptualizing Kinship in American Indian Studies Research," *American Indian Culture and Research Journal* 34, 2 (2010): 27–46; and "The Importance of Family Ties to Members of the Cowessess First Nation," PhD dissertation, University of Arizona, 2007.

20. Bethel Saler and Carolyn Podruchny, "Glass Curtains and Storied Landscapes: Fur Trade Historiography in Canada and the United States," in Andrew Graybill and Benjamin Johnson, eds, *Bridging National Borders in. North America* (Durham, NC: Duke University Press, 2010), 275–302. Also see Brian Slattery, "Our Mongrel Selves: Pluralism, Identity and the Nation," in Ysolde Gendreau, ed., *Community of Right / Rights of the Community* (Montreal, QC: Editions Themis, 2003), 3–41.

21. Fur traders and Great Lakes Métis communities were not the only ones shifting westward. See John P. Bowes, *Exiles and Pioneers: Eastern Indians in the Trans-Mississippi West* (Cambridge, UK: Cambridge University Press, 2008).

22. Susan Sleeper-Smith, *Indian Women and French Men: Rethinking Cultural Encounter in the Western Great Lakes* (Amherst: University of Massachusetts Press, 2001), 42–4.

23. Susan Sleeper Smith, "Furs and Female Kin Networks: The World of Marie Medeleine Réaume L'archevêque Chevalier," in Jo-Anne Fiske, Susan Sleeper-Smith, and William Wicken, eds, *New Faces of the Fur Trade* (East Lansing: Michigan State University Press, 1998), 56; and Sleeper-Smith, *Indian Women and French Men,* 46–7.

24. Sleeper-Smith, "Furs and Female Kin Networks," 54; and Sleeper-Smith, *Indian Women and French Men,* 45–9.

25. Sleeper-Smith, "Furs and Female Kin Networks," 56; and Sleeper-Smith, *Indian Women and French Men,* 46.

26. Sleeper-Smith, "Furs and Female Kin Networks," 58; and Sleeper-Smith, *Indian Women and French Men,* 48.

27. Sleeper-Smith, "Furs and Female Kin Networks," 55.

28. Sleeper-Smith, *Indian Women and French Men,* 50.

29. For an overview of Racette's life, see Podruchny, *Making the Voyageur World,* 294–5.

30. George Nelson's Journal, 3 November 1807–31 August 1808, 14 May 1808, and 22 May 1808, pp. 31, 34, Baldwin Room, S13, Metropolitan Reference Library, Toronto; George Nelson's Journal, 1 September 1808–31 March 1810, entitled "Journal for 1808 &c &c &c," 14 September 1809, in ibid.; George Nelson's Journal, 1 April 1810–1 May 1811, 9 July 1810, in ibid.; George Nelson's Journal and reminiscences, 1 December 1825–13 September 1836, entitled "St. Judes, Dec 1st 1825," p. 82, in ibid.; and Cox, *Adventures on the Columbia River,* 15 July 1817, p. 276.

31. George Nelson's Journal and reminiscences, 1 December 1825–13 September 1836, entitled "St. Judes, Dec 1st 1825," p. 82, Baldwin Room, S13, Metropolitan Reference Library, Toronto, ON.

32. John E. Foster, "Wintering, the Outsider Adult Male and Ethnogenesis of the Western Plains Métis," *Prairie Forum* 19, 1 (Spring 1994): 1–13.

33. Gerhard J. Ens, "Introduction," in John Francis Grant, *A Son of the Fur Trade: The Memoirs of Johnny Grant,* Gerhard J. Ens, ed. (Edmonton; University of Alberta Press, 2008), vii–xxxix; at p. x.

34. Grant, *A Son of the Fur Trade,* 1; and Gerhard J. Ens, "Métis Ethnicity, Personal Identity and the Development of Capitalism in the Western Interior," in Binnema et al. eds, *From Rupert's Land to Canada* (Edmonton: University of Alberta Press, 2001), 161–77; at pp. 164–5.

35. For example, one of her brothers, Pascal Breland, married Maria Grant, daughter of the settlement's founder and "warden of the plains," Cuthbert Grant (Grant, *Son of the Fur Trade,* 1).

36. Rowand's second country marriage was to Lisette or Louise Umfreville, likely Marie Ahne's mother, who had separated from Pierre Breland prior to 1812 (ibid., p. xlvii).

37. Ens, "Introduction," 165.

38. Grant, *Son of the Fur Trade,* 135–6.

39. Ibid., 152–64.

40. Ibid.; 170; Ens, "Introduction," xiv; and Ens, "Métis Ethnicity,"167–8.

41. Grant, *Son of the Fur Trade,* 180–4; and Ens, "Métis Ethnicity," 168–9.

42. Ens, "Introduction" pp. xiv–xxxili; and Ens, "Métis Ethnicity," 168–71.

43. Ens, "Introduction," pp. xxiii–xxxix; and Ens, "Métis Ethnicity," 172.

44. Ens, "Métis Ethnicity," 172–73.

45. Ens, "Introduction," p. vii; and Ens, "Métis Ethnicity," 161–4, 174.

46. Abraham Leon, *The Jewish Question: A Marxist Interpretation* (Mexico City: Pioneras, 1950). Leon sees the Jews as constituting a "people-class."

47. Gerhard J. Ens, "The Battle of Seven Oaks and the Articulation of a Métis National Tradition, 1811–1849," in Nicole St-Onge, Carolyn Podruchny, and Brenda Macdougall, eds, *Contours of a People: Métis Family, Mobility, and History* (Norman: University of Oklahoma Press, 2012), 93–119.

4 From Gerhard Ens, "Prologue to the Red River Resistance: Pre-liminal Politics and the Triumph of Riel," *Journal of the Canadian Historical Association* 5, 1 (1994): 111–23. Reprinted with permission from the author and from the Journal of the Canadian Historical Association.

The Red River Resistance of 1869–70 is usually thought to have begun in October of 1869 with the stopping of the Canadian survey, the formation of the Métis "National Committee" led by Louis Riel, and the blockade of the road to Pembina. As well, most historians credit Riel with taking the initiative in formulating a Métis response to the Canadian plan to acquire Rupert's Land. What these accounts miss is the vibrant debate and conflict within the Métis community about what their response to Confederation should be. The first coherent plan of assuring Métis rights was formulated in July 1869 and was opposed by Riel. It was not until Riel had defeated this first plan and its leaders that he assumed leadership of the movement against annexation.

It is this early "pre-liminal"[1] phase of the Red River Resistance—July through October

1869—that this paper proposes to examine in some detail. During this period, two Métis groups, one led by William Dease and the other by Louis Riel, were locked in a power struggle. It was a struggle on a symbolic level in which the two sides offered different paradigms of Métis "communitas"[2] as the basis on which to present their case to the Canadian government. The struggle occurred at the grass roots level involving such tactics as negotiation and coalition formation. It was not until Riel had defeated William Dease for the leadership of the Resistance and consolidated his basis of support among the French Métis that he felt strong enough to initiate the breach of October 1869. The analysis offered here concentrates on the activities of individuals vying for power within very limited political settings, and is interested in how those who achieved power carried out the consciously held goals of the group.

It is my contention that the initial Métis conflict between Dease and Riel not only set the tone for the larger Resistance to come but determined, to a large extent, the problems Riel and his faction would have in building a consensus in the Colony. To this end, the paper will explain the nature of this power struggle, the opposing paradigms of Métis communitas, the tactics Riel used to defeat his rivals, and the implications that this power struggle had for Métis unity in the Colony after October 1869.

The few historians who have examined this early period of the Red River Resistance in any detail have tended to denigrate the Métis that opposed Riel. W.L. Morton, in his extended introduction to Alexander Begg's journal, tried to show that the true nature of the Resistance was revealed in the conflict between the Métis "half-articulated demand for corporate rights . . . and the intention of the Canadian authorities to grant individual rights in due course."[3] In his view, it was the "new nation" of the Métis which was "the central and dynamic protagonist of the

Red River Resistance."[4] To make this argument Morton downplayed the role the Catholic clergy had in championing Riel's leadership,[5] and implied that those Métis opposed to Riel were dupes of the Canadians in Red River.[6] To have accorded the Métis opponents of Riel some volition and legitimacy would have undercut his argument that Riel was the undisputed leader of the French Métis in Red River.

Philippe Mailhot's account of the same period provides a much more accurate account of the role the Catholic clergy, especially that of Father Ritchot. Based on a detailed reconstruction of Ritchot's journal, Mailhot details the active part he played in directing Riel's Resistance.[7] Mailhot's account, however, closely follows Ritchot's partisan perspective. While Mailhot does not completely endorse Ritchot's argument that Dease's actions were directed by John Christian Schultz,[8] he does note that Dease's proposals mirrored those of the Canadian Party,[9] and that Dease and his party were not up to the task of directing the Resistance to annexation.[10] What both Morton and Mailhot overlook are the antecedents to the Dease proposals, and the active role the Catholic clergy had in discrediting the Dease party.

The first major Métis response to the news of the impending transfer of Rupert's Land to Canada came during the summer of 1869. In response to the vitriolic demonstrations of the Canadians in the Colony,[11] and in order to protect their land rights, a number of Métis called a large public meeting. This group included some of the traditional Métis leadership in the Colony such as William Dease, Pascal Breland, and William Hallet. Dease was the son of John W. Dease and Jenny Beignoit, and had been born in 1827 at Calling Lake. He settled at Red River and married Marguerite Genthon. The couple and their large family lived and farmed in both St Vital and St Norbert. By 1869 Dease was a prominent French-Métis trader and farmer, and member of the Council of Assiniboia.

An indication of Dease's close connection to the various Native communities around Red River was his fluency in French, English, Ojibwa, and Sioux.[12] Pascal Breland, a son-in-law of Cuthbert Grant, was a hunt and trading chief of numerous hivernant villages, the patriarch of St François Xavier, and was also a member of the Council of Assiniboia in 1869. William Hallet was the most prominent English-Métis chief of the annual buffalo hunt with close family ties to numerous French-Métis families.[13]

These men placed an advertisement in the Nor'Wester inviting all Métis to meet at the Court House on 29 July 1869 to discuss what the Métis response should be to the proposed transfer of Rupert's Land to Canada.[14] At this meeting, William Dease quickly took the initiative and advanced what might be termed an "Aboriginal Rights" paradigm for Métis rights.[15] Dease called on the Métis to defend their rights to land in the Settlement, and disputed the validity of the Earl of Selkirk's purchase of the same from the Indians. The Métis, he said, should demand the £300 000 that Canada was about to pay to the Hudson's Bay Company. To this end the Métis should form a new government in the Colony to displace the HBC, and make their case to the Canadian government. While the first proposal elicited considerable support, the call to form a new government did not and the meeting broke up with no clear plan of action decided.

Historians have generally regarded this first initiative as a failure and attributed its lack of success to the notion that Dease and Hallet were dupes of John Christian Schultz and that their program too closely resembled that of the Canadians in the Settlement—perceptions which apparently put the Métis on guard and restrained them from supporting Dease and his proposals.[16] However, this view is based on an entirely uncritical acceptance of the comments of Fathers Dugast and Ritchot,[17] both of whom were themselves not only steadfast partisans

in the conflict but had also been the first to draw attention to the similarity between Dease's proposal and the Canadians' plans in order to undermine the former. The meeting of July 29, consequently, was not a failure, but merely the opening round of a debate that would continue until early October.

Looking at the history of the Red River Settlement in a little longer perspective, it is also clear that the Dease proposal, far from being inspired by Schultz's Canadian faction in Red River, was an Aboriginal rights position designed by the traditional leadership of the Métis. Indeed, the Métis position as presented by Dease had been worked out nearly a decade earlier, in 1860, when it seemed likely that Red River would become a Crown Colony, a possibility which raised questions about Indian title, Hudson's Bay Company jurisdiction, and individual land rights in Red River.[18]

Debate over who had title began in 1860 when Peguis, the Saulteaux Chief, challenged the HBC claim to land in the Red River Settlement with the simple argument that the Indians had never sold it to Lord Selkirk and the Hudson's Bay Company.[19] That prompted the Métis, under the chairmanship of Pascal Breland, to hold a large meeting at the Royal Hotel near Fort Garry to discuss their position. The most eminent Métis traders and hunters—William Dease, Urbain Delorme, Pierre Falcon, William Hallet, George Flett, and William McGillis—all spoke, and all agreed that, the treaty being one of friendship, not sale, the HBC had not received title to the Red River Settlement by treaty with Peguis in 1817. Indeed, it was their view that the Métis had a legitimate claim to the land and, moreover, that their claim should have priority; they were descendants of the Cree, the first residents of the area, while the Saulteaux had arrived in the Red River region only shortly before 1817. Accordingly, the meeting concluded with an agreement by all present that since no proper arrangements had been made with the Native tribes of the region and since the Métis were now on the land and the immediate representatives of the first tribes in the region, the Métis should use every legitimate means to advance their claim for consideration in any arrangement which the Imperial Government might see fit to make. The meeting then adjourned until May, when the various Indian chiefs and wintering Métis would be in the Colony.[20]

This second gathering confirmed the conclusions of the first, and a statement was taken from André Trottier, one of three witnesses to the 1817 Selkirk Treaty, who swore that the Chiefs had not sold the land but only rented it to Selkirk for 20 years.[21] The controversy died down when it became clear that Crown Colony status was not forthcoming, but it subsequently flared up again in 1861 when the HBC decided to exact payment for all lands occupied in the Colony at the rate of 7s 6d per acre. If this payment was not received, the HBC warned, these lands would be sold to the first purchaser, in which case all improvements would be lost to the present occupiers. While the threat was soon withdrawn, it provoked an indignant reaction in several parishes where the Métis reaffirmed that no monies would be paid, that the HBC had no right to the land (never having purchased it in the first place), and that it was the Métis themselves who had a very palpable right to it, being the "descendants of the original lords of the soil."[22] While arguably minor incidents, these indignation meetings illustrate that the traditional Métis leadership had worked out a theory of Aboriginal rights as early as 1861 and were already using it to defend their land claims in Red River. It was a position that owed nothing to the Canadians in Red River, and it was this theory that Dease reiterated in July 1869.

Given Riel's opposition to Dease and his party, it is important to delineate Riel's paradigm of Métis communitas and the sources for it. That Riel should have assumed leadership of the Métis in 1869 is somewhat surprising. His father, who had been a leader

of the free trade movement in 1849, was fondly remembered in Red River, but Louis Riel Jr had no natural constituency among the Métis. He had left the Settlement at the age of 13 in 1858 to attend school in Montreal and had only returned to the Colony in the summer of 1868. He did not farm; he did not participate in the buffalo hunt; he did not trade; and, on his return to Red River, he refused his friend Louis Schmidt's suggestion to begin freighting to St Paul. Indeed, from his return to Red River until he assumed leadership of the Resistance, it is not clear that Riel did very much of anything. The one report of his activities, albeit from an unsympathetic observer, George R. Winship, gives the impression that he was just an ordinary town loafer who lived entirely off his mother. Winship, who had arrived in Red River about the same time as Riel, also noted that Riel was never known to earn anything himself by manual labour, preferring to hang around saloons a good deal "waiting for something to turn up for him to do suitable to his tastes."[23] Those historians who even bother to question why Riel rose to the leadership of the Métis usually point to his education as putting him naturally in the forefront. While this reasoning is plausible, it would not have carried much weight with the Métis buffalo hunters, merchant traders, or Métis councillors of Assiniboia.[24]

In fact, Riel's true constituency in 1869 was the Catholic Church, and it was through the Church that most of his influence would come. The most recent study of the Catholic Church's role in the Resistance leaves off deciding whether Riel or Catholic priests directed the Resistance, but clearly proves that Father Dugast (the main teacher at the St Boniface College) and Father Ritchot (the parish priest of St Norbert) were close partners with Riel in deciding Métis strategy in 1869–70.[25] With Archbishop Taché out of the Settlement, Dugast and Ritchot took the lead in guiding their Métis flock. Both men were secular priests who had been born in Quebec and shared a French-Canadian nationalism that saw the French Métis sharing a common history, language, and culture with the *Canadiens*. Ritchot in particular felt very threatened by the recent arrivals from Canada and feared for the religious rights of the Métis.[26] Furthermore, both men condemned the traditional buffalo-hunting economy of the Métis, hoping to win them over to a settled agricultural way of life.[27] It is therefore not surprising that the two men distrusted the traditional Métis leadership and their Aboriginal-rights justification for Resistance in 1869. For his part, Ritchot personally disliked William Dease (though Dease was a Catholic) and regarded him as a man "sans princippe et aussi hignorant qu'orgueilleux."[28] Father Dugast, meanwhile, criticized Dease's Aboriginal-rights justification of Resistance in a report to Taché, calling Dease a fool and adding that if the details of the assembly of July 29 were heard in Canada, the Métis would all be taken for a band of lunatics.[29]

For Dugast and Ritchot, then, Riel most closely represented their ideal for the Métis of Red River. Attending the College of Montreal, he had been educated by the Sulpician fathers (who trained their students "as a Catholic and French-Canadian elite, proud of their difference from the English majority of North America"[30]) and so was steeped in the twin tenets of patriotism and religion. As Riel wrote in 1874, "The French-Canadian Métis of the North (West) are a branch of the French-Canadian tree. They want to grow like that tree, with that tree; they never want to be separated from it, they want to suffer and rejoice with it."[31] Accordingly, it is easy to understand why Ritchot viewed Riel as a "jeune homme du pays (et de talent)."[32]

With this paradigm of Métis communitas in mind, the events during and after the Assembly of July 29 become more explicable. Following Dease's speech, John Bruce, who would later become the first president of Riel's "National Committee," took the floor

and castigated Dease for advocating revolt. As a magistrate and member of the Council of Assiniboia, Dease should be the first to defend the government of the country, Bruce contended, and all such intrigues should be opposed. Apparently Bruce's arguments found their mark and the assembly broke up without endorsing Dease's plan of action. Father Dugast's lengthy report of this meeting makes it clear that Bruce had been carefully coached in his address.[33] Most of the evidence suggests that Ritchot, Dugast, and possibly Riel, had done the coaching and, indeed, Ritchot later admitted that he had advised his parishioners to be on their guard, and that he considered the object of the meeting to be of a dangerous character.[34] As well, both Ritchot and Dugast went out of their way to paint the Dease initiative as being inspired by John Christian Schultz.

Further meetings followed in August as the Métis continued to debate the position they should take to protect their rights considering the proposed transfer to Canada.[35] The Dease initiative, however, had collapsed by early October and with it the aboriginal-rights paradigm of Métis communitas. Writing later, Ritchot attributed the collapse of this early movement to a failure of leadership (the leaders being bought off by Canadian transportation contracts), to the Protestant clergy's interceding with the English Métis to accept the transfer, and to the greed of some French-Métis merchants who saw Confederation as an economic opportunity.[36] While there was some truth to Ritchot's assessment, more important was the determined opposition of Riel, Ritchot, and Dugast, and their elaboration of another paradigm of Métis communitas that carried more emotional weight with the French Métis.

By the end of August, the French Métis had increasingly come to see Confederation as the annexation of Red River by Protestant Orange Ontario and, consequently, as a threat to their religious rights.[37] News that

William McDougall would be the new governor of the territory only raised the fears of the French-Catholic clergy and the many French Métis who viewed him as one with the other Canadians in the Colony (John Schultz, Charles Mair, John Snow, and J.S. Dennis), all of whom were widely distrusted.[38] Moreover, by this time there were also rumours circulating that McDougall was a "priest murderer".[39]

Dugast, writing to Taché, recounted a conversation between the Métis and John Snow that clearly showed the mindset of the time. Snow, who had been sent from Canada to build a road from Fort Garry to Lake of the Woods, tried to calm the fears of the Métis of Pointe-de-Chêne, but they would have none of it. They replied that he was friendly now that he was weak, but that they knew how the English had treated the Catholics of Upper Canada. "You are orangemen and you are all alike."[40]

How these sentiments and rumours were spread remains unclear, but these sentiments were undoubtedly shared by the Catholic clergy who, by October 1869, increasingly justified resistance to Canada in terms of protecting French and Catholic rights in Red River and who closely supported Riel, clearly the ascendent Métis leader. Thirty-five years later Dugast was to write:

In reality he [Ritchot] was the soul of the movement. It was he who launched it and without him the movement would not have taken place. . . .

It was M. Ritchot and I who not only guided but who drove on that opposition to the Canadian government—this is the real truth. I did not say it in my book because all truth is not suitable for publication. I say it to you. The ignorant métis would never have thought of vindicating their constitutional rights if M. Ritchot and I had not made them aware of them. Without M. Ritchot and me the movement remains inexplicable.[41]

With Dease's initiative in disarray, and with the active support and encouragement of Ritchot and Dugast, Riel moved to take the lead. Along with Baptiste Tourond and a few other Métis, he stopped the Canadian survey on 11 October as it approached the river lots of the Parish of St Vital, an action which, given the increasing fears and paranoia of the French Métis, won him considerable support. Then, when news arrived of the imminent arrival of McDougall in Pembina, Riel and his faction—which by this time included many of the younger and more militant boatmen of the Colony—took steps that would breach the established order, and initiate a period of crisis in the Red River Settlement. On October 20, Riel and his men met in the home of John Bruce where they organized a "National Committee" and made plans to stop McDougall from entering the Settlement. All was planned with the approval and knowledge of Ritchot.[42] The next day "la barrière" was erected across the Pembina trail at St Norbert, and all incoming and outgoing traffic was stopped and searched.

This act overturned the status quo, directly challenged the Council of Assiniboia's legitimacy, and threw the Colony into an uproar. Already humiliated by the combined efforts of Riel, Ritchot, and Dugast, and aware that most Métis still did not agree with the precipitous and resolute action Riel and his men had taken, William Dease now took an uncompromising stand against Riel, arguing that McDougall should be permitted to enter the territory and hear the Métis complaints. Sensing that support for Riel's course of action was slipping, Ritchot called for an assembly of Métis to meet in St Norbert on October 24 to resolve the divisions among the people. At this meeting, Dease and his supporters threatened to dismantle the barricade across the Pembina trail and only the intercession of Ritchot quieted the following uproar. Ritchot calmed the assembly by asking if they did not agree that Canada had treated the Colony with a lack of respect, and if it was not proper that some resistance be made. Even Dease's men could not disagree with this, and Ritchot eventually persuaded the majority of the Métis at the assembly to agree to back the path taken by Riel. Most of the rest agreed to stay neutral.[43] Dease, however, was not satisfied and continued his opposition.

The following day Riel was summoned before the Council of Assiniboia and asked to abandon his plans to prevent McDougall from entering the Colony. When Riel refused, the Council approached Dease and asked if he could raise enough French Métis to overturn the decision taken on October 24 and force Riel's men to disperse.[44] Dease moved quickly to raise a group of men to attend another meeting at St Norbert on October 27, at which both sides repeated their arguments for or against Riel's strategy. While Ritchot later claimed that he had not taken a leading role, another account, almost surely based on intelligence supplied by Dease, noted that Ritchot had declared "in favour of the stand taken, and called upon the insurgents to maintain their ground."[45] Still another of Dease's party testified that Ritchot had "raved and tore his gown addressing the assemblage in the most frantic and excited manner."[46] The appeals of Ritchot and Riel together convinced even 20 of Dease's 80 supporters that Riel was right, Ritchot observing later (with an almost palpable disdain) that Dease had been supported by only George Racette, six Indians, and a handful of others.[47] Defeated, Dease and his supporters left the ground to Riel.

Riel had won. While Dease would continue to oppose Riel throughout the winter and spring of 1869–70, and other prominent French Métis would slide back and forth between neutrality and opposition, Riel never again lost the support of most of the French Métis. The Council of Assiniboia met for the last time on October 30, agreeing there was nothing more they could do.

Usually treated as a minor and almost inconsequential interlude, the Dease/Riel conflict played a major role in defining the nature of the Métis Resistance in 1869–70. On a symbolic level, it was a battle over whether the Resistance would be grounded broadly on a concept of Métis Aboriginal rights and led by the traditional Métis leadership, or whether the Resistance would be more narrowly a defence of French and Catholic rights in the settlement and led by the young Riel. To be sure, the Resistance had many other facets not touched upon here, and there were other reasons (class, economic, familial, and generational) why many French Métis opposed Riel;[48] however, unless one understands the symbolic nature of the Dease/Riel conflict, one cannot understand how key participants understood the events in which they were involved. Those Métis leaders who had been upstaged by Riel, and sometimes badly mistreated,[49] were never able to accept his leadership.

Later in the Resistance, Riel tried to bridge the chasm that had developed between his followers and those of Dease, who continued to enjoy a good deal of support among the Métis in both Red River and in St Joseph[50] and whose help Riel needed if he hoped to build a consensus around his leadership. Writing to Dease in St Joseph, where he had sought refuge from Riel's men after they had surrounded his house, Riel pleaded with his opponent to join forces:

We have been in hostility till now, but I am certain it was not our intent to have bloodshed, among friends and relatives, or to strike terror or mourning in the lives of the Métis along the R.R. . . . .

Mr. Dease when have I ever done you any harm. If just recently our soldiers surrounded your home, it was with the intention of bringing you here to accept our word of honour and assuring us that you would do all in your power to restore peace & public safety. . . . I beg you this favour, let us re-unite and join hands. . . . Mr. Dease, I beg of you, why are you so opposed to us, after we have already discussed and aired these problems. My personal ambition is a thing not in my heart, and if I am capable of doing something it will be for the good of all. I do not ask for a reward, but only for that support and sustenance before all Métis.[51]

Dease, however, remained unmoved.

Riel also tried to broaden the scope of the Resistance after October 1869 to win over the support of the English Métis, but it never lost the French and Catholic tinge it had acquired in the period from July through September. This made it extremely difficult for Riel to build any settlement-wide consensus. After Riel and his men seized Upper Fort Garry in November of 1869, they raised a flag adorned with the fleur-de-lis and the Irish Shamrock. This ceremony was carried out by a Catholic priest who was attended by 60 of the scholars of the Roman Catholic seminary in St Boniface.[52] This symbolism was not lost on the English Métis. By allying himself so clearly with the Catholic clergy to defeat the Dease faction, Riel would never be acceptable as a leader to anything more than a small minority of English-Protestant Métis.

The Riel/Dease conflict also has some implications for the question of whether the Métis of 1869 were concerned with their Aboriginal rights. Thomas Flanagan, in a useful study of the political thought of Louis Riel, has argued that the question of Aboriginal rights played no role in the public debates of the 1869–70 Resistance. Riel's strategy in 1869, he argued, was to present the Métis as civilized men with rights equal to those of any British subject.[53]

Riel wanted the Colony to enter Confederation as a Province with institutions modelled on those of Quebec: local control of land and natural resources, responsible government, a bilingual Governor, bilingualism in the legislature and courts, and a tax-supported system of Protestant and Catholic schools.[54]

This is an accurate assessment of Riel's paradigm of Métis communitas in 1869. It does not, however, accurately describe competing paradigms that were part of the public debates on resistance before October 1869.

This paper has argued that the idea of Métis Resistance in 1869 did not spring from the brow of Riel alone and that, as early as July 1869, other Métis leaders such as William Dease had proposed another paradigm of resistance that was based on a theory of Aboriginal rights. This Aboriginal-rights paradigm, however, was opposed by Riel and his clerical advisors, Fathers Ritchot and Dugast, in their struggle to gain the leadership of the Métis Resistance. Their strategy consisted of stressing a defence of French and Catholic rights threatened by the Canadians in the Colony. With the triumph of Riel and defeat of Dease in the Assembly of October 27, the Aboriginal-rights paradigm disappeared from public view in Red River. It is interesting to note, however, that once Riel was in control of the Resistance in Red River, Father Ritchot utilized an Aboriginal-rights argument to rationalize the Métis Children's land grant (section 31 of the Manitoba Act) in his negotiations with the Canadian Government in Ottawa in 1870.[55]

NOTES

The author would like to acknowledge and thank John Foster, Tom Flanagan, Gerald Friesen, Paul Chartrand, and Allen Ronaghan, who read an earlier draft of this paper and made a number of useful comments and suggestions.

1. This term is borrowed from the anthropologist Victor Turner who pioneered a processual approach to studying political conflict as social drama. From his study of symbol and ritual, Turner outlined a three- or

four-stage process by which social dramas unfold. In this process, the first phase of a social drama was a period of "separation" or "breach" that Turner refers to as a pre-liminal phase. This phase is comprised of symbolic behaviour signifying the detachment of the individual (or group) from either an earlier fixed point in the social structure or from an established set of cultural conditions. This is a period when the norms that govern social relations between persons or groups within the same social system (village, chiefdom, university department) break down. Such a breach is signalled by an overt or deliberate non-fulfillment of some crucial norm governing the intercourse of the parties. See Victor Turner, *Dramas, Fields, and Metaphors: Symbolic Action in Human Society* (Ithaca, 1974), 13–42.

2. This is a term that Turner uses to describe the bond uniting a people over and above any formal social bond.

3. W.L. Morton, Introduction to *Alexander Begg's Red River Journal and other papers relative to the Red River Resistance of 1869–70* (Toronto, 1956), 3. Morton's introduction runs from page 1 to 148. The section dealing with the events from June through October 1869 are found on pages 31 to 55.

4. Ibid., 3.

5. Ibid., 50–1. Morton argues that some of clergy approved of Riel's aims, but only followed the Métis and did not instigate or lead the Resistance. It is interesting to note that while Morton included one of Father Dugast's letters of 1869 (29 August 1869) in his collection of documents, he left out the more interesting ones (those of 14, 24, and 31 August 1869) which deeply implicated Dugast and Ritchot in the actual planning of Riel's campaign for the leadership of the Métis.

6. Ibid., 33.

7. See Philippe R. Mailhot, "Ritchot's Resistance: Abbé Noël Joseph Ritchot and the Creation and Transformation of Manitoba," (PhD diss., University of Manitoba, 1986), 14–62.

8. Schultz had arrived in the Red River Settlement in 1861, and was the acknowledged leader of the Canadian faction openly advocating annexation to Canada.

9. Philippe R. Mailhot, "Ritchot's Resistance," 21–2, 48.

10. Ibid., 29–30, 47.

11. Among other activities that were alarming the Métis, the Canadians were staking out land, they freely denounced the Americans, Fenians, and Métis in the Colony, they ran up the Canadian flag as if a symbol of conquest, and the Métis were openly and contemptuously spoken of as cowards. Hudson's Bay Company Archives (HBCA), A12/45, William McTavish to W.G. Smith, 24 July 1869, fo. 269–70. HBCA, RG 1, Series 4/8, William McTavish to Joseph Howe, 14 May 1870, 2.

12. State Historical Society of North Dakota, A26, Albert E. Dease Papers.

13. Two of William Hallet's sisters married French Métis and converted to Catholicism.

14. *Nor'Wester*, 24 July 1869. It was later reported that Pascal Breland had not given permission to use his name on the invitation.

15. While no minutes exist for this meeting it can be reconstructed using the various accounts that do exist. See Archives de l'archevêché, Saint-Boniface (AASB), Dugast to Taché, 29 juillet 1869, T6695–6698; HBCA, A12/45, William McTavish to W.G. Smith, 10 August 1869, fos. 282–3; and Provincial Archives of Manitoba (PAM), MG3 B14, M151, Ritchot's Narrative of the Resistance, volume 1.

16. George F.G. Stanley, *Louis Riel* (Toronto, 1963), 56–7. W.L. Morton, "Introduction," to *Alexander Begg's Red River Journal*, 32–4.

17. AASB, Dugast to Taché, 29 juillet 1869, T6695–6698; PAM, MG3 B14, M151, Ritchot's Narrative of the Resistance, volume 1.

18. See "Red River a Crown Colony," *Nor'Wester*, 28 February 1860.

19. This debate can be followed in the pages of the *Nor'Wester*. See "Native Title to Indian Lands," 14 February 1860; "Peguis Refuted," 28 February 1860; "The Land Question," 14 March 1860; "The Political Condition of the Country," 28 April 1860; "Peguis Vindicated," 28 April 1860; "The Peguis Land Controversy," 14 May 1860; "The Land Question," 14 June 1860; "The Halfbreed Meeting," 28 June 1860; "Paketay-Hoond on the Land Question," 28 June 1860; "The Land Controversy," 28 June 1860; "The Last Half-Breed Meeting," 28 September 1860.

20. "The Land Question," *Nor'Wester*, 14 March 1860.

21. "The Land Question," *Nor'Wester*, 14 June 1860.

22. "Indignation Meetings," *Nor'Wester*, 15 June 1861.

23. PAM, MG 3 B15, George B. Winship Account of 1869–70 (typescript).

24. See, for example, Philippe Mailhot, "Ritchot's Resistance," 30.

25. Ibid., 31.

26. A.G. Morice, *History of the Catholic Church in Western Canada*, Vol II (Toronto, 1910), 10.

27. Philippe R. Mailhot, "Ritchot's Resistance," 9–10.

28. PAM, Ritchot's Narrative of the Resistance, volume 1, 16.

29. ASSB, Dugast to Taché, 29 juillet 1869, T6695.

30. Thomas Flanagan, *Louis "David" Riel: Prophet of the New World* (Toronto, 1979), 7.

31. Louis Riel writing to the President of the Saint Jean-Baptiste Society of Montreal, 24 June 1874. Quoted in Thomas Flanagan, "The Political Thought of Louis Riel," in A.S. Lussier (ed.) *Riel and the Métis: Riel Mini-Conference Papers* (Winnipeg, 1979), 140.

32. PAM, Ritchot's Narrative of the Resistance, volume 1.

33. AASB, Dugast to Taché, 29 juillet 1869, T6697.

34. Canada. Parliament, House of Commons, *Sessional Papers*, 1874, No. VII, "Report of the Select Committee on the Causes of the Difficulties in the North West Territories in 1869–70," Appendix No. 6, Testimony of Noël Joseph Ritchot, 20 April 1874.

35. AASB, Dugast to Taché, 31 aout 1869, T6778–6780.

36. PAM, Ritchot's narrative, volume 1.

37. HBCA, A12/45, W. McTavish to W.G. Smith, 2 November 1869, fo. 313–14.

38. This sentiment is clearly visible in the letters written by Father Dugast to Taché in the AASB. See his letters of 14 Aout 1869, T6734–37; 24 Aout 1869, T6764–67; and 31 Aout 1869, T6778–80.

39. HBCA, RG 1, Series 4/8, W. McTavish to Joseph Howe, 14 May 1870, 13. The basis of this rumour had to do with McDougall's role in the Manitoulin Island Incident of 1862–3 in Canada. For an explanation of this incident and its bearing on McDougall's reputation among the Métis, see Neil Edgar Allen Ronaghan, "The Archibald Administration in Manitoba, 1870–1872" (PhD diss., University of Manitoba, 1987), 61–85.

40. AASB, Dugast to Taché, 31 Aout 1869, T6781.

41. Archives du Collège Sainte-Marie, Fonds-Immaculée-Conception, Dugast to Fr. Joseph Grenier, 15 April 1905. Quoted in W.L. Morton (ed.) *Alexander Begg's Red River Journal*, 51n. Morton quotes this letter only to dismiss it as inaccurate citing as reasons that it was written 35 years after the fact, that Dugast possessed a flair for inaccuracy, and that Dugast was a vain and garrulous man. A close reading of Dugast's correspondence written in 1869, along with Ritchot's Narrative, suggests exactly the opposite.

42. See Ritchot's narrative, vol. 1. These events and Ritchot's influence on them is described in some detail in Philippe Mailhot, "Ritchot's Resistance," 31–9.

43. PAM, Ritchot's narrative, vol. 1, 22–5.

44. PAM, Minutes of the Council of Assiniboia, 25 October 1869.

45. Canada. Parliament, House of Commons, *Sessional Papers* 1870, No. 12, "Correspondence and Papers Connected with Recent Occurrences in the North West Territories." Letter of J.S. Dennis to William McDougall, 27 October 1869. That Ritchot took an active role at this meeting is also backed up by Ritchot's subsequent actions during the Resistance. In December of 1869, after Riel and his men had seized Fort Garry, they began to run low on supplies and approached the Hudson's Bay Company for an advance. William McTavish, the presiding HBC officer, refused the request and told the Métis to leave the fort. This caused a dilemma for the Métis Council and Riel. Their choices at this point were to either abandon the Resistance or forcibly seize HBC property. In the meeting held to decide their course of action, Ritchot took a prominent role advising the Métis to continue their course. Their case was already before the Canadian government, he argued, and soon the present ministry would fall and the demands of the Métis would be secured. With this encouragement the Métis decided not to disperse and the

HBC stores and safe were broken into. See HBCA, A12/45, William McTavish to W.G. Smith, 11 December 1869, fos. 328–9.

46. Canada. Parliament, House of Commons, *Sessional Papers* 1870, No. 12, "Correspondence and Papers Connected with Recent Occurrences in the North West Territories."

47. PAM, Ritchot's Narrative, vol. 1.

48. See Chapter 5 of Gerhard J. Ens, "Kinship, Ethnicity, Class and the Red River Métis," (PhD diss., University of Alberta, 1989).

49. Many of the Métis who opposed Riel were later imprisoned by Riel including William Dease, Baptiste Charette, William Gaddy, William Hallet, and Gabriel Lafournaise. Hallet was kept in chains in an unheated room through the worst of the winter.

50. St Joseph was a Métis community just across the US border near the present-day town of Walhalla, North Dakota.

51. Louis Riel to William Dease, 15 February 1870. Reprinted in G.F.G. Stanley (general editor) *The Collected Writings of Louis Riel/Les Ecrits Complets de Louis Riel, Vol. 1* (Edmonton, 1985), 52.

52. HBCA, A12/45, William McTavish to W.G. Smith, 11 December 1869, fo. 328–9.

53. Thomas Flanagan, "The Political Thought of Louis Riel," 150–2. See also his "Political Theory of the Red River Resistance: The Declaration of December 8, 1869," *Canadian Journal of Political Science* XI, 1 (March 1978): 153–64; and "The Case Against Métis Aboriginal Rights," *Canadian Public Policy* IX, 3 (September 1983): 316–7.

54. Ibid., 139.

55. For Ritchot's use of this argument see his Ottawa journal published in W.L. Morton (ed.) *Manitoba: The Birth of a Province* (Winnipeg, 1965), 140–2.

Chapter 14

Confederation and Anti-Confederation

READINGS

Primary Documents

Historical Interpretations

INTRODUCTION

Confederation is the worst-kept secret in Canadian history. We have referred to it in earlier topic introductions, and students frequently foreshadow it in essays focusing on the 1840s or even earlier. We know the outcome, and want to dissect the past so that we can better explain how predictable (or perhaps shocking) the result was. We do this regardless of how important the constitutional changes brought about in 1867 actually were for people living in the newly confederated colonies. For some, like those who got access to a railway as part of the package, Confederation was life-changing. It affected their livelihoods, their prospects, and their sense of being linked to the rest of the world. For others, such as those who remained relatively isolated from the reconfigured state's gifts or demands, life went on much as it had before.

The debate surrounding Confederation was passionate and continued well beyond the 1860s. Its proponents believed that the scheme could solve many of British North America's persistent problems and pave the way for future expansion. Among them, George Brown was perhaps the keenest expansionist. He argued that Confederation would bring justice to the inhabitants of the future province of Ontario, who suffered, he believed, under a grievous "French domination" in the Province of Canada and that it would allow for the annexation of the northwest. Others were more wary. Many of Confederation's opponents indeed regarded the scheme as undemocratic or unwieldly. A.A. Dorion, in particular, mentions several reasons why the arrangements for Confederation seemed to be rather too hastily made.

We should acknowledge, as Ged Martin does, that opposition to Confederation was not based on a lack of vision but on different *kinds* of visions. "Progress" was one of the most powerful watchwords of the age, and Confederation, because it was so strongly linked to progress and to a sense of destiny for British North America, acquired a momentum of its own. And yet the process was only completed in 1949, when Newfoundland entered the Dominion of Canada. In the 1860s, most Newfoundlanders believed that their island possessed the resources to support an independent destiny. Nonetheless, as James Hiller notes, the threat of financial collapse in the 1890s forced the Newfoundland government to resume Confederation talks with Canada. Negotiations failed, however, and the prospect of union was not raised again at an official level for several decades.

QUESTIONS FOR CONSIDERATION

1. Was Brown right to argue that the Confederation scheme would bring justice to both English- and French-speaking Canada and that it had been endorsed by the electorate?
2. Dorion's speech introduces us to some of the potential problems associated with the creation of a new nation from the provinces of British North America. What were some of these?
3. What are the advantages and disadvantages of being linked politically (e.g., as part of a federation like Canada) with distant places that might not share the value systems that predominate in your community?
4. Ged Martin outlines some of the case against Confederation. Where would you have stood on the issue? Would it have mattered where you lived?
5. Why did Confederation talks fail between Canada and Newfoundland in 1895?

SUGGESTIONS FOR FURTHER READING

Philip Buckner, "The Maritimes and Confederation: A Reassessment," *Canadian Historical Review* 71, 1 (1990): 1–30.

Guy Laforest, Eugénie Brouillet, Alain-G. Gagnon, and Yves Tanguay, eds, *The Constitutions that Shaped Us: A Historical Anthology of Pre-1867 Canadian Constitutions* (Montreal and Kingston: McGill-Queen's University Press, 2015).

Ged Martin, *Britain and the Origins of Canadian Confederation, 1837–67* (Vancouver: UBC Press, 1995).

———, ed., *The Causes of Canadian Confederation* (Fredericton: Acadiensis Press, 1990).

Christopher Moore, *Three Weeks in Quebec City: The Meeting that Made Canada* (Toronto: Allen Lane, 2015).

W.L. Morton, *The Critical Years: The Union of British North America 1857–1873* (Toronto: McClelland and Stewart, 1964).

Patrick O'Flaherty, *Lost Country: The Rise and Fall of Newfoundland, 1843–1933* (St John's: Long Beach Press, 2005).

Paul Romney, *Getting It Wrong: How Canadians Forgot Their Past and Imperilled Confederation* (Toronto: University of Toronto Press, 1999).

I.A. Silver, *The French-Canadian Idea of Confederation, 1864–1900* (Toronto: University of Toronto Press, 1997).

Andrew Smith, *British Businessmen and Canadian Confederation: Constitution-Making in an Era of Anglo-Globalization* (Montreal and Kingston: McGill-Queen's University Press, 2008).

Peter B. Waite, *The Life and Times of Confederation, 1864–1867: Politics, Newspapers, and the Union of British North America* (Toronto: Robin Brass Studio, 2001).

Primary Documents

1   From George Brown, in *Parliamentary Debates on the Subject of the Confederation of the British North American Provinces* (Quebec: Hunter, Rose and Co., 1865), 84–6.

LEGISLATIVE ASSEMBLY

Wednesday, February 8, 1865

The Order of the Day for resuming the debate on the Resolution for a Union of the British North American Colonies, having been read,—

Hon. GEORGE BROWN rose and said: Mr. SPEAKER, it is with no ordinary gratification I rise to address the House on this occasion. I cannot help feeling that the struggle of half a life-time for constitutional reform—the agitations in the country, and the fierce contests in this chamber—the strife and the discord and the abuse of many years,—are all compensated by the great scheme of reform which is now in your hands. (Cheers.) The Attorney General for Upper Canada, as well as the Attorney General for Lower Canada, in addressing the House last night, were anxious to have it understood that this scheme for uniting British America under one government, is something different from "representation by population,"—is something different

from "joint authority,"—but is in fact the very scheme of the Government of which they were members in 1858. Now, sir, it is all very well that my honorable friends should receive credit for the large share they have contributed towards maturing the measure before the House; but I could not help reflecting while they spoke, that if this was their very scheme in 1858, they succeeded wonderfully in bottling it up from all the world except themselves— (hear, hear)—and I could not help regretting that we had to wait till 1864 until this mysterious plant of 1858 was forced to fruition. (Hear, hear, and laughter.) For myself, sir, I care not who gets the credit of this scheme,—I believe it contains the best features of all the suggestions that have been made in the last ten years for the settlement of our troubles; and the whole feeling in my mind now is one of joy and thankfulness that there were found men of position and influence in Canada who, at a moment of serious crisis, had nerve and patriotism enough to cast aside political partisanship, to banish personal considerations, and unite for the accomplishment of a measure so fraught with advantage to their common country. (Cheers.) It was a bold step in the then existing state of public feeling for many members of the House to vote for the Constitutional Committee moved for by the last session—it was a very bold step for many of the members of that committee to speak and vote candidly upon it—it was a still bolder thing for many to place their names to the report that emanated from that committee,—but it was an infinitely bolder step for the gentlemen who now occupy these treasury benches, to brave the misconceptions and suspicions that would certainly attach to the act, and enter the same Government. And it is not to be denied that such a Coalition demanded no ordinary justification. But who does not feel that every one of us has to-day ample justification and reward for all we did in the document now under discussion? (Cheers.) But seven short months have passed away since the Coalition Government was formed, yet already are we submitting a scheme well-weighed and matured, for the erection of a future empire,—a scheme which has been received at home and abroad with almost universal approval.

Hon. Mr. HOLTON—(Ironically) hear! hear!!

Hon. Mr. BROWN—My hon. friend dissents from that, but is it possible truthfully to deny it? Has it not been approved and endorsed by the governments of five separate colonies?—Has it not received the all but unanimous approval of the press of Canada?—Has it not been heartily and unequivocally endorsed by the electors of Canada? (Cries of hear, hear, and no, no.) My honorable friend opposite cries "no, no," but I say "yes, yes." Since the Coalition was formed, and its policy of Federal union announced, there have been no fewer than twenty-five parliamentary elections—fourteen for members of the Upper House, and eleven for members of the Lower House. At the fourteen Upper House contests, but three candidates dared to show themselves before the people in opposition to the Government scheme; and of these, two were

rejected, and one—only one—succeeded in finding a seat. (Hear, hear.) At the eleven contests for the Lower House, but one candidate on either side of politics ventured to oppose the scheme, and I hope that even he will yet cast his vote in favor of Confederation. (Hear, hear.) Of these twenty-five electoral contests, fourteen Upper House elections embraced no fewer than forty counties. (Hear, hear.) Of the 130 constituencies, therefore, into which Canada is divided for representation in this chamber, not fewer than fifty have been called on since our scheme was announced to pronounce at the polls their verdict upon it, and at the whole of them but four candidates on both sides of politics ventured to give it opposition. (Cheers.) Was I not right then in asserting that the electors of Canada had, in the most marked manner, pronounced in favor of the scheme? (Hear, hear.) And will honorable gentlemen deny that the people and press of Great Britain have received it with acclamations of approval?—that the Government of England have cordially endorsed and accepted it?—aye, that even the press and the public men of the United States have spoken of it with a degree of respect they never before accorded to any colonial movement? Sir, I venture to assert that no scheme of equal magnitude, ever placed before the world, was received with higher eulogiums, with more universal approbation, than the measure for the acceptance of the Canadian Parliament. And no higher eulogy could, I think, be pronounced than that I heard a few weeks ago from the lips of one of the foremost of British statesmen, that the system of government we proposed seemed to him a happy compound of the best features of the British and American Constitutions. And well, Mr. SPEAKER, might our present attitude in Canada arrest the earnest attention of other countries. Here is a people composed of two distinct races, speaking different languages, with religious and social and municipal and education institutions totally different; with sectional hostilities of such a character as to render government for many years well-nigh impossible; with a Constitution so unjust in the view of one section as to justify any resort to enforce a remedy. And yet, sir, here we sit, patiently and temperately discussing how these great evils and hostilities may justly and amicably be swept away forever. (Hear, hear.) We are endeavoring to adjust harmoniously greater difficulties than have plunged other counties into all the horrors of civil war. We are striving to do peacefully and satisfactorily what Holland and Belgium, after years of strife, were unable to accomplish. We are seeking by calm discussion to settle questions that Austria and Hungary, that Denmark and Germany, that Russia and Poland, could only crush by the iron heel of armed force. We are seeking to do without foreign intervention that which deluged in blood the sunny plains of Italy. We are striving to settle forever issues hardly less momentous than those that have rent the neighboring public and are now exposing it to all the horrors of civil war. (Hear, hear.) Have we not then, Mr. SPEAKER, great cause of thankfulness that we have found a better way for the solution of our troubles than that which has entailed on other countries such deplorable results? And should not every one of us endeavor to rise to the magnitude of the occasion, and earnestly seek to deal with this question to the end in the same candid and conciliatory spirit in which, so far, it has been discussed? (Loud cries of hear, hear.) The scene presented by this chamber at this moment, I venture to affirm, has few parallels in history. One hundred years have passed away since these provinces became by conquest part of the British Empire. I speak in no boastful spirit—I desire not for a moment to excite a painful thought—what was then the fortune of war of the brave French nation, might have been ours on that well-fought field. I recall those olden times merely to mark the fact that here sit to-day the descendants of the victors and the vanquished in the fight of 1759, with all the differences of language, religion, civil law, and social habit, nearly as distinctly marked as they were a century ago. (Hear, hear.) Here we sit to-day seeking amicably to

find a remedy for constitutional evils and injustice complained of—by the vanquished? No, sir—but complained of by the conquerors! (Cheers by the French Canadians.) Here sit the representatives of the British population claiming justice—only justice; and here sit the representatives of the French population, discussing in the French tongue whether we shall have it. One hundred years have passed away since the conquest of Quebec, but here sit the children of the victor and the vanquished, all avowing hearty attachment to the British Crown—all earnestly deliberating how we shall best extend the blessings of British institutions—how a great people may be established on this continent in close and hearty connection with Great Britain. (Cheers.) Where, sir, in the page of history, shall we find a parallel to this? Will it not stand in an imperishable monument to the generosity of British rule? And it is not in Canada alone that this scene is being witnessed. Four other colonies are at this moment occupied as we are—declaring their hearty love for the parent State, and deliberating with us how they may best discharge the great duty entrusted to their hands, and give their aid in developing the teeming resources of these vast possessions. And well, Mr. SPEAKER, may the work we have unitedly proposed rouse the ambition and energy of every true man in the continent of America, and mark that island (Newfoundland) commanding the mouth of the noble river that almost cuts our continent in twain. Well, sir, that island is equal in extent to the kingdom of Portugal. Cross the straits to the main land, and you touch the hospitable shores of Nova Scotia, a country as large as the kingdom of Greece. Then mark the sister province of New Brunswick—equal in extent to Denmark and Switzerland combined. Pass up the river St. Lawrence to Lower Canada—a country as large as France. Pass on to Upper Canada,—twenty thousand square miles larger than Great Britain and Ireland put together. Cross over the continent to the shores of the Pacific, and you are in British Columbia, the land of golden promise,—equal in extent to the Austrian Empire. I speak not now of the vast Indian Territories that lie between—greater in extent than the whole soil of Russia—and that will ere long, I trust, be opened up to civilization under the auspices of the British American Confederation. (Cheers.) Well, sir, the bold scheme in your hands is nothing less than to gather all these countries into one—to organize them all under one government, with the protection of the British flag, and in heartiest sympathy and affection with our fellow subjects in the land that gave us birth. (Cheers.) Our scheme is to establish a government that will seek to turn the tide of European emigration into this northern half of the American continent—that will strive to develop its great natural resources—and that will endeavor to maintain liberty, and justice, and christianity throughout the land.

Mr. T.C. WALLBRIDGE—When?

Hon. Mr. CARTIER—Very soon!

Hon. Mr. BROWN—The hon. member for North Hastings asks when all this can be done? Sir, the whole great ends of this Confederation may not be realized in the lifetime of many who now hear me. We imagine not that such a structure can be built in a month or in a year. What we propose now is but to lay the foundations of the structure—to set in motion the governmental machinery that will one day, we trust, extend from the Atlantic to the Pacific. And we take especial credit to ourselves that the systems we have devised, while admirably adapted to our present situation, is capable of gradual and efficient expansion in future years to meet all the great purposes contemplated by our scheme. But if the honorable gentleman will only recall to mind that when the United States needed from the Mother Country, and for many years afterwards their population was not nearly equal to ours at this moment; that their internal improvements did not then approach to what we have already attained; and that their trade and commerce was not then a third of what ours has already reached; I think he will see that the fulfillment of our hopes may not be so very remote as at first sight might be imagined—(hear, hear.) And he will be strengthened in that conviction if he remembers that what we propose to do is to be done with the cordial sympathy and assistance of that great Power of which it is our happiness to form a part. (Hear, hear.) Such, Mr. SPEAKER, are the objects of attainment to which the British American Conference pledged itself in October. And said I not rightly that such a scheme is well fitted to fire the ambition and rouse the energies of every member of this House? Does it not lift us above the petty politics of the past, and present to us high purposes and great interests that may well call forth all enterprise to be found among us? (Cheers.)

2 From A.A. Dorion, in *Parliamentary Debates on the Subject of the Confederation of the British North American Provinces* (Quebec: Hunter, Rose and Co., 1865), 245–69, 690–5.

HON. MR. DORION—But, sir, I may be asked, granting all this, granting that the scheme brought down is not the scheme promised to us, what difference our bringing in the provinces at once can make? This I will endeavor to explain. When they went into the Conference, honorable gentlemen opposite submitted to have the votes taken by provinces. Well, they have now brought us in, as was natural under the circumstances, the most conservative measure ever laid before a Parliament. The members of the Upper House are no longer to be elected, but nominated, and nominated by whom? By a Tory or Conservative Government for Canada, by a Conservative Government in Nova Scotia, by a Conservative Government in Prince Edward Island, by a Conservative Government in Newfoundland, the only Liberal Government concerned in the nomination being that which is controlled by the Liberal party in New Brunswick, whose fate depends on the result of the elections that are now going on in that province. Such a scheme would never have been adopted if submitted to the liberal people of Upper Canada. When the Government went into that Conference they were bound by the majority, especially since they voted by provinces, and the 1,400,000 of Upper Canada with the 1,100,000 of Lower Canada—together 2,500,000 people— were over-ridden by 900,000 people of the Maritime Provinces. Were we not expressly told that it was the Lower Provinces who would not hear of our having an elective Legislative Council? If, instead of going into Conference with the people of the Lower Provinces, our Government had done what they pledged themselves to do, that is, to prepare a Constitution themselves, they would never have dared to bring in such a proposition as this which is now imposed upon us by the Lower Colonies—to have a Legislative Council, with a fixed number of members, nominated by four Tory governments. Why, taking the average time each councillor will be in the Council to be fifteen to twenty years, it will take a century before its complexion can be changed. For all time to come, so far as this generation and the next are concerned, you will find the Legislative Council controlled by the influence of the present Government.

HON. MR. DORION—The honorable member for Lambton says that makes no difference. It makes just the difference that we are to be bound by the scheme or by a Constitution enabling the Council to stop all measures of reform, such as would be desired by the Liberal party; if the honorable member for Lambton thinks that makes no difference, I beg to differ from him, and I believe the Liberal party generally will. The Government say they had to introduce certain provisions, not to please themselves, but to please the provinces below, and they have pledged themselves to those provinces

that this House will carry out the scheme without amendment. Does not the honorable member see the difference now? If the two Canadas were alone interested, the majority would have its own way—would look into the Constitution closely—would scan its every doubtful provision, and such a proposal as this about the Legislative Council would have no chance of being carried, for it is not very long since the House, by an overwhelming majority, voted for the substitution of an elected for a nominated Upper Chamber. In fact, the nominated Chamber had fallen so low in public estimation—I do not say it was from the fault of the men who were there, but the fact is, nevertheless, as I state it—that it commanded no influence. There was even a difficulty in getting a quorum of it together. So a change became absolutely necessary, and up to the present moment the new system has worked well; the elected members are equal in every respect to the nominated ones, and it is just when we see an interest beginning to be felt in the proceedings of the Upper House that its Constitution is to be changed, to return back again to the one so recently condemned. Back again, did I say? No, sir, a Constitution is to be substituted, much worse than the old one, and such as is nowhere else to be found. Why, even the British house of Lords, conservative as it is, is altogether beyond the influence of the popular sentiment of the country. Their number may be increased on the recommendation of the responsible advisers of the Crown, if required to secure united action or to prevent a conflict between the two Houses. From the position its members occupy, it is a sort of compromise between the popular element and the influence or control of the Crown. But the new House for the Confederation is to be a perfectly independent body—these gentlemen are to be named for life—and there is to be no power to increase their number. How long will the system work without producing a collision between the two branches of the Legislature? Suppose the Lower House turns out to be chiefly Liberal, how long will it submit to the Upper House, named by Conservative administrations which have taken advantage of their temporary numerical strength to bring about such a change as is now proposed? [. . .] I venture to prophesy, sir, that before a very short time has elapsed a dead-lock may arise, and such an excitement be created as has never yet been seen in this country. (Hear, hear.) Now, if this Constitution had been framed by the members of our Government, we could change some of its provisions. [. . .] But no, the Constitution is in the nature of a compact, a treaty, and cannot be changed. (Hear.)

I now come to another point. It is said that this Confederation is necessary for the purpose of providing a better mode of defence for this country. There may be people who think that by adding two and two together you make five. I am not of that opinion. I cannot see how by adding the 700,000 or 800,000 people, the inhabitants of the Lower Provinces, to the 2,500,000 inhabitants of Canada, you can multiply them so as to make a much larger force to defend the country than you have at present. Of course the connection with the British Empire is the link of communication by which the whole force of the Empire can be brought together for defence. (Hear, hear.) But the position of this country under the proposed scheme is very evident. You add to the frontier four or five hundred more miles than you now have, and an extent of country immeasurably greater in proportion than the additional population you have gained; and if there is an advantage at all for the defence of the country, it will be on the part of the Lower Provinces and not for us. And as we find that we are about to enter into a very large expenditure for this purpose of defence—this having been formally announced in a speech delivered by the President of the Council at Toronto—and as Canada is to contribute to that expenditure to the extent of ten-twelfths of the whole, the other provinces paying only two-twelfths, it follows that Canada will pay

ten-twelfths also of the cost of defence, which, to defend the largely extended country we will have to defend, will be much larger than if we remained alone.

[. . .]

This I contend, then, that if the military and naval defences of all the provinces are to be provided for by the General Government, and if you have to increase the militia for this purpose, the Lower Provinces will pay only their proportion of two-twelfths, and Canada, while obtaining no greater defensive force than at present, will have to pay five times as much as we are now paying. (Hear, hear.) Why, sir, take the line dividing New Brunswick from Maine and you find it separates on the one side 250,000, thinly scattered over a vast territory, from 750,000 on the other, compact and powerful. These 250,000 Canada will have to defend, and it will have to pledge its resources for the purpose of providing means of defence along that extended line. (Hear, hear.) And, if rumor be true, the Intercolonial Railway, this so-called great defensive work, is not to pass along Major ROBINSON'S line. The statement has been made—I have seen it in newspapers usually well informed—that a new route has been found that will satisfy everybody or nobody at all; and while I am on this point I must say that it is most singular that we are called upon to vote these resolutions, and to pledge ourselves to pay ten-twelfths of the cost of that railway, without knowing whether there will be ten miles or one hundred miles of it in Lower Canada, or whether it will cost $10,000,000 or $20,000,000.

HON. MR. DORION—In 1862, when the question of the construction of this road was before the country, what was the cry raised by honorable gentlemen opposite? Why, that the MACDONALD-SICOTTE Government had pledged itself to build a railway at whatever cost it might come to; and those who were loudest in these denunciations, were the very gentlemen who have now undertaken to build the road without knowing or even enquiring what the cost of it will be. (Hear, hear.) This, if I remember right, was the purport of a speech made by the Hon. Attorney General West at Otterville. (Hear, hear.) I was satisfied, sir, at that time, to press my objections to the scheme and retire from the Government; but my colleagues were denounced without stint for having undertaken to build the railway and pay seven-twelfths of its cost, and now the House is asked by the very men who denounced them to pay ten-twelfths of it, without even knowing whether the work is practicable or not. (Hear, hear.) [. . .] It is folly to suppose that this Intercolonial Railway will in the least degree be conducive to the defence of the country. We have expended a large sum of money—and none voted it more cordially and heartily than myself— for the purpose of opening a military highway from Gaspé to Rimouski; and that road, in case of hostilities with our neighbors, would be found of far greater service for the transport of troops, cannon and all kinds of munitions of war, than any railway following the same or a more southern route possibly can be. That road cannot be effectually destroyed; but a railway lying in some places not more than fifteen or twenty miles from the frontier, will be of no use whatever, because of the readiness with which it may be attacked and seized. An enemy could destroy miles of it before it would be possible to resist him, and in time of difficulty it would be a mere trap for the troops passing along it, unless we had almost an army to keep it open. [. . .] Sir, I say it here candidly and honestly, that we are bound to do everything we can to protect the country— (hear, hear,)—but we are not bound to ruin ourselves in anticipation of a supposed invasion which we could not repel, even with the assistance of England. [. . .] The best thing that Canada can do is to keep quiet, and to give no cause for war. (Hear, hear.) Let the public opinion of this country compel the press to cease the attacks it is

every day making upon the Government and people of the United States; and then if war does come between England and the States—even if from no fault of ours—we will cast our lot with England and help her to fight the battle; but in the meantime it is no use whatever to raise or keep up anything like a standing army.

[. . .]

Now, sir, when I look into the provisions of this scheme, I find another most objectionable one. It is that which gives the General Government control over all the acts of the local legislatures. What difficulties may not arise under this system? Now, knowing that the General Government will be party in its character, may it not for party purposes reject laws passed by the local legislatures and demanded by a majority of the people of that locality. This power conferred upon the General Government has been compared to the veto power that exists in England in respect to our legislation; but we know that the statesmen of England are not actuated by the local feelings and prejudices, and do not partake of the local jealousies, that prevail in the colonies. The local governments have therefore confidence in them, and respect for their decisions; and generally, when a law adopted by a colonial legislature is sent to them, if it does not clash with the policy of the Empire at large, it is not disallowed, and more especially of late has it been the policy of the Imperial Government to do whatever the colonies desire in this respect, when their wishes are constitutionally expressed. The axiom on which they seem to act is that the less they hear of the colonies the better. (Hear, hear.) But how different will be the result in this case, when the General Government exercises the veto power over the acts of local legislatures. Do you not see that it is quite possible for a majority in a local government to be opposed to the General Government; and in such a case the minority would call upon the General Government to disallow the laws enacted by the majority? The men who shall compose the General Government will be dependent for their support upon their political friends in the local legislatures, and it may so happen that, in order to secure this support, or in order to serve their own purposes or that of their supporters, they will veto laws which the majority of a local legislature find necessary and good. (Hear, hear.) We know how high party feeling runs sometimes upon local matters even of trivial importance, and we may find parties so hotly opposed to each other in the local legislatures, that the whole power of the minority may be brought to bear upon their friends who have a majority in the General Legislature, for the purpose of preventing the passage of some law objectionable to them but desired by the majority of their own section. What will be the result of such a state of things but bitterness of feeling, strong political acrimony and dangerous agitation? (Hear, hear.) [. . .] But, sir, respecting the defences of the country, I should have said at an earlier stage of my remarks that this scheme proposes a union not only with Nova Scotia, New Brunswick, Prince Edward Island, and Newfoundland, but also with British Columbia and Vancouver's Island. Although I have not been able to get the information from the Government—for they do not seem to be very ready to give information—yet I understand that there are despatches to hand, stating that resolutions have been adopted in the Legislature of British Columbia asking for admission into the Confederation at once. I must confess, Mr. SPEAKER, that it looks like a burlesque to speak as a means of defence of a scheme of Confederation to unite the whole country extending from Newfoundland to Vancouver's Island, thousands of miles intervening without any communication, except through the United States or around Cape Horn. (Oh!) [. . .]

So far as Lower Canada is concerned, I need hardly stop to point out the objections to the scheme. It is evident, from what has transpired, that it is intended eventually to form a legislative union of all the provinces. The local governments, in addition to the General Government, will be found so burdensome, that a majority of the people will appeal to the Imperial Government for the formation of a legislative union. (Hear, hear.) I may well ask if there is any member from Lower Canada, of French extraction, who is ready to vote for a legislative union. What do I find in connection with the agitation of this scheme? The honorable member for Sherbrooke stated at the dinner to the delegates given at Toronto, after endorsing everything that had been said by the Honorable President of the Council:—

> We may hope that, at no far distant day, we may become willing to enter into a Legislative Union instead of a federal union, as now proposed. We would have all have desired a legislative union, and to see the power concentrated in the Central Government as it exists in England, spreading the aegis of its protection over all the institutions of the land, but we found it was impossible to do that at first. We found that there were difficulties in the way which could not be overcome.

Honorable members from Lower Canada are made aware that the delegates all desired a legislative union, but it could not be accomplished at once. This Confederation is the first necessary step towards it. The British Government is ready to grant a Federal union at once, and when that is accomplished the French element will be completely overwhelmed by the majority of British representatives. What then would prevent the Federal Government from passing a set of resolutions in a similar way to those we are called upon to pass, without submitting them to the people, calling upon the Imperial Government to set aside the Federal form of government and give a legislative union instead of it? (Hear, hear.)

Perhaps the people of Upper Canada think a legislative union a most desirable thing. I can tell those gentlemen that the people of Lower Canada are attached to their institutions in a manner that defies any attempt to change them in that way. They will not change their religious institutions, their laws and their language, for any consideration whatever. A million of inhabitants may seem a small affair to the mind of a philosopher who sits down to write out a constitution. He may think it would be better that there should be but one religion, one language and one system of laws, and he goes to work to frame institutions that will bring all to that desirable state; but I can tell honorable gentlemen that the history of every country goes to show that not even by the power of the sword can such changes be accomplished. I am astonished to see the honorable member for Montreal West helping a scheme designed to end in a legislative union, the object of which can only be to assimilate the whole people to the dominant population. In that honorable gentleman's own country the system has produced nothing but a dissatisfied and rebellious people. Is it desirable that in this country then we should pass a measure calculated to give dissatisfaction to a million of people? You may ascertain what the cost of keeping down a million of dissatisfied people is by the scenes that have been and are now transpiring on the other side of the line, where a fifth of the people of the United States has risen and has caused more misery and misfortune to be heaped upon that country than could have been wrought in centuries of peaceful compromising legislation. Sir, if a legislative union of the British American Provinces is attempted, there will be such an agitation in this portion of the province as was never witnessed before—you will see the whole people of Lower Canada clinging together to resist by all legal and constitutional means, such an attempt at wresting from them those institutions that they now enjoy. They would

go as a body to the Legislature, voting as one man, and caring for nothing else but for the protection of their beloved institutions and law, and making government all but impossible. The ninety Irish members in the British House of Commons, composed as it is of nearly seven hundred members, by voting together have caused their influence to be felt, as in the grants to the Maynooth College and some other questions. It would be the same way with the people of Lower Canada, and a more deplorable state of things would be the inevitable result. The majority would be forced by the minority to do things they would not, under the circumstances, think of doing. This is a state so undesirable that, although I am strongly opposed to the proposed Federal union, I am still more strongly opposed to a legislative union. Those who desire a legislative union may see from this what discordant elements they would have to deal with in undertaking the task, and what misery they would bring upon the country by such a step. (Hear, hear.) I know there is an apprehension among the British population in Lower Canada that, with even the small power that the Local Government will possess, their rights will not be respected. How, then, can it be expected that the French population can anticipate any more favorable result from the General Government, when it is to possess such enormous powers over the destinies of their section of the country? Experience shows that majorities are always aggressive, and it cannot well be otherwise in this instance. It therefore need not be wondered at that the people of Lower Canada, of British origin, are ready to make use of every means to prevent their being placed at the mercy of a preponderating population of a different origin. I agree with them in thinking that they ought to take nothing on trust in this matter of entering upon a new state of political existence, and neither ought we of French origin to do so, in relation to the General Government, however happy our relations to each other may be at present.

[...]

I contend that the local constitutions are as much an essential part of the whole as the general Constitution, and that they both should have been laid at the same time before the House. (Hear, hear.) We ought, besides, to have a clear statement of what are the liabilities specially assigned to Upper and Lower Canada. (Hear, hear.) It is well that Upper Canada should know if she has to pay the indebtedness of Port Hope, Cobourg, Brockville, Niagara, and other municipalities which have borrowed from the municipal loan fund, and what these liabilities are; and it is important for Lower Canada to be told what are the amounts they will be required to tax themselves for. We ought, besides, to obtain some kind of information upon the subject of the Intercolonial Railway, what is the proposed cost, and what route is to be followed; and before these facts are before the House, we ought not to take it upon ourselves to legislate on the subject. Still further, the people of the country do not understand the scheme. (Hear, hear.) Many members of this House, before hearing the explanations which have been offered, were, and others are still, in doubt as to the bearing of many of these resolutions. [...] I owe an apology to the House for having offered such lengthened remarks on this question, and I have to thank honorable members for having so kindly listened to them. (Cries of "go on".) I will simply content myself with saying that for these reasons which I have so imperfectly exposed, I strongly fear it would be a dark day for Canada when she adopted such a scheme as this. (Cheers.) It would be one marked in the history of this country as having had a most depressing and crushing influence on the energies of the people in both Upper and Lower Canada—(hear, hear)—for I consider it one of the worst schemes that could be brought under the consideration of the House; and if it should be adopted without

the sanction of the people, the country would never cease to regret it. (Hear, hear.) What is the necessity for all this haste? The longer this Constitution is expected to last, the greater the necessity for the fullest consideration and deliberation. [...] There are three modes of obtaining the views of the people upon the question now under discussion. The most direct one would be, after debating it in this House, to submit it to the people for their verdict, yea or nay. The second is to dissolve the House and appeal to the people. The third is to discuss and pass the resolutions or address to a second reading, and afterwards leave it open to the public to judge of its merits, by meeting and discussing it, and sending in petitions and instructing their representatives how to vote upon it when they came to Parliament at the next session. Any one of these methods would elicit the views of the people. But to say that the opinions of the people have been ascertained on the question, I say it is no such thing. (Hear, hear.) We have heard one side of the question discussed, but we have heard none of the views on the other side; and yet the feeling, as exhibited in some parts of the country, has been unmistakeably in favor of an appeal to the people. Some fifteen counties in Lower Canada have held meetings and declared for an appeal before the scheme is allowed to pass; and when honorable gentlemen on the other side have held second meetings, they have been condemned more conclusively than at first. (Hear, Hear.) [...]

There is no hurry in regard to the scheme. We are now legislating for the future as well as for the present, and feeling that we ought to make a Constitution as perfect as possible, and as far as possible in harmony with the views of the people, I maintain that we ought not to pass this measure now, but leave it to another year, in order to ascertain in the meantime what the views and sentiments of the people actually are. (The honorable gentleman was loudly cheered on resuming his seat.)

Historical Interpretations

3   From Ged Martin, "The Case Against Canadian Confederation," in Ged Martin, ed., *The Causes of Confederation* (Fredericton: Acadiensis Press, 1990), 19–49.

The men who met at Charlottetown and Quebec in 1864 to design the Dominion of Canada live in legend as the "Fathers of Confederation". They gaze at us, from sombre photographs and dignified portraits, with a grave demeanour which makes it hard to believe that any of them could ever have called an opponent a liar or promised to build a bridge to win an election. We need not begrudge them their mythic status in Canadian history, for our real difficulty lies in reconciling the claim for their far-sighted wisdom with the equally patriotic efforts of Canada's historians, who have related the saga of the coming of Confederation as if it were the inevitable outcome of the problems of the 1860s.[1] "Only a general union, balanced with all the care and precision of a cantilever, was practical in 1864," wrote W.L. Morton a century later. If Confederation was indeed the inescapable solution in 1864, how can we attribute such superior wisdom to the Fathers? Surely they were no more than the unconscious instruments of historical inevitability? Morton implicitly confronted the issue by describing the cabinet headed by John Sandfield Macdonald, which immediately preceded the Confederation Coalition in the province of Canada, as "provincial politicians who had failed to sense the new currents which had begun to flow in Canadian politics since 1857."[2] Confederation, then, was inevitable, but perspicacity and vision were needed to grasp this evident fact. By implication, those who failed to see the necessity for Confederation got it wrong.

Such an approach can hardly encourage an unprejudiced analysis of the arguments advanced between 1864 and 1867 by those who opposed the new constitutional system.[3] The scheme drawn up at Quebec in 1864 was rejected by the voters in New Brunswick in 1865, would probably have been decisively rejected had there been an election in Nova Scotia, and might even have failed to win a majority in Lower Canada. Indeed, it is at least possible that Confederation was ultimately accepted in spite of the case against it rather than because of the arguments in its favour. Consideration of the objections raised by opponents may enable us to decide whether Confederation really was the logical deduction from interlocking circumstances, or whether we should look to other explanations for its adoption. [. . .]

The two major sources on which this paper is based are the *Confederation Debates* of 1865 in the province of Canada, and the Nova Scotia petitions of 1866 in the *British Parliamentary Papers*. The Canadian parliament had not previously printed its debates, and we may echo the lament of Dr Joseph Blanchet, four weeks and 545 pages after discussion began on 3 February 1865, that the decision "to have the speeches of this House printed in official form certainly did no good service to the country." Yet vast as was the eventual volume, it does not necessarily do justice to the opposition case. In the early phases of the debate, there was a tendency to demand further information, for the Quebec plan required much fleshing-out of practical details on which the ministers were unforthcoming—and it was tempting to debunk the visionary orations of Macdonald and McGee by trumpeting that there was no case to answer. Luther Holton replied to the first great onslaught of explanations with the flourish that if the government's speeches "contain all that can be said in favour of this scheme, we have no fear of letting them go unanswered." As the Canadian debate was getting into its stride, so news arrived of Tilley's defeat in New Brunswick which, A-A. Dorion claimed, caused the issue "to lose much of its interest."[4] Much of the debate was taken up with members taunting each other with inconsistency, which often provoked elaborate apologetics. Some speeches were intended to drag matters out while petitions were circulated:[5] Cartier embarrassed Eric Dorion, by reading into the record a circular letter he had sent to supporters requesting them to have anti-Confederation petitions "signed as soon as possible by men, women and children."[6] Similar devices were used to produce petitions in Nova Scotia, as the governor general, Lord Monck, and a former lieutenant-governor, the Marquess of Normanby, assured the House of Lords in 1867.[7] It is certainly hard to believe that the 210 inhabitants of the district of Port Medway who signed their names to a massive, 2000-word petition against Confederation were entirely unprompted,[8] and it may be doubted if any of the petitions emerged from the sober atmosphere of a political science seminar. [. . .]

"I do not know of any one opposed to union in the abstract," said New Brunswick's Timothy Warren Anglin. "But my impression is that the time has not arrived for any kind of union, and I will oppose it to the last."[9] This was a common theme among the critics: intercolonial union in principle, union one day, but not this union, not now.[10] As Edward Whelan put it, the critics accepted the principle of ploughing the field, but objected to destroying the daisies and field mice.[11] How sincere were these protestations— by some, but by no means all the critics of Confederation—in favour of an eventual British North American union? Perhaps they were gestures of open-mindedness merely to win over waverers. David Reesor found it "extraordinary" that so many members of the Canadian Legislative Council spoke "strongly and emphatically against many of the resolutions" while declaring their reluctant intention to vote for the package.[12] Yet even A-A. Dorion, who went to some lengths to clear his name of the slander of having ever spoken favourably of the idea, could leave open a faint and distant possibility: "Population may extend over the wilderness that now lies between the Maritime Provinces and ourselves, and commercial intercourse may increase sufficiently to render Confederation desirable."[13] As late as August 1864, admittedly at a social occasion, Joseph Howe proclaimed: "I have always been in favour of uniting any two, three, four, or the whole five of the provinces."[14] [. . .]

If some of the opponents subscribed to the idea of an eventual intercolonial union, most of the critics in the province of Canada argued that Confederation was not a solution to present difficulties, and it would itself require a far greater degree of political wisdom than was necessary to rescue the existing system. Henri Joly felt that the various provinces would meet in a confederated parliament "as on a field of battle." Christopher Dunkin referred to the airy dismissals of such warnings by ministerial supporters: "Oh! there won't be any trouble; men are in the main sensible, and won't try to make trouble." If public men were so reasonable as to be able to work the new system, why then had the province of Canada had "four crises in two years"? In any case, even if it were accepted that Upper and Lower Canada were not living together in harmony, the answer was surely for them to work out a new system of government and not to claim that only through a wider union could they get along.[15] [. . .]

While some critics of Confederation admitted that the Canadian Union had its problems, others felt them to have been exaggerated. Henri Joly contrasted Taché's claim that "the country was bordering on civil strife" with the ministry's throne speech, which thanked "a beneficent Providence for the general contentment of the people of this province."[16] Joseph Perrault asked "have we not reason to be proud of our growth since 1840, and of the fact that within the past twenty-five years, our progress, both social and material, has kept pace with that of the first nations in the world"?[17] [. . .]

The core of the case against Confederation was that there was no crisis sufficient to justify so large a change. Consequently, critics largely refused to enter the trap of offering alternative solutions. "We are asked, 'what are you going to do? You must do something. Are you going to fall back to our old state of dead-lock?,'" Dunkin reported, adding that whenever he heard the argument "that something must be done, I suspect that there is a plan on foot to get something very bad done." Henri Joly took the same line. "I am asked: 'If you have nothing to do with Confederation, what will you have?' I answer, we would remain as we are."[18] "Now my proposition is very simple," Joseph Howe told the people of Nova Scotia. "It is to let well enough alone."[19] Not surprisingly, the opponents of Confederation indignantly rejected the argument that they were—wittingly or otherwise—working for annexation to the United States. They replied that the campaign for Confederation itself contained the germ of an annexationist threat. Matthew Cameron, one of the few prominent Upper Canada Conservatives to oppose the scheme, warned that the delusive arguments of material gain from Confederation with the tiny Maritimes "are arguments ten-fold stronger in favour of union with the United States."[20] [. . .] Joseph Howe similarly predicted that the imposition of Confederation on unwilling provinces would lead to "undying hatreds and ultimate annexation."[21]

[. . .]

Coupled with resentment at the rejection of any possibility of amendment was anger at the total refusal of a popular vote on so major a constitutional change. An exasperated Hamilton paper exclaimed that if there was to be no general election on Confederation, the polling booths "may as well be turned into pig-pens, and the voters lists cut up into pipe-lighters."[22] In Nova Scotia, where petition after petition dwelt on the province's long tradition of representative and responsible government, the people of Shelburne put the issue in more fundamental and sober terms: "whilst Your Majesty's petitioners freely admit the right of their representatives in Provincial Parliament to legislate for them within reasonable limits, they cannot admit the right of such representatives to effect sudden changes, amounting to an entire subversion of the constitution, without the deliberate sanction of the people expressed at the polls." As Joseph Howe put it in more succinct and homely terms, the local legislature had "no right to violate a trust only reposed in them for four years, or in fact to sell the fee simple of a mansion of which they have but a limited lease." Even if the scheme were beneficial, which the people of Queen's County flatly doubted, "the means employed to force it upon the country without an appeal to the people, and with full knowledge of their intense dislike of the measure" were enough to discredit it.[23]

Both in Canada and the Atlantic provinces, opponents of Confederation attacked the scheme as "very costly, for the money is scattered on all sides in handfuls."[24] Simply listing the promised commitments left critics breathless with horror. Joseph Howe recounted that with a debt of $75 million, "the public men of Canada propose to purchase the territories of the Hudson's Bay Company, larger than half Europe," take over British Columbia and Vancouver Island, "provinces divided from them by an interminable wilderness," as well as absorb the Atlantic provinces, "countries severally as large as Switzerland, Sardinia, Greece, and Great Britain."[25] Dunkin similarly warned that with "a promise of everything for everybody," the scheme could only "be ambiguous, unsubstantial and unreal."[26] Others feared not disappointment but jobbery. "The proposed Constitution framed by arch jobbers is so devised as to provide for the very maximum of jobbing and corruption," Arthur Gordon assured Gladstone.[27] Unfortunately, responses to the threat of corruption depended on assessments by individuals of whether they would be victims or gainers from it. [. . .] Christopher Dunkin warned that the representatives of each province would seek popularity back home by inching up federal subsidies or by taking special arrangements for one province as a benchmark and precedent for comparable concessions. They would prove to be "pretty good daughters of the horse-leech, and their cry will be found to be pretty often and pretty successfully—'Give, give give!'"[28] His warning can hardly be dismissed as inaccurate.

Related to the general question of cost were various predictions about the effect of Confederation on tariffs. James Currie predicted that Canada's tariff would have to rise by 50 per cent to produce the necessary revenue to pay for Confederation. Other Canadian critics recognized that the province's existing tariff, which leaned toward protectionism, would have to be cut in order to meet the free-trading Maritimers halfway. This would reduce revenue at a time when more, not less, money was needed to meet increased costs. Letellier de St Just predicted that "the deficit which that reduction of our revenue will produce will have to be filled up by the agriculture and industry of Canada" and Dunkin thought it "rather strange" that a government should propose to cut its tariff income and "at the same time, so to change our whole system as to involve ourselves in the enormous extravagances here contemplated." Dunkin felt that no plan of direct taxation could possibly meet the cost, and that the only alternative was a reckless policy of borrowing, except that "we cannot even borrow to any large amount unless

under false pretences."[29] The argument that Confederation would create a larger credit base and make it easier to attract investment evidently did not convince everybody.

If Canadian critics feared the consequences of lowering the tariff at the dictation of the lower provinces, Maritimers feared even the compromise increase that Confederation seemed to imply. "Unless Canada consents to economize and curtail its expenses to a very considerable degree, which is not likely to happen," explained the Fredericton *Headquarters*, "the Lower provinces will have to raise their tariffs to that standard, as they will require a greater revenue to meet the expenses of government under the new confederation."[30] Whereas the Canadian tariff was intended to protect industry, Nova Scotia's commercial policy was aimed at fostering the province's worldwide carrying trade.[31] Thus raising the tariff would destroy trade rather than increase revenue—pointing to direct taxation which, Ambrose Shea warned, was "a point on which it is easy to alarm the masses everywhere." It certainly had that effect on Prince Edward Island, where the despairing Edward Whelan reported that it scared "the asses of country people, who can't see an inch beyond their noses."[32] A British journalist who visited Charlottetown in 1865 reported that taxation was regarded as "an evil which not only the Prince Edward Islanders, but the British colonies generally throughout North America, seem to consider as the greatest which can befall a community."[33] [. . .]

Textbook explanations of the coming of Confederation assume that it was necessary for the construction of the Intercolonial Railway, and that the Intercolonial was necessary both for defence and to give Canada a winter outlet, freeing its trade from the twin strangleholds of a frozen St Lawrence and a capriciously hostile United States. Opponents accepted neither argument and indeed found much to object to in the whole scheme. First, to reassure Maritimers who had not forgotten the Canadian bad faith of 1862, the railway project was actually written into the Quebec Resolutions, and would thus form part of the British legislation and the constitution of the Confederation—"a novelty, perhaps, that might not be found in the constitution of any country."[34] It certainly gave an unusual status to a mere railway line, the more so as its route had yet to be agreed. [. . .]

Canadian critics were less concerned by the constitutional impropriety of giving a railway the same status as peace, order, and good government as by the fact that the Intercolonial would gain an advantage over their own preferred projects, especially hopes for improved communications to the Red River.[35] Suspicions were further fuelled by ministerial reluctance to say where the Intercolonial would run or how much it would cost, thus prompting the prediction that "it will be a piece of corruption from the time of the turning of the first shovelful of earth."[36] It was widely appreciated that the reason for vagueness lay in the local politics of New Brunswick, where military security pointed to a route along the thinly populated North Shore, but political expediency required a vote-pulling line up the Saint John valley, never far from the American border. [. . .] The question of the cost of the Intercolonial was a sore point to Upper Canada critics of Confederation. In 1862, the Sandfield Macdonald-Sicotte ministry had withdrawn, abruptly and in an unedifying manner, from an interprovincial agreement backed by an imperial loan guarantee, by which the province of Canada undertook to pay five-twelfths of the cost of the line—which, as Henri Joly pointed out, meant that the railway could be built if required without an accompanying political union. Now Canada, with three-quarters of the population, was accepting a *pro rata* obligation to shoulder double the share envisaged in 1862. "This will involve five to seven millions of dollars of an expense more than we had any occasion for incurring," complained David Reesor, "for the other

provinces were all [sic] willing to have been responsible for the rest, and there is very good reason why they should."[37] Indeed, Gall had assured Maritimers at a banquet in Halifax in September 1864, "you will get the best of the bargain." Yet, ironically, Canada's sudden outburst of generosity aroused counter-suspicions. In New Brunswick, Albert J. Smith hinted darkly that Canada must have some hidden motive for increasing the very offer it had so recently dishonoured.[38]

Fundamentally, opponents argued that the Intercolonial was no more attractive a project in 1865 than it had been when rejected in 1862. "I have not heard any reason why we should pledge our credit and resources to the construction of the Intercolonial Railway, even previous to any estimate of its cost being made, that was not urged in 1862 when the question was before the country," A-A. Dorion asserted. [. . .] Henri Joly also doubted whether the Intercolonial could be used to send flour to the Maritimes, for "the cost of transport over five hundred miles of railway would be too great."[39]

The critics did not simply doubt whether trade could profitably flow along the Intercolonial; they also wondered whether Canada and the Maritimes were likely to have any trade at all. "Let us not . . . be lulled with fallacies of the great commercial advantages we shall derive from a Confederation of these provinces," intoned Eric Dorion. "We have wood, they produce it; we produce potash, and so do they."[40] "With regard to timber," said Henri Joly, "the Gulf Provinces have no more need of ours than we of theirs." Canada imported its coal direct from Britain, as ballast on returning timber ships. If that supply should ever fail, "Upper Canada will probably get its coal from the Pennsylvania mines, which are in direct communication with Lake Erie."[41] Yet, at the same time, Canadian critics could argue that free trade with the Maritimes could be achieved without "this mock Federal union," just as the provinces had enjoyed a decade of closer economic relations with the United States through the Reciprocity Treaty.[42] [. . .]

The critics were no more convinced by the argument that the Intercolonial was necessary for the defence of the provinces. A-A. Dorion argued that "a railway lying in some places not more than fifteen or twenty miles from the frontier, will be of no use whatever. . . . An enemy could destroy miles of it before it would be possible to resist him, and in time of difficulty it would be a mere trap for the troops passing along it, unless we had almost an army to keep it open." However far the Intercolonial snaked away from the American border, there was an existing stretch of the Grand Trunk "at places within twenty-six miles of the boundary of Maine," and thus easily vulnerable to American attack. Far from transporting large numbers of troops, the Intercolonial would need large forces simply to guard it. "Unless with a strong force to defend it, in a military point of view, it would be of just no use at all." In summary, the Intercolonial, centrepiece of so many textbook explanations of the causes of Confederation, was comprehensively dismissed by James L. Biggar: "Looking at it from a military point of view, it is well known that part of the proposed line would run within twenty-six miles of the American frontier, and that communication could be cut off at any moment by an American army; and that as a commercial undertaking it could never compete with the water route during the season of navigation; and in winter it would be comparatively useless on account of the depth of snow."[43]

The opponents of Confederation were unconvinced that the political union of the provinces would strengthen their defences in any way. "We do not need Confederation to give us that unity which is indispensable in all military operations—unity of headship. A commander-in-chief will direct the defence of all our provinces," argued Henri Joly. Defence had remained outside the orbit of colonial self-government until very recent times, and Canada's record on militia reform was hardly impressive. Consequently, the argument that unity meant strength is one which appeals more to the twentieth century observer than it did to contemporaries, especially when the unity proposed involved such tiny provinces. John S. Sanborn was simply bewildered. "How the people of New Brunswick could be expected to come up to Canada to defend us, and leave their own frontier unprotected, he could not comprehend." Conversely, Matthew Cameron asked why Canada should be taxed to build fortifications in the Maritimes: "Fortifications in St. John, New Brunswick, would not protect us from the foe, if the foe were to come here."[44] [. . .]

In the Atlantic colonies, the arguments were inverted. Petitioners from Nova Scotia's Digby County were ready to rally to "the defence of their country and their flag" but were "not disposed to adopt, as a means of ensuring their more efficient defence, a union with a Province which in 1862 refused to sanction a measure involving increased outlay for the better and more elaborate organisation of their militia."[45] Joseph Howe deftly alluded to Canadian complicity in border raids by Southern sympathizers, and the resulting threats of Northern retaliation, proclaiming: "let those who provoke these controversies fight them out."[46] He objected to a system under which Nova Scotia's militia "may be ordered away to any point of the Canadian frontier."[47] Prince Edward Islanders feared that they would be "marched away to the frontiers of Upper Canada" or, as John Hamilton Gray put it with vivid bitterness, "drafted for slaughter."[48] [. . .]

In three of the four Atlantic provinces, insularity was a physical as well as a mental factor. "We are surrounded by the sea," proclaimed Joseph Howe and—what was more to the point—"within ten days' sail of the fleets and armies of England."[49] J.C. Pope of Prince Edward Island echoed Canadian critics in predicting that an American attack would make it "necessary to retain all available strength in each of the provinces for the defence of their respective territories." His emphasis differed in his confidence that local efforts would be powerfully seconded by the British navy and army.[50] Many critics argued that Confederation would actually make the defence of British North America more difficult. Henri Joly argued that there was "no need" of political union to warn "our neighbours" not to pick on a single province.[51] [. . .]

"With Confederation, neither the number of men in the several provinces, nor the pecuniary resources now at their disposal, will be increased." The kernel of the Canadian opposition case on defence was that Confederation involved too much territory and no additional manpower. "Can you alter the geographical position of the country?" asked Benjamin Seymour. "Will you have any more people or means?" "If nature were to make the necessary effort and move their territory up alongside of us, and thus make a compact mass of people, I would at once agree that it would strengthen us in a military point of view," Philip Moore ironically conceded. In reality, however, Confederation "will weaken instead of strengthen us," since "the union will give an extension of territory far greater in proportion to the number of the population than [sic] now exists in Canada." The planned massive extension into empty and inaccessible territory westward to the Pacific struck A-A. Dorion as "a burlesque" in terms of defence. In short, critics found the defence argument literally laughable: "If we could attach the territory possessed by the moon to these provinces, and obtain the assistance for our joint defence of the man who is popularly supposed to inhabit that luminary, we might derive strength from Confederation."[52]

Critics were equally unimpressed by ringing talk of a "new nationality" in British North America. "I cannot see that the Federation of these provinces has anything of a national phase in it," commented Thomas Scatcherd. "When you speak of national existence, you speak of independence; and so long as we are colonists of Great Britain we can have no national existence."[53] Some Nova Scotian petitions protested that British North America was "incapable of forming a new nationality,"[54] but the loyal people of Barrington township had an each-way bet in wanting no part of "new nationalities too feeble to stand alone, yet difficult to be controlled."[55] [. . .]

In fact, critics feared that Confederation would actually provoke Americans into hostilities. Howe warned: "let this guy of 'new nationality' be set up . . . and every young fellow who has had a taste of the license of camp life in the United States will be tempted to have a fling at it."[56] Christopher Dunkin even expressed alarm at the tone of the Confederation debates, asking "how is the temper of the United States going to be affected . . . by the policy here urged on us, of what I may call hostile independent effort—effort made on our part, with the avowed object of setting ourselves up as a formidable power against them[?]." The Northern States, A-A. Dorion pointed out, had put into the field an army of 2 300 000, "as many armed men as we have men, women and children in the two Canadas." Military expenditure on any large scale would be useless and "we are not bound to ruin ourselves in anticipation of a supposed invasion which we could not repel." Public opinion should force the Canadian press to cease its anti-American outbursts: "The best thing that Canada can do is to keep quiet, and to give no cause for war."[57] [. . .]

Given their overwhelming rejection of the case for Confederation as a defence measure, it is hardly surprising that this aspect of the scheme produced some of the most colourful imagery among critics. Joining with the Maritimes, said James Currie, "was like tying a small twine at the end of a long rope and saying it strengthened the whole line." Incorporating the vast Hudson's Bay Territories, said Henri Joly, would create "the outward form of a giant, but with the strength of a child."[58] John Macdonald, member for Toronto West, thought "the casting of the burden of defence upon this country is like investing a sovereign with all the outward semblance of royalty, and giving him a dollar per day to keep up the dignity of his court." Macdonald has been overshadowed by his namesake to the point of invisibility, but he had a homely touch in his comments, telling the legislators as they met for the last year in Quebec City that Confederation was like taking the engine from the Lévis ferry and using it "to propel the *Great Eastern* across the Atlantic."[59] In a far smaller town, an angry young Rouge editor denounced Confederation in less whimsical imagery. As a defence against the United States it was like being "armed with an egg-shell to stop a bullet . . . a wisp of straw in the way of a giant."[60] The writer's name was Wilfrid Laurier. [. . .]

There was little direct contact between Canada and Maritimes prior to Confederation: during a visit to Montreal in 1860, T. Heath Haviland of Prince Edward Island had encountered "the utmost difficulty" in finding "so much as a newspaper from the Lower Provinces."[61] It is therefore surprising to discover the extent of their mutual antipathy. The "plain meaning" of the Canadian ministry's desire to force through the Quebec Resolutions without amendment was "that the Lower Provinces have made out a Constitution for us and we are to adopt it," said A-A. Dorion. Voting at the Quebec Conference had been by provinces, which "made Prince Edward Island equal to Upper Canada." Dorion complained of "the humiliation of seeing the Government going on its knees and begging the little island of Prince Edward to come into this union."[62] Only by appreciating the existence of this sentiment of disdain for the Maritimes among Canadian critics can we understand why Macdonald and his colleagues had no alternative but to outface and outmanoeuvre opposition in Nova Scotia and New Brunswick.

Maritimers returned the hostility. James Dingwell of Prince Edward Island thought "Canadians had not been able to manage the business of their country as we have been to manage ours; and why should we trust the management of our own affairs to people who have never been able to manage their own with satisfaction?"[63] With colourful exaggeration, Joseph Howe claimed that Canadians were "always in trouble of some sort, and two or three times in open rebellion."[64]

Despite Howe's suspicions that Lower Canadian solidarity in the federal parliament would entrench French power, hostility to Confederation in the Atlantic colonies seems to have been directed against the whole of what later became the monster of "central Canada" and was relatively free of explicit francophobia. There was a hint of it an open letter to the British Colonial Secretary in January 1867, when a recitation of Nova Scotia's loyal service to the Empire in wars against France was followed by the waspish comment: "We are now asked to surrender it to Monsieur Cartier."[65] Although francophobia was so endemic that it was not necessary to articulate it, inter-communal flashpoints in the mid-nineteenth century were more likely to concern sectarian schooling than the politics of language. Memories of their homeland's forced unification with Britain led many Irish Catholics to oppose Confederation. If anti-Confederates had warned of the danger of French power, Irish Catholics might have concluded that Confederation could bring benefits for their church. In any case, Acadians were as suspicious of Confederation as their anglophone neighbours, and it suited Howe to portray them as one of the contented minorities—along with Mi'kmaq and blacks—who had flourished under the benign institutions of an autonomous Nova Scotia.[66] [. . .]

Behind these mutual suspicions, there surely lay something deeper than the cussedness which we normally dismiss as parochialism. Even in the superheated provincial politics of the mid-nineteenth century, it seems exaggerated that Cartier could have been accused of "la lâchéte la plus insigne dans la trahison la plus noire," merely for forming a coalition with George Brown, or that Prince Edward Island representatives at the Charlottetown conference were pointed out in the street as "the men who would sell their country."[67] The fact that such remarks were made suggests that the different provinces felt themselves to possess distinct social and political cultures. This was most obvious in predominantly French-speaking and Catholic Lower Canada. [. . .] The complication in Lower Canada was the existence of a minority-within-a-minority, equally suspicious of those aspects of the new constitution which guaranteed provincial autonomy under a local francophone majority. Principal Dawson of McGill thought that "scarcely anyone among the English of Lower Canada desires Confederation, except perhaps as an alternative to simple dissolution of the Union."[68] This was a case where clashing objections had a reinforcing effect, for every reassurance offered to the Lower Canada English was a confirmation of French-Canadian fears.[69]

The separate identity of French-Canadian society on an Anglo-Saxon continent was obvious enough. What may be less obvious is that in the Maritimes—and especially in Nova Scotia—there was as great a sense of being different from the province of Canada as modern Canadians would today feel separates themselves from their neighbours in the United States. True, Joseph Howe could welcome a party of Canadian visitors to Halifax in August 1864 with the sentiment: "I am not one of those who thank God that I am a Nova Scotian merely, for I am a Canadian as well."[70] Yet the picture which emerges from his subsequent anti-Confederation campaign is of a province not simply resentful of losing its autonomy, but fearful of being subordinated to the capricious and unattractive values of "those who live above the tide," "the administration of strangers."[71] A recurrent theme of

Nova Scotian opposition was loss of its historic self-government. Behind the issue of high principle, there lay practical and local fears. The petitioners of Digby County pointed out that "while that portion of this county which borders on the sea is thickly inhabited and rapidly increasing in population and wealth, there are still considerable districts but lately reclaimed from the primaeval forest," which required grants of public money for the development of roads and bridges. They regarded "with dismay" the transfer of control over public expenditure "to a Government by which they would necessarily all be expended for widely different purposes."[72] Canada was as distant from Nova Scotia as Austria from Britain.[73] "You cannot . . . invest a village on the Ottawa with the historic interest and associations that cluster around London," wrote Joseph Howe—and he emphatically preferred "London under the dominion of John Bull to Ottawa under the dominion of Jack Frost."[74] [. . .]

Another theme common to the critics, whatever their regional loyalty, was rejection of both the proposed provincial governments and the confederate upper house as safeguards for their rights. [. . .] George Coles predicted that under Confederation, the legislature of Prince Edward Island "would be the laughing stock of the world," left "to legislate about dog taxes, and the running at large of swine."[75] While some critics concluded that the whole plan of union should be abandoned, others argued from similar premises that the union should be strengthened. The Halifax *Citizen* agreed that the Quebec scheme "has given these local legislatures very little to do," and predicted that they would occupy themselves in mischief, preserving local loyalties which would prevent "the fusion of the British American population in one actual indivisible nationality."[76] "One of the worst features of the Union plan proposed by Canada is, that it will leave our local legislature still in existence," lamented the Saint John *Globe*, which would have preferred to see outright unification.[77] Even the fervent anti-Confederate, T.W. Anglin, writing in the rival *Freeman*, agreed that if they had to have Confederation, "it would be better to abolish the local Legislatures at once in appearance as well as in reality."[78]

The critics were not reassured by the fact that both lieutenant-governors and members of the upper house were to be appointed by the central government. The prospect of lieutenant-governors drawn from provincial politics aroused little enthusiasm. "Let any one of our dozen or twenty most prominent Canadian politicians be named Lieutenant-Governor of Upper or of Lower Canada, would not a large and powerful class of the community . . . be very likely to resent the nomination as an insult?" asked Christopher Dunkin.[79] In Canada, where the Legislative Council had become elective in 1856—with life members retaining their seats—there was resentment at the reintroduction of nomination, "because the Maritime Provinces are opposed to an elective Chamber, and hence we in Canada—the largest community and the most influential—must give way to them."[80] There was also resentment at the provision in the Quebec Resolutions by which the first Confederate legislative councillors would be appointed from the existing Legislative Councils (except in Prince Edward Island)—a transparent bribe to curb the opposition in the upper houses. Worse still, the first Confederate upper house was to be appointed for life, on the nomination of the existing provincial governments—with the central government not even possessing a veto. A-A. Dorion's objection was not to the principle but to the unlucky fact that most British North American governments were Conservative. "For all time to come, as far as this generation and the next are concerned, you will find the Legislative Council controlled by the influence of the present government."[81] Future appointment by the central government aroused no more enthusiasm, since as Dunkin suggested, a government might be formed in which an

entire province "either is not represented, or is represented otherwise than it would wish to be."[82] [. . .]

The arguments of the critics of Confederation must be conceded to have been at least plausible. Why then did they fail to prevent the passage of the British North America Act in 1867? First, of course, their arguments did not pass unchallenged. Just as conventional studies of the causes of Confederation tend to underplay the opposition case, so a study of the critics necessarily distorts the debate in their favour. Indeed, arguments which high-minded posterity may find irrefutable could perhaps have produced diametrically opposite responses among contemporaries: Upper Canadian critics, in damning the Intercolonial as an irresponsible waste of money, might have convinced some Lower Canadians of its pork-barrel value.[83] Even if the opposition case against the Intercolonial Railway had been overwhelming, Confederation might still have been supported on general grounds as the most practicable solution to a range of problems. The Confederation package mattered more than the interlocking detail, and not everybody bothered with those details. [. . .] In any case, even if the argument were won inside the provinces, there remained that "atmosphere of crisis" over the North American continent. "Look around you to the valley of Virginia," McGee challenged those who wanted to know why Confederation was necessary, "look around you to the mountains of Georgia, and you will find reasons as thick as blackberries."[84] Perhaps the fundamental mistake of the opponents of Confederation was to ask people to react logically to the activities of Macdonald and Cartier in the conference chamber rather than to the operations of Grant and Sherman on the battlefield. The question for explanation then becomes why it should have been intercolonial union—rather than, say, neutrality or annexation—which met the psychological need for a dramatic response to continental crisis. One explanation may be that the idea had been around for a long time, answer looking for a question. "Everybody admits that Union must take place sometime," said John A. Macdonald, "I say now is the time."[85] In seeking to account for the adoption of so vast a scheme as Canadian Confederation, historians have naturally turned to the arguments of its supporters, and have been tempted to conclude that the arguments put forward *for* Canadian Confederation equal the reasons *why* Canadian Confederation came about. Certainly hindsight finds it easy to draw neat lines of causation linking argument to outcome: the lines may be straight, but the process itself is circular, since it identifies the winners of history as—in Morton's terms—those who sensed the currents of events. Yet we should not forget that the case against Confederation was argued as tenaciously, as eloquently and—we must assume—as sincerely as the arguments in its favour. However much historians may admire the "Fathers

of Confederation," only by recognizing not just the strength of opposition to Confederation but also the plausibility of some of the arguments put forward, can we begin to see that the outcome was by no means inevitable. Of course, some historians believe that posterity is not entitled to second-guess past controversies, that a century later we cannot award points to individual arguments, for or against, since we cannot make ourselves fully part of the atmosphere of the time. Yet such an attitude is tantamount to an uncritical abdication of our own judgement to each and every claim made by those who were on the winning side perhaps for reasons other than the simply intellectual. "La raison du plus fort, c'est toujours la meuilleure," is not the most appropriate explanatory strategy for the historian to adopt. Hindsight may yet conclude that while the Antis lost the battle, they won at least some of the arguments.

NOTES

1. The major accounts of the coming of Confederation remain D.G. Creighton, *The Road to Confederation: The Emergence of Canada 1863–1867* (Toronto, 1964); W.L. Morton, *The Critical Years: The Union of British North America 1857–1873* (Toronto, 1964) and P.B. Waite, *The Life and Times of Confederation 1864–1867: Newspapers, and the Union of British North America* (Toronto, 1962). My debt to Waite's study of press sources is obvious from the footnotes below, in which the book is cited as *Life and Times*.

2. W.L. Morton, *The Kingdom of Canada: A General History from Earliest Times* (2nd edn, Toronto, 1969), pp. 317, 314–15.

3. Paradoxically, given the relative lack of general overviews, opposition to Confederation in individual provinces and sections has been widely studied, conveying the impression that parochialism predominated. For bibliographies, see D.A. Muise, ed., *A Reader's Guide to Canadian History: I, Beginnings to Confederation* (Toronto, 1982), pp. 237–48, and *Life and Times*, pp. 342–52.

4. Christopher Dunkin, *Parliamentary Debates on the Subject of the Confederation of the British North American Provinces* (3rd Session, 8th Provincial Parliament of Canada, Quebec 1865) [hereafter cited as CD], pp. 545 (Blanchet); 147 (Holton); 682 (Dorion).

5. *Life and Times*, p. 154.

6. Not reported in CD, but see Waite ed., *The Confederation Debates in the Province of Canada 1865* (Torono, 1963), pp. xv–xvi.

7. *Hansard's Parliamentary Debates* (3rd series), CLXXXV, 19 February 1867, cols. 579–80, 577.

8. *British Parliamentary Papers* [cited as BPP], 1867, XLVIII, *Correspondence Respecting the Proposed Union of the British North American Provinces*, pp. 75–7.

9. Speech of 7 April 1866, quoted in William M. Baker, *Timothy Warren Anglin 1822–1896: Irish Catholic Canadian* (Toronto, 1977), p. 103, and see also p. 58. Anglin was editor of the

Saint John *Morning Freeman*. According to
Creighton, Anglin was "an unsubdued ex-
rebel" who "flung the full force of his abusive
and mendacious journalism against Confederation" (*Road to Confederation*, p. 251, and
see also p. 247). It is unlikely that Anglin
took part in the Irish rising of 18 48 and
there is no reason to think that his journalism was unusually abusive or mendacious by
contemporary standards, which were admittedly low. Thus have critics of Confederation
been dismissed.

10. Similar views were expressed in the Canadian
Legislative Council by James G. Currie, Bill
Flint and David Reesor and in the Assembly
by Christopher Dunkin, Joseph Perrault,
Thomas Scatcherd and T.C. Wallbridge. CD,
pp. 46, 164, 319, 483, 585, 749, 660.

11. Charlottetown *Examiner*, 30 January 1865,
quoted in *Life and Times*, p. 186.

12. CD, p. 328.

13. CD, p. 248. In May 1860, Dorion had said that
he regarded a federation of the two Canada
as "le noyau de la grande confédération des
provinces de l'Amérique du nord que j'appelle
de mes voeux." Quoted by Joseph Cauchon,
*L'Union des Provinces de l'Amérique Britannique
du Nord* (Quebec, 1865), p. 7.

14. Speech in Halifax, 13 August 1864, in J.A.
Chisholm, ed., *The Speeches and Public Letters of
Joseph Howe* (2 vols, Halifax, 1909), II, p. 433.

15. CD, pp. 352 (Joly); 508, 485 (Dunkin).

16. CD, p. 357.

17. CD, p. 586.

18. CD, pp. 543 (Dunkin); 356–57 (Joly).

19. Open letter, 10 April 1866, in Chisholm, ed.,
Speeches and Public Letters of Joseph Howe, 11,
p. 463.

20. CD, p. 456.

21. Howe to Isaac Buchanan, 20 June 1866, in
Chisholm, ed., op. cit., II, p. 464. In his 1866
pamphlet, *Confederation Considered in Relation
to the Interests of the Empire*, Howe complained
that in the New Brunswick election that year,
"one half of an entirely loyal population were
taught to brand the other half as disloyal."
Quoted in ibid., II, p. 484.

22. Hamilton *Times*, November 1864, quoted
in *Life and Times*, p. 122. See also Bruce
W. Hodgins, "Democracy and the Ontario

Fathers of Confederation," in Bruce Hodgins
and Robert Page, eds, *Canadian History Since
Confederation: Essays and Interpretations*
(2nd edn, Georgetown, Ontario, 1979),
pp. 19–28.

23. BPP, 1867, XLVIII, *Correspondence*, pp. 70, 75;
Howe et al. to Carnarvon, 19 January 1867,
p. 18.

24. CD, p. 179 (L.A. Olivier, MLC for the
Lanaudière).

25. Quoted in Chisholm, ed., op. cit., II, p. 473.

26. CD, p. 490.

27. Gordon to Gladstone, private, 27 February
1865, in Paul Knaplund, ed., *Gladstone-Gordon
Correspondence, 1851–1896* (Transactions of
the American Philosophical Society, n.s., LI,
Pt 4, 1961), p. 46.

28. CD, p. 520.

29. CD, pp. 50 (Currie); 188 (Letellier); 524
(Dunkin).

30. Fredericton *Headquarters*, 19 October 1864,
quoted in A.G. Bailey, "The Basis and Persistence of Opposition to Confederation in
New Brunswick," *Canadian Historical Review*,
XXIII (1942): 375.

31. "We have the trade of the world now open
to us on nearly equal terms, and why should
we allow Canada to hamper us?," Yarmouth
Herald, 15 December 1864, quoted in *Life and
Times*, p. 202.

32. Shea to Galt, 15 December 1864 and Whelan
to Galt, 17 December 1864, in W.G. Ormsby,
"Letters to Galt Concerning the Maritime
Provinces and Confederation," *Canadian
Historical Review*, XXXIV (1953): 167, 168.

33. Charles Mackay, "A Week in Prince Edward
Island," *Fortnightly Review*, V (1865): 147.

34. CD, p. 17 (Holton).

35. Article 69 of the Quebec Resolutions offered
only that improved communications to the
Red River "shall be prosecuted at the earliest
possible period that the state of the Finances
will permit." According to T.C. Wallbridge, this
meant "that the North-West is hermetically
sealed." CD, p. 453 and cf. Matthew Cameron,
pp. 452–3.

36. CD, p. 759 (Scatcherd).

37. CD, pp. 356 (Joly); 164 (Reesor). The 1862
agreement involved only the two provinces of
New Brunswick and Nova Scotia.

38. C. Wallace, "Albert Smith, Confederation and Reaction in New Brunswick, 1852–1882," *Canadian Historical Review*, XLIV (1963): 289. The Nova Scotian deputation to London in 1867 could "scarcely bring themselves to discuss" the Intercolonial, "so selfish and unfair at all times has been the conduct of the public men of Canada in regard to it." BPP, 1867, XLVIII, Howe et al. to Carnarvon, 19 January 1867, p. 8. For Galt's Halifax speech, see Edward Whelan, comp., *The Union of the British Provinces* (Charlottetown, 1865), p. 48.

39. CD, pp. 263 (Dorion); 356 (Joly).

40. CD, p. 863, Canada took 1.11 per cent of its imports from the other British North American territories, and sent them 2.2 per cent of its exports. New Brunswick took 2.3 per cent of its imports from Canada, to which it sent 0.87 per cent of its exports. Prince Edward Island took 2.1 per cent of its imports from Canada, to which it sent 0.6 per cent of its exports. Newfoundland took 3.9 per cent of its imports from Canada, to which it sent 0.68 per cent of its exports. (Calculated from BPP, 1866, LXIII, *Colonial Trade Statistics*, pp. 132, 152, 170, 177.) Nova Scotia figures are less helpful, but in 1866 the province took 5.5 per cent of its imports from Canada, and sent 7.15 per cent of its exports (1865 figures being 3.5 per cent and 4.96 per cent). (Calculated from BPP, 1867–68, LXXI, *Colonial Trade Statistics*, p. 144.)

41. CD, p. 355.

42. CD, pp. 356 (Joly) and 528 (Dorion).

43. CD, pp. 257 (Dorion); 750 (Scatcherd); 521 (Dorion); 883 (Biggar).

44. CD, pp. 355 (Joly); 123 (Sanborn); 456 (Cameron).

45. BPP, 1867, XLVIII, *Correspondence*, pp. 69–70.

46. Halifax *Morning Chronicle*, 11 January 1865, quoted in Chisholm, ed., op. cit., II, p. 435 (the first of the celebrated "Botheration Scheme" letters).

47. Speech at Dartmouth, 22 May 1867, quoted in ibid., II, p. 512.

48. Islander, 6 January 1865 and J.H. Gray to Tupper, 7 January 1865, quoted in *Life and Times*, pp. 186, 183.

49. Quoted in Chisholm, ed., op. cit., II, pp. 435–36.

50. Quoted in Bolger, ed., *Canada's Smallest Province*, pp. 175–76.

51. CD, pp. 354 (Joly).

52. CD, pp. 176 (Olivier); 203 (Seymour); 229 (Moore); 263 (Dorion); 234 (John Simpson, MLC for Queen's). The Halifax *Citizen* alleged that Tupper was perfectly capable of campaigning for federation with the Moon if he thought it would divert public attention. Quoted in *Life and Times*, p. 200.

53. CD, p. 748. Critics dismissed appeals to Italian and German unity as proving that the spirit of the times pointed to wider unions. Henri Joly gave a list of federations which had failed (CD, pp. 346–48), while the imperially minded Howe likened Confederation to a handful of small states withdrawing from the North German Confederation, or "a few offshoots from Italian unity" attempting to form "an inferior confederation." BPP, 1867, XLVIII, Howe et al. to Carnarvon, 19 January 1867, p. 21.

54. E.g. Petition from King's, BPP, 1867, XLVIII, *Correspondence*, p. 67.

55. Ibid., p. 71.

56. Quoted in Chisholm, ed., op. cit., II, p. 487.

57. CD, pp. 529 (Dunkin); 257 (Brome).

58. CD, pp. 46 (Currie); 353 (Joly). Henri Joly doubted comparisons between the Hudson's Bay Territories and European Russia, doubting that the West could ever support a large population. It may be noted that he ended his public career by serving as lieutenant-governor of British Columbia, 1900–1906. John A. Macdonald believed in 1865 that the prairies were "of no present value to Canada" which had "unoccupied land enough to absorb the immigration for many years." To open Saskatchewan would be to "drain away our youth and strength." Macdonald to E.W. Watkin, 27 March 1865, in J. Pope, *Memoirs of the Right Honourable Sir John Alexander Macdonald* (Toronto, 1894), pp. 397–8.

59. CD, p. 753.

60. Quoted in J. Schull, *Laurier: The First Canadian* (Toronto, 1966), p. 57.

61. Speech at Montreal, 28 October 1864, in Whelan, comp., *Union*, p. 115.

62. CD, pp. 252, 47, 656.

63. Quoted in Bolger, ed., *Canada's Smallest Province*, II, p. 177.

64. Howe to Earl Russell, 19 January 1865, quoted in Chisholm, ed., op. cit., II, p. 437.

65. BPP, 1867, XLVIII, *Howe et al. to Carnarvon*, 19 January 1867, p. 16. See also ibid., p. 12 for an unsubtle reference to the Hundred Years' War.

66. Ibid., p. 17. Cf. Leon Thériault, "L'Acadie, 1763–1978: Synthèse Historique," in Jean Daigle, ed., *Les Acadiens des Maritimes: Etudes Thématiques* (Moncton, 1980), pp. 63–8.

67. *Le Pays*, 27 June 1864, quoted in Creighton, *Road to Confederation*, p. 78, and ibid., p. 122.

68. Dawson to Howe, 15 November 1866, quoted in *Life and Times*, p. 135.

69. CD, p. 351 (Joly).

70. Speech, 13 August 1864, in Chisholm, ed., op. cit., II, p. 433. Howe rose to speak at ten minutes to midnight. "Who ever heard of a public man being bound by a speech on such an occasion as that?," he asked three years later. J.M. Beck, *Joseph Howe: II, The Briton Becomes Canadian 1848–1873* (Kingston, 1983), p. 182. In fact, Howe spoke before the Charlottetown conference.

71. Speech at Dartmouth, 22 May 1867, in Chisholm, ed., op. cit., II, p. 511.

72. BPP 1867, XLVIII, Correspondence, pp. 69–70.

73. Port Medway petition, BPP, 1867, XLVIII, *Correspondence*, p. 76; Howe et al. to Carnarvon, 19 January 1867, p. 7.

74. BPP, 1867, XLVIII, Howe et al. to Carnarvon, 19 January 1867, p. 15. J.W. Longley, *Joseph Howe* (Toronto, 1906), p. 202, and cf. Beck, op. cit., II, p. 202. The reference to "a village" was, of course, unfair, but Dunkin was concerned that the federal capital was to remain "within the jurisdiction of a subordinate province." CD, p. 507.

75. Quoted in Bolger, ed., op. cit., p. 174.

76. Halifax *Citizen*, 19 November 1864, quoted in *Life and Times*, p. 203. The lieutenant-governor, Sir Richard MacDonnell, used the same argument a few days later in a despatch: "I do not believe that so long as the boundaries of the different Provinces are maintained and Local Legislatures and petty politics fostered, the Confederation can rise to that status, and that dignity of national feeling, which creates and maintains a national military spirit and self-reliance." PRO, CO 217/235, MacDonnell to Cardwell, 22 November 1864, fos 187–212.

77. Saint John *Daily Evening Globe*, 17 October 1864, quoted in *Life and Times*, p. 136.

78. Saint John *Freeman*, 3 November 1864, quoted in Baker, *Anglin*, p. 65. Joseph Howe also condemned the duplication of legislatures as "cumbrous and expensive." Howe to Earl Russell, 19 January 1865, in Chisholm, ed., op. cit., II, p. 437.

79. CD, p. 504. Perrault alleged that some politicians were influenced by hopes of "being governor of one of the Federated Provinces," as did Letellier, who subsequently became a lieutenant-governor himself. CD, pp. 626, 188.

80. CD, p. 157 (James Aikins).

81. CD, p. 253. Dorion chose to overlook the provision in Article 14 of the Quebec Resolutions that "in such nomination due regard shall be had to the claims of the Members of Legislative Council in Opposition in each Province, so that all political panties may as nearly as possible be fairly represented."

82. CD, pp. 494–5.

83. Support for the Intercolonial might not translate into support for Confederation, as in the case of J.B. Pouliot, MPP for Témiscouata.

84. Speech at Montreal, 29 October 1864, in Whelan, comp., op. cit., pp. 122–3.

85. Speech at Halifax, 12 September 1864, in ibid., p. 46.

4 From James K. Hiller, "The 1895 Newfoundland–Canada Confederation Negotiations: A Re-consideration," *Acadiensis* XL, 2 (2001): 94–111.

The Canada–Newfoundland negotiations, which took place in Ottawa in April 1895, represent the only occasion between 1869 and 1948 when official delegations from each country met formally to discuss the possibility of Newfoundland's entry into Confederation. The episode has received attention from historians narrating the history of late-nineteenth-century Newfoundland, and particular interest was shown during the years immediately before and after Newfoundland's becoming a province in 1949.[1] This note should be read as a supplement to these earlier accounts. It is based on a wider range of sources, provides a substantial amount of additional detail, and seeks to explain more fully the attitudes of the major players. The central argument is that the negotiations failed because neither government wanted to be at the table and because the Colonial Office experienced a fit of ambivalence—concluding that imperial interests would be better served if Newfoundland became a Crown colony rather than a Canadian province. If the three parties involved had possessed the necessary political will, terms of union might well have been agreed upon.

The possibility of joining the Canadian Confederation was a subject of discussion and dispute in Newfoundland from the mid-1860s onwards. It was the central issue in the general election of 1869, when Frederic Carter's confederates were overwhelmingly defeated by Charles Bennett's anti-confederates. Thereafter Newfoundland governments adopted policies based on the assumption that Confederation with Canada was not a realistic alternative, and that the colony should pursue its interests as it chose to define them. The centerpiece policies in this regard, adopted in the 1880s, were the building of a trans-island railway to open up the island's interior and the attempt to bargain improved access to North American fish markets by asserting control over the supply of bait fishes needed by French, American, and Canadian vessels fishing for cod on the offshore banks. These were assertive and expensive policies adopted at a time when the saltfish trade, centrally important to the Newfoundland economy, was experiencing serious problems.

The 1890s were a difficult decade. The fish trade faced low prices and severe market competition, railway construction was steadily increasing the public debt, and the government's financial position was insecure. The year 1894 was particularly troubled. The Liberal party, led by Sir William Whiteway (now in his late 60s), had won the November 1893 general election with an overall majority of 10 seats. But early in 1894, on the last day allowed by law, the Tory opposition filed petitions in the Supreme Court against the election of 15 Liberals and the single independent member, alleging corrupt electoral practices under an 1887 Corrupt Practices Act that had not yet been tested in the courts. The Liberals could not counter-petition, and had to wait for what the Supreme Court might decide. The first decision arrived on 31 March; finding that the two Liberal members for the district of Bay de Verde had committed bribery under the act, Judge Sir James Winter—formerly a prominent Tory politician—unseated them and disqualified them from running again during the life of the current Assembly.

Political chaos ensued. Whiteway demanded a dissolution, and when Governor Sir Terence O'Brien refused it the government resigned without passing supply. Abandoning any pretence of impartiality, O'Brien promptly installed a minority Tory government (officially led by Augustus F. Goodridge) and prorogued the legislature. Over the following months all those accused of corrupt practice, including Whiteway and other senior Liberals such as the Colonial Secretary Robert Bond, were unseated and disqualified. The legislature remained prorogued, even after supply legislation expired. Eventually a sufficient number of Liberals lost their seats to give the Tories a majority in the House of Assembly. They also manoeuvred a majority in the Legislative Council, and the money bills finally passed in early August. Between mid-September and mid-November, though, there were by-elections in the districts where members had been unseated, and all but one of them were won by Liberals. This put the Tory government in a minority once again, but it refused to resign and Governor O'Brien—by now severely compromised politically—did not object.

It was obvious by this time that the colony was approaching an economic and financial crisis precipitated by the extraordinary political shenanigans of the previous months. [. . .] Newfoundland bond issues had become unsaleable, there were many enquiries about the state of local firms, and rumours about Whiteway's allegedly irresponsible behaviour while out of office created fear in some quarters about what might happen if and when he returned to power. The by-elections over, speculation mounted that the London and Westminster Bank, the primary London bank supporting the financing of the Newfoundland fishing industry, would refuse further accommodation to the locally owned Commercial Bank, and might also refuse to float a loan authorized by the legislature in August. Either occurrence could have had disastrous consequences. On 8 December it became known that the London and Westminster had made a call on the Commercial that the bank could not meet, and that London and Westminster would indeed refuse to accept any further bank or commercial exchange from Newfoundland. On 10 December, which became known as "Black Monday," the Commercial Bank closed its doors, soon followed by the Union (the other local private bank). The government-owned Savings Bank was now in a very precarious position, and the government itself faced bankruptcy. Merchant houses, with fish on hand but no credit, also began to close up. When immediate aid was refused by the British government, the Tories finally resigned. They were succeeded, on 13 December, by a Liberal administration led by Daniel J. Greene. To this inexperienced government fell the task of starting to clear up the wreckage.

The new government was obviously an interim one, given that Whiteway and other unseated and disqualified Liberals were waiting in the wings. However, it did manage to stabilize the situation to some degree by guaranteeing Union and Commercial banknotes at 80 and 20 cents respectively. Other legislation legalized Canadian currency, and the arrival of Canadian banks in St John's almost immediately after the "bank crash" helped as well. The government managed to scrape up enough cash to pay the debt interest due on 1 January 1895, thus staving off bankruptcy for six months. On the political front, the government put through legislation removing the disqualifications imposed on the unseated members. An unhappy O'Brien desperately resisted giving royal assent, but was eventually ordered to do so by the Colonial Office.[2] Greene resigned as premier on 1 February; he understood he was temporary, and in any case wanted to step down. Whiteway took a seat in the Legislative Council and formed a new government, but only with some difficulty given dissension over which ministers were to lose their portfolios as well as the prospect of Confederation.

At this nadir in the colony's fortunes there seemed to be three options. The government could try and raise a loan on the open market, it could seek imperial assistance (which would mean an imperial royal commission of enquiry), or it could open Confederation negotiations with the Canadian government. Commercial loans seemed to be out of the question, but the Bank of Montreal, which had sent a representative to St John's after the crash, did provide short-term financial life support. This was no doubt because Robert G. Reid, the contractor building the as yet-unfinished railway and who was being paid in Newfoundland government bonds, was closely associated with that bank. As for financial help from the British government, this had already been refused and there was little interest at the Colonial Office in changing course.

The starting point for discussion in London about Newfoundland's future, which began soon after the bank crash, was the expectation (and hope) that the colony would collapse. John Anderson, the Colonial Office official who handled Newfoundland affairs, thought recovery "impossible." For him, "a strong and honest government" in the colony was unlikely, "debased as the constituencies are by the truck system, and indiscriminate use of public money for political purposes." There was no point in directly assisting the government, since this would be tantamount to throwing good money after bad. The aim of British policy should be to obtain a "free hand" with the constitution. The imperial government should seek to become, in effect, the receiver in bankruptcy and administer the estate. If Canada was prepared "to assume the burden" on certain conditions, then well and good.[3] The permanent and assistant under-secretaries, Sir Robert Meade and John Bramston, generally agreed, noting that given the French Treaty Shore factor, Canada might well be reluctant to get involved.[4]

French fishing rights on Newfoundland's Northern Peninsula and west coast derived from eighteenth century treaties, and had for many years been the cause of friction between the colony and the imperial government.[5] The central problem in the 1890s was treaty enforcement. The original imperial legislation had expired, and the British government took the position that if the Newfoundland legislature did not pass the necessary enforcement legislation, it would do so in London. There followed an extended and highly charged exchange between the Newfoundland and British governments over where the legislation should be enacted, and what it should contain. In the end the Newfoundland legislature agreed to enact temporary enforcement legislation, pending agreement on permanent legislation. A draft permanent bill was negotiated by Whiteway in 1891 but rejected by the legislature in 1892, and temporary legislation continued to be enacted locally. The Colonial Office wanted permanent legislation but did not

like the 1891 draft, which it had come to see as clumsy and inefficient.[6] A central concern in London during the crisis of 1894–95, therefore, was that French rights should be both protected and enforced, and in this context Crown colony status for Newfoundland made some sense since London would have a free hand and would not have to deal with a fractious colonial government. If there was to be Confederation, then Canada had to be prepared to handle the French Shore—hardly a welcome prospect to Canadian politicians grappling with the Manitoba Schools question.

In London, Meade took soundings at the Treasury—where there was some concern that if Newfoundland went bankrupt and reverted to Crown colony status the British taxpayer might lose out. Meade thought not: "Administering the bankrupt affairs of Nfland out of its assets so far as they are available throws no charge on the British taxpayer." As for a royal commission, Meade thought it would be a useless exercise "unless we had cleared the ground by getting the Colony to place themselves in our hands. There was no intention to coerce them to surrender their constitution, except that no help would be given unless they consented to do so. The cost of the Commission of Enquiry would be part of the advance on account of [the] Savings Bank and for the cost of the immediate administration." Meade's suggestion, then, was that the Treasury should allow the Secretary for the Colonies, Lord Ripon, to offer a royal commission and a temporary advance on condition "that they surrender their constitution which will be settled hereafter when the report of the R.C. is received."[7] He elaborated a few days later: "Our policy should be to get Nfland off our hands into the Dominion as soon as possible . . . . My idea is that we should pass a Treaties Bill and then endeavour to get the Dominion to take them over." Crown colony government should last "just sufficiently long for this to be done." And if Confederation was indeed possible, then a royal commission might not be needed: "We have no desire to cry stinking fish if we can get the matter settled [and] off our hands to our satisfaction, and the publication of the full horrors of the situation might lead Canada to raise their terms, in fact it is certain to do so."[8] In summary, the Colonial Office was only prepared to endorse direct financial assistance if the colony agreed to an open-ended royal commission of enquiry that could recommend the suspension or abolition of responsible government. Meade's minute also suggests that help might be given to the Savings Bank if necessary. In March 1895 a retired British Customs official, Sir Herbert Murray, arrived in St John's to administer a relief fund for the benefit of fishermen and others in severe need; it was, significantly, not entrusted to the colonial government.

There was some support in Newfoundland for imperial intervention, even if this meant the end of responsible government. The idea had first emerged in April 1894, when the Tory ministry was hanging on to power and trying to avoid an election. One argument the ministry put to Governor O'Brien was that given the revelations in the election trials and the difficult financial situation there should be a thorough investigation by an imperial royal commission. Since the Liberals could be trusted to oppose any such enquiry, the existing ministry should stay in power and, if necessary, the money bills could be passed by the imperial parliament.[9] O'Brien naturally thought this an excellent idea, political wheeze though it was, but at that stage the Colonial Office was not interested.[10] The Tories raised the idea again after the bank crash, requesting immediate aid and applying for a royal commission. Once more, the Colonial Office refused.[11] When the Greene government asked whether, in the event Newfoundland agreed to a royal commission of enquiry, the imperial government would give immediate assistance and on what terms, the Colonial Office replied that while it would appoint such a commission if asked by the legislature—not just the government—there could be no pledge in advance as to what actions might be taken.[12] A petition, calling for a royal commission collected 3000 signatures in St John's, and similar petitions arrived from outlying districts—often signed by clergy and those whom O'Brien (who strongly supported the movement) was pleased to call "the responsible public."[13] The clergy's role annoyed the (pro-Liberal) *Evening Telegram*: prejudice overcame their discretion, it thundered, and "they wandered from the path of religious and clerical rectitude."[14] That all the signatories understood the constitutional implications of a royal commission is doubtful, and there seems to have been an optimistic impression abroad that the royal commissioners would arrive, as Anderson put it, "laden with bread and butter and various other good things for promiscuous distribution."[15]

Others promoted annexation to the United States. How far this was a serious movement reflecting a genuine current of local opinion is hard to judge. Despite the colony's difficulties with the imperial government, and a widespread feeling that it had been harshly treated over the years by the mother country, Newfoundlanders generally took great pride in being part of the British Empire whatever their ethnic roots. At the same time there were many, like Robert Bond, who favoured closer relations with the United States, where thousands of Newfoundlanders had emigrated. There were especially strong links between the colony and the New England states, where relief efforts following the bank crash were both energetic and successful. The *Telegram* proclaimed that "America Has More Sympathy . . . Than Has England!" and printed a long piece by John Fretwell, a US citizen who strenuously advocated annexation.[16] Posters featuring the Stars and Stripes were plastered around St John's at the end of January.[17] It was widely suspected, though, that the annexation movement was largely political, designed to whip up support for Confederation.[18] The *Evening Herald* dismissed it as a sham, pointing out that it was not supported by any leading citizens.[19]

Far more important was the vigorous anti-confederate campaign that emerged early in 1895, which included many royal commission supporters. Its leader was James Murray, a former merchant and politician.[20] He was prominent in the Anti-Confederate League, and in May he registered *The Anti-Confederate* newspaper. Many businessmen and local farmers were sympathetic, and there were large meetings in St John's and nearby towns.[21] Murray and others argued that Canada and Newfoundland had nothing in common, trading patterns would be upset, food prices would increase, Crown lands would be alienated to strangers, and the island depopulated.[22] Moreover, the current problems were merely temporary. Also involved in the anti-confederate campaign was the Political Reform and Labor Association, which represented working men in St John's and in a number of outports.[23]

Amidst this growing controversy, the Whiteway government opted in late February to open the question of Confederation. The Canadian government had refused a request for loans to the colony and the Savings Bank,[24] and the Colonial Office had refused a loan guarantee.[25] In these circumstances, given the government's opposition to a royal commission, this seemed to be the only option—and time was short, since terms of union would have to be decided before the next interest payment (due on 1 July). The Canadian government agreed on 1 March to receive a delegation,[26] but it did not leave immediately. First, Whiteway had to be sure of his party's support. According to Alfred B. Morine, a leading Tory and a confederate, Whiteway told his supporters at a secret meeting on 7 March that there was no other course. The government should try and obtain the best terms possible. He had always been a confederate, Whiteway declared, and if there was dissension the party should find another leader. Those at

the meeting agreed that the terms of union should be put to the electorate—assuming, one supposes, that they were minimally satisfactory to the government and party.[27] Secondly, both Robert Bond and Whiteway had "severe colds," and the latter something worse: it was reported that he was suffering from "severe nervous depression and internal complications caused by overwork and excessive mental strain."[28] As a result, the delegation was led by Bond while the other members were Liberal lawyers Edward P. Morris, George H. Emerson, and William H. Horwood.[29] When the delegation finally left on 27 March, Murray led a demonstration at the wharf. There were about 500 people present, carrying the Union Jack, the "native flag" draped in crepe, and a banner with a map of Newfoundland on one side and a seal on the other.[30] The delegates were jeered, and annexationists paraded with a band.[31] No prominent Tories were there. Some of them had lobbied for a bi-partisan delegation, to which Sir Mackenzie Bowell, the Canadian prime minister, did not object. The Liberals, though, did oppose such an approach, with the result that the Tories retreated into self-righteous neutrality.[32]

How far were the delegates genuinely interested in or supporters of Confederation? Morris, a prominent Roman Catholic politician, had spoken against it in the late 1880s, and represented a district (St John's West) that was largely anti-confederate. He was not identified with either camp, liked to keep his head low, and it was highly unlikely that he would risk his political career for the cause. The views of Emerson and Horwood are not known. Bond's usual response when questioned was to say that Confederation was a matter of terms, which suggested an open mind. But he was first and foremost a Newfoundland patriot, a colonial nationalist who hoped that the colony could remain politically independent and its economy bolstered by a separate reciprocity treaty with the United States (which he saw as more useful than closer links with Canada while deeply resenting Ottawa's opposition to such a separate treaty). In short, none of the delegates (so far as is known) were committed confederates, and all must have been very much aware they were only going to Ottawa because there seemed to be no other option. They must also have been aware of the extent of anti-confederate feeling.

The Canadian government was also not enthusiastic about the negotiations. A man of some vanity, Bowell no doubt hoped to glory in completing the confederation of British North America.[33] Others, though, were worried by two factors. First, there was the French Shore issue. When writing to the Canadian government in support of Confederation in early February, Ripon had warned that this would have to become a federal responsibility: "One of my principal reasons for wishing to see Newfoundland united to the Dominion is that in Canadian Ministers we should deal with men of a higher class, of wider minds, and of more statesmanlike vision than the men who have misgoverned and ruined Newfoundland." The Newfoundland legislature would have to renew indefinitely the existing enforcement legislation before the terms of union were settled, pending a decision on the nature of a permanent replacement. Possibly the federal government could then administer the French Treaty Shore as it did the North West Territories.[34] For a weak and poorly led government mired in the highly divisive Manitoba schools controversy, the last thing it needed was another issue which could provide Quebec and French Canadian MPs with another cause of resentment. Indeed, the Liberal leader, Wilfrid Laurier, stated that the settlement of the French Shore question should be an essential precondition for Newfoundland joining Canada—a position that had been adopted by Sir John Thompson and the Conservative government in 1892.[35] A French diplomat reported that the three French-Canadian ministers in the government were not sympathetic to Newfoundland

joining Confederation, but that Bowell believed that "la question du 'sentiment' doit dominer toute autre consideration."[36] Secondly, it was assumed that Newfoundland would be a financial burden. The federal government was itself not in the best financial shape. Generous financial terms could strain the federal purse and, moreover, cause trouble with the existing provinces, which might well demand better treatment for themselves.

Another important factor was that, from the Canadian perspective, there was no diplomatic urgency to conclude successful negotiations. In the 1880s the Canadian government had actively sought to bring Newfoundland into Confederation, mainly to ensure that there would be a united front in trade and fishery negotiations with the United States. Sir Charles Tupper visited St John's in 1887, and there followed a considerable amount of political manoeuvring. But no formal talks took place, and no delegation went to Ottawa. Instead, the colony tried to arrange a separate reciprocity treaty with the United States, a move that sparked outrage in Ottawa. In the controversy over what was known as the Bond-Blaine treaty (1890), the Colonial Office sided with Canada, and it was established that Newfoundland could not impose sanctions on Canadian fishermen. There were further talks—with the Prince Edward Island Senator G.W. Howlan in 1891, and in Halifax in 1892—but relations between the two countries remained frosty, and it was a cause of some resentment in the colony that London obviously placed Canadian interests above those of Newfoundland. The two countries might technically have the same status within the British Empire, but they certainly did not have the same stature.

Not surprisingly in this context, Robert Bond made it very clear in a speech at a banquet tendered to the delegates in Ottawa, where they arrived on 3 April, that he did not want Canadian condescension and that the delegation was not begging for help on bended knee. Canada was not negotiating with a financial and economic basket case, but with a fellow member of the British Empire that possessed valuable assets. Newfoundland had been "looked upon as a kind of worthless fragment of creation . . . that was left over after this great continent was formed. A mere barren rock . . . ." But it was "not that wretched, worthless island that some would have you believe." It had great economic potential in its forests, minerals, and agricultural land, and the fisheries employed 36 000 people—"men who hardened by the storms that rage along our coast would be able and willing to defend our common country should occasion ever require it . . . . Newfoundland has been the nursery for the [British] navy (cheers) and there are just as [many] brave and true hearts beating in the fishery hamlets of Newfoundland to-day, and just as strong British national sentiment as there was a century ago (loud cheers)." Moreover, Newfoundland was "the key to Great Britain's possessions in North America" and should be "the natural terminus of that short line of communications that the trade of both hemispheres demand. . . . Mr. Sandford Fleming [had] . . . pointed to the day when Newfoundland would be the connecting link between the old world and the new." Addressing the current situation, Bond denied that Newfoundland was bankrupt: "When this crash occurred . . . there were nearly four millions and a quarter of dollars on deposit in our banks." He then addressed the reason for being in Ottawa: "We are anxious to learn what Canada is prepared to offer us if we accept her invitation [to join the Confederation]. If we are offered that which will enable us to build up a community that will withstand the winds and storms of the future, then Newfoundland will come in and join you, and aid you too, in completing a structure which, bound together by the bounds of patriotism, will add greater prestige to that Empire upon which the sun never sets . . . ." The press report also noted "at the conclusion of Mr. Bond's speech he was cheered heartily for several minutes."[37]

The talks began on 4 April. The federal government was represented by Bowell, Sir Adolphe-Philippe Caron (Postmaster General), George E. Foster (Finance), and John Haggart (Railways). The Newfoundland delegation—not unreasonably—based its initial proposals on the terms discussed with Tupper in 1887 and with Howlan in 1891. Tupper had spoken of an increase in the amount to be paid for Crown lands over the sum offered in 1869, and of a federal willingness to spend generously on railways and public works. Howlan had indicated that the loss of Customs revenues to Ottawa would be made up for by federal expenditures, and that the colony could expect more generous terms than those offered in 1869. Howlan had also said that the railway would be completed at federal expense and, estimating the Canadian per capita debt at $66 (the Newfoundland equivalent was then $26), thought there would be a substantial payment to recognize the difference. Overall, Newfoundland would receive approximately $1.25 million in federal subsidies.[38]

Given these precedents, the Newfoundland delegation expected generosity and flexibility. But times had changed. Sir John A. Macdonald was gone, the political atmosphere in Ottawa was tense and unstable, and the Newfoundland debt had more than doubled since the talks with Howlan in 1891 (thanks to railway expenditures). It now stood at approximately $55 per capita. Indeed, how to deal with the debt was the central and crucial issue. The funded and floating debt stood at $11 247 534, but contractual obligations relating to the railway amounted to $4 582 300 for a total of $15 829 834. The delegation argued that since the railway was an asset, the entire cost of construction, estimated at $9 553 000, should be deducted, leaving a net debt of $6 276 534.[39] Assuming that Canada would agree to take over the debt to the extent of $50 per head, as had been the case with Prince Edward Island in 1873, then the debt allowance would amount to $10.35 million. Canada should therefore pay 5 per cent annually on $4 073 466 (or $203 673.35)— the difference between the net debt and the debt allowance. Newfoundland would start its life as a province with no debt as well as a useful source of income. In addition, the Newfoundland delegation proposed:

1. Canada would pay Newfoundland an annual subsidy of 80 cents per head— $165 000 assuming a population of 207 000.
2. Canada would pay a fisheries bounty of $150 000.
3. Canada would pay $862 858 in other subsidies.
4. There should be a special allocation for the Newfoundland Constabulary that "could be trained and equipped as a military force."
5. Canada would undertake all major public works.
6. Canada would pay $250 000 annually for ungranted Crown lands in both Newfoundland and Labrador, with Newfoundland retaining precious metals.
7. The federal government would make similar fisheries expenditures in Newfoundland as in the other provinces, channelling the money through the Newfoundland Fisheries Commission.
8. Steamer subsidies would apply to the following: a) a weekly mail and passenger service between Newfoundland and Canada, and to a Port aux Basques ferry when the railway was complete; b) coastal steam services; and c) the direct steamer service between St John's and Liverpool.
9. Newfoundland fishermen would not pay licence fees.
10. Since some local industries might be harmed by confederation, some compensation should be provided "for a limited period."
11. A naval training ship should be established in Newfoundland.
12. $50 000 should be allowed "for legislation."

Overall, then, the delegation envisaged federal payments of about $1.5 million annually (close to Howlan's figure), while estimating the annual cost of services to be delivered by the Newfoundland government at $738 594.[40]

The Canadian delegation refused to contemplate such munificence. It would not accept as a precedent the terms discussed with Tupper (nor, presumably, those discussed with Howlan), arguing that they were unofficial,[41] nor would it accept the railway as an asset or pay for its completion. Taking the Prince Edward Island terms of union as a guide, the Canadians offered to assume the Newfoundland debt up to $10 350 000, based on $50 per head of population, and pay "a yearly allowance" of $465 000:

Allowance for legislation	$ 50 000
Subsidy at 80 cents per head	165 000
Crown Lands allowance	150 000
Interest on $2 M excess debt[42]	100 000
TOTAL	**465 000**

In addition, Canada would maintain services that "fall under the head of general or Dominion services" as well as steamship services. There would be a militia grant of $40 000. Newfoundland fishermen would not receive special treatment. The new province would have four senators and ten members of Parliament. Overall, the Canadian government estimated that the provision or subsidization of services might cost $862 858 annually, when it had hoped not to go above $600 000. Overall, it could be a net financial loser to the extent of $657 000 annually.[43] From this perspective, Newfoundland was being treated fairly—even generously—compared to the existing provinces, and to go further would cause federal-provincial problems and trouble in Parliament.

The Newfoundland delegation was therefore faced with a situation where the new province, having lost the Customs revenues on which it had traditionally relied, would have to service a debt of approximately $5.4 million, and provide services that it estimated would cost over $700 000 annually. From this point of view the federal offer was inadequate, especially as there was no mention of how the railway was to be completed or operated. The delegation responded that a special fishermen's bounty was justified, since Newfoundland fishermen would have to pay licence fees for the first time under Canadian regulations, and that Confederation would probably damage the south coast herring trade. A better offer was also justified because Newfoundland would lose the advantages negotiated in the 1890 Bond-Blaine convention and, if a general reciprocity treaty was achieved, Newfoundland would be the loser because Canadian products would enter the United States at lower cost. Moreover, Newfoundland's control of bait meant that it held "the key to the North American fisheries, and . . . neither Canada nor the United States can successfully prosecute these fisheries without drawing on these supplies." Thus Confederation would place a powerful bargaining chip in the federal government's possession. The delegation also complained about the proposed debt allowance and the small payment for ungranted Crown lands, but did reduce its estimate of the cost of provincial services to $650 000.[44]

Such arguments were futile. The Bowell government was not willing to take any risks, financial or political, to bring Newfoundland into the Dominion. Nevertheless, the delegation (but not the Newfoundland government as a whole) seems by 10 April to have just about accepted the Canadian terms,[45] even though these implied a massive reorganization of internal services and the imposition of direct municipal and local taxation. While there is no surviving record of any discussions concerning the French Treaty Shore problem, it is clear that the Canadian government recognized its responsibilities in the event of Confederation, and that the Newfoundland delegation pledged that the legislature would pass the 1891 draft permanent enforcement bill—but only if there was help from London to bridge the financial impasse. Somehow the entire Newfoundland debt would have to be taken over and the railway completed.

Lord Aberdeen, the Canadian Governor General, informed the Colonial Office about the situation on 11 April. There was a "prospect of reaching [a] basis of agreement" but "much . . . if not everything, will depend on whether HM's Gov[ernmen]t will supplement [the] allowance to be given by Canada to Newfoundland."[46] In another despatch, Aberdeen raised the spectre of Newfoundland drifting into the orbit of the United States. If the talks failed, he wrote, it would be most unfortunate, "for there may not probably be soon again so much disposition on each side to unite." [. . .] Moreover, anti-confederates in Newfoundland could raise the cry that the imperial government could not reasonably prevent a separate reciprocity treaty with the US.[47] The negotiators suspended the talks sine die on 16 April to await a decision from London.[48] The delegates arrived back in St John's on 21 April.

It had been suspected at the Colonial Office that some financial aid might be necessary, but the nature of the draft terms of union and the amount of money requested caused officials to become decidedly unsympathetic. The idea of Britain contributing to the annual subsidy was rejected out of hand. Bramston noted that the proposal amounted "to an offer by Newfoundland to pass a permanent act if England will grant her an annual sum forever in aid of the expenses of Government," and predicted that the House of Commons would object.[49] In general, the impression at the Colonial Office was that the Canadian government was driving an unnecessarily hard bargain and that it should improve the financial terms.[50]

In a lengthy minute, Anderson questioned the Canadian debt proposal. The actual debt, he agreed, was nearer $10 million than $15 million, and he found it unreasonable that the cost of completing the railway should be treated "as an actual accrued obligation of the Nfdld Govt."[51] [. . .] "The passing of such a measure is not worth paying for," he concluded, "and we must stand out for the existing temporary Act."[52]

The financial arguments were expanded upon in Anderson's minutes on Aberdeen's despatch of 16 April.[53] Canada was driving a hard bargain. The debt allowance per capita was less than that given other provinces, and Canada should remember that the railway would become Dominion property. Other allowances were poor as well, and he did not think that Britain would be justified in doing any more than to guarantee a Canadian loan to finish the railway. Another suggestion was that the holders of Newfoundland bonds should take Canadian stock guaranteed by the imperial government in its place—lower interest, but higher market value.[54] The official reply to Canada on 4 May addressed the debt allowance and the railway issue, and urged Canada to absorb the whole debt. The suggestion about debt conversion was added in a secret appendix.[55]

That same day a telegram arrived from Aberdeen to the effect that Confederation could happen only if the imperial government provided a lump sum of approximately £1 million.[56] This amount, noted Anderson, could set Newfoundland on its feet for many years, "but this is intended as a gift to be divided between Canada and the Nfdld bondholders." Meade thought the demand "preposterous. Desirable as Confederation is, one can pay too high a price for it." Tellingly, he added that, for a fraction of this sum, Newfoundland would accept "some form of control."[57] On 8 May, Aberdeen transmitted another message. Canada would not assume the Newfoundland

debt over $50 per capita, and could not absorb $5 million more to complete the railway as this would be unfair to the existing provinces. The trade gain was estimated at only $1 million, and that would be balanced by a loss in revenue. Unless $5 million was forthcoming, there was no possibility of Confederation.[58] Anderson repeated his arguments. In his view, Newfoundland was being treated less generously than Prince Edward Island had been, and Canada was in effect asking to be paid for annexing the colony. He thought that Canada would benefit from union—thus questioning Bowell's figures—while Britain would actually lose. In February, Newfoundland had asked for a guarantee on £20 000 for 25 years. This was refused, "and now we are asked not for a guarantee but an actual payment of over £40 000 a year and for what?" If Newfoundland would accept an inquiry and control if necessary, concluded Anderson, Britain would be better off. It could then handle the French treaties question without relying on Ottawa, which was "rather a broken reed, as we have found in other fisheries questions." It had to be remembered that Canada had a large deficit, taxes were increasing, and the Liberals wanted a settlement of the French question before Confederation, "so that no doubt unless Canada can shew it has made a very good bargain—as it [would] if we agreed to their terms—they could not hope to carry it through."[59]

At this point Sir Charles Tupper, now the Canadian high commissioner in London, entered the affair. Ripon told him on 10 May that "it would not be possible to establish so dangerous a precedent as that the Imperial Government should be obliged to come to the rescue of any of the autonomous colonies from bankruptcy." Tupper urged the Canadian case but Ripon was adamant, going so far as to suggest "the best interests of Newfoundland might be met by the Colony going bankrupt and thus being in a position to settle its present indebtedness and engagements upon very reduced terms."[60] Tupper then urged Bowell to consider the possibility of an imperial guarantee on a £1 million loan to facilitate the Newfoundland arrangement,[61] but Bowell had had enough; his government had gone as far as it could and still obtain parliamentary support. Anything more would have opened up the question of subsidies to the other provinces. As it was, Newfoundland's demands entailed an expenditure of $1 million over the estimated income. The colony had alienated 2.5 million acres to R.G. Reid, which would not come to the Dominion, and relief estimates were high: "In short," Bowell declared, "they seem to be a kind of paternal Government, paying for everything they can out of Customs and Excise revenue, the latter being very small." Then there was the French Shore question, and there would also be difficulties with the municipality of St John's. Nothing but "an ardent desire to unite the whole of British North America . . . would justify the offer which Canada has made." In sum, Bowell concluded, "they ask us to give them a clean sheet, to assume all the services which we do for the other Provinces and to pay them $650 000 p.a."[62]

On 1 May, Whiteway had told Bowell that his government could not accept the terms unless Canada assumed the full Newfoundland debt, completed the railway, and provided a subsidy of $650 000.[63] This resulted in an offer of $6000 a mile toward the cost of the railway and a subsidy increase of $35 000.[64] This was rejected as insufficient. Conscious of the extent of anti-confederate feeling, the government needed generous terms so that it could have a hope of carrying Confederation at the polls. The colony began to look for other solutions, and the Colonial Office revived the idea of Newfoundland becoming a Crown colony. On the day that Bowell's final telegram arrived (11 May), Bond left for Montreal with R.G. Reid, authorized to try and float a loan. As O'Brien wrote, it was "the proverbial last straw left."[65] The Newfoundland government was taking a considerable risk, but one that was necessary if the indignities of a royal commission and possible constitutional change were to be avoided.

Given Bond's absence, it was Morris who reported on the negotiations to the House of Assembly on 16 May. The delegation, he said, had not expected that the terms discussed with Tupper would be repudiated, and the refusal to assume the entire public debt had made agreement impossible.[66] In Montreal, Bond stated that the Canadian government had taken advantage of the colony's predicament to try and drive a hard bargain and, moreover, the repudiation of the previous offer justified "mistrust." Bond added that the completion of the railway had also been a problem, alleging that the Canadian government wanted it either stopped or completed at Newfoundland's expense.[67] [. . .]

Under criticism in the Senate, Bowell denied that there had been any attempt to "screw them down, as the expression has been." He also denied that previous draft terms had been repudiated: "We were willing not only to consider the terms which were indirectly offered to them in the past, but we were quite willing to go much beyond that." The terms offered were more generous than those negotiated with any province, Bowell maintained, but the whole Newfoundland debt could not be absorbed, and Britain for good reasons had refused to create a precedent by financial intervention. As for the 1890 reciprocity agreement, Bowell thought that Bond and other Newfoundlanders overestimated its potential value. In terms of the future, Canada remained favourable to Newfoundland's joining the Dominion and the colony would face "a day of reckoning" sooner or later; imperial aid would be needed, certainly in the short term.[68] There does not seem to have been any serious discussion of the Newfoundland issue in the House of Commons, and there was no formal statement there either. The issue was pressed by L.H. Davies, a Liberal MP from Prince Edward Island and an acquaintance of Whiteway,[69] and other Liberals entered the fray; but Minister of Finance George Foster, who had been a member of the Canadian delegation, refused to provide any details. The longest exchange (on 10 May) degenerated into a partisan slanging match.[70]

What are we to make of the charges and counter-charges? It is clear enough that neither side was particularly anxious to negotiate Confederation, and that the Newfoundland delegation made a tactical though understandable mistake by treating the Tupper and Howlan discussions as "official." Moreover, Bowell's government was shaky; he could not afford to precipitate a round of federal-provincial arguments and, given the federal government's financial problems, the Newfoundland debt looked enormous.[71] As for Britain, Lord Rosebery's government was in political trouble while at the Colonial Office there existed a stubborn line of thought that granting Newfoundland responsible government had been a mistake and that Crown colony status would be the best solution. In both Ottawa and London there was a distinct lack of flexibility and imagination.

But were the Canadian proposals as mean-spirited as many thought? The debt allowance and the per capita subsidy offered were the same as in the case of Prince Edward Island, but the Island's debt had been much smaller and could therefore be absorbed in full. In addition, the federal government had agreed to take over PEI's railway system and, recognizing the Island's special circumstances, had included a grant in lieu of Crown lands and offered to advance up to $800 000 to buy out remaining absentee proprietors. In Newfoundland's case the $50 formula did not cover the (much larger) debt, and other financial transfers were inadequate. The federal government showed no interest in the railway, and was unwilling to recognize the colony's special circumstances—such as the fact that its economy was almost wholly based on the fisheries.

Certainly, a chance was missed, but the difficulty of the task should not be underestimated. Bowell was quite right to point out that it was very difficult to fit Newfoundland into the framework established by the 1867 British North America Act: "To-day the Newfoundland Government practically assumes the whole burden of poor-relief, educating the people, building the roads and bridges, and performs other services which, in the Provinces of Canada, are dealt with exclusively by the Municipalities and in no case by the Federal Government."[72] In effect, Newfoundland had a single level of government that was responsible for all government services and relied entirely on indirect taxation. In Canada there were three levels of government: the federal level relying on indirect taxation, the provinces on direct taxation, and the municipalities on property taxes. Services were shared. Since Newfoundland would lose its Customs and Excise revenues, it would have to impose direct taxation which, given a small and scattered population, would be difficult and expensive to collect. And, as in 1948, serious problems were raised by federal control of the fisheries, which was the colony's major industry. There were good reasons for skepticism and ambivalence on both sides.

The colony survived as an independent entity, thanks to Bond's success, with Reid's help, in raising loans for the government and the Savings Bank. The failure of the Confederation talks in 1895 probably reinforced many Newfoundlanders' suspicion of Canada and Confederation, and the relative prosperity of the early twentieth century marginalized the issue. There were sporadic manoeuvrings, which intensified when the Great Depression brought the country once again to the edge of bankruptcy. However, Canada had its own difficulties and was not then interested in Confederation. The result was an imperial royal commission, the suspension of responsible government, and the imposition in 1934 of a species of Crown colony rule. The parallels with the events of 1894–1895 are striking.

NOTES

1. A.M. Fraser, "Relations with Canada," in *Newfoundland: Economic, Diplomatic and Strategic Studies*, ed. R.A. MacKay (Toronto: Oxford University Press, 1946), 411–83; George G.F. Stanley, "Further Documents Relating to the Union of Newfoundland and Canada, 1886–1895," *Canadian Historical Review* 29, 4 (1948): 370–86.

2. Ripon to O'Brien, 21 January 1895 (tgm.) and 31 January 1895 ("confidential"), CO 194/230, pp. 40, 70–1, United Kingdom National Archives (UKNA).

3. Minute by Anderson, 12 December 1894, CO 194/228, pp. 516–18, UKNA.

4. Minutes by Bramston and Meade, 12 and 14 December 1894, CO 194/228, p. 518, UKNA.

5. The French, British, and Newfoundland governments each interpreted the wording of the treaties differently, and in Newfoundland the French presence (though seasonal) and French pretensions were deeply resented.

6. F.F. Thompson, *The French Shore Problem in Newfoundland: An Imperial Study* (Toronto: University of Toronto Press, 1961), chap. 6. See also James Hiller, "A History of Newfoundland, 1874–1901," (PhD diss. Cambridge University, 1971), 232–55.

7. Meade to Ripon, 26 December 1894, Ripon Papers, Add. MSS 43558, vol. LXIX, pp. 53–8, British Library (BL).

8. Meade to Ripon, 28 December 1894, Ripon Papers, Add. MSS 43558, vol. LXIX, p. 69, BL. The "Treaties Bill" was a bill to enforce the French Shore treaties.

9. O'Brien to Ripon, 10 April 1894 ("confidential"), and 17 April 1894 (tgm.), CO 194/227, pp. 496, 555–60, UKNA.

10. Ripon to O'Brien, 18 April 1894 (tgm.), CO 194/227, p. 564, UKNA.

11. Ripon to O'Brien, 12 December 1894 (tgm.), CO 194/228, pp. 498–9, UKNA.

12. O'Brien to Ripon, 18 December 1894, and Ripon to O'Brien, 9 January 1895, CO 194/228, pp. 547–51, UKNA.

13. O'Brien to Ripon, 4 and 26 January 1895, CO 194/230, pp. 36, 141–70, UKNA.

14. *Telegram*, 27 February 1895.

15. Minute by Anderson, 15 January 1894, CO 194/228, p. 590, UKNA.

16. *Telegram*, 9 January 1895. Fretwell had visited Newfoundland in 1894, and was the author of *Newfoundland and the Jingoes: An Appeal to England's Honor* (Boston: G.H. Ellis, 1895). See also *Encyclopedia of Newfoundland and Labrador* (*ENL*), 2:423.

17. *Herald*, 31 January 1895.

18. Harvey Mitchell, "Canada's Negotiations with Newfoundland, 1887–1895," *Canadian Historical Review* 29, 4 (1948): 257.

19. *Herald*, 1, 5, 7, and 11 February 1895.

20. *ENL*, 3:657.

21. *Telegram*, 20, 23, and 25 March 1895; Patrick O'Flaherty, *Lost Country: The Rise and Fall of Newfoundland, 1843–1933* (St John's: Long Beach Press, 2005), 192–3.

22. Murray, letter to the *Telegram*, 13 February 1895.

23. *Telegram*, 30 March 1895.

24. Whiteway to Bowell, 14 January 1895 ("private and confidential"), and Bowell to Whiteway, 14 January 1895 (tgm.), printed in George G.F. Stanley, "Further Documents Relating to the Union of Newfoundland and Canada, 1886–1895," *Canadian Historical Review* 29, 4 (1948): 376–8.

25. O'Brien to Ripon, 11 February 1895 (tgm.), and Ripon to O'Brien, 19 February 1895 (tgm.), CO 194/230, pp. 253, 264, UKNA.

26. Aberdeen to O'Brien, 1 March 1895 (tgm.), *Documents Relating to the Proceedings of the Conference at Ottawa upon the Subject of Confederation with Canada* (DRPC), p. 4, Robert Bond Papers (RBP), Col 237, 8.02.013, Archives and Manuscripts Division (AMD), Memorial University Library (MUL).

27. "Draft History of Newfoundland," chap. 9, p. 15, A.B. Morine Papers, MG 271, The Rooms Provincial Archives Division (TRPAD).

28. *Telegram*, 6 and 21 March 1895.

29. Horwood had been colonial secretary in the Greene administration, and the membership of the delegation was suggested by Whiteway. See Whiteway to Bond, 21 March 1895, RBP, 8.03.020, AMD, MUL.

30. *Herald*, 27 March 1895; *Telegram*, 27 March 1895.

31. But O'Brien reported that the steamer left amid "complete silence." See O'Brien to Ripon, 4 April 1895 ("confidential"), CO 194/230, p. 473, UKNA.

32. Bowell to Whiteway, 15 February 1895, G21, 194, vol. 1, Library and Archives Canada (LAC); *Herald*, 14, 15, and 29 March 1895.

33. On Bowell, see Peter Waite's entry in *The Dictionary of Canadian Biography* (*DCB*), XIV:120–5.

34. Ripon to Governor General Lord Aberdeen, 6 February 1895 ("confidential"), copy in Ripon Papers, Add. MSS 3558, vol. LXIX, pp. 115–18, BL. See also Ripon to Aberdeen, 13 February 1895 ("confidential"), CO 194/230, pp. 280–90, UKNA.

35. Lord Stanley to Ripon, 5 November 1892 ("private"), Ripon Papers, Add. MSS 43558, vol. LXVI, p. 1, BL.

36. Kleczkowski to Hanotaux, 11 March 1895, Correspondance consulaire politique— Angleterre, Québec et Montréal, vol. 99, p. 381, Archives du Ministère des Affaires Étrangères (AAE), Paris.

37. *Montreal Gazette* report, printed in the *Telegram*, 23 April 1895; see also RBP, 8.03.021, AMD, MUL. The banquet was on 9 April.

38. Mitchell, "Canada's Negotiations," reprinted in G.A. Rawlyk, ed., *Historical Essays on the Atlantic Provinces* (Toronto: McClelland and Stewart, 1967), 244, 246–7; Fraser, "Relations with Canada," 447–8.

39. This calculation presumably did not include the line from St John's to Harbour Grace via Whitbourne, which was still owned by the Newfoundland Railway Company (in receivership).

40. *DRPC*, pp. 38–45, RBP, Col 237, 8.02.013, AMD, MUL; Fraser, "Relations with Canada," 451–3.

41. Morris in House of Assembly, 16 May 1895; see *Telegram*, 5 June 1895. It is not known why the discussions with Howlan were never specifically mentioned.

42. The Canadian government put the Newfoundland debt at $8 350 000, or approximately $40 per head. In order to bring this amount up to $50 per head, Canada would assume "an excess of debt" of $2 million on which it would pay interest at 5 per cent.

43. *DRPC*, pp. 46–7, RBP, Col 237, 8.02.013, AMD, MUL; Fraser, "Relations with Canada"; "Memo of Terms Proposed by Canada," Mackenzie Bowell papers, MG 26E, vol. 100, file 1, LAC. This appears to be the only document relevant to the 1895 talks in the Bowell papers. The bolding is in the original.

44. Untitled and undated memorandum, RBP, 8.01.015, AMD, MUL.

45. J.T. Saywell, ed., *The Canadian Journal of Lady Aberdeen* (Toronto: Champlain Society, 1960), 216.

46. Aberdeen to Ripon (tgm.), 11 April 1895, Ripon Papers, Add. MSS 43558, vol. LXVIII, p. 125, BL.

47. Aberdeen to Ripon ("confidential"), 10 April 189, and Aberdeen to Ripon (tgm.), 11 April 1895, Ripon Papers, Add. MSS 43558, vol. LXVIII, p. 128, BL. See also Aberdeen to Ripon ("secret"), 16 April 1895, CO 42/829, p. 76–9, UKNA, as well as Stanley, "Further Documents," 385.

48. *DRPC*, pp. 13–14, RBP, Col 237, 8.02.013, AMD, MUL.

49. Minutes by Bramston and Meade, 11 April, and reply telegram, 13 April 1895, CO 537/113, pp. 84–8, UKNA.

50. Minutes by Anderson, 27 April 1895; Ripon to Aberdeen (tgm.), 4 May 1895; CO 42/829, pp. 862–4, 869–72, 885, UKNA.

51. Presumably this was the Territorial Waters Jurisdiction Act, 1878, 41 & 42 Vic., c. 73. Anderson did not specify what amendments would be necessary.

52. Minute by Anderson, 24 April 1895, CO 537/113, pp. 91–2, UKNA.

53. See note 40 above.

54. Minutes by Anderson, 27 April 1895, CO 42/829, pp. 862–4, 869–72, UKNA.

55. Ripon to Aberdeen (tgm.), 4 May 1895, CO 42/829, p. 885, UKNA.

56. Aberdeen to Ripon ("confidential" tgm.), 4 May 1895, CO 537/113, p. 95, UKNA.

57. Minutes by Anderson and Meade, 4 May 1895, CO 537/113, p. 94, UKNA.

58. Aberdeen to Ripon (tgm.), 8 May 1895, CO 537/113, p. 100, UKNA.

59. Minute by Anderson, 8 May 1895, CO 537/113, pp. 97–9, UKNA.

60. Tupper to Bowell, 11 May 1895, Canada House Records, RG 25, series A7, vol. 538, file 237, LAC.

61. Tupper to Bowell, 20 May 1895 (listing telegrams exchanged), Canada House Records, RG 25, series A7, vol. 538, file 237, LAC.

62. Bowell to Tupper, 21 May 1895, Canada House Records, RG 25, series A7, vol. 538, file 237, LAC.

63. Whiteway to Bowell (tgm.), 1 May 1895, in Stanley, "Further Documents," 365–6.

64. Bowell to Whiteway (tgm.), 11 May 1895, in *Journal of the House of Assembly,* 1895, Appendix, 422; See also copy in RBP, 9.01.018, AMD, MUL.

65. O'Brien to Ripon ("confidential"), 13 May 1895, CO 194/231, p. 53, UKNA.

66. *Telegram,* 5 June 1895.

67. *Montreal Star,* 12 May 1895, printed in *Telegram,* 27 May 1895.

68. Bowell in Senate, 20 June 1895; *Proceedings of the House of Assembly,* 350–2.

69. Davies later became the chief justice of Canada.

70. House of Commons Debates 1895, I, pp. 270–2, 344–54, 840–60.

71. P.B. Waite, *Canada 1874–1896: Arduous Destiny* (Toronto: McClelland and Stewart, 1971), 244–5.

72. Memorandum, "Canada and Newfoundland as to Debt," n.d., RBP, 8.03.016, AMD, MUL (annotated in Bond's handwriting, "The Story of 'No!'").